SOCIOLOGY
IN FOCUS
for AQA A2 Level

Edited by
Michael Haralambos and Peter Langley
Written by
Michael Hara... ...ew Pilkington,
Pa... ...Yeo

Dedication
To Jackie with thanks

Acknowledgements

Cover and page design	Caroline Waring-Collins (Waring-Collins Ltd)
Graphic origination	John A. Collins (Waring-Collins Ltd)
Graphics	Tim Button (Waring-Collins Ltd)
Author index and typing	Ingrid Hamer (Causeway Press Ltd)
Readers	Jackie Dickinson, Mike Kidson

Picture credits
Advertising Archives 205; Andrew Allen 55 (ml, mr, mb); Art Directors & TRIP Photo Library 129;
Associated Press 4, 6 (tl, tr), 8 (bl), 9 (bl), 11 (tl), 16 (tr), 18 (tl, tm, tr, br), 22 (ml), 28 (bl), 30 (bl), 34, 38, 46, 50, 72 (bl), 77 (tl), 84, 95 (tm, tr), 107 (ml), 179 (ml), 194 (ml), 199 (mr), 203 (tr), 209 (br), 233, 249 (br), 254 (tl); BBC Photograph Library 126 (bl); Chris Garratt/Pierrot Productions 199 (t); Guardian Newspaper 254 (tr); John Collins 146; Kurdish Organisation for Culture and Education 96 (ml); Mary Evans Picture Library 138 (m, b), 157, 168, 266 (bl, br), 267 (tl, tr), 270 (bl, br), 271 (tl); National Museums of Canada 149; North News and Pictures 199 (ml); Photofusion 6 (ml), 22 (mr), 39 (mr), 59, 64 (bl), 68 (mr, br), 79 (bl, br), 99, 118 (br), 194 (br), 200, 202 (br), 206 (ml, mr, bl), 236 (tl, br), 246 (ml, mr); Popperfoto.com 14 (tr), 194 (tl); Rex Features 6 (bl, br), 9 (br), 11 (bl), 36, 37, 39 (tr), 42 (mr), 64 (tr), 82 (br), 95 (tl), 96 (tr), 107 (br), 118 (tr), 122 (t), 171 (mm), 175 (tr, ml, mr), 190, 199 (br), 203 (mr), 204, 225 (tr), 236 (tr, mr, bl), 238, 249 (mr), 262 (tl, tr), 267 (mr); Robert Yager 228 (tl, tr); TopFoto 6 (mr), 8 (ml, mr), 14 (tl), 16 (tl), 26 (tl), 28 (tr), 30 (mr), 31, 56, 62, 66 (tr, mr), 68 (ml, bl), 72 (br), 75, 77 (tr), 86 (tl, tr), 113, 116 (mr), 118 (m, b), 165, 171 (mr), 175 (tl), 179 (br), 195, 202 (bl), 203 (tl, ml), 206 (br), 221 (tl), 225 (tl), 232, 246 (tr, bl), 258, 262 (mr); Women's Aid 209 (tr).

Cartoons
Unless otherwise credited, the cartoons in this book have been specially drawn by BRICK www.brickbats.co.uk

Cover picture
Hundertwasser
THE END OF THE GREEKS, 1964
© J. Harel, Vienna

Every effort has been made to locate the copyright owners of material used in this book. Any omissions brought to the attention of the publisher are regretted and will be credited in subsequent printings.

British Library Cataloguing in Publication Data
A catalogue record for this book is available from the British Library.

ISBN 1 902796 75 6

Causeway Press Limited
PO Box 13, Ormskirk, Lancs L39 5HP

Contribution © Michael Haralambos, Peter Langley, Andrew Pilkington, Paul Taylor, Alan Yeo

First impression 2004
Printed and bound by Scotprint, Haddington, East Lothian

Contents

1 Religion

Introduction

In 1854, a French poet, Gerard de Nerval, published history's most sensational obituary. 'God is dead,' he proclaimed. 'Heaven is empty. Weep, children, you no longer have a father.' Twenty-eight years later, the German philosopher, Friedrich Nietzsche, added his agreement. The age of God and of religion had passed.

In 2004, 150 years after the poet's claim, sociologists are divided about the state of religion. Some look at countries like Britain and see religion in decline. Others point to worldwide evidence of religious belief and religiously-inspired activity.

In the world's richest, most technologically advanced society, the USA, thousands of young Christian women publicly pledge to remain virgins until marriage. Meanwhile, thousands of Christian men vow to take back from their wives the man's 'God-given responsibility' to be head of the family. In many countries, religiously-inspired groups shoot and bomb people of another religion, or of another tradition within the same religion, or of no religion at all. Yet, at scenes of disaster or conflict around the world, people motivated by religious belief give aid and comfort – sometimes at risk of their lives – via such organisations as the (Muslim) Red Crescent and Christian Aid. And far from God – or belief in God – being dead, one of the world's fastest-growing movements consists of people who publicly 'witness' to the greatness of their God. Their God's name is Jehovah, their organisation is called Jehovah's Witnesses.

This chapter looks at the part played by religion in society, its relationship to social change, the various forms that religious organisations take and the debate about whether or not religion is declining in today's world.

Over two million Muslim pilgrims gather in Mecca to perform the annual hajj ceremony.

chaptersummary

▶ **Unit 1** examines sociological theories of religion.

▶ **Unit 2** assesses the role of religion, both as a conservative force which maintains things the way they are and as a radical force which encourages social change.

▶ **Unit 3** discusses different types of religious organisation, including churches, denominations, sects, cults and

New Religious Movements.

▶ **Unit 4** looks at explanations of the relationship between religious beliefs, religious organisations and social groups.

▶ **Unit 5** investigates the secularisation debate – whether or not societies are becoming increasingly secular or non-religious.

Unit 1 Theories of religion

keyissues

1 What is religion?
2 What are the main theoretical approaches to religion?

1.1 Defining religion

Religion has been defined in many ways:
- As a belief in some kind of supernatural power
- As an expression of this belief in collective worship

- As a set of moral values which guide action
- As a force which brings people together and unifies society.

These definitions let in a variety of activities under the heading of religion. For example, people talk about football as 'the new religion'. Many fans are devoted to the game. They are united in support of their team and, in some ways, a football match can be seen as a religious ritual.

There are many activities which can be seen as

supernatural – astrology, palmistry, fortune telling, witchcraft and a belief in ghosts. Should these be regarded as religious?

As a starting point, most sociologists would probably agree that religions typically involve:

- an organised collectivity of individuals, with
- a shared system of beliefs and
- a set of approved activities and practices.

There are, of course, serious questions about the extent to which members of any of the world's religions agree with fellow members' beliefs and practices. Indeed, Judaism, Christianity, Islam, Hinduism, Buddhism and Sikhism all experience divisions into often rival groupings. There are even questions about how organised a collectivity of individuals has to be to constitute a religion – especially since the advent of the Internet.

Most sociological definitions of religion focus on what religion is – *substantive* definitions – or the roles religions play in society – *functional* definitions.

Substantive definitions of religion

Belief in the supernatural Sociologists adopting substantive definitions have tried to identify what is distinctive about religious *beliefs*. For example, Max Weber saw religion as involving a belief in the *supernatural*, that is some power above the forces of nature. This suggests a belief in a being or beings, powers or forces, which are in some ways superior to humans, and which cannot be verified or explained by Western science.

Relating to the sacred An alternative substantive definition is provided by Emile Durkheim. For him, the key to religious beliefs is not that they relate to a supernatural power or being, but that they relate to things which a society's members perceive as *sacred*.

Durkheim argued that, in all societies, people divide the world about them into things which are regarded as sacred and those which are considered *profane* – non-sacred, worldly, ordinary. Sacred things are 'things set apart and forbidden'. Things, or people, seen as sacred evoke strong emotions of awe, respect and deference. For instance, in some societies, the monarch has inspired a sense of what Durkheim calls the sacred. Things regarded as sacred both draw the believer towards them while at the same time maintaining their distance. Part of the appeal of Princess Diana was that she was seen by many admirers both as someone 'ordinary' and as someone who was 'very special' (Jones, 1998).

In practice, a supernatural being (such as a god) is likely to be regarded as sacred. However, it seems as though anything could be regarded as sacred, however ordinary and mundane it may appear to outsiders – the Black Hills of South Dakota to the Dakota Sioux, the bone of a saint to medieval Christians, a cow to a Hindu. People or things regarded as sacred do not, therefore, have to be supernatural.

Functional definitions of religion

Functional definitions stress the ways religions contribute to societies. They focus on the *role* or *function* of religion in society. For Durkheim, as we have seen, religion refers to beliefs and practices concerning sacred things. These religious beliefs and practices 'unite into one single moral community … all those who adhere to them'. Thus, a key component of religion, he suggests, is that it encourages *social solidarity* or *social unity* between the fellow-believers who make up a society.

That, of course, isn't the only function that religion may perform in society. Other suggested functions are discussed shortly. Nevertheless, in Durkheim's view, it is because religion plays this crucial role of strengthening social solidarity that it occurs in all societies.

Definitions of religion – some criticisms

Supernatural beings or forces One criticism made of the widely-held view that religion involves belief in the supernatural is the recognition that not all cultures see a distinction between the 'natural' and the 'supernatural'. Angels, spirits and gods can be a 'real', 'lived' and 'natural' part of people's experience. Indeed, it can be argued that what is meant by supernatural may be nothing more than what is currently beyond Western scientific understanding.

Also, if religion always involves belief in the supernatural, is every supernatural belief, by definition, religious? For example, are astrology, fortune telling and witchcraft religious?

The sacred Durkheim's notion of the sacred has also been challenged as not universally applicable – that is, not present in every society. For example, anthropologists found that no distinction was made between the sacred and non-sacred amongst the Azande of southern Sudan and in some West African societies (Hamilton, 2001).

It has also been pointed out that what people regard as sacred does not always command respect and awe. For instance, as Hamilton (2001) notes, 'In Southern Italy, a saint who does not respond in the desired manner after long and repeated prayers may be severely admonished, the statue turned upside down, even whipped or discarded and replaced with that of another saint'.

key terms

Supernatural A being or beings, power or force beyond the laws of nature.

Sacred According to Durkheim, things which are 'set apart and forbidden', things which evoke feelings of awe, respect and deference.

Social solidarity Social unity which results from the bonds that draw members of society together.

activity1 defining religion

Item A Saluting the flag

President Clinton flanked by athletes saluting the American flag at the Atlanta Olympics in 1996

Item B A Christian saint

Catholics carry a statue of their neighbourhood's patron saint in Havana, Cuba.

Item C A clairvoyant

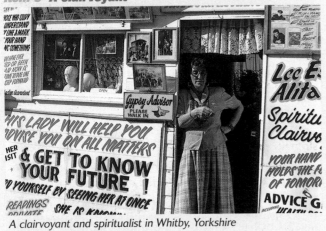

A clairvoyant and spiritualist in Whitby, Yorkshire

Item D Witchcraft

A white witch conducts a ceremony at the Long Man of Wilmington, Sussex.

Item E Remembrance Sunday

Remembrance Sunday service at the Cenotaph, London to remember Britain's war dead

Item F The World Cup

England vs Argentina, World Cup, Japan, 2002

questions

1 How can the activities illustrated in Items A and B be seen as religious? Refer to the definitions of religion outlined in the text.

2 Briefly criticise the view that all of the activities pictured above should be seen as religious.

Durkheim's view of the sacred has been criticised for being too broad and including too much. It allows other belief systems, such as nationalism or communism, to be seen as religious. For example, a nation's flag can be defined as 'sacred' when it is regarded with respect, deference and devotion. Even sport can be seen as 'sacred' – for example, the hallowed turf of certain football and cricket grounds and the respect and devotion given to the team's colours.

Functional definitions – a criticism Functional definitions have also been criticised on precisely the same grounds as Durkheim's focus on the sacred. Such definitions would again include belief systems such as communism and nationalism, and even activities such as sports, where shared beliefs and rituals also encourage unity among 'believers'.

1.2 Functionalist interpretations of religion

Functionalists see society as a system – a set of parts which work together to form a whole. These parts are the institutions of society – for example, the family, the religious system and the political system.

Functionalists assume that society has certain basic needs which must be met if it is to survive. First and foremost is the need for social order. It is assumed that social order requires a certain degree of cooperation and social solidarity. This is made possible by shared norms and values – a consensus or agreement about society's norms and values. Without this consensus, people would be pulling in different directions and conflict and disorder would result. Because of this emphasis on consensus, functionalism is also known as *consensus theory*.

When analysing any part of society, functionalists often ask, 'What is its function?' By function, they mean what is its contribution to the maintenance and wellbeing of the social system.

The functionalist approach can be seen clearly in the French sociologist Emile Durkheim's analysis of religion – *The Elementary Forms of the Religious Life*, first published in 1912.

Emile Durkheim – religion and the worship of society

As noted earlier, Durkheim recognised that things held 'sacred', which often appear 'ordinary' to non-believers, evoke in believers powerful emotions of awe, deference and respect. Therefore, he inferred, it seems their significance is as symbols – they must represent something. And what they represent, he concluded, is the *collective consciousness* – the basic set of shared beliefs, values, traditions and norms which makes social life possible. And in worshipping a society's sacred symbols, its members are unwittingly worshipping the society of which they are a part.

Durkheim's analysis was largely drawn from studies of the religion of Australian Aborigines, which he called *totemism*. Aboriginal society was divided into clans, whose members shared various duties and obligations towards each other. Each clan had a totem – a symbol, usually either an animal or plant – by which it distinguished itself from other clans. The totem was regarded as sacred and was carved on the bullroarer, the most sacred of Aboriginal objects. According to Durkheim, the totem was both the symbol of the Aborigines' god and of the clan. Though the Aborigines consciously worshipped their god, the society was the real object of their veneration. And, Durkheim surmised, 'Primitive man comes to view society as something sacred because he is utterly dependent on it'.

Reinforcing the collective consciousness Without a collective consciousness, a society cannot survive. And for Durkheim, regular acts of collective worship and shared ritual play a crucial role in ensuring society's survival. In effect, the society's members are repeatedly re-affirming their support for their shared values and beliefs.

Strengthening social solidarity Durkheim also claimed that the shared experience of the community's oft-repeated rituals further functions to unify and bind together a society's members. Whether celebrating the group's myths or history in commemorative rites, or coming together in marriage or mourning rituals, society's members are renewing their sense of membership and unity. The very act of communal worship and the practice of rituals raises people's awareness of their common situation and strengthens the bonds between them.

Although participants in societal rituals are unlikely to be consciously aware of it, Durkheim claimed that they are also expressing their sense that the society, the collective, is of supreme importance. The shared, ritualised experiences encourage an awareness that they, as individuals, are relatively insignificant and dependent. But together they are strong. In this respect, one of the main functions of religious is to strengthen social solidarity.

Supporting individuals' adaptations Though he saw the social functions of religion as of primary importance, Durkheim was not blind to its importance for individuals. Hence, he recognised that religious belief and practice can provide individuals with a sense of renewed strength, confidence, serenity and enthusiasm, and help them 'either to endure the trials of existence, or to conquer them' (Durkheim, 1968).

Conclusion In Durkheim's view, therefore, all religions fulfil certain functions for the individual and for society. For the individual, religion provides continuing motivation to face up to life, and social support based upon a sense of belonging. For society, religion unifies members around the shared values, norms, meanings and traditions of the collective consciousness and thereby encourages social integration and social solidarity. The symbols which members of the group worship may or may not be regarded as supernatural. But, to committed believers, they inspire the devotion and awe appropriate to sacred things.

Bronislaw Malinowski – religion and situations of emotional stress

Malinowski was one of the first anthropologists to live for a long period in a small-scale society. His interpretation of religion placed more emphasis on its psychological functions for the individual. He accepted that religion played a central role in promoting social solidarity, but argued that it had developed as a response to the psychological needs of individuals in specific situations of emotional stress. Situations which provoke anxiety, uncertainty and tension threaten social life and it is with such potentially disruptive situations that religion is typically concerned. In particular, Malinowski identified two types of event with which religion is characteristically involved.

In all societies – but perhaps most acutely in small-scale societies with few members – *life crises* such as birth, puberty, marriage and death are potentially disruptive and typically involve religious ritual. In particular, religion minimises the potential disruption of death by creating 'valuable mental attitudes' towards it. Religion's forceful assertion of immortality comforts the bereaved, and the religious rituals of the funeral ceremony bind together the survivors and counteract the sense of meaninglessness which might otherwise undermine social life.

The second type of event which Malinowski identified as creating anxiety and involving religion concerns activities whose outcome is important but uncertain and uncontrollable. In his study of the Trobriand Islanders in the western Pacific, Malinowski noted that when they fished in the calm, safe waters of the lagoon, where they used the reliable method of poisoning the fish, they felt no

activity2 the functions of religion

Item A The Promise Keepers

A Promise Keepers' rally in Denver, Colorado. The Promise Keepers are dedicated to introducing men to Jesus Christ.

Item C Bar Mitzvah

A Jewish boy carries the Torah, a scroll containing God's laws, during his Bar Mitzvah (initiation ceremony) at the Wailing Wall in Jerusalem.

Item B Christmas blessing

The Pope gives his annual Christmas blessing in St Peter's Square.

question

How might the activities shown in Items A, B and C reinforce the collective consciousness and strengthen social solidarity?

need for religious ritual. But, when they fished beyond the barrier reef in the open sea, where success and even survival were much less certain, fishing was preceded by rituals. Again, Malinowski suggested the use of religious ritual increases people's sense of control, diminishes anxiety and unifies the group (Malinowski, 1954).

Talcott Parsons – religion and 'problems of meaning'

Another influential interpretation of religion in the functionalist tradition was developed by Talcott Parsons (1965). In his view, religion is the primary source of meaning for members of a society. In addition, it provides and legitimises the core values of a culture and thereby promotes social solidarity and stability.

Religion provides meaning by furnishing answers to the 'eternal' questions about humanity and the world, such as those concerning suffering, justice and death. Why do people suffer? Why do villains prosper? Why do some people die at an early age? Often there appears no justice in such happenings. As a result, they threaten to undermine people's sense that life has meaning. Yet religion offers answers. Suffering tests a person's faith, punishes them for their sins and gives dignity to those who struggle on in the face of adversity. Villains get their just desserts in the afterlife, and so on. By providing explanations of events –

particularly those which threaten our sense of meaning – religion makes sense of the apparently meaningless, helps people adjust to their situation, and promotes social stability.

Religion also provides core values and norms, which it sacralises (makes sacred) and legitimises. For instance, Parsons argues that Protestantism in the United States encouraged and sacralised values such as individualism, democracy, self-discipline and equality of opportunity. Religion also sacralises and supports the web of norms which are derived from such values – norms such as universal access to legal rights and life-chances and the formal separation of the state and religion. So, by establishing and legitimising values and social norms, religion further promotes the social consensus which Parsons argues is essential for order and stability in society.

key terms

Core values The central values of society.
Life crises Events which are common to most people, which can disrupt both their lives and the wider society – for example, birth, puberty, marriage and death.

activity3 further functions of religion

Item A Individual and social stress

Soldiers of the Irish Guards praying during the Gulf War, 2003

Item B The problem of meaning

Funeral of Princess Diana, 1997

Buddhism

'Bad human beings think it is to their advantage to prevail over their fellow men, to use any method which seems expedient, no matter how cruel, in order to achieve this advantage. The advantage will not last – the methods used only create more problems, more suffering, more mistrust, more resentment, more division. The result is not good for anyone.'

'Better it were to swallow a ball of iron, red-hot and flaming, than to lead a wicked and unrestrained life eating the food of the people!'

Christianity

'You who oppress the poor and crush the destitute, the Lord has sworn by his holiness that your time is coming.'

Judaism

'The righteous suffer for the sins of their generation.'

Hinduism

'Great souls who have become one with Me have reached the highest goal. They do not undergo re-birth, a condition which is impermanent and full of pain and suffering.'

Islam

'Or do you think that you shall enter the Garden (paradise) without such trials as came to those who passed away before you?'
'For those nearest to God will come rest and satisfaction and a garden of delights, and peace. But if you are one of those who have gone wrong, then your entertainment will be boiling water and hellfire. Truly, this is the absolute truth and certain.'

Adapted from Cole, 1991

questions

1 Malinowski argued that certain situations threaten psychological and social stability. Using the examples in Item A, show how religion might function to reduce this threat.

2 According to Talcott Parsons there are situations which can make life appear meaningless. Using Item B,

a) Give examples of these situations.
b) Show how religion addresses them.
c) Suggest how, in doing so, religion contributes to the wellbeing of the individual and society.

Robert Bellah – civil religion

Durkheim's interpretation of religion's traditional function – to bind together members of a society by encouraging awareness of their common membership of an entity greater then themselves – was largely based on an analysis of small-scale, pre-industrial societies. However, it may still provide a powerful insight into the collective rituals of people in modern societies.

The concept of *civil religion* was popularised in sociology by the American Robert Bellah (1967), who drew upon the ideas of both Durkheim and Parsons. Parsons had argued that Americans were unified by values and orientations derived from Protestantism, such as individualism and self-discipline. Durkheim's insight – that any human group may be unified by a shared system of 'sacred' beliefs and practices – led Bellah to conclude that, despite America's social divisions, what largely unified them was an overarching 'civil' religion: a faith in Americanism. Unlike the 'conventional' religions of Catholicism, Protestantism and Judaism, which are unable to claim the allegiance of all Americans, civil religion generates widespread loyalty to the nation state. And, though a nation's civil religion would not necessarily involve supernatural beliefs, in American civil religion, Bellah argues, it does.

God and Americanism appear to walk hand in hand. American coins tell the world 'In God We Trust', American Presidents swear an oath of allegiance before God, and the phrase 'God Bless America' ends speeches given by dignitaries across the USA. This is not the particular God of Catholics, Protestants or Jews – it has a more general

application as 'America's God'. In this respect, the faith in Americanism helps to unite the American people.

Does the UK have a civil religion?

According to Gerald Parsons (2002), 'the most widespread and visible expression of British civil religion' is probably the events and ceremonies which annually surround Remembrance Sunday – the Sunday closest to November 11th, on which day, in 1918, the armistice ended the appallingly bloody First World War. On that Sunday, in thousands of communities across the country, people gather to remember and honour those killed in all of Britain's wars since that 'Great War'. And at the Cenotaph in Whitehall, London, the royal family leads the nation's official, nationally broadcast, act of remembrance. The previous evening, there is a now-traditional Festival of Remembrance at the Royal Albert Hall, also televised, 'culminating in the emotional intensity of the descent of a million poppy petals on the heads of a new generation of young servicemen and women' (Parsons, 2002). Millions wear red or white poppies and observe a short period of silence at 11am. Taken together, such rituals and symbols function 'as a means of transcending divisions and unifying what might otherwise be a deeply divided national community' (Parsons, 2002).

Clearly, in the UK, the monarchy has provided a focus for sentiments of what may be called civil religion. This has perhaps been most evident at times of war and national threat – for example, when King George VI and Queen Elizabeth the Queen Mother went walkabout in bomb-blasted, Second World War London. However, changes in attitude towards the royal family raise questions about the extent to which the monarchy is now capable of playing such a role.

James Beckford (2003) recognises that there are occasions when the nation is drawn together by rituals and observances such as the funeral of Princess Diana in 1997 and the Queen's Golden Jubilee in 2002. However, he believes 'it is doubtful that these occasions can compensate for the UK's deep social divisions and high rate of religious diversity and indifference. If the country has a civil religion, it is at best occasional – and at worst weak.'

activity4 civil religion in America

Item A Symbols of Americanism

A modern commemoration of a wagon train heading West

In the 19th century there was a vast migration to new lands in the West. Many migrants travelled in wagon trains, pushing back the American frontier and opening up new land to White settlement. These 'heroic treks' are pictured in books, paintings and on postage stamps, featured in films and commemorated in statues. Sometimes the 'virgin territory' of the West is pictured as the 'promised land' and the settlers as the 'chosen people'.

The Lincoln Memorial, Washington DC

Every American knows the story of Abraham Lincoln who was born in a log cabin and rose from these humble origins to live in the White House as President of the United States before dying from an assassin's bullet in 1865. Pictured on coins, sculpted in marble in the Lincoln Memorial, he has become an almost mythical figure.

Item B America's national faith

While some have argued that Christianity is America's national faith, few have realised that there actually exists alongside the churches and synagogues an elaborate and well-institutionalised civil religion in America – a collection of beliefs, symbols and rituals with respect to sacred things which are an established part of American society. This religion – there seems no other word for it – while not opposed to, and indeed sharing much in common with, Christianity, is not in any specific sense Christian.

Behind this civil religion at every point lie Biblical models – the Exodus, Chosen People, Promised Land and New Jerusalem, Death and Rebirth. But it is also genuinely American and genuinely new. It has its own prophets and its own martyrs, its own sacred events and sacred places, its own solemn rituals and symbols.

Adapted from O'Toole, 1984

Item C Shrines, saints and ceremonies

Many American civil ceremonies have a marked religious quality. Memorial Day, which remembers Americans killed in war, the Fourth of July, which commemorates the American Declaration of Independence from Britain, and the anniversary of presidential inaugurations, all celebrate national values and national unity. There are national shrines such as the Lincoln Memorial in Washington DC, the birthplaces of key presidents, war memorials and other 'special' places. It is not their age or even historical significance that inspires awe and reverence, but their ability to symbolise the nation as a 'people'.

Likewise, there are sacred objects of the civil religion – especially the flag. The extent to which these ceremonies, shrines and objects are set apart as sacred can be seen in the intensity of outrage at inappropriate behaviour or 'desecration'. Some people were arrested during the 1960s for wearing or displaying a copy of the American flag improperly, for example, on the seat of their pants.

American civil religion also has its myths and saints. Lincoln is an historical figure who particularly symbolises the civil religion, and his life from humble birth to martyrdom, typifies its values. Other 'saints' include key presidents such as Washington and Kennedy, folk heroes such as Davy Crockett, who died in 1836 fighting for Texan independence from Mexico, and military heroes such as Eisenhower, commander-in-chief of the Allied Armies in World War Two, who defended democracy and freedom against the fascist governments of Germany and Italy. Similarly, there are stories that enshrine American values such as individual achievement and upward social mobility. Lincoln's story of log cabin to White House is one. So is Davy Crockett's earlier history when, after years of hunting bears and fighting Indians on the frontier, he was elected to Congress where he was known as the 'Coonskin Congressman'. Socially important myths include America as the land of plenty, unlimited social mobility, economic consumption and achievement.

While these shrines, saints and ceremonies are not religious in the same sense as, for example, Greek Orthodox shrines, saints and ceremonies, they are still set apart as special and not to be profaned.

Adapted from McGuire, 1981

questions

1 Read Items A and B.
   a) How are the symbols of Americanism linked to Biblical models? Why might this make them more effective?
   b) Why have the wagon train and Abraham Lincoln become symbols of Americanism?

2 How can the symbols of Americanism in Item C be seen as 'religious'?

3 What are the social functions of civic religion in America?

Functionalist views – an evaluation

Positive functions From a functionalist perspective, religion is good for society and good for individuals. It performs positive functions for society – reinforcing social solidarity and value consensus – and for the individual – reducing anxiety and stress. This emphasis on positive functions ignores the many examples of religion as a negative force – as an instrument of oppression – and as a divisive force – conflict between Catholics and Protestants in Northern Ireland being a case in point.

The origins of religion Functionalism fails to explain the origins of social institutions. Where does religion come from, how did it arise in the first place? Identifying the functions of religion does not necessarily tell us anything about its origins.

Religion today Durkheim examined religion in small-scale, non-literate societies. Today's large-scale, complex societies usually contain a variety of different religions – a situation known as *religious pluralism*. It is difficult to see how religion can perform its traditional functions of reinforcing social solidarity and value consensus in modern societies with a plurality of religions.

The idea of civil religion gets round this problem. Robert Bellah (1967) makes a strong case for civil religion providing social unity and integration in societies characterised by religious pluralism. But is civil religion really religion? Does it involve worship and the supernatural? Can Abraham Lincoln and Davy Crockett be compared to saints in the Catholic Church? This brings us back to the problems of defining religion outlined in Section 1.1.

1.3 Marxist views of religion

In contrast to consensus or functionalist perspectives, Marxist theories are sometimes known as *conflict theories*. This is because they see a basic conflict of interest between the two main classes in industrial society – the capitalist or ruling class, and proletariat or subject class. From a Marxist perspective, religion is one of the institutions which maintains capitalist rule – it is an instrument of domination and oppression which keeps the proletariat in its place.

For Marx, people's religious beliefs reflect their *alienation*. In pre-communist societies, people are alienated or cut off from their work, from the products of their work and from each other. For example, in capitalist societies, they work for capitalists rather than for themselves. They do not own the products of their labour, and they work as individual wage earners rather than with each other for the benefit of the community. They have little control over their work and are exploited and oppressed by the capitalist ruling class.

Religious beliefs and practices arise in response to, and as a protest against, people's lack of control of their destiny and their dehumanisation and oppression. In a much-quoted passage, Marx argues that religion is both 'the expression of real distress and the protest against real distress. It is the sigh of the oppressed creature, the heart of a heartless world, just as it is the spirit of a spiritless situation. It is the opium of the people.'

In Marx's view, 'Man makes religion, religion does not make man. In other words, religion is the self-consciousness and self-feeling of man who has either not yet found himself or has already lost himself again.' Truly liberated individuals have no need of religion. Thus, if the alienation and exploitation associated with classes are eradicated, and people are freed to develop their human potential and 'find themselves', religion will no longer be needed and will cease to exist.

Religion and ideology Although religion represents a protest against a dehumanising social world and human alienation, it leads people in a false direction – the hopes and 'solutions' it promises are illusory. Religion, for Marx, is part of *ideology* – a pattern of beliefs which obscures and distorts the true nature of reality in ways which benefit the ruling class. Insofar as members of subject classes accept religious ideas, they suffer *false consciousness*. Thus, although religious ideas appear to express social consensus, those ideas are essentially tools in the domination of one class by another.

Religion and social control The argument that religion functions to maintain ruling class domination may be developed in a number of ways. First, religion distorts reality by encouraging the belief that people are dependent upon supernatural beings or sacred powers. For example, the belief that events are controlled by supernatural powers means there is little people can do to change their situation, apart from trying to influence the supernatural powers by prayer, sacrifice or some other means. In this way, religion obscures the human authorship of, and responsibility for, social inequality and thereby discourages the realisation that working for social change may be possible and desirable.

Second, religion often appears to lend sacred support to the current social order, and in so doing reinforces prohibitions against actions which would challenge those in power. Thus, in his letter to Christians in Rome, St Paul wrote:

'Let every soul be subject unto the higher powers. For there is no power but of God: the powers that be are ordained of God.'

'Whosoever therefore resisteth the power, resisteth the ordinance of God: and they that resist shall receive to themselves damnation.'

(*Romans*, Ch13, vs 1-2)

Likewise, in medieval Europe, the Church taught that the various unequal 'estates of the realm' – monarch, barons and bishops, knights, freemen and serfs – were God's creation. This meant that attempts to change the social order would not only be acts of treason against the monarch, but also a rejection of God's plan, punishable by eternal damnation.

In modern capitalist societies, however, in which change, innovation and high rates of social mobility are required for the success of capitalist enterprises, such religious teachings have been largely abandoned. Nevertheless, it can still be argued that mainstream religion continues to legitimise privilege and inequality – by giving its blessing to rituals involving royalty, such as the Coronation, and by the continuing presence in the House of Lords of the Archbishops and Bishops of the Church of England. Indeed, the relationship between the supernatural, inequality and national wellbeing may be neatly summarised in the phrase 'God, Queen and Country'.

Religion as compensation While religion operates primarily as a means of social control for the exploiters, for the exploited it has psychological functions as a source of solace and compensation for the misery of their alienation. So, where Durkheim sees religion as an expression and celebration of people's solidarity, Marx sees it as a consolation for experience which lacks the genuine solidarity of which people are capable.

The specific compensations religion offers vary. In Christianity, Judaism and Islam, for example, religion offers the fantasy escape of heavenly rewards – and, in Christianity, the intriguing promise that the poor would have less difficulty gaining access to heaven than the wealthy. In Hinduism and Buddhism, followers are taught that life may be better in later incarnations.

Many religions offer their followers hope by promising supernatural intervention into human affairs. In the religious history of the Jews, for instance, God is believed to have intervened many times to assist or protect his chosen people – as in parting the Red Sea to allow the Jews to escape their Egyptian pursuers.

According to Marx, religion promises happiness, but the happiness it promises is an illusion. True happiness and fulfilment are possible only when the exploited shake off the chains of their oppression and seize and practice their freedom.

key terms

Alienation A key Marxist idea which states that the nature of work in capitalist society cuts the worker off from themselves, from others, from their work and what they produce.
Ideology As used by Marx, a pattern of beliefs which obscures and distorts the true nature of reality in ways which benefit the ruling class.
False consciousness Seeing the world in terms of ideology, which presents a false picture of reality.

1.4 Neo-Marxist interpretations of religion

For Marx, religion, as part of the superstructure of society, is largely shaped by the infrastructure or economic base. As such, it reflects the interests of those who own and control the economy – the ruling class. Some neo-Marxists ('new' Marxists) have modified this view.

Antonio Gramsci

One of the most influential figures in the neo-Marxist reassessment of religion is the Italian, Antonio Gramsci. He rejected the traditional Marxist view that the cultural superstructure merely reflected society's economic base. In his view, the superstructure is more autonomous and independent than Marx acknowledged, and beliefs are no less real or important than economic forces.

For Gramsci, if the communist age were to come, it would require proletarian (working-class) action. But this action must be guided by theoretical ideas. And, just as intellectuals of the Roman Catholic Church had shaped the minds of its followers over centuries, so must the industrial working class produce its own intellectuals who can articulate working-class experience and help shape working-class consciousness.

activity5 monarch and God

Item A The divine right of monarchy

Henry IV at his coronation in 1399 receiving a blessing from archbishops

'Kings are called Gods by the prophet David because they sit on God's throne on earth. Kings exercise divine power on earth. They have the power of life and death, they are judges over all their subjects and yet are accountable to none but God only.'
James 1, King of England from 1603-1625.

Medieval monarchs ruled by divine right – they were seen to have a God-given right to rule. Although modern British monarchs no longer claim divine right, Elizabeth II's coronation in 1953 was in many ways similar to that of Henry IV. She too was crowned and blessed by archbishops.

questions

1 Analyse the information in Item A from a Marxist view.

2 Why does Birnbaum (Item B) argue that it is 'the very absence of shared values in Great Britain' which accounted for the attention paid to the Coronation?

3 How and why, in Birnbaum's view, did the press encourage false class consciousness through their coverage of the Coronation?

Item B The Coronation of Queen Elizabeth II

Queen Elizabeth II shortly after she was crowned by the Archbishop of Canterbury in Westminster Abbey, 1953

Although it is often assumed that there is a moral consensus in society, and that this consensus is personified in the person of the monarch, our evidence shows that societies like our own are arenas for conflicts of belief and moral standards unmatched in history.

I would argue that it was the very absence of shared values in Great Britain which accounts for some of the attention paid to the Coronation. The Coronation provided, for some sections of the populace, some measure of respite and relief from that condition of conflict which is more or less permanent for complex societies of a capitalist type.

From this viewpoint, the role of the press in stirring up popular enthusiasm for the Coronation is understandable. In response to the class interests it generally represents, the press continually seeks to minimise awareness of the real conflicts characteristic of British society. In this context, the personality of the Queen and her family functioned as the object of various fantasies and identifications in a way not much more 'sacred' than the cult of adulation built up around certain film stars. But the tawdry baubles of the Coronation celebration constitute no adequate substitute for the lost faith of millions.

Adapted from Birnbaum, 1955

As an Italian, Gramsci was well aware of the control over consciousness which the Catholic Church had traditionally exercised over its members. This control he referred to as *hegemony*. He was highly critical of what he regarded as the Church's characteristic subservience to the state and ruling-class interests. Nevertheless, he did not assume that religion must inevitably play such a role. He argued that, at different historical times, popular forms of religion had emerged which expressed and supported the interests of oppressed classes. Thus, he accepted the possibility that religious beliefs and practices could develop and be popularised, particularly by working-class intellectuals, to challenge the dominant ruling class ideology and support

working class consciousness and liberation.

Otto Maduro

The possibility that religion may play a progressive role in the political struggles of oppressed classes has been taken up by a number of modern Marxists, including Otto Maduro (1982). Writing about developing countries, Maduro argues that, in societies in which religion remains a dominant and conservative institution, social liberation can only be achieved if significant change occurs within the churches. This could occur if the oppressed, finding that all possible forms of protest are blocked by the central power, take their discontent to the churches – as in certain

Latin American societies, in South Africa, and in Poland before the abandonment of communism. In this situation, Maduro argues, the anguish and aspirations of the oppressed may be reflected and voiced by members of the clergy. Thus, the clergy may then fulfil the functions of Gramsci's proletarian intellectuals, by expressing the discontents of the oppressed, by shaping their consciousness of the situation, and by working with them to devise strategies of action. Evidence to support this view is given in Activity 6.

Marxist views – an evaluation

Religion as ideology Marx saw religion as a form of ideology which helped to maintain ruling class power. Critics agree there is evidence to support this view from certain times and places. However, they reject the claim that this is the primary role of religion.

To some extent, neo-Marxists avoid this criticism by admitting the possibility that religion can open the eyes of the oppressed to the reality of their situation. And this, in turn, can encourage them to take action to end their oppression.

Religion as compensation Is religion simply a compensation for oppression, a crutch which helps people to live with their situation, a balm for their wounds and a drug to give them false happiness? Again, there is plenty of evidence that can be used to support this view.

But, critics argue that this is a very one-sided view – that there is a lot more to religion than compensation. For

example, as Parsons states, religion can give meaning to and make sense of birth and death – events which affect *all* people in *all* societies.

Marxism and values To some extent, the reader must 'buy into' Marxist value judgements to fully accept Marxist views. Capitalism, and the class societies which went before, are seen as unjust and evil. Communism is the ideal society – a society in which social classes disappear, oppression ends and, as a result, religion disappears. However, there are plenty of examples of religion thriving in the communist societies of the 20th century – for instance, Poland under communism was a strongly Roman Catholic country.

Advantages of Marxism Despite these criticisms, Marxism has provided important insights. Religion has often supported the interests of the powerful. It has often provided solace and comfort for the oppressed. It has often been influenced by economic factors. And Marxism has provided a useful balance for functionalist perspectives which have tended to take a one-sided view of religion as a positive force in society.

key term

Hegemony The dominance of a ruling group exercised not only by political and economic control, but also by beliefs and ideas.

activity6 liberation theology

Item A Liberating the poor

Liberation theology is a religious justification for the liberation of oppressed peoples. It developed in Latin America in the 1950s and 60s as an alternative to the standard view of the West's duties towards the Third World. It criticised the view that the West could end the poverty of the Third World by transferring economic resources from one to the other. The theology of liberation said that, far from being the passive objects of aid, it was essential that the poor take control of their situation and accept the responsibility for ending their poverty.

That meant understanding their own condition and the reasons for it, and responding accordingly. In liberation theology's purest form, the sort the Vatican was most worried about, those conditions and the reasons for them are analysed in Marxist terms, and so is the remedy.

What the theology of liberation has to say is that the only escape from poverty which does justice to human dignity is that engineered and struggled for by the poor themselves.

Adapted from Longley, 1986

Item B Father Camilo Torres

Father Camilo Torres was a Roman Catholic priest in Colombia in South America. The vast majority of Colombian people are desperately poor. Sixty-five per cent of the land is owned by a handful of powerful families. Father Torres believed this was unjust – his solution was a Christian revolution. In his words: 'Revolution is necessary to feed the hungry, give drink to the thirsty, clothe the naked and procure a life of wellbeing for the needy majority of our people. I believe that the revolutionary struggle is appropriate for the Christian and the priest. Only by revolution, by changing the concrete conditions of our country, can we enable men to practise love for each other.'

The Catholic Church did not support Torres. Believing that the government would crush peaceful protest, he joined a guerrilla movement. Torres was killed fighting government forces in 1966. The peasants saw him as a martyr and in 1968 many priests followed his example and pledged their support for revolutionary struggle against the state.

Adapted from Jenkins, 1987

Item C *Archbishop Romero*

Mourners in El Salvador gather round the corpse of Archbishop Romero. He was shot dead in his cathedral in 1980 by four gunmen, allegedly members of a right-wing death squad. Archbishop Romero was a champion of social and economic reforms to improve the lot of the poor.

Item D *Father Rogelio Cruz*

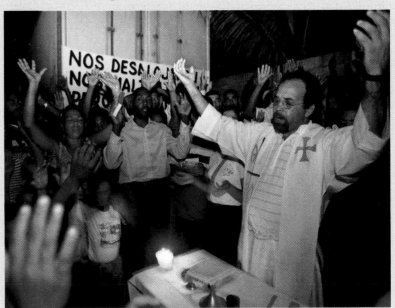

Father Rogelio Cruz, a Catholic priest, leads 200 families, left homeless in December when police bulldozed a squatters' village, in a nightly protest mass at a temporary tent camp in Santo Domingo, Dominican Republic, 2000.

questions

1 'Liberation theology sounds like a Christian version of Marxism.' Comment on this statement.

2 Use the information in this activity to assess the differing views of Marx and Maduro on the role of religion in society. Does the information disprove Marx's view?

1.5 Feminist views of religion

There are several versions of feminism, but they have a number of things in common. Most use *patriarchy* as a key idea. This refers to a social system which is organised for the benefit of males, a system in which male dominance is supported by beliefs, values and norms.

Many feminists claim that religion is a patriarchal institution. Teachings and practices from a range of religions suggest that they systematically benefit males over females. Here are some of the main feminist concerns.

The sacred texts

- In almost all the world religions, the gods are male. Hinduism comes closest to being an exception, with its female goddesses.

- The sacred texts overwhelmingly feature males and male activity.

- They were also written, and have been interpreted, by males. They incorporate many traditional male stereotypes and biases. For instance:

1) In the creation story (shared by Judaism and Christianity) God created Adam and then 'the fowl of the air' and 'the beasts of the field'. Only later did he decide to create Eve, as a 'helpmate' for Adam, observing that 'It is not good that the man should be alone'. And, as is well known, Eve was created out of one of Adam's ribs.

2) Having been commanded by God not to eat the fruit from the 'tree of the knowledge of good and evil', it was Eve whom the serpent persuaded to disregard God's command. Having also fed it to Adam, Eve and he both then experienced sin and shame and covered their naked bodies (*Genesis*, Ch.2, v.15-Ch.3 v.7).

3) In the Christian tradition, the two central women – the Virgin Mary and Mary Magdalene – are typical female stereotypes. The 'Holy Mother' Mary is chaste (a virgin), giving, caring, self-sacrificing, suffering. Mary Magdalene, a prostitute who became one of the few women very close to Jesus, represents woman as temptress and seductress.

Religious professionals In all world religions, the majority of religious professionals are male. In Christianity, females are not eligible to become priests in the Roman Catholic, Greek or Russian Orthodox churches, and only became eligible since 1992 in the Church of England. Nor can they become rabbis in Orthodox Judaism.

Worship In most religions, women are likely to be the main attenders. Yet their role tends to be secondary – they don't often participate actively in the service. Orthodox Jewish women, for instance, can't read from the Torah scroll or participate in symbolic actions at festivals.

Limitations and exclusions In many religions, females are limited in where they may go, both at home, and outside the home, and in centres of worship. In Orthodox Judaism, the women sit in the balconies at the back of, and above, the main space, or behind screens, so as not to distract the males. Sometimes they can't see or hear properly (Swale, 2000).

In everyday life, too, female followers of world religions are often significantly more limited than males with regards to where they can go, and with whom they may associate.

Differential treatment In a number of religions, or in cultures heavily influenced by religion, women have fewer options or receive less favourable treatment than men in daily life.

- In Western Christianity, for a significant part of its history, a wife was the property of her husband. She lost her property to him on marriage, was required to promise him life-long obedience, and was unable to divorce him.

- In some versions of Islam, the male is allowed up to four wives. In some Islamic countries, a male may divorce a wife by declaring so three times, though the female may not divorce her husband.

- In Islamic Iran, though such practices have significantly diminished since Ayatollah Khomeini was in power, females may still be flogged for dress-code violations and stoned to death for adultery. In Afghanistan, 'girls are still given away in marriage against their will, women who "dishonour" their families are routinely murdered and, although rape is widespread, offenders usually go unpunished as few women dare speak out' (Amnesty International, 2003).

- However, such inequalities are by no means found solely in some Islamic countries. They exist, too, in some predominantly Christian and Hindu cultures. For instance, in parts of (Christian) South America, (Hindu) India and the (Muslim) Middle East, sexual norms are more strict for females. Also, the transgression of such norms results in more frequent, and more severe, punishment for females than males. Moreover, such punishment is often applied unofficially – not infrequently physically, sometimes fatally – by males, who are often family members.

Feminist views – an evaluation

Goddesses According to many feminists, religion has been a major institutional means for controlling women –

perhaps, for much of history, *the* major means. Yet, in many ancient and folk religions, females have had key positions. In ancient Greek and Roman religion, for example, goddesses were neither uncommon nor unimportant. The Greek goddess Athena, for instance, was god of war, wisdom and the arts. Goddesses remain important in Hinduism. And modern followers of pagan Wicca (witchcraft) worship a goddess of the moon and of the woodlands, whom they claim was worshipped throughout Celtic Europe.

Leadership roles Religion has also been a means through which some women have developed leadership roles. In Christianity, a few have created religious faiths and organisations, some of which now number millions of followers around the world. In 19th century America, Ellen White founded the still-flourishing Seventh Day Adventist Church, and Mary Baker Eddy, the Church of Christ, Scientist (Christian Science).

Today, thousands of women around the world have assumed positions of leadership in the fast-growing Christian Pentecostal movement and in other apparently patriarchal and conservative religious movements. Moreover, these important roles – at least within the Pentecostal movement – often lead on to leadership roles in the wider community (Martin, 2003).

Freedom within religion In all religions, there are those who argue that freedom and fulfilment for women can only be found *within* a religious tradition. Evidence which may provide support for this view is provided in Activity 7.

Advantages of feminism Feminists have often been criticised for being preoccupied with gender inequality and ignoring other aspects of society. While there is some truth in this, the sharp focus of feminism does have some advantages. In terms of religion, it highlights those aspects of belief and practice which support male dominance and keep women in their place.

key term

Patriarchy A social system which systematically benefits males over females.

1.6 Weber's views on religion

Marx paid little attention to the specific religious beliefs of different groups and cultures. Durkheim based his general statements about religion on a small number of examples. The German sociologist Max Weber's studies, however, involved an ambitious series of detailed analyses of major religions – Confucianism and Taoism (in China), Hinduism and Buddhism (in India) and ancient Judaism (in Palestine). Additionally, in his most famous work, *The Protestant Ethic and the Spirit of Capitalism* first published in 1904, he analysed the influential Calvinist tradition within Christianity.

activity7 women and religion

Item A Religious leaders

Pope John Paul II

Rev. Sun Myung Moon, founder of the Unification Church (the 'Moonies')

Former Iranian leader Ayatollah Khomeini

Item B Gender roles and Orthodox Jews

Instead of the feminist programme of broader gender definitions and options, sexual liberation, an emphasis on careers, and the acceptance of a variety of family patterns, Orthodox Judaism proposed clear and firm gender norms, the control of sexuality, assistance in finding partners, and explicit guidelines for nuclear family life.

In the USA, many women were converted to Orthodox Judaism because it supported and legitimated their desires for the 'traditional' identity of wives and mothers in nuclear families. The rabbis told the recruits that women's role was highly valued in Orthodoxy and that women's primary place in the home, where a majority of the rituals took place, gave her special status within the Jewish religious world. In addition, women gained an extra benefit – strong support for a view of men's roles that placed great stress on men's involvement in the home and with their families.

Adapted from Davidman, 1991

Item C The veil

Increasing numbers of women in Islamic countries are wearing the veil in public places. At the same time, growing numbers of women are entering university and the professions and participating in life outside the home.

The veil can be seen as a restriction on their freedom. On the other hand, it can be seen as a way of making the transition into the public sphere more comfortable. From this perspective, Islamic dress can be seen as the uniform of transition.

Adapted from Ahmed, 2000

An Afghan woman in Kabul

questions

1 What support do the pictures in Item A provide for feminist views on religion?

2 How can Items B and C be used to a) support and b) criticise feminist views?

Although Weber accepted that religion often functioned to justify social inequality, as Marx had argued, he was also concerned to show that religion did not inevitably function in this conservative manner. Religion existed, he believed, because people everywhere needed a system of basic beliefs to make sense of their existence and to have a sense of their identity. Religion provided people with *meaning*. However, Weber's major argument was that societies developed differently partly because the religious beliefs and ideas about the ethical conduct of their members were different. In other words, religious beliefs and religious movements *can* help shape social change.

Calvinism and the 'spirit of capitalism'

The major question which Weber addressed in much of his writing about religion was why the capitalism which had developed in some Western countries had not also emerged in the East. He concluded that while Eastern religions, for example Hinduism and Buddhism, embodied certain key teachings and values which had discouraged the development of capitalism, Judaism and Christianity, and especially the Calvinist and Puritan varieties of Christianity, had encouraged it.

Protestantism and capitalism Weber argued that although individual greed and the pursuit of gain may be found in all societies, only in the West did entire societies develop, and come to accept, *rational capitalism* – a system which encouraged the methodical pursuit of profit by legal means, involving calculation, book-keeping and long-term planning, and which relied on the creation of free markets and a free labour force. In Weber's view, modern capitalism had been able to develop in the West, and particularly in predominantly Protestant areas, because it was compatible with the Calvinist teachings which guided many of the early Protestant movements such as the Puritans, Presbyterians, Baptists and Quakers. And it was among these movements, he argued, that capitalism flourished. It was much less compatible with religions such as Hinduism which taught that if believers accept their lot in this life and act in accordance with tradition, they will gain the reward of a higher caste position in the next life. Such beliefs discourage rational calculation and innovation and therefore the development of capitalism.

A question of salvation The most significant teaching of John Calvin (1509-64) was that of *predestination*. According to this doctrine, even before their birth, God has selected some for *salvation* and others for eternal damnation. Neither the saved nor the damned could influence the decision, either by the strength of their faith or by their earthly actions. And moreover, no-one could be sure whether he or she had been pre-selected for heaven or for hell.

Such terrifying beliefs could well have driven followers into an attitude of helpless fatalism, resignation and inactivity. Instead, Weber argued, the 'salvation anxiety' with which they were plagued, provoked the opposite response. Despite Calvin's teaching that people's behaviour could not influence God's decision, some followers developed doctrines which held out a measure of hope that individuals could discover reassuring 'signs' that they were among those chosen for salvation.

Work as a 'calling' While none could be sure of their salvation, all were required to pursue an intensely active life of labour. Work was a 'calling', and God was most effectively worshipped through a rigorously disciplined life of work, and a denial of indulgence. Any activity which unnecessarily detracted from work was evil. Mere socialising, sleeping longer than strictly necessary, or even religious contemplation if it interfered with a person's daily labours, were regarded as sins, for they detracted from the active performance of God's will. But if a person's work was rewarded with material success, this may be a sign of God's grace and indicate that they were among the elect – that they had been chosen by God for salvation.

Thus, to cope with the chronic anxiety of damnation, Calvinists energetically threw themselves into highly disciplined economic activity and a lifetime of 'good works'. Those in business pursued profit and wealth, not as ends in themselves, but as Christian obligations to make the best use of their God-given gifts and talents and as indications of God's favour. And, because they were limited in how they could spend their wealth – they could not 'waste' it on expensive 'luxuries' – they tended to save and reinvest in their businesses.

According to Weber, the Calvinist idea of the calling affected not just the employer but also the worker. For capitalism to take root, drastic changes were needed in the attitudes of workers who traditionally were concerned merely to earn the wage necessary to meet their modest expectations and otherwise to spend their time in leisure. The Calvinist notion of the calling transformed the traditional, easy-going, undisciplined workforce into 'sober, conscientious, and unusually industrious workmen, who clung to their work as to a life purpose willed by God' (Weber, 1958). Thus, the Protestant ethic encouraged not merely the 'spirit of capitalism' but a new 'spirit of labour' as well, without which the spirit of capitalism could not have been translated into action.

Religion and rationality In these ways, Weber concluded, Calvin's influential religious teachings, popularised and interpreted by generations of Puritan successors, had significant, though unintended, consequences for the economic system of capitalism. For, alone among the teachings of the world's major religions, they encouraged among believers a rational, calculating, efficient and highly committed approach to work which provided capitalism with a fertile soil in which to take root. And it is the growth of *rationality* which provides a key, perhaps *the* key, to understanding the nature of modern societies.

In developing his argument about the significance of Calvinist teachings for the development of capitalism, Weber believed that he had successfully challenged Marx's somewhat deterministic view that religious ideas merely reflect a society's economic base. Weber was careful to make clear that he was not claiming that Calvinism was the sole cause of capitalism – he acknowledged that, even in countries with a significant Calvinist population, such as Scotland or Switzerland, capitalism would not develop if economic conditions were not right (for example, if there was a shortage of skilled labour or investment capital, as was the case in Scotland). Nevertheless, he could reasonably claim to have demonstrated that religious beliefs can have a significant role in influencing a society's economic system and development.

Evaluation of Weber's argument

Which came first, Calvinism or capitalism? There are a number of challenges to Weber's argument. The most central is the challenge to Weber's claim that Calvinism preceded capitalism. Eisenstadt (1967) argues that the first great upsurges of capitalism occurred in Catholic Europe – in Italy, Belgium and Germany – *before* the Protestant Reformation. The historian Tawney (1938) claims that society had already changed radically, in a capitalist direction, before the advent of Calvinism. New technologies had been invented and introduced, a capitalist class had emerged and new ways of viewing society had developed. In this view, as Calvinism emerged, it was adopted by the rising capitalist class and, with some changes in emphasis, provided a religious justification for a rational capitalism which was already established and developing.

Other religions and capitalism Another important criticism, voiced by some writers on Hinduism and Islam, is that Weber misunderstood those religions and failed to recognise the many elements in them which could have been supportive of rational economic action. Weber has also been criticised for underestimating the capitalist spirit of the Jews. Because they were openly interested in profit, would trade in anything, would compete and try to undercut the competition, and would lend money at interest, Jews proved formidable business competitors, and were probably more capitalist than Weber suggested.

Interpreting Calvinism Doubt has also been cast on Weber's interpretation of the attitudes of influential Calvinists to wealth and the pursuit of gain. As Weber himself recognised, many Calvinist preachers taught that wealth was a great danger, providing unending temptations, and that its acquisition was morally suspect. Moreover, it is not clear why Calvinists should come to regard economic success as the major benchmark which God might use to indicate his favour. Nor is it clear why Calvinists should have had to reinvest the profits they accumulated. Could they not have been given away to the poor (for which practice there seems some scriptural support) or used to boost employees' wages?

There is also the puzzling question of why and how Calvinism was able to attract converts – or, even more baffling, succeed as a major religious movement. As depicted by Weber, Calvinism had little to offer its followers. It did not promise them salvation and made it

disconcertingly clear that membership made not the slightest difference to their prospects either in this life or the next.

Conclusion The debate about the relationship between Calvinism and capitalism still continues. It will probably never be settled. The historical documents tell us little about the way Calvinist teachings 'were received, understood and interpreted by ordinary believers', or how they were translated into behaviour (Hamilton, 2001).

key terms

Predestination The idea that people's destination after death is predetermined by God.
Salvation The saving of the soul and its admission to heaven.
Protestant ethic Moral beliefs based on Protestantism which led to self-denying, self-disciplined lives of labour which, in turn, encouraged the development of capitalism.
Rationality Action directed by reason rather than emotion or tradition.

1.7 An interpretivist view of religion

Peter Berger – religion, rationalisation and 'the problem of modernity'

Rationalisation Weber's analysis of Calvinist Protestantism forms an important part of a broader argument. Weber believed that the modern world was characterised by a process of *rationalisation*. This involved systematically working towards a clearly defined goal by precisely calculating the way to reach that goal. This can be seen in the rise of capitalism which emphasised rational calculation in business activity and rationally organised work practices in order to maximise efficiency and profit. In particular, it can be seen in the spread of bureaucracy, the characteristic institution of modern society. Bureaucratic institutions are rational – they systematically and efficiently organise people in order to attain particular goals.

Weber believed that rationalisation has its costs. Reason replaces faith, and the support which faith provides disappears. This leads to disillusionment, to *disenchantment*. The world is 'demystified', its richness, mystery and magic taken away. It now appears cold. And social relationships, particularly in bureaucratic settings, become increasingly impersonal.

These themes have been taken up since the 1960s by the Austrian-born American sociologist Peter Berger. Berger's main concern has been with what he calls 'modernity' – in particular, with questions of how changes in social structure and social interaction in modern society are experienced by individuals, and how they strive to create a meaningful reality. He takes an interpretivist approach, seeking to discover the meanings which people impose upon the world in order to make sense of it.

activity8 the protestant ethic

Item A A pre-capitalist view

It is much sweeter to spend money than to earn it. I think that I have done more by having spent money well than by having earned it. Spending gave me a deeper satisfaction, especially the money I spent on my house in Florence.

(An example, from a medieval Florentine, of a pre-capitalist attitude towards money).

Item B The Protestant ethic

From a pamphlet published in 1653. Father Christmas is driven out of town by a Puritan.

A Puritan family meal in the early 17th century. Their dress is simple and their food is plain. The children are standing at the table to eat their food. This was considered good discipline by Puritan parents.

The Godly and hardworking man shall have prosperity, but he that follows pleasures shall have much sorrow. Don't be too concerned about being popular and sociable – it can waste a lot of valuable time.

(John Browne, a 16th century Protestant)

Even if you are called to the poorest labouring job, do not complain because it is wearisome, nor imagine that God thinks any the less of you. But cheerfully follow it, and make it your pleasure and joy that you are still in your heavenly master's services, though it be the lowest thing.

(Richard Baxter, a prominent 17th century English Puritan)

Items A and B quoted in Kitch, 1967

Religion must necessarily produce hard work and discourage the wasting of money. We must encourage all Christians to gain what they can and to save all they can – that is, in effect, to grow rich.

(John Wesley, 1703-1791, English founder of Methodism)

Quoted in Weber, 1958

questions

1 Read Item A. How does this view differ from Calvinist attitudes?

2 a) What attitudes, identified by Weber as characteristic of Calvinism, are expressed in Item B?

   b) Using Weber's argument, show how these attitudes could encourage the growth of capitalism.

Berger begins by elaborating on Weber's argument that Protestantism has played a unique role in rationalising attitudes and social structures, particularly in the spread of bureaucracy. And, like Weber, he believes that the process of rationalisation, encouraged by Protestantism, has tended to 'demystify' the modern world and has led to modern people's 'disenchantment of the world'.

Plurality of life-worlds The spread of rationalisation – and associated disenchantment – Berger argues, has been accompanied by other changes in the conditions and experiences of people in modern societies. Significantly, the high levels of social and geographical mobility, combined with widespread exposure to the electronic media, have given people an unprecedented awareness of alternative social worlds, lifestyles and belief systems. As a result, each person's life-world has become pluralised. It is no longer a single, unified and integrated world. Instead it is fragmented and diverse.

Homelessness In this situation, traditional religion is plunged into a crisis of credibility as individuals are faced with any number of competing belief systems and ways of living. In today's pluralistic and multicultural societies, each religion becomes one among many. It becomes increasingly difficult to maintain that *any* religion has a monopoly of truth. And all religions have to compete with a rapidly growing diversity of secular belief systems. This undermines traditional religious teachings, it erodes past certainties about morality and people's identity, it encourages a sense of meaninglessness. The result is *anomie* or loss of confidence in the norms, whereby people lack direction and guides to action. Using Berger's

term, people are 'homeless', cut off from traditional supports and comfort and sense of self, all of which made them feel 'at home'. And religion – whose main function, Berger believes, has been as a shield against anomie – has been rendered largely impotent. It no longer has the power to give meaning to life.

activity9 problems of modernity

Item A Social diversity

Christian belltowers and a Muslim mosque in Bethlehem

People at Respect Festival, 2001

Item B Homelessness

Many of the discontents of modern society stem from the pluralisation of social life-worlds. These discontents can be characterised as 'homelessness'. The pluralistic structures of modern society have made the life of more and more individuals migratory, ever-changing, mobile. Not only are an increasing number of individuals in a modern society uprooted from their original social settings, but, in addition, no subsequent setting succeeds in becoming truly 'home' either. A world in which everything is in constant motion is a world in which certainties of any kind are hard to come by. The age-old function of religion – to provide ultimate certainty – has been severely shaken.

The problem becomes most clearly apparent when one looks at that ancient religious function which Weber called 'theodicy'. This means any explanation of human events that gives meaning to the experiences of suffering and evil. Modern society has threatened the plausibility of religious theodicies, but it has not removed the experiences that call for them. Human beings continue to be stricken by sickness and death. They continue to experience social injustice and deprivation. What modernity has accomplished is to seriously weaken those definitions of reality that previously made the human condition easier to bear. This has produced an anguish all its own.

Adapted from Berger, Berger & Kellner, 1974

questions

1 a) With reference to Items A and B, explain what you understand by the 'pluralisation of social life-worlds'.

b) What sort of 'discontents' may pluralisation encourage?

2 How might the pluralisation of social life-worlds undermine religion?

1.8 Postmodernism and religion

A number of sociologists have tried to identify the main developments in human society. Some distinguish between *premodern society* and today's *modern society*. Others believe we have moved beyond modernity and are now living in *postmodern society*.

Sociologists who take this view are known as *postmodernists* and the theory they have developed is known as *postmodernism*.

Postmodern society

Sociologists have identified various characteristics of postmodern society. They include:

ICT The development and spread of information and communication technology (ICT), including television and the Internet. As a result of this development, people are increasingly exposed to images, ideas and information from around the world.

Consumerism The growth of consumerism – buying goods and services is becoming increasingly central to people's lives. What we buy says who we are. A range of branded goods from Nike trainers to Gucci sunglasses and Armani fragrance allows us to select items to fit our chosen identities.

Movement of people Mass travel and migration – people are increasingly exposed to different societies and different ways of life. Countries are becoming more and more multicultural.

Risk and uncertainty A sense of growing social and environmental risk. People's lives are increasingly insecure. Few can look forward to a job for life. Relationships are more at risk as the rise in divorce indicates. And with global warming and worldwide pollution, the environment we live in appears increasingly dangerous and uncertain.

Globalisation We live in an increasingly global society. The boundaries between nation states are breaking down with transnational organisations, such as the European Union, and transnational companies, like the Ford Motor Company, Nestlé and Coca-Cola. Interaction between nation states becomes more frequent and intense as goods, capital, people, brands, images, fashions and beliefs flow across national boundaries.

The cultural impact

Postmodernists believe that the changes outlined above have had a major impact on the culture of societies in the postmodern age. According to David Lyon (2000), this involves changes in people's attitude to *authority*, to their sense of *identity*, and to their ideas of *time* and *space*.

Authority According to Lyotard (1984), postmodern culture is characterised by a widespread loss of confidence in the grand explanations – the 'big stories' or *metanarratives* – traditionally provided by science, religion and politics. People are less likely to accept that there are absolute truths, whether religious, scientific or political. And, along with an increased pessimism that science and reason will provide solutions, comes a declining confidence in the inevitability of *progress*. Thus, sources previously regarded as authoritative, such as the scientific community, the clergy and politicians, are regarded with increasing scepticism.

To some extent, these developments are consequences of the global spread of information, which exposes growing numbers to competing interpretations of 'reality', and claims to the truth. As diverse worldviews – religious, ethnic, political, scientific – penetrate societies around the globe, knowledge in postmodern society comes to be seen as *relative*. There is no longer a single truth. It has been replaced by a multitude of truths which are relative to particular times and places.

Identity In modern society, people's identities are largely shaped by their occupation, gender, social class and nationality. In postmodern society, their identities are constructed more by personal choice. As a result, they are more fluid and flexible. However, they are also more under threat.

According to Manuel Castells (1996), this is primarily a result of the information technology revolution and globalisation. Individuals' destinies and their sense of themselves are largely at the mercy of a dynamic, globalised capitalism, which can rapidly create and destroy jobs and change communities in ways beyond political control. In this insecure, postmodern world of sudden flows of power, employment, and wealth, trying to construct an identity, either as an individual or a community, becomes of central importance (Castells, 1996).

And increasingly, according to Zygmunt Bauman (1992), individuals in postmodern societies are constructing their identities primarily through what they choose to *consume*. As David Lyon (2000) puts it, 'self-esteem and our recognition by others may be purchased over the counter'.

Time and space Postmodern society has seen a restructuring of time and space. Distance no longer provides a barrier to communication – people can talk to or email each other almost instantly across the world. This provides immediate access to cultures, practices, ideas and belief systems which were once remote and inaccessible.

Postmodernity and religion

Postmodern society has resulted in:

- A decline of previously dominant religious organisations
- A growth of fundamentalism in all world religions
- The spread of new types of religious organisations, movements and networks.

The decline of dominant religious organisations Modernity is associated with authoritative institutions which provide a metanarrative in which to believe. In modernity, the metanarratives of the world religions were transmitted via sacred texts and interpreted by highly-regarded religious authorities.

However, globalisation – in particular, the spread of people and ideas around the world – has resulted in a greatly increased exposure to rival metanarratives, including a wide range of contradictory religions and philosophies. Repeated exposure to alternative versions of the truth may undermine people's confidence in them all, and encourage a view of truth as relative. Hence, one consequence of postmodernity may be a decline in the authority of both established religious institutions and religious metanarratives. (This suggestion is discussed further on page 58.)

The rise of fundamentalism While postmodern relativism may undermine some religious institutions and diminish their support, it may at the same time encourage a counter-response. The last few decades have witnessed a rise in religious *fundamentalism* in all major world religions. For example, the worldwide membership of the Jehovah's Witnesses grew from 44,080 in 1928 to over six million in 2000. This is expected to at least double by 2020.

Fundamentalism is seen by its followers as a return to the basics or fundamentals of religion. It often involves a literal interpretation of religious texts and strict moral codes of behaviour. People tend to look to the past, to a 'golden age' of religion, and use this as a template for the present and the future.

One interpretation of the growth of fundamentalist movements such as Jehovah's Witnesses is that they offer hope, direction and certainty in a world which seems increasingly insecure, confusing and morally lost (Holden, 2002).

In poorer societies, whose traditional cultures and religions are subjected to the forces of Westernisation and globalisation, fundamentalism can also provide a defence against cultural and religious dominance. Perceiving a threat to their faith and identity, people may respond by looking backward to traditional truths. Thus, for Bauman (1992), 'fundamentalist tendencies' may 'reflect and articulate the experience of people on the receiving end of globalisation'. Similarly, Castells (1996) sees fundamentalism as a way in which people construct 'resistance identities', as globalisation undermines their traditional sense of self.

However, although fundamentalism may reject aspects of globalisation, it is not necessarily against science and technological progress. For instance, in Egypt and other Islamic societies, while conservative Islam has grown in influence in politics, law, education, and on the street, it has nevertheless embraced modern science and technology. It has stressed the 'complementary' relationship between science and Islam in its education system and in its literature (Herbert, 2001). Similarly, as Starrett (1998) notes, it has accepted many modern medical technologies (including in-vitro fertilisation, plastic surgery and birth control), as long as they are applied within certain limits. And, as Castells (1996) shows with regards to Christian, Hindu and Islamic fundamentalism, such groups are highly dependent on ICT to mobilise ideas, money and social links.

The spread of new religious movements As noted earlier, personal identity in postmodern society is increasingly constructed by individuals rather than shaped by the groups to which they belong. And identity is increasingly reflected by personal consumption – the goods and services a person chooses to buy. This emphasis on identity and consumption can be seen in people's choice of religion and the uses they make of it.

Postmodern society encourages people to select religious beliefs and practices to suit their chosen identities. Traditional religious metanarratives have lost much of their authority. As a result of travel, migration and the 'information explosion' from the new electronic media, people are exposed to a vast array of religions. Postmodern consumers are already well-prepared to select those items which appeal to them. This freedom of, and desire for, choice has led to a spread of new religious movements.

Those interested can dip in and select a 'pick and mix' assortment from the beliefs and practices on offer at the 'spiritual supermarket'. These can then be tested out to see if they 'work' for the consumer. If the experience proves rewarding, the beliefs and practices can be incorporated into the individual's identity. If not, they can be dropped.

Postmodernism – an evaluation

While accepting some of the trends identified by postmodernists, many sociologists argue that they have gone too far. Have we really entered a brand new age of postmodernity? Are all truths relative? Is fundamentalism a response to postmodern society?

The relativisation of truth Steve Bruce (2002) rejects the view that faith in science and reason is dead and all truths carry equal weight.

Although people nowadays are much more cautious about the consequences of science, for example, genetic modification and nuclear power, Bruce denies that this amounts to a wholesale rejection of the metanarrative of science and to the relativisation of thought. Not all the ways of viewing the world have become equally plausible. For instance, most still see 'a difference in kind between astronomy and astrology, or between surgery and aura healing'. And 'most practitioners of spiritual medicine defer to conventional doctors for more serious ailments' (Bruce, 2000).

Consumption and individualism Bruce (2002) accepts that greater wealth and consumer choice have allowed people to create what they see as their own particular identities. However, he criticises postmodernists for ignoring the possibility that consumers may be manipulated by advertising to purchase items of mass consumption and to see this as an expression of their individuality.

Postmodernists present a picture of individuality based on consumption – of the individual constructing their identity based on personal choice. Bruce argues that this view underestimates the power of *group* identities. For instance, social class, ethnicity, gender and age all continue to shape our identities in important ways.

key terms

Metanarratives The grand explanations or big stories of modern society provided by science, religion and political ideas.
Fundamentalism Movements within established religions which seek a return to the basic texts or beliefs – the 'fundamentals' – of religion.
Relativism The idea that there is no single or absolute truth. Truth is therefore relative.

Fundamentalism Is the growth of religious fundamentalism a response to the particular changes brought about by postmodern society? This may be the case. But fundamentalism has a long history. For example, Abdullahi An-Na'im (2003) identifies many instances of Islamic fundamentalism over the past thousand years. He sees them as a response to social, political and economic crises. As such, there is nothing particularly new about today's Islamic fundamentalism.

summary

1. Substantive definitions ask what religion is. For example, religion is a belief in the supernatural.

2. Functional definitions ask what are the functions or roles of religion in society. For example, religion strengthens social solidarity.

3. Durkheim's functionalist analysis states that religion reinforces the collective consciousness and strengthens social solidarity.

4. Malinowski argues that religion reduces the disruption caused by life crises and the anxiety produced by activities whose outcome is uncontrollable and uncertain.

5. Parsons claims that religion deals with the 'problem of meaning' by providing answers to universal questions such as why do people die unjustly. Religion also sacrilises and legitimates core values which, in turn, strengthens social consensus.

6. Bellah argues that civil religion – a faith in Americanism – unites American society.

7. For Marx, religion reflects the alienation and exploitation of class-based society. It acts as a system of social control, it justifies social inequality, it produces false consciousness, and provides compensation for alienation and oppression. In doing so, religion discourages political action by the subject class to improve their situation.

8. Some neo-Marxists argue that religion can challenge ruling-class dominance – for example, liberation theology in Latin America.

9. Many feminists claim that religion is a patriarchal institution. Supernatural beings and religious professionals are overwhelmingly male. And in many religions, women play a secondary role in worship. In strongly-religious societies, women tend to have fewer options and less favourable treatment.

10. Weber argues that at certain times and places religion can be a force for social change. He claims that early forms of Protestantism, particularly Calvinism, encouraged the rise of capitalism. The Protestant ethic, with its emphasis on hard work, self-discipline and self-denial, provided the basis for the spirit of capitalism.

11. Weber's views have been widely criticised. For example, some critics argue that capitalism preceded early forms of Protestantism.

12. Peter Berger agrees with Weber's view that rationalisation has led to disenchantment. He argues that the pluralisation of people's life-worlds has produced an unprecedented awareness of different belief systems. This undermines traditional religious teachings. The result is anomie. Religion no longer has the power to give meaning to life.

13. According to postmodernists, the metanarratives of modern society have been undermined in postmodern society. As a result, knowledge and beliefs are increasingly seen as relative. This has led to a decline in traditional religion which can no longer claim a monopoly of the truth.

14. Some researchers have seen the rise of religious fundamentalism as a response to this development. They see people going 'back to basics' in an age of uncertainty.

15. People are seen to increasingly construct their own identities in postmodern society – largely on the basis of what they consume. The growth of new religious movements reflects this – people can select a mix of beliefs and practices to suit their desired identity.

activity 10 religion in postmodern society

Item A Mixing to taste

Glenn Hoddle

Glenn Hoddle, the former England football coach, is a controversial figure. He made no secret of his strong Christian beliefs. He used a faith healer for counselling his team. And he was forced to resign in 1999 as a result of his statement about karma which was seen as offensive to people with disabilities. In Hoddle's words, 'You and I have been given two hands and two legs and half-decent brains. Some people have not been born like that for a reason. The karma is working from another lifetime. I have nothing to hide about that. It is not only people with disabilities. What you sow, you have to reap.'

Statements of mixed religious belief are becoming more commonplace. Hoddle's apparent Hinduism (belief in karma) is hitched to a (Christian or Jewish) Biblical phrase about reaping what you sow. And how does this square with his consulting a New Age faith healer? The evidence shows that more and more people can both claim some fairly conventional religious positions and cheerfully add on other elements – Feng Shui, yoga, mysticism, astrology, Shiatsu, Reiki and the rest. It has been likened to cocktail mixing – mixing divine drinks to individual taste.

Adapted from Lyon, 2000

Item B What works for me

In postmodern religion, truth is relative to what people imagine will satisfy their requirements. People have what they take to be 'spiritual' *experiences* without having to hold religious *beliefs*. Instead of authoritative texts providing truth, 'truth' is seen in terms of 'what works for me'.

Adapted from Heelas, 2000

Item C Religious shopping mall

Item D Islamic fundamentalism

Today, *Sharia* law – a legal system based on Islamic teachings – has been adopted in a number of Islamic countries – for example, parts of Pakistan and Islamic areas of Nigeria. This is often seen as a recent development and as an example of fundamentalism. However, there is nothing new about this. For example, it occurred in 10th century Morocco and 11th century Moorish Spain.

Fundamentalist *jihad* movements developed in Islamic areas of West Africa in the 17th, 18th and 19th centuries. Some of these resulted in the creation of Islamic states – for example, Ivory Coast and Guinea.

Adapted from An-na'im, 2003

questions

1 How do Items A, B and C illustrate postmodernists' claims about the nature of religion in postmodern society?

2 How can Item D be used to criticise postmodernists' views?

Unit 2 *Religion and social change*

keyissues

1 Is religion a conservative force?
2 Is religion a radical force?

One of the major debates in the sociology of religion concerns the relationship between religion and social change. Is religion a conservative force? Does it maintain things the way they are and discourage social change? Or is religion a *radical force*? Does it initiate social change, does it encourage new ideas and new ways of behaving? Or does it do both at certain times and places? Is religion sometimes a conservative force discouraging social change and sometimes a radical force encouraging social change?

Some of the main sociological theories of religion deal with these questions. The answers they provide will now be examined.

2.1 Social change and theories of religion

Marxism

From a traditional Marxist view, religion is a conservative force. According to Karl Marx, it justifies the dominance of the ruling class and provides consolation for the subject class. As a result, religion discourages social change.

Religion and the ruling class Religion often legitimates – defines as right – the position of the ruling class. For example, monarchs in medieval Europe ruled by divine right. How can human beings change what is ordained by God? To do so would be punishable by eternal damnation. Justifying ruling-class domination as God-given discourages attempts to change the situation.

Religion and the subject class According to Marx, religion is 'the opium of the people'. It provides consolation for the misery of oppression by offering the false promise of eternal happiness in the next life. This illusion of happiness makes life appear bearable and therefore discourages attempts by the subject class to change their situation. Again, religion acts as a conservative force which maintains things they way they are.

Alternative Marxist views Marx's friend and co-writer Friedrich Engels saw glimmers of a demand for change in some religious movements which looked forward to change in the here-and-now rather than in the afterlife. For example, he saw aspects of communism in early Christianity. However, because of religion's emphasis on the supernatural, Engels felt that these movements were doomed to failure – they would not lead to political revolution.

As noted in Unit 1, some Marxists argue that religion can contribute to radical change. For example, Antonio Gramsci and Otto Maduro claim that, at certain times and places, religion can directly support the liberation of the subject class and help them to become aware of their true situation.

Evaluation As outlined in Unit 1, there is evidence to support the standard Marxist view that religion is a conservative force – that it supports the powerful and helps to keep the masses in their place. However, there is plenty of evidence which suggests that religion can sometimes encourage social change. For example, Roman Catholicism in Eastern Europe in the 1970s and 80s supported resistance to the domination of the Soviet Union (Hunt, 2002).

Feminism

A number of feminists have seen religion as a conservative force. Where Marxists have seen religion as maintaining the power of the ruling class, feminists have seen it as maintaining patriarchy – the domination of women by men.

Christianity provides evidence to support this view.

- The Christian God – 'our father' – has traditionally been seen as male.
- Eve was created as a 'helpmate' for Adam.
- Christianity traditionally defined a wife as the property of her husband. She owed him life-long obedience.
- Until recently, women could not become clergy in Christian churches. This changed in 1992 in the Church of England. But women are still barred from becoming religious professionals in the Roman Catholic Church.

These examples support the view that religion serves to keep women in their traditional place – subordinate to men.

Evaluation There is plenty of evidence to support the view that religion reinforces patriarchy and discourages change. As such, religion is a conservative rather than a radical force. However, there is evidence to question this view. As noted in Unit 1, goddesses played a significant part in ancient Greek and Roman religion. And today, thousands of women have positions of leadership in the rapidly growing Christian Pentecostal movement.

Functionalism

In general, functionalist theories have seen religion as a force for stability rather than change. It reinforces value consensus, it strengthens social solidarity, it deals with life crises which threaten to disrupt society. As such, religion is seen as a conservative force which maintains the status quo – keeping things the way things are.

Emile Durkheim According to Durkheim, religion reinforces the collective conscience – the norms and values of society. Religious rituals strengthen social solidarity by binding together members of society. In these respects, religion is a force for stability rather than change.

Bronislow Malinowski According to Malinowski, religion serves to reduce the anxiety and tension which result from events which threaten to disrupt social life. Such events

activity 11 religion in Black America

Item A Gospel music

Throughout the USA, Black churches have resounded with the sound of gospel music. In Detroit, the Reverend C.L. Franklin, father of the famous soul singer Aretha Franklin and pastor of the Bethel Baptist church, has raised congregations to fever pitch with his preaching and gospel singing. So intense is the feeling that he arouses that nurses are regularly on hand to tend members of his flock overcome with emotion. People leave the church feeling cleansed, their burdens lifted, recharged and ready to face the problems of a new week.

At a Madison Square Garden gospel concert in New York City, Mahalia Jackson, the Queen of Gospel, sings *Just Over The Hill*, a song about going to heaven. As she sinks to her knees, singing with intensity and jubilation, women in the audience shriek and faint. Gospel music, in the words of one of its singers, 'stirs the emotions'.

Gospel singers

A member of the Ward Sisters, a famous Black gospel group states, 'For people who work hard and make little money, gospel music offers a promise that things will be better in the life to come'. According to Thomas A. Dorsey, one of the founders of modern gospel music, 'Make it anything other than good news and it ceases to be gospel'. Many gospel songs ring with joy, excitement, anticipation and conviction about reaching the 'blessed homeland' and 'waking up in glory'. Life on earth might be hard and painful with little hope for improvement, but life after death is nothing but good news.

God not only promises eternal salvation and perfect happiness, he also provides support and direction for life on earth. Typical lines from gospel songs include, 'Take your burdens to the Lord and leave them there', 'God will carry you through', 'Since I gave to Jesus my poor broken heart, he has never left me alone', and 'What would I do if it wasn't for the Lord?'

Adapted from Heilbut, 1971 and Haralambos, 1995

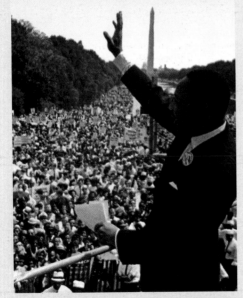

Martin Luther King giving his 'I Have a Dream' speech during the March on Washington in 1963.

Item B Protest

In the late 1950s and early 1960s, some Black preachers came out of their churches and on to the streets. Led by the Reverend Martin Luther King, the Southern Christian Leadership Council, an organisation of Black churches in the southern states of the USA, directed mass protest against racial discrimination. Partly due to their campaign, the American government passed civil rights laws which declared discrimination on the basis of skin colour to be illegal.

Adapted from Franklin and Starr, 1967

questions

1 How does Item A support the traditional Marxist view of religion as a conservative force?
2 How does Item B question this view?

include life crises – birth, puberty, marriage and death. For example, a funeral ceremony checks the disruptive emotions which follow the death of a loved one. It promises life after death and brings together family and friends to support the bereaved. In doing so it reintegrates society.

Again, religion is seen to bring social stability rather than change.

Talcott Parsons Like Durkheim, Parsons sees religion as reinforcing value consensus – for example, the Christian Ten Commandments back up the norms and values of Western societies. In addition, he sees religion as giving meaning to and making sense of life. This helps people to adjust to and accept their situation which, in turn, promotes social stability. Again, the emphasis is on stability rather than change.

Evaluation Functionalists have been criticised for presenting what many see as a one-sided view of religion – for their emphasis on religion promoting social solidarity and value consensus and for neglecting instances of religion as a force for social change. This criticism is not entirely fair. For example, Talcott Parsons (1951) argued that Christianity not only reinforced, it also helped to produce, the norms and values which shaped modern societies and were essential to their economic development.

Max Weber

From a Marxist view, religion is largely shaped by economic factors. As part of the superstructure of society, religion reflects the infrastructure or economic base. Max Weber argued that in certain cases, the opposite was true – religion can help to shape entire economic systems and bring radical changes to society as a whole.

Weber argued that human action is directed by meanings. As a result, social change can result from a change in meanings, from a change in world view – the way people see the world. And these new meanings can be generated by religion.

This was the argument Weber used in his most famous work, *The Protestant Ethic and the Spirit of Capitalism* (see pages 17, 19-20). He claimed that a number of Protestant religions which developed in 16th century Europe produced the ideas which were essential for the development of capitalism.

As outlined in Unit 1, these ideas included self-discipline, rational thinking, a 'calling' in life which the individual must follow in a determined and single-minded way, and a condemnation of time-wasting, laziness, luxuries and entertainment. From these ideas developed the 'spirit of capitalism' which was a major factor in the creation of the capitalist system.

Evaluation If Weber is correct, religion can sometimes be a significant force for social change. However, as noted in Unit 1, a number of researchers claim that early forms of capitalism preceded the new Protestant religions. In terms

of their argument, Weber got it the wrong way round – capitalism came first and helped to produce Protestantism.

2.2 Religious fundamentalism

In recent years, there has been a rise in religious fundamentalism – in particular, Christian fundamentalism in the USA and Islamic fundamentalism in North Africa, the Middle East and the Far East.

Religious fundamentalism is seen by its followers as a return to the basics or fundamentals of religion. It usually involves a literal interpretation of religious texts and strict moral codes of behaviour. Its followers often see it as turning the clock back to true religion, to a time when religion was not watered down, tarnished and corrupted by the evils of modern society.

Some researchers see fundamentalism as a particularly conservative form of religion – it looks backward, it rejects many of the changes in modern society, it tries to return to a former time.

This is a somewhat different view of religion as a conservative force. Rather than maintaining things the way they are, fundamentalists aim to make things the way they were. In one respect they are conservative, in another respect they are not because they seek to change the existing society.

Christian fundamentalism in the USA

In the 1970s, there was a revival of Christian fundamentalism in the United States. In 1979, Jerry Falwell and a small group of preachers founded the Moral Majority – a conservative political movement which aimed to return to traditional values. Basing their views on a literal interpretation of the Bible, their goal was to restore God to the centre of American society. In his book *Listen America*, Jerry Falwell urged Americans to come 'back to God, back to the Bible, back to reality'.

The Moral Majority pointed out what they saw as the ills of American society – high divorce rates, widespread juvenile delinquency, pornography on the Internet, adultery in the White House, abortion on demand and increasing tolerance of homosexuality. This, in their view, was not God's way (Ammerman, 2003).

The election of Ronald Reagan as President of the United States has been seen by some as an indication of the Moral Majority's power. Reagan shared many of their views. However, by the 1990s, many members felt that the movement had failed. Two prominent members published *Blinded by Might* stating that, 'Today, very little that we set out to do has gotten done. In fact, the moral landscape of America has become worse' (quoted in Ammerman, 2003).

Despite this apparent failure, there is evidence that Christian fundamentalism had a significant influence on the election of George Bush in 2000 and on his policies from then on. Bush himself is a fundamentalist, born-again Christian. Shortly after his election, he created the Office of

Faith-Based Programs which encourages religious groups to take over welfare services for the homeless, unemployed, drug addicts and alcoholics. This is part of Bush's 'compassionate conservatism', a phrase borrowed from his close advisor, the fundamentalist Christian Marvin Olasky, who wrote a book entitled *Compassionate Conservatism*. Olasky's message for dealing with the poor is summed up by his statement: 'What we've found is the most useful kind of poverty-fighting is spiritual. And we forgot that in the 20th century' (quoted in Saunders, 2001).

Islamic fundamentalism

Although Islamic fundamentalist movements vary due to local history and circumstances, they have certain things in common. Islamic fundamentalists see themselves as the saviours and moral guardians of their societies. They are the chosen few who must restore true religion in an immoral and decadent society which has abandoned God's design for living. They have a duty to translate God's will into practice in line with a literal reading of the Qur'an – the Muslim bible (An-Na'im, 2003).

The Iranian revolution The following case study on the revolution in Iran in 1979 highlights some of the main features of Islamic fundamentalism.

In the 1920s and 30s, the Shah (ruler) of Iran felt that traditional Islamic culture was holding back the modernisation of his country. He introduced a Western curriculum into schools, secular (non-religious) laws into courts and invited Western companies into Iran to develop agriculture and industry. The development of the oil industry brought considerable wealth to a small elite, while leaving the mass of the population in poverty.

By the 1970s, parts of Iran, particularly the capital Tehran, were becoming increasingly Westernised with bars, cinemas, discos, night clubs, and Western dress, food, music and films. Many people resented both the wealthy

activity 12 *fundamentalism in the USA*

Item A Pat Robertson

One of the leaders of the Moral Majority, TV evangelist and former presidential candidate Reverend Pat Robertson outlines his vision of America after fundamentalist Christians have taken control. 'When the Christian majority takes over this country, there will be no satanic churches, no more free distribution of pornography, no more abortion on demand, and no more talk of rights for homosexuals.'

Pat Robertson at an anti-abortion demonstration in Wichita, Kansas

Item B President Bush

According to George Bush, the greatest hope for the poor is not a reform of government welfare services but 'redemption' – in other words, religious belief. Welfare is a poor alternative to the power of religion. Like all fundamentalists, Bush takes the Bible literally as the word of God. He sees the world in religious terms. When he talks about the 'axis of evil', referring to states like Iraq under Sadham Hussein, he is identifying his enemies as literally satanic, as possessed by the devil.

Adapted from Saunders, 2001 and James, 2003

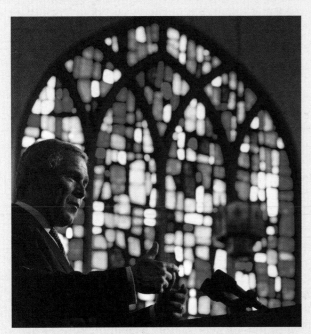

George Bush in the pulpit in New Orleans, claiming that the 'miracle of salvation' is the answer to many of society's problems.

question

With some reference to Items A and B, how can Christian fundamentalism be seen both as conservative and as a movement for social change?

elite and the influence of the West.

The ayatollahs – religious leaders – blamed the poverty of the masses on the decline of Islam and on Western influence. They saw the solution as a return to a truly Islamic society based on the Qur'an and a rejection of Western capitalism and Western ways. This would cure the disease of 'westoxicification' and restore God's design for living (Bruce, 2001).

In 1979, the people overthrew the Shah and an Islamic state was established under the leadership of Ayatollah Khomeini. Bars were looted and burned, cinemas destroyed, casinos and nightclubs closed down, and alcohol and Western music banned. Women were encouraged to stay at home and study the Qur'an, and in public they were required to cover themselves with the *chador* – veil. Islamic law – the *sharia* – was reinstated, and schoolchildren now recited the Qur'an rather than singing the national anthem.

Religious fundamentalism – conclusion

In one respect, fundamentalist movements are conservative forces. They look backwards for their inspiration for the future, they attempt to turn the clock back to a time of true religion. But no movement can hope to completely restore the past. And there are often many new features in fundamentalist movements. Steve Bruce (2001) gives the following picture of fundamentalism in Iran. 'Although Islamic fundamentalists typically portray their task as a return to the past, the Islam they promote is not the traditional rather easy-going rural religion of a nomadic tribal people who gave a high place to the magical powers of the cults of local saints. It is a puritanical "reformed" Islam that places unusually strict requirements on individuals and replaces the magic of the saint cult with rigorous self-discipline.'

Although the aim of religious fundamentalists is a return to the past, they also aim to change existing society.

activity13 *fundamentalism in Iran*

Item A Westoxification

In the words of an Iranian ayatollah:

'Islam was defeated by its own rulers, who ignored Divine Law, in the name of Western-style secularism. The West captured the imagination of large sections of our people. And that conquest was far more disastrous for Islam than any loss of territory. It is not for the loss of Andalusia (a reference to the Moors being driven out of Spain) that we ought to weep every evening – although that remains a bleeding wound. Far greater is the loss of sections of our youth to Western ideology, dress, music and food.'

Quoted in Taheri, 1987

Item B An Iranian woman

'Once we thought that Western society had all the answers for successful, fruitful living. If we followed the lead of the West we would have progress. Now we see that this isn't true. They are sick societies, even their material prosperity is breaking down. America is full of crime and promiscuity. Russia is worse. Who wants to be like that? We have to remember God. Look how God has blessed Saudi Arabia. That is because they have tried to follow the (Islamic) Law. And America, with all its loose society, is all problems.'

Quoted in *History of the 20th Century*, Vol. 8, 1994

Item C Anti-American demonstration

Anti-US demonstration outside the American Embassy in Tehran, 1979. The poster on the right shows a picture of the religious leader, Ayatollah Khomeini.

question

In what ways do the items illustrate Islamic fundamentalism?

Christian fundamentalism in the USA aims to change the moral landscape of America. Fundamentalism in Iran aimed to rid the country of Western influence and create an Islamic society. These are radical aims. And sometimes they can lead to radical social change – in the case of Iran, they led to a revolution.

2.3 Religion and social change – conclusion

The first section in this unit looked at theories of religion. Most theories see religion as a conservative force, as a force which maintains the status quo. Weber, however, argued that at certain times and places, religion could be a radical force, helping to change society in significant ways.

The second section looked at religious fundamentalism arguing that though conservative in their outlook, fundamentalist movements can sometimes lead to radical change in the wider society.

This section examines further evidence and ideas about the relationship of religion and social change.

Religion as a force for change

Geoffrey K. Nelson (1986) argues that there are many instances in history when social change and even revolution have been directed by religious beliefs. He gives the following examples.

- One of the leaders of the Peasants' Revolt in England in 1381 was a priest called John Ball. He claimed that God had given the land to all men equally, and that the peasants should rise up against the lords who had stolen the land from them.

- Churches played an important part in the civil rights movement in the USA during the 1960s. Protests led by the Reverend Martin Luther King influenced the government to pass civil rights laws which banned segregation on the basis of skin colour.

- From the 1960s, a number of radical individuals and groups have emerged from the Roman Catholic Church in Latin America. They argued that Christians have a duty to help liberate the poor and oppressed. They developed a set of teachings known as *liberation theology* and sometimes joined movements to overthrow oppressive regimes. For example, in 1979 Catholic revolutionaries played a part in the overthrow of the right-wing government in Nicaragua.

Nelson argues that examples such as these indicate how religion 'can spearhead resistance and revolution'. However, he also notes that in each case there are examples of religion encouraging the opposite response. During the Peasants' Revolt, many churchmen supported the lords and condemned the rebellion. In the USA, some Black religious groups discouraged civil rights protest. And in Latin America, many Roman Catholic churchmen supported the position of the ruling groups.

Nelson's point is that in certain times and places, religion can be either a conservative or a radical force.

Stability and change

Nelson's research suggests that the question should not be, 'Is religion a conservative or a radical force?' Instead, it should be, 'Under what circumstances does religion encourage or discourage change?' This is the approach taken by Meredith McGuire (1981) who asks, 'In what way and under what conditions does religion promote rather than inhibit change?' She answers this question in the following way.

Beliefs Religions with strong moral codes are more likely to be critical of the wider society. As a result, their members are more likely to demand changes in society. Religions which focus on the social conduct of their members in this world are more likely to produce change than religions which focus on spirituality or other-worldly concerns. In terms of this view, Protestantism is more likely to produce change than Buddhism with its spiritual goal of eliminating the self and earthly desires.

Culture Where religious beliefs are central to the culture of society, they are more likely to be used to justify or legitimate demands for stability or change. This can be seen in Central and South American countries with a strongly Roman Catholic tradition.

Social location If religious institutions are closely integrated with other parts of the social structure – for example, the political and economic systems – they have greater power to produce stability or change. For example, the Roman Catholic Church in Poland was closely linked to Solidarity, a trade union organisation which played an important role in the overthrow of communism.

Internal organisation Religious institutions with a strong, centralised authority will have more power to affect stability or change. For example, the Roman Catholic Church has a powerful centralised authority and a strict hierarchy of religious professionals. They tend to speak with one voice. And when they don't, they are disciplined from on high and even expelled from the church. This happened to some Latin American churchmen who supported liberation theology.

Evaluation McGuire has outlined factors which influence whether religion acts as a force for stability or change. In many cases, however, she does not indicate *why* the same religion with the same beliefs, the same relationship to culture and the same social location and internal organisation, sometimes promotes change and sometimes inhibits change. Why, for example, after years of emphasising the joys of the afterlife, did Black congregations in the USA take to the streets in protest under the leadership of Martin Luther King? Answers to this question require an examination of the social context and circumstances which led to this change of direction.

summary

1. Marx saw religion as a conservative force which justified the position of the ruling class and provided consolation for the subject class. As a result, it tended to keep the subject class in its place, so discouraging social change.

2. Some neo-Marxists argue that religion can sometimes help to make the subject class aware of their situation and support their liberation. In this respect, religion can sometimes act as a radical force.

3. Some feminists have argued that religion is a conservative force, seeing it as maintaining patriarchy – keeping women in their traditional place as subordinate to men.

4. In general, functionalists have seen religion as a force for stability rather than change. By reinforcing value consensus and strengthening social solidarity, religion tends to maintain society the way it is.

5. On the basis of his analysis of the relationship between early Protestantism and capitalism, Weber argued that religion can sometimes be a significant force for social change. In his view, early Protestantism provided the meanings and guides for action which were an important factor in the rise of capitalism.

6. Some researchers see fundamentalism as a particularly conservative form of religion – it looks backwards, it rejects many of the changes in modern society and tries to return to a former time.

7. Despite this, fundamentalism can be seen as a force for change – fundamentalists do try to change society even though their model for change is based on the past.

8. There is evidence that religion can act in some circumstances as a conservative force and in others as a radical force.

9. In view of this, some researchers argue that the question should not be, 'Is religion a conservative or a radical force?' Instead, it should be, 'Under what circumstances does religion encourage or discourage change?'

10. Meredith McGuire has attempted to answer this last question. She has outlined factors which influence whether religion acts as a force for stability or change.

Unit 3 Religious organisations and movements

keyissues

1 What are churches, sects, denominations and cults?

2 What are New Religious Movements?

3 What is the New Age movement?

Religious organisations differ in many ways. Some are organised in terms of a rigid hierarchy – for example, the Roman Catholic church with the Pope at its head and a chain of officials leading down to local priests. Others lack a clearly defined hierarchy and official positions.

Religious organisations also differ in terms of their relationship to the wider society. Some generally accept society's norms and values, others reject them.

Sociologists have used such differences to classify religious organisations into types. This unit looks at the main types they have identified. It begins with four concepts – church, sect, denomination and cult. It is important to note that these are *ideal types* – they are models of 'pure types' of religious organisations. In the messy real world, no organisation will exactly fit an ideal type – it will only tend to fit one type better than others.

3.1 Church and sect

Max Weber introduced the distinction between *church* and *sect* in the early 20th century. His friend, Ernst Troeltsch (1931) developed this idea, seeing churches and sects as very different types of organisation.

Church

Membership A church aims to be the 'spiritual home' of everybody in society. Membership is open to all and easily obtained. The church is the dominant religious organisation in a society and people qualify for membership simply by being born into that society – though there are formal rituals such as baptism which officially signify membership.

In its most developed form, a church seeks to be universal and all-inclusive – to include members of all social groups in all societies.

Organisation Churches have a complex, formal hierarchy made up of professional clergy. In the Roman Catholic church, for example, the Pope heads an organisational pyramid of cardinals, archbishops, bishops and priests.

Worship and ritual Worship in churches tends to be restrained. Rather than being spontaneous, it is often based on traditional ritual – for example, a fixed order of service, standing for hymns, and regular repetition of prayers.

Sense of legitimacy This refers to the legitimacy or 'rightness' of religious beliefs. Churches claim to have a monopoly of truth – only their teachings offer the truth, they provide the only legitimate religion.

Relationship to the wider society Churches generally accept the norms and values of the wider society. They are often closely linked with society's major institutions – for example, church and state were closely linked in medieval Europe.

Involvement and commitment Although churches encourage members to play an active role – to regularly attend services and participate in church functions – there is no compulsion to do so. Those who show low levels of involvement and commitment are still regarded as members.

Sect

Membership Unlike churches, the attitude of sects to the world outside is highly exclusive – they erect strong boundaries between themselves and the wider society and exclude people considered 'unworthy'. Gaining membership is not a right, but has to be earned by personal merit. This might be indicated by a knowledge of doctrine, a conversion experience, or the recommendation of existing members. There is therefore a clear distinction between members and non-members. Jehovah's Witnesses, Seventh Day Adventists, Christadelphians and the Amish of the United States are examples of sects.

Organisation Sects generally lack a professional clergy and a complex hierarchy. Instead, they depend for leadership upon the special, God-given talents of members.

Worship and ritual There is little use of ritual, and worship is typically emotional, expressive and spontaneous. For example, members of Christian sects often cry out phrases such as 'Hallelujah' and 'Praise the Lord' as the spirit takes them.

Sense of legitimacy Historically, church and sect have seen the other as rivals and, often, as dangerous enemies. Significantly, both claim that they have a monopoly of the truth and that they are the only true religion.

Sects often look forward to an event of great significance – for example, the second coming of Jesus, the anticipated battle of Armageddon between God's forces and Satan's, the Day of Judgement, and 'life' in heaven or hell. Members are encouraged to think of themselves as an elite who possess special enlightenment or spiritual insight, with salvation reserved for them alone, while non-believers are rejected.

Relationship to the wider society Sects are generally critical of the wider society and expect members to stand apart from it. Contact with non-members is generally discouraged except in an attempt to convert them. Sects are also critical of the mainstream religious bodies – whom they regard as too worldly – and distance themselves from them.

Involvement and commitment of members Sects demand high standards of behaviour from their members and high levels of commitment. Much of the members' spare time is spent in sectarian activities – for example, in Bible study, trying to gain converts, or socialising with sect members. However, if members fail to meet the sect's high standards, they may be punished, and even expelled – a powerful sanction when their whole way of life has been built around the group.

activity14 church and sect

Item A The Roman Catholic Church

The Roman Catholic Church is the largest Christian grouping. Its followers accept the authority of the Pope – the Vicar of Christ – as Christ's representative on earth. When he defines matters of faith or morals, the Pope's statements are regarded as infallible (incapable of error) and binding on all Catholics.

The Pope stands at the head of a complex hierarchy. Below him are the cardinals, who are responsible for electing and advising the Pope. Next come the 'greater' patriarchs (eg of Jerusalem), and 'minor' patriarchs (eg of Lisbon). Then come archbishops and bishops followed by priests, deacons and subdeacons.

Worship is based on traditional rituals. It is governed by detailed rules and regulations, including strict dress codes for the various religious professionals. Here are part of the instructions for the Roman Catholic Mass.

Bishops in the foreground and cardinals in red robes attend a Mass inside St. Peter's Basilica at the Vatican.

The procession comes to the altar. The procession consists of the incense bearer, attendants, master of ceremonies, subdeacon, deacon, and officiating priest, all dressed in the appropriate vestments. First, the preparatory prayers are said at the foot of the altar. The altar is 'incensed'. The officiating priest reads – and the choir sing – the *Introit* and *Kyrie*. The priest, the deacon and subdeacon recite the Gloria in excelsis (Glory in the highest) which is also sung by the choir.

Adapted from *Catholic Encyclopaedia*

Item B Jehovah's Witnesses

Jehovah's Witnesses believe that only they have the true faith, that only they can offer the path to salvation. In the words of their official publication, *The Watchtower*, Witnesses 'do not share in the divisive politics of this world, although they subject themselves to human governments as long as God patiently allows these to function. Instead, they patiently await the Day of Judgement and the unfolding of God's Plan for men on Earth.'

Jehovah's Witnesses separate themselves from the wider society which they regard as corrupt and immoral. They are hostile to other religions, particularly mainstream Christianity which they see as heretical – as contrary to God's teachings. Life revolves around the sect with Bible study groups, meetings, social events and door-to-door visits with the aim of gaining converts.

The Watchtower organisation, based in New York, imposes strict control on members. It is the supreme authority – its word, which appears in The Watchtower, is the only truth. Those who take contrary views are excluded from the sect and shunned by members.

Only Jehovah's Witnesses are morally pure, only they will be saved on the day of judgement when God will overturn the existing social order and transform the world.

Adapted from various issues of *The Watchtower* and www.apologeticsindex.org

question

With reference to Items A and B, why is Roman Catholicism defined as a church and Jehovah's Witnesses as a sect?

3.2 Denomination and cult

Denomination

The concept of *denomination* was introduced to sociology by the American Richard Niebuhr in 1925. Denominations are usually described as part-way between church and sect. Though widely seen as conventional, respectable and mainstream, they often have a history of challenging authority. Unlike the sect, they tend to be tolerant of others' beliefs. Examples of denominations in the UK include Methodists, Baptists and United Reformed.

Membership Unlike the church, the denomination is not 'universalistic' in that it does not seek to make members of the whole population. Although membership is open to all, there is no sect-like test of merit. Denominations tend to be disproportionately middle class.

Organisation Denominations have a professional clergy but their organisational hierarchy is much less complex than that of a church. They have no bishops, archbishops, patriarchs or popes. But the hierarchy is more developed than that of a sect, which typically has no professional clergy. Laypeople play a more direct role than in a church – as non-professional lay-preachers, for instance – but less than in a sect.

Worship and ritual Worship is relatively formal, with less ritual than a church but less spontaneity than in a sect.

Though most stand to sing and sit to pray, there is no crossing oneself, incense or bells, as at a church service, nor cries of 'Hallelujah' or 'Praise the Lord' as in a sect. Most sociologists would agree that in the USA, the so-called churches are closer to denominations.

Sense of legitimacy Unlike churches and sects, denominations do not claim an exclusive monopoly of the truth. As a result, they are more tolerant of alternative beliefs and less demanding of their members. And, because they accept that there are other paths to salvation, they will more readily cooperate with other religious organisations.

Relationship to the wider society While churches tend to be closely associated with the state, denominations are explicitly separate from the state. However, unlike many sects, they do not reject the state or the wider society. Hence, in Britain, clergy of such denominations as the United Reformed and the Methodists appear at national occasions, such as Remembrance Sunday, alongside Church of England clergy who usually officiate as representatives of the national church.

Involvement and commitment Although denominations wish to increase their members, they put relatively little pressure on potential recruits to commit themselves to a particular set of beliefs, to regular attendance, or to membership. In part, this reflects a fundamental value of *individualism*. The right of individuals to interpret the scriptures themselves, without priests as intermediaries, has been central to the 'non-conformist' Protestant traditions such as Methodism, Baptism, Presbyterianism and Unitarianism.

Cult

In everyday language, the terms *cult* and sect are often used interchangeably to refer to relatively small religious groups whose beliefs and practices deviate from those of mainstream religions and appear strange to most people. However, some sociologists make a distinction between sects and cults.

According to Roland Robertson (1970), the key difference between cults and sects is as follows. Sects believe they have a monopoly of the truth, while cults believe their teachings are just one of many paths to the truth. Cults are therefore more tolerant of the beliefs of others and of the behaviour of their members.

Roy Wallis (1974) developed this distinction between sects and cults. Where sects are exclusive, closed, tightly-knit organisations, cults are more loosely organised and open to the outside world. Where sects demand membership tests and strict codes of behaviour which apply to all their members, cults have none of these restrictions. Cults are more individualistic in that they allow individual members to decide what they will or will not accept.

While sect members usually believe in a God who is external to human beings, many cults emphasise the 'power', 'divinity' or 'real self' which is said to reside within individuals. A main aim of such cults is to help people experience their 'inner power' or 'inner divinity'.

Membership Cults are usually open to all and welcome those with a sympathetic interest. There may be no concept of membership – people may simply join in or drop out as they wish.

Organisation Cult organisation is likely to be loose. There may be a charismatic leader, but hierarchies and ideas of seniority are usually discouraged.

Sense of legitimacy Unlike sects, cults do not claim to have a monopoly of the truth. As a result, cults are relatively tolerant – sometimes even welcoming – of followers' involvement with other groups.

Relationship to the wider society Because of the wide range of cults, there is no common orientation to the wider society. Followers generally expect to live 'in the world' and cult-related activity is likely to be part-time.

Involvement and commitment Many cults do not demand high levels of commitment from their followers. Nor do they demand acceptance of their teachings. They simply ask that people be open to the experiences they offer. If people find these experiences rewarding, then they will be likely to learn more about the cult's teachings and increase their involvement.

3.3 Church, sect, denomination and cult – an evaluation

Problems of classification As noted at the start of this unit, the categories or concepts used to classify religious organisations are ideal types or 'pure' types. Their fit with real organisations will not therefore be exact. But is the fit close enough to be useful? Some researchers have their doubts. For example, Stark and Bainbridge (1987) argue that the long list of characteristics used to define each type

activity 15 cults

Item A Dianetics

In early 1950, L. Ron Hubbard published an article which developed a psychological theory claiming that there were two sectors of the mind – the analytical and the reactive mind. The analytical mind was the basis of intelligent reasoning, and when its functioning was not constrained, it had much greater power than normally available. When a person was fully 'cleared' of 'engrams' – the recordings of traumatic incidents suffered by an individual – they would be completely free of any psychological problems or psychosomatic illnesses and would have a vastly increased IQ. Following a best-selling book which elaborated these ideas, thousands tried out the technique and hundreds enrolled for short courses of 'auditing' (Dianetic therapy), or training.

L. Ron Hubbard

The movement, known as Dianetics and later as Scientology, developed rapidly all over America. Local enthusiasts formed groups to pursue the study and practice of Dianetics and recruited others. However, Hubbard's work was seen as a starting point, to be developed further by others. The view that many held was that Dianetics was a science to which any individual could contribute. One editor of a Dianetics newsletter emphasised this individualistic orientation: 'There is no reason to take what I say as the "truth", as the "right way". Your way is the best for you.' And Dianetics practitioners claimed: 'There are many, many roads to a higher state of existence. No man can say "This is the route for all to follow".'

Adapted from Wallis, 1975

Item B 'Is there anybody out there?'

The Raelians were founded in 1973 after a young Frenchman, out walking in wild countryside, came upon a flying saucer from which emerged a benign, four-foot tall, humanoid alien. Over a few afternoons, the extraterrestial (ET), who could speak any human language, dictated his messages to Rael, messages which provide humanity with a revolutionary account of its origins, and offer guidance and hope for our future. In a nutshell, long ago a group of ETs had settled Earth and perfected their ability to create life in forms like their own. We Earthlings were the result. Thereafter, they withdrew, but kept a kindly eye on us and sent periodic messengers, such as Buddha, Christ and Joseph Smith of the Mormons, to inform us of our origins and – with limited success – to try to guide us. Although they created us, we mistook them for gods.

However, suddenly aware of the scale of our ability for destruction at Hiroshima (where the first atomic bomb was dropped), they became very alarmed and felt an urgent, and perhaps final, urge to help before we ran out of time. Unsurprisingly, however, they are not entirely confident of their likely reception by the Earthlings. Our reactions to Rael and the messages he conveys are the litmus test. Rael is the messenger for this 'Age of Revelation'. But he also comes bearing a set of meditative techniques taught him by his ET contact which can remove the root causes of most of our earthly ills. It's called 'Sensual Meditation' and proposes to 'awaken the mind by awakening the body'.

Though humanity is not perhaps inevitably doomed to self-destruct without their guidance, Rael's task is to persuade us to ponder our unexpected origins, practice the meditative

The spacecraft which brought the ETs to Earth to speak to Rael.

techniques taught to him, and demonstrate that we are capable of wisdom and benevolence by building the aliens a home, an embassy, in which to welcome them. Then they will return.

Worldwide, the Raelians claim between 15,000 and 25,000 followers. In Britain there are about 300 names on the mailing list but only a dozen or so whom the British representative regards as really committed. Enquiries are welcome and no commitment is required.

Adapted from Yeo, 1988

question

Using Items A and B, show how a cult differs from a sect.

of religious organisation can be a recipe for confusion. When a researcher looks at an actual religious organisation in the real world, they may find that some of its characteristics fit a sect, others a cult and yet others, a denomination. Clearly this makes classification extremely difficult.

A possible solution is to limit the defining characteristics of religious organisations to a relatively few essential or key characteristics. For example, Stark and Bainbridge (1987) define sects as breakaways from established religious organisations and cults as entirely new movements.

Problems of general application Can the classification of church, sect, cult and denomination be applied universally to all religious organisations and movements? Troeltsch's classification of church and sect indicates some of the problems of general application. It was based on the

history of sects within Christianity. While it may offer insights into some religious traditions – perhaps Judaism and Islam – it is doubtful whether it can be applied to others such as Hinduism and Buddhism.

In addition, Troeltsch's classification may only be applicable to a particular time period and place. Churches may well be a thing of the past – in particular, medieval Europe. Steve Bruce (1995) argues that today's so-called churches, such as the Church of England, are more like denominations.

Problems of stigma As Hadden (2003) points out, the terms sect and cult are problematic for research because of their associations in everyday thought. They are often seen as 'weird', 'freaky', and sometimes as 'threatening' and 'dangerous'. No member of an unconventional religious organisation would want to be labelled by such terms.

3.4 New Religious Movements

Sociological interest in unconventional religious movements increased dramatically throughout the West in the 1960s and 1970s. As more and more groups emerged, sociologists increasingly found the terms sect and cult inadequate to describe, categorise and analyse the new movements. For instance, although some, such as the meditative, Hindu-based Siddha Yoga movement, appeared to be cult-type religions – emphasising inner experience and the divine within – they quickly developed complex organisational structures quite untypical of cults. Gradually, in addition to the still useful concepts of sect and cult, a new concept was introduced – the *New Religious Movement* (NRM).

One influential attempt to identify types of NRM was made by Roy Wallis (1985). Wallis noted that they mainly drew upon Christian traditions (such as the Jesus People), on non-Western religions (usually Hindu, Buddhist or Muslim), or from Western psychology and psychotherapy, as in organisations such as the Ehrhard Seminars Training (Est).

His main point, however, was that NRMs also differed significantly in how they are 'orientated to the world'. He proposed that NRMs are either primarily *world-affirming*, *world-rejecting* or *world-accommodating*.

World-affirming NRMs broadly accept the world. Many do not appear conventionally religious at all and their language may be much more akin to business. What they offer their members or 'clients' are techniques to enable them to live more satisfactorily or successfully in the world.

In Transcendental Meditation, for instance, each person is assured that they will relax and cope better with life if they meditate on a secret mantra (chant), or sacred word, given to them personally during initiation to the movement.

World-accommodating NRMs encourage their members to remain within the wider society, though they are dissatisfied with and critical of the secular (non-religious) nature of society. They try to help their followers cultivate their awareness of their inner power or inner divinity. However, like the denomination, they claim to be merely one of a variety of paths to truth or salvation. In Siddha Yoga, for instance, meditation and chanting are practised regularly, not primarily to help people cope with or succeed in life, but as a spiritual experience in which they come into contact with their own spiritual core or inner self. The churches and denominations are seen not as corrupt, but as failing to help people have such spiritual experiences.

World-rejecting NRMs are sect-like organisations, often founded by a charismatic leader. They are critical of or even hostile to the wider society – they keep their distance from it and often from other religious organisations. Like sects, they are seen by their members as uniquely legitimate – as the sole means of access to truth or salvation. They therefore draw clear boundaries between members and non-members, set strict conditions for entry and continuing membership, and require a high level of commitment. For instance, the Jesus People lived in group houses, sometimes on the land in agricultural communes, and abandoned in their thousands the drugs, drinking and promiscuous sex of their former lives to devote themselves to bringing others to Jesus.

activity 16 New Religious Movements

Item A Scientology and Transcendental Meditation

Psychologically-based movements such as Scientology typically place little emphasis on collective ritual or worship but focus instead on the problems of individuals. They market themselves as a service which individuals can purchase and consume at their convenience. Their practices are directed more to reducing the problems of this life than to achieving salvation in the next. Such movements often draw upon ideas from the fringes of modern psychology or from Eastern thought.

Even some of the new religions which draw more directly from an existing religious tradition, such as Transcendental Meditation, also appear to be orientated to enabling people to achieve the conventional goals of this life – such as better jobs, a higher IQ, or greater success in personal relationships. These movements seem to form a type, sharing the common characteristics of accepting most of the goals and values of the wider society but providing new means to achieve them. Their organisational form is also distinct from traditional religion. Rather than organising as churches or chapels, they typically organise themselves in the form of multinational business corporations and employ the techniques of modern marketing and advertising.

Adapted from Wallis, 1985

John Travolta, a follower of Scientology, attending an exhibition of the works of its founder, L. Ron Hubbard.

Item B Neo-Pentecostalism and Charismatic Renewal

Some religious movements neither fully accept the norms and values of the surrounding society, nor entirely reject them by cutting themselves off in communities of the like-minded. Rather, they feel that the secular world and even many religious bodies have slipped away from God's design for human life. However, individuals can overcome this problem in their own lives without separating entirely from the secular world. Believers will normally continue in conventional jobs and family life, their religious practice reinvigorating and re-equipping them to face a degenerating secular world. This group includes Evangelical Christian movements such as Neo-Pentecostalism and the Charismatic Renewal. They claim that the Holy Spirit is still alive in the world and can be experienced through various divine 'gifts' – for example, through the gift of 'speaking in tongues'.

An Evangelical prayer meeting

Such groups are essentially a protest against the loss of vitality in existing religious institutions and their abandonment of a living spirituality. The new movement restores this spirituality and returns to traditional certainties in a world where religious institutions have become colder, more bureaucratic and less certain of their role and even of their fundamental beliefs.

Adapted from Wallis, 1985

Item C ISKCON and the Children of God

Some religious movements reject the world around them, seeing it as utterly corrupt. The world has to be abandoned or totally transformed. Such movements separate themselves from the wider society in communities of the faithful. Some look forward to a spiritual revolution. Members of the International Society for Krishna Consciousness (ISKCON) spend much of their lives in ritual prayers and chants, seeking spiritual truth to escape the illusion and corruption of the outside world.

Other movements look forward to a supernatural intervention. The Children of God live in a state of high expectation, awaiting the imminent return of Christ who will transform the world around them.

Adapted from Wallis, 1985

Hare Krishna festival, London

question

Each of the items provides an example of one of Wallis's types of NRM – world-affirming, world-accommodating, world-rejecting. Match each item to one of these 'orientations to the world'. Give reasons for your choices.

NRMs – an evaluation

Nothing new Critics have argued that there is nothing particularly new about so-called New Religious Movements. They've been regularly appearing over the last 200 years (Hunt, 2002). The only difference over the past 50 years has been an acceleration in their rate of growth – the data bank of NRMs at the London School of Economics estimates that there are now nearly 2600 'new religions' (Barker, 1999).

Former terms OK Many sociologists feel that the term New Religious Movement adds little or nothing to the existing classification of religious organisations. For example, Hadden (2003) doubts that it adds anything of importance to existing terms such as sect and cult.

Some NRMs are 'new' Other sociologists claim that some of the new movements are sufficiently different from existing religious organisations to justify the term NRM. They point to movements like the Unification Church, often known as the Moonies, which draw from a variety of belief systems and are difficult to classify in terms of the existing types. The founder of the Unification Church, Sun Myung Moon, has integrated aspects of Christianity, Taoism and Confucianism along with a liberal sprinkling of new ideas which he has concocted (Hunt, 2002).

Orientations to the world Wallis's claim that NRMs have distinctive orientations to the world has been criticised. The same movement may have a different character and orientation to the world at different organisational levels or when facing different publics. Thus, a movement's elite may be living largely world-rejecting lives in a sect-like refuge, while ordinary followers may be living world-accommodating or even world-affirming lives in the community. We cannot therefore assume that each movement has only one distinctive orientation to the world.

3.5 The New Age movement

Alongside the variety of religious organisations discussed above, new movements have emerged which seem to lack even the degree of coherence and organisational structure of many cults. Although cults are often precarious and short-lived, they at least have some organisational structure and common belief system. That does not seem to be the case with the so-called 'New Age movement'.

The New Age movement has certain things in common with cults. It draws together people who are engaged in an individualistic quest for spiritual experience. However, even sociologists who describe it as a movement, acknowledge that it has few of the attributes normally associated with social or religious movements (Sutcliffe, 2003). And few of those interviewed by researchers use the term New Age movement to describe the groups or ideas in which they are interested.

Why is it so difficult to characterise the New Age movement? First, because the groupings which are commonly identified with the New Age are so diverse, it is difficult to identify common characteristics. Indeed, there is no agreement about which groups are part of New Age. So, while Hunt (2002) identifies neo-Pagans as a strand 'of major importance', Sutcliffe's detailed study of British New Agers includes very few references to pagan groups (Sutcliffe, 2003).

Second, as Sutcliffe points out, the so-called New Age movement lacks a leader, headquarters, a prescribed text, organisational boundaries, a public policy and common goals. Nor has it common doctrines or beliefs. In short, it lacks precisely the qualities one would expect of religious or other movements. Yet sociologists commonly refer to it as if it is a movement (Sutcliffe, 2003).

Rather than New Age being a movement, Sutcliffe argues, it is more a collection of individuals, most of whom gather, when they choose, in loose and egalitarian groups. These individuals and groups commonly link into wider networks of people – in the region, in other regions, in other countries – who share similar spiritual interests. And,

as Sutcliffe points out, people will 'seek' along different paths at the same time – what he calls *multiple seeking*. Those interested, for instance, in 'holistic healing' may dip into any number of practices – 'astral projection, guided visualisation, iridology, reflexology, chromotherapy, rebirthing, shiatsu, pyramids and crystals (Sutcliffe, 2003). Each of these attract enthusiasts, and through them individuals are able, if they wish, to contact other groups and networks of people with complementary or related interests. And the Internet has, of course, facilitated such individualistic contacts between seekers.

Membership Interested individuals can attend and participate in any activities. There is no concept of membership. What unifies seekers – insofar as they feel they have anything in common – is the quest for spiritual experience or growth, though each will take their own individual paths.

Organisation Like the cult, the primary concern of those interested in New Age groupings is highly individualistic – often, some form of mystical or spiritual personal experience. The most important organisational form is the network, whereby individuals or couples come into contact with like-minded people in small groups and learn the groups' beliefs, norms, values and practices. People are likely to meet in private houses or rented premises and come together for special 'workshops' or more regular contact.

Worship and ritual Although individual New Agers may believe in some kind of God, the sacred is likely to be seen as within. As a result, there is unlikely to be worship as such, though there may be some ritual behaviour – such as chanting, incense burning or sitting in the lotus position – to assist the 'inner quest'.

Sense of legitimacy Whereas churches and sects believe that there is one truth, which they alone have access to, those involved in New Age believe that there are many truths which may come from a whole range of sources. People should be open to truth whatever its source. In an important sense, the source of legitimacy for New Age groupings is located within individuals. What is important is what 'works' for the individual in their spiritual quest. However, New Age seekers tend to be critical of 'religion' which they see in terms of dogma, organised belief and church control. As such, it discourages genuine spirituality (Sutcliffe, 2003).

Relationship to the wider society New Age seekers live 'in the world'. In Britain, the most significant exceptions are those who live or stay at Findhorn in Scotland, Britain's only New Age settled 'colony'. Ecological and environmental concerns are widespread throughout New Age, in line with the concept of the Earth as Gaia, a living – and perhaps dying – organism. Many are, therefore, active in 'Green' campaigns.

Involvement and commitment The commitment of New Age seekers is primarily to their own spiritual growth or progress. Groups usually stay together only as long as they satisfy the needs of participants, for the group is essentially just a convenient source of support and encouragement. However, Heelas (1996) identifies three levels of commitment among seekers.

- 'The fully engaged' who have given up conventional lifestyles for a spiritual quest – for example, residents of Findhorn and some New Age travellers.
- 'Serious part-timers' who lead otherwise conventional lives but devote serious time and effort to spiritual concerns.
- 'Casual part-timers' who experiment with 'exotic' things as consumers.

Evaluation – the New Age movement

The New Age and religion This chapter began with a review of definitions of religion. For example, religion has been defined as:

- A belief in some kind of supernatural power
- An expression of this belief in collective worship
- A set of moral values which guide action
- A force which brings people together and unifies society.

In terms of each of these definitions, it can be argued that New Age spirituality falls short of religion. In many cases, there is no evidence of a supernatural power. For example, what have herbalism, crystal healing, meditation, Tarot cards and shiatsu massage got to do with the supernatural?

Nor is there much evidence of collective worship or common values which guide action. And apart from the Findhorn Community – around 200 people – and a visit to the annual Festival for Mind-Body-Spirit, there is little evidence that New Age beliefs and practices bring people together and unify society. In fact, the opposite seems the case – the 'movement' is individualistic rather than social, self-centred rather than group-centred. According to Steve Bruce (2002), its social impact is insignificant.

It can therefore be argued that the New Age movement fits none of the definitions of religion outlined above.

A movement? As noted earlier, critics have argued that New Age groupings are so diverse and loosely organised that they cannot be said to be a movement. In addition, those identified by sociologists as New Agers rarely see themselves as part of a movement, nor label themselves as such.

Spirituality Despite these criticisms, it would be unwise to dismiss the whole idea of New Age spirituality. Since the late 1960s, there has been a growth in self-orientated, spiritually-concerned groups which don't seem to fit the existing typologies of church, sect, denomination and cult, or even New Religious Movement. It appears that increasing numbers of people in the West are seeking their inner self, are searching for their true nature, for spirituality, vitality, wisdom, tranquillity, love and creativity, all of which are to be found and developed in their inner life (Heelas, 1996). But whether this spiritual seeking can be called religion is another question.

summary

1. In their analysis of religious organisations, sociologists have used four main ideal types – church, sect, denomination and cult.

2. Churches and sects are seen as opposite ends of the religious spectrum. Churches are open to all members of society, accept the state and the political and economic systems, are hierarchical and have a professional clergy. Limited demands are made on members and worship is ritualised and restrained. Both churches and sects are likely to claim a monopoly of the truth.

3. Sects, however, are widely perceived as unconventional and deviant. They distance themselves from – and are critical of – the wider society. They generally lack a professional clergy and place high demands on members. Worship lacks formal rituals, and emphasises spontaneity.

4. Denominations tend to be seen as conventional and respectable. Unlike churches and sects, they do not claim a monopoly of the truth. They place fewer demands on their members compared to sects. Denominations are separate from the state and tolerant of the wider society. They have a professional clergy but a less complex hierarchy than a church. Worship is less ritualised than a church but less spontaneous than a sect.

5. Cults, like sects, are often regarded as deviant by the wider society. Unlike sects however, they claim no monopoly of the truth and are therefore more tolerant of other paths. Many emphasise an 'inner divinity' or 'power within', and try to help seekers to experience and develop it. They make few demands – they simply ask people to be 'open' to their teachings.

6. With the emergence in the West of large numbers of new movements that did not fit existing classifications, the term New Religious Movement (NRM) was coined. NRMs mainly draw on Christian or other world faith traditions or Western psychotherapy. Wallis identified world-affirming, world-accommodating and world-rejecting NRMs.

7. The New Age movement is not a religious organisation as such. It is more like a loose network of more-or-less like-minded 'seekers' who dip into a variety of beliefs and practices. Insofar as followers share a common characteristic, it is a quest for spiritual experience and personal growth.

8. It can be argued that New Age spirituality falls short of religion. For example, in many cases there is no evidence of a supernatural power.

activity 17 the New Age movement

Item A The Company of Avallon Society

The Company of Avallon Society (COAS) was formed in 1985 by student researchers of esoteric philosophy, occult science, and Earth Mystery phenomena. The COAS publicly revealed its existence in 1989 so as to expand and advance its aims, work and contact with others of like mind and interest.

The society takes its name from the group of spiritual entities who supplied archaeological data to Frederick Bligh Bond during his work at Glastonbury Abbey from 1907 to 1922. Glastonbury folklore and legends are of especial interest to the COAS, particularly those concerning the origins of Celtic Christianity and its links with Druidism. Study is focused mainly on the Western Mystery Traditions, and 'areas of linkage' between these and other Mystery Traditions, especially those of Ancient Egypt.

COAS overall aims include:

- Rational understanding, development, plus beneficial use of those extraordinary faculties and functions of the human psyche ('soul-powers'), that result in telepathy, telekinesis (movement of objects using the power of the mind), precognition, intuition, and the like.
- To establish and develop contact and rational communication with:
  a) those 'organising intelligences' at work in the Kingdom of Nature who are known as Devas, Nature Spirits, Angels, etc.
  b) intelligent entities and 'souls' existing in alternative, complementary and/or parallel dimensions of consciousness or reality that are empathetic and supportive to the wellbeing, evolution and needs of the human race and its environment.

Adapted from introductory circular letter to enquirers, undated

Item B Smudging

Eleni Santoro is a New Age practitioner. She offers a 'smudging service' to New York estate agents which removes 'bad vibes' by 'balancing energies'.

The tools of her trade include objects from all over the world – silver Tibetan bells, a statue of Ganesh (the Hindu God of prudence and wisdom), an antique Chinese bell, an African necklace of yellow, red and green beads and a silver bowl containing three limes.

Having meditated for several minutes, shuffling a slim pack of 'angel cards', she picks three. Or rather, as she later explains, it is the angels who pick the cards – Light, Release, Humour – best suited to this interior. The smudging session also has a soundtrack – sounds of mountain streams or Japanese drums.

Adapted from Fowler, 1997

Item C Getting through the day

Ellen was a member of a spiritual healing group. She used mini-meditations during her hectic moments at the office, applied acupressure and visualisation to counter a headache and employed breathing techniques and visualisation at each stoplight to handle the stress of a difficult commute home. At home, she used a mantra (chant), crystal and visualisation to 'centre' herself during and

A crystal after work

after an argument. Most days, she spent one hour on exercise followed by stress-reducing visualisations in the sauna. Later she had a cup of herbal tea and meditated for half an hour.

Adapted from McGuire, 2003

Item D Picking and mixing

The New Age ransacks myths, legends, rituals and symbols from different times, places and cultures – from Celtic Christianity, from Eastern religions, from ancient Norse and Germanic religions, from Australian Aborigines and Native Americans.

The 'movement' uses a wide range of practices and techniques picked up from all over the world – meditation, aromatherapy, crystals, mantras, self-hypnosis, reflexology, herbalism, spiritual healing.

Followers pick and mix from this cornucopia of beliefs and practices, concocting a DIY 'religion' which fits their individual requirements.

Adapted from Bruce, 2002 and Hunt, 2002

Kindred Spirit, a New Age magazine

questions

1   With reference to the items, how would you evaluate the claim that the New Age is:

a)   a movement

b)   a religion?

2   How can the items be used to support the claim that the New Age reflects postmodern society?

Unit 4 *Explaining religious movements*

keyissues

1   What explanations have been given for the origins of sects, cults, denominations, New Religious Movements and the New Age movement?

2   What explanations have been given for their development?

As the key issues state, this unit is concerned with explanations. It focuses on the relationship between religious beliefs, religious organisations, social groups and social contexts. Why for example, do members of certain social groups join particular types of religious organisations? What is it about their social situation which attracts them to certain religious beliefs?

4.1 Sects

As noted in the previous unit, sects are close-knit religious groups whose members claim to have a monopoly of the truth. Life often revolves around the sect – high standards of behaviour and levels of commitment are demanded. Members tend to cut themselves off from the outside world and exclude those considered 'unworthy'. This section examines various explanations for sects – how they arise, why they appeal to particular groups, and what social situations encourage their growth.

Social marginality

According to Max Weber (1963), those on the margins of society are most likely to join sects. They are on the outside looking in – for example, the poor and members of some ethnic minority groups. Many feel they have been denied the prestige, the occupational status, income and opportunities which they deserve.

Sect membership can address this problem. In Weber's terms it can offer members a *theodicy of disprivilege* – a religious explanation for their situation and a promise of a 'sense of honour' either in this life or the next. Sect members now become the 'chosen few' rather than outsiders relegated to the margins of society.

The Black Muslims, an African-American sect which rose

to prominence in the 1960s, illustrates these points. Its objective was to recruit 'the Negro in the mud' – the unemployed, the homeless and the destitute. It stated that Blacks are 'by nature divine', and that Whites are inferior and evil. It prophesied that Whites and their religion will be destroyed and that Blacks will then rule forever under Allah's guidance. Members claim that belonging to the sect gave them self-respect and hope for the future.

Relative deprivation

Deprivation refers to a lack of something – for example, a lack of prestige, employment, income or decent housing. From the point of view of the individual concerned, deprivation is *relative* – it is relative to an expectation that is not fulfilled, to a position they feel they deserve but have been unable to attain, to a comparison between themselves and other members of society which leaves them wanting. Relative deprivation refers to the deprivation or loss that people perceive or feel (Glock, 1964).

Sects offer a religious solution to relative deprivation. As one of the chosen few, sect members are no longer deprived. Following the strict code of behaviour laid down by the sect, and provided with the support of fellow members, they may gain self-respect and a sense of community. And the self-discipline demanded by many sects may improve their material situation – for example, they may find a job or get a better paid job (Hamilton, 2001).

Again, the Black Muslims provide an illustration. In most large cities, they operate small businesses – barber's shops, clothing stores and restaurants. Their *Economic Blueprint for the Blackman* advocates economic independence from White America. They are encouraged to work hard, save and abstain from luxuries. A strict moral code forbids the use of alcohol, tobacco and narcotics, sexual intercourse outside of marriage, dancing, dating and many forms of sport. In particular, the responsibilities of the man as husband, father and breadwinner are emphasised. Members take courses on self-improvement and look after the welfare of their fellow members.

The idea of relative deprivation does not just apply to those at the bottom of the class system or to those who experience racial discrimination. It can also apply, for example, to members of the White middle class – for instance, those who feel disillusioned with the materialism of Western society and the teachings of mainstream religion can sometimes find what they're looking for in the beliefs and community of a sect (Wallis, 1984).

Social change and relative deprivation The experience of relative deprivation may become more intense as circumstances change. For example, the Black Muslims came to prominence in the 1960s. This was a period which promised change and improvement for African Americans – for example, laws were passed banning discrimination and segregation in many areas of public life. As a result, expectations rose rapidly. However, for many, particularly those in low-income, inner-city areas, those expectations were not met – things were as bad as ever. As a result, the experience of relative deprivation became more intense.

For some, the Black Muslims offered a means of translating rising expectations into reality. Statements by members indicate that the sect gave them purpose, direction, pride and hope.

The relationship between social change and the development of sects is examined in detail in the following section.

Social change and social dislocation

Sects tend to emerge during periods of rapid social change. Such circumstances can lead to *social dislocation*, to a feeling of being uprooted. This can result in *anomie* – a sense of normlessness, a feeling that traditional norms have broken down and that guidelines for action are no longer in place.

Sects with their clearly defined belief systems and strict moral codes can provide certainty in a time of uncertainty and anomie. They often contain a promise that life will improve if members follow the guidelines they provide. This can give direction and hope. And the close-knit ties of sect life can provide a community where none exists on the outside.

Circumstances that lead to anomie Research suggests that the normative breakdown and insecurity which encourages the development of sects can result from a variety of factors.

First, the experience of disasters, whether natural or man-made. As Norman Cohn's studies of medieval Europe illustrate, sects may be preceded by outbreaks of plague, devastating fires, long droughts, serious economic slumps or calamitous wars, any of which may lead to a deep sense of doom and a fervent desire for salvation (Cohn, 1957).

Sects may be a response to unsettling contact with a powerful alien culture, especially if accompanied by the experience of being occupied and colonised. For example, the colonisation of Palestine by the Romans saw the birth of a sect which later became known as Christianity. In such contact between cultures, traditional norms, values and institutions may be shaken and undermined. And the contact often demoralises those who find themselves confronted by a more powerful society.

People who feel that their way of life is threatened or has collapsed experience a sense of disorientation, frustration,

deep anxiety and even rage. They will be predisposed to follow a messianic leader, such as Jesus Christ, who promises the coming of a new age.

A number of sociologists have argued that the social changes involved in the process of industrialisation and modernisation encouraged the emergence of sects. These changes can lead to social dislocation and a crisis of meaning and identity. People are less able to make sense of the world, they are increasingly unsure about who they are.

Sects can help some people to adjust to and make sense of a new situation. Bryan Wilson (1970) gives the example of Methodism which began as a sect. He sees the emergence of Methodism as a response by the new urban working class to the 'chaos and uncertainty of life in newly settled industrial areas'. Sects can provide a sense of community, clearly defined guidelines for living and a feeling of certainty.

Evaluation

The examples outlined in this section appear to support the view that sects are a response to social marginality, relative deprivation, rapid social change and social dislocation. However, there is evidence to question these explanations.

Beckford's (1975) study of Jehovah's Witnesses in Britain questions the significance of social marginality and relative deprivation. He found that most were upper working class and lower middle class. They showed no obvious signs of deprivation either financially or in terms of social status. Most had a religious upbringing and became disillusioned with mainstream religion. Sect membership offered an alternative religious direction which made sense and provided fulfilment.

Stark and Bainbridge (1985) examined the percentages of sects formed in the USA in different time periods during the first three-quarters of the 20th century. Sixteen per cent were formed in the 1950s, a period of social stability, 14% in the 1960s and only 3% from 1970 to 1977. The 1960s and early 1970s were a time of social unrest with student demonstrations, the hippie movement, Black riots and the Vietnam War. These findings cast doubt on the view that sects are most likely to emerge during periods of social change and social dislocation. However, it is important to note that Stark and Bainbridge use a fairly limited definition of a sect – a breakaway movement from an established religion. A broader definition may result in different figures and a different conclusion.

---

key terms

Theodicy of disprivilege A religious explanation for 'disprivilege' and a promise that things will get better in this life or the next.

Relative deprivation Deprivation which is relative to what people expect and feel they deserve.

Social dislocation A feeling of being uprooted, which can lead to a sense of anomie.

4.2 Cults and New Religious Movements

As outlined in the previous unit, cults are small religious groups which, unlike sects, believe that their teachings are just one of many paths to the truth. Compared to sects, cults are more tolerant of and open to the outside world. Many cults aim to develop the inner self and help people to experience their inner power.

Sociological explanations of cults are usually included within explanations of world-affirming New Religious Movements (NRMs), most of which can be classified as cults. They are also included within explanations of the New Age movement which contains many cult-like features. These explanations tend to focus on movements which developed in the West from the 1960s onwards.

The origins of NRMs

Rationalisation Roy Wallis (1984, 1985) draws on Max Weber's idea of *rationalisation* to explain the origins of NRMs. According to Weber, the meanings and motives which direct action in modern industrial society are rational. They are based on cold and deliberate reasoning, on precise calculations of the most effective ways of

activity 18 *the origins of sects*

Item A *The Ghost Dance*

By 1890, the traditional way of life of the Native American Sioux had ended. They had been defeated by the US army, rounded up, and confined to reservations. The buffalo, their main source of food, had all but disappeared, slaughtered by professional White hunters such as Buffalo Bill.

The US government was determined to stamp out the Sioux way of life. Traditional customs such as the Sun Dance, an important religious ceremony, were banned. The reservation authorities tried to force the Sioux to become farmers – an occupation despised by Sioux warriors.

Farming was doomed to failure. The land was unsuitable, there was a drought and the cattle became diseased. Undernourished, the Sioux had little

The frozen body of Chief Big Foot, leader of the ghost dancers at Wounded Knee

resistance to the measles and whooping cough which swept through the reservations in 1890. On one reservation, the death rate rose to 45 a month in a population of 5,550.

In 1890, the Sioux received news of a messiah, a Paiute called Wovoka. He had been visited by Christ and founded a new religion – the Ghost Dance. This was his message.

In the beginning, God made the earth and then sent the Christ to earth to teach the people. But White men treated him badly, leaving scars on his body, and so he went back to heaven. Now he has returned to earth as a Native American. He will renew everything as it used to be and make it better.

In the next springtime, when the grass is knee-high, the earth will be covered with new soil which will bury all the White men. The new land will be covered with sweet grass and running water and trees. Great herds of buffalo and wild horses will come back. The Native Americans who dance the Ghost Dance will be taken up in the air and suspended there while a wave of new earth is passing, and then they will be set down among the ghosts of their ancestors on the new earth. There they will follow their traditional way of life, forever free from death, disease and misery. Only Native Americans will live on this regenerated earth – the White race will disappear.

About half the Sioux nation believed in the new religion. They danced the ghost dance and wore 'ghost shirts' which they believed made them invulnerable to White men's bullets. Fearing trouble, the authorities called in the army. Troops surrounded a group of ghost dancers at Wounded Knee Creek. Fighting broke out and 150 Sioux including 60 women and children, were massacred. The Ghost Dance was over.

Adapted from Utley, 1963 and Brown, 1975

Item B The Rastafarian movement

The Rastafarian religion originated in the West Indies and was based on the ideas of Marcus Garvey, who preached that the only way for Black people to escape their poverty and oppression was to return to Africa. When Haile Selassie was crowned emperor of Ethiopia in 1930, and took the title 'Lion of Judah' (Ras Tafari), this was seen as a fulfilment of prophecy and followers claimed him as the Messiah, the incarnation of God. Rastafarians see themselves as the ancient lost tribe of Israel, enslaved and transported from Africa by Whites. They will remain forever oppressed and suffering, even in Jamaica, until they return to Africa. In Jamaica, its appeal has been greatest among the most disadvantaged sections of the Jamaican populace – the urban underclass. Some key beliefs are included in the 'Charter of the Rastafarians' below.

Rastafarian priests, Kingston, Jamaica

From the Rastafarian Charter

3 The Rastafarian Movement consists of the most advanced, determined and uncompromising fighters against discrimination, ostracism and oppression of the Black people of Jamaica.

4 The Rastafarian Movement stands for freedom in its fullest sense and for the recovery, dignity, self-respect and sovereignty of the Black people of Jamaica.

11 The Rastafarian Movement has as its chief aim the complete destruction of all vestiges of White supremacy in Jamaica, thereby putting an end to economic exploitation and the social degradation of the Black people.

Adapted from 'Charter of the Rastafarians' quoted in Williams, 1981

question

Give a sociological explanation for a) the Ghost Dance and b) Rastafarianism.

---

attaining goals such as making money and producing goods and services.

As a result of this process of rationalisation, mystery and magic, prophecy and the sacred have been pushed into the background. This has led, in Weber's words, to the 'disenchantment of the world', to *desacralisation* – the removal of the sacred, of religious meanings, guidelines and explanations. According to Wallis, many NRMs developed in response to this loss of the sacred.

Wallis is primarily concerned with explaining world-rejecting NRMs (many of which are similar to sects) and world-affirming NRMs (many of which are similar to cults).

World-rejecting NRMs

Wallis argues that the loss of the sacred was most acutely felt by young people in America and Europe during the 1960s and early 1970s. These were the years of political protest, counter-cultures and alternative lifestyles, when many young people sought to transform society. Their efforts largely failed. As a result, some young people believed that their lives and the wider society could not be transformed by human effort alone. They were therefore open to movements which claimed they could change the world by supernatural means, which claimed that a divine

power would intervene to transform society.

Some disillusioned and disenchanted young people joined world-rejecting NRMs – sect-like organisations, often founded by a charismatic leader. Such movements were critical or even hostile to the outside world, seeing it as corrupt and lacking in spirituality. Examples of these movements are Krishna Consciousness (ISKCON) and the Children of God. Their members were usually middle-class young adults. For example, one survey found that 85% of Krishna Consciousness members in the USA were under 26 (Judah, 1974). And a number of studies found that many members of world-rejecting NRMs had previously been involved in hippie counter-cultural movements (Downton, 1979).

World-affirming NRMs

Many world-affirming NRMs can be classified as cults. They are concerned with self-realisation, self-improvement and the development of the inner self. As their name suggests, world-affirming NRMs generally accept the wider society.

According to Wallis, world-affirming NRMs have their origins in the values and concerns of advanced capitalist societies. These societies place a high value on status, achievement, self-confidence, personal attractiveness, happiness and self-fulfilment. For many people, these values are difficult to translate into reality. Some find an answer in world-affirming NRMs which offer them recipes, techniques and knowledge to find what they're looking for.

Movements such as Transcendental Meditation and Scientology promise success in personal relationships and in employment, a higher IQ and a route to personal fulfilment. The Human Potential Movement and Est offer personal and spiritual growth, self-realisation and happiness.

Members of world-affirming NRMs are usually older, more affluent and even more middle class than members of world-rejecting NRMs. One study found that the average age of participants in Human Potential groups was 35 (Stone, 1976). According to Wallis, they have paid a high price for their successful careers and lifestyles – a single-minded focus on work, a high level of self-control, and a repression of their inner selves. In Wallis's words, world-affirming NRMs can provide 'a context and method of liberating spontaneity, of contacting the "real" self behind the masks and performances, of feeling and sharing intimacy and love (if only for a weekend before a return to the harsh reality of urban industrial life)' (Wallis, 1985).

Evaluation

Much of the research on NRMs has focused on movements in the West from the 1960s onwards. It has looked at NRMs which were formed or developed during these years and tended to explain them in terms of the context of Western society at the time. There is a major problem with this approach.

NRMs are not just recent developments confined to the West. Both sects and cults are examples of NRMs and both have a long history and a global spread. It is therefore inappropriate to simply explain them as a response to specific developments in Western society during the second half of the 20th century (Hunt, 2002).

key term

Desacralisation The removal of the sacred – of religious meanings, explanations and guides to action.

4.3 The New Age movement

A number of sociologists have looked for an explanation of the New Age movement in the social context of the late 20th and early 21st centuries. Some have seen it as a reflection of *late modernity*. This is defined as a phase rather than a new era, the development of an existing type of society – modernity – rather than a new type of society. Others have seen it as an expression of *postmodernity*, a new era which is distinct from and follows modernity.

Who participates?

Survey data indicates that New Agers are mainly female, predominantly middle class and well-educated. There is a fairly even spread across the age groups with the highest percentage – 42% according to one survey – in the 35-49 age group (York, 1995).

According to Steve Bruce (2001), the New Age movement appeals to those who work in 'expressive professions' – teachers, social workers, nurses, counsellors, artists, writers and actors. People in these professions tend to be individualistic, and concerned with 'personal development' and 'human potential'. These concerns are reflected in many aspects of the New Age movement.

Late modernity and postmodernity

Individualism and the self *Individualism* and *social reflexity* have been identified as characteristics of late modernity. Increasingly, the individual selects their own identity and designs their own lifestyle. They are more likely to be reflexive – to reflect on the self and what they are doing (Giddens, 1991, 2001).

Similarly, a concern with self has been identified as a feature of postmodernity. In the postmodern age, the individual has greater freedom to construct their own identity.

The New Age movement reflects these concerns. According to Paul Heelas (1996), it is a 'self-religion'. According to Steve Bruce (2002), it is concerned with self-discovery, personal choice, and the development of individual potential, freedom and autonomy.

Relativism Late modernity has been described as a time of uncertainty when traditional norms and values are breaking down at an increasingly rapid rate.

Postmodernity has been characterised as an era of *relativism* – as an era in which there are no absolute truths, in which no one belief system has a monopoly of the truth. *Metanarratives* – grand explanations – such as those of science and established religions have been undermined (Lyotard, 1984).

New Age spirituality is seen to thrive in this social context. Paul Heelas (1998) argues that the disintegration of the certainties of modernity has left a vacuum of meaning within which 'self-religions' emerge as individuals struggle to make sense of the situation.

Postmodernists argue that an age of relativism means that there is no longer a single truth – instead, there are many truths. This allows people to combine ideas, symbols and beliefs from the past and present, from a variety of cultures and from many parts of the world. This is exactly what New Age spirituality does. The relativism of postmodern society opens the door for the New Age movement and the individual construction of religion.

According to Bauman (1992), postmodernity has produced a 'crisis of meaning'. For some, the New Age movement provides answers.

Choice and consumption Both late modernity and postmodernity have been seen as times which emphasise individual choice and consumption. In particular, postmodernity has been characterised as an era in which people are preoccupied with choosing and consuming symbols, images, brands and goods in order to construct their own identities and lifestyles.

The New Age movement has been seen as a reflection of this concern. New Agers pick-and-mix from a vast range of ideas and beliefs – they select, match and construct to fit their image of self and their chosen lifestyle. According to Steve Bruce (2002), the individual consumer 'will decide what to believe' and 'the crucial test is personal experience'. If it works, if it provides meaning, satisfaction and fulfilment, the individual will 'buy into' New Age spirituality. If it doesn't work, they won't.

Life-as to subjective-life

According to Paul Heelas and Linda Woodhead (2004), there has been a 'massive turn' in Western culture from *life-as* to *subjective-life*. Life-as is life lived in terms of external roles, duties and obligations – for example, roles such as employer and employee, husband and wife, which are accompanied by a range of duties and obligations. These external roles, duties and obligations are 'higher authorities' which direct people's lives and give meaning to their existence. They are often supported by religion, by tradition and by the law.

Increasingly, people are moving from a focus on life-as to subjective-life which sees the inner feelings of each unique individual as primary. In Heelas and Woodhead's (2004) words, 'The goal is not to defer to higher authority, but to have the courage to become one's own authority. Not to follow established paths, but to forge one's own inner-directed … life'.

Assuming that Heelas and Woodhead are correct in their identification and description of recent changes in Western culture, then this 'cultural turn' helps to explain the growing attraction of New Age spirituality. With its focus on the inner-self, on subjective-life, on the unique individual, New Age spirituality can be seen as a reflection of broader cultural changes.

Evaluation

Relativism For Steve Bruce (2001), postmodernists take the argument too far. While he agrees that traditional authorities and established religions have been undermined, Bruce rejects the claim that the scientific 'metanarrative' has been abandoned. Scientific knowledge is still valued, and the idea that most people in Western societies now regard science as on a par with, for instance, the findings of palmistry or the reading of tea leaves, is nonsense.

Romanticism How new is the New Age movement? For Bruce (2001), New Age seekers' preferences for the more culturally alien and exotic religions and therapies is part of a romantic Western tradition 'as old as industrialisation

itself'. There is a long tradition of 'romanticising the underdeveloped and finding true humanity and spirituality in the rural peripheries of the urbanising world'.

Tautology Explanations which see the New Age movement as shaped by late modernity and postmodernity are somewhat tautological. A tautology is a circular argument. For example, postmodern society is characterised by a concern with individualism and the self, choice and consumption and the relativity of beliefs and ideas. To argue that postmodern society shapes the New Age movement is a tautology because the New Age movement is part of postmodern society. What we need to know is what caused postmodernity *and* the New Age movement.

A similar criticism can be made of Heelas and Woodhead's explanation of New Age spirituality as a reflection of a more general cultural change. Again, what we need to know is what caused these more general changes *and* New Age spirituality.

key terms

Individualism An emphasis on the individual rather than the social group.
Reflexivity Reflecting and looking back on the self.
Life-as Life lived in terms of external roles, duties and obligations.
Subjective-life An approach to life which sees the inner feelings of each unique individual as primary.

4.4 The development of religious movements

So far, this unit has focused on the origins of religious movements. This section looks at their development.

Sects and denominations

From sect to denomination H. Richard Niebuhr (1929) argued that sects are shortlived – they must either evolve into a denomination or die. He gave the following reasons for this claim.

Members of sects tend to come from the margins of society. On joining the sect, they usually lead frugal and ascetic (strict, self-denying) lives. As a result, their social status is likely to rise and their wealth increase. Their new situation no longer fits with their rejection of the wider society – and it brings greater public acceptance. As their contact with mainstream society grows, they modify their more unconventional beliefs.

This process is accelerated by the next generation. They were not converted into the sect, they were merely born into it. As a result, they are unlikely to show the same enthusiasm and commitment as their parents. They are more likely to make compromises with, and be less critical of, the wider society.

The very success of a sect can lead to its downfall. The

more its membership grows, the greater the need for full-time officials to manage the organisation. This, coupled with the toning down of its more 'extreme' views and the rise in its members' status, leads the sect down the road to a denomination. The once radical sect now becomes a respectable denomination, sitting comfortably within mainstream society.

There is evidence that some sects follow the route outlined by Niebuhr. For example, the Quakers began as a sect in the 17th century. Within a few generations they had moderated their beliefs and entered mainstream society. So much so that several Quaker families played a major part in the development of the British banking system – Barclays Bank still bears the name of one of these families. Similarly, the Methodists began as a sect, moderated their strict beliefs and their criticisms of the wider society, and developed into a denomination.

Evaluation Death or denomination are not the only alternatives open to sects. Some survive as sects – they become *established sects* (Yinger, 1970). They often do so by isolating themselves from the outside world – for example, the Amish in Pennsylvania, isolate themselves from the rest of American society. And the Exclusive Brethren keep outside influences at bay by banning their members from watching television and using computers (Hunt, 2002).

The path to salvation According to Bryan Wilson (1970), the crucial factor which determines whether a sect develops into a denomination or remains a sect is the way it answers the question, 'What shall we do to be saved?'

The answer from some sects is to convert as many people as possible. These *conversionist sects* are likely to develop into denominations. They are typically found in the USA where they use large-scale revivalist meetings to generate conversions. They can become a denomination without compromising their primary aim – they can still save souls.

Other types of sect cannot maintain their basic position in a denominational form. The primary aim of *adventist sects*, such as Jehovah's Witnesses, Seventh Day Adventists and Christadelphians is to prepare themselves for the Day of Judgement. To do this, they must separate themselves from today's sinful and corrupt society and await the second coming of Christ. Only membership of the sect will guarantee them a place in the new world order. Becoming a denomination would compromise their position which

demands separation from, rather than integration with, the wider society.

Wilson concludes that whether or not a sect becomes a denomination is largely determined by its prescription for salvation.

Cults and New Religious Movements

World-rejecting NRMs As noted earlier, most world-rejecting NRMs are similar to sects. Researchers who don't use the term NRM would classify many of them as sects.

Wallis (1984, 1985) sees two main routes for world-rejecting NRMs. The first is similar to the route described by Niebuhr. This involves a relaxation of the strict demands on members, a less critical view of the wider society, and a more conventional organisational structure. They move from world-rejecting to world-accommodating or world-affirming NRMs (see Activity 19, Item B).

Some world-rejecting NRMs take the opposite route, moving further inwards rather than outwards. According to Wallis, this is due to the intensity of their rejection of the wider society and the hostile reaction of the wider society to this rejection. In rare cases, this can lead to self-destruction where members of the movement commit suicide – the ultimate act of world-rejection (see Activity 19, Item A). In other cases, the movement goes underground – as in the case of the Children of God (Wallis, 1985).

World-affirming NRMs As noted earlier, world-affirming NRMs are similar to cults. Many support the norms and values of the mainstream culture and offer recipes for self-fulfilment and success in the wider society. They can be seen as serving clients or customers in a religious marketplace. From this point of view, their survival and development depend on the demand for the services they offer. To flourish, they must be sufficiently flexible to adapt their services to new demands and to compete with new brand names entering the market (Wallis, 1985).

Some do well when the economy is buoyant, but go to the wall during a recession – as did the Human Potential Movement. Others, such as Scientology and Est, vary their product to meet changing demands and attract a new clientele (Wallis, 1985).

key terms

Established sects Sects which survive over a relatively long period of time.
Conversionist sects Sects whose primary aim is to convert people.
Adventist sects Sects whose primary aim is to prepare themselves for the Day of Judgement, for the transformation of the world.

summary

1. The following explanations have been put forward for the origin of sects.

   - Social marginality – Sects tend to recruit those on the margins of society. Their new status as the 'chosen few' provided by a theodicy of disprivilege can bring self-respect and hope for the future.

   - Relative deprivation – Sects can provide a sense of community, mutual support and self-respect. The self-discipline and self-denial demanded by many sects can improve people's material situation.

   - Social dislocation – This can result in anomie (a sense of normlessness). Sects, with their clearly defined belief systems and strict moral codes, can provide certainty and direction.

2. Circumstances which can lead to anomie include:

   - Natural or man-made disasters

   - Contact with, or colonisation by, a powerful alien culture

   - The process of industrialisation and modernisation.

3. Wallis sees NRMs resulting from the processes of rationalisation and desacrilisation. He sees world-rejecting NRMs during the 1960 and 70s as a response to the failure of young people to change society by protest and alternative lifestyles. He sees world-affirming NRMs as a response to the values of capitalist society – as a means of realising them or as compensation for the price paid for living up to them.

4. Some sociologists have seen the New Age movement with its emphasis on individualism, relativism, choice and consumption as a reflection of late modernity, while others have seen it as a reflection of postmodernity.

5. According to Heelas and Woodhead, the increasing emphasis on subjective-life, as opposed to life-as, accounts for the growth of New Age spirituality.

6. Niebuhr argued that sects are short-lived – they must develop into denominations or die.

7. But some sects survive – as established sects. They often do so by isolating themselves from the outside world.

8. According to Bryan Wilson, conversionist sects are likely to develop into denominations because they can still save souls in this form. Adventist sects cannot become denominations, because only membership of the sect will guarantee them a place in the new world order.

9. Wallis sees two main routes for world-rejecting NRMs. First, they can develop into either world-accommodating or world-affirming NRMs. Or second, they can turn further inwards and increase their isolation from the wider society.

10. Wallis argues that the survival and development of world-affirming NRMs depends on the demand for the services they offer. To flourish, they must respond to new demands.

activity 19 the development of NRMs

Item A The People's Temple

The People's Temple was founded in the USA by the Reverend Jim Jones. He promised to create a utopia – a perfect society in which everybody worked for the common good. Most members were recruited from the poor.

As his following grew, Jones demanded more and more discipline and dedication, along with absolute loyalty to himself. He became a messiah-like figure, claiming at various times to be God, Buddha and Lenin. He forecast the destruction of the world and claimed that only members of the Temple would survive.

Jones and his followers grew increasingly hostile to the outside world. He vehemently criticised the 'enemies' of the People's Temple. Rumours of human rights abuses led to an investigation of the movement. Jones responded by leading around 1000 of his followers to Guyana in South America, where they hacked a settlement, known as Jonestown, out of the jungle.

Jonestown after the mass suicide

Concerned relatives of the movement's members demanded an investigation which was led by Congressman Leo J. Ryan. Jones sent gunmen to ambush Ryan as he returned to his plane. The Congressman and several of his party were killed.

Next day, November 18, 1978, Jones announced that the community would soon be attacked. He ordered his followers to commit suicide as a sign of their dedication. They had rehearsed this many times. They drank a mixture of Kool-Aid (a soft drink) and cyanide. According to the few survivors, most people took their lives willingly, with mothers giving the cyanide to their children, then drinking it themselves. Over 900 people died.

Adapted from *Chronicle of America*, 1989 and www.apologeticsindex.org

Item B 3HO and Vajradhatu

3HO

According to their website, the 'Healthy, Happy, Holy Organisation (3HO) is a worldwide association of people dedicated to the excellence of the individual. The basic philosophy of 3HO affirms that you, as a human being, are so perfectly created that by using exercise, breathing and meditation, you can balance and revitalise the physical body, nervous and glandular systems and bring balance and peace to your life.

3HO brings to the public the ancient science of Kundalini Yoga. It offers complete lifestyle guidelines on nutrition and health, interpersonal relations, child rearing and human behaviour. You may choose from a wealth of knowledge to find the exact techniques you are looking for to become healthy, happy and holy.'

Vajradhatu

Vajradhatu is based on the teachings of Buddha. According to their website, 'Buddhism is taking an increasingly prominent role in contemporary Western society as interest increases in this approach to life. A unique quality of the Buddhist teachings is that they can be expressed through existing cultural norms, making use of them rather than destroying or replacing them. This allows many Westerners to practice Buddhism today without renouncing their cultural heritage or radically changing their lifestyles. A careful sequence of group practice programmes ensures that students can develop according to their own interests and commitments.'

Sociological comment

New Religious Movements such as 3HO and Vajradhatu – whose members are mainly well-educated, middle-class, White Americans – have become increasingly world-affirming. This was a response to changing social and economic conditions. It provided a strong foundation on which the movements can grow. As Khasala (1986) states, 'What better way to become an accepted part of American society than by embracing some of the values that this country holds most dear: utilitarian individualism, capitalistic enterprise, and most definitely, financial success.'

Adapted from Hunt, 2002; Khasala, 1986; www.3HO.org; www.shambhala.org

questions

1 Discuss Item A in terms of Wallis's view of the development of world-rejecting NRMs.

2 Discuss Item B in terms of Wallis's view of the development of world-affirming NRMs.

3 The movements in Item B appear to be taking the route to denominationalism. What evidence is there for this statement?

Unit 5 Secularisation

keyissues

1 What is secularisation?

2 What is the secularisation thesis?

3 What are the arguments for and against secularisation?

Has the importance of religion changed over time? In some countries, such as Britain, religion is often seen as less important than in the past. The question of the changing significance of religion in modern societies has been central to sociology. Marx, Durkheim, Weber and many other sociologists have regarded it as an issue of major importance.

This unit looks at the argument that religion is declining in modern society – a process known as *secularistion*.

5.1 Defining secularisation

The word secular means not sacred, not spiritual, not religious. So, secularisation refers to the process of becoming less religious. And the claim that religion is declining in importance is known as the *secularisation thesis*.

However, defining secularisation is not as simple as this. Sociologists cannot agree on a definition of religion. As a result, they cannot agree on how to define – and measure – secularisation.

Two views of secularisation

Woodhead and Heelas (2000) identify two versions of the secularisation thesis – the *disappearance thesis* and the *differentiation thesis*.

The disappearance thesis This thesis states that modernity is bringing about the death of religion. The significance of religion both for society *and* for individuals is steadily declining. This process will continue until religion disappears.

The differentiation thesis This thesis states that religion is declining in *social* significance. It no longer plays an important part in society – for example, it no longer influences major social institutions such as the family and the educational, legal and political systems. It has become separated or differentiated from the wider social structure. However, it is likely to retain some significance in people's private lives.

Evaluation The distinction between the disappearance thesis and the differentiation thesis is important. Early sociological theorists such as Marx and Weber believed that religion would disappear. However, more recent British sociologists, such as Bryan Wilson, Roy Wallis and Steve Bruce state that their version of the secularisation thesis does *not* suggest that religion will disappear and everyone will eventually become an atheist. Instead, it means that the social significance of religion is declining (Bruce, 2002). In Bryan Wilson's (1982) words, 'It does not even require that most individuals have relinquished all their interest in religion. It maintains no more than that religion ceases to be significant in the working of the social system.'

The Broad and Narrow Approach

Sharon Hanson (1997) makes a distinction between religion on a social and individual level. She states there are two levels to the secularisation debate, and that these levels are often confused.

- The Broad Approach asks whether religion has lost significance on the level of the social system.
- The Narrow Approach focuses on religion at the level of individual consciousness.

Making this distinction is important. As noted earlier, secularisation may be occurring on the societal level, but not on the individual level.

Secularisation and the West

Most supporters of the secularisation thesis focus on the West – they do not see it as a global process. One of its main supporters, Steve Bruce (2002), limits the secularisation thesis to Europe, North America and Australasia. He sees the secular West as an exception in the sweep of human history.

key terms

Secular Not sacred, not spiritual, not religious.
Secularisation The process of becoming less religious.
Secularisation thesis The claim that religion is declining in importance.
Disappearance thesis The claim that religion both on a societal and an individual level will eventually disappear.
Differentiation thesis The claim that religion is declining in social significance, that it no longer plays an important part in society.
The Broad Approach Focuses on the significance of religion on a societal level.
The Narrow Approach Focuses on the significance of religion on an individual level.

5.2 Evidence for secularisation

The evidence in support of the secularisation thesis can be organised in terms of Bryan Wilson's (1966) definition of secularisation as 'the process whereby religious thinking, practice and institutions lose social significance'. So, compared to past ages:

1 What power, prestige and influence do religious institutions have?

2 What influence does religion have on people's beliefs, thinking, attitudes and consciousness?

3 How widespread are religious practices?

The power and influence of the church There can be little doubt that the power and influence of the church in Western Europe has declined over the last 1000 years. As a social institution, the Roman Catholic Church in medieval Christendom had power to rival that of kings. At its peak in the 12th and 13th centuries, the Roman Catholic Church was central to the political life of Western societies. It was the major employer, with its own courts and its own judges and lawyers, and its own physicians. In its heyday, it has been estimated that throughout Western Europe one out of every thirty adult males was in the service of the Church.

And it could shape and dominate the imagination. It provided one of the very few opportunities for literacy. And 'at a time when not one man in a thousand could read, the Church taught its story in stone, painting, glass and embroidery, in buildings which – in an age when most people lived in huts little bigger or cleaner than pigsties – towered above the landscape and blazed within with colour and wealth' (Bryant, 1953).

Today, in Western Europe, the power and prestige of religious institutions have long since shrunk. Church buildings can be seen in ruins or put to secular use. During the 20th century when the country's population almost doubled, the number of full-time clergy halved (Bruce, 2002). And, where once the churches played a major role as providers of information and guidance, this function has largely passed on to the media and to the medical profession.

Religious beliefs Supporters of the secularisation thesis claim that people's thinking and attitudes are no longer based on religious beliefs. To accept that secularisation has occurred, Wilson argues, 'All that needs to be assumed is that society was much more preoccupied with supernatural beliefs and practices, and accorded them more significance, than it does now' (quoted in Wallis & Bruce, 1989). Wilson accepts that superstitious and magical beliefs, indifference and unbelief were common in the Middle Ages. Nevertheless, he argues that those concerned were 'believers'. All shared a belief in the reality of the supernatural, even if they did draw on beliefs defined as deviant by the established church. Their beliefs were not secular in any modern sense.

The historian Peter Laslett came to similar conclusions. He studied evidence of the villagers living in Clayworth, Nottinghamshire in 1676 and concluded that they were 'literal believers, all of the time', though they might combine their Christian beliefs with others such as witchcraft (Hanson, 1997).

Surveys from the second half of the 20th century suggest a decline in religious belief. In 1947, 45% of British respondents said they believed in a 'personal God'. By 1981 this figure had dropped to 41%, by 1990 to 32% and by 2000 to 26% (Bruce, 2002).

Religious practices With regard to the mainstream churches and denominations in Western Europe, there is general agreement that religious practices have declined. The evangelical revivals of 18th and 19th century Britain (Methodism, Salvation Army, and others), led to gains in membership until perhaps the 1930s. Thereafter, most Protestant organisations declined. Church membership, church attendance, church marriage, church funerals, christenings, Sunday School and Bible reading are all down. According to Steve Bruce (1992), 'The high point for the British churches was between 1860 and 1910 when around 28% of the adult population were active members'. By 2002, only 17% claimed to be members and only about 8% attended church (Bruce, 2002). Even Roman Catholics – whose numbers grew until the early 1960s through immigration from Ireland and a high birth rate – appear to be part of this general decline in religious practice.

The decline might be greater than the figures suggest. A survey by Leslie Francis indicated that clergy in rural areas were overestimating Sunday attendances by an average of 40% (Morgan, 1997).

For most people, it appears that churches and denominations offer little more than ceremonial for the rites of passage of birth, marriage and death.

Privatised religion There is evidence of a decline in religious beliefs, particularly traditional Christian beliefs – for example, the belief in a personal God. And there is evidence of a decline in collective religious practices.

Some researchers argue that religion is becoming a 'private affair'. And this means a range of different beliefs rather than overarching, society-wide beliefs. Thomas Luckmann (1970) states, 'Once religion is defined as a "private affair", the individual may choose from the assortment of "ultimate" meanings as he sees fit'. And privatised religion does not encourage public, collective religious practice.

Grace Davie (1994) argues that there has been a separation of 'belief and belonging'. She claims that religious belief remains widespread but is less likely to be expressed in an institutional setting. People no longer feel they belong to a religious organisation.

If privatised religion is widespread, then, in terms of Hanson's Narrow Approach – religion at the level of individual consciousness – secularisation may not be occurring. However, in terms of the Broad Approach, secularisation may well be occurring. Religion appears to be losing its significance on the level of the social system. It no longer forms part of the mainstream culture. The major institutions of religion – churches and denominations – are declining in importance as their membership dwindles. This also provides support for the differentiation thesis which is an example of the Broad Approach. It states that secularisation is occurring if the *social* significance of religion is declining.

Beyond church and denomination Some religious groups outside the Christian mainstream have grown in Britain. Non-Trinitarian groups, such as the Christadelphians, Christian Scientists, Mormons and Jehovah's Witnesses have grown from 71,000 in 1900 to 533,000 in 2000. However, the 2000 figure is just one-sixth of the numbers lost to the main Christian Trinitarian churches over the same period (Brierley, 2000). (Trinitarian refers to a belief in the Trinity – God as Father, Son and Holy Spirit. Non-Trinitarian refers to a number of alternative views of God.)

As discussed in Unit 3, the last 40 years of the 20th century saw the emergence of a large number of New Religious Movements (NRMs) and the New Age movement. Eileen Barker (1983) estimated that the numbers involved in many of these NRMs in Britain were only in the hundreds. And, at any point in time during a 25 year period, the total involved in all NRMs was no more than 100,000. Socially as well as numerically, Steve Bruce (2002) regards NRMs as insignificant. Unlike earlier NRMs such as Methodism, they only affect the lives of their followers and make little or no difference to the wider society.

Bruce is equally dismissive about the New Age movement. He sees it as having minimal effect on society as a whole. And the commitment of New Age 'seekers' is slight as they flit from one spiritual novelty to the next. With the most popular aspects of New Age being relaxation techniques, meditation, yoga and massage, Bruce (2002) regards it not so much as an alternative to traditional religion as 'an extension of the doctor's surgery, the beauty parlour and the gym'.

Ethnic religions and secularisation In the UK, there has been a steady growth in the membership of ethnic minority group religions – for example, membership of the Muslim faith rose from 130,000 in 1970 to 675,000 in 2000 (Brierley, 2000). This reverses the trend shown by the majority population. Does this indicate a resurgence of religion amongst ethnic minorities – an opposite trend to secularisation?

At least part of this increase is due to continued immigration – for example, there are growing numbers of migrants from a Muslim background. Even this, however, does not fully account for the higher levels of religious participation amongst ethnic minorities. Steve Bruce (2002) suggests the following explanations.

Religion can remain a powerful social force when it provides resources for *cultural defence*. For example, in cases of ethnic conflict, it can be a positive source of ethnic identity and solidarity. Similarly, religion can provide a vehicle for *cultural transition* when an immigrant population settles in a new, and often unwelcoming, world. Religion can offer a sense of community and a sense of self-worth and support.

In the case of ethnic minority groups, religion may provide resources for cultural defence and cultural transition. However, it appears that this is only a short-lived adaptation. As Bruce (2002) notes, the third generation of Muslims is approaching 'the English level of religious indifference'. If this is so, ethnic religious enthusiasm is simply a blip in the overall trend to secularisation.

key terms

Cultural defence The strategies used by a group to defend its culture and group identity.
Cultural transition The change in culture when people – for example, immigrants – move from one social setting to another.

Evidence for secularisation – evaluation

Problems of measurement Does the data used to support secularisation provide a valid – a true and accurate – measure of the process? Different religious organisations measure membership in different ways. Many don't record attendance figures and those that do, don't always record them all year round and for all services. As noted earlier, some exaggerate attendance levels, as do many members of their congregations when asked how often they attend services.

Similarly, when people say they believe in God in response to a questionnaire-based survey, what does this mean? Is this belief of major significance to their lives? Or, is it something they rarely think about, something they regard as unimportant?

Religious beliefs are extremely difficult to measure. For example, over 37 million people in England and Wales described themselves as Christian in the 2001 census. They were asked to respond to the question 'What is your religion?' by ticking one of a number of options (*Social Trends*, 2004). For many, this statement of religion may mean little or nothing. It may simply be seen as a follow-on from being English.

David Martin (1969) argues that church attendance in Victorian Britain, particularly for the middle classes, was as much a sign of respectability as of religious conviction.

Belief and belonging As noted earlier, Grace Davie (1994) makes the distinction between belief and belonging. Some forms of religious belief still appear widespread. For example, European Values surveys from the 1980s to 2000 show that nearly 60% of Europeans describe themselves as 'a religious person' and around 50% claim that God plays a significant part in their life (Cook, 2000).

While belief may be fairly high, belonging – membership of and attendance at religious institutions – is low and getting lower. As discussed earlier, a decline in institutional religion does not necessarily indicate secularisation. Private or personal religion may remain relatively strong. Whether secularisation is occurring depends, in part, on how the process is defined – in terms of the Broad Approach or the Narrow Approach.

Historical comparisons Going to church is often assumed to be a valid indicator of religiosity. However, it may have different meanings at different times. For example, in the past it may have been an expression of community – a normal part of community life which had little to do with religion as such. Today, with the breakup of close-knit communities, collective worship may well be an expression of religious faith rather than a normal part of social life.

A 'golden age' of religion There is a tendency for some researchers to look back to a supposedly 'golden age' of religion in the Middle Ages as a point of comparison for today. There are a number of problems with this view.

- First, the religious practices of the land-owning nobility are much better documented than those of the peasantry.

- Second, there is some evidence that the peasantry were largely indifferent or even hostile to the Catholic Church.

- Third, although some supporters of the secularisation thesis accept that there was some apathy or indifference to religion in the Middle Ages, their critics argue that they have underestimated the extent of these views (Hamilton, 2001; Hunt, 2002).

Beyond major religious institutions Secularisation theorists have tended to focus on mainstream, institutional religion – on churches and denominations. They have dismissed NRMs as numerically and socially insignificant. And their tone is often scornful when it comes to the New Age movement. Yet the significance and potential of such movements may be much greater than they suggest (Heelas & Woodhead, 2003; 2004 – see pages 58-59).

The USA Compared to Europe, both belief and belonging in the USA are high. For example, surveys indicate that 90% of people believe in God and over 40% regularly attend a religious institution (Hunt, 2002). Does this evidence go against the secularisation thesis? This question will be discussed in Section 5.5, pages 59-61.

Further evaluation of the evidence used by secularisation theorists is contained in later sections.

activity20 evidence for secularisation

Item A Medieval religion

The God in whom medieval people believed was an intensely personal God, forever appearing in acts of nature, visions and apparitions, plagues and cures, storms, fires and miracles. And not only God, but the whole hierarchy of Heaven, angels and saints, apostles and martyrs, lay on the frontiers of the visible, tangible world, ready at any moment to reveal themselves.

So too did the Devil and the fiends, witches and ministers of evil. A flight of crows seemed a swarm of demons, the howling of the wind was the cry of some wicked lord, borne through the middle air to Hell. At a time when people knew little of the laws of nature or the world outside their village homes, they accepted such ideas with no more question than their twentieth century descendants did of the latest scientific marvels.

Beyond all this lay a conception shared by rich and poor alike, educated and ignorant. It was that divine law governed the universe, from its greatest to its minutest part. Everything that happened in the world – everything that had happened, was happening and was going to happen – was a part of God's plan, only partly intelligible to people's puny intellect. The Church existed to help explain the plan, to help people obey it and, through Christ's love and sacrifice, to obtain forgiveness for them when they broke God's law.

Adapted from Bryant, 1953

Part of a medieval painting called the Great Doom. It shows some of the horrors of hell – a miser is being roasted and cheating traders are suspended over the fire on a bridge of spikes.

Item B From sacred to secular

Former churches in Preston, Lancashire, converted into a radio station, an antique centre and a printers.

Item C Membership of religious groups (UK, thousands)

Group	1970	1980	1990	2000
Christian: Trinitarian of whom:	9,272	7,529	6,624	5,917
Anglican (C of E)	2,987	2,180	1,728	1,654
Catholic	2,746	2,455	2,198	1,768
Free Churches	1,629	1,285	1,299	1,278
Presbyterian	1,751	1,437	1,214	989
Orthodox	159	172	185	235
Christian: Non-Trinitarian	276	349	455	533
Buddhist	10	15	30	50
Hindu	80	120	140	165
Jewish	375	321	356	383
Muslim	130	305	495	675
Sikh	100	150	250	400
Others	20	40	55	85

Adapted from Brierley, 2000

Item D Religious beliefs

Beliefs	1947	1981	1990	2000
There is a personal God	45	41	32	26
There is some sort of higher power, spirit or life force	39	37	41	21
There is something there	n.a.	n.a.	n.a.	23
I don't really know what to think	16	16	15	12
I don't really think there is any sort of God, spirit or life force	n.a.	6	10	15
None of these	n.a.	n.a.	1	3

Note: n.a. = not asked.

Adapted from Bruce, 2002

Item E The social significance of New Age spirituality

Although New Agers often use words like 'radical' and 'alternative', the effect is anything but. The anxious, repressed merchant banker who learns to meditate and gets his regular shiatsu massage, does not throw up banking and become a youth worker or an eco-warrior. He just becomes a happier and more relaxed merchant banker.

But even if the merchant banker does decide to throw it all in, buy a farmhouse in Wales and start a pottery with a side-line in horoscopes, the impact on the rest of the world is minimal. In the 18th and 19th centuries, the Methodists were responsible for a vast amount of social reform. They put a stop to child labour in factories and mines. They stopped young boy sweeps being forced to climb up the chimneys of Georgian houses. They restricted the length of the working day. They put an end to a system by which men were paid their wages in pubs. They ended slavery. They also founded schools, penny savings banks and public libraries.

Adapted from Bruce, 2002

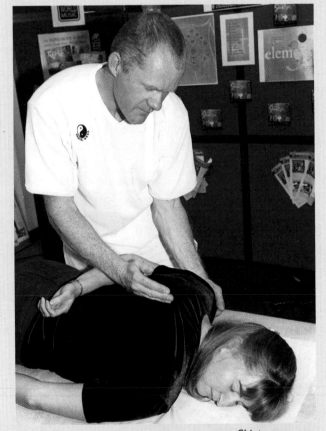

Shiatsu massage

questions

1 In what ways do Items A and B support the secularisation thesis?

2 a) Briefly describe the trends shown in Items C and D.

   b) What support do they provide for the secularisation thesis?

3 Using Hanson's concepts of the Broad Approach and the Narrow Approach, explain why Bruce (Item E) argues that the rise of New Age spirituality does not contradict the secularisation thesis.

5.3 Sociological theories and secularisation

This section looks at secularisation in terms of broader sociological theories of social change. Most of the sociologists examined here assume that secularisation is occurring in one form or another. Their aim is to explain the process. Others are less sure about the secularisation thesis. Some see a transformation of religious expression rather than a decline in religion as such.

Karl Marx

Marx believed that capitalism was the penultimate era of human society. The final era, communism, would follow the overthrow of capitalism.

As outlined earlier (see pages 12-13), Marx saw religion as a reflection of class society – it justified the position of the ruling class and provided compensation for the oppression of the subject class. Social classes and oppression would disappear in communist society. Since these are the social forces which generate religion, religion too would disappear.

Marx believed that capitalism itself contained the seeds of secularisation. It presented a materialist view of the world – its aim was to produce goods and make profits. And the social order was seen to be based on contracts rather than being ordained by God – for example, the wage contract between employer and employee.

Marx saw the death of religion as inevitable. His theory is an example of the disappearance thesis of secularisation.

Max Weber

As outlined in Unit 1, Weber saw rationalisation as the key process in the development of modern society (see pages 19-20). Reason steadily replaces faith. The world becomes demystified – its magic and mystery are taken away. The meanings which direct action are increasingly rational rather than religious.

Ironically, it was religion, in Weber's view, which spearheaded this process of rationalisation. Weber claimed that the spirit of capitalism had its origins in early forms of Protestantism, particularly Calvinism. And the spirit of capitalism was one of the main factors in the development of rational capitalism. Once on its way, modern society no longer needed religion to guide action – reason was now a sufficient guide.

Malcolm Hamilton (2001) summarises Weber's views. 'Calvinistic Protestantism was its own gravedigger. In many ways, it could not help but sow the seeds of secularisation in modern society by its own promotion of worldly activity and consequent expansion of wealth and material well-being.'

Peter Berger

Like Weber, Peter Berger (1973) sees the origins of secularisation in religion itself. He notes that it is the Christian world, and particularly the Protestant world, which has experienced the greatest degree of secularisation. And it is Protestantism, more than any other branch of Christianity, which has cut out or cut down the sacramental, the sacred and the ritual elements of Catholicism, and the mystery, miracle and magic found in many other religions. In Berger's view, one of the main factors leading to secularisation is the rationality of Protestantism (see pages 20-22).

Berger argues that the process of secularisation has been accelerated by more recent changes in modern society. The growth of the media and increasing social and geographical mobility have exposed people to a range of different religions. Faced with this market place of religions with their competing sets of beliefs and practices, it has become increasingly difficult to accept the teachings of any one as the truth. This weakens the authority of all religions. And this accelerates the process of secularisation (see pages 20-22).

Bryan Wilson

The British sociologist Bryan Wilson (1966, 1976), argues for the differentiation thesis – that religion is declining in social significance. In Hanson's (1997) terminology, he takes the Broad Approach. Wilson gives the following explanations for secularisation.

Social differentiation As modern society developed, its various institutions became increasingly separate as they specialised in particular functions. This process is known as *social differentiation*. Religious institutions were once directly involved in politics, social control, social welfare, health and education. Now there are specialist institutions for each of these areas. As a result, religion is relegated to the margins of society where it 'ceases to be significant in the working of the social system' (Wilson, 1982).

Rational thinking and science Like Weber and Berger, Wilson argues that rational thinking has largely replaced religious views of the world. Like Weber, he sees early Protestantism contributing to rational thought. However, he places more emphasis on the development of science and the scientific method, which he sees as displacing religious explanations. In Wilson's (1966) words, 'Science not only explained many facets of life and the material environment in a way more satisfactory, but it also provided confirmation of its explanation in practical results'.

The decline of community Traditionally, religion has drawn its strength from close-knit communities. Communal values were expressed and reinforced in religious rituals. Events of significance to the community – from the harvest to births, marriages and deaths – were celebrated in the local church.

Industrialisation and urbanisation have led to the break-up of this type of community life. As a result, religion has lost much of its reason for being.

Emile Durkheim

The remaining views examined in this section are less sure about the secularisation thesis. Rather then seeing religion declining or disappearing, they are more likely to see a transformation of traditional religion into a new form of religion.

Looking back over the 19th century and the early years of the 20th century, Durkheim saw the rapid social changes brought about by industrialisation and urbanisation as a threat to religion. These changes led to the break-up of community and to anomie – a disruption of the norms which govern behaviour. The result was a weakening of social solidarity and collective consciousness. Since the close-knit community with its shared norms and values was the lifeblood of religion, religion itself was threatened.

Durkheim feared that religion would be relegated to a corner of life – a private matter, no longer capable of overarching society and unifying its members. However, he did not see the decline of religion as an irreversible trend, believing that all societies must have sacred symbols and communal ritual if they are to survive. So, in Durkheim's view, religion will not die, though it is likely to change its form. A possible example of this transformation of religion is the civil religion identified by Robert Bellah in the USA (see pages 10-12). If Bellah is correct, civil religion performs Durkheim's essential functions of religion – reinforcing collective consciousness and strengthening social solidarity.

Postmodernist views

According to Lyotard (1984), postmodern society is characterised by a loss of confidence in metanarratives – the big stories or grand explanations provided by science, religion and politics. Their authority and certainty have been undermined, their claim to the truth has been questioned. As a result, traditional institutional religion with its claim to universal truth has been undermined (see page 23).

According to Zygmunt Bauman (1992), this produces a 'crisis of meaning'. Traditional religious metanarratives, such as Christianity, cannot deal with this crisis, which explains their decline. However, new religions or new expressions of religiosity can restore meaning. But these new expressions are very different from the old religions. They are tailored by individuals to fit their particular identities, rather than being imposed by institutions which claim an exclusive truth which everybody should believe. This can be seen in the decline of religious monopolies, such as Christianity, and the rise of the New Age movement.

---

key term

Social differentiation The process by which social institutions become increasingly specialised and separate.

5.4 The spiritual revolution thesis

In an important study known as the Kendal Project, a team of researchers led by Paul Heelas set out to test the *spiritual revolution thesis*. This thesis states that a spiritual revolution is underway, or may have already taken place (Heelas & Woodhead, 2003; 2004).

The researchers identified two possible trends. First, a decline in traditional Christianity with its emphasis on a God-on-high, who tells people how to live their lives. This is the argument put forward by secularisation theorists. Alongside this decline in the sacred is an alternative growth in the sacred in the form of New Age spirituality. Here the emphasis is on the spirituality of the inner self rather than conforming to some externally imposed morality. This is the argument put forward by *sacralisation theorists.*

Methodology The researchers chose Kendal as the setting in which to test the spiritual revolution thesis. Kendal is a town of some 28,000 people in the Lake District in northwest England. It was small enough to investigate systematically, but large enough to have a range of traditional religious activity and New Age spiritualities.

The focus of the research was a comparison between the 'congregational domain' and the 'holistic milieu'. The congregational domain was represented by 25 Christian churches and chapels in Kendal. A head-count was taken of those who attended on Sunday, 26 November, 2000. This avoided the problem of self-reporting where people tend to exaggerate their attendance rate.

The holistic milieu refers to those who practise activities which they see as involving the whole person – as combining the mind, body and spirit. The inclusion of 'spirit' is critical. If an activity such as yoga or tai chi is not seen as spiritual, then that person is not included in the holistic milieu. A questionnaire was used to count those involved in New Age spiritualities and in-depth interviewing explored the attractions of New Age.

The findings The head-count for attendance at churches and chapels was 2207, 7.9% of the population of Kendal – exactly the same as the percentage for Britain as a whole. Attendance figures for Kendal from the 1950s onwards show a significant decline. By comparison, the holistic milieu shows strong growth. There were 95 practitioners (providers) of spiritual activities in 2000. In the 1970s, there were only three such practitioners in the *Yellow Pages*, by 1999 this had grown to almost 40. Those taking part in 2000 numbered 600, 1.6% of the population of Kendal. However, only 55% considered these activities to be of spiritual significance, 0.9% of the population of Kendal.

Conclusion In Heelas's (2004) words, 'the spiritual revolution clearly has not taken place in Kendal'. At first sight, the 0.9% involved in holistic spiritual practices seems a long way from the 7.9% involved in the congregational domain. However, the trends suggest a different picture. If present trends continue, then the revolution will take place in twenty or thirty years, when numbers involved in the holistic milieu will overtake those in the congregational domain – see Activity 21, Item A.

Evaluation The Kendal Project is an important piece of research. First, it provides a measurement of New Age spirituality. Second, it looks at trends over time.

How do its findings fit into the secularisation debate? The trends identified in Kendal suggest that New Age spirituality cannot be dismissed as easily as some secularisation theorists argue. However, the numbers involved are still fairly small.

Can New Age spirituality be directly compared to religion? Although many people believe that holistic practices have a spiritual aspect, this is very different from believing in and praying to a supernatural being.

5.5 Religion in the USA

Is America an exception to secularisation in the West? This question has often been asked because of the apparently high levels of attendance at religious institutions in the

key terms

Spiritual revolution thesis States that a spiritual revolution is underway, or may already have taken place.
Sacralisation Becoming sacred. A term used by those who see a growth of spirituality or religion.

USA and the high proportion of Americans who say they believe in God.

Statistical evidence

Various surveys over the past 50 years indicate that between 90 and 95% of Americans claim to believe in God. And, over the same period of time, around 40% of Protestants and 50% of Catholics say they attended church in the past week.

These figures are based on self-reports – that is, people reporting their religious beliefs and practices to interviewers or on self-completion questionnaires. There is evidence that they overstate their commitment to religion in order to present themselves in the best possible light. For

activity21 the spiritual revolution thesis

Item A *The timing of the revolution*

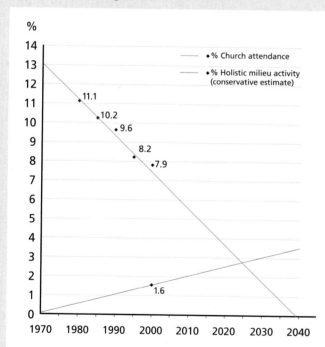

Adapted from Heelas & Woodhead, 2003; 2004

Item B *The scale of the revolution*

Findings from the Kendal Project show that 80% of those involved in holistic milieu activities are women, and 83% are over 40. Over half have attended university or college and many work in people-centred, caring jobs, such as nursing, where personal wellbeing is a major concern. Given the relatively small number of people with these characteristics, there is not much scope for expansion in the future. This means, of course, that the rate of growth of the holistic milieu is likely to slow down.

Adapted from Heelas & Woodhead, 2004

questions

1 Briefly summarise the trends shown in Item A.

2 New Age spirituality is very unlikely to become a majority concern. Discuss with reference to Items A and B.

example, Hadaway and Marler (1999) conducted a head-count of people who attended church. They found actual attendance was about half the level of self-reported attendance – 'Instead of 40% of Protestants attending church, we found 20%. Instead of 50% of Catholics attending church, we found 28%'. However, even these levels are considerably higher than those in Britain.

The secularisation of religious institutions

When it comes to secularisation, America should be in the lead. As Bryan Wilson (1966) observed, it is 'a country in which instrumental values, rational procedures and technical methods have gone furthest, and the country in which the sense of the sacred, the sense of the sanctity of life, and deep religiosity are most conspicuously absent' (Wilson, 1966). So how come there is high church attendance and widespread religious beliefs in a markedly secular society?

To Will Herberg (1960), the answer is simple. The religious content of churches, denominations and synagogues has been watered down. Religious institutions have compromised their beliefs and practices to fit in with the wider society. They have undergone a process of internal secularisation.

Herberg argues that the high level of attendance at religious institutions is directed by secular rather than religious concerns. He claims that to be an American – to demonstrate an American identity – requires a public commitment to religious beliefs within a religious organisation. Which religious organisation doesn't really matter. Either Protestant, Catholic or Jewish faiths are regarded as acceptable evidence of an American identity. Over time, these three religious traditions have become more and more alike in their teachings and in their function of supporting the nation. The central themes of American religion increasingly reflect the American Way of Life – the core values of American society such as freedom, democracy and achievement.

Herberg explains America's religious enthusiasm in terms of the unique experience of a nation which had to weld together a mix of people from across the world. In doing this, American religion has itself become secular. To a large

summary

1. There are two main versions of the secularisation thesis – the disappearance thesis and the differentiation thesis.

2. Sharon Hanson makes a distinction between secularisation on the level of the social system (the Broad Approach) and on the level of the individual (the Narrow Approach).

3. Secularisation theorists claim that the power and influence of religious institutions, religious beliefs and religious practices have all declined.

4. They accept that religion may continue on an individual level – as privatised religion. However, they take the Broad Approach, arguing that religion is losing its significance on the level of the social system.

5. The evidence for secularisation has been questioned in the following ways.

   - Are the measurements of religious beliefs and practices valid – true and accurate?

   - If privatised religion remains widespread, is it reasonable to claim that secularisation is occurring?

   - Is the comparison of a 'golden age' of religion in the past with a secular present justified?

   - Does the rise of the New Age movement and high levels of religious belief and church attendance in the USA provide evidence against the secularisation thesis?

6. Sociological theories offer the following views of secularisation.

   - Karl Marx believed that religion will disappear with the overthrow of the capitalist system.

   - Max Weber argued that rationalisation is steadily eroding religion on both an individual and societal level.

   - Peter Berger claimed that the authority of all religions is weakened as they compete for clients in the religious market place. How can their competing and contradictory beliefs all be seen as true?

   - Bryan Wilson gave the following reasons for the decline of religion on a societal level – social differentiation, rational thinking and science, and the decline of community.

   - Emile Durkheim argued that the rapid social changes brought about by industrialisation and urbanisation and the resulting anomie led to a decline in religion. He did not see this as an irreversible trend – societies must have sacred symbols and communal rituals if they are to survive.

   - Some postmodernists argue that the loss of confidence in metanarratives has led to a decline in traditional religion. This produces a 'crisis of meaning'. However, they see new types of religion offering to restore meaning.

7. The Kendal Project indicated that the New Age spiritual revolution had not taken place. However, it suggested that if present trends continue, then the revolution will take place in 20 to 30 years.

8. Evidence on religious belief and attendance at religious institutions in the USA has been used to question the secularisation thesis. Even allowing for problems of measurement, attendance levels are high compared to Europe.

9. Will Herberg argues that religious institutions in the USA have retained support by becoming more secular.

10. In view of the different definitions of religion and secularisation and the problems of measurement, it is difficult to reach firm conclusions about the secularisation thesis.

extent 'religion' has gone out of religion. Despite its apparent vigour, American religion has been secularised.

Evaluation Herberg's views have received some support. For example, Peter Berger (1970) argues that American religious institutions have maintained relatively high attendance levels by downplaying the supernatural and 'modifying their product in accordance with consumer demands' – that is, the demands of a secular society.

Whether American religion is becoming more secular depends on the researcher's view of religion. To Herberg, 'authentic religion' involves a strong belief in a supernatural power, a strong commitment to religious teachings and a refusal to compromise those teachings to fit in with the wider society. Other researchers might take a different view of religion and, as a result, reach different conclusions.

Herberg has been criticised for ignoring Christian fundamentalism in the USA. With their commitment to a literal interpretation of the Bible and to strict moral codes based on the 'word of God', the beliefs of Christian fundamentalists in many ways reflect Herberg's 'authentic religion'.

Conclusion

It is difficult to reach firm conclusions about the secularisation thesis. The term is used by different researchers in different ways. For some, it means the decline of religion on a societal level. For others, it means the decline of religion on an individual level.

Sociologists are unable to agree on a definition of religion. As a result, they will have different views of the secularisation process and how to measure it. In addition, they have their own views on 'authentic' religion. Is religion in the USA only a watered-down version of the real thing as Herberg and Berger claim? And what about New Age spirituality? Is it as real and significant as religious beliefs and practices? Or is it, as Steve Bruce (2002) claims, little more than 'an extension of the doctor's surgery, the beauty parlour and the gym'?

Even when sociologists agree on definitions of religion and secularisation, problems remain – in particular, the problem of measurement. How do you measure religious beliefs and practices? What do these measurements mean? Does a belief in God and regular church attendance reflect strong religious convictions? As this unit has indicated, we can't be sure.

In view of the different definitions of religion and secularisation and the problems of measurement, it is difficult to prove or disprove the secularisation thesis.

2 Power and politics

Introduction

For many people, politics is an activity involving middle-aged men – and a few women – at Westminster. It often appears distant and removed from their daily lives. Sociologists, however, see politics as a vital part of daily life.

From a sociological viewpoint, politics is about power – power in everyday life, power in society as a whole, and power on a global scale. The questions which follow from this are: Who has power? How do they use it? Who gains and who loses in the process?

Politics is about political parties and general elections. But it is also about the power of the rich over the poor, of men over women, of the White majority over ethnic minorities. Politics is about decisions made in Parliament. But it is also about decisions made by transnational companies with worldwide business interests.

The way power is distributed and exercised on a local, national and global level affects everybody's lives. It can create jobs or destroy them, it can raise living standards or lower them, it can improve the environment or pollute it.

This chapter looks at the way power is defined and measured, how it is distributed and how it is used.

One view of politics – Prime Minister's Question Time in the House of Commons

chaptersummary

▶ Unit 1 looks at the definition and measurement of power.

▶ Unit 2 outlines and assesses theories of power.

▶ Unit 3 examines the role of the modern state.

▶ Unit 4 looks at various political ideologies and their relationship to political parties.

▶ Unit 5 examines various forms of political participation, including voting behaviour.

▶ Unit 6 considers the roles of political parties, pressure groups, new social movements and the mass media in the political process.

Unit 1 Defining power

keyissues

1 What is power?

2 How is power measured?

1.1 Power and authority

Power is a *contested concept* – in other words there is no agreed definition. The debate about how power should be defined and measured underlies many of the broader debates about how power is distributed in society.

Max Weber – power and authority

Max Weber's (1978) work is often taken as a starting point in the study of power. Weber defined power as 'the chance of a man or a number of men to realise their own will in a communal action even against the resistance of others.' Power is unequally distributed if some are more successful than others in achieving their aims.

Imagine a group of friends discussing how they are going to spend their evening. One of the group suggests going out clubbing and is supported by a couple of others. A second person points out that there is a good film on at the cinema that they should go and see. She too receives some support. A third person complains that he is tired and would rather order a pizza and stay in and watch TV. In the end, the girl who wants to go to the cinema succeeds in persuading most of the others to join her. Those who wanted to do something else go along with the will of the majority. According to Weber's definition, this girl and her supporters are exercising power in the group as they manage to realise their will even in the face of some resistance from the others.

Weber identified two types of power, *authority* and *coercion*. Authority is the exercise of power which is regarded as legitimate. Weber regards authority as the more effective form of power as it is based on the consent of those who are subject to it. Coercion is the exercise of power which is regarded as illegitimate. Both forms of power are backed up by the threat of force, though in practice this is more important for coercion than authority. Compare a demand for money from a tax inspector and an armed robber. The former is based on authority, the latter on coercion, the threat of force being more important to the robber for the successful exercise of power.

Weber identified three types of authority.

1 Charismatic authority This type of authority is based on the charisma or personal qualities of the leader. Many religious and political leaders in history have attracted followers by the power of their personalities. Examples include Jesus Christ, Mohammed, Fidel Castro and Adolf Hitler. However, ordinary people may exercise charismatic authority, for example one teacher may be able to control her pupils much more effectively than another because her personality inspires awe, admiration or affection.

2 Traditional authority This type of authority is based on established customs and traditions which dictate that certain individuals should hold power. In the Middle Ages, the power of the king and the nobility was based on inherited positions. Tradition dictated that positions of power were passed on from father to son and that vassals or subordinates owed certain obligations to their lords. The British monarchy and hereditary peerages in the House of Lords remain as examples of this type of authority in modern Britain.

3 Rational-legal authority This type of authority derives from impersonal rules which give the holders of certain positions or offices power over their subordinates. For example, in armies in the past, a leader may have been obeyed because his soldiers admired his courage and qualities of leadership (charismatic authority) or because members of his family had traditionally been military leaders (traditional authority). However, in a modern army, an officer is obeyed primarily because he holds rational-legal authority – because rules and regulations stipulate that he has the authority to give orders.

Weber saw rational-legal authority as the dominant form of authority in modern societies. Not only armies but political, industrial, religious and educational organisations are based on rational-legal authority. They are organised on bureaucratic lines with structures of authority and rational rules designed to ensure that power is used to achieve the goals of the organisation.

Weber's types of authority are *ideal types*. Ideal does not mean best but pure. An ideal type is a model of the purest type. In reality, ideal types do not exist. For example, even in modern bureaucratic organisations where rational-legal authority is dominant, elements of charismatic and traditional authority may exist. However, ideal types are useful for describing, classifying and comparing things in the real world.

key terms

Contested concept A concept for which there is no agreed definition.
Authority Power which is recognised as legitimate.
Coercion Power which is not recognised as legitimate and which requires force, or the threat of force, to exercise it.
Charismatic authority Authority based on the charisma or personality of the person who exercises it.
Traditional authority Authority based on tradition or custom.
Rational-legal authority Authority based on rules which have been devised to achieve rational goals within an organisation.
Ideal types An ideal or pure category used for sociological analysis. It enables sociologists to match types in the real world to ideal types in order to see which one they come closest to.

1.2 Faces of power

Stephen Lukes (1974) identifies three ways in which sociologists have approached the study of power. Each involves studying a different dimension or 'face' of power. Lukes argues that an understanding of power requires an awareness of all three faces.

The first face of power – success in decision making

This approach has been adopted by *pluralists* such as Robert Dahl (1961) and Nelson Polsby (1963). Pluralist theories argue that power can be seen from the outcomes of the decision-making process (see Section 2.1). Dahl argues that 'A has power over B to the extent that he can get B to do something that B would not otherwise do' (1957).

In order to study how power is distributed, pluralists favour what is sometimes termed the *issue method*. Polsby, for example, argues that sociologists should study specific issues in order to determine who actually gets their own way in the decision-making process. Those who are most frequently successful in getting the outcomes they want will have most power. For example, if Parliament passes a law on car emissions which is supported by the AA and the RAC but opposed by environmental groups then, in this instance, the car interest groups have more power than the environmental groups. In practice, most studies based on this method suggest that no one group dominates decision making in Western democracies. Instead, they paint a picture of many groups exercising some degree of political power.

The second face of power – managing the agenda

Critics of the pluralist view, such as Peter Bachrach and Morton Baratz (1962), argue that simply studying decision making ignores a second dimension of power – the ability to control the agenda for debate. In their view, real power lies in the ability to prevent certain issues from being seriously considered. This means that those issues will never reach the point of decision making, they will remain *non-decisions*. For example, a local council might be asked to vote on a number of alternative cuts in expenditure. A pluralist would argue that the group supporting the cuts that were actually decided would hold power in this situation. However, this ignores the question of who *sets the agenda*, of who decided that the choice was between these particular cuts rather than other possibilities – such as no cuts or even increases in expenditure. In this situation, real power might lie in the hands of those who set the agenda and decided on the alternatives.

activity1 faces of authority

Item A Adolf Hitler

Item B Judge

Item D Henry VIII

Item C Headmaster

questions

1   Match each item with one of Weber's three types of authority (traditional, charismatic or rational-legal). Give reasons for your choice.

2   Weber's types of authority are ideal types. In practice, authority may be a mixture of two or three types. Briefly explain, using one or more of the items in this activity.

The third face of power – manipulating the views of others

Lukes argues that although the second view of power represents a step forward, it still ignores a third dimension. This view sees power as the ability to shape the wishes and desires of others. Those others are persuaded that both they and the powerful share the same interests – what is good for the powerful is good for everybody. And this may allow the powerful to increase their wealth, prestige and privilege at the expense of others. Marxists take this view of power when they see a ruling class exploiting a subject class. Members of the subject class are unaware of this exploitation and unknowingly contribute to it by their acceptance of the *ruling class ideology*. This imposed consensus about what is normal and reasonable may rule out a consideration of alternatives which might challenge the dominance of the powerful. (See Section 2.3 on Marxist views of power.)

Further views of power

Zero-sum approach The views discussed so far tend to see power as something which some hold to a greater extent than others. Thus if a powerful group holds 90% of the available power, this leaves only 10% for the rest of society. There is a fixed amount of power and the more one group holds, the less there is for others. This is known as the *zero-sum* approach to power.

Variable-sum approach The American sociologist Talcott Parsons (1967) rejects the zero-sum approach. He argues that power is something which resides in society as a whole and can increase or decrease according to how effectively the social system is able to achieve agreed social goals. For example, if improving living standards is a major goal, then society's power will increase to the degree that living standards improve. Or power can decrease, as in societies like Bosnia in the 1990s, where central political authority broke down and civil war prevented the achievement of many social goals. In this sense, power is not fixed or constant, it is variable – it can increase or decrease. As a result, this view is sometimes known as the *variable-sum* approach to power.

This type of approach has received renewed interest from sociologists such as Anthony Giddens (1985) and Michael Mann (1986, 1993). Mann, for example, argues that modern institutions (such as states, armies and economic organisations) have much greater power than their equivalents in the past. This is because they have greater *organisational effectiveness*. The modern state, for example, can now intervene far more extensively in people's lives because it has a large and powerful bureaucracy which can tax, supervise and police the people it governs. In this respect, societal power is variable – modern states are able to exercise far greater amounts of power than pre-modern states.

Poststructuralist views of power A further approach to power is provided by poststructuralists, such as the French writer Michel Foucault (1977). Foucault argues that power does not reside in social structures or institutions such as the state or economic organisations, but pervades all aspects of everyday life. For Foucault, power is exercised through *discourses* or ways of talking and thinking about things. Discourses lead us to take certain things for granted and think about things in a certain way, while other alternatives become unthinkable. Discourses define what is true and real for us. For example, discourses about mental illness or criminality are used to define who is 'normal' and 'abnormal' in society. Foucault does not deny that some have more power than others and that discourses may serve the interests of powerful groups in society. He points out that power is most visible when there is resistance from subordinate groups seeking to challenge dominant discourses. (See Section 2.4 on Foucault and poststructuralism.)

key terms

Issue method A method of studying power which involves analysing decisions in order to see which individuals or groups get their own way.

Agenda setting The process by which those with power manipulate the agenda or items for debate in order to exclude certain issues and prevent them from even being considered.

Ideology A set of ideas about how the world is and should be, which reflect the views and interests of a dominant group in society.

Zero-sum approach to power An approach to power which assumes that the total amount of power in society is fixed.

Variable-sum approach to power An approach to power which assumes that the total amount of power in society varies according to how effectively power can be used to achieve socially approved goals.

Discourses Ways of talking and thinking about things which encourage us to construct and categorise the social world in particular ways.

summary

1. Max Weber identified two types of power – authority and coercion – and three types of authority – charismatic, traditional and rational-legal.

2. Stephen Lukes identified three faces or dimensions of power – the power to make decisions, to manage the agenda, and to manipulate the views of others.

3. Most views of power use a zero-sum approach. The variable-sum approach provides an alternative view.

4. Michel Foucault's poststructuralist view argues that power is exercised through discourses – ways of talking and thinking about things.

activity2 studies of power

Item A *The decision-making method*

'I do not see how anyone can suppose that they have established the dominance of a specific group in a community without basing their analysis on a careful examination of a series of concrete decisions.'
Dahl, 1973

Item B *Power and non-decision making*

Matthew Crenson carried out a study in the United States to investigate how and why air pollution became a political issue in some American cities much earlier than in others. Crenson showed that differences in the politics of air pollution were not simply due to differences in the actual levels of pollution. He compared two neighbouring cities in Indiana, both equally polluted and both with similar populations. The first, East Chicago, took action to clear the air in 1949, while the other, Gary, did nothing until 1962.

Crenson argues that US Steel, which had built the town of Gary and was responsible for its prosperity, managed for many years to prevent the issue of air pollution even being raised. When a law against air pollution was finally enacted, US Steel also managed to influence its content in its own favour. US Steel did this without directly intervening in the political arena and was able to exert influence mainly by its reputation for power. Executives from the corporation took no clear stance on the air pollution issue and never directly opposed anti-pollution activists. Thus a study of the decision-making process

East Chicago

would find it very difficult to pin down what US Steel's involvement was in this issue. An examination of concrete decisions would tell us little or nothing about the company's power.
Adapted from Crenson, 1971

Item C *Challenging patriarchal ideology*

Many feminists claim that all human societies are based on a system of gender inequality which benefits men at the expense of women. Men are seen to dominate women by a combination of force and patriarchal ideology. Patriarchal ideology is a set of beliefs and values which justifies male power and female subservience. Some feminists argue that women should organise themselves independently in order to challenge male power.

In the 1980s, a group of women set up a women-only peace camp outside a United States Air Force base at Greenham Common in Berkshire. The camp was part of a wider campaign against the basing of American nuclear cruise missiles in the UK. Sasha Roseneil carried out a study of the camp based on participant observation.

Roseneil argues that the camp was only possible because of what she terms a transition from private to public patriarchy. Under private patriarchy, women were subjugated by the control of their fathers and husbands. After the Second World War, more and more women moved out of the home into the world of work where they encountered new types of male power – for example, exclusion from high status jobs. However, the financial independence gained from paid work and the weakening of private patriarchy enabled some women, such as those at Greenham Common, to escape the domestic sphere and to participate in politics, often for the first time.

Anti-nuclear protesters at Greenham Common after the arrival of cruise missiles in 1983

By mixing with others in the camp and becoming exposed to feminist ideas, many of the women became aware of the extent to which society and its institutions – including even the peace movement – were male dominated. After the camp closed in 1994, when the base itself was decommissioned, many of the women became involved in other campaigns – against war and sexual violence and to protect the environment and animal rights.
Adapted from Roseneil, 1995

(all body)## questions

1 How might Item B be used to criticise the decision-making approach outlined in Item A?

2 What problems might there be in establishing that a person or a group has power simply by virtue of their reputation? Refer to Item B in your answer.

3 a) Which of Lukes' three faces of power is represented by the feminist concept of patriarchal ideology (Item C)?

   b) How might involvement in a group such as the Greenham peace camp enable women to challenge patriarchal ideology?

Unit 2 Theories of power

key issues

1 What are the main sociological theories of power?

2 What are their strengths and weaknesses?

2.1 Pluralism

Pluralist theories of power have their origins in the work of Max Weber. Unlike Marx, Weber believed that power was not automatically linked to ownership of wealth. Ordinary people with little or no wealth could exercise power by joining *parties* – groups of people with similar political goals or interests. By parties Weber meant not only formal political parties, such as the Labour and Conservative Parties in Britain, but also *interest groups* or *pressure groups* such as trade unions and organisations such as Greenpeace and Friends of the Earth. The idea that ordinary people are able to infuence the process of decision making through many (a plurality of) different groups is the basis of the pluralist approach.

Classical pluralism

Weber's ideas were developed by American political scientists, such as Robert Dahl, into what has become known as *classical pluralism*. Classical pluralists accept that the majority of citizens in Western societies have little or no direct involvement in political decision making. However, this does not mean that these societies are undemocratic. They are seen as *representative democracies* where citizens elect political leaders who are charged with carrying out the wishes of those who elected them.

Pluralists argue that citizens in Western democratic societies have a variety of interests and concerns. These interests and concerns are represented and articulated in two main ways. First, through *political parties*, which seek to gain power by putting up candidates in elections with the aim of forming a government. Second, through pressure groups or interest groups – groups which seek to influence those in government to follow policies which they favour.

Pluralists see political parties and pressure groups as crucial for the democratic process. They are the means by which the views of sectional interests in society are articulated both inside and outside the legislature – Parliament in the UK, Congress in the USA. No one group is seen to dominate the decision-making process. Power is therefore shared among a range of groups. Pluralists reject the idea that democracy is possible in a one-party state, since there must be opposition parties and a range of pressure groups to represent the views of those who disagree with the governing party.

For pluralists, the role of the state is to arbitrate between the various interest groups which seek to influence the decision-making process. Pluralists see the involvement of groups representing all sections of society as essential for democracy. It enables the government to gauge the strength of support for different policies and gain feedback from interested parties on proposals which may affect them. Democracy only works if these concerns are reflected in government decisions.

Pluralism and the study of decision making

Pluralists argue that the decision-making process is the key to understanding the distribution of power in society. Robert Dahl argued that 'concrete decisions' must be examined to find out which groups achieve the outcomes they desire. Only then will it be possible to say who has power.

Dahl's approach is clearly illustrated in *Who Governs* (1961) – his classic study of local government in New Haven, Connecticut. He examined three major issues in local politics – urban renewal, political nominations and education. A number of groups with differing views were involved. However, few groups participated in decisions on all three issues – groups only became involved when issues directly affected their own interests. From his analysis of the decision-making process, Dahl concluded that no single group dominated New Haven politics. Instead, a variety of groups had some success in influencing, decisions, and policies were often a compromise between the wishes of competing groups. In this study, Dahl reflects the pluralists' preference for the study of specific issues and concrete decisions – Stephen Lukes' first face of power.

Evaluation of classical pluralism

Classical pluralism represents the way many people believe liberal democracies such the UK and USA operate. It suggests that such political systems are truly democratic and that power is distributed throughout society.

Classical pluralists can claim to have solid evidence for their view of the distribution of power from case studies of decision making at both local level (Dahl, 1961) and national level (Hewitt, 1974).

Studies of pressure group activity (see Section 6.2) show that a range of groups – for example, those representing ethnic minorities or opposing big business – can influence decision making. For instance, environmental groups such as Greenpeace have influenced laws to control pollution, and campaigns by groups representing ethnic minorities have resulted in legislation to outlaw racial discrimination and the incitement of racial hatred.

However, classical pluralism has also received considerable criticism.

Non-decision making Measuring power by examining decisions ignores non-decision making – that is managing the agenda so that certain issues never reach the point of decision making. This is Lukes' second face of power, which many pluralists fail to examine.

Manipulation of the wishes of others There is a failure to consider the possibility that people might accept and even welcome decisions which are against their interests. This is Lukes' third face of power. Marxists, for example, argue that most people have been persuaded to accept the capitalist system even though it is against their real interests. Lack of opposition to decisions does not mean these decisions are in everyone's interests.

The power of capital Marxists argue that the pluralists' focus on the decisions taken by local and national

activity3 the representation of interests

Item A

Business people

Item B

Bradford council estate

Item C

Striking firefighters in Glasgow

Item D

questions

1 How much influence might each of the groups illustrated above have over government policy making?

2 Why might the interests of some groups be better represented than those of others?

governments ignores the possibility that the real centre of power is elsewhere. John Westergaard and Henrietta Resler (1976) point to the failure of governments since 1945 to eradicate poverty and reduce inequalities of wealth and income. In their view, such inequalities are created by the existence of private property and a capitalist economy. Governments, even drawn from left-wing political parties, have done little to control big business.

Unequal representation of interests Even using the pluralists' own method – focusing on decision making – it can be shown that some groups exercise more power than others. Economically powerful groups and groups containing a large proportion of middle-class activists are usually more successful than those representing poorer and less educated sections of the population.

Non-representation of interests Many interests may not be represented at all. It is only in the last twenty years or so that women who are victims of domestic violence, children who are sexually abused, and schoolchildren who are systematically bullied have been brought to public notice and received any kind of representation. And the next twenty years will probably bring a new set of interests to public attention.

The 'organising out' of outsiders There are rules and conventions for influencing governments. Demands must be made in a moderate way – demands for revolutionary change backed up by violent protest are unlikely to succeed. Groups such as anti-capitalism demonstrators, environmentalists, animal rights protestors and Irish Republicans who step outside this consensus about acceptable political behaviour are likely to be branded as 'eccentric', 'extremist' or even 'subversive'. In this way, 'outsiders' are kept on the outside, their demands dismissed as inconsequential and unrealistic, their interests unrepresented.

The problem of overloaded government *New Right* theorists argue that pluralism has put too much emphasis on governments consulting widely with different interest groups and being responsive to the demands of the electorate. Writers such as Samuel Brittan (1983) claim that it is precisely this which has lead to the problem of *overloaded government*. When this happens, *every* issue becomes a concern of the government, which then makes concessions (usually by spending more money) to a whole variety of interest groups in order to buy electoral popularity. New Right theorists argue that overloaded government leads to economic inefficiency and a failure to follow clear and consistent policies.

Elite pluralism

As a result of the criticisms outlined above, many supporters of classical pluralism have modified or changed their positions. For example, Robert Dahl (1989) has accepted that the unequal distribution of wealth and income in the USA makes equal political influence impossible. David Marsh (1985) describes this position as *elite pluralism*.

Elite pluralists accept that many political interests, for example those of ethnic minorities or the unemployed, are under-represented. However, since they constitute a significant number of voters, governments will eventually be forced to take note of their interests. Elite pluralists accept the argument that some groups have greater access to government than others. However, they point out that governments must consult with a range of interest groups in order to minimise conflict.

One way they accomplish this is by consulting with different *policy communities*. Each policy community is made up of a range of interest groups concerned with a particular set of issues. For example, there are policy communities on agriculture, health services and transport. Within each policy community, the relevant government department will consult with *insider groups* (pressure groups who have regular access to government departments) and may also receive representations from *outsider groups* (who are consulted less frequently, if at all). Elite pluralists argue that although ordinary citizens may exert little direct influence on decision making, it is likely that leaders or elites within organisations such as pressure groups, trade unions and professional associations will

key terms

Parties Max Weber defined parties as groups of people who unite to pursue common political objectives. This broad definition includes interest groups and political parties.
Classical pluralism A theory of political power which claims that in Western democracies power is dispersed amongst many competing groups.
Representative democracy A system of democracy where power is exercised on behalf of the people by elected representatives.
Pressure or interest groups Groups who seek to put pressure on decision makers to favour their views on policy issues.
New Right A political movement which advocates a reduction in the role of the state and a market economy largely free from state control.
Overloaded government A concept used by New Right thinkers to suggest that government has taken on too many responsibilities in trying to please and appease different interest groups.
Elite pluralism A version of pluralist theory which accepts that power is unequally distributed. Elite pluralists see power as shared amongst a relatively small number of competing elites.
Policy community A community of interest groups who are all concerned with a common group of policies or issues, often centred on a particular government department.
Insider groups Interest groups which have access to key decision makers and are thus able to influence decision making.
Outsider groups Interest groups which do not have direct access to decision makers and therefore depend on indirect forms of influence such as protests, direct action and use of the mass media.

voice their interests within the relevant policy communities. (See Section 6.2 on pressure groups.)

Evaluation of elite pluralism

Elite pluralism provides answers to some of the criticisms of classical pluralism. It acknowledges the existence of under-represented interests and accepts that power is to some degree concentrated in the hands of a few elites.

Some critics of elite pluralism argue that this in itself undermines the pluralist position that power is widely dispersed in capitalist societies. Moreover, the assumption by elite pluralists that elites or leaders of interest groups act in the interests of their members is also open to question. In the USA, corrupt union leaders have been accused of lining their pockets with the pension funds of those who they are supposed to represent. Some British MPs have been seen as more concerned with securing lucrative directorships and consultancies than with the problems of their constituents.

Finally, elite pluralism, like classical pluralism, largely fails to take into account the third face of power – the ability to shape and manipulate the desires of others.

2.2 Elite theory

Elite theorists reject the pluralist view that power in liberal democracies is widely dispersed. Instead, they argue that power is concentrated in the hands of a small minority – an *elite*. Elite theory originally developed as a response to Marxism which claimed that democracy was only possible under communism. The classical elite theorists asserted that rule by elites was inevitable in all societies, even communist ones. However, not all versions of elite theory are so pessimistic. Many modern elite theorists argue that rule by elites results from the way societies are organised, rather than being an inevitable feature of human society.

activity4 pluralism and power

Item A *The issue method*

Christopher Hewitt's study of the distribution of power is one of the few studies of Britain using the 'issue method'. Hewitt's study covered the period 1944-1964. This included periods of both Labour and Conservative government. He analysed twenty-four issues, six under each of four policy areas – foreign policy, economic policy, welfare policy and social policy.

The table summarises his findings. It shows the issues, the policy outcome on each issue (ie, the decision made by Parliament), the views of various interest groups and public opinion (based on public opinion polls). *Pro* indicates that the interest group supported the successful policy outcome, whilst *anti* indicates they were against. *Divided* indicates that there was no clear majority for or against a particular policy. A dash (–) indicates that no data was available for this group.

Issue	Successful policy outcome	Business	White collar	Unions	Religious	Public opinion
India	Independence for India	–	–	–	–	Pro
Russia	Hard-line policy to Russia	–	–	Pro	–	–
Abadan	Sanctions against Iran	Pro	–	–	–	–
Suez	Military intervention	–	–	Anti	Anti	Divided
Nuclear deterrent	Independent deterrent policy	Anti	–	Divided	Divided	–
Central Africa	Federation	–	–	–	Anti	–
US loan	Loan negotiated	–	–	–	–	–
Road haulage	Nationalisation	Anti	–	Pro	–	–
Steel	No effective nationalisation	Pro	–	Anti	–	–
Resale price maintenance	Abolition of RPM	Anti	–	–	–	Pro
Common Market	No entry	Anti	–	Pro	–	–
Railways	Beeching's rationalisation policy	Pro	–	Anti	–	Divided
Education Act	Education Act	Pro	Pro	Pro	Pro	Pro
National Health	National Health Service	–	Pro	–	–	Pro
National Insurance	National Insurance Act	Anti	–	Pro	Pro	Pro
Rent Act	Rent decontrol	Pro	Pro	Anti	–	–
Comprehensives	No support for comprehensives	–	Divided	–	–	–
Motorways	Motorway programme	Pro	Pro	Pro	–	Pro
Town and country	Town and Country Planning Act	Anti	Pro	Pro	–	Pro
Divorce	No change in divorce laws	–	Divided	–	Pro	–
Capital punishment	Abolition of capital punishment	–	Anti	–	Pro	Anti
Television	Commercial television	Divided	Divided	Anti	Anti	Divided
Immigration	Immigration control	–	–	–	Anti	Pro
Clean air	Clean Air Act	Divided	Pro	–	–	Pro

Adapted from Hewitt, 1974

Item B *The law and order policy community*

The Home Office has overall responsibility for the police, prisons and the maintenance of public order. It also drafts new laws concerning the administration of the legal system in England and Wales.

Professional organisations such as the Prison Officers' Association (POA), the Police Federation, the National Association of Probation Officers and the British Association of Social Workers are often consulted about new legislation which will affect their areas of work. The Home Office needs the cooperation of such groups in order for the new legislation to work effectively. However, sometimes this relationship breaks down – for example, on occasions the POA has threatened industrial action because it could not reach agreement with the Home Office on working conditions for prison officers.

The Home Office also deals with pressure groups seeking reforms or protecting the rights of people who come into contact with the legal system. The National Council for Civil Liberties, for example, aims to defend civil and political rights such as freedom of speech and freedom of assembly. It organises campaigns to publicise cases of people's rights being threatened, tries to influence the drafting of new legislation, and produces pamphlets designed to inform people about their rights.

NCCL	National Council for Civil Liberties
NACRO	National Association for the Care and Resettlement of Offenders
PROP	Preservation of the Rights of Prisoners
RAP	Radical Alternatives to Prison

The Howard League for Penal Reform enjoys close relationships with the Home Office and has representatives sitting on committees concerned with the running of the prison system.

Some pressure groups have the active support of the Home Office – for example, the National Association for the Care and Resettlement of Offenders receives money from the government to aid its work. However, more radical pressure groups, such as the Radical Alternatives to Prison (RAP) and the Preservation of the Rights of Prisoners (PROP), tend to have less influence. RAP is in favour of the abolition of prisons for all but the most serious offenders, but it lacks the regular contact with government of the Howard League. PROP sees itself as a kind of prisoners' trade union, but the Home Office does not even officially acknowledge its existence. Such organisations try to mobilise the mass media and public opinion in order to put pressure on the government.

Adapted from Stradling, 1988

questions

1 How might the evidence from the table in Item A be used to support a pluralist view of the distribution of power in Britain?

2 Hewitt's study (Item A) used the 'issue method' in researching power.
   a) Explain what this method involves.
   b) What are the strengths and weaknesses of using the issue method for measuring the distribution of power?

3 How does Item B illustrate the concept of a policy community?

4 How could the working of the law and order policy community be used to:
   a) support the pluralist view of power
   b) criticise the pluralist view?

Classical elite theory

Vilfredo Pareto (1848-1923) and Gaetano Mosca (1858-1911) rejected the idea that real democracy was possible either in liberal democracies or under communism. Instead, they argued that in all societies an elite, a small minority of individuals with superior personal qualities, would monopolise power.

Pareto For Pareto, the psychological characteristics of elites separated them from the masses. He classified elites into two types – 'lions' who were distinguished by their ability to act forcefully to gain and retain power, for example, military dictators; and 'foxes' who relied more on cunning and an ability to manipulate people, for example, political leaders in Western democracies. Each type eventually replaces the other, resulting in a *circulation of elites*. Pareto claimed that 'History is the graveyard of aristocracies' – all elites are sooner or later replaced by others. Foxes lack the strength and decisiveness of lions and are eventually overthrown by a group of lions, as in a military coup. However, lions lack the subtlety and guile of foxes. They are gradually infiltrated leading to an elite dominated by foxes.

Mosca Mosca also asserted that elite rule was inevitable but, unlike Pareto, he argued that the particular characteristics which give an elite its superiority vary from society to society. For example, in the feudal societies of medieval Europe, ability as a soldier would be important for a leader, while in a capitalist industrial society, wealth and business connections would be an advantage. In his later work, Mosca accepted that elites in liberal democracies might in some way represent the people. But he always maintained that real involvement by the majority in politics was impossible. Mosca was sceptical about the ability of the masses to govern themselves and felt that real power would always be exercised by an elite.

Evaluation of classical elite theory Pareto's theory has been criticised for being too simplistic. He makes little distinction between different types of political systems,

asserting that all societies are characterised by the same process of circulation of elites. Yet, many societies have remained dominated by a single elite for centuries – for example, the ruling Brahmin caste of traditional India and the *literati,* the educated ruling class of ancient China.

Both Pareto and Mosca seem contemptuous of the mass of the population and of those who see the masses as capable of governing themselves. Mosca opposed the extension of the vote to the working classes, seeing them as unfit to participate in the political process. He and Pareto dismiss the predictions of Marxism, that the overthrow of capitalism would lead to true democracy, as nothing more than wishful thinking.

While Pareto and Mosca appear to be cynical about the possibility of democracy, some modern sociologists have argued that there is some basis for their scepticism about both Marxism and pluralist democracy. Many of the communist societies established in the twentieth century, such as the USSR, North Korea and the People's Republic of China, have been seen by their critics as virtual dictatorships dominated by a Communist Party elite. Even Western liberal democracies offer little opportunity for ordinary citizens to participate in political decision making in any meaningful way – many ordinary people now appear apathetic and uninvolved in politics. Nevertheless, it can be argued that the fact that elites often appear to dominate supposedly democratic systems does not mean that democracy cannot work. Rather it means that ordinary

*activity*5 *lions and foxes*

Saddam Hussein after being sworn in as president in 1995 for another seven years

Tony Blair after winning the 2001 general election

Saddam Hussein came to power in the 1960s in a military coup and was overthrown by US and allied forces who invaded Iraq in 2003. Tony Blair became Prime Minister when Labour won a landslide victory in the 1997 general election in the UK. He subsequently won another election in 2001.

question

How might these two leaders represent examples of Pareto's 'lions' and 'foxes'?

people need to ensure that they remain involved in decision making and do not allow their leaders to take more and more power into their own hands.

The power elite – C. Wright Mills

While Pareto and Mosca saw elite rule as inevitable, the American sociologist C. Wright Mills saw it as something which emerged in the USA less than 100 years before his book, *The Power Elite* (1956), was written. Mills saw elite rule as a result of the structure of society which allowed a disproportionate amount of power to be held by a few individuals who occupied what he called the *command posts* in key institutions.

Mills identified three key institutions as the centres of power.

- **The federal government** which has steadily taken power from the individual state governments as America became a world power.
- **The major corporations** which have increasingly dominated the economy at the expense of small firms.
- **The military** which has become more and more important in relation to foreign policy and government spending.

Mills argued that the holders of the top positions in these three institutions constituted three important elites – the political, economic and military elites. The three elites are closely connected. First, because of their similar social origins, education, kinship and other social ties. Second, because their interests are intertwined. For example, the economic elite prospers from contracts placed by the military and political elites. For these reasons Mills claimed that in reality the three elites are not separate but form a single *power elite*.

Mills claimed that key political decisions, such as the dropping of the atomic bomb on Hiroshima in 1945, were taken by the power elite with little reference to the majority of citizens. The masses are hardly involved in politics and even elections fail to provide real choice since there is little difference between the main political parties, the Republicans and the Democrats. For Mills, real democracy will only come about when the structure of society changes so that power is less centralised and is devolved to the people. This would involve a reduction in the power of the military and the large corporations and require politicians to become more responsive to the people.

Evaluation of Mills Unlike the classical elite theorists, Mills' theory was only intended to apply to the USA in the 1950s. Nevertheless, critics of Mills, such as the pluralist Robert Dahl, argued that he only showed that elites in the USA have the potential for control. He failed to show they have actual control because he did not analyse a range of concrete decisions. In addition, pluralists argue that there are many other elites such as pressure group leaders, religious leaders, trade union leaders and so on, who provide a counterbalance to the more powerful elites. This means the elites identified by Mills cannot take decisions without some reference to opposition groups.

Marxists also reject the notion of a power elite, arguing that real power in capitalist societies, such as the USA, derives not from positions in institutions, but from ownership and control of the means of production (see Section 2.3).

Despite these criticisms, Mills offers a fresh version of elite theory. Elites emerge because of the power of particular institutions in particular societies. They are not inevitable as Pareto and Mosca claim. They are not based on class divisions as Marxists insist.

The fragmented elite model

Some British elite theorists have modified and developed elite theory. One version, the *fragmented elite model*, put forward by Ian Budge and his colleagues (1983), suggests that there are a number of elites in Britain, all in competition with one another. Government ministers and their departments are included in the factions competing for power and influence. Unlike the power elite, which Mills saw as cohesive, Budge argues that the various elites in Britain are often in conflict. Government policy frequently results from a trial of strength between different government departments competing for funds or control, or between different elites competing to influence a particular aspect of policy. Budge argues that government policies are often neither rational nor consistent since they are shaped by the relative strength of competing elites.

Evaluation This model shares many features with elite pluralism. It suggests that power is concentrated in few hands but, rather than a single elite, there are a number of competing groups. Like pluralism, it tends to focus on decision making, the first face of power, and gives little consideration to the second and third faces.

Elite recruitment in Britain

Much of the research into elites in Britain up to the 1980s has been concerned with how members of elites are recruited and the social connections between elite groups. This research provided considerable evidence that many elites were largely closed to the mass of the population. A number of studies examined the educational backgrounds of elites. They showed that a high proportion of politicians, top civil servants, judges, military leaders, company directors and members of other elite groups are educated at fee-paying public schools which draw most of their pupils from wealthy families. Oxford and Cambridge Universities also appear to act as an important recruiting ground for elite positions (Stanworth & Giddens, 1974).

In recent years, sociologists have given less attention to the class background of elites. Some have even claimed that elites have become more open to entrants from all social classes. Political leaders such as Margaret Thatcher and John Major made much of the fact that they had neither attended private schools nor come from wealthy backgrounds. Recent research has focused more on the gender and ethnic composition of elites. Feminists argue that the exclusion of women from positions of power has been ignored by sociologists concerned with issues of class (see Section 2.5). Others have pointed to the under-representation of ethnic minorities in Parliament, the civil service and business elites (see Section 2.6).

Elite integration in Britain

A further aspect of elites which has received considerable attention is the degree of integration between elite groups. Mills argued that the American power elite was united by common outlooks and social connections. Studies of top decision makers, such as government ministers, top civil servants and financial leaders, show that many are related by kinship and marriage (Lupton & Wilson, 1974). Similarly, Richard Whitely (1974) showed that many large firms are linked by *overlapping directorships* (whereby someone who is a director of one company is also a director of another), or by kinship ties between directors. Such links help to create cohesion and unity between elites. Anthony Giddens (1974) notes that there is considerable movement between elites. Many civil servants and politicians come from business backgrounds, and it is common for a retiring MP to be invited to become a company director.

The similar origins and social connections of many elite members are seen by some elite theorists as evidence that some sort of power elite exists in Britain. However, it is one thing to identify these connections, but quite another to prove that they result in a united, self-interested power elite. The fragmented elite model, for example, would suggest that despite their common social origins, elite members compete for power.

key terms

Elite A small group who hold power in society, usually at the expense of the majority.
Classical elite theory A version of elite theory which argues that elites are made up of individuals with superior personal characteristics and that rule by elites is inevitable.
Circulation of elites A concept developed by Pareto. Each type of elite has inherent weaknesses which means that sooner or later it is overthrown or replaced by an elite with different characteristics.
Power elite A concept developed by Mills to describe what he saw as three interlocking elites (the political, military and economic elites) who controlled decision making in American society.
Command posts A term used by Mills to describe key positions in the federal government, the armed forces and major corporations.
Fragmented elite model A model which claims that power is concentrated in the hands of a few elites who compete for influence.
Overlapping directorships A situation where someone is a director of two or more companies.

2.3 Marxist theories of power

Marxist theories of power derive from the work of the German philosopher Karl Marx (1818-1883). Like classical elite theorists, Marx argued that throughout most of history, power has been concentrated in the hands of a few people

activity6 the social background of MPs, June 2001

Item A Occupational background of MPs

Occupation	Labour	Conservative	Lib Dem
Professions	179	64	27
Lawyer	31	31	6
Civil servant/local government	30	2	3
Teaching (all levels)	98	7	12
Other professions	20	24	6
Business	33	60	14
Manual workers	51	1	0
Miscellaneous	149	41	10
White collar	73	2	1
Politics	44	18	4
Publisher/journalist	32	14	4
Other	0	7	1

Adapted from Butler & Kavanagh, 2002

Item B Educational background of MPs

Education	Labour	Conservative	Lib Dem
State school	48	3	4
State school and degree	296	57	30
Public school	2	6	1
Public school and degree	66	100	17
Totals	412	166	52
Oxford or Cambridge	65	79	14
Other universities	210	59	22
All universities	275	138	36
%	67	83	70
Eton	2	14	2
Other public schools	66	92	16
All public schools	68	106	18
%	17	64	35

Adapted from Butler & Kavanagh, 2002

Item C **Women MPs 1983-2001**

	Labour	Conservative	Lib Dem	Others	Total
1983	10	13	0	0	23
1987	21	17	2	1	41
1992	37	20	2	1	60
1997	101	13	3	3	120
2001	95	14	5	4	118

Adapted from Roberts, 1999 and Butler & Kavanagh, 2002

Item D **Black and Asian MPs and candidates 1983-2001**

	Labour	Conservative	Lib Dem	Candidates
1983	0	0	0	18
1987	4	0	0	27
1992	5	1	0	23
1997	8	0	0	42
2001	12	0	0	66

Adapted from Sewell, 1993 and Butler & Kavanagh, 2002

Item E **Tony Blair**

A White, middle-class, middle-aged male who attended public school and Oxford University.

questions

1 To what extent are MPs representative of those who elect them? Consider the representativeness of MPs in terms of:

   a) social class

   b) gender

   c) ethnicity.

2 To what extent is it important that the social background of political leaders is representative of the population as a whole?

in society. However, for Marx they are best described as a *ruling class* rather than an elite. Unlike classical elite theorists, Marx saw the power of the ruling class as based on their ownership and control of the economic system rather than their superior personal qualities.

According to Marx, the structure of any society is primarily determined by the way its economy is organised – its *mode of production*. Particular modes of production produce particular *relations of production*. For example, under the capitalist mode, relations of production are based on private ownership and control. Capitalists invest their wealth in financing the production of commodities by workers who are paid wages for their labour. Capitalists are seen to dominate and exploit workers. This relationship produces the class system of capitalist society. For Marx, all societies, with the possible exception of *primitive communism* at the dawn of history, are made up of a ruling class which exploits and controls a subordinate class.

The state in capitalist society

Pluralists argue that in the later stages of capitalism,

universal suffrage and democratic rights gave power to every citizen. Rather than acting on behalf of a privileged class, the state now serves the interests of society as a whole. Marx rejected this argument. He accepted that the state relied less on coercion to enforce its power – in a democracy, citizens were more likely to feel that the state was serving their interests. For Marx, this was an illusion. In the *Communist Manifesto* published in 1848, Marx claimed that, 'The executive of the modern state is but a committee for managing the common affairs of the whole bourgeoisie' – the ruling class.

According to Marx, the political system, as part of the *superstructure*, is shaped by the requirements of the economic system or *infrastructure*. The institutions, beliefs and values which make up the superstructure serve to maintain and reproduce the relations of production. As with other parts of the superstructure, for example the legal system and religious institutions, Marx saw the state having an *ideological* role. The state gives the appearance of representing the interests of society as a whole yet, in reality, it serves the interests of the capitalist class. Thus Marxists, such as Westergaard and Resler (1976), point to the way in which the state identifies the 'national interest' with the need for businesses to make profits and compete internationally. In this way, the state is acting to legitimate existing economic arrangements and uphold the interests of the dominant class.

Marx argued that real democracy would only come in a communist society in which private property was abolished. Members of society could only be politically equal when they were economically equal. Marx believed that the overthrow of capitalism was inevitable. Unlike classical elite theorists, he did not accept that the masses lacked the capacity to govern themselves. Marx believed that the working class would eventually see through ruling-class ideology, break the chains which bound them and transform capitalism into communism.

Many modern Marxists argue that the relationship between the state and the ruling class is more complex than Marx outlined. The modern state is subjected to many pressures and influences and to merely see it as serving the interests of a unified ruling class is too simplistic. Modern Marxists have developed and modified Marx's ideas.

Antonio Gramsci – hegemony and the state

One writer who has considerable influence on Marxist theories of power is the Italian communist leader Antonio Gramsci (1891-1937). Gramsci rejected the *economic determinism* of many classical Marxists who saw the infrastructure as directly determining the superstructure. Gramsci argued that under certain circumstances the opposite might be true – ideas and beliefs may change the infrastructure.

Gramsci argued that the ruling class exercised power by a combination of force and consent. He saw the superstructure as divided into two main parts. On the one hand, *political society* consists of the institutions of rule by force, for example the army and police. On the other hand, *civil society* consists of the institutions of rule by consent – for example, the church, trade unions, political parties and mass media. For Gramsci, political and civil society together made up the state. He defined the state as 'the entire complex of practical and theoretical activities with which the ruling class not only justifies and maintains its dominance, but manages to win the active consent of those

activity7 *the future of communism*

Item A *Marx's vision*

The ruling class exploits the working class.

The workers' revolution overthrows the ruling class.

Communism replaces capitalism and the state eventually 'withers away'.

A successful revolution in one country leads to revolutions in other countries.

Item B *The collapse of communism*

Lenin's statue being dismantled in East Berlin in 1991. Lenin was one of the founders of Soviet communism after the Russian Revolution of 1917.

Opening the Berlin Wall after the collapse of communism in Eastern Europe in 1989. The wall divided communist East Berlin from capitalist West Berlin.

question

Using the pictures, discuss the possibility of the transition to communism.

---

over whom it rules'. Thus the state extends beyond what is conventionally regarded as 'political' into many areas of everyday life which help to sustain the ideology of the dominant class.

Hegemony A key concept in Gramsci's work is the idea of *hegemony*, which he defined as 'intellectual and moral leadership'. Gramsci argued that the ruling class exercise hegemony in capitalist society because their ideas and values are dominant. As a result, they are able to persuade other groups to consent to their rule. For Gramsci, revolution is only possible if working-class people are able to challenge the hegemony of the ruling class. This requires the emergence of working-class intellectuals who can win over hearts and minds and lead the workers' revolution.

Gramsci recognised the importance of divisions within the ruling class (for example, between financiers, industrialists and landowners), and within the subject class (for example, in Italy there was an important division between peasants and industrial workers). The ruling class could only maintain its hegemony by creating alliances or *power blocs* between different groups that made it up. And the subject class could only challenge ruling class hegemony by forming similar alliances. In this way, the subject class could occasionally force concessions from their rulers. The ruling class were prepared to make these concessions in order to maintain consent to their rule.

Gramsci's ideas had a major influence on the development of neo-Marxist ('new Marxist') theories of power (see Section 3.2). However, not all Marxists accept his views. Some see him as failing to give sufficient emphasis to economic structures as a source of power. Thus it could be argued that workers accept the control of their employers not because they believe in the capitalist system, but because they have little choice – the alternatives might include unemployment or prison.

Ralph Miliband – an instrumentalist view of the state

How does the state represent the interests of the ruling class? What is the nature of the relationship between the state and the ruling class? These questions have received considerable attention from modern Marxist writers. One approach, often termed the *instrumental view*, is associated with the British sociologist Ralph Miliband (1969).

Miliband argues that the state is run by a number of elites including the business elite. Members of these elites are often related by kinship and marriage, they have similar social and educational backgrounds and share a common interest in maintaining the status quo. Government ministers, senior civil servants and other state officials are members of the same social class as financiers and business people and they have similar values. In practice, this means that those running the state see it as their role to defend private property and to preserve the capitalist system. Because of this, the state acts in the interests of the wider capitalist class.

Nicos Poulantzas – a structural view of the state

The work of the Greek sociologist, Nicos Poulantzas provides an alternative structural version of the Marxist approach. Poulantzas criticises Miliband for placing too much emphasis on the social background of elites. For Poulantzas, the state operates in the interests of the ruling class irrespective of the personnel who run it. This is because in capitalist society the nature of economic relationships and the ideological dominance of the ruling class constrain the choices available to those running the state. This means that in the long run, they are forced to safeguard and promote capitalist interests. Thus, even left-wing governments must compromise with business and financial interests in order to ensure stability in capitalist societies. For example, in the UK in the 1970s, a Labour government attempted to pursue left-wing policies of high taxation and greater social equality. However, when the government needed to borrow money from the IMF (International Monetary Fund), it was pressured into reducing spending on public services even though it had been voted into power to follow these policies.

Relative autonomy Like Gramsci, Poulantzas recognises the existence of divisions within the capitalist class. Different groups of capitalists may disagree over the policies they wish the state to adopt. Poulantzas sees the state as acting as a partially independent representative of the capitalist class as a whole. He argues that the state must have what he terms *relative autonomy* from the ruling class. If the state has a degree of independence from sectional interests within the capitalist class, it is better able to serve the long-term interests of capital for the following reasons.

1 The state can compromise between the often competing demands of different groups of capitalists – for example, bankers may want high interest rates, which might be damaging to industrialists.

2 The state can make concessions to the working class (for example, welfare services) which may be opposed by the ruling class. However, this may serve the long-term interests of capital by reducing social tensions.

3 The state can intervene directly in the economy (for example, by providing nationalised services such as transport, which assist the process of capital accumulation) even when this is opposed to the short-term interests of some capitalists.

Evaluation Miliband argues that Poulantzas overstates the degree to which the capitalist system determines the state. To suggest that every action taken by the state is determined by the infrastructure is, for Miliband, going too far.

The concept of relative autonomy has been criticised as being too vague. It is not clear under what circumstances that state is autonomous and when it is constrained by capital.

Nevertheless, despite these criticisms, Poulantzas has had considerable influence on many neo-Marxists seeking to explore the complex relationship between society and the state.

Marxist theories – evaluation

Marxist theories of power argue that the capitalist class not only own and control the means of production but also act as a ruling class politically. A number of objections have been raised to this argument.

Separation of ownership and control Some critics argue that in advanced industrial societies there has been a *separation of ownership and control*. Control of businesses is passing from owners to salaried managers. If this is the case, there may be little justification for seeing a ruling class both owning and controlling the means of production.

Changing patterns of ownership Even in terms of ownership, the existence of a ruling class can be questioned. Ownership of wealth has now spread from a small capitalist class to other groups in society. In Britain, more and more ordinary citizens own shares and have a stake in capitalism. And around 40% of all shares in private companies are now held by institutions such as pension funds and insurance companies rather than individuals. In this situation, identifying a capitalist class becomes increasingly difficult.

Other forms of inequality Marxism focuses on class. Critics argue that it ignores other forms of inequality. Many of today's social movements are concerned with the rights of women, ethnic minorities, gays, lesbians, and people with disabilities. Such political struggles do not fit easily into a Marxist analysis of power.

Support for Marxist theory Despite these criticisms, there is still support for Marxist views of power. For example, John Scott (1991) argues that capitalists with a significant minority shareholding can still have a major say in the running of large companies. And institutions such as insurance firms, with shareholdings in large companies, are often owned and controlled by wealthy financiers.

David Coates (1984) argues that the core of the British ruling class has always consisted of financiers, such as merchant bankers. Throughout the 20th century, they have forged alliances with other groups of capitalists to maintain a dominant influence over government policy.

2.4 Poststructuralist theories of power

Most sociological theories argue that power can only be understood by examining social structures. For example, Marxists claim that power can only be explained in terms of the economic and class structures of society.

The French philosopher Michel Foucault takes a different approach. He likens power to a net which envelops all social relationships. Rather than trying to explain power in terms of social structures, he argues that power operates through *discourses*. A discourse is a way of talking about

key terms

Ruling class The dominant class who own and control the major aspects of the economy.

Mode of production The way society produces goods and services.

Relations of production The relationships between the two main classes in society, ie the ruling and subject classes.

Capitalists Those who invest money in the production of goods and services and receive the profits.

Communism A social system in which the economy is owned by all members of society. As a result, there are no social classes.

Primitive communism According to Marx, the earliest stage of social development.

Infrastructure The economic base of society which shapes the superstructure.

Superstructure The rest of society - for example, the political, legal and educational systems.

Economic determinism The view that the economic system largely shapes the rest of society.

Political society For Gramsci, those parts of society which maintain ruling class domination by force - for example, the police and army.

Civil society Those parts of society which maintain ruling class domination by consent - for example, religion and the mass media.

Hegemony A system of control by which the ruling class impose their beliefs and values on the rest of society, so gaining acceptance of their rule.

Power blocs Alliances between groups within a social class - for example, between industrialists and financiers within the capitalist class.

Instrumental approach Miliband's view which sees the state representing ruling class interests because it is largely staffed by members of that class.

Relative autonomy Poulantzas' view that the state has some freedom to act independently in order to safeguard the long-term interests of capitalism.

something which shapes the way people think, the way they define truth and the meanings through which they interpret the world.

Foucault's approach is known as *poststructuralism* which means 'after structuralism'. Much of his work is concerned with looking at how discourses change. For example, in

Madness and Civilisation (1967), he examines changing discourses of mental disorder, and in *Discipline and Punish* (1977), he looks at changing discourses of punishment. Foucault argues that as discourses change, so do the forms and mechanisms of power which operate through those discourses.

activity8 capitalism and politics

Item A **An NHS hospital**

Item B **A state school**

Item C Shareholding

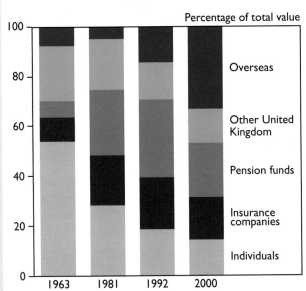

Shares held in UK companies: by sector

Percentage of total value

- Overseas
- Other United Kingdom
- Pension funds
- Insurance companies
- Individuals

1963 1981 1992 2000

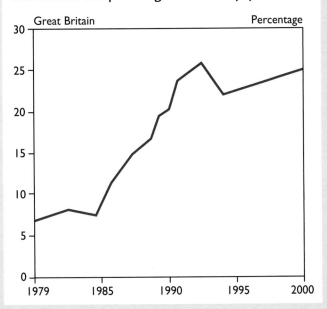

Shareholders as a percentage of the adult population

Great Britain   Percentage

1979 1985 1990 1995 2000

Adapted from Social Trends, 1993 and Office for National Statistics, 2004

questions

1 How might a Marxist interpret Items A and B?

2 a) How might Item C be used to criticise Marxist views?

   b) How might Marxists respond to this criticism?

Changing discourses of punishment and new forms of power

In *Discipline and Punish* (1977), Foucault traces the birth and development of the modern prison system from the late 18th century onwards. Before this time, he argues, rulers exercised power over their subjects by sovereign rule. Power was centred in the person of the king or queen. Those who went against their wishes were punished, often in public, by methods which involved physical assault upon the body, such as whipping, torture and execution. Such spectacles served to reinforce the sovereign's right to rule.

Foucault shows how in Western Europe this 'gloomy festival of punishment' was dying out by the end of the 18th century. Physical punishments, including public executions, were steadily replaced by imprisonment as the most common penalty for crime. In Foucault's terminology, the discourse of punishment was changing.

Although punishments still involved the body, this was only a means to an end. The goal of punishment was to instil discipline rather than demonstrating to others the dreadful consequences of breaking laws made by the sovereign. Early prison reformers experimented with regimes where the body was manipulated, for example by rationing food and regulating daily activities such as sleeping patterns. The intention was to mould and transform the body so that all prisoners functioned in a uniform and disciplined way. The idea was to change the person rather than simply make them suffer.

Disciplinary power Foucault argues that the development of modern prisons coincided with a new discourse which sought to understand and control the human body and the human mind. This gave birth to 'new sciences' such as criminology, psychiatry and modern medicine. The knowledge and technologies which derive from these new sciences formed the basis for *disciplinary power*.

Disciplinary power is applied by a whole range of authorities, for example, judges, prison officers, probation officers and psychiatrists. They assess the individual's crime in relation to his or her mind and circumstances, in order to devise the most efficient and effective methods of punishment and reform.

Normalisation Foucault argues that the aim of prison reformers was to bring criminals' behaviour in line with what they regarded a normal behaviour. He calls this process *normalisation*. From the 18th century onwards, doctors replaced priests as the definers of normality and, like those involved in the correction of criminals, they acquired considerable power over those who were defined as deviant. In the 19th century, doctors created a whole variety of categories of 'sexual deviants' including homosexuals, prostitutes, those who masturbated and those with unusual sexual fetishes. These groups were seen to be in need of treatment in order to bring them back to 'normal' sexual behaviour.

Foucault does not see doctors as a new elite, exercising power over their patients. He argues that they were just as subject to the new discourses they developed as their patients were. However, discourses are always open to resistance. In the case of homosexuals, this can be seen in the formation of a homosexual subculture which resisted the dominant discourse's definition of homosexuality as a 'perversion'.

Surveillance Foucault was also interested in how architecture and technology could be used as mechanisms of disciplinary power. In his work on prisons, he suggests that new forms of disciplinary power were based on the ideas of the philosopher, Jeremy Bentham who invented the *panopticon*. This was a circular prison building designed around a central axis. Inmates would be housed in cells around the building allowing guards in the centre to observe any inmate at any time. Bentham's ideas were reflected in the design of new prisons, such as Pentonville, from the 1830s onwards. Foucault argues that surveillance is apparent not only in the development of prisons but in other bureaucratic organisations – for example, public health services which conduct surveys and collect statistics about disease.

The issue of surveillance has become even more relevant today because of modern technology. Shoppers and football fans are monitored by closed circuit television; government agencies use computers to keep records on citizens and check whether they have paid taxes or claimed benefits; employers use computerised systems to check the hours worked by staff and to record and calculate sales and productivity. For Foucault, the type of surveillance symbolised by the panopticon developed as a means of control throughout society. Hospitals, schools, offices and shopping malls are all part of the panopticon world. The extension of surveillance and the diffusion of disciplinary mechanisms led to the formation of disciplined society.

Evaluation

Foucault offers a new approach to the study of power. For him, power is about the extent to which different claims about truth are accepted – for example, the claim that people who behave in certain ways are mentally ill or sexually perverted. This approach has considerable relevance to contemporary politics where politicians seek to convince voters about the truth of their discourses on asylum seekers, controlling crime, or financing the health service.

Foucault rejects the view that some discourses are truer than others. The Marxist concept of ideology states that the dominant ideology is a distortion of the truth which prevents the working class from realising their true interests. For Foucault, discourses which favour communism are no more 'true' than those which support

capitalism. Power can be seen when a particular discourse becomes dominant at a particular point in history. However, other versions of the truth constantly compete with dominant discourses in a power struggle.

Foucault is critical of approaches which see power residing in the structure of society – in the state, in ruling classes, or in power elites. In his view, power relationships 'go right down into the depths of society' (Foucault, 1977). As a result, all members of society are subject to the discourses of the day.

But where do the dominant discourses come from, why do they change, why do they favour some sections of society rather than others? Critics of Foucault argue that answers to these questions are to be found in the social structure. From their point of view, this is the source of real power.

key terms

Discourse A way of talking about something which shapes the way people see the world and define what is true and real.
Disciplinary power The dominant form of power in modern society. It is exercised by means of surveillance and through systems which mould individuals to standards of normality.
Normalisation The process whereby those subjected to disciplinary power are observed, measured and assessed against standards of normality, then moulded towards the norm if they are seen as deviant.
Panopticon A design for a prison by Jeremy Bentham which allowed all the inmates to be viewed at all times by the guards. Foucault uses this as a metaphor for a society based on discipline and surveillance.
Surveillance The process by which people are kept under observation to ensure conformity and discipline.

2.5 Gender and power

Traditional sociological theories gave little consideration to gender differences in power. However, the growing influence of feminism since the 1970s has changed this.

Feminist theories of power

For many feminists, the study of politics does not start with parliament, political parties or pressure groups. Nor does it start with ruling elites or ruling classes. Instead, power starts at the personal level. This is reflected in the feminist slogan – 'the personal is political'.

Feminists argue that power differences in everyday life are at their most obvious in the relationships between men and women. They see men controlling women's lives in the home, in the workplace, and in the wider society.

The public and the private spheres A number of feminists distinguish between the *private sphere* of the home and the *public sphere* beyond the home. Until the 20th century, women were excluded from many areas of the public sphere. For example, they were not allowed to vote in

activity9 normalisation and surveillance

Item A The punishment of the body

If he is judged to be a vagabond, he is to be whipped and a hole burnt in the lobe of his ear with a hot iron. If he is found guilty again, his other ear will be burnt and he will be made a servant. If he is found guilty a third time, he will be condemned to death.

William Harrison, *The Description of England*, 1586

Up until the end of the eighteenth century many punishments involved the infliction of pain upon the victim.

Item C School medical examination

After the Boer War (1899-1902), there was concern because many army recruits were unfit for military service because of malnutrition and disease. Soon after this, regular medical inspections were introduced in schools to ensure that children were developing normally.

Children being weighed and measured in a Bradford school in 1907

Item B The panopticon

The panopticon, designed by Jeremy Bentham, allowed guards to observe every prisoner without being observed themselves. It was the basis for the design of a number of new prisons in the 19th century.

Item D Electronic surveillance

Closed circuit television (CCTV) control room

questions

1 How does Item A illustrate Foucault's view of punishment before the era of disciplinary power?

2 How might Foucault's concepts of normalisation and surveillance be applied to Items B, C and D?

parliamentary elections until 1918. And it wasn't until 1928, when the voting age for women was reduced from 30 to 21, that they shared the same voting rights as men.

Laws to give women equal rights in other areas were not passed until the 1970s. The Equal Pay Act (1970) was designed to give women the same pay as men for doing the same work. The Sex Discrimination Act (1975) was intended to end gender discrimination in employment, education, accommodation, transport, entertainment and the provision of goods and services.

However, the private sphere of the home, the family and intimate relationships is, in many respects, untouched by the law. In this sphere, women tend to remain subordinate to men. For example, they are largely responsible for domestic work and childcare, and the use of domestic violence by men to control women remains widespread.

According to Carol Pateman (1988), women's subordination in the private sphere prevents them from gaining equality in the public sphere. For example, their domestic responsibilities can limit their careers and their opportunity to enter politics.

Patriarchy

Sylvia Walby (1990) argues that the concept of *patriarchy* is central to understanding gender inequality. Patriarchy refers to a social system based on male dominance. Walby identifies six structures which combine to maintain male power. These are:

Paid employment Despite legislation, many women are still denied equality in terms of pay and employment opportunities.

Household production Many women still undertake large amounts of unpaid domestic labour as housewives.

Culture Walby argues that views of femininity have changed in Western culture. In the 19th century, the hallmark of femininity was domesticity, today it is sexual attractiveness. As a result, women's bodies are exploited – for example, in advertising and pornography.

Sexuality Women today have greater sexual freedom, but a double standard still operates – they are condemned by men as 'slags' if sexually active and 'drags' if they are not.

Violence Men still use violence, or the threat of violence, to control and oppress women. This violence can take many forms including rape, sexual assault, wife beating, sexual harassment in the workplace and child abuse.

The state Walby acknowledges that the state has given women greater rights. But, it's nearly 30 years since the Sex Discrimination Act was passed and there are still far fewer women than men in positions of power and influence.

Walby argues that there has been a shift from what she calls *private patriarchy* to *public patriarchy*. In the 19th century, women were largely controlled by their husbands (or if unmarried, by their fathers) who restricted them to the private sphere. In the 20th century, women have gained greater access to the public sphere. But, this has simply led to a greater emphasis on public patriarchy. For example, in the workplace, women still tend to earn less then men and remain concentrated in low-status, low-skilled occupations. And at the other end of the scale, women are seriously under-represented in Britain's top jobs. Women now make up 45% of the workforce but only 7% of the senior judiciary, 7% of senior police officers, 9% of top business leaders and 9% of national newspaper editors (Equal Opportunities Commission, 2004).

Evaluation of feminist theories

Feminist theories have made an important contribution to understanding power. They have highlighted the importance of gender inequalities. They have pointed to the significance of power relations within the private sphere when most theories of politics have concentrated on the public sphere. However, the concept of patriarchy has been criticised for being too vague and sweeping – for ignoring the fact that increasing numbers of women are rising to the top and that the state legislates to support gender equality.

While recognising these changes, many feminists argue that patriarchy still maintains gender inequality. Although the position of women has improved in some areas over the past 30 years, male dominance remains a fact of life (Walby, 1997).

key terms

Patriarchy A social system based on male dominance.
Private sphere The home and the family.
Public sphere The world beyond home and family – for example, paid employment.
Private patriarchy For Walby, the form of patriarchy which predominated until the late 19th century – the control of women by men within the home and family.
Public patriarchy For Walby, the form of patriarchy which developed in the 20th century – women have greater freedom to come out of the home but are still controlled by men in the public sphere.

2.6 Ethnicity and power

Immigration Since the 1950s, ethnicity and immigration have been important issues in British politics. The influx of non-White immigrants from New Commonwealth countries since 1948 was often met by hostility and discrimination. The state responded in two ways – first, by tightening immigration controls, and second, by legislating against racial discrimination. As Andrew Pilkington (2003) notes, these responses sometimes appeared contradictory.

Since 1962, governments have introduced controls on immigration. Many of these controls appear designed to keep out Black people. For example, the 1968 Commonwealth Immigrants Act took away the automatic right to settle in the UK from British passport holders who did not have a 'close family connection' with Britain. This closed the door to many Black immigrants.

activity10 women in politics

Item A Women in politics, 2004

Members of Parliament	18%
The Cabinet	24%
Members of the House of Lords	17%
Members of the Scottish Parliament	40%
Members of the National Assembly for Wales	50%
Local authority council leaders	12%

Adapted from Equal Opportunities Commission, 2004

Labour's women MPs after the 1997 general election

Item B Why so few?

Women made up 18% of MPs after the 2001 general election. To discover why this percentage was so low, the Equal Opportunities Commission undertook a survey of 408 would-be and actual candidates. More than eight out of ten female Conservative candidates, six out of ten Labour candidates and one third of Liberal Democrat candidates believed that their party's selection committees were biased in favour of men. When asked to consider the most important reasons for the low number of women in Parliament, 50% of all candidates gave family commitments or childcare issues. Other reasons included:

- The hours of work in Parliament
- Women not putting themselves forward for selection
- The male culture of the House of Commons
- Sex discrimination within parties or the attitudes of parties.

Research has shown that when women and men seek selection as candidates, they have very similar levels of political experience – but more men are selected, particularly for safe seats. Both women and men say that family responsibilities can be a barrier to going into politics – but it's still the women candidates who get asked how they will manage the balance between the two.

Adapted from Bentley et al., 2002 and Equal Opportunities Commission, 2004

Item C Scotland and Wales

40% of Members of the Scottish Parliament and 50% of Members of the Welsh Assembly are women. These relatively new institutions have taken positive action in an attempt to balance the numbers of women and men – for example, 'twinning' whereby two constituencies jointly select a male and female candidate, one to contest each seat.

Adapted from Equal Opportunities Commission, 2004

question

How useful is the concept of patriarchy to explain the position of women in politics?

Since 1990, concern about immigration has turned to asylum seekers. A series of Asylum and Immigration Acts have sought to tighten controls on people seeking asylum in the UK. At the same time, Britain's membership of the EU has allowed EU citizens to live and work freely in the UK.

Discrimination The second aspect of the state's policy was to outlaw *racial discrimination,* beginning with the first Race Relations Act in 1965 and culminating in the 2001 Race Relations Amendment Act. These laws sought to ban discrimination in the workplace, housing and other areas of social life. The 1976 Act set up the government funded CRE (Commission for Racial Equality), which promotes racial equality and has powers to investigate suspected cases of discrimination. The 2001 Act requires public bodies to produce plans to promote racial equality.

Andrew Pilkington (2003) argues that government policies have been a mixture of racism (in the case of immigration controls) and liberalism (in the case of race relations legislation). He claims that government commitment to immigration control has always been stronger than to racial equality. For example, a top government department, the Home Office, is responsible for immigration control, while combating discrimination has been delegated to lesser bodies such as the CRE.

Institutional racism In recent years, a number of state institutions have been accused of *institutional racism* – racism as an in-built part of their normal routines and practices. The Macpherson Report (1999), following the murder of the Black teenager Stephen Lawrence, found evidence of institutional racism in the police. Studies of schools indicate that African-Caribbean students – especially boys – are more likely to be placed in lower ability groups than White students with similar grades, and much more likely to be excluded than their White peers (Wright, 1986; Gillborn, 1990).

Political participation by ethnic minorities

There is evidence of an increase in political participation by ethnic minorities. This suggests that growing numbers feel that involvement in mainstream politics will offer them some chance of redressing ethnic disadvantage.

Voting behaviour Surveys indicate that increasing numbers of ethnic minorities are voting in general elections. However, there are higher levels of participation by Asians than African-Caribbeans (Layton-Henry, 1990).

Local government There has been a growth in the number of local councillors from ethnic minority groups. In 1993, only 0.6% of local councillors were Black or Asian (Sewell, 1993). By 2001, this figure had increased to 2.5% (National Census of Local Authority Councillors).

Parliament In 1987, four Black MPs were elected, the first since 1924. By 2001, there were 12 ethnic minority MPs, all from the Labour Party (1.8% of MPs, while ethnic minorities make up 6% of the UK population). In 2002, Paul Boateng was appointed as Chief Secretary to the Treasury, the first Black Cabinet Minister. Although all three main parties are fielding more Black and Asian candidates, they are often selected for unwinnable seats (Saggar, 2001).

Ethnic organisations There is a long history of community based self-help and action groups in ethnic minority areas. There is some evidence of this strategy moving into mainstream society. In the 1980s and 1990s, there was an attempt to create *Black sections* within the Labour Party. However, this was not successful. Ethnic minorities have formed successful pressure groups – for example, African-Caribbeans have voiced concern over the under-achievement and school exclusions of Black children. Following the murder of Stephen Lawrence, groups supporting his parents forcefully voiced their views to the Macpherson Inquiry into institutional racism in the police. Asian communities have generally organised themselves on religious lines – for example, some Muslim groups protested over the publication of Salman Rushdie's book *The Satanic Verses* in 1988 and others contributed to the inquiries into the urban riots of 2001.

Progress? Despite evidence of increasing participation in mainstream politics, many members of ethnic minority groups feel excluded from the political process. There is considerable evidence that racial discrimination and ethnic disadvantage remain widespread in the UK. And members of ethnic minorities are rarely found in positions of power and influence.

It is not surprising that the feelings of frustration, anger and powerlessness generated by this situation sometimes lead to public disturbances and riots.

Riots There are many different ways of interpreting riots. One way is to see them as political action by those who are under-represented by political institutions. From this point of view, Jerry White (1981) states, 'Riot has classically been a collective weapon of the politically powerless – to get those with power and wealth to share a little more or to take notice'. And, as the brother of a Black man who died in police custody said after the Brixton riot of 1995, 'It took a riot to draw attention to the plight of Black people dying in custody'.

During the 1980s and 1990s, there were a series of inner city riots, mainly involving young African Caribbeans in St Paul's (Bristol), Handsworth (Birmingham), Brixton, Southall and Tottenham (London), Moss Side (Manchester) and Toxteth (Liverpool). In 2001, there were riots, mainly involving young Asians, in a number of northern English towns including Bradford, Burnley and Oldham.

key terms

Institutional racism Racism which is built into the normal practices and routines of institutions such as the criminal justice system.
Black sections The view that Black people should form 'sections' within local Labour Party branches to discuss and further their particular interests.

activity11 riots and the political process

Item A A summer of unrest, 2001

Riot in Bradford, 12 July 2001

The British National Party's Luke Smith (centre) celebrates his party's victory in the Burnley local elections.

Bradford April 14-15: Arson attacks after a racial flare-up at a Hindu wedding.

Oldham May 26: Riots after attacks on Asian homes.

Leeds June 5: 100 Asians riot after a local man says police squirted him with CS gas.

Burnley June 23: Violence sparked by a dispute over loud music, followed by a hammer attack on an Asian taxi driver by White men.

Bradford July 7: Asians fight police after a march against the National Front.

Adapted from *The Guardian*, 2001

Item B Why riot?

According to young Asians, the following factors contributed to the riots.

Racism 'If you go into a White area, you are only going to get abuse.'

The police 'I have got no confidence in the police.'

   The police are seen as racist and heavy-handed in their treatment of Asians. David Ritchie, who led an inquiry into the Oldham riots, states: 'There can be no dispute that policing and the perception of policing was a contributory factor behind the riots'.

Unemployment Some young people pointed to high levels of unemployment which they saw as partly due to racism. For example, one young man in Oldham blamed the lack of employment opportunities for Pakistanis on prejudice against their OL8 postcode. And David Ritchie sees the small numbers of ethnic minority members employed by Oldham council as 'a form of institutional racism'.

The extreme right Many blamed provocation from extreme right groups – in particular, the National Front and the British National Party (BNP). The Chief Superintendent in Oldham said: 'There is no doubt that the presence of the National Front and the British National Party in recent weeks would seem to be a deliberate ploy to exploit our racial situation'.

Adapted from *The Guardian* 28.5.2001, 30.6.2001, 28.11.2001. 12.12.2001

questions

1 Which factors could be described as long-term or underlying causes of the riots and which as short-term or immediate causes?

2 How can the riots be seen as a form of political action?

summary

1. Classical pluralism states that power is widely distributed in Western democracies.

2. It sees the interests of citizens represented by political parties and pressure groups.

3. Classical pluralism measures the distribution of power by the issue method – by examining 'concrete decisions' (Lukes' first face of power).

4. Classical pluralism has been criticised for failing to consider:

   * Lukes' second and third faces of power – non-decision making and manipulating the views of others

   * The power of capital

   * The unequal representation and the non-representation of interests

   * The 'organising out' of outsiders from the decision-making process.

5. Elite pluralists recognise that some groups have greater access to government, and greater power, than others.

6. However, they argue that, in many cases, the leaders or elites within pressure groups voice the interests of ordinary citizens in policy communities. The extent to which they do this is questionable.

7. Classical elite theorists claim that rule by elites is inevitable. Both Pareto and Mosca were sceptical about the ability of the masses to govern themselves.

8. C. Wright Mills did not see rule by elites as inevitable. He claimed that the 'power elite', made up of three key institutions – the federal government, the major corporations and the military – emerged during the first half of the 20th century in the USA. Pluralists have criticised Mills for failing to analyse actual decisions.

9. Where Mills sees the various elites forming a single power elite, the fragmented elite model sees elites competing for power and influence.

10. Studies of elite recruitment indicate that elites are relatively closed groups whose members are largely drawn from the upper levels of the class structure. In addition, they are usually male and White.

11. Marxist theories state that power is concentrated in the hands of the ruling class – those who own and control the forces of production. The state is seen to represent the interests of the ruling class.

12. Compared to Marx, Gramsci placed more emphasis on the role of ideas. He argued that working-class intellectuals must win over the hearts and minds of the workers in order to challenge ruling-class hegemony.

13. Miliband's instrumentalist view argues that those who run the state share the same social and economic background, and therefore the same values, as the capitalist class. As a result, they will promote the interests of capital.

14. Poulantzas argues that the state operates in the interests of capital, no matter what the social background of state officials. There is little alternative but to support capitalism since it is so deeply embedded in society.

15. Poulantzas argues that the state has relative autonomy – a degree of independence. This allows it to act in the long-term interests of capitalism rather than responding to the demands of sectional interests within the capitalist class.

16. The following criticisms have been made of Marxist theories.

    * There has been a separation of ownership and control in advanced industrial societies.

    * The existence of a ruling class has been questioned with the increasing spread of share ownership.

    * Marxism tends to ignore other forms of inequality – for example, ethnic and gender inequality.

17. Foucault's poststructuralist theory states that power operates through discourses rather than residing in the structure of society – in the state, in ruling classes or elites. Critics argue that power can only be understood by examining social structures.

18. Many feminists argue that the concept of patriarchy is central to understanding male dominance and female subordination.

19. While the position of women has improved in recent years, they are still largely responsible for housework and childcare and are noticeable by their absence from the top jobs.

20. Government policy towards ethnic minorities appears contradictory. On the one hand, immigration controls have been applied more tightly to ethnic minorities. On the other hand, there have been a series of Acts seeking to ban discrimination.

21. There is evidence of an increase in political participation by ethnic minorities. However, many members of ethnic minority groups feel excluded from the political process. Riots can be seen as a response to this.

Unit 3 The state

keyissues

1 What are the main theories of the state?

2 What is the future of the state?

3.1 The rise of the modern state

Defining the state

Max Weber (1978) defined the *state* as 'a human community that successfully claims the monopoly of the legitimate use of physical force within a given territory'.

The state has authority over those who live in a defined geographical area, and the right to use force to back up this authority. Other groups may use force to achieve their aims, but this is not usually seen as legitimate by the majority of the population.

More recent definitions of the state tend to follow Weber. For example, Andrew Heywood (2002) give the following definition.

- The state is sovereign – it exercises power over all other groups in society.
- That power is legitimate – it is usually regarded as right and legal. And the decisions of the state are usually accepted as binding on members of society.
- The state has the power to use force to make sure its laws are obeyed. In Weber's words, the state has a monopoly of 'legitimate violence'.
- The state governs a clearly defined geographical area and all who live within that area.
- State institutions are clearly defined as 'public'. These public bodies – for example, Parliament, the Home Office and the police force – are responsible for making and enforcing collective decisions.

The rise of the state

Some small-scale societies have been described as stateless societies since there is no centralised authority with the power to use legitimate force to support its decisions. Some early forms of state had a long history – for example, ancient civilisations such as Greece, Rome, Egypt and China had a strong centralised political authority. However, the modern nation-state is a fairly recent development, emerging during the last few centuries.

In Europe, modern states developed with the decline of the feudal system and the rise of capitalism. From the 16th century, monarchs imposed more effective controls over their kingdoms. Rule by local nobles was replaced by professional administrators who were loyal to the monarch. Customary laws were replaced by written codes of law. Authority was centralised, and only the state could legitimately use force – unlike the Middle Ages when powerful nobles had their own private armies and exercised considerable control over their estates. The borders of states were more clearly defined and a greater sense of national identity emerged.

Weber and the state For Weber, the development of the modern state was part of the process of *rationalisation* which accompanied the rise of capitalism. Rational action is based on reason rather than tradition or emotion. It sets goals and involves precise and deliberate calculation of the most effective ways of reaching those goals.

Weber saw bureaucracy as the institution of rational action. It is based on *rational-legal authority* – on written rules backed by the force of law (see page 63). Weber believed that the modern state could not operate effectively without bureaucratic control. The major institutions of the state – from the civil service and the education system to

the police and army – are all organised on bureaucratic lines. And this was a key instrument of state power. In Weber's words – 'bureaucracy has been and is a power instrument of the first order'.

Life in the modern state was increasingly governed by written rules and subject to bureaucratic control. Power was exercised by elected or appointed officials rather than leaders who inherited their positions. Rational-legal authority steadily replaced traditional authority.

key terms

The state An institution which has a monopoly of the use of legitimate force over those who live in a particular geographical area.
Stateless societies Societies without a state – they have no centralised authority with the power to use legitimate force to support its decisions.
Rationalisation A process whereby reason replaces tradition and emotion as a basis for action.

3.2 Theories of the state

Pluralist theories of the state

Pluralists see the state in Western democracies as an organisation representing the interests of members of society as a whole. They argue that direct political involvement by the mass of the population is impractical in large complex societies. However, their interests are channelled through a variety of pressure groups and through their elected representatives. In this way, every major concern is voiced and all significant groups are represented.

Using evidence from research using the issue method, pluralists argue that power is widely distributed in Western democracies. As a result, no one group dominates government decision making – there is no ruling elite, no ruling class, and power is dispersed rather than concentrated.

Dunleavy and O'Leary (1987) identify three main pluralist views of the state – the *weathervane model*, the *neutral-state model* and the *broker-state model*.

The weathervane model This view sees the state as a weathervane of public opinion. Its direction reflects public opinion and the demands of pressure groups. State policy is therefore shaped by the concerns of its citizens in general and by the requirements of sectional interests. In terms of the weathervane model, Parliament is seen as little more than a meeting place which gives the official seal of approval to decisions which have already been made in the public mind.

The neutral-state model This view argues that the state does more than simply mirror public opinion – it is more than a weathervane at the mercy of the public. Instead, the state is seen as a neutral or impartial referee, acting in the public interest. It referees and compromises between the demands of competing pressure groups, making sure that even the weakest has a voice. It takes their views on board, assesses them in terms of what's best for the country as a whole, and makes decisions on that basis.

As its name suggests, the neutral state does not favour any particular group in society – something it shares with the weathervane state. However, where the weathervane state is fairly passive – blown in directions indicated by public opinion – the neutral state is more active – it listens to a range of views, then makes decisions in the public interest. And these decisions are often a compromise between competing demands.

The broker-state model This view sees groups within the state having their own interests and concerns. For example, particular political parties or government departments are seen to have their own agendas. State officials will negotiate with a variety of pressure groups, and develop policies which compromise between the often conflicting demands of these groups. But these policies also reflect the concerns of the state officials.

The term broker state refers to deals brokered – facilitated and negotiated – by the state with a variety of pressure groups.

Marxist theories of the state

Marxist theories of the state were outlined in the previous unit. Marx saw the state as representing the interests of the ruling class. In his words, the state is 'but a committee for managing the common affairs of the whole bourgeoisie' (capitalist ruling class). As long as class societies exist, so will the state. Marx believed that the overthrow of capitalism would lead to a classless society – communism – in which the state would eventually wither away. People would then govern themselves.

Not all Marxists agree how and why the state acts in the interests of the ruling class. As outlined earlier, Miliband's instrumentalist approach argues that state officials share the same background and values as the capitalist class and will therefore promote their interests. In contrast, Poulantzas' structuralist approach argues that the state will operate in the interests of capital, no matter what the background of state officials. They have little alternative because capitalism is so embedded in the structure of society. In addition, Poulantzas argues that the state has relative autonomy – a certain degree of independence from the capitalist class. This allows it to act in the long-term interests of capital rather than responding to the sometimes conflicting demands of sectional interests within the capitalist class.

Contradictory functions The German sociologist Claus Offe (1982) argues that the state can never wholly succeed in representing capital because it is required to perform contradictory functions. According to Offe, the state has two main functions: 1) *accumulation* – assisting capitalists to create profits and accumulate capital – and 2) *legitimation* – making the system appear just and fair to all.

These two functions can conflict. In raising revenue for public services, the state threatens the profitability of capitalist businesses. This may lead to a *fiscal crisis* – insufficient revenue from taxation and borrowing to meet government spending. The state typically reacts with cuts in public expenditure in order to restore the profitability of business. However, this may lead to a *legitimation crisis* whereby citizens question whether the state is acting in their interests when benefits and public services are cut back.

The boundaries of the state Marxists often take a broad view of the state, including a variety of institutions which they see as reinforcing the dominance of the ruling class. For example, Louis Althusser (1969) refers to *ideological state apparatuses* which include the education system, the mass media, the law and religion. In his view, their main purpose is to transmit ruling class ideology which encourages the subject class to accept their position as normal, reasonable and just.

New Right theories of the state

New Right thinkers have been critical of the state in advanced capitalist societies. They make the following points.

- A *free market*, that is a market free from state interference, is essential to the efficiency and smooth-running of capitalist economies. Free and open competition between companies will increase productivity and profits.
- The state has intervened far too much in the market. This has had a negative effect, reducing efficiency, productivity and profitability. Market forces, directed by the law of supply and demand, should be the major influence on the economy, not the state.
- Similarly, the state has intervened far too much in the lives of individuals. This is a threat to personal freedom.
- The negative effects of this can be seen in state welfare policy. Welfare benefits are far too high. They reduce people's incentive to work and to compete for jobs in the labour market. And they reduce self-reliance – people become dependent on welfare rather than standing on their own two feet.

New Right thinkers argue that the state has taken on too many responsibilities, that it interferes far too much in people's lives and intervenes far too much in the economy. Their solution is to 'roll back the state'. State control should be minimised. The result would be a more dynamic economy and greater individual freedom. And, as the state shrinks, so will the money it needs, and this, in turn, will lead to lower taxation (McAuley, 2003).

However, critics of the New Right take a different view. Who would take care of the poor and the powerless in a society at the mercy of market forces? Who would protect human rights? Roll back the state and society may end up dominated by those with wealth and property.

key terms

The weathervane model A pluralist view which sees the state directed by public opinion and pressure groups.

The neutral-state model A pluralist view which sees the state as an impartial referee compromising between the demands of competing pressure groups and acting in the public interest.

The broker-state model A pluralist view which sees the state pursuing its own interests as well as negotiating with and reflecting the demands of various pressure groups.

Accumulation The process by which the value of investments in capitalist enterprises increases.

Legitimation For Marxists, the process by which the capitalist system is made to appear just and fair.

Fiscal crisis When there is insufficient revenue from taxation and borrowing to meet government spending requirements.

Legitimation crisis When the legitimation process breaks down and people begin to question whether the state really governs in their interests.

Ideological state apparatuses For Althusser, the range of institutions in capitalist society which transmit ruling class ideology.

Free market A market free from state intervention where there is open competition between companies.

activity12 views of the state

Item A

Item B

Item C

Item D

Item E

questions

1 Match each of the cartoons with one of the theories of the state given in Section 3.2.

2 Give reasons for your choices.

3.3 State-centred theories

Society-centred theories The theories of power and the state discussed so far are sometimes known as *society-centred theories* (Nordlinger, 1981). They see the state as reflecting the distribution of power in the wider society and acting accordingly. For example, pluralist theories see power as widely distributed in society – as a result, the state represents the variety of individuals and groups who share power in the wider society. By contrast, Marxist theories see power as concentrated in the hands of the ruling class – as a result, the state acts on behalf of the dominant minority in society. In each case, the activities of the state are shaped by the distribution of power in the wider society.

State-centred theories In contrast, state-centred theories argue that the state has the ability to act independently. It is not simply a reflection of the wider society. It can exercise power in its own right, develop its own policies and act in terms of its own agendas.

Eric Nordlinger – the state as a political actor

Eric Nordlinger (1981) criticises society-centred theories for ignoring the state's power to act independently. He argues that, at times, state policy is opposed to the views of powerful groups in society and the public in general. For example, in 1965, Parliament suspended the death penalty for murder and, in 1969, voted to continue this suspension indefinitely. These acts went against public opinion. Since

then, calls to re-instate the death penalty have been ignored by Parliament, again in the face of public opinion.

Nordlinger argues that the state often initiates policies for which there is little interest or support. In some instances, these initiatives are unpopular, but the state can sometimes change minds by manipulating pressure group and public opinion. Nordlinger uses evidence from Dahl's *Who Governs* (1961) which shows that when the mayor first placed urban renewal on the agenda, none of the main pressure groups in New Haven showed much interest or support. However, the mayor eventually managed to gain their support. This is an example of a political figure setting an agenda and changing minds by persuasion.

Theda Skocpol – the power of states

Like Nordlinger, Theda Skocpol (1985) argues that states have their own priorities and goals. They are concerned with perpetuating their own power and control, rather than simply representing the people or responding to the demands of the powerful.

Skocpol is particularly critical of Marxist theories. She argues that Marxists have focused almost exclusively on class relationships and ignored the state as an entity in itself. She looks at evidence from three revolutions which led to the overthrow of the state – in France (1788), China (1911) and Russia (1917). Skocpol (1979) argues that, in all three cases, class struggles were an important factor. However, she claims that the weakness of the states themselves was a major reason for their downfall.

Evaluation of state-centred theories

State-centred theories focus directly on the state. They provide evidence that the state can act independently and is not simply a mouthpiece for public opinion or the demands of the powerful. However, critics argue that this 'independence' has been exaggerated. For example, Bob Jessop (1990) argues that the state and society are so closely connected that it is impossible to separate them in any analysis of power.

> ## key terms
>
> **Society-centred theories** Theories which see the role of the state shaped by the wider society.
> **State-centred theories** Theories which see the state as having the ability to act independently from the wider society.

3.4 Globalisation and the state

Traditionally, sociologists have looked at the state in the context of individual countries. In other words, they have looked at the *nation-state*. They have analysed the role of the state within its geographical boundaries and in terms of the society over which it has sovereignty. Many of the questions sociologists asked were based on this view. For example, to what extent does the state represent the people it governs?

In recent years, sociologists have broadened their perspective. This is based on the view that we live in an increasingly global society. From this, it follows that states must be viewed in a global context. They do not exist in isolation. They increasingly operate in an international framework.

Globalisation

The term *globalisation* refers to the development of a global or world society. Nation-states are becoming more interdependent. They are more likely to be influenced by processes occurring on a global scale. Events in any one society are increasingly linked to events in other societies.

Globalisation has a number of aspects. They include the following.

Economic globalisation The economies of nation-states are increasingly part of a global economic system. There has been a rapid growth in the size of *transnational corporations* (TNCs) – companies which operate in a number of countries, for example, Ford, General Motors, Sony, Nestlé and Nike. They can move investment and production from one country to another, wherever economic conditions are most favourable. And they sell their products to world markets.

Financial transactions are increasingly global. The existence of major stock exchanges in various countries mean that the buying and selling of shares can continue round the clock. And currency dealing is now big business on an international scale.

Nation-states are joining together in economic unions. The European Union consists of 25 nation-states forming a free trade area – in effect a single home market without tariffs such as import duties. And the North American Free Trade Area has created a tariff-free zone from Mexico to Canada. In 2005, it will be renamed The Free Trade Area of the Americas and expanded to include every country in Central America, South America and the Caribbean, except Cuba.

Political globalisation More and more nation-states are becoming members of international organisations. These organisations include the UN (United Nations), NATO (North Atlantic Treaty Organisation) and the European Union. International financial institutions, such as the World Bank and the IMF (International Monetary Fund), have steadily grown. For example, the IMF, which among other things provides loans for member states, has grown from around 25 members in 1945 to 184 in 2004 (IMF, 2004).

Cultural globalisation Real-time communication systems have compressed time and space to the point where worldwide communication is virtually instant – for example, e-mail and satellite TV. The growth of TNCs has led to corporations such as Coca Cola, McDonald's, Nike and Mars going global.

The world is increasingly bombarded with Western tastes, styles and fashions via advertising directed by international advertising corporations and entertainment provided by transnational media corporations. According to some observers, one of the consequences of these developments is the emergence of a global consumerist culture (Sklair, 2003).

Nation-states as too small

Where do these developments leave the nation-state? According to some researchers, too small and with too little power. Take Wal-Mart Stores, a TNC which began in the USA and expanded worldwide. Its turnover of $220 billion in 2001 was greater than the income of all but 20 countries. And where a TNC decides to invest can make a major difference to the economy of a small country or of a region in a larger country. Yet states often have little control over these decisions. TNCs are primarily accountable to their shareholders, not to the nation-states in which they happen to have their headquarters (Sklair, 2003).

One response to this situation is to form transnational political organisations. The European Union provides an example. On the one hand, it creates a powerful economic organisation with a large home market. On the other hand, it results in a loss of political sovereignty for each of the member states. For example, the European Court of Justice makes judgements which can have a significant impact on member countries. Similarly, global financial institutions such as the World Bank and the IMF can provide support for ailing economies and in this respect, strengthen individual nation-states. But again, this can result in a reduction of national sovereignty. The terms of the loans they provide often require states to change their social and economic policies (Welsh, 1997).

Global risks According to the German sociologist Ulrich Beck (1992), we are entering a *global risk society*. Global risks transcend national boundaries – and the nation-state is too small to protect its citizens. Beck points to the explosion at the nuclear power station at Chernobyl in the former Soviet Union in 1986 (see Activity 13). Radioactive material was blown westward across Europe reaching 20 countries.

Single nation-states do not have the power to deal effectively with major environmental and social problems. These include global warming, pollution, disappearing rainforests, the depletion of fish stocks in the world's oceans, devastating accidents such as oil spills and explosions at nuclear plants, diseases such as AIDS, addictions to a range of harmful drugs, and international terrorism. Many researchers argue that these are global problems which require global solutions – nation-states are just too small to deal with them. But this raises basic issues about the powers which have traditionally been seen as belonging to individual nation-states (Welsh, 1997).

Nation-states as too big

On the one hand, nation-states have been seen as too small to operate effectively in a global context. On the other hand, they have been seen as too big to deal with some of the consequences of globalisation.

Opposing tendencies According to Anthony Giddens (1990), globalisation consists of a number of opposing tendencies. These include new identities *and* old identities, centralisation *and* decentralisation, integration *and* fragmentation, homogenisation *and* differentiation. Thus, globalisation encourages people to adopt new identities as members of larger social units such as the European Union. It can also produce an opposite response – people focus on old identities, for example, ethnic identities – as a defensive reaction to unwelcome change. As states integrate into larger social units and power is increasingly centralised, there is an opposing tendency – for fragmentation or breaking-up, as in the case of the former Soviet Union, and decentralisation as in the UK with power devolved to the regions with the Welsh Assembly and the Scottish Parliament. And as cultures become more homogeneous – the same – there is a tendency for differentiation – for people to strive for difference, for example, the attempt by many people in Wales to retain the Welsh language.

Where does this leave the nation-state? According to some researchers, it is too big to deal with some of these opposing tendencies.

Ethnicity and nationalism In recent years, there have been growing demands from ethnic and 'national' groups within nation-states for autonomy and independence. This can be seen in the break-up of the former Soviet Union and the former Yugoslavia into separate nation-states, in ethnic conflict in former colonial territories in Africa, such as the

Sudan, and in the former republics of the Soviet Union – for example, Chechnya's demand for independence from Russia.

In the UK, there has been a resurgence of Scottish and Welsh nationalism, along with demands for either regional government or independence from the UK.

These developments can be seen as reactions to globalisation. Existing nation-states are seen as too big. They must fragment, decentralise, recognise difference and accept the resurgence of old identities.

The future of the nation-states

The nation-state can be seen as threatened from without and within – from without by transnational corporations and transnational political organisations, from within by ethnic and 'national' groups. According to Daniel Bell (1987), the state is 'too small for the big problems of life, and too big for the small problems of life'.

Anthony Giddens Has the nation-state got a future? For many, the answer is yes. For example, Anthony Giddens (2001) sees nation-states as far from obsolete. Some of their powers may have been reduced, but they remain the most important unit of power in today's world. Indeed, the nation-state 'has become a universal political form'. Its rivals have dropped by the wayside – colonial empires have disappeared and the last empire, the Soviet Union, broke up in 1990. There are now more nation-states than there have ever been.

Despite forecasting a bright future for the nation-state, Giddens sees a growing need for 'global governance'. He looks forward to global organisations to deal with global problems – from the spread of AIDS, to global warming, to the regulation of financial markets, to human rights. Giddens (2001) sees the move to global governance as 'the greatest necessity and the greatest challenge facing human societies at the start of the twenty-first century'.

David Held What impact does globalisation have on democracy? Held (1993) sees many nation-states as having little say in a global society. They have little control over their own economies and are often at the mercy of transnational corporations.

Held calls for a new system of global democracy. He sees existing global organisations, such as the United Nations, as offering a model for the future. But because nation-states have maintained their sovereignty, the UN is often ineffective. Held suggests a number of transnational political organisations from regional parliaments representing a number of countries in particular areas such as Africa and Europe, through to a world parliament. This global body would become 'an authoritative international centre for the consideration and examination of pressing global issues, eg health and disease, food supply and distribution, the debt burden of the Third World, the instability of the hundreds of billions of dollars that circulate the globe daily, ozone depletion, and the reduction of the risks of nuclear war' (Held, 1993).

Leslie Sklair offers a less optimistic picture. He sees nation-states increasingly overshadowed by the power of transnational capitalists and their corporations. Transnational corporations have no real ties or loyalties to the nation-state – they reflect the interests and concerns of those who own and control them. Sklair (2003) sees transnational capitalism as the main driver of global society, and as the main cause of global problems.

There is a rapidly growing gap between the world's richest and poorest nations and between the rich and poor in every nation. And this, according to Sklair, is due to the pursuit of profit which drives global capitalism. In addition, capitalist globalisation has promoted consumerism with little thought for the environmental consequences. According to Sklair, this has led to global warming, the destruction of rainforests, over-fishing by large commercial

fleets in the world's oceans and a range of other environmental problems.

Sklair (2003) concludes that, 'Those who own and control the institutions that drive globalisation presently wield most of the power in the global system'.

key terms

Globalisation The process by which societies become increasingly interconnected in a global network.
Transnational corporations Companies which transcend national boundaries and operate in a number of countries.
Global risk society A world society in which risks transcend national boundaries.

summary

1. The modern state is a fairly recent development, emerging in Europe during the 16th century.

2. According to Weber, the modern state is part of the process of rationalisation.

3. There are three main pluralist theories of the state.
   - The weathervane model which sees the state directed by public opinion and the demands of pressure groups.
   - The neutral-state model which sees the state as an impartial referee, compromising between the demands of competing pressure groups and acting in the public interest.
   - The broker-state model which sees the state pursuing its own agenda as well as brokering deals with various interest groups.

4. Marxist theories see the state as representing the interests of the ruling class.
   - Miliband's instrumentalist theory argues that state officials share the same background and values as the capitalist class and will therefore promote their interests.
   - Poulantzas's structural theory argues the state has little option but to support the ruling class because capitalism is embedded in the structure of society.
   - Poulantzas also argues that the state has relative autonomy. This allows it to represent the long-term interests of capital rather than responding to the short-term demands of factions within the ruling class.
   - Offe argues that the state can never wholly succeed in representing ruling-class interests because it has two contradictory functions – supporting both the processes of accumulation and legitimation.

5. New Right theories are critical of the modern state for:
   - Too much intervention in the market
   - Too much intervention in the lives of individuals
   - Taking on too many responsibilities.

6. Society-centred theories see the state as reflecting the distribution of power in society and acting accordingly.

7. State-centred theories argue that the state can exercise power in its own right, develop its own policies and act in terms of its own agendas.

8. Traditionally, sociologists have looked at the role of the state within the nation it governs. Increasingly, they look at the state in a global context.

9. Globalisation has a number of aspects. They include:
   - Economic
   - Political
   - Cultural.

10. According to some researchers, the nation-state is too small, and has too little power, to deal with transnational corporations and global risks.

11. One response to this is for individual states to join larger political units. However, in the process, they lose some of their sovereignty.

12. According to Giddens, globalisation has a number of opposing tendencies.
    - New identities and old identities
    - Centralisation and decentralisation
    - Integration and fragmentation
    - Homogenisation and differentiation.

    Some researchers argue that the nation-state is too big to deal with some of these tendencies.

13. The nation-state can be seen as threatened from without (eg by TNCs) and within (eg from demands by sections of its population for autonomy or independence).

14. Giddens argues that although the power of the nation-state has been reduced, it remains the most important unit of power in today's world. However, he sees the need for global organisations to deal with global problems.

15. Held argues that new international institutions must be developed if democracy is to survive in a global society.

16. Sklair sees nation-states increasingly overshadowed by international capitalism and the power of TNCs.

activity13 the state and globalisation

Item A Pepsi

Pink, Britney Spears and Beyoncé at the launch of the Pepsi Gladiator commercial – a global ad, transmitted on global media, featuring global stars

Item B Global terrorism

Attack on the World Trade Center, September 11, 2001

Madrid train bombing, March 11, 2004

Item C Chernobyl

On 26 April 1986, the nuclear power station at Chernobyl in the Soviet Union exploded as a result of human error. 31 workers and firefighters died within days (of radiation burns) and 50,000 square kilometres of surrounding land was contaminated. The nuclear fallout reached 20 countries, including Britain. Scientists have estimated that between 280,000 and 500,000 deaths will result worldwide from this accident.

Greenpeace, *Nuclear Power*, 1992

FRG = Federal Republic of Germany (the former West Germany)
GDR = Germany Democratic Republic (the former East Germany)

Dates of first measurement of radiation fallout from Chernobyl in various countries, 27 April to 2 May 1986. Map based on information from the International Atomic Energy Agency.

Item D Destruction of the rainforest

Amazon rainforest, Brazil

questions

1 How does Item A illustrate the power of transnational corporations?

2 a) How do Items B, C and D illustrate Beck's view of a global risk society?

   b) What problems are faced by the nation-state in dealing with such risks?

   c) How might global organisations help to deal with these problems?

3 How does Item E illustrate Giddens's opposing tendencies of globalisation?

Item E Kurdistan

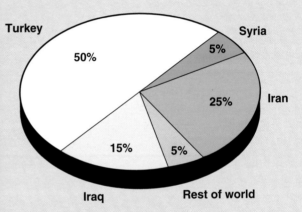

Turkey 50%

Syria 5%

Iran 25%

Rest of world 5%

Iraq 15%

The Kurdish flag. The wording reads 'Freedom for Kurdistan'. According to the Kurdish Organisation for Culture and Education, Kurdistan covers an area of 520,000 km² mainly in Turkey, Iran and Iraq and has a population of over 25 million Kurds.

Unit 4 Political ideologies

keyissues

1 What is ideology?

2 What are the main political ideologies today?

3 What is the relationship between political ideologies and political parties?

4.1 What is ideology?

A distortion of reality The word ideology has many meanings. It is often used in a negative sense to describe a set of ideas which distort reality. Marxists use the term in this way. When they refer to *ruling class ideology*, they are talking about beliefs which produce a *false consciousness*, a picture of the world which is false and distorted. Feminists use ideology in this way when they talk about *patriarchal ideology* (see page 83).

A justification for inequality From this perspective, ideology not only distorts reality, it also provides a justification for inequality. Thus ruling class ideology justifies the position of the ruling class and supports its dominance. And it blinds members of the subject class to the truth about their situation. For example, the emphasis on freedom in capitalist society – the free market, free democratic societies, individual freedoms – projects an illusion which disguises the oppression and exploitation of the subject class.

The term patriarchal ideology is used in a similar way. It presents a false picture of the characteristics of males and females. And this picture serves to justify and maintain gender inequality.

A closed system of thought The philosopher Karl Popper (1959) sees ideology as a closed system of thought. By this he means that ideologies are closed to evidence which challenges their beliefs. They refuse to consider alternative views or to tolerate opposing ideas. They are immune to rational argument. Their version of the truth has an answer for everything.

This view of ideology was largely based on the belief systems of fascist and communist totalitarian regimes in the 20th century. As a result, it also saw ideology as an instrument of social control and oppression.

Neutral views of ideology

The views of ideology outlined above are all negative. Ideology is bad, false and oppressive. Neutral views see ideology as neither good nor bad, true nor false, liberating nor oppressive. Most modern social scientific views of ideology treat it in a neutral way. Here are some examples.

- Ideology is 'an interrelated set of ideas that in some way guides or inspires political action' (Heywood, 2002).
- 'An ideology is a reasonably coherent structure of thought shared by a group of people. It is a means of explaining how society works and of explaining how it ought to work' (Dobson, 1992).

This unit is primarily concerned with political ideologies and their relationship to political parties. It focuses mainly on liberalism, conservatism and socialism.

key terms

Ruling class ideology A set of ideas which distorts reality and justifies the position of the ruling class.
False consciousness A picture of the world which is false and distorted. In Marxist terms, it presents a false picture of the relationship between the ruling and subject classes.
Patriarchal ideology A set of ideas which distorts reality and justifies male dominance.

4.2 Liberalism

Key ideas of liberalism

In its broadest sense, liberalism is the ideology of modern Western democracies. The following are some of the key ideas of liberalism.

Individual freedom The aim of liberalism is to create a society in which every individual is free to develop their own unique talents. Individual freedom is central to liberal thinking. Each person should be able to act as they please, so long as they don't threaten the freedom of others to do likewise.

Equality of opportunity Each individual should have an equal opportunity to develop their talents to the full. This does not mean that everybody should be equal in terms of wealth, income and social status, only that they should have an equal chance to attain positions of power and status.

Liberals believe in equal rights – for example, equality under the law and political equality in the sense of one person, one vote.

Government by consent Government should be based on the consent of the governed – a representative democracy translates this ideal into practice. One of the main tasks of government is to protect individual freedom. Many liberals believe in a form of limited government that protects but does not infringe on the rights and liberties of the individual.

The development of liberalism

Classical liberalism This form of liberalism became influential in British politics in the 19th century. It argued that people are rational, that they know what they want and are capable of making their own choices. Intervention (or interference) from above should be kept to a minimum – self-help was far more preferable. Wherever possible, the individual should make their own way in life rather than relying on the state.

Progressive liberalism The later years of the 19th century saw the emergence of progressive liberalism, also known as social, or welfare, liberalism. As industrialisation developed, it became clear that self-help was not the answer for many people. Poverty was widespread – and many people were poor through no fault of their own. Progressive liberalism recognised that state intervention was necessary – social welfare would give people the opportunity to live a decent life and enjoy the freedoms which were rightfully theirs.

Progressive liberalism can be seen in the policies of the Liberal governments of 1905-1915. The 1908 Old Age Pensions Act provided pensions for people over 70. The 1911 National Insurance Act provided sickness benefit and payment of medical expenses for all manual workers. It also provided unemployment benefits for workers in seven occupations which were subject to high levels of unemployment.

Progressive liberalism had a major influence on both Labour and Conservative governments from 1945 to the mid-1970s. The Beveridge Report, published in 1942, provided the blueprint for the modern welfare state created by a series of Acts passed by the post-war Labour government. State intervention in the economy was seen as a means of raising living standards and reducing unemployment.

From a progressive liberal viewpoint, state welfare provisions were a means to an end – to help individuals to stand on their own two feet and take responsibility for their own future. In other words, to give them the opportunity to exercise their individual liberties (Heywood, 2002).

Neo-liberalism In many respects, neo-liberalism shares ideas with the New Right (see page 89). It can be seen as a return to classical liberalism with its emphasis on self-help and its rejection of state intervention. It sees state intervention as a threat to individual freedom, and state welfare as sapping individual initiative and enterprise.

Similarly, state intervention in the economy is seen as harmful. A free market is essential to economic growth, high productivity and prosperity. Too much state regulation will crush private enterprise.

Neo-liberalism had a major influence on Margaret Thatcher's Conservative governments from 1979 to 1990. She scornfully referred to the 'nanny state', seeing its welfare provisions undermining initiative and freedom and creating welfare dependency. She championed the free market, privatising nationalised industries in the belief that competition would increase efficiency and productivity.

The Liberal Democrats Today's Liberal Democrats are closest to progressive liberalism. First, they are concerned with individual liberties – with civil rights and equal opportunity. Second, they see an important role for the state in guarding these rights and promoting equality of opportunity.

activity14 liberalism

Item A Classical liberalism

The spirit of self-help is the root of all genuine growth in the individual. Help from others is often weakening whilst self-help is strengthening. Whatever is done for men or groups takes away the incentive and necessity of doing it themselves. And where people are over-guided and over-governed, the inevitable tendency is for them to become comparatively helpless.

Adapted from Smiles, 1859

Item B Progressive liberalism

A mother and child crying because there is nothing for dinner, East End of London, 1912.

The working classes have done their best during the past 50 years to make provision without the aid of the state. But, it is insufficient. The old man has to bear his own burden while in the case of a young man who is broken down and who has a wife and family to maintain, the suffering is increased and multiplied to that extent. These problems of the sick, of the ill, of the men who cannot find means of earning a living are problems with which it is the business of the state to deal. They are problems which the state has neglected for too long.

From a speech made to Parliament by David Lloyd George on 15 June 1908

Item C The Liberal Democrats

The Liberal Democrats exist to build and safeguard a fair, free and open society, in which we seek to balance the fundamental values of liberty, equality and community, and in which no-one shall be enslaved by poverty, ignorance or conformity. We champion the freedom, dignity and well-being of individuals, we acknowledge and respect their right to freedom of conscience and their right to develop their talents to the full. We aim to disperse power, to foster diversity and to nurture creativity. We believe that the role of the state is to enable all citizens to attain these ideals, to contribute fully to their communities and to take part in the decisions which affect their lives.

Adapted from the *Preamble to the Constitution of the Liberal Democrat Party*

Item D *Margaret Thatcher*

The free market was like a vast sensitive nervous system, responding to events and signals all over the world to meet the ever-changing needs of peoples in different countries, from different classes, of different religions, with a kind of benign indifference to their status. Governments acted on a much smaller store of conscious information and, by contrast, were themselves 'blind forces' blundering about in the dark, and obstructing the operations of markets rather than improving them. State subsidies and direction of investment achieved progressively more inefficient industries and ever lower returns on capital.

Welfare benefits, distributed with little or no consideration of their effects on behaviour, encouraged illegitimacy, facilitated the break-down of families, and replaced incentives favouring work and self-reliance with perverse encouragement for idleness and cheating.

From Thatcher, 1993

questions

1 How does Item A illustrate classical liberalism?
2 Judging from Item B, how does progressive liberalism differ from classical liberalism?
3 Use Item C to support the view that the aims of Liberal Democrats reflect progressive liberalism.
4 Identify ideas from neo-liberalism in the excerpts from Margaret Thatcher's book in Item D.

4.3 Conservatism

Key ideas of conservatism

Conservative ideas emerged in the late 18th and early 19th centuries. They have been seen as a reaction to the rapid economic, social and political changes brought about by industrialisation (Heywood, 2002).

Edmund Burke's *Reflections on the Revolution in France*, published in 1790, provides an early illustration of conservative views. Burke saw the French Revolution as a threat to order and stability. Change should not be sudden, it should not be based on a brand new model which swept away the past. Instead, it should be gradual, built on institutions which have stood the test of time, and based on the accumulated wisdom of the past. In Burke's words, the way forward is 'change in order to conserve'.

Tradition Burke's views illustrate the key theme of conservative thought – the importance of tradition, of tried and tested ideas, experience and institutions. What has been shown to work in the past should be conserved for the present and the future.

Change It follows that change should be built on the best of the past. It should not be based on a brand new blueprint which sweeps away everything that went before. Change should proceed gradually and be approached with caution.

Human nature Conservatives tend to see human beings as imperfect and flawed. They can be selfish as well as unselfish, irrational as well as rational, greedy as well as generous.

The state In view of the imperfections of human nature, society needs a strong state to maintain law and order and ensure social stability. People need leadership and guidance from above.

Society Where liberalism tends to focus on the individual, conservative thought stresses the importance of the family and the nation. The family is seen as the cornerstone of society, transmitting shared values and contributing to social stability. The nation provides people with a common identity and a collective purpose. Symbols of the nation such as the flag, the national anthem and the monarchy help to make individuals feel part of something greater than themselves.

Varieties of conservatism

Whiteley et al (1994) identify three main types of conservatism, all of which can be seen within the British Conservative Party.

Traditional conservatism This strand of conservative thought derives from the traditional values of the aristocracy. It emphasises patriotism and authority. It opposes changes which might upset the established order – for example, women's liberation, closer ties with Europe, and easier divorce laws. Traditional conservatives are strong supporters of law and order and of longstanding institutions such as the monarchy and the House of Lords.

One-nation conservatism Sometimes known as paternalistic conservatism, this version of conservative thought developed during the mid-19th century. Spelt out in the writings of Benjamin Disraeli (1804-1881), it states that the wealthy and powerful have a duty to look after the less well-off. On the one hand, this is a moral obligation, on the other hand, it will prevent a revolution from below. Social reform is therefore right, and a means for creating a stable, cohesive and united 'one-nation'.

This 'middle way' formed the ideology of Conservative governments in the 1950s and 60s. Prime Minister Harold Macmillan described it as 'private enterprise without selfishness'. One-nation conservatism sees private enterprise and competition as a good thing, but argues that state intervention in the market is important for social reasons – for example, to reduce unemployment. And it stresses the importance of state welfare to deal with poverty.

key terms

Traditional conservatism Emphasises patriotism and authority, and opposes changes which might upset the established order.
One-nation conservatism States that the wealthy and powerful have a moral duty to look after the less well-off. This will serve to stabilise and unite society.
Liberal conservatism Argues for a free market and limited welfare, plus a strong state to maintain law and order.

Liberal conservatism This branch of conservatism became the ideological framework for the Thatcher governments of the 1980s. As outlined in the previous section, it was largely based on neo-liberalism with its emphasis on the free market and the restriction of welfare. However, unlike neo-liberalism, liberal conservatism argues that a strong state is needed to maintain public order and uphold traditional values (Bentley et al., 2004).

activity15 conservatism

Item A Benjamin Disraeli

The following is an extract from a speech given by Benjamin Disraeli, leader of the Conservative Party, in 1872. He refers to the Conservative Party as the Tory Party.

Gentlemen, the Tory Party, unless it is a national party is nothing. Now I have always been of the opinion that the Tory Party as three great objects. The first is to maintain the institutions of the country. The principles of liberty, of order, of law, and of religion are not to be entrusted to individual opinion or to the capricious whims and passion of multitudes, but should be embodied in a form of permanence and power. We associate with the monarchy the ideas which it represents – the majesty of law, the administration of justice, the fountains of mercy and of honour. Gentlemen, there is another and second great object of the Tory Party to uphold the Empire of England.

Another great object of the Tory Party and one not inferior to the maintenance of the Empire, or the upholding of our institutions, is the elevation of the condition of the people. It must be obvious to all who consider the condition of the multitude with a desire to improve and elevate it that no important step can be gained unless you can effect some reduction of their hours of labour and humanise their toil. I ventured to say a short time ago, speaking in one of the great cities of this country, that the health of the people was the most important question for a statesman. It is, gentlemen, a large subject. It has many branches. It involves the state of the dwellings of the people. It involves their enjoyment of some of

Disraeli

the chief elements of nature – air, light and water. It involves the regulation of industry, the inspection of their toil. Upon you depends the issue. You have nothing to trust to but your own energy and the sublime instinct of an ancient people.

Item B The Conservative Party manifesto, 2001

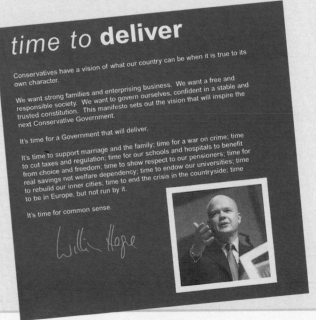

time to deliver

Conservatives have a vision of what our country can be when it is true to its own character.

We want strong families and enterprising business. We want a free and responsible society. We want to govern ourselves, confident in a stable and trusted constitution. This manifesto sets out the vision that will inspire the next Conservative Government.

It's time for a Government that will deliver.

It's time to support marriage and the family; time for a war on crime; time to cut taxes and regulation; time for our schools and hospitals to benefit from choice and freedom; time to show respect to our pensioners; time for real savings not welfare dependency; time to endow our universities; time to rebuild our inner cities; time to end the crisis in the countryside; time to be in Europe, but not run by it.

It's time for common sense.

questions

1 a) Identify the conservative ideas in Disraeli's speech (Item A).

   b) Which type of conservatism does Disraeli represent? Give reasons for your answer.

2 Identify the conservative ideas in Item B.

4.4 Socialism

Key ideas of socialism

Socialism emerged in the early years of the 19th century in response to the development of capitalist industrial society. Some of the key ideas of socialism are outlined below.

Collectivism The ideal society is based on collectivism, where everybody works for the common good rather than individual self-interest. To this end, private property should be abolished and economic resources used for the benefit of the whole community.

Equality This is a guiding principle of socialism. The extremes of wealth and income between the rich and poor are seen as evil. Equality brings out the best in human nature. And it brings cooperation, stability and cohesion in human society.

Capitalism Capitalism exploits and dehumanises wage earners. It generates widespread social inequalities, and a range of social problems including poverty, unemployment and crime.

Social class Socialists see social class as the main division in society – for example, the capitalist ruling class who own and control private industry and the subject or working class who sell their labour in return for wages. Socialists tend to support the working class who they see as exploited and oppressed.

Human nature Socialists, as their name suggests, see humans as social beings. They see people as shaped by their social situation rather than being essentially good or bad, generous or selfish. They look forward to a society based on cooperation rather than competition, on collectivism rather than individualism. This will bring out the best in people (Heywood, 2002).

Varieties of socialism

Revolutionary socialism or communism is best known from the 19th century writings of Karl Marx and his collaborator, Friedrich Engels. They saw a basic conflict of interest between the ruling and subject classes in capitalist society. They believed that class conflict would lead to the revolutionary overthrow of capitalism and its replacement by communist society. In this communist utopia (ideal society) the means of production (land, raw materials, factories) would be communally owned. As a result, there would be no social classes, no oppression or exploitation, and none of the social problems which capitalism generated. People would work together in harmony for the common good. (For further details of Marxist views, see pages 75-78 and 89.)

Democratic socialism Rather than looking forward to a workers' revolution, democratic socialists see the existing political system as a way to gain power and transform society. Their aims are the same as revolutionary socialists, but the means they choose to achieve them – the ballot box – are different.

Social democracy Social democrats do not expect to change the basic structure of capitalist society. Instead, they aim to achieve greater social equality and social justice – for example, by introducing measures to redistribute wealth and income from the rich to the poor. As this suggests, a major concern is for the weak and vulnerable. This can be seen in the establishment of the modern welfare state by the Labour government of 1945-1950. In addition, this government nationalised – brought into public ownership – the railways and the coal and steel industries. Their reasons were not only ideological. These were ailing industries which were vital to the economy – and bankruptcy would mean widespread unemployment.

Socialism and the Labour Party The British Labour Party was formed in 1900 to represent the working class in Parliament. Until recently, there have always been two wings in the party – democratic socialists and social democrats. In practice, however, Labour has acted as a social democratic party seeking to reform rather than completely transform capitalist society.

New Labour and the Third Way From 1979 to 1997, the Labour Party failed to win a general election. Many party members felt that Labour's socialist beliefs were no longer attractive to the electorate.

In 1994, under Tony Blair's leadership, the Labour Party – increasingly referred to as New Labour – abandoned many of its traditional socialist ideas, including Clause 4 of its constitution which committed the party to the 'common ownership of the means of production' (see Activity 16, Items C and D).

Socialist ideology was partly replaced by the Third Way which is seen as an alternative to both neo-liberalism and traditional socialism. The Third Way focuses on equality of opportunity rather than equality. It places a high value on local communities with its policies of devolution and elected mayors. There is an emphasis on citizens' responsibilities and duties to their communities. Welfare reform offers the unemployed opportunities to work and encourages them to be responsible for their own actions rather than being dependent on benefits. People are encouraged to be 'stakeholders' – to have a stake in society by participating more in local and national affairs. The Third Way has no commitment to public as opposed to private ownership. Its main concern is to support what works best in specific cases.

4.5 Other political ideologies

So far, this unit has looked at ideologies which have formed the basis for the main political parties in Western democracies. These ideologies are often seen on a continuum from left to right. Thus socialism is referred to as left-wing, conservatism as right-wing, with liberalism in the centre.

activity16 socialism

Item A

Item B

A Soviet poster of 1919 showing a bloated capitalist

Item C　*Clause 4*

The old Clause 4
The Labour Party's object is to secure for the workers by hand or by brain the full fruits of their industry and the most equitable distribution thereof that may be possible upon the basis of common ownership of the means of production, distribution and exchange, and the best obtainable system of popular administration and control of each industry or service.
From the Labour Party constitution, 1993

The new Clause 4
The Labour Party believes that by the strength of our common endeavour we achieve more than we achieve alone, so as to create for each of us the means to realise our true potential and for all of us a community in which power, wealth and opportunity are in the hands of the many not the few, where the rights we enjoy reflect the duties we owe, and where we live together, freely, in a spirit of solidarity, tolerance and respect.
From the Labour Party constitution, 1998

Item D Tony Blair and the Third Way

The new progressive politics has two driving concepts behind it. First, it defines a new role for collective action – national and local government, voluntary and community organisations, trade unions – which advances the interests of the individual. The purpose of such action is to empower individuals to fulfil their potential and meet their responsibilities. It is not about dictating to the individual; it is not about the supremacy of the collective good over individual aspirations. It is there to help people make the most of themselves, recognising that in unequal societies, in the absence of such collective help only the privileged few will get the chance to succeed.

But it does not stand for rigid forms of state ownership or provision. It is pragmatic (practical) as to whether public or private means are the best delivery mechanism. This is why reform of public services and of the role of government are high on the policy agenda of every progressive government.

Secondly, the Third Way represents a historic realignment of economic and social policy, at a time when the old boundaries between economy, state and society are breaking down. For years, the economic framework of the British left was dominated by questions of public ownership. Markets were poorly understood, their obvious limits leading the left to neglect their great potential for enhancing choice, quality and innovation. Effective markets are a pre-condition for a successful modern economy. The question is not whether to have them, but how to empower individuals to succeed within them. What used to be socially important is now an economic imperative. Individuals need opportunities as well as safeguards within the market – above all opportunities to gain new knowledge and skill to develop their potential. Without the assertion of equal worth, without the extension to all of basic entitlements at work, and without investment in their talents, both economy and society are impoverished. Social exclusion, poor education, high unemployment, racism and sexism, are not just socially wrong but economically inefficient.

questions

1 What basic principle of socialism is illustrated in Item A?

2 Russia became a communist society – the Soviet Union – after a revolution in 1917. Why is the capitalist portrayed in this way in the Soviet cartoon in Item B?

3 Compare the views of socialism in Item C. Which comes closest to democratic socialism and which to social democracy? Give reasons for your answers.

4 Which aspects of traditional socialist ideology does Tony Blair accept and reject in Item D?

Other ideologies do not fit easily into this left-right continuum. Two such ideologies – feminism and environmentalism – will now be briefly examined.

Feminism

Feminism starts from the idea that we live in male-dominated societies, that this is wrong and should be changed.

First-wave feminism Feminist ideas developed from the mid-1800s with the emergence of the women's suffrage movement which campaigned for political equality with men. In 1918, 'women of property' over 30 gained the right to vote in parliamentary elections. In 1928, the vote was extended to women over 21 – the first time they had the same voting rights as men.

Second-wave feminism The so-called second-wave of feminism emerged in the 1960s with the rise of the Women's Liberation Movement. Feminist demands for equal rights had an important influence on government legislation. The Equal Pay Act (1970) stated that women and men doing the same job should have equal pay. And the Sex Discrimination Act (1975) stated that women should have the same rights as men in employment, education, accommodation, transport, entertainment and the provision of goods and services.

Liberal feminism Various types of feminism have been identified. Liberal feminists see equal rights guaranteed by law as the main route to gender equality. As outlined above, this view has had an important influence on government legislation. And today, all political parties in Western democracies accept the main principles of liberal feminism.

Socialist feminism Liberal feminists argue that equal rights under the existing system will eventually end the subordination of women. Socialist feminists see this as wishful thinking. They argue that capitalism is *the* major cause of women's subordination. For example, they claim that women in their domestic roles as mothers and housewives service the capitalist system by reproducing labour power – rearing and socialising future generations of workers – and supporting male workers with domestic labour. And all this at no cost to the capitalist. Socialist feminists argue that the exploitation of women will only end in a socialist society.

Radical feminism Radical feminists see gender inequality as the basic feature of all human societies. They claim that patriarchy – male dominance – permeates every aspect of society – values, beliefs, relationships, family life, religion, education, work, leisure and politics. Radical feminists call for fundamental change in all these areas – the private as well as the public world. In their view, 'the personal is the political'.

Environmentalism

Environmentalism, also known as the ecological or green movement, developed in the 1960s. It was a result of a growing concern about the impact of industrialisation, modern technology and population growth on the environment. It rejected the idea that progress meant economic growth, and that materialism was a value worth pursuing.

The ecosystem Where other political ideologies are about relationships between people, environmentalism is about relationships between people and the environment. Environmentalists argue that the very existence of the *ecosystem* – living organisms and their physical environment – is threatened by the demands made upon it by human beings. They claim that current social and economic policies are destroying the environment – by pollution, by the destruction of natural habitats and by the depletion of natural resources which cannot be renewed.

Environmentalists call for policies of *sustainability* – resources should only be used if they can be sustained, that is renewed or recycled.

Political influence Since the 1960s, the environmental movement has influenced both public opinion and the major political parties. And, in some cases, its candidates have been elected to national legislatures. For example, the Green Party holds a small number of seats in the German Bundestag. In the UK, the Green Party has yet to gain a seat in Parliament, due partly to the first-past-the-post (as opposed to proportional representation) electoral system which favours the main parties. As a result, environmentalists have tended to focus on pressure group politics. Groups such as Friends of the Earth and Greenpeace have had some success – every major political party now claims a concern about the environment.

Conclusion

The ideologies of liberalism, conservatism and socialism have been major influences on political parties in Western democracies. However, their influence may be declining for a number of reasons.

- First, as the following unit shows, class is declining as an influence on party politics. Traditionally, the Labour Party was seen as representing the working class and the Conservative Party as representing the middle and upper classes. This class-based view of politics is declining, especially since the emergence of 'New' Labour.
- Second, ideologies such as feminism and environmentalism are increasingly coming to the fore. These ideologies are not class-based. And they have influenced all political parties.
- Third, the traditional left-wing/right-wing view of party politics is no longer as clear-cut as it once was. The newer ideologies do not fit easily into this continuum. And, judging from the ideas broadcast by a growing variety of pressure groups, neither will the ideologies of the future.
- As a result, governments will have to listen to and act on the demands of a growing range of pressure groups and social movements, many of which operate outside mainstream politics.

key terms

Ecosystem The system made up of living organisms and their physical environment.
Sustainability Sustaining resources by renewing or recycling them.

summary

1. Negative views of ideology see it as:
   - A distortion of reality
   - A justification for inequality
   - A closed system of thought.

2. Neutral views see ideology as a set of ideas which guides political action.

3. Liberalism emphasises individual freedom, equality of opportunity and government by consent.

4. Classical liberalism states that state intervention should be kept to a minimum. Wherever possible, the individual should rely on self-help.

5. Progressive liberalism argues that state intervention – particularly state welfare provision – is necessary to ensure equal opportunity and individual liberty.

6. Neo-liberalism rejects state intervention, seeing it as harmful to the economy and to individual initiative and freedom.

7. Liberalism has influenced all the major political parties. In particular, progressive liberalism influenced the Liberal governments of 1905-1915 and both Labour and Conservative governments from 1945 to the mid-1970s. Neo-liberalism had an important influence on Margaret Thatcher's Conservative governments from 1979 to 1990.

8. The key ideas of conservatism include:
   - An emphasis on tradition
   - Gradual change based on the best of the past
   - A strong state to maintain law and order and ensure social stability
   - The importance of the family and the nation.

9. Traditional conservatism emphasises patriotism and authority and support for longstanding institutions such as the monarchy.

10. One-nation conservatism states that the wealthy and

powerful have a duty to look after the less well-off. This is both a moral obligation and a means to unite and stabilise society.

11. Liberal conservatism emphasises the free market, limited welfare provision and a strong state to maintain law and order.

12. One-nation conservatism was the ideology of Conservative governments in the 1950s and 1960s. Liberal conservatism provided the ideological framework for the Thatcher governments of the 1980s.

13. The key ideas of socialism include:

   ● Collectivism – working collectively for the common good

   ● Equality – which brings out the best in human nature

   ● A rejection of capitalism and the classes it generates

   ● The view that human beings are shaped by their social situation rather than being essentially good or bad.

14. There are various types of socialism. They include:

   ● Revolutionary socialism, which looks forward to a workers' revolution overthrowing capitalism.

   ● Democratic socialism, which argues that the existing political system can be used to end capitalism and establish socialism.

   ● Social democracy, which argues that it is possible to achieve greater social equality and social justice within the framework of capitalism.

15. Socialism has been the major ideology of the Labour Party. In practice, Labour has acted as a social democratic party, seeking to reform rather than end the capitalist system.

16. Since 1997, New Labour, under Tony Blair, has seen the Third Way as an alternative both to neo-liberalism and traditional socialism.

17. Ideologies such as feminism and environmentalism have had an important influence on all the major political parties.

18. Such ideologies do not fit easily into the traditional left-wing/right-wing continuum.

19. The growing numbers of pressure groups, each with their own ideology, suggest that governments will be increasingly influenced by a variety of new ideologies.

Unit 5 *Political participation*

keyissues

1 What are the main forms of political participation?

2 How and why have they changed?

3 To what extent do social factors affect voting behaviour?

4 How and why have voting patterns changed in recent elections?

5.1 Political participation in representative democracies

People can participate in politics in a variety of ways – from voting in local and national elections to becoming an active member of a political party or pressure group. For most people, however, political participation is limited to voting in national elections. This section looks at political participation in democratic societies.

Modern democracies are known as *representative* or *indirect democracies*. This means that citizens do not participate directly in the machinery of government, they do not have a direct say in political decision making. Instead, their views, concerns and interests are represented by those they elect. Whether democracies actually work like this is a matter for debate. As previous sections have shown, the view that elected politicians actually represent the people is sometimes dismissed as an illusion.

How much participation? For democracy to work effectively, how much participation is required? For some, the answer is the more participation the more democracy. This means that citizens need to do more than put a cross on a ballot paper in general elections. For example, they should join a pressure group, go on a demonstration, sign a petition, write to their MP. From this viewpoint, the more they participate, the more likely their voices are to be heard and their interests represented. A healthy democracy therefore requires active participation in the political process by large numbers of citizens.

Other researchers disagree. They argue that the average citizen knows little about politics and should let their elected representatives get on with the job. Other than voting, they should leave governing to the experts (Parry & Moyser, 1993).

Forms of political participation

Voting Voting in national elections is usually seen as the most important form of political participation in democracies. In recent years, the percentage of the adult population who voted in general elections in the UK has declined. In the 2001 general election, only 59.3% of those eligible to vote actually voted – the lowest turnout since 1945 (see Activity 17, Item A). Figures for local elections are much lower. For example, estimates for the May 2003 local elections indicate around one-third of the electorate voted.

Party membership and activity Membership of political parties has been steadily declining. For example, in 2003, the Labour Party had around 250,000 members, compared to 400,000 in 1997. Most members are not particularly active, doing little more than placing an election poster in their window or delivering party leaflets (Broughton, 2000).

Pressure groups and other organisations Large numbers of people are members of organisations which, in varying degrees, participate in the political process. These include pressure groups which are directly concerned with influencing government policy. In some cases, for example Friends of the Earth, membership has grown in recent years, in other cases it has declined. Some organisations, such as trade unions, which perform a range of services for their members, see influencing government policy as only one of their aims. In some cases, membership of such organisations is growing, in other cases declining. For example, trade union membership in the UK has steadily declined over the past 25 years.

Demonstrations There is evidence that participation in demonstrations has increased in recent years (see Activity 17, Items C and D). One survey found that 10% of respondents said they took part in a demonstration in 2000 compared to 6% in 1986 *(British Social Attitudes Survey, 2001-02)*. Recent demonstrations include the Countryside Alliance's 400,000 strong march in London in 2002 and over one million people protesting in London against the war in Iraq in 2003.

Demonstrations appear to be an addition rather than an alternative to other forms of political participation. For example, people who attend demonstrations are more likely to vote than those who do not attend *(British Social Attitudes Survey, 2001-02)*.

Other forms of political participation Few people take part in forms of participation which take up considerable amounts of time and effort. For example, the most common type of political action in 2000 was signing a petition. Details of other forms of political participation are given in Activity 17, Item B.

Who participates?

Political participation is not spread evenly across the population – some sections of the population are more politically active than others.

Age There is some evidence which indicates that young people are increasingly withdrawing from political participation. In the 2001 general election, turnout in the 18-24 year old age group fell to 35%, an all time low. And membership of the youth wings of the main political parties has declined in recent years. However, young people are more likely to take part in more unconventional forms of political participation – for example, demonstrations. It may be that young people simply participate differently than their elders (Evans, 1997).

Social class Most political activists come from the upper levels of the class system. They are more likely to have the resources – money, education and 'know-how' – to enter

the political arena (Parry & Moyser, 1993).

Gender There appears to be no significant gender difference in political activism. However, fewer women than men become MPs and local councillors.

Political outlook Political activists tend to hold more 'extreme' views – they are more likely to be left-wing or right-wing than in the middle of the political spectrum (Parry et al, 1991).

Changes in political participation

Between 1945 and the 1970s, there was a growth in membership of traditional political organisations such as political parties and trade unions. Since then, membership has declined. In recent years, voting in national elections has also declined. However, according to the *British Social Attitudes Survey, 2001-02*, there is little indication that other forms of political participation are declining, and some evidence that suggests a growth (see Activity 17, Item B).

Mark Evans (1997) sees a 'dramatic upsurge in single-issue protest activity'. This includes fairly shortlived one-off protests – for example, against the closure of a local hospital or the siting of a new airport runway. It also includes single-issue pressure groups concerned with a particular issue such as animal rights or global capitalism. Evans suggests five reasons for changes in political participation. They are:

1 Globalisation There is a growing perception that power has shifted from national legislatures, such as the UK Parliament, to wider political groupings such as the European Union. Many issues are now seen as global rather than national. As a result, pressure groups such as Greenpeace now operate on a global level. And social movements, such as the anti-capitalist movement, are international in terms of their membership, vision and activity.

2 Post-industralisation This refers to the view that Western societies have moved from a reliance on traditional industries such as iron, steel, coal and manufacturing to a growth in the service sector. This has led to a move away from traditional forms of representation such as political parties and trade unions. In post-industrial society, people are looking for more participatory forms of representation – hence the growth of single-issue pressure groups.

3 The 'strong' state Some researchers argue that the state in Britain is becoming increasingly centralised and insensitive to public opinion. A 'strong state' means fewer opportunities for people to be heard. As a result, there has been a rise in unconventional forms of political protest.

4 Changes in the class structure Older forms of political protest reflected the traditional class structure of industrial society. Political protest was associated with trade unions and political parties representing the working class. With a shrinking working class and a growing middle class, new concerns and forms of protest are emerging. Many of the more recent single-issue pressure groups – for example, environmental groups such as Earth First! and Friends of the Earth – are led and supported by university-educated people from middle-class backgrounds.

5 Party loyalty There is evidence that people's loyalty to and identification with a particular political party has declined in recent years. As a result, they are more open to the appeal of a range of single-issue pressure groups.

activity17 political participation

Item A *Turnout in UK general elections, 1945-2001*

Year	% turnout
1945	72.8
1950	83.9
1951	82.6
1955	76.8
1959	78.7
1964	77.1
1965	75.8
1970	72.0
1974 (Feb)	78.8
1974 (Oct)	72.8
1979	76.0
1983	72.7
1987	75.3
1992	77.7
1997	71.4
2001	59.3

Adapted from Craig 1989, Butler & Kavanagh 1997, 2002

Item B *Political action, 1986-2000*

% saying they had	1986	1989	1991	1994	2000
Signed a petition	34	41	53	39	42
Contacted their MP	11	15	17	14	16
Contacted radio, TV or newspaper	3	4	4	5	6
Gone on a protest or demonstration	6	8	9	9	10
Spoken to an influential person	1	3	5	3	4
Contacted a government department	3	3	4	3	4
Formed a group of like-minded people	2	3	2	3	2
Raised the issue in an organisation they already belong to	5	4	5	4	5
None of these	56	48	37	53	47

Adapted from *18th British Social Attitudes Survey, 2001-02*

Item C *The anti-capitalist movement*

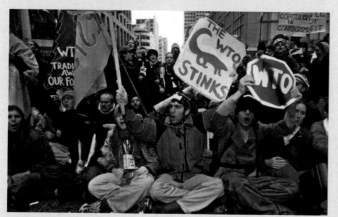

Anti-capitalist demonstration against the World Trade Organisation (WTO), Seattle, 1999

The late 1990s saw the emergence of a global anti-capitalist movement. Those opposed to capitalism believe that the pursuit of profit involves the exploitation both of people and of the world's natural resources. They are particularly worried about the growing power of transnational corporations.

The anti-capitalist movement has no leadership and no established headquarters. It consists of a loose collection of dissatisfied people and groups including environmentalists, socialists, anarchists and those demanding debt relief for Third World countries. A visible focus of the movement has been a series of mass demonstrations held in major cities including Seattle (USA), Gothenburg (Sweden), Prague (the Czech Republic), Genoa (Italy) and London. Several of these demonstrations have been organised to coincide with meetings of the leaders of the world's most powerful countries.

Adapted from Bentley et al, 2002

Item D *Anti-war protest*

Demonstration against war in Iraq, London, February 15, 2003

questions

1 Describe the trends shown in Items A and B.
2 Suggest reasons for these trends. Refer to Items C and D in your answer.

5.2 Class and voting behaviour

Why do people vote for particular political parties? Sociologists have argued that there is a tendency for people with similar social characteristics to vote for the same party. In the UK, social class has been seen as the main social influence on voting behaviour. However, evidence from more recent general elections questions this view.

Partisan alignment

From 1945 to 1970, most voters in Britain saw themselves as Labour or Conservative and voted accordingly. This identification with and loyalty to a particular party is known as *partisan alignment.*

Class alignment There is evidence that social class formed the basis for partisan alignment. Traditionally, Labour was seen as the party of the 'working man' and the Conservatives as the party of the middle and upper classes. And this view was often translated into voting patterns. For example, in the 1964 general election, 64% of manual workers (working class), voted Labour and 62% of non-manual (middle and upper class), voted Conservative (Denver, 1994). This link between class, party identification and voting behaviour is known as *class alignment.*

Political socialisation What accounts for partisan alignment and class alignment? According to Butler and Stokes (1974), the answer is *political socialisation.* Children were socialised to follow their parents' party identification and party loyalty. Similarly, their class identification was learned from their parents.

Dealignment

Dealignment refers to a weakening of party loyalty and identification *(partisan dealignment)* and/or a weakening of class-based voting *(class dealignment).*

Partisan dealignment There were four general elections in the 1970s. Less than half the voters consistently voted for the same party in these elections. According to Bo Sarlvick and Ivor Crewe (1983), this is evidence of partisan dealignment – of a reduction in loyalty to a particular party. As a result, the electorate has become more *volatile* – more changeable, less consistent.

Class dealignment Sarlvick and Crewe (1983) argue that the main reason for partisan dealignment is a process of class dealignment – a decline in class-based voting. For example, in the 1979 general election, only 50% of manual workers voted Labour compared with 64% in 1964 (Denver, 1994).

Reasons for dealignment Sarlvick and Crewe (1983) suggest two reasons for dealignment. First, changes in the class structure, which have weakened class identification and class loyalty. There has been a decline in sectors of employment where Labour support has traditionally been strongest – heavy industries like coal, steel and shipbuilding which were highly unionised and state owned until the 1980s. Increasing numbers of working-class voters no longer belong to trade unions. And they are more likely

to own their own houses. Factors such as these tend to weaken class identification. This leads to class dealignment and, in turn, to partisan dealignment.

Second, and partly as a result of these changes, Sarlvick and Crewe (1983) argue that people are increasingly guided by party policy rather than party loyalty when casting their vote. This *policy preference model* states that people base their vote on an evaluation of parties' policies on a range of issues – for example, education, health, the economy, foreign policy.

The policy preference model rejects the view that political socialisation is mainly responsible for voting behaviour. Rather than tending to follow in the footsteps of their parents, voters are pictured as assessing the policies of the various parties and voting for those which best match their own preferences.

Class, ideology and voting

Class A study of the 1983 general election by Anthony Heath and his colleagues questioned both the findings and explanations of Sarlvick and Crewe (Heath, Jowell & Curtice, 1985). Heath et al. argue that the two-class division of manual and non-manual workers is too crude and simple to adequately represent the class system. Using a five-class model, they find that the link between class and voting is stronger than the findings of Sarlvick and Crewe indicate. However, in a study of the 1997 election, Heath accepts the view that, from 1964 to 1997, there has been an overall decline of class-based voting. He therefore accepts the general view that class dealignment is occurring (Evans, Heath & Payne, 1999).

Ideology On the basis of their study of the 1983 election, Heath et al (1985) reject the policy preference model. They asked voters which issues they thought most important and for their assessment of parties' policies on those issues. Unemployment and inflation were seen as the most important issues and Labour's policies were judged to be the best. Yet the Conservatives won the election.

Heath et al (1983) argue that voters' perception of parties' ideological position is more important than parties' actual policies when deciding who to vote for. Their research indicates that, despite having the most popular policies, Labour lost the 1983 election because its ideology was seen as too left-wing, as too 'extreme', by many voters. In terms of this argument, *party image* – the general picture of what the party stands for – is more important than specific party policies.

Continuing dealignment – the 1997 and 2001 elections

Partisan dealignment In 1997, Labour swept to victory gaining the largest majority in its history. Is there any evidence here of strong loyalty to the party? Or is the process of partisan dealignment still continuing? A study by Ivor Crewe and Katrina Thompson (1999) looked at the strength of party identification from 1964 to 1997. They argue that 'very strong' identification indicates a strong commitment to the party – in other words partisan alignment. Evidence from the 1964 to the 1997 election shows a steady decline in the percentage of voters who 'very strongly identify' with a political party – from 44% in 1964 to 16% in 1997. On the basis of this evidence, Crewe and Thompson claim that the process of partisan dealignment is continuing.

Evidence from the 2001 election shows a further decline in 'very strong' party identification, suggesting a continuation of partisan dealignment (Evans, 2003). In addition, the 2001 election had the lowest turnout – 59% of the electorate – since the 1918 election. This can be seen as further evidence of partisan dealignment – loyal party supporters are most likely to vote.

Class dealignment Is continuing partisan dealignment linked to continuing class dealignment? In other words, is the decline in party loyalty linked to a decline in class-based voting? Yes, according to a study by Evans, Heath and Payne (1999). Looking at the trend from 1964 to 1997, they find an overall decline in class-based voting – in other words, continuing class dealignment. And this trend continued in the 2001 election – for example, Conservative support from the middle class (their traditional supporters) declined from the 1997 election (Norris, 2001).

Reasons for continuing dealignment By 1997, Tony Blair and New Labour had moved from the left of the political spectrum to the centre. According to David Sanders (1997), Labour's resounding election victory in 1997 was a result of convincing 'middle Britain' that it had shed most of 'the baggage of old Labour's socialist past'.

By 1997, the ideological gap between Labour and Conservative had narrowed considerably. There were few major differences between their policies. And voters recognised this. In 1987, 84% of voters thought there was a 'good deal of difference' between Labour and Conservative. In 1997, this figure dropped to 33% (Budge, 1999).

Labour had successfully transformed itself into a 'catch-all' party, a party which appealed to all social classes. As a result, Labour's share of the middle-class vote in 2001 was only slightly below the Conservative share.

This move to the political centre by the Labour Party is seen by a number of researchers as the main reason for the recent continuation of partisan and class dealignment. Similar parties with similar ideologies do not encourage strong loyalties. And, 'catch-all' parties which do not directly appeal to particular classes do not encourage class-based voting (Evans et al., 1999; Norris, 2001).

Conclusion

There is general agreement that processes of partisan dealignment and class dealignment have been occurring since the 1970s. And there is a close link between the two – strong loyalties to a political party are often based on class, with voters seeing that party as representing their class.

A process of dealignment does not mean that partisan loyalty and class-based voting have ended, only that they are declining. For example, in the 1997 and 2001 elections, Labour had a significantly larger share of the working-class vote than the Conservatives.

Will dealignment continue? Not necessarily, according to some researchers. Evans et al. (1999) argue that if the ideological gap between the two main parties widens, and they appeal directly to their traditional supporters, then this may strengthen party loyalty and increase class-based voting. As a result, the processes of partisan and class dealignment may be halted or reversed.

key terms

Partisan alignment Identification with and loyalty to a particular political party.
Class alignment A link between class, party identification and voting behaviour – class-based voting.
Partisan dealignment A weakening of partisan alignment. A reduction in the proportion of the electorate with strong loyalties to a political party.
Class dealignment A reduction in class-based voting.
Political socialisation The process whereby individuals learn political values and party loyalties from their parents.
Volatility of electorate Voters are inconsistent and changeable in their voting behaviour.
Policy preference model States that people base their vote on an assessment of the parties' policies – they vote for the party whose policies they prefer.
Party image A general picture of what a political party stands for.

5.3 Other social influences on voting

Sociologists have focused on the relationship between class and voting behaviour. However, they have also examined a number of other social factors which might be linked to voting.

Gender

From 1945 to 1992 women were more likely to vote Conservative than men. Over this period, the gender gap declined and, by 1997, it had virtually disappeared. In the 2001 election, there were hardly any gender differences in support for the two main parties. What accounts for these changes?

The changing position of women in society As full-time wives and mothers, women tended to be more traditional in their outlook. As a result, they were more likely to be attracted to traditional views of the home and family – which used to be a cornerstone of Conservative policy.

Woman have increasingly moved into paid employment. Their experience in the workplace and participation in the trade union movement has, so the argument goes, exposed them to pro-Labour ideas and values.

New Labour Labour's move to the political centre has made the party more attractive to women. New Labour's focus on health, education and childcare in 1997 and 2001 reflected the concerns of many women.

Gender and age Older people are more likely to vote Conservative than younger people. And the life expectancy of women is higher than that of men. As a result, there are more older women than men and this partly accounts for the gender differences in voting. However, the age-effect appears to be declining. In 1983, 53% of voters over 65 voted Conservative. By 2001, this figure reduced to 42% (Bentley et al., 2002).

Ethnicity

In the 2001 election, as in previous elections, around four out of every five ethnic minority voters supported the Labour Party. There is some variation between different ethnic groups – for example, in the 1997 election, 86% of African-Caribbean voters supported Labour compared to 70% of Asian voters (Saggar, 1997). Two main reasons have been suggested for this high level of ethnic support for Labour.

Class Surveys indicate that the most common reason given for Labour support is that Labour represents the working class. However, class-based voting is only part of the picture. The Labour vote from African-Caribbeans and Asians is much higher than the White working-class Labour vote.

Party policy and party image The Labour Party is usually seen as more sympathetic towards issues such as 'race' and immigration. This image is reflected in the party membership of ethnic MPs. The 12 ethnic minority MPs in 2001 were all from the Labour Party.

Age

There is a tendency for younger people to vote Labour and older people to vote Conservative. For example, in the October 1974 election, 42% of 18-24 year old voters supported Labour and 24% Conservative. There are exceptions – in the 1983 and 1987 elections, the Conservatives obtained a majority of the young vote. However, by 1997, the traditional pattern was re-established and, in 2001, 47% of the 18-24 year old voters supported Labour compared to 29% who supported the Conservatives. Support for the Liberal Democrats was spread fairly evenly across all age groups.

In the 2001 election, only the 65+ age group gave the Conservatives a majority of their votes. However, the gap between Conservative and Labour support in this age group has narrowed over the years. For example, in 1983, 53% of 65+ voters supported the Conservatives and 28% Labour. In 2001, these figures were 42% and 37%.

Young people are the least likely to vote. In 2001, only 39% of the 18-24 age group voted.

*activity*18 *dealignment*

Item A *Party identification*

Adapted from Evans, 2003

Item B *Class and voting*

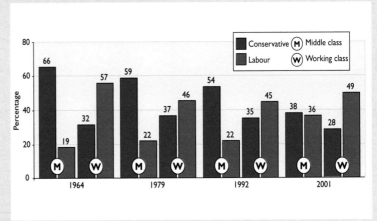

Adapted from Bentley et al., 2002

questions

1. What support does Item A provide for partisan dealignment?

2. What support does Item B provide for class dealignment?

3. Provide brief explanations for the trends shown in Items A and B.

Explaining age and voting behaviour Some researchers argue that older people are more conservative with a small 'c' – more committed to traditional norms and values. As a result, they are more likely to see the Conservative Party as representing their views. However, the diminishing gap between Conservative and Labour voters in the 65+ age group throws some doubt on this argument.

At the other end of the age spectrum, so the argument goes, young people are more radical, more open to change and to new ideas. They tend to see Labour as closer to their views.

Why are young people less likely to vote? Some researchers see them as alienated – cut off – from the political process because of cynical MPs, spin doctors and politicians' focus on the negative aspects of youth. Alternatively, they are more interested in particular issues – for example, environmentalism and animal rights. As a result, they tend to look to pressure groups rather than political parties to represent their concerns (Evans, 2003).

Regional differences

There have always been regional differences in party support in Britain. During the 1980s, these differences became sharper and researchers began to use the term 'North-South divide' to describe them. Election results in the 1980s showed that support for the Conservatives declined in Scotland, Northern England and Wales, whilst support for Labour declined in the South of England. Various reasons have been given for these developments.

Class and region Although class dealignment has occurred, there is still a link between class and voting behaviour. And there is also a link between class and region – for example, the South of England has the highest proportion of middle-class home owners. However, class only accounts for part of the regional differences in party support.

Cultural differences It appears that, to some extent, different regions have their own political cultures. For example, from 1979-1992, Labour gained more votes from the middle class in its industrial heartlands of Scotland, Northern England and Wales than from the middle class in other areas. Similarly, the Conservatives gained more votes from the working class in the South of England – where Conservative support was traditionally strong – than from the working class in other parts of Britain (Johnston & Pattie, 1992).

Economic factors Variations in the economic situation of different regions appear to influence voting behaviour. For example, the Conservative vote in the 1980s dropped in areas experiencing an economic decline (Johnston & Pattie, 1992).

Nationalist parties Regional differences in party support are most clearly seen in Scotland and Wales with the rise of nationalist parties from the 1970s – the Scottish National Party (SNP) and Plaid Cymru. However, support for nationalist parties appears to have peaked. For example, the SNP reached its highest point in October 1974 with 30% of the Scottish vote. In 2001, its vote was down to 20% (Bogdanor, 2003).

The 1997 and 2001 elections Labour won landslide victories in the 1997 and 2001 elections. This was partly due to significantly increased support from middle-class voters in the South of England. According to one estimate, around a quarter of regional differences in voting behaviour disappeared between 1987 and 1997. Reasons suggested for this include further partisan and class dealignment and New Labour's ideological shift to the centre of the political spectrum (Curtice & Park, 1999).

Conclusion

Overall, the effect of social factors on voting behaviour appears to be declining. Although class-based voting remains, the process of class dealignment is well underway. Gender differences have all but disappeared. Ethnicity is still important, with significant differences between African-Caribbean and Asian voting patterns and those of the White majority. Age remains important in the 18-24 age group. However, it is becoming less important in the 65+ age group. And although regional differences continue, they are becoming less marked.

As the effect of social factors declines, the influence of party images, ideologies and policies on voting behaviour tends to increase.

summary

1. Some researchers argue that an effective democracy requires varied and active participation in the political process by a large number of citizens. Others argue that citizens need to vote and little else.

2. There are various forms of political participation in democracies. They include:
   - Voting in local and national elections
   - Membership of a political party
   - Support for pressure groups
   - Taking part in demonstrations.

3. Some sections of the population are more politically active than others. For example, age and class appear to influence the extent and type of political participation.

4. Since the 1970s there has been a decline in membership of trade unions and political parties and of voting in national elections. During the same period, there has been a rise in single-issue pressure groups and protest activity.

5. Mark Evans gives the following reasons for changes in political participation.
   - Globalisation
   - Post-industrialism
   - An increasingly 'strong' state

- Changes in the class structure

- A decline in party loyalty.

6. From 1945 to 1970 party identification and party loyalty were strong. This is known as partisan alignment.

7. Social class formed the basis for partisan alignment – members of different classes identified with different political parties and voted accordingly. The link between class, party identification and voting behaviour is known as class alignment.

8. Since the 1970s there has been a process of partisan dealignment and class dealignment. A number of reasons have been suggested for this.

   - Changes in the class structure which have weakened traditional class loyalties to political parties.

   - A growing focus on policy preference voting based on an evaluation of party policies.

   - Increasing concern with party ideology and party image.

9. Labour's landslide victories in 1997 and 2001 were largely due to its move to the centre of the political spectrum and its rejection of left-wing socialism. There was further evidence of partisan and class dealignment with an increasing proportion of middle-class voters supporting Labour.

10. Gender differences in voting behaviour have all but disappeared. Reasons suggested for this include:

   - The changing position of women in society

   - Labour's move to the political centre

   - A decline in the age-effect on the 65+ age group voters, the majority of whom are women.

11. Ethnicity has an important effect on voting behaviour with around 4 out of 5 Black and Asian voters supporting Labour. Reasons suggested for this include:

- Class

- Party policy and image.

12. There is a tendency for older people to vote Conservative and younger people to vote Labour. However, the gap between Conservative and Labour support in the 65+ age group has narrowed in recent years.

13. Reasons suggested for age-group differences in voting behaviour include:

   - Older people are more committed to traditional norms and values.

   - Younger people are more radical – more open to change and new ideas.

14. Younger people are less likely to vote. Reasons suggested for this include:

   - Alienation from the political process

   - A concern with specific issues, therefore more likely to look to pressure groups rather than political parties.

15. Regional differences in party support increased during the 1980s. Reasons suggested for this include:

   - Class differences between regions, which, despite dealignment, still affected voting

   - Differences in political culture between regions

   - Economic differences

   - Nationalist parties.

16. Regional differences declined in the 1997 and 2001 elections. Reasons suggested for this include:

   - Further partisan and class dealignment

   - New Labour's ideological move to the political centre.

17. Overall, the effect of social factors on voting behaviour appears to be declining.

*activity*19 *social factors and voting behaviour*

Item A *Age*

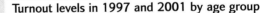

How people aged 65+ voted, 1983-2001 (%)

	1983	1987	1992	1997	2001
Conservative	53	50	49	44	42
Labour	28	27	36	34	37
Lib/Lib Dems	19	23	14	16	18

Adapted from Dorey, 2002

Turnout levels in 1997 and 2001 by age group

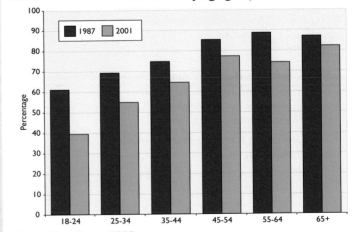

Adapted from Evans, 2003

Item B *Gender*

Year		Con %	Lab %	Lib Dem %
1964	Men	40	48	11
	Women	46	42	12
1966	Men	38	53	8
	Women	45	46	9
1970	Men	44	49	8
	Women	51	41	8
1974 (Feb)	Men	40	41	19
	Women	40	38	22
1974 (Oct)	Men	34	46	19
	Women	40	39	21
1979	Men	47	39	13
	Women	46	39	14
1983	Men	46	30	24
	Women	43	28	28
1987	Men	44	33	22
	Women	44	31	25
1992	Men	41	40	19
	Women	45	36	19
1997	Men	31	44	17
	Women	32	44	17
2001	Men	32	42	18
	Women	33	42	19

Adapted from Denver & Hands 1990, Crewe 1992 and Butler & Kavanagh 1997, 2002

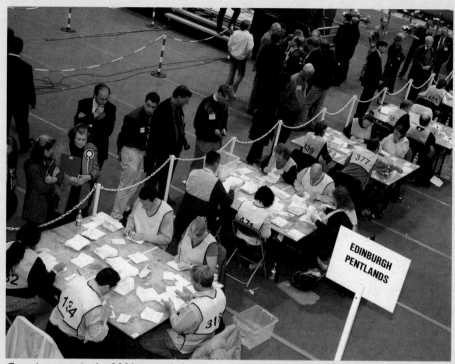

Counting votes in the 2001 general election

Item C *Ethnicity*

	1974 (Oct)	1979	1983	1987	1992	1997
Labour	81	86	83	72	81	78
Conservative	9	8	7	18	10	17

This table shows the percentage of Black and Asian voters who voted for the two main parties between 1974 and 1997.

Adapted from Saggar, 1997

questions

1 Describe the trends in the voting behaviour of the 65+ age group shown in Item A.

2 Suggest explanations for the difference between turnout of the younger and older age groups shown in Item A.

3 a) Describe the trends in gender and voting behaviour shown in Item B.

b) Suggest reasons for these trends.

4 Suggest explanations for the pattern of ethnic voting shown in Item C.

Unit 6 Political parties, pressure groups and social movements

key issues

1 What is the role of political parties in democratic societies?

2 What are the main types of pressure groups and what methods do they use?

3 What are new social movements and why have they become increasingly important?

4 What role do the mass media play in politics?

6.1 Political parties

Before the 19th century, political parties consisted of loose groupings of MPs linked by family connections and similar views. Only a small minority of the population – wealthy male property owners – were entitled to vote.

Between 1832 and 1928, the vote was gradually extended to all adult men and women. This led to the development of modern political parties. In the mid-19th century the Conservative and Liberal Parties evolved from the Tory and Whig Parties and, in 1900, the Labour Party was established.

To appeal to a mass electorate, parties had to present a clear set of policies. To stay in government, they had to translate those policies into laws and respond to changes in public opinion. This required an efficient and disciplined organisation whose members could unite behind the parties' policies, fight an election campaign, and govern as a team.

For many researchers, political parties form the cornerstone of democracy – 'democracy without political parties is unthinkable' (Dalton & Wattenburg, 2002). Marxists, however, see mainstream politics as little more than an illusion of democracy. Political parties give the impression of representing the interests of the people, but, in reality, they simply serve the interests of the capitalist ruling class. Some Marxists, however, do see a positive role for revolutionary socialist parties – they can unite the working class and direct its members towards the overthrow of capitalism.

For elite theorists, political parties are simply a means of persuading the masses that they have some political influence. But, in reality, society is governed by and for the ruling elite.

For pluralists, political parties are essential for democratic government. Competing parties offer a real choice to the electorate. They are the link between the mass of citizens and the state. And, to gain power and form a government, they must represent the interests of the people.

Functions of political parties

Pluralists argue that political parties have a number of important functions in modern democracies. They include the following.

Fighting elections In a democracy, two or more political parties compete to form a government. Political parties present a set of policies to the electorate. They choose their candidates and fund election campaigns. And the existence of political parties provides a way of making those who govern accountable. Parties can be held responsible for policy successes and failures – and rewarded or punished for these at the next election.

Policy making Each party offers a set of policies from which voters can choose. These are communicated to the electorate through party conferences, party political broadcasts, election manifestos and campaign leaflets. No party can win an election by appealing to a single, sectional group – for example, the working class. Policies must therefore reflect a range of interests in society.

Forming a government In Britain, the government is formed by the political party with an overall majority in the House of Commons, or occasionally by the largest single party, or very occasionally by a coalition of parties. The leader of the governing party becomes prime minister. He or she selects government ministers and members of the cabinet.

Representing the people This is often seen as the main function of political parties. Although parties have tended to appeal to particular sections of the population, ideally they should represent the nation as a whole once they form a government.

From a pluralist viewpoint, representative government is the only way that democracy can function in a large, complex modern society. Direct participation by the mass of the population in the day-to-day business of government is not possible. The only feasible alternative is some way of representing the views, concerns and interests of the population. And the main means of doing this is political parties.

6.2 Pressure groups

Like political parties, pressure groups put forward policies and seek support for them. Unlike political parties, they do not aim to form a government. Instead, they try to achieve their objectives by putting pressure on those in government.

Where political parties have a programme covering a wide range of issues, pressure groups focus on a narrower range or even a single issue.

Pluralists argue that pressure groups play a vital role in democracies. They articulate and publicise issues which may be ignored or overlooked by the main political parties. And they represent groups in society whose voices might otherwise go unheard.

Protective and promotional groups

Protective groups Pressure groups differ widely in their aims, organisation, membership and methods of operation. A distinction is often made between *protective* and *promotional groups*. Protective groups – sometimes described as *sectional groups* – primarily aim to protect their own members' interests. Many economic organisations come under this heading – for example, trade unions (Unison and the GMB), professional associations (the Law Society and the British Medical Association) and employers' organisations (The British Road Transport Association, the Association of Engineering Employers). Other protective groups are based on a variety of common interests – sharing the same leisure activity (Surfers against Sewage), living in the same area (local residents' associations), or experiencing the same illness or disability (British Diabetic Association).

Membership of protective groups is usually 'closed' – that is limited to a particular section of society, occupational or professional group.

Promotional groups Promotional groups are often referred to as cause groups – they seek to promote a cause which they see as neglected by government. Groups concerned with environmental issues provide examples – Greenpeace, Friends of the Earth, the Royal Society for the Protection of Birds and the Council for the Protection of Rural England (CPRE).

Many promotional groups are concerned to promote their own values and morality. For example, there are groups for and against abortion rights (National Abortion Campaign and LIFE), for and against smoking (FOREST and ASH), and for and against media censorship (National Viewers and Listeners Association and the Campaign against Press and Broadcasting Censorship).

Some promotional groups campaign on behalf of others in society who they see as unfairly treated and in need of help. Examples include Shelter (for the homeless) and the Child Poverty Action Group.

Evaluation The distinction between protective and promotional pressure groups is not always helpful. Some groups fit under both headings. For example, the Child Poverty Action Group not only promotes the cause of children living in poverty, it also seeks to protect them. And the British Medical Association not only seeks to protect the interests of its members, it also supports campaigns to improve the health of the population as a whole – banning smoking, improving diet and reducing alcohol abuse.

The overlap between protective and promotional groups has led some researchers to develop an alternative classification – *insider groups* and *outsider groups*.

Insider and outsider groups

Insider groups This distinction is based on the relationship between pressure groups and the government. Insider groups are regularly consulted by ministers and civil servants. They are invited to contribute their views to the policy-making process. There are a number of reasons why certain pressure groups become insider groups.

- Their expertise is useful for policy making. For example, the British Roads Federation regularly advises the Department of Transport.

- Ministers need the cooperation of certain pressure groups to translate their policies into action. For example, teachers' unions are often consulted about changes in educational policy since their support is needed to put those changes into practice.

- The aims of the pressure group are seen by government as reasonable and realistic. For example, government ministers are unlikely to invite members of the anti-capitalist movement to contribute to a policy discussion.

- The activities of the pressure group are seen as reasonable. Groups who rely on confrontation, direct action or breaking the law to make their point are unlikely to become insider groups.

- Insider groups are usually seen by government to be representative of their membership. For example, 90% of farmers belong to the National Farmers Union. Governments recognise the union as the voice of farming and consult them on this basis (Bentley et al., 2004).

Outsider groups As their name suggests, outsider groups have less access to ministers and government departments. Many have none at all. There are various reasons why some pressure groups remain 'outside'.

- Their aims are seen as unreasonable, unrealistic and extreme. The anti-capitalist movement is an obvious example.

- Their methods are seen in the same light – for example, the direct and sometimes illegal action of the Animal Liberation Front.

- The issues they promote are seen as insignificant or unpopular – there are few votes to be won by consulting them.

- They lack the expertise policy-makers require. Nor is their cooperation needed to implement policies (Bentley et al., 2004).

Some former outsider groups have become insiders and vice versa. For example, Friends of the Earth were an outsider group in the 1970 and 1980s. They became an insider group in the 1990s due partly to the increasing importance given to environmental issues by governments, partly to the increasing professionalism and expertise of the pressure group, and partly because they moved away from direct action (Bentley et al., 2004).

Pressure group methods

Pressure groups use a variety of methods to further their aims. To a large extent, the methods they use depend on the nature of the group and their relationship with government. For example, an insider group with an established relationship with a government department may not need to mount a high profile campaign to gain media attention and raise public awareness. Here are some of the methods used by pressure groups to influence governments.

Contacts with MPs and civil servants Many pressure groups attempt to directly influence government legislation by communicating their views to MPs and civil servants.

activity20 *insider and outsider groups*

Item A The CBI

The Confederation of British Industry (CBI) is the main group representing the interests of employers in the British manufacturing industry. Since 1997, the CBI has established close links with New Labour governments. And New Labour has been keen to emphasise its support for big business.

Labour governments have consulted the CBI on a range of economic issues, seeking their views at every opportunity and utilising their expertise. For example, when New Labour introduced the minimum wage, there was widespread consultation with employers' organisations such as the CBI. As a result, the minimum wage was set at a level that business could accept.

And the CBI has played its part in the relationship, stating that it does not intend to adopt a confrontational strategy towards New Labour's employment policy. Labour ministers have been invited and have accepted invitations to the CBI's annual dinner. Speaking at the 2001 annual dinner, the chancellor, Gordon Brown, made it clear that support for private industry and wealth creation was a central feature of New Labour policy.

Adapted from Bently et al., 2002

Chancellor Gordon Brown speaking at the 2001 CBI conference

Item B The Barbed Wire Britain Network

New Labour is determined to take a strong stance on asylum seekers. Some of its methods are opposed by the Barbed Wire Britain Network to End Refugee and Migrant Detention. The group's main demand is to end the holding of asylum seekers in detention centres and prisons. The group's activities include:

- demonstrations at the main detention centres
- local public protest meetings
- visiting detainees
- the printing of publications
- the launch of a campaigning website
- national events to draw attention to the problem
- support for hunger strikes and roof-top protests by detainees.

Despite the group's campaign, the Home Secretary announced plans to increase the numbers held in detention centres and prisons from 1,500 in 2002 to 4,000 in 2003.

Adapted from Bentley et al., 2002

A Barbed Wire Britain Network leaflet

This is often done through departmental select committees and backbench committees. For example, in 2001-02, 32 pressure groups submitted evidence to the Home Affairs Select Committee's inquiry into government drug policy. Some pressure groups have established links and regular contact with particular government departments – for example, the British Medical Association and the Royal College of Nursing with the Department of Health.

Expertise and cooperation Pressure groups realise that they are more likely to influence MPs and civil servants if they have something to offer them. The main things on offer are expert knowledge and advice, and cooperation. Often, pressure groups have more specialist expertise than MPs and civil servants. And governments often need the cooperation of pressure groups to implement new legislation. For example, the cooperation of trade unions and employers' associations is needed to implement new working practices.

Using the courts Pressure groups can challenge government decisions by taking a case to court. For example, in 2004, Animal Aid and the National Anti-Vivisection Society took legal action in an attempt to overturn the government's decision to allow Cambridge University to build a research laboratory to conduct experiments on monkeys. A court case is expensive, but, even if the pressure group loses, it can raise public awareness about the issue.

Using the media Pressure groups often use the media to publicise their cause and gain public support. Larger and well-financed pressure groups have press offices and public relations departments. For example, Greenpeace's press desk is open 24 hours a day to deal with media organisations around the world. Pressure groups sometimes use publicity stunts and direct action in order to attract media attention. Most groups now have their own website, and publish their own material. Many place advertisements in newspapers and magazines.

Direct action This refers to a range of activities outside the formal political process – legal and illegal, violent and non-violent. Sometimes direct action is designed to prevent activities which the group is opposed to. Examples include disrupting fox hunts, lying in the path of trucks transporting nuclear missiles, and using speed boats to prevent the dumping of waste at sea.

Direct action includes protest marches and demonstrations, boycotts (for example, of imported food from a country with a poor human rights record), publicity stunts, blockades and occupations (for example, of a company whose activities the protesters oppose), damage to property and violence. Violence can range from scuffles with the police during a protest march, to IRA violence in Northern Ireland, to the global violence of Al Quaeda (Grant, 2000).

Direct action can show the strength and extent of opposition. It sometimes attracts considerable media attention. It can put considerable pressure on governments or particular organisations. It may bring public support, but it may bring just the opposite.

Pressure groups and democracy – the case for

Pluralists see pressure groups as an essential part of a representative democracy. The following points support this view.

Representation of particular interests Without pressure groups, many interests might be unrepresented and unheard. For example, pressure groups representing victims of domestic violence and gays and lesbians have only emerged over the past 30 years or so. Before then, their concerns were rarely voiced.

Regular influence on government Voting every five years in general elections is a minimal form of political participation. Situations change, new issues arise, public opinion changes. Pressure groups provide a means of influencing politicians between general elections, and of voicing concerns and responses to new situations.

Alternative forms of opposition In Parliament, the government is faced by opposition parties. Pressure groups provide alternative forms of opposition. This is particularly important when the government has a large majority in the House of Commons and opposition parties are ineffective. It is also important when opposition parties support government policy – for example, the Conservatives supported Labour's decision to go to war with Iraq. In February 2003, over one million people marched through London in opposition to the war. Although this did not prevent British troops from taking part in the invasion of Iraq in March, it did indicate that large numbers of people were against the war.

Protection for minorities Pressure groups can provide some protection for minorities who may experience discrimination and whose interests may be overlooked. In this respect, they can help to check what the political philosopher John Stuart Mill called 'the tyranny of the majority' (Bentley et al., 2004).

Alternative viewpoints To operate effectively, a democracy needs an informed citizenship – citizens who are aware of the issues, debates and a variety of viewpoints. Pressure groups can raise issues and offer alternative viewpoints which are not available from politicians or the media.

Pressure groups and democracy – the case against

Marxist views From a Marxist viewpoint, power is concentrated in the hands of the capitalist class. Pressure groups operate within the framework of capitalist society.

activity21 pressure group politics

Item A The People's Fuel Lobby

In protest against high fuel taxes, a relatively small group of lorry drivers and farmers blockaded Britain's oil refineries in September 2000. Within five days they nearly brought the country to standstill. Garages ran out of petrol and panic-buying emptied supermarket shelves.

Despite the chaos and inconvenience, the People's Fuel Lobby enjoyed considerable public support. The tabloid press portrayed the government as arrogant and out of touch, particularly when ministers refused to surrender to those 'holding the country to ransom'.

Within a week, the protestors called off their action, but issued the government with an ultimatum – cut fuel duty or face further blockades. In November 2000, the Chancellor offered just enough to prevent a repeat performance.

The government was clearly shaken. Its popularity had plummeted. It was faced with widespread disruption and a campaign backed by considerable public and media support. It responded to the action of a self-appointed, unelected pressure group whose leaders were not publicly accountable.

Adapted from Bentley et al., 2002

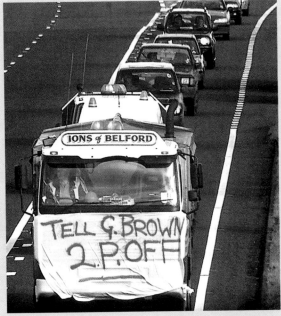

A message to the Chancellor, Gordon Brown, from the People's Fuel Lobby

Item B Greenpeace and Brent Spar

In 1995, the Department of Trade and Industry granted Shell a licence to dump the Brent Spar oil storage structure over the edge of the continental shelf in the North Atlantic. Environmentalists, including the pressure group Greenpeace, argued that this would contaminate the ocean bed and threaten marine life. Greenpeace International has over 3 million members worldwide (including 350,000 in the UK).

Greenpeace activists attempted to occupy the Brent Spar as it was towed into the Atlantic. This was filmed by Greenpeace ships and included scenes of a Greenpeace helicopter being attacked with water cannons by Shell vessels. As no television companies were prepared to charter ships, the only images available were those provided by Greenpeace. Pictures of a plucky little helicopter flying into a barrage of water cannons were broadcast by television channels throughout Europe.

The British Prime Minister, John Major, came under increasing criticism from other European states, including Germany, Sweden, the Netherlands and Denmark. In Germany and some other countries, there was a massive consumer boycott of Shell petrol stations. Shell was losing £2.5 million a day because of the boycott. Finally, in June 1995, Shell backed down and agreed to abandon the dumping, causing considerable embarrassment to the British government which had supported them. The Brent Spar was towed to a Norwegian fjord and left to rust.

Adapted from Welsh, 1997 and Grove-White, 1997.

Water cannons spraying Greenpeace Brent Spar protesters

questions

1 Outline the methods used by the pressure groups in Items A and B.

2 Suggest reasons for the success of these groups.

They may win small victories on behalf of ordinary people but these are little more than sops or minor concessions. They do not alter the basic structure of society.

New Right views Some New Right thinkers have seen pressure groups as unrepresentative, as reflecting minority interests, and raising unrealistic expectations. Samuel Brittan (1983) argues that the constant and vocal demands of pressure groups force governments to give in to them in order to gain votes. Since almost every group has a rival putting in a counter-claim, governments can never satisfy all their demands. But they spend more and more money in the vain hope of doing so. In this way, pressure group, politics weakens governments and drains the nation's income through excessive government spending.

Inequality between pressure groups Some pressure groups are large, well-organised and well-financed. Others are just the opposite. As a result, pressure groups do not have equal influence. For example, it is often claimed that pressure groups representing business interests, such as the Confederation of British Industry (CBI) have greater influence than groups representing less powerful sections of the population such as the low-paid and lone-parent families. For instance, when Labour decided to introduce a statutory minimum wage, the CBI argued for no more than £3.50 an hour, whilst the trade unions called for £4.15 to £4.50. The government settled for £3.60, a sum which was much closer to the CBI's figure (Bentley et al., 2004).

A number of researchers have argued that pressure group politics merely serves to reinforce the position of wealthy and powerful. This view is critical of the pluralists' claim that pressure groups are essential to a representative democracy.

Non-legitimate power Pressure groups often bypass the normal representative processes. Unlike politicians, their leaders are not publicly accountable. Sometimes they break the law – a clear example of non-legitimate power (Heywood, 2002).

Pressure groups can be seen as a threat to democracy – as the 'tyranny of the minority'. A small, well-organised pressure group which 'holds the country to ransom' can be more effective than a less well-organised majority.

6.3 New social movements

Definitions and classifications

Social movements According to Anthony Giddens (2001) a *social movement* is a 'collective attempt to further a common interest or secure a common goal through actions outside the sphere of established institutions'. For example, the environmental movement involves large numbers of people drawn together by a common goal – to protect the natural environment. In pursuit of this goal, they often act outside established political institutions – for instance, they take direct action.

Old social movements Sociologists often distinguish between *old social movements* and *new social movements*. Old social movements were mainly concerned with

material or economic issues and were usually class based. They campaigned on issues such as higher wages, better working conditions and improvements in housing, education, health and welfare services for the working class. For example, in the 19th and 20th centuries, movements such as Chartism, socialism and the trade union movement played an important part in extending democracy and improving the lives of working people.

New social movements (NSMs) Examples of NSMs include feminism, environmentalism, the anti-capitalist movement and the peace movement. They differ from old social movements in the following ways.

- They are more concerned with non-material issues.
- They tend not to be class based – they draw their support from across class lines and their concerns are not solely directed to improving the position of a particular class.
- They are likely to focus on a single issue.
- Many are international in their outlook and activity. They have supporters across the world and are concerned with global issues (Giddens, 2001).

Classifying NSMs Simon Hallsworth (1994) identifies two types of NSM based on the issues they promote. The first type is concerned with defending aspects of the 'natural and social environment' which are seen as under threat. This category includes environmentalism, the peace movement and animal rights groups.

The second type is concerned with gaining equal rights for groups who have been discriminated against and marginalised in society. This category includes feminists, civil rights movements, gay rights groups and disability rights groups.

New issues and new approaches

Extending the political agenda Many NSMs seek to extend the boundaries of what is generally seen as political (Hallsworth, 1994). Feminism, one of the most influential social movements of the 20th century, provides an example. Feminists have achieved formal political and civil rights for women in most democratic societies. And they have put new issues on to the political agenda – contraception, abortion, childcare for working mothers, sexual harassment in the workplace and domestic violence.

Environmentalists have also helped to create new political agendas. Political parties can no longer ignore green issues. Environmental pressure groups in the UK have succeeded in eliminating lead from petrol, persuaded governments in the 1990s to cut back on the building of new roads, and encouraged greater research and investment in renewable sources of energy such as wind and wave power.

Universal morality and new values Many NSMs are concerned with moral issues which affect everybody. Issues such as the environment, peace, human rights and animal rights transcend national boundaries – they are not limited to a particular group in a particular society (Crook et al., 1992).

Organisation Compared to political parties and traditional pressure groups, NSMs tend to be informal and fragmented movements. For example, the feminist movement includes self-help groups, consciousness-raising groups and pressure groups. Similarly, the environmental movement consists of well-established pressure groups such as Greenpeace and Friends of the Earth and one-off protest groups whose supporters have come together to prevent a particular development or protect a particular forest.

NSMs tend to be suspicious of elected politicians, bureaucratic organisations, hierarchies of power and control, and full-time officials. Members of NSMs emphasise communication and participation, rather then direction from above. For example, the anti-capitalist movement has no clearly defined leadership, no paid officials and no established headquarters. Members form a network linked by common concerns and values. The Internet can be crucial in establishing and maintaining this global network and in directing action. For example, the massive anti-capitalist demonstration in Seattle in 1999 involving tens of thousands of protesters from over 80 countries against the World Trade Organisation was largely organised through the Internet (Giddens, 2001).

Methods Pressure groups which form a part of NSMs sometimes act like traditional pressure groups – for example, giving evidence to parliamentary committees and establishing links with government departments. However, they often become involved in various forms of direct action – demonstrations, protests, and high profile activity that attracts the attention of the media and the public. And, the same applies to many people within the movements – participation and direct action often go together.

The methods adopted by NSMs reflect their concern not only to change government policies but also to change culture. The causes they promote require not only governments but also people in general to change their values and behaviour.

Explaining new social movements

Late modernity and risk According to Anthony Giddens (2001), NSMs are a response to the changing risks which have arisen in late modern society. Many of these risks are global, they transcend national boundaries and present challenges which national governments are unable to deal with. They include a variety of threats to the environment – global warming, disappearing rainforests, depleted fish stocks in the world's oceans, and accidents such as oil spills and explosions at nuclear plants. And many of these threats are seen to result from the actions of the rich and powerful – for example, transnational corporations whose concern is profit rather than the environment.

Faced with these risks, people feel insecure, isolated and powerless. Many have lost faith in national political institutions. For some, the way forward lies in NSMs. In the UK today, the main environmental pressure groups have a combined membership which is far larger than that of the main political parties.

The politics of postmodernity Stephen Crook, John Pakulski and Malcolm Waters (1992) claim that a process of postmodernisation is occuring in advanced societies. Part of this process involves a move towards a 'new politics'. They see NSMs as central to the new politics.

Crook et al. suggest the following reasons for this change. A process of *class decomposition* is occurring – class identity and class solidarity are breaking down. As a result, politics is less concerned with sectional class interests. This can be seen from the decline in class-based voting. Class decomposition is accompanied by *social differentiation* – people are becoming increasingly different in terms of their lifestyles and consumption patterns. And lifestyle and consumption, rather than class, are becoming the basis for identity. NSMs reflect these changes. They are concerned with ways of living rather than more narrow economic issues.

The mass media are becoming increasingly influential in postmodernising societies. And the media often deals with issues on a global scale – for example, the pollution caused by oil spillages off the coast of Spain and Alaska and on land in Nigeria and Iraq. As a result, people become increasingly global in their outlook and concerns. And this too is reflected in NSMs – for example, by the environmental movement.

Post-industrial society and post-materialist values Some sociologists see a move in the West from *industrial* to *post-industrial society*. The majority of people are no longer employed in manufacturing industry – in the production of goods. Most are now employed in so-called 'people work' which involves leisure and tourism, catering, banking, education, the media and care and welfare services.

This change to post-industrial society has been accompanied by a change in values – from *materialist* to *post-materialist values*. The new values are less concerned with material progress and higher living standards. They are more concerned with self-expression, individual freedom, personal identity and chosen lifestyles.

Post-materialist values are reflected in NSMs. For example, movements promoting the rights of ethnic minorities, women, gays and lesbians, and the disabled are concerned with establishing positive identities, freedom of expression, freedom from discrimination and freedom for individuals and groups to develop their own lifestyles. A study by Manuel Castells (1983) of the gay movement in San Francisco showed how they developed districts organised around their own values and lifestyles – with gay bars and clubs, gay rights organisations and gay representation in local politics.

Post-materialist values are also concerned with the negative effects of economic growth and materialism – for example, their effect on the environment and on relationships between nations. Again, this is reflected in NSMs – for instance, the environmental movement and the anti-nuclear and peace movements (Touraine, 1983, 1995).

The significance of NSMs

Revitalisation of the political process Anthony Giddens (2001) argues that NSMs have revitalised the political process. With membership of political parties and the turnout at general elections declining, it appears that people are losing faith in traditional politics. Giddens sees the growth of NSMs as evidence that people are not apathetic towards politics, that they have not lost interest in participating in the wider world and in decisions which affect their lives. He sees support for NSMs 'as a way of highlighting complex moral issues and putting them at the centre of social life'.

Global politics Many NSMs are global in their outlook and activities. They transcend the nation state. Their networks are maintained and their causes promoted by information technology. They sometimes engage in *netwars* – using the Internet to attack corporations and governments. To the powers that be, this can be a serious threat. A US Army report warned that, 'A new generation of revolutionaries, radicals and activists are beginning to create information-age ideologies in which identities and loyalties may shift from the nation state to the transnational level of global civic society' (quoted in the *Guardian* 19.01.2000).

As globalisation proceeds, NSMs may well develop into significant players on the global stage.

Questioning the significance of NSMs Paul Hirst (1990) argues that NSMs only produce major change when the legitimacy of the state is questioned by the majority of the population. This happened in Eastern Europe in the late 1980s with the overthrow of communist regimes. In Western democracies, most people accept the legitimacy of the state. As a result, Hirst argues, only organisations which work within the state – for example, political parties, trade unions and business organisations – can achieve real influence. This excludes many NSMs. According to Hirst, NSMs can only achieve influence at local level or in single-issue campaigns.

A Marxist viewpoint Alex Callinicos (1989) rejects the view that there is a move to a post-industrial or postmodern society in which class is becoming increasingly insignificant and class politics are dying.

He argues that capitalism now operates on a global scale. As a result, the exploitation of workers is worldwide. Callinicos believes that only working-class organisations can overthrow capitalism. In his view, the only significant political conflicts are those which are part of the wider class struggle. Since NSMs do not fall into this category, their significance is minor. However, there is an outstanding exception – the anti-capitalist movement.

Callinicos (2003), believes that the anti-capitalist movement has revitalised the class struggle on a global scale. It has attacked global capitalism, transnational corporations and the worldwide exploitation of workers. And it has attacked organisations – such as the World Trade Organisation – which it sees as representing the interests of global capitalism. It has drawn together a range of groups concerned with a variety of issues – for example, socialists, anarchists and environmentalists. And it has revived radical politics with its concern for social justice.

key terms

Social movement A collective attempt to further a common interest or secure a common goal through actions outside the sphere of established institutions (Giddens, 2001).

Old social movement A social movement mainly concerned with economic issues such as wages and living standards. Old social movements are usually class based.

New social movement A social movement which draws support from across class lines and is more concerned with non-material issues. Many such movements are global in their outlook and activity.

Class decomposition The breakdown of the class system, of class identity and class solidarity.

Social differentiation A growing difference between people in terms of their lifestyles and consumption patterns.

Post-industrial society A society in which employment in the service sector exceeds employment in manufacturing industry.

Post-materialist values The values of post-industrial society. The concern with material progress and higher living standards is partly replaced by a concern with individual freedom, personal identity and chosen lifestyles.

activity22 *the anti-capitalist movement*

Item A Direct action

Protest against the World Trade Organisation (WTO), Seattle, 30 November, 1999

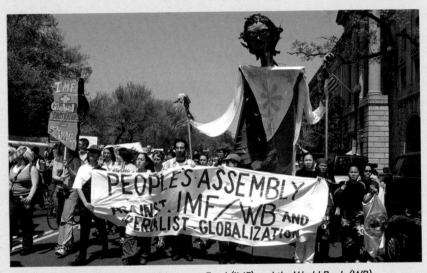

Protest against the International Monetary Fund (IMF) and the World Bank (WB), Washington DC, 16 April, 2000

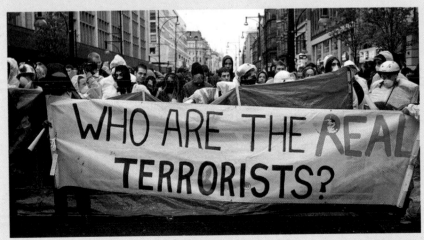

London, 1 May, 2001

Item B Aims of the movement

'I think the great majority of people who have joined this movement started off with a vague sense that something was wrong and not necessarily being able to put their finger on what it was. Having a sense that power was being removed from their hands, then gradually becoming more informed, often in very specific areas because what you find in our community of activism is some people who are very concerned about farming, those who are very interested in the environment, or labour standards or privatisation of public services, or Third World debt. These interests tie together and the place they all meet is this issue of corporate power.'

George Monbiot, writer and activist in the anti-capitalist movement quoted in T*he Observer* 14.7.2002

Item C Organisation of the movement

A distinguishing feature of the new protest, according to leading activists, is synergy between different groups. One activist, Anne says: 'We are totally interconnected, like a big family'.

Websites play a key role in bringing so many people together. But activists say it is e-mail which has really revolutionised the movement. You can start with a very small distribution list, but then as everyone on that list forwards a message to everyone on their own personal mail list, it cascades down to an enormous number of people. This makes it almost impossible for the police to estimate the level of any threat, or to guess at the number involved.

The groups say they have no leaders and no hierarchy, though the police dispute this. The truth is probably somewhere in between – the structure of the groups means no one can be sure what others are doing. No one has overall control. But there are some people who have more power, more say, by virtue of their experience and credibility.

Adapted from Reeves, 1999

Item D *Impact of the movement*

It was the appearance of the anti-capitalist demonstrators in Seattle in November 1999 that first made business leaders take notice of their concerns. Company chairmen forced to cower behind police lines cannot help but be impressed by the strength of feeling and the powers of organisation of people who might be ignored if they contented themselves with polite protest. The force of the attack has been strengthened because it has penetrated the system. Socially responsible investors, such as those putting pressure on BP and other oil companies, bring the arguments to the boardroom.

One response has been a drive within business for greater responsibility and openness. For example, the EU has backed a new organisation, CSR Europe, which was behind the European Parliament's first conference on corporate responsibility. Self-interest is a significant driver of this growing concern. For example, companies with strong brands (such as Nike and Adidas) have realised they must protect their reputations. That means, among other things, trying to ensure suppliers do not employ children or pay low wages.

Adapted from Cowe, 2001

questions

1 In what ways can the anti-capitalist movement be seen as a new social movement? Refer to Items A, B and C in your answer.

2 Judging from Item D, how significant is the anti-capitalist movement?

6.4 The mass media and politics

The mass media are 'the means through which content, whether fact or fiction, is produced by organisations and transmitted to and received by an audience' (McCullagh, 2002). The mass media include newspapers, magazines, television, radio, the Internet, advertisements, books and films.

This section looks at the relationship between the media and politics. It outlines various theories of media effects – the effects the media are seen to have on audiences. It then considers the possible effects of the media on voting behaviour.

Pluralist theories

From a pluralist position, the media are seen to reflect the various views and interests in the wider society. As a result, they present a broad spectrum of political ideas and ideologies. In doing so they inform the public and act as a means of political communication.

Members of the audience tend to be drawn to those aspects of media output which reflect their interests and opinions. As a result, media effects on the audience are seen as fairly limited. They tend to reinforce rather than change people's political attitudes and behaviour.

Evaluation The pluralist model assumes that media output is diverse – it covers a range of viewpoints and offers the audience considerable choice. Other theories take a very different view. They argue that the media broadcast a dominant ideology which offers little choice of alternative viewpoints.

Marxist theories

Marxists reject the pluralist claim that the media present a diversity of political views. Instead, they argue that the media transmit ruling class ideology – a false view of reality which supports the interests of the capitalist ruling class.

Ralph Miliband (1969) describes the media as the new 'opium of the people', adapting Marx's famous phrase, 'religion is the opium of the people'. Miliband likens the media to a hallucinatory drug which creates illusions and produces a feeling of wellbeing. It is not only political reporting that supports the system. The content of entertainment programmes from soaps to chat shows portrays the capitalist system in a favourable light and diverts attention from the inequalities and exploitation it produces.

The media offer no challenge, no alternatives to the status quo – to the way things are.

Evaluation Marxist views are based on a value judgement – that capitalism is an evil, exploitative system. Agreement with their views involves an acceptance of this judgement.

From a pluralist viewpoint, the absence of real challenge to capitalism in the media simply reflects an absence of real challenge in the wider society. If people wanted radical and revolutionary ideas, the media would provide them.

Postmodernist views Postmodernists argue that we live in a media-saturated society – that we are constantly bombarded with media images. As a result, the line between image and reality becomes increasingly blurred. Some postmodernists take this argument even further – media images actually become reality.

The media do not simply present a single version of reality – they offer multiple realities. News, documentaries, advertisements, soaps and movies provide often conflicting views set in the past, present and future, in this world and in other worlds. And these multiple realities are open to multiple interpretations – people interpret them in a variety of ways (Strinati, 1992).

Exposure to the multiple realities broadcast by the media results not in one 'truth' but many. People become increasingly sceptical. Truth becomes relative. There is no way to judge whether one truth is any more valid than others.

In terms of politics, this suggests that people will become increasingly sceptical of the policies and promises of political parties. They will become disenchanted and detached from the political process.

Evaluation Postmodernists have produced little concrete evidence to support their views. Greg Philo and David Miller (2002), on the basis of many years of research, argue that audiences are well aware that there is a reality behind media images. And their research indicates that audiences recognise that the images and accounts given by TV news sometimes present a one-sided and distorted picture.

Early theories of media effects

The two-step flow model This approach argues that most people are not directly influenced by the mass media – for example, the media do not directly affect their decisions on how to vote. Instead, their views are developed in *primary groups*, such as family, friends and work colleagues. Within these groups are opinion leaders who are influential in forming opinions.

Where does this leave the media? On the basis of a survey in an American city, Katz and Lazarsfeld (1955) argue that opinion leaders are more exposed to and influenced by the media and it is through them that media effects are transmitted to other members of the group – hence the term two-step flow. In this way, voters are influenced by opinion leaders who, in turn, have been influenced by the media.

The uses and gratifications model This approach argues that audiences use the media in different ways for different purposes. For example, Blumler and McQuail (1968) found that some people watched party political broadcasts simply to reinforce their existing views, while others watched to help them decide how to vote. The uses and gratifications model places the audience in the driving seat – they decide how to use the media and what they want from the media.

Evaluation Early research into media effects has two main problems. First, it focuses on short-term effects – for example, the effects of election campaigns on voting behaviour. Critics argue that the media is more likely to influence people over long periods of time. Second, it looks at deliberate attempts to influence people – for example, the effects of party political broadcasts. Critics argue that the media is likely to be most influential when no attempt is made to influence – as in the transmission of a dominant ideology which is taken for granted both by those who work in the media and the audiences they reach.

Cultural effects theory

This approach argues that the media can have important effects on audiences. These effects are not the short-term

changes of opinion that earlier researchers claimed. Instead, they are a slow, steady, long-term build-up of ideas and attitudes in terms of which people understand the world.

A study of the effect of newspapers on voting behaviour interviewed the same people on a number of occasions during a 12 month period before a general election (Miller, 1991). The results indicate that the constant repetition of the same political viewpoints did influence people's voting behaviour.

Evaluation The basic problem faced by cultural effects theory is how to separate the effects of the media from all the other factors which influence people's attitudes and behaviour. Was it the newspapers which affected their political views or were other factors more important?

The media and elections

Do the media affect voting behaviour and the results of general elections? Judging by the claims of the *Sun* newspaper, the answer is yes. The *Sun* boasted that it was primarily responsible for the Conservatives' victory in the 1992 election. Sociologists are not so sure.

The press

Most people in Britain read a national daily and a Sunday newspaper. And most newspapers support one of the main political parties.

Until the mid-1990s, the majority of newspapers supported the Conservative Party. In the 1992 election, 70% gave their support to the Conservatives, 27% to Labour (Linton, 1996). Things changed by the 1997 election when 11 national daily and Sunday newspapers backed Labour compared with 7 for the Conservatives. For the first time in its history, the *Sun* – with the largest circulation of daily newspapers – urged its readers to vote Labour. After his landslide victory in 1997, Tony Blair was quick to show his gratitude – he thanked the *Sun* for 'its magnificent support' which 'really did make the difference' (Scammell & Harrop, 1997).

By the 2001 election, press support for Labour was even higher with the *Times* and the *Daily Express* switching to Labour. And again, Labour won by a landslide. But this time support for Labour was not as strong as in 1997 – in some cases it was barely lukewarm (Scammell & Harrop, 2002).

Does the press make a difference? It is tempting to conclude that press support for the Conservatives from 1979 to 1992, and for Labour in 1997 and 2001, contributed to their election victories. The traditional view is that newspapers reinforce rather than change voting intentions. Apart from anything else, people tend to read papers which reflect their own political views. However, in recent years, with increasing dealignment and a more volatile electorate, media influence on voting behaviour may be increasing (Bentley et al., 2004).

There are a number of reasons to question press influence.

- It is difficult to isolate the influence of the press from all the other factors which might affect voting behaviour.
- The press may be responding to the same influences as the electorate. If this is the case, the majority of newspapers will support the winning party.
- Surveys suggest that the influence of the press during election campaigns is not significant. In the 2001 election, there was a swing of 2% from Conservative to Labour during the campaign. This swing was 5.5% among *Daily Mail* readers, despite the paper's support for the Conservatives. The swing was 6.5% among *Guardian* readers – the paper supported Labour. Swings to Labour among readers of other newspapers were less dramatic (Deacon et al., 2001). On the basis of this evidence, it appears that the political standpoint of newspapers had little effect on the result of the 2001 election.

Might newspapers have an influence over the longer term? As noted earlier, one study interviewed people over a 12 month period before an election. The findings suggested that newspapers can influence voting intentions (Miller, 1991).

Election campaigns are fairly short and sharp. Mass communication is steadily growing. The periods between elections provide continuing definition and discussion of political issues by the media. Focusing on election campaigns may not reveal the influence of newspapers or the media in general (Deacon et al., 2001).

Broadcasting

Surveys indicate that during the 2001 election campaign, 89% of the electorate obtained information about election issues from television, 74% from newspapers and 39% from radio (Lilleker et al., 2003).

Unlike newspapers, broadcasting media – TV and radio – are bound by legislation to provide impartial coverage of news and current affairs. The extent to which they do this is debatable. At various times the BBC has been accused of left-wing bias by the Conservatives and right-wing bias by Labour.

Compared to newspapers, television is extremely visual, colourful, and it has sound. These differences may be very important for the portrayal of party leaders. A number of commentators have noted a growing focus on party leaders in recent years, a process sometimes referred to as the 'presidentialisation' of election campaigns. In the 2001 campaign, the three main party leaders accounted for 41% of broadcast coverage and 34% of newspaper coverage (Deacon et al., 2001). As a result, parties need leaders who are 'telegenic' – come across well on TV.

In 1997, Tony Blair exuded charisma as he bounded across TV screens, while the Conservative leader John Major appeared bland and dull. And in 2001, the then Conservative leader William Hague suffered by comparison with Tony Blair in his TV appearances. If the trend towards presidentialisation continues, then television may have a significant effect on election results.

Conclusion

The relationship between politics and the media is not clear-cut. Most of the research has focused on short-term media influence during election campaigns. It is extremely difficult to isolate the effects of the media from other factors which influence voting behaviour. It is even more difficult to isolate the long-term effects.

summary

1. There are various theories of the relationship between the mass media and politics.
2. Pluralists argue that the media reflect the diversity of political views in society. In general, the media are seen to reinforce people's existing political views.
3. Marxists argue that the media transmit ruling class ideology – a false view of reality which supports the capitalist system.
4. Postmodernists claim that the line between media images and reality is becoming increasingly blurred. The media are seen to transmit 'multiple realities' – not one 'truth' but many.
5. The two-step flow model argues that opinion leaders pass on media messages to members of the groups to which they belong.
6. The uses and gratifications model states that audiences use the media in different ways for different purposes.
7. The above two models focus on the short-term effects of the media – for example, changing voting intentions during an election campaign.
8. Cultural effects theory looks at the possible long-term effects of the media. It claims that the media can have important effects if audiences are exposed to a steady, long-term build-up of ideas and attitudes.
9. The traditional view is that newspapers reinforce rather than change voting intentions. However, the increasing volatility of the electorate may increase their influence.
10. The growing focus on party leaders may increase the influence of TV on voting behaviour.
11. It is extremely difficult to isolate the effects of the media from other factors which might influence voting behaviour.

activity23 the media and elections

Item A Newspapers

Newspaper	Circulation (000s)		Preferred winner	
	2001	1997	2001	1997
Dailies				
Sun	3,288	3,935	Lab	Lab
Daily Mail	2,337	2,127	Con	Con
Mirror	2,056	2,390	Lab	Lab
Daily Telegraph	989	1,126	Con	Con
Express	929	1,208	Lab	Con
Times	667	772	Lab	Eurosceptic
Daily Star	585	660	Lab	Lab
Guardian	362	402	Lab	Lab
Independent	197	256	Not Con	Lab
Financial Times	176	304	Lab	Lab
Sundays				
News of the World	3,675	4,365	Lab	Lab
Mail on Sunday	2,238	2,112	Con	Con
Sunday Mirror	1,761	2,238	Lab	Lab
Sunday People	1,277	1,978	Lab	Lab
Sunday Times	1,206	1,310	Lab	Con
Sunday Express	870	1,159	Lab	Con
Sunday Telegraph	767	909	Con	Con
Observer	408	454	Lab	Lab
Independent on Sunday	211	276	Lab	Lab
Sunday Business	53	-	Lab	-

Adapted from Bentley et al., 2002

Item B Switching back

The Daily Express *returns to its traditional support of the* Conservatives (22.04.2004).

Item C Television

The three main party leaders Tony Blair (Labour), William Hague (Conservative) and Charles Kennedy (Liberal Democrat) pictured on BBC TV News shortly before the 2001 election.

questions

1 Assess the influence of newspapers on election results. Refer to Items A and B in your answer.

2 Look at Item C. Why might TV portrayal of party leaders influence election results?

3 Methodology

Introduction

Methodology refers to the whole research process – to the methods used to collect data, to the analysis of the data, and to the theories which underlie both.

At its simplest, methodology refers to research methods such as interviews and questionnaires. What are their strengths and weaknesses, how good is the data they produce? These questions were examined in *Sociology in Focus for AQA AS Level*.

At the other extreme, methodology deals with philosophical questions such as the nature of knowledge. How can we say that one statement is true and another false? How can we 'know' anything? This chapter examine some of the attempts to answer such questions.

The scientific method - one view of methodology

chaptersummary

▷ Unit 1 looks at ways of assessing the validity and reliability of research data.

▷ Unit 2 examines various views of science and their application to sociological research.

▷ Unit 3 looks at interpretivist methodology.

▷ Unit 4 looks at postmodernist methodology.

▷ Unit 5 looks at feminist methodology.

▷ Unit 6 considers the relationship between values and sociological research.

▷ Unit 7 examines the relationship between sociology and social policy.

Unit 1 Assessing research findings

keyissues

1 How valid and reliable are research findings?

2 Do researchers affect the data they collect?

3 What are the advantages of combining various research methods and types of data?

Sociological research methods were outlined and evaluated in *Sociology in Focus for AQA AS Level*. This unit takes a more general view of the research process. It asks how good are research findings and how do we know?

1.1 Quantitative and qualitative methods and data

Quantitative data is data in a numerical form - in the form of numbers. Official statistics are an obvious example. Questionnaires and structured interviews are the usual research methods used to obtain quantitative data. Their responses can often be fairly easily translated into numbers.

Some researchers argue that unless human behaviour is expressed in numerical terms, it cannot be accurately measured. Without accurate measurement conclusions will be based on impressions and as such will be little more than unsupported opinion.

Qualitative data covers a range of material from the descriptions of social life provided by participant observation and unstructured interviews to information from written sources such as diaries, autobiographies and novels. Some researchers argue that qualitative data provides greater depth, a richer and more detailed picture of social life. It is more likely to capture the subtleties, nuances and shades of meaning than the numerical data provided by quantitative methods.

Use of the contrast quantitative/qualitative implies either/or and better/worse – that researchers use and favour either one or other type of data. In practice, most researchers use both kinds of data, recognising their strengths and weaknesses and seeing them as suited to different purposes. For example, the findings of a small-scale participant observation study can form the basis for a questionnaire used in a large-scale social survey. And, as we shall see shortly, quantitative and qualitative data can be used together as 1) a means of checking the other and 2) building up a more complete picture of social life.

1.2 Validity and reliability

Validity refers to the accuracy of a description or measurement. Data is valid if it gives a true picture of a way of life or an accurate measurement of something. For example, official statistics on crime are valid if they provide an accurate measurement of the extent of crime.

Some researchers argue that qualitative data with its depth and richness is more likely than quantitative data to provide a valid picture of social life. However, methods used to collect qualitative data, such as participant observation, rely heavily on the interpretive skills of the researcher. It is therefore difficult to assess the validity of the data they produce. Possible ways of doing this will be examined shortly.

Reliability Research methods and data are reliable when different researchers using the same methods obtain similar results. For example, if the same questionnaire and the same sampling procedure produce similar results when used by different researchers, then the methods and the data are reliable. A reliable method allows studies to be replicated, ie repeated.

1.3 Triangulation

Triangulation is a term used to describe various ways of assessing the validity and reliability of research methods and data (Denzin, 1970). It looks at the topic under investigation from different angles and vantage points. Triangulation can take various forms. These include:

1 Investigator triangulation This involves the use of different researchers, eg different observers and interviewers. The aim is to check for observer and interviewer bias by, for example, using interviewers from different social backgrounds.

2 Data triangulation This involves collecting data at different times from different people in different places. It can also involve combining primary and secondary data. Data triangulation serves as a cross-check for validity. It can also serve as a means of assessing researchers' interpretations and conclusions.

3 Methodological triangulation This takes two forms. 'Within-method' triangulation uses a variety of techniques within the same method, for example open and closed questions within a questionnaire. Asking similar questions in a variety of ways can check on the validity of the answers and the reliability of the method. 'Between-method' triangulation refers to the combination of a number of research methods, for example questionnaires, unstructured interviews and participant observation. The

data produced by each method can be checked by comparing it with the data produced by the other methods.

The idea of triangulation is illustrated by the following quotation from *Belfast in the 30s: An oral history* (quoted in Macdonald & Tipton, 1993).

'In the first place we carried out ... "investigator triangulation". That is, each transcript was checked by two or three researchers to ensure that it said what people had meant to say. In the second place, we systematically did a cross-method triangulation, in that every piece of oral evidence that could be, was checked against a range of written sources: newspapers, parliamentary reports, documents etc. Finally, there was a considerable amount of data triangulation possible within the oral sources themselves' (Munck & Rolston, 1987).

1.4 Reflexivity

A White male middle-class researcher – and most of them are – will tend to see the social world he studies through White male middle-class eyes. And, to some extent, he will be seen by those he studies in terms of his social identity which will influence the way they respond to him. In these respects social research is *reflexive* – it reflects and is shaped by the researcher.

As a researcher, our findings will be coloured by our social background, our experiences and our culture. What we see and how we interpret it will be influenced by the fact that we are social beings. Social research involves social relationships. To some extent those being studied will be influenced by the presence of the researcher.

The idea of reflexivity also refers to a recognition, an awareness, that research is reflexive. This awareness means that, as researchers, we should be critical of ourselves, our research and our findings. We should examine ourselves in order to discover to what extent our findings reflect our own beliefs and values. We should question whether our presence affects the actions of those we study. This critical awareness will help us get nearer to our goal – a valid picture of social reality. (The influence of values on research is examined in Unit 4.)

Assessing validity How do sociologists attempt to minimise their influence on research? How do they try to ensure the validity of their data? Some of the ways of assessing research findings have been discussed under the heading of triangulation. Some others will now be examined.

Asking the researched In his study of an Italian American gang in Boston, William Whyte (1955) discussed his findings with Doc, the leader of the gang. Doc assessed Whyte's interpretation of the gang's behaviour from an insider's viewpoint.

Playing the part Aaron Cicourel (1976) spent four years studying probation officers in California. Part of this time was spent as an unpaid probation officer. His aim was to discover the meanings used by probation officers to define young people as delinquent. Cicourel claimed that by learning to play the part of a probation officer, he was able to identify the same young people as delinquents as his full time colleagues. This provided support for his interpretation of the meanings that *they* used to define delinquency.

Presenting the data In *The Social Organisation of Juvenile Justice*, the published report of his findings, Cicourel presents lengthy extracts from conversations between probation officers and juveniles along with detailed descriptions of their interaction. Although this presentation is selective – it represents only a small part of his field notes – it gives others some opportunity to assess Cicourel's interpretation of the data.

Comparing results Researchers often compare their findings with those of others who have conducted similar research. This comparison encourages them to question their results and to assess to what extent their findings reflect their research methods and their own beliefs and values.

Critical self-awareness None of the above methods is foolproof but they do encourage a critical self-awareness which can only assist the quest for validity. Recognising the reflexive nature of social research is an important step forward. (Unit 4 develops this point.)

Dialogic research

Awareness of reflexivity has led some sociologists to examine the relationship between researchers and those they research. They argue that this relationship is unequal. The researcher directs operations, decides what's important, what questions to ask, who to ask, and who to observe – when, where and for how long. The voices of the researched can be lost in this process, and so can the validity of the research findings. A possible solution to this problem is *dialogic research*.

Dialogic research involves a dialogue between researcher and researched. It is about the researcher letting go of power and inviting the researched to set the agenda, to decide what's important and how to express it (Puwar, 2001).

Phil Cohen's (1996-97) research on youth in East London provides an example of the dialogic method. Some of the young people were given cameras and tape recorders and asked to record their social world in their own way. As a result, the researched also became the researchers.

activity1 triangulation

Carolyn Hoyle's research examined how the police dealt with domestic violence. She used a variety of methods – 'interviews with police officers and victims, observation of officers on duty, and examination of official records were all used to understand the police response to incidents of domestic violence'.

She interviewed victims *after* she had interviewed police officers 'partly to ensure that the police officers had given me an accurate version of the incident and of the wishes of the victims'. She used semi-structured interviews which produced 'quantitative data and qualitative descriptions'.

In discussions with the researcher and talking amongst themselves, police officers sometimes trivialised domestic violence. Dealing with 'domestics' was more trouble than it was worth, it was exasperating because they were 'so griefy'. These comments may reflect the 'canteen culture' of police stations where officers get things off their chests and put on a show of bravado. But, when asked about specific incidents, their replies contradicted these comments. They said they listened carefully to both sides in the dispute and had done their best to deal sympathetically and effectively with the situation. These claims were supported by Carolyn Hoyle's direct observation of officers dealing with domestic violence.

Adapted from Hoyle, 2000

Canteen culture

question

1 In what ways can Hoyle's research be seen as an example of triangulation?
2 With reference to Hoyle's research, outline the advantages of triangulation.

Dialogic research offers an opportunity to capture people's outlook, priorities, hopes and anxieties with a minimum of intrusion by the 'official' researcher. This concern is often reflected in feminist research – see pages 143-145.

1.5 Methodological pluralism

Methodological pluralism is similar to triangulation and can serve a similar purpose. However, its aim is not so much as a means of checking validity and reliability but rather to build up a fuller picture of social life by combining different research methods and different types of data. It recognises that each method and type of data has its particular strengths and weaknesses. Combined they are seen to produce a more comprehensive and rounder picture of social reality. And their combination can also provide new insights and new directions for research.

Some of the strengths of methodological pluralism can be seen from Eileen Barker's (1984) study of the Moonies – the Unification Church. She conducted in-depth interviews, each lasting 6-8 hours, with a number of Moonies. The interviews dealt with their background, why they became a Moonie, their life in the church and the meaning of religion as they saw it. Barker also lived as a participant observer in several centres with the Moonies at various times during the six years of her research. This enabled her to gain the trust of many members of the church, resulting in information which would not have been given to an outsider. Two years after the start of her research, she constructed a large (41 page) questionnaire based on her findings from interviews and observation. This provided

information from a larger sample and was intended to reveal 'social patterns, trends and tendencies and gain a more reliable understanding of regularities between variables - of "what goes with what"'.

Barker claims that combining different methods of investigation gave her a much fuller picture than any one method or data source could have provided.

summary

1. Many researchers use both quantitative and qualitative data, while recognising the strengths and weaknesses of each.

2. Triangulation provides a way of assessing the validity and reliability of research findings. It takes three main forms:
   - Investigator triangulation
   - Data triangulation
   - Methodological triangulation.

3. Social research is reflexive – to some extent it reflects and is shaped by the researcher. This can seriously affect the validity of research findings.

4. Dialogic research may improve the validity of research findings. It offers research participants the opportunity to take part in the direction of the research – to set the agenda, to decide what's important and even conduct their own research. This allows the voices of the researched to be heard.

5. Apart from triangulation and an awareness of reflexivity, there are various ways of assessing the validity of research findings. They include:
   - Asking research participants if the researcher has got it right
   - Playing the part – successfully acting out the role of those being studied
   - Presenting the data – providing sufficient data for others to make a judgement about its validity
   - Comparing research findings with the results of similar studies.

6. Methodological pluralism combines different research methods and different kinds of data with the aim of producing a more detailed, in-depth and comprehensive picture of social life.

Unit 2 Sociology and science

keyissues

1 What is science? What are scientific methods?

2 Are the methods and assumptions of the natural sciences appropriate to the study of human behaviour?

Sociology is often referred to as a *social science*. Whether or not it can be seen as a scientific discipline is one of the major debates within the subject. The founding fathers of sociology in the 19th century were, however, in no doubt. By following the rules and logic of the scientific method, sociology could discover the laws underlying the development of human society. And, in this respect, it was a science just like the *natural sciences* of physics and chemistry which seek to discover the laws underlying the behaviour of matter.

2.1 Auguste Comte – positivism

Auguste Comte (1798-1857) is credited with inventing the term sociology. He argued that sociology should be based on the methodology of the natural sciences. This would result in a 'positive science of society' which would reveal the 'invariable laws' which governed the evolution of human society. Comte's approach is known as *positivism*.

Comte insisted that only directly observable 'facts' were acceptable as evidence in his science of society. Anything that couldn't be directly measured, such as subjective meanings and purposes, was ruled out. The facts of society must be objectively measured and quantified, ie put into a numerical form. It would then be possible to identify cause and effect relationships and discover the laws underlying social evolution.

2.2 Emile Durkheim – the rules of sociological method

Social facts In *The Rules of Sociological Method*, first published in 1895, Durkheim outlined the logic and methods to be followed for sociology to become a science of society. The starting point, 'the first and most fundamental rule is: Consider social facts as things'. Social facts are the institutions, beliefs and values of society. As things, social facts can be treated in the same way as the objects, events and processes of the natural world. They can be objectively measured, quantified and subjected to statistical analysis. Correlations can be drawn between social facts, cause and effect relationships established and theories developed to explain those relationships. In this way 'real laws are discoverable' in the social world as in the natural world.

But how can social facts be treated as things? Aren't beliefs, for example, part of human consciousness? And aren't human beings, because they have consciousness, fundamentally different from the inanimate objects which make up the natural world? In view of this, is natural science methodology appropriate for the study of human behaviour?

External reality Durkheim accepted that social facts form part of our consciousness – they have to for society to exist. Without shared norms and values, for example, society could not operate. But, although they are a part of us, social facts also exist outside of us. In Durkheim's words, 'collective ways of acting and thinking have a reality outside the individuals'. Members of society do not simply act in terms of their particular psychology and personal beliefs. Instead they are directed to act by social facts, by values and beliefs which are over and above the individual and part of the wider society. In this respect social facts 'have a reality outside the individuals' and can therefore be studied 'objectively as external things'.

Thus just as matter is constrained to act by natural forces, so human beings are constrained to act by social forces. Given this, social facts can be studied using the methodology of the natural sciences.

The social facts of suicide Durkheim's *Suicide: A Study in Sociology* was published in 1897. This study exemplified his rules of sociological method. Durkheim argued that the causes of suicide rates (the number of suicides per million of the population) are to be found in society, *not* in the psychology of individuals. Suicide rates are social facts. They are also a product of social facts, of 'real, living, active forces which, because of the way they determine the individual, prove their independence from him'.

Statistical evidence Durkheim examined official statistics on suicide from a number of European countries (see Item A, Activity 2, p135). He found that 1) suicide rates within each country were fairly constant over a number of years and 2) there were significant differences in the rates both between societies and between social groups within the same society.

Correlation and analysis Durkheim found correlations between suicide rates and a wide range of social facts. For example, he found statistical relationships between suicide rates and religion, location, age and family situation. Some of these are illustrated in the following table. In each of the pairs, the group on the left had a higher suicide rate than the group on the right.

Protestants	-	Catholics
City dwellers	-	Rural dwellers
Older adults	-	Younger adults
Unmarried	-	Married
Married without children	-	Married with children

Causation Having established correlations between social facts, Durkheim's next task was to see if he could discover causal connections. He argued that variations in suicide rates were caused by variations in levels of social integration that is the extent to which individuals are part of a wider social group. In the case of the examples given above, the groups on the left have lower levels of social integration than the groups on the right. For example, older adults are less socially integrated than younger adults because their children have grown up and left home, many of their friends and relatives have died, and if they have retired from work they may well have lost touch with their workmates. Using examples such as this, Durkheim claimed that 'suicide varies inversely with the degree of integration of the social groups of which the individual forms a part' – that is, the higher an individual's social integration the less likely they are to take their own life.

Theory and explanation Durkheim's final task was to explain why suicide rates vary with levels of social integration. Part of his explanation runs as follows. As members of society, people are social beings – they have been socialised to play a part in society. The greater their social isolation the less they can participate in society. Their lives lack meaning and purpose unless they are shared with others. In Durkheim's words, 'The individual alone is not a sufficient end for his activity. He is too little.' In a situation of social isolation, 'the individual yields to the slightest shock of circumstance because the state of society has made him ready prey to suicide'.

Durkheim doesn't claim to explain all aspects of suicide. For example, he does not explain why only a small minority of socially isolated individuals commit suicide. He sees this as the job of the psychologist because it concerns individual behaviour rather than social facts.

Durkheim believed that his research on suicide proved that scientific methodology was appropriate for the study of society, because it had shown that 'real laws are discoverable'. (For further discussion of Durkheim's study of suicide see pages 264-268. For a broader discussion of Durkheim's view of society, see pages 164-167).

2.3 Karl Popper – deduction and falsification

Induction vs deduction Durkheim argued that theories should come from evidence, from gathering data, from describing, classifying and analysing social facts. It is from this process that theories are generated. This is known as an *inductive* approach.

A *deductive* approach reverses this process. It begins with a theory and uses data to test that theory. This is the approach advocated by Karl Popper. From his viewpoint it is the only way science can proceed.

Falsification According to Popper rather than looking for evidence to confirm their theories, scientists should do their best to disprove or falsify them. This is the distinguishing characteristic of science – the development of theories which can be tested against evidence and be capable of *falsification*.

This means that theories must be constructed in such a way that falsification is possible. Popper argues that Marx's theory of history fails in this respect – it cannot be falsified and is therefore non-scientific. In particular, it fails to specify precisely what has to happen before the proletarian revolution occurs in capitalist society. And when the revolution does not happen, Marxists simply push its coming further and further into the future, thus preventing the possibility of falsification.

Popper rejects the search for laws governing the evolution of human society, which he sees as a 'unique historical process' (1959). However, he sees no reason why the methodology of the natural sciences cannot be applied to the social sciences. Theories of human behaviour which are open to the possibility of falsification can be developed.

Theories that survive falsification tests, however, are not necessarily true. They have simply not been falsified. The following oft-quoted example illustrates this point. 'All swans are white' is a scientific statement because it can be falsified. But, however many times it is confirmed by observation, it cannot be accepted as true because the very next swan might be black, red, blue or yellow. In this respect, there are no absolute truths in science.

Sociology and falsification Despite Popper's claim to the contrary, there are real problems in applying his model of scientific methodology to the study of human society. In the closed system of the laboratory where variables such as matter, temperature and pressure can be controlled, it may be possible to falsify a theory. However, human societies are open systems which means it is impossible to control variables. Because of this, it is difficult to see how a theory can be falsified.

2.4 Thomas Kuhn – normal science

For Durkheim, science consists of accumulating evidence and developing theories from that evidence. For Popper, science consists of creating testable theories and attempting to falsify them. For Thomas Kuhn 'normal science' – the vast majority of work which is called science – differs from both these views. Kuhn's *The Structure of Scientific Revolutions* (1962) argues that the way science has developed bears little relationship to conventional views of the scientific method.

Paradigms According to Kuhn, most of the time scientists are busily preoccupied with 'normal science'. Normal science operates within a *paradigm*. A paradigm is a framework of concepts and theories which states how the natural world operates. It identifies appropriate methods for studying that world and specifies what questions to ask and how to answer them. A paradigm is shared by members of the scientific community. It shapes the way they see the world they study.

In some respects paradigms are like blinkers – they place limits on inquiry, they erect barriers to alternative views, they restrict the scientific imagination. This is because normal science operates within the confines of a paradigm – developing and refining it but not challenging it. For example, until the 16th century Western astronomy was based on the theory of terracentricity – the idea that planets and the sun move around the earth. It is perfectly possible to confirm this idea with observations and measurements. And it is also possible to ignore or explain away contradictory evidence which might challenge it. So committed are scientists to the existing paradigm that they operate within it rather than attempting to falsify it.

Scientific revolutions Kuhn rejects the conventional view which sees science as a progressive accumulation of knowledge based on the testing and proving and disproving of hypotheses. Change does occur, but only when one paradigm is replaced by another. Kuhn calls this process a *scientific revolution* – it is sudden and revolutionary as a whole way of thinking about the world is swept away within a relatively short period of time. An example is the replacement of Newton's paradigm in physics with Einstein's. Once a new paradigm is established, normal science resumes and any real change has to wait until the next scientific revolution.

Scientific revolutions occur when evidence accumulates which cannot be explained in terms of the existing paradigm. This evidence accumulates to the point where it cannot be ignored, dismissed as an anomaly or as the result of incorrect observation and measurement. This happened with the Copernican revolution in astronomy in the 16th century. Copernicus stated that the sun, not the earth was the centre of the universe and that the planets orbited the sun. This view of the universe appeared to make sense of observations that could not be explained in terms of the previous paradigm.

Kuhn's view of paradigms and scientific revolutions has been criticised as a distortion of the history of science. For example, Lakatos (1970) rejects the view that normal science is dominated by a single paradigm. Instead, he sees the development of science as a history of constantly competing paradigms.

Sociology and paradigms In terms of Kuhn's view of science it has been argued that sociology is in a pre-paradigmatic and therefore pre-scientific situation. There is a range of competing sociological perspectives and there is little indication that this variety will develop into a single paradigm which will be acceptable to the sociological community. However, in terms of Lakatos' view, this does not disqualify sociology from being a science. In fact, sociology's history of competing perspectives largely accords with his view of the history of science.

2.5 The realist approach to science

The realist view of science, while accepting that there are basic differences between the social and natural worlds, maintains that a social science is possible. It argues that events in both the social and natural worlds are produced by underlying structures and mechanisms. According to Roy Bhaskar, the essential task of realism is to uncover and explain these structures and mechanisms (Bhaskar, 1978).

Open and closed systems Andrew Sayer (1992) distinguishes between open and closed systems as arenas of study. The laboratory is the prime example of a *closed system*. Sciences like physics and chemistry have the advantage of being able to create closed systems in which conditions can be fixed and variables controlled. This allows them to reveal 'more clearly the operation of mechanisms' (Sayer, 1992).

However, a large body of scientific research takes place within *open systems* where it is not possible to control variables. Meteorology is an example of a natural science where closed systems are rare. As a result, it is unable to predict the weather with any degree of accuracy, as daily weather forecasts indicate. However, it is able to offer an explanation of the weather after the event in terms of underlying mechanisms. In much the same way, geology is able to provide explanations for the occurrence of oil deposits. However, geologists' attempts to predict its presence have only limited success as the billions of dollars spent on unsuccessful oil exploration show.

One of the most famous non-predictive explanations is the theory of evolution, which specifies mechanisms such as natural selection and mutation which are seen to underlie the evolutionary process. But, because evolution takes place within an open system it is not possible to predict its future.

Human behaviour takes place in open systems. Because of this it is not possible to predict its course with any degree of accuracy. There is no way of controlling all the variables which affect human action. However, from a realist viewpoint, this does not rule out a social science. It is still possible to explain human behaviour in terms of underlying structures and mechanisms, just as

The landlord-tenant structure

From Sayer, 1992

meteorologists, geologists and evolutionary biologists explain behaviour in the natural world.

Structures, mechanisms and consciousness From a realist point of view, human behaviour operates within structures. Sayer (1992) defines structures as 'sets of internally related objects and practices'. He gives the following example using the landlord-tenant relation. The diagram illustrates the necessary relations for its existence. In Sayer's words, 'The landlord-tenant relation itself presupposes the existence of private property, rent, the production of economic surplus and so on; together they form a structure'. There are of course structures within structures. For example, the landlord-tenant structure forms part of the wider class structure in capitalist society.

Structures constrain human behaviour, they place limits on human action. However, this does not mean that human beings are simply directed by structural constraints. In the open system which is human society, they have varying degrees of freedom to direct their own actions. Realists include consciousness as part of the explanation for behaviour. They accept the interpretivist view of social reality as socially constructed. And they also accept the Marxist view of false consciousness – that socially constructed meanings can distort reality (Blaikie, 1993).

Mechanisms operate within structures. It is part of the scientist's job to identify these mechanisms and explain how they work. And in this respect the social scientist's job is the same as the natural scientist's. So just as an evolutionary biologist identifies mechanisms such as natural selection to account for biological change, so a sociologist identifies mechanisms such as the class struggle to account for social change.

Realism, sociology and science From a realist viewpoint, events in both the natural and social worlds are produced by structures and mechanisms. Given this, social science is based on the same principles as natural science. Both are concerned with the identification and explanation of structures and mechanisms. (For an analysis of Durkheim as a realist, see page 268.)

2.6 Sociology and science – conclusion

Objectivity The traditional picture of a scientist is of a rational, logical researcher who collects and explains 'facts'. In terms of the research process, he or she is objective, value-free and unbiased. The 'facts' are undistorted and uncontaminated – they are not coloured by the beliefs, experiences and values of the researcher.

Unit 1 has argued that, as far as sociology is concerned, this view of the researcher and the research process is a myth. Whether this disqualifies sociology as a science is a matter of opinion. Researchers in the natural sciences are also influenced by their beliefs and values. Kuhn's view of science suggests that the concepts and theories which make up paradigms are, in part, articles of faith – they include many of the common-sense beliefs of the time, for example, the belief that the earth is the centre of the universe.

These points are developed in Unit 6, Sociology, Methodology and Values, which asks:
● Is an objective, value-free sociology possible?
● And, is it desirable?

Natural and social science The natural and social sciences study different things. The natural sciences study matter which behaves in a predictable manner in a given situation. Matter simply reacts to a particular stimulus. There is no need for the natural scientist to interpret meanings and motives and discover beliefs and values in order to explain the behaviour of matter.

The same is not true for sociologists. Human beings define situations and act accordingly. They give meanings to events and act in terms of those meanings. And the beliefs and values they hold direct their behaviour. In view of this, sociologists have to discover definitions, meanings, beliefs and values in order to understand human action.

This has led many sociologists to argue that natural science methods are not suitable for the study of human behaviour. Interpreting meanings is very different from observing inanimate objects. And if sociology is seen as a science, then it is a very different science from the likes of physics and chemistry.

These points are developed in the next two units – Unit 3 Interpretivist Methodology and Unit 4 Postmodernist Methodology.

Views of science There are many views of science and scientific methods. As a result, there are many views about the relationship between sociology and science, and about the appropriateness of applying the assumptions and methods of the natural sciences to the study of human

key terms

Positivism In Comte's view, a method of study based on directly observable facts, objectively measured, from which it is possible to identify cause and effect relationships and discover laws underlying social evolution.
Social facts In Durkheim's view, the institutions, beliefs and values of society, which although they exist within individuals also exist outside of them and direct their behaviour.
Inductive approach Developing theories from evidence.
Deductive approach Beginning with a theory and using evidence to test that theory.
Falsification The process of testing a theory against evidence and showing the theory to be false.
Normal science Science which operates within an established paradigm.
Paradigm A framework of concepts and theories which states how the natural world operates.
Scientific revolution The overthrow of an established paradigm by a new paradigm.
Realist approach Assumes that events in both the natural and social worlds are produced by underlying structures and mechanisms.
Closed system A system in which all the variables can be controlled.
Open system A system in which it is not possible to control all the variables.

summary

1. Comte believed that sociology should be based on the methodology of the natural sciences.

2. Durkheim argued that social facts have a reality outside individuals. Social facts can therefore be studied as 'things'. This means that the methodology of the natural sciences can be used to study human society.

3. Durkheim argued that his study of suicide supported this view. He claimed to have discovered cause and effect relationships between social facts.

4. According to Popper, science is based on the development of theories which can be tested against evidence and be capable of falsification. It is difficult to see how sociology can fit this view of science. Human societies are open systems which means that it is impossible to control variables. Because of this, it is difficult to see how a theory can be falsified.

5. According to Kuhn, 'normal science' operates within a paradigm. A scientific revolution occurs when the existing paradigm is overthrown by a new paradigm.

6. Sociology has a range of competing perspectives rather than a single paradigm. In terms of Kuhn's view of science, it is in a pre-paradigmatic and, therefore, pre-scientific situation.

7. From a realist viewpoint, events in both the social and natural worlds are produced by underlying structures and mechanisms. In view of this, there is no reason why sociology cannot be a science.

8. Human society is an open system. So is the world in which natural sciences such as meteorology and geology operate. Again, there is no reason why sociology cannot be a science.

9. In view of the differences between the natural world and the social world, many researchers argue that natural science methodology is inappropriate for the study of human society.

activity2 views of science

Item A Suicide statistics

Rate of suicides per million inhabitants in European countries

		Period		Numerical position in the		
	1866-70	1871-75	1874-78	1st period	2nd period	3rd period
Italy	30	35	38	1	1	1
Belgium	66	69	78	2	3	4
England	67	66	69	3	2	2
Norway	76	73	71	4	4	3
Austria	78	94	130	5	7	7
Sweden	85	81	91	6	5	5
Bavaria	90	91	100	7	6	6
France	135	150	160	8	9	9
Prussia	142	134	152	9	8	8
Denmark	277	258	255	10	10	10
Saxony	293	267	334	11	11	11

Adapted from Durkheim, 1970 (originally published in 1897)

Item B An open system

Man-made pollution and climatic change are threatening the survival of the world's great whales. Nine years after commercial whaling was banned, the effects of global industrialisation now pose as great a threat to the world's largest mammals as the huge factory whaling fleets of the past. The hazards are outlined in scientific papers submitted to the International Whaling Commission. The authors argue that chemical pollution, ozone depletion and global warming are hindering the recovery of whale populations hunted almost to extinction in the 60s and 70s.

A separate report by biologist Dr Kevin Brown, commissioned by the London-based Environmental Investigation Agency, estimates that at least 150,000 man-made chemicals, increasing by 2,000 a year, are dumped in the oceans. He warns that damage to marine life caused by global warming and a thinning ozone layer could worsen the effects of chemicals through complex interactions which scientists are unable to predict.

'There are vast gaps in our knowledge ... but I wouldn't be surprised if there is a spiralling effect and whale numbers start crashing,' said Dr Brown, of Durham University.

His fears are echoed by Dr Mark Simmonds, of the University of Greenwich, who points out that six mass deaths of seals and dolphins have been recorded since 1987 – all in highly contaminated waters such as the North Sea – compared with only four over the previous eight decades.

Although viruses were the immediate cause of death, he argues that pollution must have played a major role.

Adapted from *The Observer*, 28.5.1995

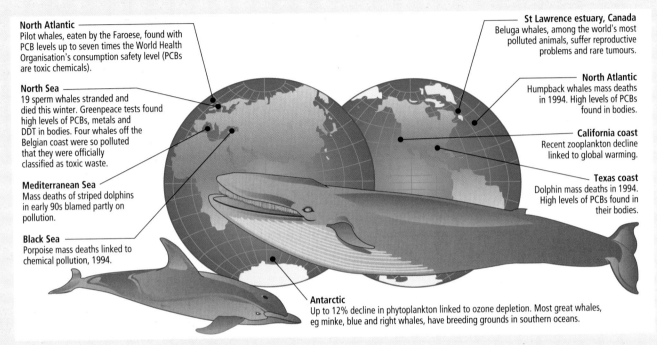

North Atlantic
Pilot whales, eaten by the Faroese, found with PCB levels up to seven times the World Health Organisation's consumption safety level (PCBs are toxic chemicals).

North Sea
19 sperm whales stranded and died this winter. Greenpeace tests found high levels of PCBs, metals and DDT in bodies. Four whales off the Belgian coast were so polluted that they were officially classified as toxic waste.

Mediterranean Sea
Mass deaths of striped dolphins in early 90s blamed partly on pollution.

Black Sea
Porpoise mass deaths linked to chemical pollution, 1994.

St Lawrence estuary, Canada
Beluga whales, among the world's most polluted animals, suffer reproductive problems and rare tumours.

North Atlantic
Humpback whales mass deaths in 1994. High levels of PCBs found in bodies.

California coast
Recent zooplankton decline linked to global warming.

Texas coast
Dolphin mass deaths in 1994. High levels of PCBs found in their bodies.

Antarctic
Up to 12% decline in phytoplankton linked to ozone depletion. Most great whales, eg minke, blue and right whales, have breeding grounds in southern oceans.

questions

1 Durkheim claimed that 'each society is predisposed to contribute a definite quota of voluntary deaths'.
   a) What support for this statement is provided by Item A?
   b) Use Item A to support Durkheim's claim that a science of society is possible.

2 Use Item B to support the realist view that:
   a) both the social and natural sciences operate in open systems
   b) conclusive verification or falsification are not possible in open systems
   c) in view of this, there are basic similarities between the methodologies of the natural and social sciences.

Unit 3 *Interpretivist methodology*

keyissues

1 How significant are meanings for understanding social action?

2 What are the similarities and differences between the main interpretivist perspectives?

Interpretivist sociology covers a range of theoretical perspectives which see fundamental differences between the natural and social worlds. From an interpretivist perspective, the social world is essentially a world of meaning. Human beings construct their own social reality.

Their actions are directed by meanings, their experience is based on meanings. Any understanding of human action must therefore involve an understanding of those meanings. And for many researchers, this means employing methodologies which are very different from those used in the natural sciences.

3.1 Max Weber – social action

Social action Max Weber (1864-1920) defined sociology as 'a science which attempts the interpretive understanding of social action in order thereby to arrive at a causal explanation of its course and effects' (1964). Social action is action which involves other members of society. It is based on meanings in the minds of social actors which direct their actions. Weber was particularly concerned with motives – the intentions and purposes which direct social actors to achieve certain goals.

Verstehen Motives are an important part of any explanation of social action. Weber's method of interpreting motives is known as *verstehen* which roughly translates as empathetic understanding. Researchers put themselves in the place of social actors and attempt to see the world through their eyes. The problem of course is whether verstehen produces a true picture of the actor's world view. Weber's solution to this problem will be examined shortly.

The Protestant ethic Weber's methodology can be illustrated with his most famous work, *The Protestant Ethic and the Spirit of Capitalism* (see also pages 17, 19-20). Weber was interested in the meanings and motives - the 'spirit of capitalism' – which, he believed, led to the rise of capitalism. On the basis of a wide range of historical documents, he claimed that they developed from early forms of Protestantism which preceded capitalism. Weber identified a Protestant work ethic in terms of which work became a 'calling' which must be pursued with a single mind. Making money is an indication of success in one's calling, it shows that a person has not lost favour in God's sight. Weber argues that the Protestant work ethic is a major cause of the rise of capitalism.

The comparative method How does Weber know that his interpretation of motives – in this case the Protestant work ethic – is correct? His answer is to use the *comparative method* which compares different societies and different groups within the same society. In the absence of a laboratory in which variables can be manipulated and controlled, Weber attempts to find 'natural' laboratories which allow the influence of variables to be measured.

If Weber's interpretation of the Protestant work ethic is correct, then Protestants should have spearheaded the rise of capitalism. He produces evidence which indicates that early capitalism developed within predominantly Protestant rather than Catholic societies, and within those societies the 'business leaders and owners of capital are overwhelmingly Protestant'. From this, Weber claims that his interpretation of the motives of social actors is validated. (For further discussion of Weber's methodology, see pages 167-169).

3.2 Herbert Blumer – symbolic interactionism

Weber investigated meanings on a wide canvas, often drawing on information from across the world and from different time periods. Symbolic interactionists tend to focus on meanings in the context of small-scale interaction situations. From this point of view, the meanings which direct action are developed and negotiated during the process of social interaction. The job of the sociologist is to discover these meanings.

Discovering meaning Herbert Blumer (1962) has developed a methodology for the study of social interaction. The first step is for researchers to immerse themselves in interaction situations, to observe and interpret the actions of others and attempt to see the world through their eyes. In Blumer's words, this involves 'feeling one's way inside the experience of the actor' in order to 'catch the process of interpretation through which they construct their action'. Blumer is refreshingly honest when discussing how this might be achieved. 'It is a tough job requiring a high order of careful and honest probing, creative yet disciplined imagination, resourcefulness and flexibility in study, pondering over what one is finding, and constant readiness to test and recast one's views and images of the area.'

Structure and meaning Symbolic interactionists accept that to some extent social interaction is structured. Meanings are not constantly reinvented, social interaction is often routine and repetitive rather than creative and spontaneous. But this does not mean that negotiation and interpretation aren't still important aspects of interaction. Nor does it mean that human action is shaped by the structures and mechanisms of the social system, as some sociologists would argue.

Blumer gives the example of family structure and industrialisation to illustrate this point. It has been claimed that industrialisation leads to the replacement of extended families by nuclear families. Blumer objects to this view which tends to see human action as a product of structures and mechanisms. Where in the equation are the meanings people give to family life, where are the interpretations they place on industrialisation? Without these meanings and interpretations sociologists have little chance of grasping social reality.

Blumer argues that the research process must be as systematic, rigorous and objective as possible. Equally important, however, are qualities such as sensitivity and sympathy. Both the tone and substance of Blumer's methodology are a long way from many of the views of science outlined in previous sections. (For further discussion of Blumer's methodology, see pages 181-182).

3.3 Phenomenology

Phenomenological perspectives take the logic of a social reality to its furthest point. They argue that as human beings our only reality consists of meanings. The job of the sociologist is to discover these meanings and nothing more – for the logic of this argument states there is nothing more to discover. The methodology that results from this view will now be examined using the example of suicide.

Discovering suicide In *Discovering Suicide* J. Maxwell Atkinson's basic question is 'How do deaths get categorised as suicide?' When he has answered this question he can go no further because suicide is simply a meaning and has no reality beyond this. Classifications of suicide are not right or wrong, they just are. For example, there is no such thing as a 'real' or objective suicide rate waiting to be discovered. The official statistics are the rate, full stop.

Atkinson's research attempts to discover the meanings used by coroners to classify deaths as suicide. He held discussions with coroners, attended inquests, observed a coroner's officer at work and analysed a coroner's records. He argues that coroners have a 'commonsense theory of suicide' which they use to both classify and explain deaths as suicide. In terms of this theory, the following evidence is seen as relevant for reaching a verdict.

1 Whether suicide threats have been made or suicide notes left.

2 The type of death – hanging, gassing and drug overdose are seen as typical suicide deaths.

3 The location of death – death by gunshot at home is more likely to be seen as suicide than in the countryside where it may well be interpreted as a hunting accident.

activity3 suicide

Item A Suicide in 1870

SUICIDE OF TWO LOVERS BY LEAPING OVER THE TAFFRAIL OF THE AMERICAN PASSENGER SHIP "BLOOMENTHORPE" ON THE PASSAGE TO SAN LUIS.

DISTRESSING SUICIDE AFTER WARWICK RACES.

Item B Retired coroner

During the War it was something of an understanding that you didn't bring in suicide verdicts unless you really had to. 'Bad for National Morale' – and of course I think most people felt responsible for keeping morale up. I think with suicide at that time we felt it was a kind of 'defeatism', defeatism in the face of the enemy, and that was a cardinal sin, letting the side down, you know. So when there was a verdict of suicide, lots of coroners couldn't resist reading a sermon about moral cowardice. I expect I did.

Quoted in Langley, 1988

Item C No more suicides

Suicide has been officially abolished in the Irish Republic – not because people have stopped taking their own lives, but because coroners are forbidden to say that they did.

A decision by the High Court in Dublin last April means that verdicts of suicide cannot be brought in by coroners. As a result, the Republic has officially had a nil suicide rate since then.

This situation came about when relatives of a person recorded as having committed suicide challenged the coroner's verdict. The law has always prevented coroners from apportioning blame: verdicts on road accident victims, for example, could not say who was to blame.

The High Court ruled that this prohibition extended to suicide: coroners could not blame victims for their own deaths either.

Adapted from *The Guardian*, 4.11.1985

questions

1 Use Items A, B and C to support a phenomenological view.
2 Do you believe there is a 'real', 'objective' suicide rate? Give reasons for your answer.

4 The biography of the deceased – a recent divorce, the death of a close friend or relative, a history of depression, problems at work, financial difficulties, lack of friends are seen as typical reasons for suicide.

The closer the deceased fits this commonsense theory of suicide, the more likely his or her death will be defined as suicide. In Atkinson's words, coroners 'are engaged in analysing features of the deaths and of the biographies of the deceased according to a variety of taken-for-granted assumptions about what constitutes a "typical suicide", "a typical suicide biography", and so on'.

Having uncovered to his satisfaction the meanings used to classify deaths as suicide, Atkinson's research is finished. There are no more questions to ask.

Causation As outlined in a previous section, Durkheim's research on suicide was concerned with causation, in particular with the causes of variations in suicide rates. Phenomenologists see this as a pointless and misguided exercise. Suicides are not objective 'social facts' with causes that can be explained, they are meanings. To try and discover the 'causes' of suicide will simply result in uncovering the meanings used to classify a death as suicide. Thus it comes as no surprise that the 'typical suicide biography' – the friendless, divorced loner – is very similar to Durkheim's socially isolated individual. Suicides, like any other aspect of social reality, are simply constructions of meaning.

Conclusion Phenomenology rejects the entire scientific enterprise as it is normally understood. It is a distortion of social reality to treat it as 'social facts', as 'things'. There are no 'structures' or 'mechanisms' operating in human society. There are no objective facts with causes which can be explained. There are only meanings to be uncovered and understood.

3.4 Two sociologies?

It is sometimes argued that there are 'two sociologies' (Halfpenny, 1984). The first is based on 'scientific methodology', using 'hard' quantitative data and concerned with discovering causal relationships. This approach is sometimes labelled 'positivism'. The second is based on 'interpretivist methodology', using 'soft' qualitative data and concerned with understanding the meanings which make up social reality. This approach is sometimes labelled 'interpretivism', sometimes 'phenomenology'.

Supporting the distinction Some sociologists find this distinction between the two sociologies useful. They claim that there is a tendency for some researchers to adopt a positivist view and see the methods of the natural sciences as the most effective way of acquiring knowledge. And they see a real distinction between this group and those who adopt an interpretivist approach.

Those who support this distinction also claim to detect a tendency for positivists to favour certain research methods, for example survey research based on questionnaires, and certain forms of data, for example quantitative data. On the other hand, those who adopt an interpretivist approach are said to favour methods such as participant observation and unstructured interviews which are seen to produce rich, in-depth qualitative data.

These differences are seen to reflect the aims of the 'two sociologies'. Positivism aims to discover cause and effect relationships. This requires quantitative data so that the strength of relationships between variables can be measured. Interpretivism aims to understand human action. This requires rich, qualitative data in order to discover the meanings which lie behind action.

Opposing the distinction Ray Pawson (1989) rejects this view of the 'two sociologies'. He argues that it gives a false

key terms

Interpretivist sociology A range of theoretical perspectives which emphasise the importance of meanings for understanding human action.

Verstehen A term used by Weber for interpreting motives. Roughly translated it means empathetic understanding – ie, attempting to understand motives by putting yourself in the actor's place.

Comparative method Comparing different societies, and different groups within the same society.

Phenomenology A view which states that phenomena – things or events – must be studied in their own right, not as representing something else. Thus, meanings must be studied as meanings – they have no other reality.

summary

1. Interpretivist perspectives emphasise the importance of meanings for understanding social action.

2. However, there are important differences between interpretivist perspectives. Some look for causal explanations of social action, others seek only to discover the meanings used to construct social reality.

3. Some sociologists make a distinction between two sociologies – positivism and interpretivism. They argue that these sociologies differ in terms of theory and methodology.

4. Other sociologists argue that this distinction is false. They see sociology as far more varied in terms of theory and methodology than the idea of two sociologies suggests.

picture of the relationship between theory, research methods and the actual practice of doing sociology.

Pawson describes the idea of 'two sociologies' as a 'methodological myth'.

In other words, the two sociologies don't exist. Instead, there is a whole range of different views, different assumptions and different methodologies. As previous sections have shown, there are various views of science and its application to the study of human society. And sociologists who are primarily concerned with meanings use a variety of research methods and types of data and often start from different theoretical perspectives. This variety cannot be reduced to 'two sociologies'.

Unit 4 Postmodernist methodology

keyissues

1 How does postmodernism challenge sociological research methodology?

2 What alternatives does it offer?

The challenge

Postmodernists directly challenge the entire basis of research methodology in the social sciences. They reject the whole idea of collecting data to support or reject hypotheses or theories. They question the possibility of making any definite statements about social reality. They reject the idea that there is an objective reality 'out there' waiting to be discovered. They argue that the 'facts' and 'knowledge' that fill sociological research reports and textbooks are nothing of the sort. They are simply sociologists' constructions of reality rather than a valid description and analysis of the social world 'out there'.

The following discussion of postmodernist methodology is largely based on Mats Alvesson's excellent book *Postmodernism and Social Research* (2002).

A postmodernist view of reality

From a postmodernist perspective, any description, analysis, view or picture of the social world is simply one view amongst many. And this applies to sociologists as much as anybody else.

Nothing is certain – everything is tentative, doubtful, indeterminate. Take yourself. In one sense you are one person, in another sense you are lots of people. In one sense you have one identity, in another sense you are made up of multiple identities. In various situations you adopt different identities, see things in different ways, operate with different meanings. What you see or say in one situation may contradict what you see or say in another situation.

This applies both to the sociologist and those who participate in his or her research. Nothing is fixed, everything is fluid; nothing is whole, everything is fragmented; there is no single reality, only multiple realities.

Objectivity and research

Sociologists aim to be objective, to present the social world of those they are studying as it really is, to give us the 'facts'. Many sociologists accept that complete objectivity is an ideal that is unattainable. However, they do their best to get there. And they believe their research reports are a lot better than the view of the person in the street.

From a postmodernist view, research reports are not objective. Instead, they are constructions which are designed to persuade, to give the impression of rational, analytic thinking, and to convince the reader that the researcher's view is 'the truth'. And often, the persuasion works. In the words of Mats Alvesson (2002),

'This is made possible through the skilful denial of any relevance of the pre-structured understanding of the researcher, his or her class, gender, nationality, his or her paradigmatic, theoretical and political preferences and biases, the vocabularies employed, the dynamics of the research process, the expectations and more or less politically skilled operations of the informants, the more or less arbitrary decisions about informants, the selective presentation of evidence and rhetorical tricks and conventions of writing.'

Sociologists are a bit like conjurers. They deceive, they play tricks, they create illusions. For example, they skilfully present an illusion of objectivity where none exists.

Sociological categories

Think of the following terms – culture, subculture, norm, value, social class, ethnicity, social structure, social status, social role. These are all categories used by sociologists to order, organise and make sense of the social world. According to postmodernists, the social world is forced into these categories, wedged into these pigeonholes. In this respect, the social world becomes a construction built by sociologists. In this way, researchers impose their own order and framework on the social world.

From a postmodernist viewpoint, the social world is ambiguous rather than clear-cut, fluid rather than fixed, open rather than closed. It cannot be rammed into fixed, predetermined categories.

Is there any alternative to researchers imposing their reality on the social world? Do they have to make sense of human action by using pre-set categories?

Categories as problematic A starting point is to see all categories as problematic, to be aware that they create order where none may exist, that they impose a particular view of reality, that they structure the social world in a particular way.

Defamiliarisation This offers the possibility of getting away from a sociological construction of the social world. *Defamiliarisation* means looking at the familiar in new and novel ways. Instead of assuming human action is natural, rational, patterned, ordered, the observer should try and see it from other viewpoints – as exotic, random, irrational, contradictory, arbitrary, crazy. For example, look back on your schooldays and family life and try and look at them in a fresh and novel way – for example, as an alien from another planet or somebody from the distant past or future.

Multiple interpretations

Postmodernists are particularly scathing and dismissive of *metanarratives* – literally 'big stories' such as Marxism and functionalism which offer a single explanation, a single perspective on social reality. Metanarratives have their own set of categories, their own vocabulary (or jargon), they are based on particular values, they define the social world in a particular way, and they wrap it all up in a neat, tidy, rigid framework. A metanarrative is a total package into which all social reality can be accommodated.

But if you buy into one metanarrative, that's all you get. All your research will be coloured by it. What you look for, how you interpret it, will be guided by the big story you believe.

From a postmodernist viewpoint, there are multiple, if not infinite, interpretations of the social world. Who is to say which is 'right' or the 'best'?

Where does this take us? Some would say nowhere – what's the point of doing research if it's no better or worse than any other view – for example, no better or worse than the view of the journalist, novelist, comedian, child, grandparent, Christian, Muslim or Jew?

key terms

Defamiliarisation Looking at the familiar in new and novel ways.

Metanarratives Big stories or pictures of how the world works. Grand theories produced by the natural and social sciences.

Multiple interpretations Looking at the social world from different vantage points and in terms of different perspectives.

For some, there is a halfway house. Sociologists should be more humble. They should accept the idea of *multiple interpretations*. They should look at the social world from different vantage points, in terms of different perspectives. And they should allow other voices to be heard in their research publications, particularly the voices of those they are researching.

Evaluation

Much of what postmodernists have to say about sociological methodology is negative. Taken to its extreme, it suggests that sociological research is a waste of time. Worse, it can be seen as an illusion which distorts the social world and deceives the audience.

But have postmodernists got it right? Using their arguments, there's no way of judging whether they're right or wrong. The voice of postmodernism is simply one voice amongst many – neither better nor worse.

Despite this criticism, postmodernism has made sociologists more aware of the problems and pitfalls of research. It has made many researchers more sensitive, more questioning and more humble. Mats Alvesson (2002) presents the following evaluation. Postmodernism 'offers a challenge and an inspiration to revise and make qualitative research more sophisticated and creative. This is not bad, and a strong reason for taking it seriously. But not too seriously.'

summary

1. From a postmodernist perspective, any description or analysis of the social world is simply one view amongst many.
2. As a result, it is not possible to make any definite statements about social reality. Sociological research is not, and cannot be, objective.
3. Researchers impose their own order and framework on the social world by using pre-set categories.
4. Researchers should regard all categories as problematic. And they should defamiliarise themselves from the social world in order to open their eyes to a variety of interpretations.
5. Postmodernists reject metanarratives, arguing they should be replaced by multiple interpretations of the social world.
6. Using their own arguments, there is no way of judging whether postmodernists are right or wrong.
7. Postmodernism has made sociologists more aware of the problems and pitfalls of research. And it has encouraged them to be more creative and innovative.

activity4 postmodernism and research

Item A The research process – a simple version

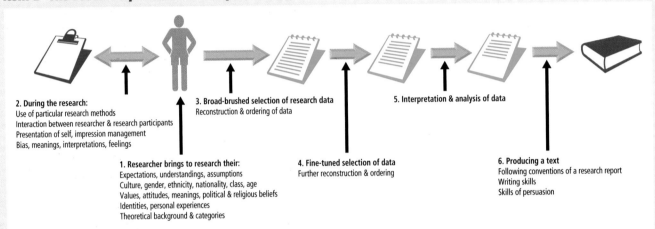

1. Collection of data

2. Production of a wealth of information eg, writing up observations and transcribing interviews

3. Structuring the data, reducing mess

4. Analysis and further reduction of material

6. Creating an order and logic to the report

6. Producing a text

Adapted from Alvesson, 2002

Item B The research process – a complex version

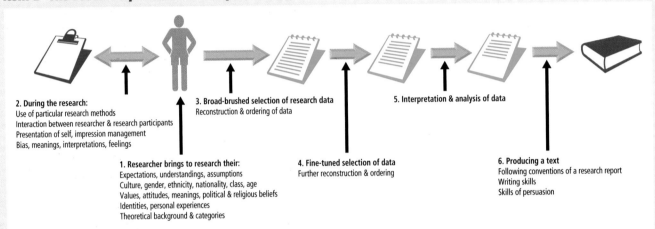

2. During the research:
Use of particular research methods
Interaction between researcher & research participants
Presentation of self, impression management
Bias, meanings, interpretations, feelings

3. Broad-brushed selection of research data
Reconstruction & ordering of data

5. Interpretation & analysis of data

1. Researcher brings to research their:
Expectations, understandings, assumptions
Culture, gender, ethnicity, nationality, class, age
Values, attitudes, meanings, political & religious beliefs
Identities, personal experiences
Theoretical background & categories

4. Fine-tuned selection of data
Further reconstruction & ordering

6. Producing a text
Following conventions of a research report
Writing skills
Skills of persuasion

Adapted from Alvesson, 2002

Item C Body ritual among the Nacirema

The Nacirema spend a large part of the day in ritual activity. The focus of this activity is the human body. The basic belief underlying their rituals is that the human body is ugly and has a natural tendency to debility and disease. Every household has a shrine where the body rituals take place.

The focal point of the shrine is a box or chest which contains many charms and magical potions. Beneath the charm-box is a small font where they perform the daily mouth ceremony. The Nacirema have a horror of and fascination with the mouth. Were it not for the rituals of the mouth, they believe that their teeth would fall out, their gums bleed, their friends desert them and their lovers reject them.

Once or twice a year, the Nacirema seek out a holy-mouth-man. The ceremony involves almost unbelievable ritual torture. The power of the holy-mouth-man is evident from the fact that his clients return year after year, despite the fact that their teeth continue to decay.

Adapted from Miner, 1965

Unit 5 *Feminist methodology*

keyissues

1 What is feminist methodology?

2 What contribution has it made to sociology?

Over the past 30 years 'women's studies' has become a major growth industry. In university bookshops, shelves are stacked with books about women and their place in history and society. And most of these books are written by women.

What does this mean? Clearly it means that women are seen as more important than before. The growth of women's studies can be seen as a reflection of the rise of feminism and changes in perceptions of women's roles in Western society. There is little doubt that social change and the changes in values which accompany it influence choices about what to study. For many feminists, however, the effects of these changes are a lot more fundamental than simply choice of subject matter.

5.1 Feminism – the weak thesis

Ray Pawson (1992) distinguishes between the 'weak thesis' and the 'strong thesis' of feminist methods. In terms of the 'weak thesis', research methods in sociology are essentially sound. The problem is that in practice they are shot through with sexism. The solution is to purge them of sexism. Eichler's *Non-Sexist Research Methods* (1988) is an example of this approach. She identifies major areas of sexism which infuse the research process. These include:

Androcentricity This means viewing the world from a traditional male perspective, with its assumptions of male dominance and superiority – for example – seeing women as passive objects rather than active subjects. As a result, women are largely 'invisible' – in Sheila Rowbotham's (1973) words, they are 'hidden from history'.

Overgeneralisation Many studies deal only with men but present their findings as though they applied to both men and women. For example, until recently social mobility

studies in Britain were based solely on men. Since women's social status was seen to derive from the status of their husbands, there seemed little point in looking at women in their own right. Their class position could be simply 'read off' from the position of their husband.

Research methods

According to Eichler, the sexist assumptions outlined above are found in all aspects of the research process. This can be seen from her examples of questions taken from questionnaires. The first is an example of a sex specific term when talking about people in general.

● If someone wanted to make a speech in your community claiming that Blacks are inferior, should he be allowed to speak or not?

The next question reflects common assumptions about male dominance.

● Is it acceptable for women to hold important political offices in state and national government? Yes/No.

The solution is to reformulate the questions in a non-sexist way.

Eichler's argument suggests reform rather than radical change. Research methods, in and of themselves, are not sexist. Once researchers learn to use them in a non-sexist way, then the problem will be solved.

5.2 Feminism – the strong thesis

The changes advocated by the strong thesis are more fundamental. Something of their flavour is provided by Ann Oakley's article 'Interviewing Women: A Contradiction in Terms' (1981).

Feminist interviewing

Oakley (1981) argues that the standard approach to interviewing has the following characteristics. '(a) its status as a mechanical instrument of data-collection; (b) its function as a specialised form of conversation in which one person asks the questions and another gives the answers; (c) its characterisation of interviewees as essentially passive individuals and (d) its reduction of interviewers to a question asking and rapport-promoting role'.

Oakley sees this approach as clinical, manipulative, exploitive and hierarchical. The interviewer 'uses' the respondent for 'his' purposes, controlling the content and direction of the interview. The relationship is unequal – the interviewer takes and the respondent gives. A feminist methodology would replace this by a non-hierarchical relationship, with the researcher giving as well as receiving. For example, an interviewer must 'be prepared to invest his or her personal identity in the relationship' which means honesty, sincerity, understanding and compassion between equals. It means that both parties have a say in the content and direction of the interview. Only with this personal involvement will 'people come to know each other and admit others into their lives'.

This example argues for a change in research methods – a new type of interviewing – rather than simply cleansing existing methods of sexism. It argues that research techniques are so imbued with male assumptions and practices that they must be radically changed. These changes are not only morally correct, they will also result in better data.

One reaction to Oakley's views is summed up by Ray Pawson's (1992) query, 'What's new?'. There is a long tradition of interviewing which emphasises sensitivity and non-directive approaches. Whether Oakley's views are significantly different from this is questionable.

Gender politics and methodology

Some feminists argue that the 'women's struggle' and feminist methodology are inseparable. 'Malestream' sociology is so saturated with assumptions of male dominance that a feminist alternative is required. Maria Mies (1993) provides an example of this approach. She argues that a feminist methodology must have the following features.

1 **Conscious partiality** The idea of so-called value free research has to be replaced by conscious partiality, which in practice means that female researchers must positively identify with the women they study.

2 **View from below** This replaces the 'view from above', with its assumptions of male dominance, which supports the existing power structure. Researchers must take the 'view from below' because it is more likely to reflect women's experiences and more likely to empower women in their struggle for liberation.

3 **Action research** Rather than being a detached spectator, a dispassionate observer, the researcher should actively participate in the struggle for women's liberation.

4 **Changing the status quo** From this involvement in their own emancipation, both researchers and the women they study will develop a better understanding of their situation. This is based on the idea, 'If you want to

know a thing, you must t change it'. Only by challenging and changing patriarchy will its true nature be revealed.

5 **Raising consciousness** Both researchers and the researched must raise their consciousness – become aware of their oppression. In particular, it is the job of the researcher to give women the means to gain insight into and change their situation.

6 **Individual and social history** Part of the process of raising consciousness requires a study of women's individual and social history. This will allow women to reclaim their history from its appropriation by men.

7 **Collectivising experience** Women must collectivise their experience and join together and cooperate in their struggle for liberation. They must overcome the individualism, competitiveness and careerism which characterise the male world.

In terms of these propositions, Maria Mies is claiming that valid knowledge can only emerge from the struggles waged by the oppressed against their oppressors. The journey to truth involves just the opposite of value freedom. In Mies's case it requires a wholehearted commitment to women's liberation.

Mies's views are not new. Marxists have produced similar arguments for the liberation of the working class, as have African Americans for Black liberation in the USA. Whatever the virtues of this point of view, it is unlikely to offer a recipe for sociology as a whole since there is more to human society than oppressors and oppressed.

5.3 The primacy of experience

A number of feminists have argued that the only way to know something is to experience it. Given this, it is crucial for feminist research to capture the experience of women and to express it as directly as possible with a minimum of reinterpretation on the part of the researcher.

Too often researchers see the experience of others in terms of their own values and preconceptions. In particular, they force this experience into theoretical frameworks and categories which only serve to distort it. This argument was put forcibly by Kaluzynska (1980) when she rejected the whole Marxist debate about domestic labour – whether it was 'productive' or 'non-productive', whether it created 'surplus value', whether it was 'alienating' and so on. She objects to the imposition of concepts which, she argues, distort the experience of housework. In her words, 'Why did we have to get to grips with value theory to appreciate what a drag housework was?'.

There are, however, problems with giving primacy to personal experience. It makes the assumption that if we dig hard enough and deep enough we'll get to the 'real thing' – the direct experience of others. But, as the section on reflexivity indicated, recording the experience of others will always to some degree be coloured by the values and theoretical concepts of the researcher.

5.4 Postmodern feminism

Women as a category

Feminism is not a single perspective. In its early days, things were fairly simple. Women were the oppressed, men were the oppressors, the target was patriarchy, the aim to liberate women. There was a tendency to see women as a single, undifferentiated category. Groups of women objected to this approach – for example, Black women and lesbian women. OK, they were women, but, they argued, their experiences and social situation distinguished them from women in general. As a result, many of the generalisations about women did not apply, or only partly applied, to them.

Postmodern feminism takes this argument a step further. It rejects the standard feminist metanarrative ('grand story') of women as a homogeneous, undifferentiated category, faced with an oppressive patriarchal system. And it even rejects categories which subdivide the category 'women', such as Black women, lesbian women and working-class women. Instead, postmodern feminists emphasise diversity and variation. They argue that researchers should be open to this diversity rather than approaching it with pre-set, preconceived categories.

Evaluation This approach has been criticised by a number of feminists. Breaking down or rejecting the category 'women' prevents the possibility of making generalisations which apply to most or all women. It also blunts the force of feminist protest and threatens the unity of women as a group. Emphasising variation and uniqueness may lead to 'divide and conquer', so serving male dominance (Alvesson, 2002).

The research process

Research as a construct Postmodern feminists favour interpretivist research methods such as participant observation. They are particularly aware that the results of research are a social construct – they are largely constructed by the researcher from fieldnotes which document their observations. This awareness leads them to revisit, reopen and reinterpret their fieldnotes. As Sara Delamont (2003) states,

> 'fieldnotes are not a closed, completed, final text: rather, they are indeterminate, subject to reading, rereading, coding, recording, interpreting, reinterpreting.'

This is in line with the postmodernist view that there are multiple interpretations of any observation.

Multiple voices As outlined in Unit 4, postmodernists argue that researchers should allow the voices of those they research to be heard. Again, in Sara Delamont's (2003) words, this means 'the text will reproduce the actors' own perspectives and experiences. This may include extended biographical and autobiographical accounts, extended dialogues between the researcher and informants, and other "documents of life". Typically, there is an emphasis on the kinds of narratives or stories through which social actors construct their own and others' experiences.'

Reflexity The researcher's own voice should be heard loud and clear, expressing her or his thoughts and feelings about the research. This will be a reflexive voice, reflecting on the research process, the author's interpretations, emotions and relationships with the research participants. This reflects the researcher's awareness that they are a part of the social world they are researching, that the results of their research may say as much, if not more, about them as about the research participants they are studying.

Presenting research Postmodernists' focus on multiple identities and multiple interpretations is reflected in their writing styles. Descriptions of social action and social scenes vary from 'cold' to 'hot', from dispassionate to passionate, from clinical to evocative. There is a mix of styles from poetic to descriptive, from the researcher's words to those of the research participants. The intention is to allow the reader to move through a variety of interpretations and observe from a variety of standpoints (Delamont, 2003).

key terms

Androcentricity A male-centred view of the world which assumes male superiority and dominance.

Overgeneralisation Generalising further than the evidence allows. For example, generalising from a male sample to both males and females.

Conscious partiality Positively identifying with and favouring a particular group.

Multiple voices Many voices. In this case, it refers to the view that many voices should be heard in the research report.

summary

1. There are a number of feminist methodologies.

2. The 'weak thesis' states that androcentricity and overgeneralisation are found in all aspects of the research process.

3. Research methods, in and of themselves, are not sexist. Once researchers learn to use them in a non-sexist way, the problem will be solved.

4. The 'strong thesis' states that feminism requires its own research methods – for example, feminist interviewing.

5. Some feminists see the women's struggle and feminist methodology as inseparable. The feminist researcher should be consciously partial and actively participate in women's liberation.

6. Postmodern feminism rejects pre-set, pre-determined categories. It emphasises diversity and variation.

7. It argues that there are multiple interpretations of any observation and that this should be reflected by multiple voices in research reports.

Conclusion

Sociology used to be a male subject, run by males and concerned with males. Women were largely absent from sociology departments and in a minority among research participants. When sociologists studied workers, they usually studied male workers. When they studied social mobility, it was men who went up and down the class system – women didn't even make it into the supposedly representative sample. And women's concerns and issues were unlikely to be heard and researched.

Thanks in large part to feminists, women now feature in every area of sociology – as workers, members of ethnic minorities, as voters, as students, as mothers and housewives, as participants in the class system and as members of religious organisations. Women are no longer invisible.

The research process has been largely cleansed of sexism. Researchers are increasingly aware that sexism will produce invalid results.

Feminists have been in the forefront of recent developments in methodology. Many have argued that sociology is not, should not and cannot be value free. They have emphasised the importance of capturing the experience of research participants and of expressing that experience directly. They have argued that emotion has an important part to play in the research process. And they have opened up, questioned, and presented alternatives to, established research methodology.

activity5 feminism and methodology

Item A Sexist questionnaires

A study of the lifestyles of adolescent girls and boys included sets of questions about the roles they might identify with (Murdock & Phelps, 1973). Both girls and boys were given a list of roles to choose from, which included 'good pupil', 'rebel', 'good friend' and 'pop fan'. Boys were given a separate list which included 'sports fan' and 'natural leader'. Girls were also given their own list with roles such as 'homemaker' and 'fashion follower'. The girls had no opportunity of choosing from the boys' options and the boys' had no opportunity of choosing from the girls' options.

Adapted from Jones, 1974

Item B Woman-to-woman

Janet Finch describes herself as a feminist sociologist. She conducted two studies based on in-depth interviews in which all the interviewees were women – 1) clergyman's wives and 2) women who used and ran preschool playgroups. She talked to the women in their own homes about marriage, motherhood and childbearing.

She preferred a woman-to-woman discussion in an informal setting 'on both methodological and political grounds'. In her view 1) it works better and 2) it's morally better. Finch found that she gained their trust because she was a woman and because, as a feminist, she treated them as equals. Sharing their gender, both parties shared a subordinate position in society and, as a result, were likely to identify with each other. And, in an equal relationship, the interviewees felt they could talk freely. The women welcomed the interviews and were enthusiastic during the discussions.

As a feminist sociologist, Finch was 'on the side' of the women she studied. In her words, this 'inevitably means an emotional as well as an intellectual commitment to promoting their interests'. Does this bias her research? No more than any other research, since, in her view, 'all social science knowledge is intrinsically political in character'.

Adapted from Finch, 1993

questions

1 a) How can the questions in Item A be seen as sexist?
   b) How might the results of this study simply reproduce traditional gender stereotypes?
2 a) In what ways does Finch's woman-to-woman interviewing style reflect Oakley's 'feminist interviewing'?
   b) What are the advantages of this style of interviewing?

Unit 6 *Sociology, methodology and values*

keyissues

1 Is an objective, value-free sociology possible?
2 Is it desirable?

What we see, the questions we ask and the way we interpret data are influenced by a range of social and personal factors. They include our class, gender, ethnicity, nationality, culture and our personalities, experiences and life histories. These points will now be developed, focusing on the influence of values on social research.

Values are strongly held beliefs about what is right and wrong, what is good and bad, what is worth fighting for and fighting against, what is worth having and not having, who is worthy of respect and support and who is not.

Can the research process in particular and sociology in general be *value free*? And, going one step further, is a value-free sociology desirable?

The founding fathers of sociology believed that an objective, value-free science of society was both possible and desirable. Despite their many differences, not least in terms of personal values, Comte, Marx and Durkheim each believed his work to be uncontaminated by value judgements. Today's sociologists are a lot less certain. A brief look at the debate about values and the study of deviance illustrates this.

6.1 Values and the study of deviance

In an article entitled 'Whose Side Are We On?' the American sociologist Howard Becker (1970) argues that it is impossible to conduct research 'uncontaminated by personal and political sympathies'. Becker's sympathies lie with the underdog, those who have been labelled deviant. He is critical of the agents of social control who, in his eyes, create deviance by selectively applying labels to the poor and powerless (see page 234). Becker argues that not only the research process but the theories which lie behind it – in his case interactionism – are infused with value judgements. From his standpoint 'interactionist theories look (and are) rather left'.

Like Becker, the American sociologist Alvin Gouldner (1975) believes that a value-free sociology is impossible. However, his values are a lot further to the left than Becker's. From his standpoint, Gouldner accuses the interactionists of adopting a 'bland liberal position' (liberalism advocates reform within the existing structure rather than radical social change). A more radical position would lead to a critical examination of the relationship between deviance and the unequal distribution of power in society.

Gouldner pictures Becker and his interactionist

colleagues as White middle-class liberals who 'get their kicks' from a 'titillated attraction to the underdog's exotic difference'. Their sympathies result in no more than mild criticism of the agents of social control. Their bland liberalism prevents a radical critique of the structure of social inequality which creates deviance.

Gouldner argues that values underlie every sociological perspective. And these values influence the way sociologists picture and explain the social world.

Functionalism has often been seen as reflecting a conservative position which advocates the maintenance of the status quo – the way things are. In doing so, it is seen to justify existing social structures. With its view that order, stability and consensus are essential for the smooth running of society and its emphasis on the positive functions of social institutions, it implies that radical change is harmful to society.

Alvin Gouldner (1971) argues that in terms of the logic of functionalism, 'only "evil" – social disorder, tension or conflict – can come from efforts to remove the domination of man by man or make fundamental changes in the character of authority'.

Marxism The values which underlie Marxism are plain for all to see. Marx was committed to socialism. His vision of communism is utopian – a perfect society. He looked forward to an egalitarian society free from the evils of capitalism – free from oppression, exploitation and alienation, with wealth and power shared by all rather than concentrated in the hands of the few. And it is partly in terms of this vision that Marxists see capitalist society. For example, J.C. Kincaid's (1973) solution to poverty states, 'Poverty cannot be abolished in a capitalist society but only in a socialist society under workers' control, in which human needs and not profits determine the allocation of resources'. Marxism replaces the functionalist commitment to the status quo with a commitment to revolutionary change.

6.2 Sociological theory and values

Feminism The previous unit looked at feminist methodology and made the point that most feminist researchers argue that sociology is not, should not, and cannot be value free.

Many feminists wear their hearts and values on their sleeves. They place a high value on gender equality. They regard the present system of patriarchy as unjust and oppressive. They identify with the women they study and seek to empower them in their struggle for liberation. Patriarchy is wrong – the injustices of the system must be spelt out as a first step to overthrowing it.

Feminist research is directed by values which define what is right and wrong and what should be done.

6.3 The question of relativism

If we accept that to some degree value judgements underlie all sociological perspectives, where does this leave the search for 'truth'? Since all perspectives are value based it can be argued that there is no way – apart from our own value judgements – of deciding whether one is superior to another. Some would agree with this argument. They would take a *relativist* position, seeing all knowledge as relative. In terms of this view, there is no such thing as objective knowledge since everything is seen through the lens of our values and culture.

Others argue that just because a perspective is based on values does not necessarily negate its insights and its findings. Taking a relativist view is like dismissing the research findings of Greenpeace and the nuclear industry simply because of the differing values and vested interests of those organisations. And since any view of society can only be partial, differing perspectives in sociology may add breadth to that view. It is this breadth that allows Melvin Tumin (1967) to make the following statement about social stratification. 'The evidence regarding the mixed outcomes of stratification strongly suggests the examination of alternatives. The evidence regarding the possibilities of social growth under conditions of more equal rewarding is such that the exploration of alternatives seems eminently worthwhile.' And here Tumin is referring to evidence produced from a variety of sociological perspectives.

Views of reality

At one extreme, there is the position that objectivity and value freedom are possible. At the other extreme, all knowledge is seen as relative and there is no way of deciding between opposing views of reality. The most radical version of relativism rejects any possibility of objective knowledge, seeing in its place only subjective experience. In this respect, there is no reality outside human perception. What we see is what there is and there is nothing else.

Few, if any, sociologists accept this position – if they did there would be little point in doing sociology. Here is an elegant rejection of relativism by Julia O'Connell Davidson and Derek Layder (1994).

'But the idea that there is no reality separate from the conceptual systems employed by people to grasp it accords quite ludicrous powers to human thought (Trigg, 1989). A tree that falls in a forest falls regardless of whether a person is there to witness and conceptualise the event, children in Somalia die of starvation regardless of whether the governments of the Western world believe that they are providing adequate aid. Many people in Britain and the United States fondly imagine that they live in a meritocratic, post-racist, post-sexist society, but this does not mean that a working-class child or a Black child or a female child is truly blessed with the same chances of obtaining wealth and social power as the middle-class, White, male child. Of course one person's freedom fighter

is another person's terrorist. And of course you can never know with absolute certainty that another person understands what you say in exactly the same way that you understand it. And of course language, concepts and beliefs affect our perception of social reality. But this does not mean that there really is no solid world out there separate from human beings' concepts and beliefs. In practice, as King Canute is purported to have discovered, the object world has a nasty habit of intruding no matter what people may believe about it.'

key terms

Value-free research Research that is free from the values of the researcher. Research that is objective.

Relativism The idea that there can be no objective, value-free knowledge.

summary

1. There is evidence to suggest that values underlie every aspect of the sociological enterprise from the gathering of data to the construction of theories.

2. It can be argued that feminism, functionalism, Marxism and other theories are, at least in part, value based.

3. A relativist position states that an objective, value-free sociology is impossible. Carried to its extreme, this means that there is no way of judging whether research findings are valid or invalid.

4. Many sociologists, while accepting that a value-free sociology is not possible, still retain the ideal of objectivity. This means that research which is rigorous, systematic and reflexive is better than research which is sloppy, unsystematic and uncritical.

activity6 thinking about values

Item A *Taking sides*

To have values or not to have values: the question is always with us. When sociologists undertake to study problems that have relevance to the world we live in, they find themselves caught in a crossfire. Some urge them not to take sides, to be neutral and do research that is technically correct and value free. Others tell them their work is shallow and useless if it does not express a deep commitment to a value position.

This dilemma, which seems so painful to so many, actually does not exist; for one of its horns is imaginary. For it to exist, one would have to assume, as some apparently do, that it is indeed possible to do research that is uncontaminated by personal and political sympathies. I propose to argue that it is not possible and, therefore that the question is not whether we should take sides, since we inevitably will, but rather on whose side we are on.

Adapted from Becker, 1970

Item B *Better ways of conducting research*

Social researchers draw on their everyday knowledge and on their political and moral values in the process of research; they use them to set the research agenda and to design classification systems; they use their social, as well as professional, skills to obtain information; they employ their knowledge as members of society and their political values to analyse and interpret their findings. But accepting this inevitable and indissoluble link between scientific and everyday thinking and between social theories and moral and political values does not make critical investigation impossible. As Geerz (1973, p30) comments in relation to ethnographic and anthropological work:

'I have never been impressed by the argument that, as complete objectivity is impossible ... one might as well let one's sentiments run loose. As Robert Solow has remarked, that is like saying that as a perfectly aseptic (germ free) environment is impossible, one might as well conduct surgery in a sewer.'

Research that is rigorous and reflexive produces knowledge that is more objective than research which is sloppy and uncritical. Researchers who, as well as being technically competent, consider the impact of their own gender, 'racialised' and class identity upon the research process and who understand that research is itself a form of social interaction will produce a more reliable picture of the social world. In short, there are better and worse ways of conducting research.

From O'Connell Davidson & Layder, 1994

Item C *The value of money – a Blackfoot view*

One day White men came into our camp to buy our land for dollar bills and put us on reservations with other Indians.

When the White chief had laid all of his money down on the ground and shown how much he would give all of us for signing a treaty with him, our chief took a handful of clay and made a ball of it and put it on the fire and cooked it. And it did not crack. Then he said to the White chief:

'Now, give me some of your money; we will put the money on the fire and the clay alongside of it, and whichever burns the quickest is the cheapest.'

The White chief said:

'My money will burn the quickest, because it is made of paper; so we can't do that.'

Our chief then reached down into his belt pocket and took out a little buckskin bag of sand, and he handed it to the White chief, and said: 'Give me your money. I will count the money, while you count the grains of sand. Whichever can be counted the quickest will be the cheapest.'

The White chief took the sand and poured it out into the palm of his hand, and as he looked at it, he said:

'I would not live long enough to count this, but you can count the money quickly.'

'Then,' our chief said, 'our land is more valuable than your money. It will last forever. It will not even perish by the flames of fire. As long as the sun shines and the waters flow, this land will be here to give life to men and animals. We cannot sell the lives of men and animals; therefore we cannot sell this land. It was put here for us by the Great Spirit, and we cannot sell it because it does not belong to us. You can count your money and burn it within the nod of a buffalo's head, but only the Great Spirit can count the grains of sand and the blades of grass on these plains. As a present to you, we will give you anything we have that you can take with you; but the land, never.'

From Long Lance, 1956

Blackfoot Indians performing a religious ceremony

Item D King Canute

King Canute ordering the waves to go back

questions

1 Do you agree with Becker's view in Item A? Give reasons for your answer.
2 'There are better and worse ways of conducting research.' Discuss with reference to Item B.
3 It is useful to look at social life from a variety of standpoints and vantage points. Discuss with some reference to Item C.
4 How does the cartoon in Item D support O'Connell Davidson's and Layder's rejection of relativism? (See page 148.)

Unit 7 Sociology and social policy

keyissues

1 What is the relationship between sociology and social policy?

2 To what extent has sociology influenced governments in recent years?

Social policy refers to government policy on a range of social issues – for example, education, the family and poverty. Have sociologists a contribution to make? After all, they study these areas. Should they be consulted by government and join the working parties which shape social policy? Or, should they stand apart from government, criticising social policy and developing alternatives to existing policy?

7.1 The founding fathers

Many of the founding fathers believed that sociology had a central part to play in society – in reforming social institutions, solving social problems and improving the human condition.

Auguste Comte (1798-1857) Comte saw sociology as a practical subject. It shouldn't remain in the universities, it should be applied to the wider society. Comte believed in order and progress – he saw sociology providing the ideas to reinforce social order and direct social progress. In his words, the purpose of sociology is 'to know, in order to predict, in order to control'.

Emile Durkheim (1858-1917) Like Comte, Durkheim focused on the question of order in society. He was concerned with the political upheaval and civil unrest which he believed resulted from industrialisation and a breakdown of value consensus. He saw sociology as providing ways of restoring order and strengthening the integration of society.

Durkheim believed that sociology pointed to a need for a new moral order in industrial society, whereby people would be bound together by a sense of duty and obligation to the community as a whole.

Karl Marx (1818-1883) Where Durkheim saw sociologists working with governments to improve existing societies, Marx looked forward to the overthrow of governments and their replacement with communist societies.

Marx hoped that his work would inspire and direct working-class movements in capitalist societies. However, it was only after his death that his ideas shaped history. For example, Lenin's interpretation of Marxism provided a practical framework for the establishment of a communist state after the Russian Revolution of 1917.

Sociologists today Today's sociologists tend to be a lot less ambitious than the founding fathers. Many feel that sociology can make important contributions to social policy. However, they tend to see these contributions as limited to specific areas such as family policy or education policy. They are unlikely to see sociological ideas or research findings reforming society as a whole, as Durkheim hoped, or spearheading revolutionary change as Marx anticipated.

7.2 Shaping social policy

Before looking in detail at the relationship between sociology and social policy, it is important to have some indication of the factors which shape social policy.

David Donnison, one of the UK's leading experts on poverty, makes the following points about how social policy is shaped.

'As in all debates about important issues of social policy, the questions posed and the concepts used in debates about poverty are shaped partly by changing circumstances and growing knowledge, but also by the changing political agendas of the societies concerned.' (Donnison, 2001)

Changing circumstances Societies change. To some extent social policy is shaped by changes in society. This is illustrated by the following example.

The aftermath of a war often brings changes. People have made great sacrifices, their lives have been disrupted and they are often not prepared to accept their old status – they want something better. This can be seen in the expansion of social services after the First World War (1914-1918) when the then Prime Minister, Lloyd George, promised the troops 'homes fit for heroes'.

During the Second World War (1939-1945) a committee chaired by Sir William Beveridge produced the famous *Beveridge Report on Social Insurance and Allied Services*. Published in 1942, it became an immediate bestseller. Popular support for its principles was widespread both at home and among the troops abroad. Its recommendations appeared to embody the very things being fought for – democracy, freedom and equality.

The Beveridge Report's recommendations were put into effect by a series of Acts from 1944 to 1948. Together they created the modern welfare state in the UK.

Growing knowledge Social policy is also shaped by a growth in knowledge. The following evidence illustrates this point.

During the 19th century, the dominant view of poverty saw it resulting from some form of character defect – the poor lacked moral fibre, they were work-shy, lazy and idle. In other words, the poor were to blame for their poverty (Page, 2001).

In 1899, Seebohm Rowntree conducted a systematic study of poverty in York. In terms of his definition of poverty – insufficient food, fuel and clothing to maintain good health – 28% of York's population were poor. In many cases, there was no evidence of individual blame. In some cases, the breadwinner's wages were simply too low to keep the family out of poverty. And in other cases, people were too old or sick to work.

Research such as this influenced governments. For example, Liberal governments in the early 1900s were increasingly likely to see poverty as a social rather than an individual problem, and as a problem for which the state should accept some responsibility. This view is reflected in their social policies. For example, the 1908 Old Age Pensions Act provided pensions for those over 70. And the 1911 National Insurance Act provided sickness benefit to all manual workers and other workers below a certain income level.

Changing political agendas This is the third major influence on social policy identified by Donnison (2001).

Different political parties have different political agendas which shape their social policies. For example, the Labour Party has traditionally been the main supporter of social welfare policies. And political agendas change. For example, the policies of New Labour in the 2000s are very different from those of Labour of 20 years ago.

To what extent does sociology influence the thinking of political parties in general and their social policies in particular? This is a difficult question to answer. An attempt will be made in Section 7.3 with reference to Tony Blair's Labour governments.

It is probably safe to say that governments listen to sociologists when it suits them and when sociological theories and research findings fit their politics. This can be seen from the Conservative governments of Margaret Thatcher (1979-1990) and John Major (1990-1997). Mrs Thatcher had no time for sociology. However, she was influenced by New Right thinkers who included sociologists like David Marsland in the UK and Charles Murray in the USA.

The New Right blamed the welfare state for creating what they saw as a dependency culture whereby those at the bottom of the class structure became dependent on welfare benefits. As a result, so the argument goes, they lost the will to work, self-reliance, initiative and individual responsibility. The Thatcher and Major governments attempted to end this 'culture of dependency' by reducing welfare benefits and introducing measures such as the Job Seekers' Allowance and the Child Support Agency (Page, 2001).

New questions David Donnison (2001) claims that 'major shifts in policy often come about, not when the old questions are finally answered, but when new questions are asked'. He gives the following example to illustrate this.

For years the question had been: Does the death penalty deter people from killing each other? Researchers researched, politicians debated and the death penalty remained in force. Around 1963, a new question was increasingly heard: Is the death penalty acceptable in a civilised society? And two years later the death penalty was abolished. A new question had led to a new policy.

Does sociology ask new questions which influence government policy? The short answer is sometimes. The following provides an example.

Rowntree's study of poverty in York, discussed earlier, was largely based on the idea of *absolute poverty*. People were defined as poor if they were unable to meet basic needs such as adequate food and shelter. In terms of this concept, it appeared that, by the 1960s, poverty was a small and dwindling problem. Then, two British sociologists, Brian Abel-Smith and Peter Townsend, developed a new concept – *relative poverty* – which led to new questions.

Relative poverty was defined as the inability to afford an acceptable standard of living and a reasonable style of life. The idea of basic needs was extended to include things that most people would see as reasonable – for example, an annual holiday and Christmas presents for the children. In terms of relative poverty, 7.5 million people, that is 14.2% of the population, were now defined as poor – a massive jump from previous estimates (Abel-Smith & Townsend, 1965). Earlier studies had seen the elderly as the largest group in poverty. This now changed to the low paid with dependent children (see Activity 7). And this suggested a change in social policy – direct more resources to the low paid with young children.

From the 1960s onwards, sociologists have used the concept of relative poverty. This concept leads to new questions and new answers. Governments have increasingly seen poverty in relative terms and reflected this view in their policies.

7.3 Sociology, social policy and New Labour

The influence of sociology on government can probably be seen most clearly in Tony Blair's New Labour – both in the general philosophy of the party and in its social policy.

When New Labour came to power in 1997, they offered a 'Third Way' in politics – neither the traditional left-wing policies of 'old' Labour, nor the right-wing policies of the Conservatives. The Third Way sought new directions and new solutions to old and new problems.

Much of this was influenced by one of Britain's leading sociologists, Anthony Giddens, who has been described as Tony Blair's favourite guru. Giddens' *The Third Way: The Renewal of Social Democracy* was published in 1998.

Giddens and the Third Way

In *The Third Way*, Giddens stressed the importance of social solidarity and social cohesion. He argued that a strong society needed active citizens who were concerned not just about their rights but also their duties and obligations to the community.

Giddens called for a renewal of civil society. He saw it as the job of government to promote this renewal. Community-based organisations who have a sense of civic duty should be encouraged. This would strengthen social integration.

Giddens saw *social exclusion* as the main threat to social order and social solidarity. Society would tend to fracture and disintegrate if groups became excluded from the mainstream. For example, if the poor or ethnic minorities were detached from the wider society, they would not feel part of the national community.

What can governments do to prevent social exclusion? In the case of the poor, for example, exclusion can be prevented by raising welfare benefits, improving public services – especially health and education – and providing opportunities to move out of poverty. Without measures such as these, the poor would be excluded from mainstream society and social solidarity would be threatened (Giddens, 1998, 2000; Bennett, 2001).

New Labour and the Third Way

Social Exclusion Unit Giddens's Third Way is reflected in New Labour's social policy. In their first year of government, Labour set up the Social Exclusion Unit to find solutions to the problem of exclusion. The Unit is directly responsible to the Cabinet and it attempts to ensure that all policies – health, education, poverty, crime, urban renewal – are part of a coordinated strategy to deal with social exclusion (MacGregor, 2001).

Poverty Living in poverty means exclusion from many of the activities that most people take for granted. The largest group in poverty are low-paid workers and their dependent children. Labour's policy to reduce poverty has focused on this group. It has introduced the following:

● A minimum wage
● The Working Families Tax Credit to top up the wages of low-paid workers
● A significant increase in Child Benefit allowances
● The National Childcare Strategy which provides money for the development of childcare centres
● The Sure Start programme which provides health and support services for low-income families with children under four (Donnison, 2001; Page, 2002).

Unemployment Labour's New Deal, introduced in 1998, was part of their programme for social inclusion. The New Deal offered education and training for young people between the ages of 18 and 24 who had been out of work for more than six months. It was later extended to older people.

The New Deal provided personal advisors who offered direction and support to the unemployed, guiding them through the various options – academic courses, vocational training, self-employment, or voluntary work.

The New Deal emphasised the duties of citizenship. It was the duty of unemployed people to take up work and training opportunities. If they didn't, their benefits might be withheld until they did.

Education Shortly after their election in 1997, Labour promised to 'overcome economic and social disadvantage and make equality of opportunity a reality' (*Excellence in Schools*, 1997).

The focus was reaching out to the excluded and providing them with opportunities to enter mainstream society. This involved finding new ways of motivating young people in deprived inner-city areas and of improving 'underachieving schools'. For example, Education Action Zones were set up in urban areas which had low levels of educational attainment.

Citizenship Labour has made the teaching of citizenship a compulsory part of the secondary school curriculum. One of the aims is to encourage 'active citizenship' – to develop young people who are public-spirited, who recognise their social responsibilities and who translate this into action in their local communities (Chitty, 2002).

Conclusion There is plenty of evidence here to suggest that sociology has had an important influence on Labour's social policy. However, this is only one perspective in sociology, and to some extent, only one person – Anthony Giddens. Other sociologists are critical of both the perspective and the person. For example, Stuart Hall has criticised *The Third Way* for attempting to smooth over basic contradictions and conflicts in society. And Angela McRobbie accuses both Giddens and New Labour of giving insufficient attention to the situation of women in society (Bennett, 2001).

Conclusion

It is not possible to establish with any certainty the relationship between sociology and social policy. The following points can be made.

- Sociology has some influence on social policy. However, it varies from government to government. As noted earlier, sociology was out of favour during the Conservative governments of Margaret Thatcher and John Major. However, in the person of Anthony Giddens, it has had a significant influence on Tony Blair and New Labour.

- Governments tend to select particular perspectives within sociology when forming social policy. They are rarely influenced by radical perspectives.

- Sociology provides a range of ideas and evidence which can inform social policy. Sociologists often sit on government committees and working parties which develop social policy. Some are employed by pressure groups such as the Low Pay Unit and the Child Poverty Action Group.

- People with a background in sociology are often employed by government departments. For example, the Home Office, which carries out its own research, sometimes employs people with qualifications in sociology.

- Some sociologists see themselves as problem raisers rather than problem solvers. They should be critical, they should identify problems, they should open governments' eyes rather than helping to solve problems which governments have identified and selected as deserving of solution.

- Other sociologists see sociology simply as an academic subject. Their job is to conduct research and present their findings, not to apply their research skills to solving problems defined by government. In fact, standing apart from government is a virtue – it helps sociologists to maintain their independence.

- Sociology is only one of many influences on social policy.

key terms

Social policy Government policy on social issues – for example, education, the family and social inequality.

Absolute poverty The inability to meet basic needs such as adequate food and shelter.

Relative poverty The inability to afford an acceptable standard of living and a reasonable style of life.

Third Way A new direction in politics which differs from traditional left-wing and right-wing policies.

Social exclusion Exclusion from the mainstream of society.

summary

1. Many of the founding fathers believed that sociology had an important part to play in changing society for the better.

2. According to David Donnison, social policy is shaped by a variety of factors. These include:
   - Changing circumstances in society
   - A growth in knowledge
   - Changing political agendas.

3. The influence of sociology on social policy varies from government to government. For example, the Conservative governments of the 1980s and 1990s had no time for sociology. However, Tony Blair's Labour governments were strongly influenced by Anthony Giddens' writings.

4. New Labour's concern with social exclusion reflects Giddens' view that social exclusion is the main threat to social solidarity and social order.

activity7 sociology and social policy

Item A Two views of poverty

Rowntree conducted three studies of poverty in York – in 1899, 1936 and 1950. Based mainly on a concept of absolute poverty, they indicated a steady reduction in poverty. The table compares Rowntree's 1950 study with a study by Abel-Smith and Townsend in 1960 based on a concept of relative poverty.

Percentage of those in poverty Rowntree 1950	Cause of poverty	Percentage of those in poverty Abel-Smith and Townsend 1960
4.2	Inadequate wages and/or large families	40
68.1	Old age	33
6.4	Fatherless families	10
21.3	Sickness	10
0	Unemployment	7
1.5	Percent of sample population in poverty	14.2

(Wages are adequate or not depending on the number of dependent family members who require support.)

Adapted from Coates & Silburn, 1970

Item B Tony Blair on social policy

- 'For too long, the demand for rights from the state was separated from the duties of citizenship and the imperative for mutual responsibility on the part of individuals and institutions.'
- 'A key challenge of progressive politics is to use the state as an enabling force, protecting effective communities and voluntary organisations and encouraging their growth to tackle new needs, in partnership as appropriate.'
- 'Our historic aim will be for ours to be the first generation to end child poverty, and it will take a generation.'
- 'The sight of a rough-sleeper bedding down for the night in a shop doorway or on a park bench is one of the most potent symbols of social exclusion in Britain today.'

Quotations from May et al., 2001

questions

1 Read Item A. How might an acceptance of the idea of relative poverty change government social policy?
2 Judging from the quotes in Item B, what influence has Anthony Giddens had on Tony Blair's social policy?

4 Sociological theory

Introduction

Throughout your sociology course, you have been examining specific topics with the help of sociological theories. You may have considered, for example, functionalist theories of education and the family, or Marxist theories of power and religion. Whilst these theories certainly do have a lot to say about such specific issues, they are in fact much more general theories about the nature of society, individuals, and the relationship between the two. The aim of this chapter is to explore these general theories in more depth, and to evaluate their contribution to our understanding of the nature and development of human societies and the individuals who comprise them.

chaptersummary

▶ **Unit I** outlines the nature of sociological theory and the ways in which sociological theories can be evaluated.

▶ **Unit 2** discusses the origins of sociological theory and the work of three major 19th century theorists.

▶ **Unit 3** examines the establishment of three major

schools of sociological theory which emerged during the first half of the 20th century.

▶ **Unit 4** looks at the ideas of structure and action in sociological theory.

▶ **Unit 5** examines two recent challenges to sociological theory.

Unit 1 What is sociological theory?

keyissues

1 What is sociological theory?
2 How can sociological theories be evaluated?

The topics you have looked at so far have been viewed from a number of differrent perspectives – for example, Marxism, functionalism and symbolic interactionism. These, together with several others, are sociological theories, and they are fundamental to the whole discipline of sociology. Before we go on to examine what the various sociological theories say, it will be helpful to explain what a sociological theory actually is. There are essentially two elements to this – sociological theories as *models* and sociological theories as *propositions*.

1.1 Sociological theories as models

If we try to create a model of something, we attempt to create a *representation* of it. The sorts of models with which most of us are familiar are models of objects such as boats or aircraft. When we make models of such objects,

we attempt to represent their main features in such a way that they are recognisable, without actually building another whole boat or aircraft. Inevitably, when we build such a model, we emphasise some features of the real object at the expense of the others – one model of the Q.E.II might have a particularly realistic passenger deck, whilst another a very realistic funnel. When we see a good model of the Q.E.II, we recognise it as a model of the Q.E.II, but do not mistake it for the real thing. We can also recognise two different models as being equally good models, even though each has different strengths and weaknesses.

Sociologists do something rather similar when they attempt to represent society. In creating models of society they attempt to represent its important features. Just as with building a model ship, some features of society are inevitably emphasised at the expense of others. So, for example, Marxism places particular emphasis on the conflicts in society whilst functionalists tend to emphasise the degree of consensus in society. Neither gives a complete representation of society, but each draws attention to some of its important features.

A difficulty with this view of sociological theories as

models concerns how we can choose between them. Although sociological theories can often be directly compared with features of the society they represent, and judgements made about their accuracy, sometimes this is not the case. Some theories are rather like a hall of mirrors at a seaside resort. A hall of mirrors is a collection of distorting mirrors, some of which make you appear very thin, some very fat and others which grossly distort the proportions of your body. Of course, we know that our bodies are being distorted by these mirrors because we have seen our reflections in ordinary mirrors.

Similarly, sociological theories can function like a hall of mirrors. Each provides a different representation of society. But, since we do not know which mirror gives the true representation, it is very difficult, if not impossible, for us to select the most accurate image. For this reason, choosing between competing sociological theories can be one of the most challenging, but also one of the most interesting, tasks facing the sociologist.

1.2 Sociological theories as propositions

Although it might be difficult to choose which competing sociological theory gives us the best representation of society, it is important that we try to find ways of doing so. If we did not, and simply decided to regard each theory as a different but equally valid representation of society, we would face some serious difficulties.

The idea that competing theories are merely different but equally valid views is often called *relativism*. The chief difficulty with relativism is that it can lead to conclusions which are logically impossible. This is sometimes referred to as the problem of *incoherence*. Consider the following example of a relativist argument: 'the feminist claim that the most fundamental divisions in society are those of gender is a different but equally valid argument as the Marxist claim that the most fundamental divisions in society are those of class'.

The problem is this – the most fundamental divisions in society cannot be *both* those of class and gender. One must be, by definition, more fundamental than the other. We could claim the following: 'divisions of class and gender are equally fundamental'. In so doing, however, we would in fact be contradicting both claims in the original argument, because each insists that one division is more fundamental than the other. This shows us that when we are faced with contradictory theories – theories which cannot both be right – we must reject either one or both of the theories.

The question is, therefore, on what basis should we reject or accept any given sociological theory? To begin to see the answer to this, it is important to notice that sociological theories – like other types of theory – usually contain within them what we might call *propositions*. Essentially, a proposition is any statement which purports to say something which is true. Both of the theories we considered above purported to say something which was

truthful – that gender was the most fundamental division in society and that class was the most fundamental division in society. Both theories therefore contained propositions. There are basically two ways in which we can evaluate propositions.

Logical evaluation The first of these we could call *logical evaluation*. This concerns the internal validity of the argument we are examining. Do the various elements of the theory fit together in a logically coherent way, or do they contradict each other? We have already examined one example of logical evaluation. We saw that to simultaneously accept the different claims of Marxists and feminists about which divisions in society are the most fundamental is simply illogical. It should therefore be rejected before we even begin to examine the available evidence.

Sometimes a theory might be perfectly logical, but contradicted by some piece of evidence. Consider the following example:

All sociologists vote Labour.
Basil is a sociologist.
Therefore, Basil votes Labour.

Logically, the conclusion, 'Therefore Basil votes Labour' follows from the premises of this argument. It may well be, however, that each statement within the argument is untrue – not all sociologists vote Labour and Basil could be an accountant who votes for the Natural Law Party.

Similarly, some or all of the elements of an argument could be perfectly true, but the argument itself is logically flawed. Consider the following:

The first professor of sociology was French.
Durkheim was the first professor of sociology.
Therefore Durkheim wrote a book called Suicide.

Each one of these statements is perfectly true, but taken together the conclusion simply does not follow from what went before. In fact, logically, this 'argument' is nonsense, even though each of its elements is perfectly true.

These examples show us is that it is just as important to pay attention to the form of an argument as it is to the truth of its various elements. Clearly, however, the logical validity of any particular sociological argument is not the only criterion by which it should be evaluated.

Empirical evaluation As well as a theory's logical validity, we should also be concerned about the truth of the specific propositions it contains. If we cannot accept on logical grounds the argument that Marxism and feminism present equally valid views of which are the most fundamental social divisions, then we are still left with the need to decide which divisions are in fact most fundamental. Somewhat obviously, we need to do this by comparing the various claims being made with the social reality they are purporting to describe. This task we can call *empirical evaluation*.

As you will have seen in the chapter on methodology, sociologists have devised many ingenious methods of gathering data about social phenomena. Let us take just one to illustrate the example we are considering. Imagine we decide to try to settle the dispute between Marxists and feminists by conducting a series of interviews with a carefully selected sample of individuals. Imagine we ask working-class women which group they feel they have most in common with – working-class men, or upper-class women. If the majority choose upper-class women, then we might conclude that the feminist theory is the most accurate, in that gender is being identified by the respondents as the most important variable. If the majority choose the working-class men, then we would perhaps conclude that the Marxist point of view is the most accurate, since class has been identified as the most important variable.

Whilst at first sight this appears to be a straightforward way of settling disputes between theories, there is in fact a serious problem with it. Marxists, faced with the evidence that most people regard gender as the most important division in society, could easily argue that this result has arisen from the false consciousness of the respondents. In other words, those people interviewed falsely believed gender to be most important because such a belief serves the interests of the capitalist ruling class. Marxists might therefore argue that in reality it is class which is most important, even though people do not generally recognise this.

This last example illustrates a very important point about the relationship between sociological theories and empirical evidence. Whilst theories certainly make statements about the real world which they claim to be true, they also often contain their own standards by which these statements should be evaluated. In other words, some piece of empirical evidence might be accepted as valid by supporters of one theory, but not by supporters of another. What this means is that sociological theories cannot always be straightforwardly tested by obtaining empirical evidence, as the validity and relevance of this evidence may always be challenged by supporters of the theory in question.

We have tried in this section to show that sociological theories need to be evaluated both logically and empirically, but that the latter may not always be straightforward because there exists a complex relationship between theories and empirical evidence. We now turn to a consideration of the origins of sociological theory in the ideas of the Enlightenment, and the writings of Karl Marx, Emile Durkheim and Max Weber.

key terms

Model A representation of something.
Proposition A statement which claims to be true.
Relativism In this context, the view that theories are different but equally valid.
Logical evaluation Evaluating a theory to see if its logic is sound. For example, do its propositions contradict each other?
Empirical evaluation Evaluating a theory in terms of evidence. For example, does the evidence support the theory?
False consciousness A false or distorted view of the world.

activity1 life of Galileo

Brecht wrote *Life of Galileo* in 1938. Galileo was a 17th century scientist whose discoveries challenged the Ptolemaic model of the universe which placed the earth at the centre of the universe, a view supported by the Church. Galileo's discoveries also challenged the ideas of the ancient Greek philosopher Aristotle which were still influential. In this extract from Scene 4, Galileo is trying to persuade court scholars of the significance of his discoveries.

GALILEO *at the telescope:* As your highness no doubt realises, we astronomers have been running into great difficulties in our calculations for some while. We have been using a very ancient system which is apparently consistent with our philosophy but not, alas, with the facts. Would you gentlemen care to start by observing these satellites of Jupiter, the Medician stars?

ANDREA (the housekeeper's son) *indicating the stool by the telescope:* Kindly sit here.

PHILOSOPHER: Thank you, my boy. I fear things are not quite so simple. Mr Galileo, before turning to your famous tube, I wonder if we might have the pleasure of a disputation?

Galileo displays his telescope to Florentine nobles.

Its subject to be: Can such planets exist?

MATHEMATICIAN: A formal dispute.

GALILEO: I was thinking you could just look through the telescope and convince yourselves?

ANDREA: This way, please.

MATHEMATICIAN: Of course, of course. I take it you are

familiar with the opinion of the ancients that there can be no stars which turn round centres other than the earth, nor any which lack support in the sky?

GALILEO: I am.

PHILOSOPHER: Moreover, quite apart from the very possibility of such stars, which our mathematicians – he turns towards the mathematician – would appear to doubt, I would like in all humility to pose the philosophical question: are such stars necessary? The universe of the divine Aristotle, with the mystical music of its spheres and its crystal vaults, the orbits of its heavenly bodies, the slanting angle of the sun's course, the secrets of the moon tables, the starry richness catalogued in the southern hemisphere and the transparent structure of the celestial globe add up to an edifice of such exquisite proportions that we should think twice before disrupting its harmony.

GALILEO: How about your highness now taking a look at his impossible and unnecessary stars through this telescope?

MATHEMATICIAN: One might be tempted to answer that, if your tube shows something which cannot be there, it cannot be an entirely reliable tube, wouldn't you say?

GALILEO: What d'you mean by that?

MATHEMATICIAN: It would be rather more appropriate, Mr Galileo, if you were to name your reasons for assuming that there could be free-floating stars moving about in the highest sphere of the unalterable heavens.

PHILOSOPHER: Your reasons, Mr Galileo, your reasons.

GALILEO: My reasons! When a single glance at the stars themselves and my own notes makes the phenomenon evident? Sir, your disputation is becoming absurd.

MATHEMATICIAN: If one could be sure of not over-exciting you, one might say that what is in your tube and what is in the skies is not necessarily the same thing.

PHILOSOPHER: That couldn't be more courteously put.

FEDERZONI: They think we painted the Medicean stars on the lens.

GALILEO: Are you saying I'm a fraud?

PHILOSOPHER: How could we? In his highness's presence too.

MATHEMATICIAN: Let's not beat about the bush. Sooner or later Mr Galileo will have to reconcile himself to the facts. Those Jupiter satellites of his would penetrate the crystal spheres. It is as simple as that.

FEDERZONI: You'll be surprised: the crystal spheres don't exist.

PHILOSOPHER: Any textbook will tell you that they do, my good man.

FEDERZONI: Right, then let's have new textbooks.

PHILOSOPHER: Your highness, my distinguished colleague and I are supported by none less than the divine Aristotle himself.

GALILEO almost obsequiously: Gentlemen, to believe in the authority of Aristotle is one thing, tangible facts are another. You are saying that according to Aristotle there are crystal spheres up there, so certain motions just cannot take place because the stars would penetrate them. But suppose those motions could be established? Mightn't that suggest to you that those crystal spheres don't exist? Gentlemen, in all humility I ask you to go by the evidence of your eyes.

MATHEMATICIAN: My dear Galileo, I may strike you as very old-fashioned, but I'm in the habit of reading Aristotle now and again, and there, I can assure you, I trust the evidence of my eyes.

GALILEO: I am used to seeing the gentlemen of the various faculties shutting their eyes to every fact and pretending that nothing has happened. I produce my observations and everyone laughs. I offer my telescope so they can see for themselves, and everyone quotes Aristotle.

FEDERZONI: The fellow has no telescope.

MATHEMATICIAN: That's just it.

PHILOSOPHER grandly: If Aristotle is going to be dragged in the mud – that's to say an authority recognised not only by every classical scientist but also by the chief fathers of the church – then any prolonging of this discussion is in my view a waste of time.

Adapted from B. Brecht, *Life of Galileo*, 1980

questions

1 a) What reasons does Galileo give for believing his model of the universe?

   b) What reasons do the court scholars give for rejecting this model?

2 When sociologists evaluate theories are they likely to draw upon the type of evidence Galileo uses or the type of evidence the court scholars use? Give reasons for your answer.

summary

1. There are two essential elements to sociological theories – models and propositions.

2. Theories can be evaluated in two ways – logical evaluation and empirical evaluation.

3. These types of evaluation are necessary to avoid relativism.

Without them, it is not possible to decide between competing theories.

4. Empirical evaluation is problematic because people may have a false consciousness. As a result, evidence based on their statements may not be valid.

Unit 2 *Classical sociology and the advent of modernity*

keyissues

1 What are the origins of sociological theory?

2 How significant is the work of Marx, Durkheim and Weber to the development of sociological theory?

Modernity Sociology, as a distinct form of enquiry, emerged in the 19th century in the wake of 'the so-called "twin revolutions" – the Industrial Revolution of England (and later elsewhere) which occurred roughly between 1780 and 1840 and the Democratic Revolutions of the United States of America in 1776 and France in 1789' (Lee & Newby, 1983). These revolutions signalled a radical transformation in society and the advent of *modernity*. Although the early sociologists characterised the transformation in different ways, they recognised that the modern world – which they saw emerging in their lifetimes – represented a significant break from the past.

There is now widespread agreement over the major features of modernity. They can be grouped under three headings – the economic, the political, and the cultural. Economically, modernity involves the dominance of industrial capitalism; politically, it involves the consolidation of the nation state and, typically, liberal democracy; culturally it involves a stress on reason as opposed to tradition (Jones, 1993).

Responses to modernity The dramatic changes which occurred in North America and Northern Europe in the second half of the 18th century and the first half of the 19th century generated very different political responses. For liberals, the changes were welcome. Individuals are naturally rational and should be free to pursue their own interests. The removal of traditional restraints and the emergence of governments which guaranteed the rights of individuals were therefore seen as progressive developments. For socialists, the changes were not unwelcome, but were seen as not going far enough. Human beings are naturally communal and their interests can, therefore, only be met collectively. This necessitates the replacement of capitalism, which divides people, by socialism which enables people to cooperate. In contrast to these two optimistic responses to social change, conservatives exhibited horror. Human beings are naturally members of a social organism – unequal but dependent on each other. The revolutions, in their disregard for tradition and their rupture of the natural order, were seen as dangerous developments.

Liberalism, socialism and conservatism have all influenced the development of sociology. Much 19th century sociology took up the conservative concern with the threat to social order and much subsequent sociology

has involved a debate with the ghost of Marx, exhibiting in the process the influence of socialism (Zeitlin, 1971). Liberalism, however, was the most significant in the emergence of sociology as a distinct form of enquiry, because this was the dominant political philosophy of the Enlightenment.

2.1 The Enlightenment

The Enlightenment refers to 'a period in European intellectual history which spans the time from roughly the first quarter to the last quarter of the 18th century. Geographically centred in France, but with important outposts in most of the major European states, the "Enlightenment" is composed of the ideas and writings of a fairly heterogeneous group, who are often called by their French name philosophes' (Hamilton, 1992).

Whatever differences there were between the philosophes, they recognised that they were engaged on a common project. This is evident in their cooperative enterprise – the publication over twenty years of the *Encyclopédie*. This work reflected two shared principles – confidence in the ability of human reason to provide an understanding of the world, and faith in the ability of human beings to use this understanding to improve the world.

The radical nature of these two principles should not be underestimated. They constituted a direct challenge to the traditional conception of the world propagated by the Roman Church. Reason was no longer seen as subservient to divine revelation as interpreted through the teachings of the Roman Church. And history was no longer seen as 'synonymous with God working his purpose out' (Smart, 1992). Instead, stress was placed on the power of human reason to create knowledge, which in turn can be used to improve the human condition. In the process, the Enlightenment brought about a cultural change in what constitutes knowledge and what the purpose of knowledge is. A distinctly modern conception of knowledge was born.

The Enlightenment philosophes systematically developed and popularised among influential members of society ideas which had been originally formulated in an earlier era. Scientific discoveries in the 16th and 17th centuries challenged the traditional religious world view which placed the earth at the centre of the universe. The problem of deciding what constituted the truth was therefore raised in an acute form. Philosophers in the 17th century grappled with this question and came up with two broad answers.

For the *rationalists*, true knowledge was logically deduced from a few basic premises which could not be doubted. Descartes, for example, concluded that however much he doubted, he could be sure of one thing, 'cogito ergo sum' (I think therefore I am). This constituted for him a firm foundation for knowledge. For the *empiricists*, true knowledge was induced from, that is derived from observations. Berkeley, for example, concluded that 'esse est percipi' (to exist is to be perceived). This constituted for him a firm foundation for knowledge.

Although the rationalists and empiricists (and indeed many of the Enlightenment philosophes) continued to believe in a God, the basis of knowledge was no longer seen as the word of God (as interpreted through the Church) but reason or sensory observation. What the Enlightenment philosophes did was to synthesise these two traditions. 'An understanding or knowledge of natural and social reality was deemed to depend upon a unity of reason and observation, made possible by the practice of scientific methods of inquiry' (Smart, 1992).

Indeed, when 18th century writers talk of the power of human reason they 'meant the scientific method: the deductive reasoning of the mathematical sciences and the inductive, empirical reasoning of the sciences of nature' (Dunthorne, 1991).

The 17th century also witnessed a dispute between the 'ancients' and the 'moderns' over the respective merits of the works of classical antiquity and the more recent thinking of an emerging modern Europe. The view of the 'moderns' that knowledge had grown over time eventually gained ascendancy and paved the way for the Enlightenment to argue that there existed a more general process of social development and that knowledge could be used to promote further progress.

The Enlightenment belief that science was a force for enlightenment and progress generated tremendous optimism. The success of the natural sciences encouraged a belief 'that in the struggle of man against nature the balance of power was shifting in favour of man' (Gay, 1973). Science would enable human beings to gain mastery over nature. And the application of the scientific method to social arrangements would justify the reform of social institutions. In both cases, the result would be the enhancement of human freedom.

The emergence of a sociological perspective can be detected in the Enlightenment. 'For the first time, man could "dare to know" about the social arrangements under which he lived, rather than have them presented to him through the obscuring haze of a religious ideology. By knowing about these social arrangements, their operation would become clear, and thus open to change' (Hamilton, 1992). The philosophes tended not to have a clearly worked out model of society, however. Wedded to the notion that individuals are essentially rational and self sufficient, society was seen as a collection of individuals. It was therefore left to later writers in the 19th century to develop more coherent models of society and to give birth to sociology as a distinct form of enquiry. What is significant is that these writers built on the cultural change which the Enlightenment brought in ways of thinking about society. It is to the work of the three who above all others have established the principal frames of reference of modern sociology – Marx, Durkheim and Weber – that we now turn.

key terms

Rationalists They believed that true knowledge was logically deduced from a few basic premises or statements which were clearly true.

Empiricists They believed that true knowledge was derived from observations – from empirical evidence that could be directly observed.

activity2 the individual and society

Item A A medieval model of the individual and society

Society, like the human body, is an organism composed of different members. Each member has its own function - prayer or defence or merchandise or tilling the soil. Each must receive a means suited to its station and must claim no more. Within classes there must be equality. If one takes into his hand the living of two, his neighbour will go short. Between classes there must be inequality, or otherwise a class cannot perform its function or enjoy its rights.

Adapted from Tawney, 1936

Item B The view of a sixteenth century writer

God made all the parts of the body for the soul and with the soul to serve him and all the subjects in the kingdom to serve their King and with their King to serve him. If the head of the body ache, will not the heart be greatly grieved and every part feel his part of the pain of it. And if a King in his world be displeased then the heart of his kingdom (the hearts of his subjects) will have a feeling of it.

Nicholas Bretton, a 16th century writer

Item C The rise of individualism

The transformations which ushered in modernity tore the individual free from their stable moorings in traditions and structures. Since these were believed to be divinely ordained, they were held not to be subject to fundamental change. One's status, rank and position in the 'great chain of being' - the secular and divine order of things - overshadowed any sense that one was a sovereign individual. The birth of the 'sovereign individual' represented a significant break with the past.

The sovereign individual – the idea that the individual is the centre of the universe, that all things can be traced back to the individual, that the individual sets things in motion, makes the world go round and is the motor of social action and change – was a new idea which only gradually emerged.

Many major movements in Western thought and culture contributed to the emergence of this new conception: the Reformation and Protestantism, which set the individual conscience free from the religious institutions of the Church and exposed it directly to the eye of God; Renaissance humanism, which placed Man at the centre of the universe; the scientific revolutions, which endowed Man with the faculty and capacities to inquire into, investigate and unravel the mysteries of Nature; and the Enlightenment, centred on the image of rational, scientific Man, freed from dogma and intolerance, before whom the whole of human history was laid out for understanding and mastery.

Adapted from Hall, 1992

Item D An Enlightenment model of the individual and society

Man was born free, and he is everywhere in chains. Those who think themselves the masters of others are indeed greater slaves than they. How did this transformation come about? I do not know. How can it be made legitimate? That question I believe I can answer. . . . The social order is a sacred right which serves as a basis for all other rights. And as it is not a natural right, it must be one founded on covenants – binding agreements. The problem is to determine what those covenants are.

'How to find a form of association which will defend the person and goods of each member with the collective force of all, and under which each individual, while uniting himself with the others, obeys no one but himself, and remains as free as before?' This is the fundamental problem to which the social contract holds the solution.

Whichever way we look at it, we always return to the same conclusion: namely that the social pact establishes equality among the citizens in that they all pledge themselves under the same conditions and must all enjoy the same rights.

From J. Rousseau *The Social Contract* quoted in D. Held et al ., 1983

Item E Sir Isaac Newton

William Blake's painting (dated 1795) of the scientist Sir Isaac Newton. Blake portrays him as a godlike figure drawing on a chart beside his underwater grotto.

questions

1 Read Items A and B. How do they portray the relation between the individual and society?

2 Read Item C. How does the relation between the individual and society change with the rise of modernity?

3 Read Item D. How does this Enlightenment model of society differ from that presented in Items A and B?

4 Briefly comment on the painting of Sir Isaac Newton in the light of Items A to D.

2.2 Karl Marx (1818-1883)

Marx did not see himself as a sociologist, but his ideas have been extremely influential within sociology and have in fact formed the basis for a distinct sociological perspective. This perspective is characterised by three central features. First, the starting point for analysing society should always be the material conditions of production – the way people organise the production of goods and services. Second, the motor of social change is class conflict and it is such conflict which propels society forward from one production system to another. Third, the conditions which will enable the working class to replace the modern oppressive productive system by a classless system can be scientifically identified. Marx's support for a scientific approach and his view that this approach can help society to progress indicate his debt to the Enlightenment.

The materialist conception of history

For Marx, the first priority of human beings is to ensure physical survival by producing the means of subsistence. Unless the provision of food and shelter is met, no other activity is possible. Hence, according to Marx, the way society organises its production is the most fundamental aspect of human existence and it is from this that all other aspects of human activity develop. Thus ideas, which other writers such as Hegel had seen as fundamental for social life, are ultimately dependent upon the way people organise the production of their means of subsistence.

The economic base and social superstructure

In developing his materialist conception of history, Marx distinguished between the *base* and *superstructure* of society. The base consists of the *forces of production* (the tools and machinery, the knowledge and the raw materials which people use in order to produce goods and services) and the *relations of production* (the social relationships between people involved in the production process).

Those parts of the forces of production which can be legally owned, for example land in feudal society and factories in capitalist society, are known as the *means of production*.

Together, the forces and relations of production define the way a society organises its production of goods or services, or *mode of production*. The economic base or dominant mode of production is the bedrock of society and all other social institutions and processes develop from it and are ultimately dependent upon it. As Marx put it, the economic base is 'the real foundation on which legal and political superstructures arise and to which definite forms of social consciousness correspond. The mode of production of material life determines the general character of the social, political and spiritual processes of life' (Bottomore & Rubel, 1961).

Let us take an example of one mode of production, feudalism. In societies where this was the dominant mode of production, land was the chief means of production so that ownership of land put the lords in a position of dominance over the serfs who had to work the land in order to survive. Since the serfs did not own the land, they were forced to hand over a proportion of what they produced as tithes to the lords. The rest of the social structure reflected the economic subordination of the serfs to the lords. The legal system obliged serfs to provide military service for their lords and the church justified their exploitation.

Class and social change

Marx was less concerned to offer a description of any particular mode of production than to put forward an account of how it changes and is eventually replaced by another. He distinguished four main modes of production which have succeeded each other. In chronological order they are primitive communism, ancient society, feudalism and capitalism. Apart from primitive communism where people only produce enough to subsist and there is no surplus for a particular group to appropriate, each mode of production is characterised by a particular set of class relations.

Those who own the means of production exploit the labour of those who do not own the means of production. In ancient society masters exploited the labour of slaves whom they owned; in feudal society the lords exploited the labour of serfs who were tied to the land; and in capitalist society the bourgeoisie exploit the labour power of the proletariat who are forced to work for them in order to survive. In each case exploitation leads to class conflict and the eventual replacement of each mode of production.

Class conflict leads to the overthrow of a mode of production because of underlying contradictions which develop within the mode of production between the forces of production and relations of production. The forces of production develop as people discover new ways of mastering nature and generating wealth. There comes a point, however, when their full potential is held back by the existing relations of production. It is then that the conditions are conducive for the class who own the new means of production to rise up and overthrow the old mode of production.

This process can be illustrated by the transition from feudalism to capitalism. Within feudalism, the discovery of new sources of power, such as steam, allowed human beings to master nature more effectively. For this potential to be realised, however, it was essential that people were no longer tied to the land but free to work for those who owned the new sources of power. These were the conditions which encouraged the bourgeoisie to unite and overthrow the feudal relations of production and establish a new mode of production. In Marx's words, 'With the change of the economic foundation the entire immense superstructure is more or less rapidly transformed' (Bottomore & Rubel 1961). Thus the bourgeoisie oust the feudal aristocracy from political power and the culture is transformed as concepts such as freedom replace the dominant concepts of feudalism such as loyalty. The resolution of old contradictions, however, does not mean an end to contradictions. Contradictions develop within the new mode of production – the contradictions of capitalism will eventually lead to its replacement by communism.

The transition from capitalism to communism

Marx's primary concern was to analyse capitalism and identify the conditions which will bring about its downfall. Capitalism can be defined in terms of two interrelated features: a) the production of goods and services is primarily geared to the search for profits which accrue to those people who own the means of production and b) the process is organised in terms of a market in which commodities, including labour power itself, are bought and sold. As a consequence, capitalism is characterised by two classes – those who own the means of production (the bourgeoisie) and those who do not own the means of production (the proletariat) who are therefore forced to sell their labour power and work for the bourgeoisie.

The relation between these classes is, on the surface, less exploitive than in a feudal society in which people were obliged, for example, to hand over a definite amount of produce to the lord of the manor or to work unpaid on the lord's land. In a capitalist society, workers hire out their energies and skills, in order to produce the goods and services which are eventually sold on the market, in exchange for wages. The exchange, however, is not a fair one. The wages invariably represent less in terms of value than the value realised through the sale of the products of proletarian labour and the difference between the two, which Marx called *surplus value,* is appropriated by the bourgeoisie as profit. For Marx, the relation between the bourgeoisie and proletariat is clearly one of exploitation, and has, as a consequence, the increasing *alienation* of the proletariat.

Alienation 'In what does this alienation consist?' Marx asked. 'First, that the work is external to the worker, that it is not a part of his nature, that consequently he does not fulfil himself in his work but denies himself, has a feeling of misery, not of wellbeing, does not develop freely a physical and mental energy, but is physically exhausted and mentally debased. The worker, therefore, feels himself at home during his leisure, whereas at work he feels homeless. His work is not voluntary but imposed, forced labour. It is not the satisfaction of a need, but only a means for satisfying other needs. Its alien character is clearly shown by the fact that as soon as there is no physical or other compulsion, it is avoided like the plague. Finally, the alienated character of work for the worker appears in the fact that it is not his work but work for someone else, that in work he does not belong to himself but to another person' (Bottomore & Rubel, 1961).

Crisis and contradiction As capitalism develops, Marx argued, so the conditions for its downfall and replacement become more apparent. Driven by the need to maintain the rate of profit, the bourgeoisie adopts increasingly sophisticated technology, thus creating the possibility for the population as a whole to enjoy a high standard of living and for its members to fulfil themselves. Such an outcome is, however, not possible so long as the bourgeoisie continues to appropriate surplus value for itself. In Marx's terms, the relations of production in a capitalist society prevent the promise of shared material abundance, which the developing forces of production point to, from being fully realised. What is more, the existence of a fundamental imbalance between production and consumption results in periodic crises when the market is unable to absorb all the goods and services which have been produced.

The bourgeoisie, of course, responds to such crises by seeking new markets around the world, thus encouraging

in the process European colonial expansion. Economic crises, however, recur and invariably result in bankruptcies. In order to counteract these tendencies to overproduction, capital becomes more concentrated, thus making it increasingly possible for production to be centrally coordinated and orientated to people's needs. However, such an outcome is again not possible so long as the bourgeoisie compete with each other to make profits. For these possibilities to be realised, the revolutionary action of the proletariat is needed.

Class polarisation At first the proletariat's resistance to bourgeois domination is only sporadic. Members are not united but struggle among each other as well as against the bourgeoisie. Over time, however, a combination of circumstances promotes the *class consciousness* of the proletariat. The development of capitalism tends to mean the demise of classes characteristic of the former pre-industrial society – landowners and serfs – and therefore the emergence of a more simplified class structure as the last vestiges of the previous class structure disappear. The existence of a particularly vulnerable and unorganised sector of the labour force, which can be tapped during a boom but disposed of during a slump, described by Marx as 'a reserve army of labour,' tends to mean that wages remain around subsistence levels. As a resut, the relative disparity in wealth between the bourgeoisie and proletariat increases. The introduction of machinery tends to mean the erosion of traditional craft skills and the elimination of skill divisions within the proletariat.

In short, a process of class polarisation occurs, in which the proletariat, less divided and subject to increasing relative poverty, face a clearly distinct bourgeoisie. As they live through the economic crises of capitalism with their attendant increases in unemployment and decreases in wages and as they work concentrated together in large factories, so members of the proletariat communicate to each other their increasing dissatisfaction with bourgeois exploitation. They organise themselves to begin with on a local level, and later on a national level, to improve their wages and conditions until, finally, they are strong enough to oust the bourgeoisie and set up a new society. In the process, they transform themselves from a mere category of people who happen to share the same conditions, to a group of people who, realising they share the same conditions, organise to change them. In Marx's terms, they make the transition from a *class in itself* to a *class for itself.*

Revolutionary change The bourgeoisie of course does attempt to prevent the proletariat from making this transition from a class in itself to a class for itself. Although its power rests ultimately on ownership of the means of production, such economic dominance is translated into political dominance with the result that the bourgeoisie becomes a ruling class. The state, considered by Marx to be 'the executive committee for managing the common affairs of the whole bourgeoisie' represents the interests of the class as a whole, managing its common affairs in two major ways. The first relies on its control of the means of coercion and involves being repressive. Examples here include legislation inhibiting the formation of trade unions and the use of the army to quash strikes. The second depends on the dissemination of beliefs and values throughout society and involves propagating ideologies which purport to show the justice and necessity of bourgeois domination. Particularly because, as Marx put it, 'the ideas of the ruling class are, in every age, the ruling ideas: ie the class which is the dominant material force in society is at the same time its dominant intellectual force' (Bottomore & Rubel, 1961). As a result, the development of class consciousness may be delayed.

Ultimately, Marx argued, the proletariat will see through the fog of bourgeois ideology and become revolutionary. For the revolution is inevitable. Marx went even further claiming that the proletarian revolution will be unique. Whereas past revolutions have been made by a minority for the benefit of a minority, the proletariat's revolution will be made by the majority for the benefit of the majority. This will enable a classless society to be formed in which the ideals put forward during the French Revolution will be fully realised – freedom will replace oppression; fulfilment alienation; equality inequality; fraternity self-interest. Such a society Marx called *communism*.

Evaluation

Economic determinism While it is indisputable that Marx saw economic factors as crucial in any analysis of society, it is unlikely that he ever believed, as some argue, that all social development is caused by economic changes. His famous statement 'Men make history but not under circumstances of their own choosing' suggests rather that Marx believed human beings can have an influence on the outcome of events, but that this freedom of action is constrained by the limits set by the development of the economy. Whether Marx placed an undue emphasis on economic factors still remains a contentious issue, however.

Social change The opening line of the *Communist Manifesto*, written by Marx and Engels, states that 'the history of hitherto existing society is the history of class struggle'. This suggestion that history has an overall direction and that it is governed by a dynamic principle – the class struggle – is questioned by many contemporary sociologists. What's more, there is some dispute as to whether it's possible to talk of class divisions prior to the advent of capitalism. And whether other social divisions in modern societies are at least as significant as class.

The transition to communism Capitalist societies have not developed in the direction Marx anticipated. Although the 20th century has witnessed the establishment of communist states following revolutions, these have occurred in non-capitalist societies and have failed to fulfil Marx's vision of freedom and equality. What's more, the collapse of communist regions in Eastern Europe since 1989 has led some commentators to argue that Marx's ideas are no longer relevant. Needless to say, Marxists believe that they can explain why capitalist societies have remained resistant to revolution, why communist regimes have collapsed, and why Marx's ideas remain as significant today as they ever were.

key terms

Forces of production The tools, machinery, raw materials and knowledge used to produce goods and services.

Relations of production The social relationships between people involved in the production process – for example, the relationships between employers and employees.

Means of production Those parts of the forces of production that can be legally owned – for example, factories in capitalist society.

Mode of production The forces and relations of production – the economic base of society. The way a society organises its production of goods and services.

Superstructure All other aspects of society – for example, the political and legal systems.

Class conflict The conflict of interest between the two major classes in society – those who own the means of production and those who do not.

Surplus value The difference between the costs of labour and the wealth received from that labour by those who own the means of production. In capitalist society, surplus value is the profits received by the bourgeoisie.

Alienation An alienated worker is cut off from their work, unfulfilled at work, is forced to work, and works for somebody else.

Class consciousness This occurs when the subject class, for example the proletariat, become fully aware of the truth about their situation.

Class polarisation This occurs when the gap in income and wealth between the ruling and subject classes grows steadily wider.

Class in itself People who share the same class position but are not aware of their true situation. They are blinded by false consciousness.

Class for itself People who share the same class position, are aware of their true situation, and organise to change it.

Ideology From a Marxist position, false beliefs and ideas – for example, justifications for the domination of the bourgeoisie.

Communism A classless society in which the means of production are communally owned and people are equal, free from oppression, and fulfilled as human beings.

2.3 Emile Durkheim (1858-1917)

Although the word 'sociology' and many of the discipline's founding principles had been established by Auguste Comte (1798-1857), it was Emile Durkheim who finally established sociology as a serious and respectable academic discipline. In particular, it was Durkheim who first offered a formal statement of 'sociological method' in his book *The Rules of Sociological Method* (1964; first published in 1895). Although, as we shall see, Durkheim's approach to the study of society can be subjected to a number of criticisms, its influence on sociology to this day should not be underestimated.

activity3 class and ideology

Item A Clement Atlee, Labour Prime Minister 1945

Now a new Parliament must be elected. The choice is between that same Conservative Party which stands for private enterprise, private profit and private interests and the Labour Party which demands that in peacetime as in war the interests of the whole people should come before that of a section.

Item B Harold MacMillan, Conservative Prime Minister 1959

This election has shown that the class war is obsolete.

Item C Harold Wilson, Labour Prime Minister 1964

Let us be understanding. Let us not condemn them too harshly. For remember that these are men who were sure at birth that they were ordained by providence to rule over their fellow citizens and to find themselves rudely deprived of the powers that they exercised cannot have been easy for them.

Item D Ted Heath, Conservative Prime Minister 1970

Our purpose is not to divide but to unite and where there are differences to bring reconciliation; to create one nation.

Item E Margaret Thatcher, Conservative Prime Minister 1988

In the world in which we now live, divisions into class are outmoded and meaningless. We are all working people who basically want the same things.

Item F John Major, Conservative Prime Minister 1992

I believe that in the next ten years we will have to continue to make changes that will genuinely produce across the whole of this country a genuinely classless society in which people can rise to whatever level that their own abilities and their own good fortune may take them from wherever they started.

Item G Tony Blair, Labour Prime Minister 1997

For year, the economic framework of the British left was dominated by questions of public ownership. Markets were poorly understood, their obvious limits leading the left to neglect their great potential for enhancing choice, quality and innovation. Effective markets are a pre-condition for a successful modern economy. The question is not whether to have them, but how to empower individuals to succeed within them.

Item H Your Country Needs You

questions

1 Read items A to G. What similarities can you detect in these statements by postwar British Prime Ministers. How would Marx account for these similarities?

2 Look at Item H. How does this poster illustrate a similar ideology to that in Items A to G?

Durkheim's methodology – the study of 'social facts'

Durkheim's central methodological principle, first outlined in his *The Rules of Sociological Method*, was as follows: 'Consider social facts as things'. To understand what Durkheim meant by this, and to appreciate its significance, we need to begin by defining his concept of 'the social fact'. For Durkheim, social facts are characterised by two things: first, they must be *external* to the individual, and second, they must *exercise constraint* over the individual. Some examples will help to clarify what is meant by this.

A very obvious example (when we think about it) of a social fact is language. Let us see how language fulfils Durkheim's two criteria. First, language is external to individuals. Although it is perfectly true that it is internal to us in the sense that we all possess an individual knowledge of the language(s) which we speak, it is external to us in the sense that the language we speak was in existence before any one of us was born, and will continue to be in existence after each of us has died. Language is not an individual characteristic or creation. It is shared by and produced by the social group. As such, it is external to the individual.

Second, although we might not feel that language exercises a constraint over us, a moment's reflection will reveal that it certainly does. If we wish to say something to another speaker of the same language as us, we really have no choice but to use certain words as opposed to others. It is thus no use my using the word 'cheval' if I want to talk to a fellow English speaker about a horse – I have little choice but to use the word 'horse', if I want to be understood.

Perhaps Durkheim's best known example of a social fact can be seen in his analysis of suicide. In his book, *Suicide: A Study in Sociology* (1970; first published in 1897), Durkheim shows how the apparently highly individual act of suicide can be analysed as a social fact. First suicide, or rather the suicide rate, can be shown to be external to individuals by the fact that the suicide rate varies between different social groups, and that this variation remains fairly constant over time. For example, Durkheim noticed that suicide rates were consistently lower in Catholic countries than they were in Protestant countries and that this difference remained stable over relatively long periods of time. Suicide rates thus seemed to be products of social groups, rather than of individuals. Second, the suicide rate could be seen as constraining because the probability that any individual would commit suicide could be shown to vary according to which social groups they belong.

Of course, Durkheim does not claim that the social fact of the suicide rate will tell us which members of a social group will commit suicide. This, he argued, was the proper province of the psychologist. The job of the sociologist was first to identify social facts – such as the suicide rates of various social groups – and second to explain them. (For further discussion of Durkheim's view of social facts, see pages 131-132; for his study of suicide, see pages 131-132 and 264-268).

Cause and function

One of the more important arguments advanced by Durkheim in *The Rules of Sociological* Method was that in explaining social facts it is necessary to distinguish between their causes and their *social functions*. To understand what Durkheim meant by social functions we must consider his so-called 'organismic analogy' – the idea that societies are like living organisms.

To see how this analogy works consider the following example. If I take a living organism, say a dog, each of its parts – its legs, its tail, its liver, its heart and so on – can be seen to make a contribution to the dog's overall functioning. However, if I were to take any one of these parts in isolation, say its tail, it would 'do' very little, and I would be unable to see how it makes a contribution to the overall functioning of the dog. It only makes sense, as it were, in relation to all the other parts which go to make up the dog. Even if I took all the individual parts of a dog, and placed them in a box, I still would not have something we could meaningfully call 'a dog', which barked and wagged its tail. All I would have would be a pile of lifeless limbs and organs. Similarly, Durkheim argued that only by examining the contribution which each of a society's parts makes to its overall functioning can we arrive at a complete understanding of these parts. This approach is sometimes known as holism, and can be summed up in the phrase: *the whole is greater than the sum of its parts.*

For Durkheim, the study of any social fact's functions must be different from the study of its causes. This is because unless we were to say that a particular social fact was the result of deliberate intentions, its cause cannot be the same as its functional effects. The reason for this is obvious – since functional effects occur only *after* a phenomenon has come into existence, they cannot have caused that phenomenon to come into existence in the first place. Durkheim therefore claimed that the causes of social facts should be sought in other social facts which had

occurred at an earlier point in time. If, however, we wish to explain why a social fact persists over time, we should seek to discover the contribution it makes to the overall working of society, in short, its *function*.

The division of labour

Moral regulation At the centre of Durkheim's work is a concern with morality. Morality can be seen as a classic example of a social fact. Moral codes are external to individuals in the sense that they are properties of social groups, and they are constraining over individuals in that they plainly influence our behaviour. But for Durkheim morality is also central to his understanding of how social order is possible.

At the centre of Durkheim's analysis, as with most social theorists, are a set of assumptions about 'human nature'. For Durkheim, following the philosopher Rousseau, human beings possess an innate tendency towards limitless desire. If these desires remain unchecked then, Durkheim argued, human beings could never be happy, because their desires would always outstrip their ability to satisfy them. At the same time, such limitless desires would pose an obvious threat to social order. Durkheim thus argued that human happiness, social order and social solidarity could only be achieved by the regulation of human desires to within attainable limits. It is for this reason that morality – the social fact responsible for the regulation of individual desires – was so central to Durkheim's whole approach.

Social solidarity In his first major work, *The Division of Labour in Society* (1933; first published 1893) Durkheim set out to show how, as societies developed from simple, small-scale pre-literate forms, to modern, complex and industrial forms, the basis of moral regulation, and hence of social solidarity, also underwent change. In the former type of society, Durkheim argued that social order was achieved by what he termed *mechanical solidarity*. In such societies, the extent to which different individuals perform different tasks – the *division of labour* – was very limited. Therefore, since most people shared a common set of interests and problems, a single set of moral rules to guide them was sufficient. The source of such moral regulation was religious, and Durkheim assumed that members of such societies shared a common commitment to the authority of their religion which provided appropriate moral limits in any situation they were likely to face. This he called the 'conscience collective', which roughly translates as the 'collective conscience'.

The basis of the mechanical solidarity of small-scale societies is *similarity* – the division of labour is limited and there is little role differentiation. As the division of labour becomes increasingly specialised and complex, *mechanical solidarity* is replaced by *organic solidarity*. This organic solidarity is based on *difference*. The different and specialised parts of the division of labour work together to maintain the social unit. Specialised occupational roles are interdependent – they need each other.

Anomie As societies became more complex, however, Durkheim argued that the ability of a single source of moral authority to regulate the increasingly divergent lives of society's members was gradually weakened. So much so that modern societies, which are characterised by a very highly developed division of labour, faced a chronic state of crisis as far as moral regulation was concerned. Durkheim called this lack of moral regulation *anomie*, and this is closely linked to his belief in the growth of excessive individualism – people come to see themselves first and foremost as individuals rather than as members of social groups.

Although Durkheim regarded anomie as a very significant feature of modern societies, he maintained that it could be overcome by the development of strong occupational associations which would become the source of moral regulation for their members. For example, they would regulate terms and conditions of employment and wages and salaries. These associations, Durkheim argued, would overcome the problems posed by modern societies in two main ways. First, they would counter the modern trend towards individualism by integrating their members into a social group. Second, they would set limits on the rewards which members of society could expect to receive, and hence would serve to limit desires to within attainable bounds.

Evaluation

Although there can be little doubt about Durkheim's enormous influence on the development of sociology, we need to take account of a number of criticisms of his work.

Anomie and human nature It can be argued that Durkheim's view of human nature is unrealistically pessimistic. In many ways, his argument that human beings need to be morally regulated by society is the direct opposite of Marx's view that human nature is in fact corrupted by the social relations of production in capitalist societies.

Determinism It is sometimes said that Durkheim's approach represents an extreme form of *determinism*. That is, human actions are explained purely by the effects of external forces acting upon the individual. It has been argued that this can be seen in his analysis of suicide – apparently one of the most individual choices a human being can ever make. Durkheim claims that the suicide rate is, in fact, nothing more than a product of social forces over which individuals have absolutely no control. Many sociologists, most notably perhaps symbolic interactionists whose ideas we consider later in this chapter, have argued that this presents an inaccurate picture of human action. Instead, they argue that although social forces perhaps influence individual choices, they do not determine them in a straightforward way. Human beings, they argue, possess freedom of choice, and so can always resist the influences of social forces if they so choose.

Power and inequality Durkheim was extremely concerned about the consequences of the increasingly specialised division of labour – the inequalities which it entails and the anomie it generates. However, it is sometimes argued that he failed to grasp the extent to which modern capitalist societies are composed of groups with fundamentally opposing interests. Marx considered capitalist societies to be characterised by irresolvable class conflicts. Durkheim regarded such conflicts as did occur to be temporary anomalies which could be overcome by the development of new forms of moral regulation. At no time, however, does he consider that the moral regulations which are central to all forms of social solidarity might be ideologies – that is, sets of beliefs which portray a false picture of reality and justify fundamentally unjust power relations.

Whilst each of these criticisms might be convincing to some sociologists, it is important to note that we cannot settle any of them simply by appealing to available evidence. Each point of view presented reflects, in large measure, simply different ways of 'seeing' society. To return to our earlier analogy, each is viewing society in a different distorting mirror. They do, nevertheless, sensitise us to possible weaknesses in Durkheim's approach. We shall return to some of these later in the chapter when we consider the development of functionalism after Durkheim.

key terms

Social facts Aspects of society which are external to the individual and constrain their behaviour.
Holism A view which states that the whole is greater than the sum of its parts.
Function/social function The contribution made by a social fact to the operation of society as a whole.
Mechanical solidarity A form of moral regulation based on shared values. The 'collective conscience' which unites members of society.
Organic solidarity A form of solidarity based on the interdependence of a specialised division of labour.
Anomie A lack of moral regulation, normlessness.

2.4 Max Weber (1864-1920)

Durkheim's approach to the study of society rested firmly upon his assumption of the effects of external and constraining social facts on individual behaviour, Max Weber emphasised the importance of taking into account the points of view of social actors, and the meanings which they attribute to their own behaviour and that of others. For this reason, Weber is often regarded as the founding father of *interpretivist sociology*, or of the *social action approach* within sociology.

Meaning and the concept of verstehen

As we saw in the previous section, Durkheim regarded the proper task of sociology to be the identification of relationships between social facts. It is often argued, however, that this approach ignores the *meaningful* nature of human conduct. Let us examine what is meant by this.

activity4 the case of Robinson Crusoe

Item A Shipwrecked

In 1719, the novelist Daniel Defoe published a classic story about a man on his own, called Robinson Crusoe. Crusoe went out from England to make his fortune and had many adventures before being shipwrecked on a desert island. He was the only survivor of the wreck, and though he managed to salvage many things from it and to make himself some sort of life on the island, he survived entirely alone until he discovered a single footprint in the sand. This was the mark of a native whom he discovered and named 'Friday' (after the day on which he found him) and made him his servant. Crusoe was finally rescued and taken home.

Item B Family

Born in the city of York, of a good family, though not of that country, my father being a foreigner of Bremen, who first settled at Hull. He got a good estate by merchandise, and leaving off his trade lived afterwards at York, from whence he married my mother from a very good family in that country.

Item C Education

My father had given me a competent share of learning, as far as house education and a county free-school generally goes, and designed me for the law. Being the third son of the family and not bred to any trade, my head began to be filled with early rambling thoughts.

Robinson Crusoe pictured in the first edition, 1719

Item D Religion

I frequently sat down with thankfulness and admired the hand of God's providence, which had thus spread my table in the wilderness. These reflections made me very sensible of the goodness of Providence to me and very thankful for my present condition.

Item E Power

In a little time I began to speak to him and to teach him how to speak to me; and first I made him know his name should be Friday, which was the day I saved his life. I likewise taught him to say Master, and then let him know that was to be my name.

Item F A social being

Robinson Crusoe was indeed a unique individual, making his way in the world by his own efforts, 'master of all he surveys', as the poem puts it. But this is very different from saying that he can be understood and explained in individual terms. We can't fully explain who he is, where he comes from, what he thinks and does, how he behaves, by looking at him simply as an individual. This is the problem with individualist types of explanation.

Adapted from Hall, 1993

questions

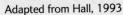

1   What social facts influenced Robinson Crusoe?
2   Is there an argument for combining social and individual explanations to understand Robinson Crusoe's behaviour?

If we are concerned to identify what it is that distinguishes human beings from either animals or inanimate objects, then perhaps the most crucial difference is that human beings are capable of intentional action. We do things on purpose, in order to reach some goal, and usually we have some choice both about the goal and the means we select to achieve it. For example, if asked why you are reading this chapter, you will probably answer with reference to some goal – to enable you to pass an examination in sociology, perhaps. You will also, presumably, have some choice about both the goal and the means you have selected to achieve it – you could always decide not to take the examination, and you could always choose to read another book. It is for this reason that

Weber would say that your action is meaningful. It is not merely the product of the operation of external forces over which you have no control, but is the result of your own interpretations of the world around you and of the conscious choices you make about your future.

Weber thus emphasised that it is not enough merely to note statistical correlations between social facts as Durkheim had done – although Weber certainly believed that such correlations were an important starting point for sociological analysis. He insisted, in addition, that explanations of human action should be grasped on the level of meaning. Whilst, methodologically, it may not be difficult to explore the meanings of actors' conduct when one has the opportunity to interview them – although

Weber did not himself practice this kind of sociological investigation – obvious difficulties are faced when one is dealing with social events which took place in the past. Since Weber's own preoccupation was with the origins of modern capitalism, he had himself to overcome this difficulty. The events he was concerned with had taken place several centuries before he was born. His solution was the method of *verstehen*.

Verstehen can be translated from the German as broadly meaning 'empathetic understanding'. In simple terms, one attempts to imagine how the world would have looked from the point of view of the actors whose actions one wishes to understand, even where such a point of view is quite alien to one's own. The classic example of the application of verstehen can be found in Weber's account of the behaviour of early Calvinists in *The Protestant Ethic and the Spirit of Capitalism* (1958). (For further discussion of Weber's methodology, see pages 136-137; for his study of Protestantism and capitalism, see pages 17, 19-20).

The ideal type

Before we move on to consider the ways in which Weber categorised social action, it will be helpful to explain his concept of the *ideal type*. Ideal types are generalisations which help researchers to organise and classify their findings. Rarely, if ever, are they found in their pure form, but they provide us with a set of categories through which we can make sense of our observations. For example, Weber produced an ideal type of a bureaucracy. He lists six 'ideal' characteristics of bureaucracies, but it is unlikely that any actual bureaucratic organisation will possess all six characteristics in pure form. We can nevertheless identify it as a bureaucracy, because it comes closer to the ideal typical bureaucracy than to any other form of organisation.

Types of action

Both the concept of verstehen, and Weber's use of ideal types can be seen in his four-fold categorisation of types of action. These categories of action begin from the assumptions of verstehen in that they adopt the point of view of the actor. They are ideal types in that they are theoretically pure forms to which real instances of action only ever approximate.

Instrumentally rational action In this type of 'purely' rational action, the actor assesses both their goals and the means by which these should be achieved. For example, if it is my goal to win a marathon, then it would be instrumentally rational for me to undergo a strict regime of training and dieting prior to the race. By contrast, it would not be rational, in relation to this goal, for me to spend the weeks prior to the race indulging in an almost incessant orgy of drinking, smoking and over-eating. However, it would still be instrumentally rational for me to decide that the costs (in terms of pain and suffering) of dieting and training were not worth the benefit of winning the marathon. Under these circumstances, I would simply reject the goal of winning the marathon, thus making my over-indulgent behaviour rational in terms of my revised goal of gaining as much immediate pleasure as possible.

Value-rational action This type of rational action is similar to instrumentally rational action in that means are judged to be rational if they are thought to be successful in reaching the goal towards which they are directed. However, in this case, the goals cannot be abandoned even if they are immensely difficult to achieve. For example, a devoutly religious person who believed that they would only enjoy salvation if they lived a life of celibacy would, if acting in accordance with value-rationality, accept a life of celibacy no matter how difficult this might prove. To reject the goal as being simply too difficult to achieve, however, would be an example of instrumentally rational action.

Traditional action This form of action does not involve the assessment of either goals or means. Instead, it is performed simply because tradition dictates that it should be. Although Weber felt that traditional action had declined in significance in modern societies, which he believed were characterised increasingly by rational action, examples of traditional conduct can still be found. In Britain, for example, it is still usual to celebrate Christmas by, amongst other things, purchasing and decorating a Christmas tree. The majority of people who engage in this behaviour, however, can give no reason for doing so other than the fact that it is 'traditional'.

Affective action This final form of action can best be expressed as being a result of emotion. Again, Weber felt that this type of action was becoming less significant in modern societies, but examples can still be found. Someone hearing the news that a close relative had been killed in an accident might burst into tears out of grief. Or, a wife discovering her husband's infidelity might assault him out of anger. No well thought out goals are involved in such actions. And since the circumstances are by definition novel, the actions can clearly not be described as traditional. They are the direct result of the unusual emotional state of the actor.

Rationalisation and disenchantment

Weber argued that modern societies are characterised increasingly by a process of *rationalisation*. As the term suggests, this means that the world is increasingly governed by rationality, in which traditional and affective forms of action are replaced by predominantly rational forms. Organisations increasingly adopt a bureaucratic form and legitimate authority is predominantly rational legal (see page 63). Corresponding to this was a trend towards what is usually translated from the German as *disenchantment*, although a more literal translation of Weber would be *the driving out of magic from things*. This can be seen partly as *secularisation*, but is in fact broader than this and includes the progressive removal of non-rational elements from all spheres of life. Weber was fearful that in the process warmth and humanity might be driven out of social life – the very things which give meaning to human existence (see pages 19-20 and 57).

Evaluation

Psychologism Whilst Durkheim has often been accused of ignoring the role of psychological factors in human behaviour, it has sometimes been said that Weber over-emphasises the role of such factors. This criticism has two aspects to it. First, it has been suggested that in using the method of verstehen, Weber is forced to go beyond available evidence and attribute motives to social actors without any means of verifying them. Taken to its extreme, this could reduce sociological enquiry to little more than guesswork. Second, it can be argued that, in giving such weight to individual motives, Weber underestimates the power of external social forces to constrain and determine behaviour.

Ambiguity Although Weber makes a great effort to be clear about exactly what he means by the ideal type, it can nevertheless be argued that the concept can lead to certain ambiguities, particularly when applied to types of action. Percy Cohen points out, for example, that many forms of traditional action may also conform to one or other type of rationality (Cohen, 1968). For instance, when people in small-scale non-literate societies give gifts to the village headman, they do so both because it is traditional *and* because they hope to receive some benefits as a result. Similarly, whilst an outburst of rage might appear to be purely affective, it could be seen, from the point of view of a psychoanalyst, as rational in that it could have been motivated by an unconscious desire to reduce one's level of stress.

Conclusion

In this unit, we have considered some of the most important early influences on the development of sociological theory. Although each has been subjected to criticism, the ideas we have discussed have had an enduring influence on the ways in which sociologists seek to understand human societies. In the unit which follows, we turn our attention to the ways in which these founding theorists' ideas have been developed by later generations of social theorists.

key terms

Verstehen Empathetic understanding. A method used to interpret the meanings and motives which guide action.
Ideal type A classification of something into 'pure' types – for example, Weber's types of action.
Instrumentally rational action Action in which both goals and the means to attain them are rationally assessed.
Value-rational action The goals are fixed and the means are rationally assessed.
Traditional action Both goals and means are fixed by tradition.
Affective action Action is directed by emotion, with no clearly defined goals.
Rationalisation A process by which the world is increasingly governed by rational thought and action.
Disenchantment The removal of religion, 'magic', warmth and humanity in an increasingly rational world.
Secularisation A process by which religion loses its power and influence in society.

summary

1. Sociology has its roots in the Enlightenment. It reflected two key aspects of Enlightenment thought.
   - The ability of human reason to provide an understanding of the world.
   - A belief that this understanding can be used to improve the world.
2. Marx saw the material conditions of production – the way people organise the production of goods and services – as the starting point for the analysis of society.
3. The mode of production largely shapes the rest of society – that is the superstructure, which includes political and legal systems, religion, and so on.
4. Apart from primitive communism, all societies have a dominant ruling class which exploits a subordinate subject class. The power of the ruling class derives from their ownership and control of the means of production.
5. Class conflict provides the motor for social change. It propels society forward from one production system to another.
6. There is increasing alienation and class polarisation in capitalist society. This will promote class consciousness and help to unite the proletariat. This, in turn, will eventually lead to the overthrow of capitalism and its replacement by communism.
7. Marx has been criticised for:
   - What some see as economic determinism
   - Overestimating the importance of class in directing social change

   - Failing to predict the development of capitalist societies.
8. Durkheim saw sociology as the study of social facts. Social facts are external to the individual and constrain individual behaviour.
9. In explaining social facts, it is necessary to distinguish between their causes and their functions. Causes should be sought in other social facts which occurred at an earlier point in time. In order to explain why a social fact persists over time, we need to discover its function – the contribution it makes to society.
10. Durkheim's work focused on moral regulation and its contribution to social solidarity and social order.
11. He distinguished between two types of solidarity – mechanical solidarity based on common values and a limited division of labour, and organic solidarity based on a specialised division of labour.
12. Durkheim saw anomie – a lack of moral regulation – as characteristic of modern society.
13. Durkheim has had an enormous influence on the development of sociology. However, he has been criticised for:
    - Over-emphasising human beings' need for moral regulation
    - Determinism – external forces shaping behaviour
    - A failure to appreciate the significance of conflict in society – particularly class conflict.
14. Weber argued that in order to understand and explain

behaviour, it is essential to discover the meanings which social actors give both to their own actions and the actions of others.

15. To discover these meanings, Weber used the method of verstehen – empathetic understanding.

16. Using this method, Weber identified four types of action. They are ideal types.
    - Instrumentally rational action
    - Value-rational action
    - Traditional action
    - Affective action.

17. Weber saw a process of rationalisation occurring in modern societies – action is increasingly rational rather than traditional or affective. Related to this is a trend towards disenchantment.

18. Like Marx and Durkheim, Weber has had a lasting and significant influence on sociology. However his approach has been criticised for:
    - Attributing motives and meanings to social actors without sufficient means of verifying them
    - Underestimating the power of external social forces to direct behaviour
    - Failing to recognise that certain forms of behaviour can be directed by two or more of the types of social action he identifies.

activity5 disenchantment

Item A Modernity and religion

Modernity is the transition from fate to choice. At the same time, it dissolves the commitments and loyalties that once lay behind our choices. Technical reason has made us masters of matching means to ends. But it has left us inarticulate as to why we should choose one end rather than another. The values that once led us to regard one as intrinsically better than another – and which gave such weight to words like good and bad – have disintegrated, along with the communities and religious traditions in which we learned them. Now we choose because it is what we want; or it works for us; or it feels right to me. Once we have dismantled a world in which larger virtues held sway, what is left are success and self-expression, the key values of an individualistic culture.

Item B Pictures of modernity

The shopping mall – a temple to materialism and consumerism

Former church, now Cottiers Bar and Restaurant, Glasgow

Max Weber delivered the famous prophetic warning that the cloak of material prosperity might eventually become an iron cage. It was already becoming an end in itself, and other values were left, in his words, 'like the ghost of dead religious beliefs'. Once capitalism consumed its religious foundations, he feared the consequences.

In the past, disadvantaged groups could find in religion what Karl Marx called 'the feeling of a heartless world'. A purely economic order offers no such consolations. A culture of success places little value on the unsuccessful.

The erosion of those bonds of loyalty and love which religion supported has left us increasingly alone in an impersonal economic and social system. Emile Durkheim was the first to give this condition a name. He called it anomie: the situation in which individuals have lost their moorings in a collective order. It is the heavy price we pay for our loss of communities of faith.

Adapted from Sachs, 1990

Item C The logical song

When I was young, it seemed that life was so wonderful,
A miracle, oh it was beautiful, magical.
And all the birds in the trees, well they'd be singing so happily,
Joyfully, playfully watching me.
But then they sent me away to teach me how to be sensible,
Logical, responsible, practical.
And they showed me a world where I could be so dependable,
Clinical, intellectual, cynical.

From *Breakfast in America* by Supertramp, 1979, words and music by Roger Hodgson

questions

1 How do Items A, B and C illustrate Weber's belief that rationalisation is resulting in disenchantment?

2 Judging from Item A, what similarities and differences are there between Weber's picture of modernity and those of Marx and Durkheim?

keyissues

1 What are the main assumptions of functionalism, Marxism and symbolic interactionism?

2 How significant are these perspectives for the development of sociological theory?

There has never been one model of society on which all sociologists are agreed. In this unit we shall be considering three competing models which have their origins in the work of Marx, Durkheim and Weber. The three models which we shall consider – functionalism, Marxism and symbolic interactionism – each make very different assumptions about the nature of human beings and the societies which they inhabit. Although these are not the only models which have emerged in sociology, and some sociologists straddle different models, they are nevertheless three of the most significant in the development of sociology as a discipline. This is evident both in this book, where continual references are made to these models, and in any of the major textbooks in sociology. Although, as we shall see in later sections, matters are now more complex than a consideration of these three models suggests, they do nonetheless form the basis of the modern discipline.

3.1 Functionalism

During the first half of the twentieth century, functionalism became the dominant theoretical perspective in sociology. Functionalism has its origins in the work of such 19th century social theorists as Auguste Comte and Herbert Spencer, but owes most to the work of Emile Durkheim. Functionalism was subsequently adopted by sociologists, but much of its early impact was through the work of British social anthropologists such as Bronislaw Malinowski and A. R. Radcliffe-Brown.

Social systems Although the views of functionalist sociologists differ in detail, they share in common a concern with studying societies as *systems*. The idea that a society is a system has a number of implications, which are central to functionalist analysis. First, is the assumption that societies should be studied as wholes, rather than as collections of independent parts. As we saw in Durkheim's work, just as a living organism is more than merely the sum of its constituent parts, so societies need to be treated as entities in their own right with, as it were, a life of their own.

Second, and following from this, is the assumption that the parts of society need to be understood in terms of the contribution which they make to the functioning of the whole. If, for example, we were to be interested in central heating systems, we could only understand the role of, say, the radiators, in relation to the system as a whole. On their own radiators do very little, and had we never seen one as part of a functioning central heating system, we would stand little chance of figuring out what they are for. In exactly the same way, functionalists assume that we can only understand the role of the constituent parts of societies in terms of their contribution to the functioning of the society as a whole.

Third is the assumption that parts of societies perform a primarily positive function in relation to the overall functioning of the society. Just as we would not expect to find parts of central heating systems which either perform no function whatsoever, or actually impair the overall performance of the system, so functionalists would not expect to find parts of societies which either do not contribute to, or actually impair their overall functioning. This means that functionalist analysis tends to search for positive functions of social institutions, whilst either denying or seriously underplaying, their negative or disruptive aspects.

Although by the 1950s, functionalism had become the dominant theoretical perspective in sociology, this dominance was not to last. From this time onwards, functionalism was subjected to a range of criticisms which ultimately led to its widespread rejection. Nevertheless, the influence of functionalism on modern sociological theory remains substantial.

Talcott Parsons (1902-1979)

Although Parsons' work is often criticised for what some see as its rather dry and obscure style, it represents the fullest and most systematic statement of functionalist theory available. For Parsons, as with Durkheim before him, the central problem for all social theory was, in the name of the 17th century philosopher Thomas Hobbes, the 'Hobbesian problem of order'. Hobbes believed that human beings were driven by passions which, if left unrestrained, would lead to social chaos, or a 'war of all against all'. The problem, therefore, was how to explain the fact that this state of affairs does not routinely occur in human societies. Indeed, human societies are, for most of the time, rather orderly and peaceful places. Hobbes' solution to this problem was to assume that, driven ultimately by the need for self-preservation, people voluntarily agree to restrain their passions and submit to the sovereign authority of the state.

As we saw in the discussion of Durkheim's work, he offered the rather different solution that social order is maintained by a shared commitment to a common morality. This, essentially, was Parsons' solution too.

The social system and its functional prerequisites

It was suggested in the introduction to this unit that the assumption that societies are systems is fundamental to functionalist theory. This assumption is made most explicitly in the work of Parsons – indeed, his major statement of functionalist theory is presented in a book entitled *The Social System* (Parsons, 1951). For Parsons, any social system inevitably faces four problems, which must be solved if the system is to survive. Parsons calls these four problems *functional prerequisites*, and they are as follows: adaptation, goal attainment, integration and pattern maintenance or latency.

Adaptation The first, *adaptation*, refers to the need for any social system to adapt to its environment. In even the most simple societies, some mechanism must exist whereby food and shelter are obtained. This could involve, for example, hunting and gathering and the production of simple shelters against the elements. Such activities might strike us as straightforward in comparison with the complex arrangements which exist in our own societies for converting the raw materials of the natural environment into produced goods for consumption and use. They do nevertheless require social organisation, and crucially for Parsons, normative regulation. Whilst in simple societies this might be achieved by the existence of customs and norms, in advanced industrial societies it tends to be achieved by legally regulated economies.

Goal attainment The second of Parsons' functional prerequisites is *goal attainment*. This refers to the need for societies to set goals towards which the activities of their members and institutions are directed. In simple societies, this might revolve around the need to obtain sufficient food, whilst in societies such as our own, it involves more complex economic goals such as seeking profit. In modern societies, goal attainment is fundamentally the responsibility of the political system, which establishes a legal and economic framework which regulates and directs the pursuit of such goals.

Integration The third functional prerequisite is *integration*. This refers to the need to maintain cohesion within the social system and to deal effectively with deviance which threatens the overall stability of the system. Whilst in simple societies this function would be fulfilled largely as a result of what Weber called traditional authority, in modern complex societies it is performed largely by the legal system – what Weber called rational-legal authority.

Pattern maintenance The final functional prerequisite is *pattern maintenance*, or *latency*. This refers to the need to maintain the pattern of value commitments amongst a society's members. Crucial to this is the process of socialisation which takes place within institutions such as the family and the education system. Socialisation serves to internalise a society's values into the personalities of individual actors.

This framework allowed Parsons to classify all the parts of any given society into one of these four categories, and in doing so, to claim that each contributes in at least one of these four ways to the overall functioning of that society.

Social evolution and equilibrium

It is sometimes said that functionalism in general, and Parsons' theory in particular, emphasise social stability to such an extent that they are in danger of failing to account for social change. We shall return to this charge in our evaluation of functionalism. For the present, it is important to note that Parsons does not ignore the issue of social change, but in fact makes its explanation a central part of his general theory.

Equilibrium An important element of Parsons' analysis of social systems is that they exist in a state of *equilibrium*. Equilibrium is best defined as 'balance', and in relation to social systems, refers to the ways in which the four subsystems are interrelated. This means, for Parsons, that a change in one part of a social system tends to produce changes elsewhere in the social system such that the system, overall, returns to a state of equilibrium. Social systems are therefore regarded as self-regulating, always tending to return to a state of equilibrium, albeit a changed one. In this way, Parsons explains social change as a dynamic and functionally necessary response to disturbances within the system. Although, for Parsons, social systems tend towards a state of equilibrium, a perfect equilibrium is never attained – instead, societies are thought to exist in a state of 'moving equilibrium'.

Social evolution A second aspect of Parsons' approach to social change is his notion of *social evolution*. Heavily influenced by such 19th century social evolutionists as Herbert Spencer, Parsons believed that all social systems are involved in an evolutionary development from more simple to more complex forms. The central concept used by Parsons to explain the patterns of social evolution is *structural differentiation*. This refers to the tendency of social institutions to become more specialised. Thus, for example, prior to the industrial revolution, the household used to be not only a domestic space, but also a place where goods were produced. After the industrial revolution, factories replaced the household as a site of production and the household came to fulfil the more specialised role as a site of domestic activity only.

This trend carries with it its own problems, however, which modern societies must solve. In particular, the development of increasingly specialised roles and institutions requires the development of an increasingly broad and general set of values capable of regulating a wider range of activities. In modern industrial societies, such values include a belief in *universalism* and in *achievement* – universal society-wide standards of achievement are applied to everyone and form the basis for allocating people to roles and fixing their rewards. Such general values are capable of regulating a very wide range of specialised activities in our societies.

Robert K. Merton

Parsons' work represents the height of functionalist theorising in sociology, and is the most systematic and abstract of functionalist approaches. Parsons' desire to explain all aspects of all societies from within a single theoretical framework has led to his theory being described as a *grand* theory. One functionalist sociologist who attempted to refine functionalist analysis, but at the same time rejected the highly abstract approach developed by Parsons, was Robert K. Merton.

Merton's modification of functionalist theory begins with a critique of the notion – fundamental to Parsons' model – that societies exhibit 'functional unity'. This is the idea that all parts of a society are interconnected such that all parts of the system work together for the benefit of the whole, and that a change in one part of the system will necessarily produce change elsewhere. Merton suggests that whilst this may sometimes be the case, one cannot assume that it will be in advance. Rather, the degree to which parts of the social system are interconnected is a matter which should be empirically investigated in each case. Indeed, Merton suggests that in modern highly differentiated societies, a relatively high degree of *functional autonomy* will exist within parts of the social system. In other words, some parts will operate as largely independent units.

Merton also challenges the idea of 'universal functionalism', that is, the idea that all parts of the social system fulfil some positive function. Again, as with the issue of functional unity, Merton suggests that whether or not a particular part of the social system fulfils a positive function is a matter for investigation and is not something which can be assumed in advance. For Merton, any part of the system might be either functional, dysfunctional or non-functional. In other words, its contribution to the social system may be positive, negative or non-existent.

Finally, Merton challenges what he terms the 'postulate of indispensability' – the assumption that the institutions or roles which actually exist within a society are the only ones which could meet that society's functional prerequisites. In other words, he challenges the assumption made by many functionalists that social institutions and roles exist by necessity and are therefore inevitable parts of that society. Instead, Merton argues that the same functional needs could just as well be met by different institutions and roles which are functionally equivalent.

These specific criticisms of grand theory advanced by Merton led him to suggest that social theorists should abandon their search for over-arching theoretical systems which specify the nature and functions of social institutions in advance. Instead, they should concentrate upon developing more concrete theories grounded in empirical evidence, which address specific social phenomena rather than entire social systems. Such theories were called by Merton, *theories of the middle range*.

Evaluation

Teleology Despite Durkheim's early caution about confusing the cause of a phenomenon with its functions, this charge can be levelled at later functionalist theorists. In particular, functionalist theories may be accused of being *teleological*. A theory is said to be teleological if it explains a phenomenon's causes in terms of its effects. Thus if functionalists argue that the cause of social stratification is to allocate the most able individuals to the most important positions in society, then their argument is teleological – it explains causes in terms of effects. This can lead to some very strange explanations. For example, if it is argued that the family exists because it has the effect of stabilising adult personalities and of accomplishing the primary socialisation of children, then it seems difficult to avoid the assumption that this is because someone sat down and invented the family for this purpose. Of course this would be absurd. As we have seen, however, functionalist explanations tend to be of this type, and so can be criticised on the logical grounds that they confuse cause and effect.

Value consensus A second criticism which can be levelled at functionalist theory is that it over-emphasises the degree of *value consensus* – agreement about values – in societies. As Merton's critique of functionalism suggests, it can be argued that the degree of value consensus in a society is an empirical matter which cannot be presumed in advance. At the very least, it seems difficult to avoid the conclusion that the degree of value consensus which exists will undergo change over time, and will vary between different social groups. In addition, it has been suggested there is no reason to assume that even if a high degree of value consensus exists, it will necessarily promote social solidarity. Collective commitment to an ethic of individualism, for example, may produce exactly the opposite effect.

Conflict A third criticism of functionalism is that in its concentration on social order and value consensus, it largely ignores the existence of coercion and conflict in society. For example, David Lockwood has pointed out that Parsons' emphasis on social order and value consensus ignores the fact that competition for scarce resources, an inherent feature of modern societies, will inevitably lead to conflict over scarce resources.

key terms

Functional prerequisites Requirements which must be met and problems which must be solved in order for the social system to survive.

Adaptation The need for the social system to adapt to its environment.

Goal attainment The need for society to set goals for its members and institutions.

Integration The need to maintain order and stability in society, and to deal with deviance.

Pattern maintenance The need for value consensus and commitment to those values.

Structural differentiation The tendency for social institutions, such as the family and religion, to become more specialised in terms of their functions.

Functional autonomy The idea that some parts of society operate as largely independent units.

Teleology Explaining the causes of something in terms of its effects.

activity6 functions and dysfunctions

Item A

Street party in Jubilee Drive, Liverpool, to celebrate the Queen's Silver Jubilee

Item B

Anti-capitalist riot, London, 2000

Item C

Glastonbury music festival

Item D

Domestic violence

questions

1 From a functionalist view, which activities in Items A to D would be seen as functional and which as dysfunctional?
2 Explain your answers in terms of functionalist theory.

3.2 Marxism

Although Marxism has a long ancestry, it did not grow to prominence within sociology until the 1960s. That decade saw a range of social movements which challenged the dominant social order and made the functionalist picture of a social system based on value consensus seem less plausible. In this context, Marxism gained converts with its picture of society as inherently riven by social conflict.

Marxism, as a sociological perspective, does not slavishly follow Marx in every particular but rather accepts three of his central beliefs – a belief that in some sense the economy is of primary importance, that class conflict is consequently central, and that ultimately this will result in a more desirable form of society. Where modern Marxists part company with Marx is over the question of whether it is possible to identify the conditions which will entail the demise of capitalism. Marx himself was somewhat vague on this issue, but a number of his followers adopted an economic determinist position whereby economic crises were seen as inevitably dooming capitalism to extinction.

The Marxists we shall be examining in this section reject this position. Impressed by the capacity of capitalism to survive crises, they pay particular attention to the role of the superstructure in maintaining it. We shall look at two very different versions of Marxism – *humanist Marxism* and *structuralist Marxism*. The first develops Marx's early work and adopts as its starting point the assumption that human beings are able to transform their environment. The second develops Marx's later work and adopts as its starting point the assumption that human beings are the product of structures.

Humanist Marxism

Gramsci Gramsci's central contribution to Marxism is his development of Marx's ideas on ideology through a theory of *hegemony* (1971). The bourgeoisie, he argues, seek to maintain their domination not only by using the state to coerce people but also, increasingly, by propagating ideologies, through the institutions of civil society such as the churches, in order to win people's consent. For the bourgeoisie to be ideologically dominant, or hegemonic, these ideologies need to be tied into the popular culture of the subordinate classes.

The extent to which such hegemony is achieved varies over time but it is unlikely ever to be complete. There are two reasons for this. First, the bourgeoisie are often divided and frequently need to forge alliances with other groups in order to constitute a *power bloc* and control the state. Second, the proletariat has a *dual consciousness*, one part of which reflects the ideas of the bourgeoisie and the other part of which reflects their everyday experience. The need to create a power bloc inhibits the propagation of a coherent ideology, while the existence of dual consciousness means that workers will at least partially see through bourgeois ideology.

For Gramsci a proletarian revolution will *not* inevitably result from economic crises. What is needed is for the proletariat to make alliances with other groups and for Marxists to win the hearts and minds of the subordinate classes by connecting Marxist ideas to popular culture. Gramsci is optimistic that in the struggle for hegemony, people will eventually be persuaded of the need for revolution. The stress Gramsci places on popular culture as the site in which ideologies compete has been taken up in cultural studies where youth subcultural styles are seen on the one hand as indicative of resistance to domination and on the other hand as an opportunity for marketing a new fashion, for general consumption and profit. (For further discussion of Gramsci, see page 76-77).

Critical theory What distinguishes critical theory is its attempt to identify what is distinctively human and to use this as a yardstick from which to criticise existing society. We shall look at two examples here – the Frankfurt School, and its three main figures, Adorno, Horkheimer and Marcuse, and the chief heir to that inheritance, Habermas.

The Frankfurt School For the Frankfurt School there are two attributes which distinguish human beings from animals – the ability, which Marx highlighted, to transform the environment, and the ability, which the Enlightenment stressed, to make rational decisions about our lives. Capitalist societies do not allow human beings to exercise their creativity and reason and thus deserve criticism for being oppressive and irrational. The Frankfurt School agrees with Gramsci that particular attention needs to be paid to ideology which is increasingly integrating people into the capitalist system. Two phenomena are highlighted as crucial here – the growth of *instrumental reason* which is seen as the dominant way of thinking in capitalist societies and the development of *mass culture*.

The stress on instrumental reason is reminiscent of Weber's emphasis on rationalisation as a central feature of modernity. It is a way of looking at the world which 'is concerned with discovering how to do things, not what should be done' (Craib, 1984). According to the Frankfurt School, the search for the most efficient means to achieve ends not only generates an uncritical attitude towards the ends pursued in capitalist societies, but also encourages us to treat people as means rather than ends in themselves. Reason does not, as the Enlightenment hoped, liberate people in capitalist societies but instead becomes a mechanism for oppressing people.

People's acceptance of instrumental reason is explained by the Frankfurt School in terms of the development of mass culture. Not only is culture now an industry, but developments in technology have meant that through various media such as newspapers it reaches the mass of the population. Adorno and Horkheimer use the term 'culture industry' to refer to the products and processes of mass culture. Such an industry does not meet people's true needs but instead produces and satisfies false needs. Our true need – to make collective rational choices about our lives – is denied and instead we are encouraged as individuals to choose which standardised products to consume. We are discouraged in the process from thinking beyond the confines of the moment. Art or high culture is different because it embodies ideals which cannot be met within capitalist societies and therefore provides us with a vision of an alternative society. This function of art, however, is increasingly lost as the culture industry turns it into another cultural commodity. While at one stage, the music of Mozart provided a vision of a harmonious world at odds with existing disorder, now it has become incorporated into mass culture. The culture industry claims that the world is already harmonious so that the critical function of art now only resides at the margins, in the work of those who challenge this supposed harmony, such as the music of Schoenberg.

Such an analysis leads the Frankfurt School to a very pessimistic conclusion. Hegemony in contemporary capitalist societies now seems almost complete. People are dominated not only at work but also in their leisure. What's more there seem to be few signs of resistance. Although Marcuse recognises that there are a few marginal groups such as ethnic minorities who are not fully integrated into the system, the overriding picture is of society as a mass of isolated individuals who are manipulated by big business. There seems to be no way out.

Habermas Habermas's starting point is different from that of the Frankfurt School. For Habermas, what distinguishes human beings is not only their ability to transform the environment but also language – the ability to use signs to communicate with each other. This has far reaching consequences. According to Habermas, when one person talks to another, that person implicitly claims that what is said is intelligible, true, justified and sincere. For there to be rational communication, speakers need to be able to defend all four claims. This presumes various conditions, ie that 'there are no external constraints preventing participants from assessing evidence and argument, and in which each participant has an equal and open chance of entering the discussion' (Giddens, 1985). Circumstances where these conditions are met Habermas calls an *ideal speech situation*. And it is this which provides him with a yardstick against which to measure existing social arrangements.

Social evolution has witnessed increasing possibilities for rational communication and at the same time the emergence of legally sanctioned institutions such as state bureaucracies and markets. In a complex society, it is not always possible for communication to settle competing claims. Instead, power and money become major mechanisms for routinely settling issues ranging from an individual's welfare entitlement to the price of bananas. A problem arises, however, when power and money 'penetrate into areas of everyday life and practice which require communicative action' (Layder, 1994). According to Habermas, this has happened with politics. Whereas politics should involve discussion and debate over what are desirable ends, increasingly it has become simply a question of who can run the economy best. In other words, communicative rationality has been displaced by instrumental rationality. Unlike the Frankfurt school, Habermas does see the glimmering of a way out, for he does not see capitalism as a stable system.

Habermas identifies four types of crisis through which the system moves. In early capitalism *economic crises* present the main problem. According to Habermas, the state reacts to economic crises by accepting an increasing level of responsibility for the management of the economy through such familiar strategies as the protection of home markets and promotion of public sector production. Such action, however, generates a *rationality crisis*. Government intervention in the economy requires heavy borrowing but this creates inflation and disrupts the normal working of the market. Government intervention ceases for a time but the shift between interventionist and laissez-faire (non-interventionist) approaches to the management of the economy makes the state appear to be acting in an irrational manner. This leads to a *legitimation crisis*. The state finds it increasingly difficult to reconcile the conflicting demands placed upon it. The switch from an interventionist to a laissez-faire approach means that people's expectations of improved welfare cannot be met. At this stage the state loses its legitimacy. This in turns leads to a *motivation crisis*. Increased state power, coupled with the seeming irrelevance of which political party forms the government, undermine people's motivation for participating in the system at all.

There is a way out, however. For new social movements may emerge, such as the environmentalist and women's movements, to challenge instrumental rationality and inject back into politics a concern with values. Although critical theory questions the link which Marx saw between the rise of the proletariat and the advent of a free society, its search for 'an emancipatory alternative to the existing order' indicates its continuing commitment to the Enlightenment ideal (Bronner & Kellner, 1989).

Structuralist Marxism

For structuralist Marxism, the notion that we are the authors of our actions is mistaken. Rather we are the products of underlying structures. Despite its opposition to humanistic Marxism on this issue, there is agreement that economic determinism needs to be rejected. This is clear(ish) in the work of Althusser.

According to Althusser, societies – which he labels social formations – comprise three levels: the economic, the political and the ideological. Although the economy is 'determinant in the last instance', the political and ideological levels are not mere reflections of the economy but have 'relative autonomy' – a degree of independence – and do have effects on the economy.

To clarify what this means, it is helpful to think of an analogy – a three storey building comprising a shop on the ground floor, offices on the second and living quarters on the third. It does not make sense to say 'that the first and second floors are caused by the ground floor, even though they rest upon it' (Craib, 1984). If we assume that the building is one enterprise, the office work which goes on on the first floor is obviously dependent upon the kind of trading conducted in the shop, but work relationships there may well develop in a quite different way. Similarly, if the owners live on the second floor their style of life is influenced by the nature of the business, but their family life has its own dynamics. The economy, in short, does set limits on the political and ideological levels but the latter are not completely dependent upon the former. What's more these levels affect the economy. Returning to our example, new information systems in the office may increase turnover in the shop, while a family bust up might force the business to close down. The interaction, in short, between the three levels is extremely complex.

Althusser's rejection of economic determinism is further apparent when he argues that different types of society can be distinguished according to the dominance of the different levels. What he means by this is that in the operation of a society, one particular level may become more important than the others. It is, however, the economic level which determines which of the levels is dominant at any particular time. 'It is as if the economic level hands over its power to one of the other levels, or keeps it to itself, for the duration of that type of society' (Craib 1984). Two examples illustrate this. Under feudalism, the landlords have to ensure that serfs hand over the surplus which they have produced. To do this, they are reliant on the state forcing the serfs to do so, or the church persuading them to do so. In this mode of production, the political and ideological levels are thus dominant. Under capitalism, by contrast, the bourgeoisie automatically receive the surplus produced by the proletariat. In this mode of production, the economic level is dominant.

Although this is the case, Althusser recognises that capitalist relations of production depend upon a number of conditions being fulfilled which cannot be guaranteed purely at the economic level. Workers need, for example, to be trained in the appropriate skills and persuaded to accept their role. For Althusser (1971), it is above all the state which ensures that these conditions are met and that 'the reproduction of the relations of production' occurs. It does this in two ways – through 'repressive state apparatuses' such as the army and the police which coerce people and through 'ideological state apparatuses' such as education and the mass media which ensure that people are socialised to fill their allotted places in the relations of production. We may think that we are the authors of our own actions but, in fact, we are the products of pre-existing structures which map out our lives for us. Capitalism can be overthrown, but this will depend not upon people changing their consciousness, but rather upon contradictions at different levels coming together to reinforce each other. Althusser calls this process *overdetermination*. This is when capitalism is most vulnerable to revolution, as in the case of the Russian Revolution in 1917.

Evaluation

What is most striking when looking at Marxism are the different approaches within it. We need really to evaluate each separately. Nonetheless, there is some agreement that central to the analysis of modern society are the concepts of capitalism and class. The main concerns of Marxism are twofold: 1) to account for the unexpected stability of capitalism and 2) to identify the factors likely to lead to the demise of capitalism. While Marxists agree that the economy is in some sense fundamental and that class conflict is therefore central, in practice they often pay particular attention to the superstructure (the state and ideology) and acknowledge the importance of social movements not based on class.

They therefore often find themselves on the horns of a dilemma. If they attempt to do justice to the complexity of the world and question, for example, the link between the proletariat and the demise of capitalism, aren't they abandoning Marxism? If they attempt to do justice to the complexity of the world and see, for example, the economy as only determinant in the last instance, aren't they putting forward a theory which is 'unfalsifiable' and in Popper's view as unscientific as the belief that God is all powerful?

key terms

Humanist Marxism Assumes that human beings can transform their environment and influence social change.
Structuralist Marxism Assumes that human behaviour is largely shaped by the structure of society and that human beings are a product of structures.
Hegemony Domination through ideology.
Dual consciousness The view that proletarian consciousness is shaped by the dominant ideology and their everyday experience.
Instrumental reason The use of reason to discover the most efficient means to achieve ends.
Mass culture A culture based on false needs which is transmitted through the media to the mass of the population.
Overdetermination When contradictions at different levels of society – the economic, political and ideological – come together and reinforce each other.

activity7 a crisis of hegemony?

Item A The Handsworth 'mugging'

In March 1973, two boys were found guilty of robbing and inflicting grievous bodily harm on a man in Handsworth, Birmingham. The boys had stolen a total of 30p, some keys and five cigarettes. They had also returned to attack the victim two hours after the initial incident. Each boy received a ten year sentence. A third boy, the 'ringleader', according to the judge on the case, was found guilty of attempted murder and robbery with regard to the same victim. He was given a twenty year sentence. All three sentences were extremely long and, arguably, harsh for the type of crimes committed.

Item B Press headline 17 August 1972

As Crimes of Violence Escalate, a Word Common in The United States Enters the British Headlines: Mugging. To our Police, it's a frightening new strain of crime.

(Daily Mirror)

Item C Press editorial 13 October 1972

WHAT ARE the British people most concerned about today? Wages? Prices? Immigration? Pornography? People are talking about all these things. But the Sun believes there is another issue which has everyone deeply worried and angry: VIOLENCE IN OUR STREETS... Nothing could be more utterly against our way of life, based on a common sense regard for law and order ... If punitive jail sentences help to stop the violence – and nothing else has done – then they will not only prove to be the only way. They will, regrettably, be the RIGHT way. And the judges will have the backing of the public.

(Sun)

Item D A judge's view

Mugging is becoming more and more prevalent, certainly in London. As a result, decent citizens are afraid to use the Underground late at night, and indeed are afraid to use the underpasses for fear of mugging. We are told that in America people are even afraid to walk in the streets late at night for fear of mugging. This is an offence for which deterrent sentences should be passed.

Judge Alexander Karmel, QC

Item E A politician's view

In my view it is absolutely essential to stop this rising tide of mugging in our cities. I have seen what happens in America where muggings are rife. It is absolutely horrifying to know that in all the big American cities, coast to coast, there are areas where people dare not go out after dark. I am extremely anxious that such a situation should never come to Britain.

Birmingham MP, Mrs Jill Knight (quoted in the Birmingham Evening Mail, 20.8.1972)

Item F Social conflict – Northern Ireland, 1972

In 1972, the IRA stepped up its bombing campaign and tens of thousands of Catholics took part in civil rights marches. On 30 January 1972, soldiers opened fire on an illegal march in Derry killing 13 and injuring 29. On 22 February, seven people were killed in an IRA attack on the 16th Parachute Brigade at Aldershot. On 28 March, 100,000 Protestants marched against direct rule from Westminster.

The Bogside, Derry, 1972. Rioting Catholic youth flee from a gas cannister fired by British troops.

Item G Social conflict – the miners' strike, 1972

In 1972, striking miners attempted to create a power crisis. In February 1972 they clashed with police as they tried to prevent trucks taking coke from the West Midland Gas Board coke depot in Birmingham. At Longannet, near Edinburgh, 2,000 miners fought with police to prevent deliveries of oil to the power station. Most power stations were working well below capacity and 12 were completely shut down by fuel shortages. The government called a state of emergency.

Striking miners face 500 police at West Midlands Gas Board coke depot, 1972.

questions

1 Read Items A to E. What common themes appear in the reactions from the press, the judiciary and the politician?

2 Look at Items F and G. How might they indicate a crisis in hegemony?

3 Why did the state respond to this crisis by focusing attention on the seemingly trivial issue of 'mugging'?

3.3 Symbolic interactionism

Although, as we have seen, there are significant differences between functionalist and Marxist theories of society, both emphasise the ways in which individual behaviour and consciousness are shaped by external forces in society. In their own ways, therefore, both may be regarded to some extent as *deterministic* theories, in which little scope is allowed for individuals to shape their own destinies by the exercise of their free will. Symbolic interactionists, by contrast, emphasise the ways in which society is actively shaped by the conscious and deliberate actions of its members. For this reason, symbolic interactionism is usually regarded as a *social action theory*, whilst functionalism and Marxism are regarded as *structural* theories.

Although a wide range of intellectual influences on the development of symbolic interactionism may be traced – including especially the work of such 18th century Scottish Moralists as Adam Ferguson, John Millar and Adam Smith, and in the 19th century, Charles Darwin's theory of evolution. Perhaps the greatest influence was the late 19th century American philosophy of 'pragmatism' developed by such men as John Dewey, William James and Charles Pierce.

At the heart of pragmatism, as with symbolic interactionism, was a concern with 'meaning'. For pragmatists, the meaning of an object was not intrinsic to that object, but depended upon the ways in which human beings behaved towards it. So, for example, there is nothing about a chair which intrinsically gives it its significance as something we sit upon – this significance derives entirely from the fact that this is indeed how human beings behave towards chairs. It would be entirely possible for us to treat chairs as objects of worship, as places for our pet canaries to perch, or as virtually anything else. And if we were to do so, the meaning of 'chair' would be quite different, even though the physical nature of the object remains unchanged. It is this pragmatist concern with the ways in which human beings actively make their environments meaningful that forms the starting point of symbolic interactionism.

George Herbert Mead

One of the most significant figures in the development of the symbolic interactionist tradition was the American philosopher and social psychologist, George Herbert Mead. Mead taught at the University of Chicago from 1893 until his death in 1931, and founded what, because of its continued association with the university and the city, became known as the 'Chicago School' of symbolic interactionism. During his lifetime Mead published very little, most of his work being published after his death on the basis of lecture notes and fragmentary manuscripts. Probably his most significant book from the point of view of symbolic interactionism is *Mind, Self and Society*, first published in 1934.

Human conduct versus animal behaviour What is the difference between the behaviour of animals and that of human beings? Mead's answer to this question gives us the clue to the whole approach of symbolic interactionism. For Mead, following the ideas of behaviourists such as John B. Watson, animal behaviour could be accounted for in terms of responses to stimuli. Such responses may either be directly instinctual, such as a cat's response to a physical threat, or learned, as was demonstrated by Ivan Pavlov in his famous experiments where he 'conditioned' a dog to salivate whenever a bell was rung, by repeatedly associating the sound of the bell with the arrival of food. Whilst Mead agreed that such processes could account for certain aspects of human behaviour, he argued that most needed to be characterised in a qualitatively different way.

To see Mead's point, consider the following situation. If I walk up to a dog belonging to one of my students and deliver a hefty kick to its rear end, its behaviour will be predictable. It will probably bark, turn around and snap at my ankles. It would do the same whoever was to deliver the kick, and under whatever circumstances. Of course, following Pavlov's principle, it is possible that if I repeat this often enough, the dog will come to associate my presence with being kicked, and will begin to bark and snap at my ankles even when I do not kick it. But even so, its behaviour remains predictable. Now, imagine that instead of kicking the dog, I kick its owner, my student. How will the student respond? An initial response might be to say that he will kick me back, but a moment's reflection reveals that things are not so straightforward as at first they might seem. Will the student kick me back? He may, but this will depend upon how he has interpreted my kick. For example, he may interpret it as simply an act of gratuitous violence, in which case he would probably feel quite justified in returning the kick. However, there are a good many other ways in which my behaviour could be interpreted. He might judge that it was the result of mental instability on my part, in which case returning the kick begins to seem not merely inappropriate, but even callous – in our society, at least, assaulting the mentally ill is generally frowned upon. He might judge that my kick was merely an over-enthusiastic attempt to explain the principles of symbolic interactionism, in which case he might consider a verbal remonstration sufficient, as at least I had intended no harm.

The point is that how the student reacts will depend upon how he interprets my behaviour, or, in other words, what *meaning* he attributes to it. For Mead, this ability involves the distinctively human capacity to put oneself in the place of others, and to see oneself from the point of view of others. This he calls *role-taking*. In assessing how to respond to my kick, my student has to imagine the situation from my point of view – in short, he has to 'take my role'.

The self In an attempt to understand this distinctively human ability to take the role of others, Mead developed the concept of the *self*. For Mead, the self is viewed as having two elements which he terms the *I* and the *Me*. To understand the distinction which Mead is making, consider the following example. Imagine that, in the course of a particularly dull lecture, you become aware of an impulse to leave the room and go for coffee. This impulse originates from the part of your personality which Mead calls the *I*. It is spontaneous and, as it were, uncensored.

However, although such impulses may be common enough, they are in fact rarely acted upon. This is because as soon as you become aware of such a desire, you cannot avoid imagining what sort of response your walking out of the lecture would provoke in those around you, and especially the lecturer! This 'imagining' of the likely responses of others originates from the part of the personality which Mead calls the *Me*. This is the internalised points of view of other people, and acts as a sort of censor of the *I's* plans.

Crucial to Mead's notion of the self, was the fact that it can only emerge as the result of social interaction. We have to learn the points of view of specific other people (*significant others* in Mead's terminology) and of society in general (for Mead, the *generalised other*). Mead identified two principal stages by which the child acquires a social self. The first he calls the *play stage*. This phase, which begins as soon as the child starts to use language, is exemplified by the tendency of young children to pretend to be someone else. For example, children will play 'doctors and nurses' or 'teachers', or pretend to be their father or mother chastising a younger sibling. Mead argues that, in doing this, children learn to see themselves from the point of view of significant others. The second stage is termed by Mead the *game stage*. This phase is exemplified by the playing of team games, in which the child has to see himself not only from the point of view of specific individuals, but of entire groups. For example, although the members of the opposing team in a game of football all have individual points of view, a player must be able to imagine himself from the collective point of view of that team, ie as their opponent. It is this process which, in Mead's view, completes the development of the social self because it leads to the ability to view oneself from the generalised point of view of one's society.

The significance of Mead's work Although Mead's work has important implications for both philosophy and social psychology, its importance to sociological theory lies principally in his view of human beings as socially self-conscious. They are not the mindless products of external social norms over which they have no control. Potentially, therefore, Mead's theory has the ability to explain how social order is maintained – by the fact that human beings possess an internalised representation of the point of view of their fellow members of society. At the same time, Mead also recognises that human beings act self-consciously in possibly unpredictable ways.

Herbert Blumer

After Mead's death in 1931, the tradition which he had helped to establish at the University of Chicago was continued by the sociologist Herbert Blumer. Indeed, although his work clearly owed an immense amount to Mead's influence, it was in fact Blumer who coined the term *symbolic interactionism*. Perhaps Blumer's greatest contribution to the development of symbolic interactionism was his working out of some of the major implications of symbolic interactionist theory for how sociologists should study society.

Blumer's critique of variable analysis As we have seen, a major assumption of a number of sociological approaches is that human behaviour can be understood in terms of the influences of external causes which are amenable to measurement. A classic example of this is Durkheim's study of suicide, in which a society's suicide rate is correlated with certain other features of that society, such as the degree of integration or regulation which prevails. Such explanations take the form, variable X (say a low level of integration) produces variable Y (say a high suicide rate). Individual consciousness as such is deliberately ignored in such explanations.

For Blumer, this was unacceptable. First of all, he emphasises the fact that variables are in fact creations of sociologists, and can usually only be identified and measured if the sociologist makes some quite arbitrary and groundless assumptions. Consider the example of social class. Imagine that a sociologist wishes to demonstrate a relationship between being working class and experiencing relatively poor health. Before this can even be meaningful, the sociologist must define and operationalise 'social class'. She may define social class in terms of occupation and classify her sample accordingly. Next she must define and operationalise the second variable, 'relatively poor health'. She may choose to use the incidence of longstanding illness. Finally, she must examine the relationship between the two variables – does being working class increase one's risk of experiencing poor health? The crucial point for Blumer, however, is that the answer to her question will depend almost entirely on how the variables have been defined and operationalised. They could, quite legitimately, have been defined and operationalised quite differently, and this would inevitably have produced a different answer to the question being addressed.

Second, and most importantly for Blumer, is the fact that even if social class does influence health, the process by which this occurs needs to be examined. Following Mead's theoretical lead, Blumer emphasises the fact that human behaviour does not result from the blind operation of external social forces (or, in other words, variables). Instead, behaviour (or *conduct*) results from how a social actor interprets or attributes meaning to a situation. Thus, to continue the same example, the central question would be, what meanings do people attach to their class position, and how do these meanings contribute to subsequent conduct which either promotes, or damages, their health? Crucial for Blumer, as for Mead, is the fact these meanings are not inevitable and pre-determined, but will change over time and vary between individuals.

Blumer therefore uses symbolic interactionist theory to challenge certain other sociological approaches on methodological grounds. In Blumer's view it is simply not legitimate to see human behaviour as resulting from the operation of measurable variables. Instead, individual actions need to be examined from the point of view of the actor's interpretation of the situation in which they find themself. It is for this reason that symbolic interactionists have tended to rely upon such qualitative research techniques as participant observation in an attempt to discover these meanings. (See page 137 for further discussion of Blumer's methodology.)

Erving Goffman – the dramaturgical analogy

All the world's a stage,
And all the men and women merely players;
They have their exits and their entrances,
And one man in his time plays many parts.

(*As You Like It*, Act II, Scene VII, Shakespeare)

Impression management Erving Goffman (1959), the most influential symbolic interactionist, uses a *dramaturgical analogy* – society as drama – to illuminate social interaction and explore 'the way in which the individual in ordinary work situations presents himself and his activity to others, the ways in which he guides and controls the impression they form of him'. Goffman argues that in everyday social interaction individuals are not only constantly expressing themselves to others, but also are trying to create certain impressions of themselves in the mind of an audience. This process of *impression management* is central to behaviour, as social actors attempt to control the impressions others have of them.

Goffman pays most attention to the non-verbal aspects of interpersonal communication and this is illustrated by the example he quotes from his research into rural life in the Shetland Islands. The crofter's wife, when serving local dishes to tourists, would check on the stated feelings of liking the food by watching how quickly the tourists ate the food and how eagerly it was consumed. In social interaction, we constantly watch for these non-verbal 'signs given off' as the ways in which a person's true feelings might be revealed. We do not always take things at face value, but we check the whole performance for any discrepancies, and for signs of the underlying motivations of the performer.

Performance The idea of performance is very important to Goffman's analysis. It refers to any activity of a participant in a social interaction which influences other participants. When playing a part, the individual is implicitly asking the others in an interaction to believe in their performance. And to achieve this, the social actor must create the appropriate impression. For example, some teachers take the view that it is important to get the upper hand in a new class – starting out tough and letting the students know who's boss. Any bumbling around or signs of weakness will not create the desired impression and the performance

will fail, endangering future performances before that class. Goffman recognises that we can believe in the roles we play, or perform them with no real conviction. Deluding an audience may be out of self-interest, or it may be because the audience demands to be deluded. An illustration of the latter is the way doctors may give placebos (something which will have no medical effect) to hypochondriacal patients in the knowledge that there is nothing wrong with them, but simply because they demand treatment.

To be effective, performances need to be cohesive and sustained. Some of the techniques used to confirm an impression are considered next.

Front and regions Social actors employ the equivalent of theatrical 'props' to assist in the creation of a particular impression or definition of a situation. Anything which is intentionally or unintentionally used to enhance the effectiveness of a performance, Goffman refers to as 'front'. Furniture, decor and specialised equipment may be used to create the right setting for a performance and these are allied to the personal 'front' of clothing, speech, facial expressions and body language in order to create a cohesive impression, consistent with the role being expressed. The budding young executive, keen to create an impression of dynamism, will go in for 'power dressing' and is likely to develop the leisure interests and activities associated with that image. Many of the 'props' we carry or utilise have an apparently practical purpose, but their real value lies in the way they contribute to creating a desired impression. Solicitors' case papers are usually tied with ribbon, ostensibly to prevent the contents from falling out, but the social impact is one of setting aside legal papers from other kinds of material, inferring a special and superior status to them and to the person carrying them.

Just as a theatre has a 'frontstage' where the performance takes place, and a 'backstage' where actors can relax out of their roles, so there are separate 'regions' in social interactions. A 'region' is any area which is bounded to some degree by barriers to perception. Performances take place in a 'front region' whilst in the 'back region', a performance can be knowingly contradicted by out-of-role behaviour. In a school or college, the classroom, corridors, dining areas, etc form the 'front region' for adults performing the role of teacher and for younger people presenting the role of student. However, both teachers and students can relax from their respective roles in either the staff room, or in areas where teachers tend not to visit. Even in these 'back regions' however, a performance of a different kind has to be maintained as colleagues or friends now form a different audience to the 'frontstage' one. So the 'back region' for one performance becomes the 'front region' for another.

When performances fail Goffman notes that sometimes discrepancies appear in our performances which affect the audience's impressions of us. Sometimes an individual fails to maintain their expressive control, the mask slips and the whole performance can be jeopardised in the same way as a jarringly wrong note can spoil an entire concert.

Goffman suggests that examining occasions when this happens tells us a great deal about the nature of performances. For example, an audience, or part of an audience, sometimes colludes with a role player to cover up or ignore discrepancies in a performance and this illustrates the way social actors can work in 'teams', helping to maintain expressive control. Sometimes, however, discrepant behaviour can be more damaging to attempted impression management, culminating in embarrassment and even retirement from that role.

Role distance Goffman creates a strongly humanistic version of social role. The roles we perform in social interaction are not scripted for us by society, but are actively created and defined by our performances. Individuals often distance themselves from the role they are occupying by making communications out of character with the role, thus showing themselves to be more than the role being performed. Elements of the individual's self, made up from other roles they occupy, may appear in the performance of a role, and it is this which allows for spontaneity and creativity in a performance. In acting out the role of teacher for example, an individual may allow other roles – of parent, 'ordinary person' or friend – to enter their performance. Similarly, a civil servant, even when turning down a request because it doesn't fit the rules, may show a 'human face', to indicate that they are more than the role they are performing. We are not programmed into a role, straight-jacketing our behaviour, but through the use of 'role distance', actively create the roles we occupy.

Roles and power Analogies in sociology have to be used with care. It is one thing to point to apparent similarities between social behaviour and acting on a stage, and another to suggest that the two are identical. Goffman recognises the limitations of the dramaturgical analogy, pointing out that the stage presents activity which is imaginary and rehearsed, whilst social behaviour is real and frequently unplanned. Furthermore, in social life the audience often takes a very much more active role than it does in the theatre. For Goffman, therefore, the dramatic analogy is only a framework with which to begin to understand behaviour and many parts of his analysis, for example the idea of role distance, go much further.

Unlike some of the early symbolic interactionists, Goffman does pay specific attention to the ways in which inequalities in power are played out in face-to-face interaction. Without attempting to analyse the structural location and causes of inequality, Goffman nevertheless identifies the way hierarchies create problems of self-respect and opportunity. In *Asylums*, a study of the experience of inmates in a mental hospital, Goffman (1968) explores the problem posed for individual social actors by the imposition on them of a complete regime in a 'total institution' – an institution, such as a prison or mental hospital, in which inmates live, eat and sleep. Even in this, the most extreme case of apparent powerlessness, the individual is still capable of employing strategies which ensure that some self-determination can be retained. Inmates who fool the staff to get extra food or cigarettes are

maintaining their sense of self-determination. In this respect, Goffman's work carries the important message that power is not merely the creation of a hierarchy of positions in society, but the constant acting out in face-to-face interaction of that inequality.

Whilst Goffman rejects the structural view that the individual is what their place in an organisation defines them to be, he does not, unlike some of the early symbolic interactionists, ignore the effect of external constraints. The individual's self does not arise solely out of their interaction with others, but within the context of the limitations imposed by social institutions. The self constantly moves between the limitations of external society and the needs of inner individuality. Goffman concludes that, 'it is against something that the self can emerge'. That 'something' is society. From this, it can be seen that Goffman is acknowledging the impact on our individuality of external social constraints. Our individual 'self' is created in the context of hierarchical organisations which, although they do not rigorously define the way we are, play a part in forging our individuality.

Evaluation

As noted above, symbolic interactionism has a number of strengths. First, it moves away from the deterministic assumptions of much sociological theory, and emphasises the conscious involvement of the actor in social life. Second, it recognises that human conduct is meaningful, and hence that a grasp of actors' meanings and interpretations is essential to an understanding of their actions.

Equally, however, symbolic interactionism can be criticised. The most fundamental and persistent difficulty is its tendency to ignore the influence of social structures. It is possible to acknowledge Blumer's criticisms of variable analysis whilst still recognising that an individual's

key terms

Role-taking Putting oneself in the place of others and seeing oneself from the point of view of others.

Self In Mead's view, the self consists of two elements, the *I* and the *Me*.

Significant others Specific other people who matter to the individual.

Generalised other Society in general.

Play stage The first stage in which a child acquires a social self. Involves seeing themselves from the point of view of significant others.

Game stage The second stage in this process, where they see themselves from the point of view of groups rather than just individuals.

Dramaturgical analogy Seeing a similarity between society and drama, and using this to illuminate social interaction.

Impression management The attempt by social actors to shape and control the impressions others have of them.

Performance Any activity of a participant in social interaction which influences other participants.

Role distance Distancing ourselves from the roles we are playing.

economic position (their class, however this is defined) will affect their behaviour whether they recognise it or not. Poverty, for example, would seem to be real enough, and its effects will be obvious whether or not an actor defines himself as poor. A second, and related, criticism is that symbolic interactionism exaggerates the extent to which human actors do in fact consciously interpret their environments. It may be argued that whilst self-conscious interpretation does occur, this tends to be only when some unusual situation is encountered. For most of the time, human beings seem to act as though on 'automatic pilot', or merely out of habit. The notion of habit seems closer to the view of action advanced by systems and structural theorists than to that advanced by symbolic interactionists.

summary

1. Functionalists argue that societies should be studied as systems – as wholes made up of interconnected parts.

2. The function of any part is the contribution it makes to society as a whole.

3. Talcott Parsons identifies four functional prerequisites which must be met if the social system is to survive – adaptation, goal attainment, integration and pattern maintenance.

4. Parsons explained social change in two ways.
   - As a response to disturbances in the system in order to restore it to equilibrium.
   - In terms of social evolution. As societies evolve, institutions become increasingly specialised – a process known as social differentiation.

5. Robert Merton questions the assumption that all parts of the social system are closely interconnected and work together for the benefit of the whole.

6. Merton argues that:
   - Some parts may have functional autonomy – they may operate as largely independent units.
   - Any part of society may be functional, non-functional or dysfunctional.

7. Criticisms of functionalism include the following.
   - Its theories are teleological – it tends to explain the causes of parts of society in terms of their effects or functions.
   - It overestimates the degree of value consensus in society.
   - Its focus on social order and value consensus downplays the importance of conflict in society.

8. There are two main versions of modern Marxism – humanist Marxism and structuralist Marxism.

9. Gramsci's humanist Marxism argues that the proletariat have a dual consciousness which means they will partially see through bourgeois ideology.

10. According to the Frankfurt School, instrumental reason and mass culture produce and satisfy false needs. Hegemony in capitalist societies is now almost complete.

11. Habermas sees capitalism as an unstable system which moves through a series of crises. He sees hope for the future in the emergence of new social movements which challenge instrumental rationality.

12. According to Althusser's structuralist Marxism, capitalism can be overthrown when contradictions at different levels of society – the economic, political and ideological – come together and reinforce each other.

13. The central concern for modern Marxism is to explain the unexpected stability of capitalism and to identify factors that will lead to its downfall.

14. Symbolic interactionism focuses on small-scale interaction situations and the meanings which direct action.

15. According to Mead, people react to others in terms of the meanings they give to the actions of others. This involves role-taking.

16. The self emerges from social interaction. The child acquires a social self as they pass through the play stage and the game stage.

17. Mead sees human beings as socially self-conscious – they do not simply behave in terms of social norms.

18. Blumer criticises variable analysis, arguing that it sees human beings as shaped by forces beyond their control. This ignores how social actors define and give meaning to their situation. And it fails to discover the meanings which direct action.

19. Goffman uses a dramaturgical analogy to interpret social action. Just like actors in a play, people in society are seen to create performances by the skilful use of impression management.

20. Social actors are seen as creative – negotiating the meanings which direct their actions and adapting and developing the roles they play.

21. Goffman accepts that there is an external society which can constrain human behaviour. However, there is still plenty of room for people to express their creativity and individuality.

22. Critics of symbolic interactionism argue that:
   - It largely ignores the influence of social structures on human behaviour.
   - It exaggerates the extent to which people consciously interpret their situation – often they act out of habit with little thought.

activity8 defining the situation

Henderson Dores is out with his girlfriend Irene Stein. They are trying to locate his car after spending the evening in a restaurant. It is central New York, just after midnight and Henderson has just noticed three men coming towards them. Irene is searching in her handbag for a tissue and has noticed nothing.

Henderson looked round again in what he hoped was an unconcerned natural way. The figures – dark, lithe-looking – had crossed to their side of the street with what looked like more urgency.

Jesus Christ, Henderson thought, they say it happens to everybody sooner or later – like a car crash or a burglary.

He felt a surging panic begin to overwhelm him. It's only when you haven't got any money that they kill you. Or pour petrol over you and set you alight. Or rape you. Gang-sodomise you. They were only ten yards away.

'RUN!' Henderson screamed, simultaneously flinging away the umbrella and giving Irene a mighty push. His hand closed around his wallet, fat with credit cards and dollars.

'You can have it, you bastards!' he yelled at the muggers and with all his strength bowled his wallet in their direction. He saw it fly open and notes and cards shower out, then he turned and ran.

Henderson races off, pursued by two of the men who eventually catch up with him.

'OK,' he bellowed in mingled rage and terror as he was hauled to a stop, 'Kill me, kill me, I don't care!'

Both his hands were firmly gripped. 'Sir,' a quiet voice came. 'Relax, please, sir. We have your wallet and your money here.'

Later, Henderson was able to reconstruct what happened. The three men were returning theatre-goers who had been surprised by Henderson suddenly throwing his girlfriend to the ground, throwing his wallet at them and running off in panic-stricken flight!

Adapted from Boyd, 1985

questions

1 Make a list of the ways in which meanings are transmitted in the situation described above.

2 How does this extract illustrate the view of one symbolic interactionist, W. I. Thomas, that 'if men define situations as real they are real in their consequences'?

Unit 4 *Structure and action in sociology*

keyissues

1 What are the main assumptions of structuralism, ethnomethodology and structuration theory?

2 How have they seen the relationship between structure and action?

Although functionalism, Marxism and symbolic interactionism have been central to the establishment of sociology as a discipline, alternative approaches have developed. In this unit, we shall look at three which present very different ways of looking at the relation between 'structure' and 'action'.

4.1 Structuralism

As the name implies, *structuralism* is concerned with structures. It has been an influential way of looking at the world, not only in sociology and the social sciences, but also in the arts, literary studies and history. The origins of structuralism lie in linguistics – the study of language – and in particular in the work of a Swiss linguist, Ferdinand de Saussure. In order to understand how structuralism has been of relevance as a sociological theory, it will be helpful to begin by considering the distinctive approach adopted by Saussure to the study of language.

Ferdinand de Saussure

Central to Saussure's analysis of language, and indeed to structuralism in general, is the observation that it is possible to study a language in two dimensions. First, we can study what individual people actually write and say. If a person utters a sentence like 'elephants are bigger than apples' we can pay attention to the meaning of this particular utterance, consider its truth, their reasons for saying it and so on. This dimension of language – the dimension of what people actually write and say – is called the *diachronic*. Contrasted with this, however, is the fact that it is only possible for anyone to utter this sentence, or indeed any other, because there are *rules* which go to make up the language which is being spoken. Most obviously, there are rules governing the relationship between words and things (or what Saussure calls *signifiers* and *signifieds*). In English, the word elephant (the signifier) is attached by convention to the large animals with trunks which are indigenous to Africa and India. Of course, there is no absolute reason why we should call them elephants (the word itself is quite arbitrary), but once the convention is established we must use it if we are to make sense.

Second, there are rules of grammar. In English, for example, there are particular rules governing tenses. So the sentence 'elephants were bigger than apples' has a different meaning from our original sentence, 'elephants are bigger than apples', by virtue of the grammatical rules governing past and present tenses. Saussure's point is that we can also study language in this way – as a system of rules governing what we can and cannot say. This second dimension, which concerns itself with the structure of language itself, is called the *synchronic*.

This distinction between the diachronic and the synchronic is fundamental not only to structuralist linguistics, but to the whole structuralist approach. To see how the distinction works, let us consider an example of human activity. Let us take lunch. When we have a meal, we are most likely to be concerned with its diachronic dimension – that is, what we are actually going to eat, and in what order. Imagine we go into a restaurant. Our order may well look something like this. We begin with soup of the day; we then move on to roast chicken, with potatoes, carrots and peas, and finally we choose strawberries and cream followed by coffee and mints. However, as with uttering individual sentences, this meal as it appears in the diachronic dimension depends upon rules which exist in the synchronic. First there are rules, often specific to cultures, about what we can and cannot eat. It is not generally permitted in our culture, for example, to eat parrots, whilst chickens are perfectly acceptable. Second, there are rules about what we can eat together from the same plate, and in what order – the grammatical rules of eating in fact. In our culture, for example, it is not really permissible to begin a meal with dessert and coffee, or to round it off with a bowl of soup. What is clear from this example, as with the example of language, is that the diachronic dimension – the element of action – depends upon the synchronic dimension – the element of structure. It is this concern with the synchronic, or structural elements of human activity, which is characteristic of structuralism.

Claude Lévi-Strauss

As you will by now have noticed, many of the sociological theorists considered in this chapter could be called structuralist. Certainly, Durkheim's concern with social facts, or Marx's emphasis on the underlying logic of capitalism, could win them the label of structuralist. However, the theorist who did most to formulate the implications of the structuralist approach for the social sciences was the Belgian anthropologist Claude Lévi-Strauss. Lévi-Strauss was concerned to apply structuralist methods to the analysis of human culture. One of his most famous analyses was of myths.

Myths exist in all societies. Although, superficially, the myths which different societies possess are quite different from each other, Lévi-Strauss's analysis emphasises that this is only so when considered in a diachronic sense. When viewed synchronically, he argues that myths possess certain common structural features. One can, according to Lévi-

Strauss, and indeed he spends much time attempting to demonstrate this, place a large number of myths (theoretically all myths) alongside each other, and detect a common set of underlying rules which govern their structure. Lévi-Strauss attempts to explain this deep structure in terms of fundamental properties of the human mind. The underlying structure of culture, he says, is ultimately produced by the biologically determined structures of the human brain.

Oppositions Here is a brief illustration of Lévi-Strauss's approach. Myths are based on *oppositions*. Typical oppositions are good/evil; male/female; life/death; night/day; land/sea. For example, these and many other oppositions are found in the creation myth in *Genesis* which tells the story of the creation of the world, of life, and of human beings.

Many of these oppositions cause unwelcome contradictions for human beings. For example, death contradicts life. Myths can resolve this contradiction by stating that death is not a necessary consequence of life. They can introduce a new possibility, a new form of existence which is neither life nor death. Thus myths often contain 'mythical beings' such as angels, ghosts and other supernatural creatures who are neither alive nor dead as we normally understand these terms. In this way, myths mediate between the opposition of life and death, they resolve the contradiction.

Lévi-Strauss argues that all myths have the same basic structure – opposition and mediation or, put another way, contradiction and resolution. Only when this structure is revealed are we in a position to interpret the function of myths. In Lévi-Strauss's (1965) words, 'the purpose of myth is to provide a logical model capable of overcoming a contradiction'.

Semiotics

Derived from the theoretical basis of structuralism, *semiotics*, or the study of signs, was developed most famously in the work of Roland Barthes. Semiotic analysis concentrates upon the central structuralist principle that the relationship between signifier and signified is arbitrary, and hence determined only by convention and applied according to rules. For example, consider a red rose. A red rose can be considered a signifier, in the sense that it has a meaning beyond its mere physical existence as a flower. We know this from the fact that if a man gives a bunch of red roses to a woman, she will interpret this in a quite different way than if he had given her a bunch of daffodils. Red roses, in our culture, signify love, whilst daffodils do not. There is no necessary reason for this – it could just as easily be the other way round. The task of semiotics is to interpret the meanings of signs in our culture.

Barthes was also heavily influenced by Marxism, and one of his central tasks was to analyse the deep ideological meanings of signs in modern popular culture. He argued that very often such signs, whilst appearing on the surface trivial enough, betray deeper ideological 'myths', which are often invisible to ordinary people and can only be seen when subjected to semiological analysis. One of Barthes' own examples will serve to illustrate this point. The example is of a Black soldier saluting the French flag on the cover of the magazine *Paris Match*. At face value, this is just what it appears to be – a Black soldier saluting the French flag. However, at a deeper level, Barthes argues, this picture signifies a strongly ideological message, namely, 'that France is a great Empire, that all her sons, without colour discrimination, faithfully serve under her flag, and that there is no better answer to the detractors of an alleged colonialism than the zeal shown by this Negro in serving his so-called oppressors' (Barthes, 1973). In other words, this seemingly straightforward picture of a Black soldier saluting the flag contains a hidden justification of French imperialism and a denial of racial discrimination.

As with other structuralist writers, Barthes' approach rests upon his analysis of the synchronic dimension, and specifically upon the systems of rules which govern the relationship between signifiers and that which they signify. It is only in relation to these systems of rules, which link certain signs with deeper ideological meanings, that the specific products (that is the diachronic dimension) of popular culture can be understood.

Evaluation

There can be no doubt that structuralism provides a powerful method for the analysis of virtually any aspect of human culture. More specifically, it has encouraged sociologists to recognise that 'what appears to us as solid, normal or natural, is in fact the end result of a process of production from some form of underlying structure' (Marshall, 1994). It has nevertheless been subject to criticisms.

One is that in reducing the diachronic to the synchronic – or, interpreting actual utterances, myths, pictures or whatever in terms of underlying systems of rules – we are in danger of losing the uniqueness and subtlety of actual human action. Subtle differences in meaning between myths, for example, are in danger of being lost sight of in the eagerness of the structuralist to find some underlying pattern which all myths have in common.

Second, it can be argued that structuralism has an inevitable difficulty in explaining change. If particular instances of action are to be explained with reference to some underlying structure, then it is difficult to see how changes in that structure are to be explained.

Despite these criticisms, as we shall see, the insights of structuralism have nevertheless been important in shaping modern sociological theory.

key terms

Diachronic The part of language people actually write and say.
Synchronic The structure of language – the rules governing language.
Oppositions Opposites such as good/evil, male/female.
Semiotics The study of signs.

4.2 Ethnomethodology

Ethnomethodology is an approach to sociological theorising developed during the 1960s by the American writer, Harold Garfinkel. Ethnomethodology can be seen largely as a reaction to the highly structural and systematic theorising in sociology which reached its climax with the work of Garfinkel's teacher, Talcott Parsons. The

activity9 semiotics

Item A

Do women have to be naked to get into the Met. Museum?

Less than 5% of the artists in the Modern Art Sections are women, but 85% of the nudes are female.

GUERRILLA GIRLS Box 1056 Cooper Sta. NY, NY 10276 CONSCIENCE OF THE ART WORLD

Item B

World War I poster

Item C

World War II poster

question

Interpret the ideological significance of Items A, B and C.

philosophical underpinnings of ethnomethodology lie in a branch of European philosophy known as phenomenology, and in particular in the work of Edmund Husserl (1859-1938) and Alfred Schutz (1899-1959). Before we undertake an examination of ethnomethodology, therefore, it will be helpful to briefly consider the essence of phenomenology.

Phenomenology

The central point of phenomenology, first outlined by its founder Edmund Husserl, is that human beings do not experience the world at first hand, but rather interpret the world through their senses in a way which is meaningful to them. Imagine that you are looking at a table. How do you know that it is a table? At first sight, of course, that sounds like an absurd question, but a moment's thought reveals that it is in fact more profound than it seems. What you are in fact looking at is not intrinsically a table, but a solid

object of a certain shape and size. You only call it a table because you know about tables – in other words, because you possess the category of table in your mind, and when you see objects of a certain shape and size, you place them into this category. Had you never encountered the concept of table you would not describe the object as a table – indeed to you, it would not be a table. It is this concern with how human actors make sense of the world around them that is at the centre of phenomenology.

This fundamental concern was applied specifically to the subject matter of sociology by Husserl's student, Alfred Schutz. Schutz emphasised the fact that the ways in which human beings classify objects in the world is not an individual process, but rather a collective process. The categories we use are not peculiar to ourselves, but are shared with other members of our society. Such categories are called by Schutz *typifications*.

Typification refers to any shared concept – golf ball, democracy, Church, armchair, etc – and forms the basis of communication. Collectively, Schutz says that our typifications build up into what he calls a stock of 'commonsense knowledge'. Of course, one consequence of this notion is that there is no guarantee that any two individuals will perceive the world in the same way, as there may always be differences in the typifications which they adopt as a result of different experiences of life. Yet Schutz argues that, in order for communication to be possible at all, we must assume that the typifications which we adopt are shared with others. We thus get by in the social world by creating and sustaining a sort of illusion of shared understanding.

Harold Garfinkel and ethnomethodology

An approximate meaning of the term 'ethnomethodology' is 'the methods used by people'. Specifically, it refers to the study of the methods which social actors (or 'members' as ethnomethodologists usually refer to them) use to make sense of their social world. It thus begins from the phenomenological assumption that the world does not present itself with an already meaningful and clearly demarcated order. Rather this order is actively constructed through the activities of members. Ethnomethodology seeks to understand how they do this.

The documentary method For Garfinkel, members employ the *documentary method* to make sense of and account for the social world which they inhabit. The documentary method involves taking certain aspects of a situation from an infinite number which could have been selected, defining them in a particular way, and then using this definition to provide evidence for some underlying pattern. New situations are then themselves interpreted in relation to this underlying pattern.

An example of this is Atkinson's study of the practices of coroners (see pages 137-139 and 269-270). The underlying pattern here was the coroner's commonsense view of what constituted a suicide, and on this basis individual deaths were deemed either to be or not to be suicides. However, the very act of classifying deaths itself gives further support to the belief in the existence of an underlying pattern. Identifying particular examples of the pattern and the belief in the existence of the pattern itself are therefore mutually reinforcing. This mutual reinforcement was termed by Garfinkel *reflexivity*, and he felt that this was an essential element of social life. Members constantly seek to explain events in terms of underlying patterns, and use these explanations to justify and reinforce their initial belief in the existence of the underlying patterns. There is no reason to believe, however, that these patterns refer in any direct way to some external social reality.

Indexicality A central part of Garfinkel's analysis was the observation that members make interpretations of situations on the basis of context. Two members, acting in precisely the same way, may be subject to quite different interpretations depending upon the contexts of their actions. For example, if the action concerned is telling an off-colour joke, then if it is performed by a comedian in a night club it is likely to elicit a different interpretation than if it is told by a nun in a convent. This is what Garfinkel meant by *indexicality* – the meaning of the action in each case is not derived from intrinsic features of the action, but rather from the social contexts in which it takes place.

Rules and social order Parsons and many other sociologists assumed that rules were simply learned in the process of socialisation and were capable of guiding conduct in most situations. Garfinkel emphasises that it is the assumption of the existence of rules, rather than rules themselves, which is responsible for the maintenance of social order. Garfinkel illustrates this with reference to a simple game. His point is that even in a simple game, where the rules are written down in an unambiguous fashion, it is easy to find what he calls 'monsters', or possibilities not covered by the rules. Here is his illustration of how easy it is to find such monsters in even the simplest of games.

> Say we are going to propose a game of ticktacktoe. Two persons play ticktacktoe. Any two persons? When, today? Tomorrow? Do we have to be in sight of each other? Can we play by mail? Can one player be dead? (cited in Heritage, 1984).

The point of this illustration is that we assume that our activities are guided by clearly understood rules. However, in reality this is not the case. The extent to which the maintenance of social order is based upon such fragile assumptions is illustrated in Garfinkel's so-called 'breaching experiments'. Here, he asked his students to go into familiar situations and behave in unexpected ways. For example, some went into a department store and started to haggle over the price of goods, whilst others went home to their families and behaved like lodgers. In each case, the behaviour could not be easily accounted for, and produced reactions such as confusion and anger. What these experiments illustrate is that social order is in fact very fragile and only maintained by the mutual assumptions of members.

Ethnomethodology and sociology

As well as being a radically different approach to understanding social order, ethnomethodology also offers a general critique of sociological theory. Garfinkel argued that 'man' is usually represented by sociology as a 'cultural dope' – that is someone who unthinkingly and compliantly acts out the norms of their society. In contrast, ethnomethodology regards the individual as a skilled member of society, who is constantly engaged in interpreting and giving meaning to situations, and maintaining a sense of social order. For Garfinkel, then, social order is not an objective pre-given determinant of human action, but rather is the active accomplishment of members.

Ethnomethodologists have argued that conventional sociology employs very similar procedures to members living their everyday lives. Specifically, just as members employ the documentary method to identify and justify underlying patterns, so do professional sociologists. Social class is one example. Because sociologists assume that there is an underlying pattern of social class relationships, particular instances of behaviour – such as voting patterns, educational achievements and so on – are interpreted in the light of this underlying pattern. This interpretation, in turn, gives further support for the existence of the underlying pattern. For ethnomethodologists, however, this would just be another example of a mutually reinforcing fiction. The realities of sociologists, therefore, are seen as just as 'constructed' as those of any other members.

Evaluation

There can be no doubt that ethnomethodology constituted a radical critique of conventional sociology. Its emphasis upon interpretation and social order as the active accomplishment of members did indeed offer a new way of looking at social order. It can nevertheless be subjected to various criticisms.

First, Alvin Gouldner has accused ethnomethodology of being preoccupied with trivia. In concentrating upon the mundane elements of everyday life, it ignores the wider inequalities in power and wealth which prevail in modern societies. Even granting Garfinkel's emphasis on the active construction of social reality by members, he seems to

key terms

Typification Any shared concept – for example, bacon, grass, liberalism, death.

Documentary method The method used by members of society to make sense of the world around them. It involves selecting certain aspects of a situation, then using them as evidence of an underlying pattern. New situations are then interpreted in terms of this pattern.

Reflexivity As used by Garfinkel, explaining events in terms of underlying patterns and using these explanations to justify the existence of those patterns.

Indexicality The meaning of an action is derived from the context in which it takes place.

ignore the ways in which different groups in society might find it easier than others to have their view of reality adopted by the majority.

Second, ethnomethodology's critique of mainstream sociology could very easily be directed back on itself. Surely, if all other actors – including sociologists – employ the documentary method, then why should ethnomethodologists themselves be exempt? If they are not, then ethnomethodology becomes just another self-reinforcing account of an ultimately unknowable social world.

activity10 ethnomethodology

Item A An experiment in counselling

In an experiment conducted in a university department of psychiatry, students were invited to take part in what was described as a new form of psychotherapy. Students were told to summarise a personal problem, and then ask the counsellor a series of questions which could be answered either 'yes' or 'no'. The counsellor sat in an adjoining room, and communicated with the student by intercom. Unknown to the students, the 'counsellor' was not who they claimed to be, and the answers were randomly divided in a predetermined sequence between 'yes' and 'no'. Despite the fact that the answers were completely random, and indeed that some contradicted previous answers, the students felt that the advice received was helpful and sensible.

Adapted from Garfinkel, 1967.

Item B A streaker

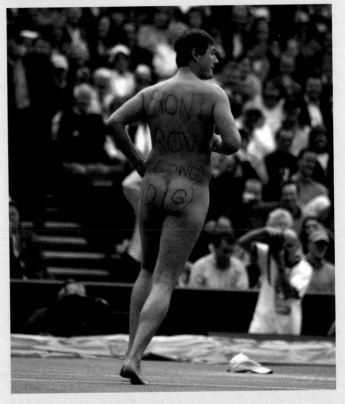

questions

1 Read Item A. In what ways does this experiment demonstrate the documentary method?

2 Item B is a picture of a streaker. How does this statement illustrate Garfinkel's concept of indexicality?

4.3 The unification of structure and action

As we have seen in this chapter, sociological theories tend to come closer to one of two general approaches – one which emphasises social structure, and the other which emphasises social action. It would be wrong to say that any theory in sociology completely ignores either structure or action, but it would be fair to say that whilst Marxists, functionalists and structuralists tend to emphasise the role of social structures, Weber, symbolic interactionists and ethnomethodologists tend to emphasise the creative and interpretivist nature of social action. This tendency for sociological theories to emphasise one aspect at the expense of the other has led some writers on sociological theory to suggest that structure and action represent alternative ways of looking at society which cannot be brought together. In this section, we shall consider one influential approach to this problem, that of the British sociologist Anthony Giddens.

Anthony Giddens and the theory of structuration

The duality of structure At the centre of Giddens' concern to overcome the division between structural and action approaches within sociology is his concept of the *duality of structure*. In simple terms, action (or 'agency' as he usually calls it) and structure are just two ways of looking at the same thing. For Giddens, structures are produced by social action, and it is only through social action that they are maintained over time. However, at the same time, it is only by the existence of structures that actions are made possible. Let us take the example of speech and language to illustrate this.

Language can be regarded as a structure. It is a set of rules for communication which exists independently of any particular individual who uses it. It therefore exerts constraint over individual language users (like Durkheim's social facts) in that if I wish to say something, I am obliged to use certain words in a certain order – if I want to be understood, that is. However, language (the structure) only exists because people use it correctly when they speak and write – in other words, through action. Indeed, it is only because people speak and write according to the rules of their language, that the language continues to exist. This should not be taken to imply that languages are simply reproduced by the act of speaking and writing, however. Although this will usually be the case, it is quite possible for new words to be introduced, old ones to be forgotten, and even new grammatical rules to enter the language as a result of the ways in which people write and speak. Thus for Giddens, although structure clearly influences action, action may also independently influence structure.

Structure, rules and resources Giddens identifies two important elements of structure: *rules* and *resources*. Rules refer to the range of regulatory principles which influence action. They could refer to unwritten rules such as how one proposes marriage, or to laws regulating how one is to

drive a motor car. The second element of structure for Giddens is *resources*. Giddens identifies both *allocative* and *authoritative* resources. Allocative resources refer broadly to what Marx identified as the 'forces of production', whilst authoritative resources refer to the distribution of social power. For Giddens, each of these elements of structure may be reproduced through the agency of social actors, but equally they may be transformed by social actors.

Agency and the reproduction of structures Although Giddens allows the possibility that structures can be transformed through agency, he also seeks to explain their reproduction. According to Giddens, much human action is 'mundane', and draws upon stocks of shared commonsense knowledge which is routinely applied with little conscious thought. Agents draw upon their knowledge of rules, and make use of available resources to accomplish their goals. Giddens, in fact, suggests that human beings have an innate desire for predictability in their social lives. He believes that we share a basic need for what he calls 'ontological security'– a confidence that the world is in fact as it appears to be. This tends to produce social stability and persistence rather than social change.

Reflexity Although Giddens does emphasise the degree to which structures are reproduced through human agency, he also allows the possibility that they may change. Drawing on the insights of writers such as Goffman, Giddens points out that actors do not merely react to external stimuli, but engage in the 'reflexive monitoring of action'. This means that they can reflect upon their own actions and their consequences, and have the ability to choose new courses of action. However, Giddens acknowledges that structures do not only change as a result of deliberate actions by actors, but can change as the result of the unintended consequences of actions. For example, the decision by sufficient numbers of actors to visit a particular holiday resort may produce major changes in the local economy which no one intended, but which nevertheless resulted from these actions.

Evaluation

There can be no doubt that Giddens' work represents a major attempt to solve an apparently intractable problem in sociological theory – the relationship between structure and agency. Whilst Giddens' theory of structuration does indeed appear to offer a way out of this theoretical cul-de-sac, his work has nevertheless been subjected to criticism.

Margaret Archer has criticised Giddens for failing to give sufficient attention to the extent to which structures themselves influence the degree to which they can be changed through agency. She emphasises the fact that actors cannot simply change the world as they wish, and that very often structures will constrain action and systematically frustrate the transformative efforts of actors.

On a different theme, Ian Craib has argued that Giddens' model of the personality is in fact rather confused, and rests upon certain basic misunderstandings of psychoanalytic theory. Specifically, Craib suggests that the important notion of ontological security – an inborn desire for predictability – is based upon a 'fundamentally oversimplified notion of the individual' (Craib, 1992).

key terms

Duality of structure Action and structure are two ways of looking at the same thing. Structures are produced by action and action maintains structure.
Agency Giddens' term for social action.
Reflexivity As used by Giddens, the ability of human beings to monitor and reflect on their own actions, and to choose new courses of action.

summary

1. Structuralism is concerned with the structures which underlie behaviour.

2. Lévi-Strauss applied structuralism to the study of culture. He argued that all myths have the same basic structure – opposition and resolution.

3. Barthes applied structuralism to the study of signs – semiotics. He claimed that 'deep' ideological meanings lie beneath the relatively trivial surface appearance of signs.

4. Phenomenology is concerned with how human actors make sense of the world around them. It argues that actors use typications – shared concepts – to build up a stock of 'commonsense knowledge'.

5. Ethnomethodology argues that members of society actively construct meanings and impose them on the world. This gives a sense of meaningful order.

6. According to Garfinkel, people use the documentary method to make sense of the world. This involves creating underlying patterns of meaning and imposing them on events and situations in order to make sense of them.

7. The meaning of an action is derived from the context in which it takes place, not from the intrinsic or essential features of the action.

8. According to Garfinkel, social order is maintained because members of society assume that rules exist. It is this assumption, rather than the rules themselves, which creates social order. In reality, social order is very fragile.

9. Ethnomethodology has been criticised for ignoring inequalities of wealth and power in the wider society, and for not considering the possibility that the powerful may impose their meanings on others.

10. According to Giddens, structure and action are two ways of looking at the same thing. Structures are produced by social action, and it is only through social action that structures are maintained over time.

11. Human behaviour is not completely determined by structures. Human beings are reflexive – they can reflect on their own actions and choose new courses of action.

12. Giddens' theory of structuration offers a way out of the opposition between structural and social action approaches.

13. Critics argue that Giddens fails to recognise the power that structures have to shape and constrain action. Actors cannot simply change the world as they choose.

Unit 5 Challenges to sociological theory

keyissues

1. What are the main assumptions of globalisation and postmodernism?

2. How do they challenge more traditional sociological theories?

New approaches are constantly emerging which challenge the conventional wisdom of sociologists. Feminism, for example, questioned the male bias of the discipline and opened up new areas for investigation (see pages 143-145). In this unit we shall look at two recent approaches which challenge the taken-for-granted assumptions of many sociologists.

5.1 Globalisation

At various stages in this chapter we have talked about society and indeed, if pushed to define the subject matter of sociology, many sociologists would say 'modern society'. Society, in turn, is often visualised as a social system with distinct boundaries separating it from other social systems. And this 'society' is usually equated with the nation-state. This is not surprising. For it reflects the nineteenth century origins of sociology when 'nation-states become supreme because they won at war, were economically successful and, subsequently, achieved a significant degree of legitimacy in the eyes of their populations and other states' (Held, 1992).

Beyond the nation-state There are two problems with picturing the subject matter of sociology in this way. First, human behaviour has never been explicable purely in terms of particular societies or nation-states. The influence of major religions, patterns of trade and indeed war and conquest extend well beyond the boundaries of nation-states.

Second, we live in a 'shrinking' world. In this context, human behaviour is increasingly influenced by global forces. While *globalisation*, in the sense of the growing interconnectedness of societies, has always been a feature of modernity, a number of theorists have suggested that in the last two decades we have entered a qualitatively new phase of globalisation. One of its main features has been described as 'time-space compression', in recognition of the fact that our lives are increasingly, and remarkably quickly, influenced by distant events. David Harvey puts it well: 'As space appears to shrink to a "global" village of telecommunications and a "spaceship earth" of economic and ecological interdependencies – to use just two familiar and everyday images – and as time horizons shorten to the point where the present is all there is, so we have to learn to cope with an overwhelming sense of compression of our spatial and temporal words' (Harvey, 1989).

Let us take each of these images of globalisation in turn. The Live Aid movement of the mid-1980s provides a good example of the way the world 'has come to seem like a village' (Tester, 1995). The movement, founded by the singer Bob Geldof, emerged in order to raise money to relieve an appalling famine in Ethiopia. It culminated in a day long concert, held at venues in Britain and America 3,000 miles apart but linked by satellite into one programme. The mass media was central. For it was television which allowed people in Britain and America to become aware in their living rooms of a famine miles away, and it was television which broadcast the concert around the world.

A dramatic illustration of our ecological interdependence on 'spaceship earth' was the explosion in 1986 at the Chernobyl nuclear power station in the former Soviet Republic of Ukraine. The consequences were not foreseeable but were felt as far away as Cumbria. The explosion provides an example of the way globalisation is producing what Ulrich Beck (1992) calls a 'risk society', in which the survival of the planet is threatened by technological developments. While natural hazards such as floods, hurricanes and volcanoes threatened people in the past, the risk environment which now confronts us 'is structured mainly by humanly created risks' (Giddens, 1990).

Opposing tendencies While there is widespread agreement that we are in a period of increasing globalisation, there is no agreement about what has brought it about, or what it will lead to. Indeed some aspects of globalisation appear contradictory.

In Giddens' (1990) words, globalisation does not bring about 'a generalised set of changes acting in a uniform direction, but consists of mutually opposed tendencies'. Here are some examples of these opposed tendencies.

- **First, cultural homogenisation versus differentiation**. Globalisation encourages cultural homogenisation – a uniform global culture. We can now drink Coca Cola at McDonald's, wear trainers and watch Hollywood films on television across the world. At the same time, there is a fascination with difference so that ethnic food, dress and music are also available around the world.

- **Second, old identities versus new identities.** Globalisation makes us increasingly aware of cultural differences. For some, this may be experienced as a threat to the familiar certainties of the past. Racism and religious fundamentalism are examples. They can be seen as defensive reactions which attempt to preserve or recreate a perceived past. For others, however, an awareness of other cultures may be interpreted as an opportunity to construct new identities which fuse different cultural traditions.

- **Third, centralisation versus decentralisation.** Globalisation enables organisations to develop which transcend national boundaries. Transnational corporations and the European Union are examples. At the same time, it generates a powerful decentralising force as communities seek to control their own fate. Hence the resurgence of nationalism in Eastern Europe with the break up of the Soviet Union.

The effects of globalisation are not only complex but there is also an unevenness with which globalisation has been experienced across space and time. It has quickened recently, but its consequences are not uniform across the globe. 'In the latest form of globalisation, it is still the images, artifacts and identities of Western modernity, produced by the cultural industries of "Western" societies (including Japan) which dominate the global networks' (Hall, 1992).

Evaluation The concept of globalisation does capture an important phenomenon and it does challenge the idea of society as a well-bounded system. While this means that we need to be highly sceptical of sociological theories which visualise societies as discrete social systems, it does not mean that we should abandon the idea of society. For societies can still exist within the framework of a global society. They are still recognised as societies by their members. And their boundaries are sufficiently clear for sociologists to recognise and study them as social units. (For further discussion and examples of globalisation see pages 92-94).

key terms

Globalisation The process by which societies become increasingly interconnected.
Cultural homogenisation The process by which cultures become increasingly similar.
Cultural differentiation The process by which aspects of one culture enter another.

activity11 globalisation

Item A Global products and global icons

Jakarta, Indonesia

Vietnamese edition
of 8 Mile

David Beckham
escorted through
a cheering crowd
in China. It is
estimated that a
billion Chinese
watched his debut
for Real Madrid
against the all-star
Chinese Dragons
in Beijing on
August 3, 2003.

Russian edition of Lord of the Rings

Item B Global risks – the world's fish

Last month a fleet's annual quota of fish was caught in eight minutes. The sea cannot stand it.

The world's fisheries are hurtling towards commercial extinction as hi-tech supertrawlers become ever more efficient at hoovering up their prey. The oceans, covering 70% of the globe, should – and could – adequately meet the needs of humanity without unbalancing the marine ecosystem. But greed, rather than commonsense or conservation, is driving exploitation of the seas.

Last month, the United Nations Food and Agriculture Organisation (FAO) warned 9 of the world's 17 major fishing grounds had been devastated by over-fishing, with four more under serious threat. The global fish catch, which rose five-fold between 1950 and 1989, has now levelled out at around 100 million tonnes a year.

Nobody knows for sure what effect chronic over-fishing will have on other marine wildlife. Just as worrying is the effect on the human beings who rely on fish to stay alive. But, for the developing world, the disappearance of commercial fisheries

Danish industrial fishing vessel, North Sea

would spell disaster. In Asia alone, a billion people rely on fish as their main source of animal protein. And apart from the spectre of starvation, a fishing crash would cost an enormous number of jobs.

Adapted from the Observer, 2.4.1995

Item C Global risks – Chernobyl

In 1986, the nucular power station at Chernobyl in the Ukraine exploded. It provided a stark lesson about the huge sum which a single major nuclear accident can cost the world.

Nine years after the radioactive cloud released from Chernobyl passed over Wales, long-suffering farmers 1,500 miles from the scene of the accident still face controls on their sheep flocks.

In the Ukraine and Belarus, which took the brunt of the radiation, 1.3million hectares of land is contaminated, and estimates put the final clean-up bill at between £1.25 billion and £3.75 billion.

This figure includes resettlement of 2.5 million refugees living on contaminated land, medical treatment for victims, and the clean-up of the plant and surrounding irradiated countryside.

The trouble is that no matter how we generate energy, we create problems. The burning of coal, gas and oil plays havoc with our atmosphere, just as surely as the abuse of nuclear power devastates the ground.

It is an issue that transcends national borders. Global economic growth needs global energy planning. We do not have that, and there are precious few signs we will ever get it. The human mind seems almost incapable of dealing with the time scales and geography which are required when dealing with nuclear power. Yet we must face up to the issues. The alternative is short-term manoeuvring, and long term disaster.

Adapted from the *Observer*, 30.4.1995

Radiation check, Chernobyl

questions

1 How do the pictures in Item A illustrate globalisation?

2 How do Items B and C suggest that we live in a global 'risk society'?

3 Globalisation requires institutions for global government. Discuss with reference to Items B and C.

5.2 Postmodernism

Postmodernism as theory

Postmodernism is a new way of looking at the world. It questions all the key ideas of the Enlightenment. It rejects the view that it is possible to build either a natural or social science on the basis of observable facts. It argues that there is no objective or indisputable way of distinguishing truth from falsity. It sees no firm foundation for knowledge. And it rejects the Enlightenment belief that human beings are capable of achieving a rational understanding of social reality and can use this understanding to create a more rational and just society.

As such, postmodernism is a direct challenge to sociology.

Postmodernity and postmodern society

Postmodernists believe that we are now living in a new era – postmodernity – and a new form of society – postmodern society. This represents a clear break from the previous era – modernity – and the previous form of society – modern society.

Before examining postmodernist theory in more detail, here is a short sketch of how postmodernists see postmodern society.

A diversity of images and values Postmodern society is dominated by new information and communication technologies which bring the world into our homes and into our consciousness. Websites, e-mails, chat rooms, computer games, DVDs, CDs, and terrestrial, satellite and cable TV bombard us with sounds, symbols and images from across the globe. They expose us to an increasingly diverse range of ideas and values, many of which have little connection with our present or past lives. This can cut us off from our past, make our present seem rootless and unstable, and our future unpredictable.

This myriad of diverse images and values is constantly changing. New lifestyles come and go, new styles of music and fashion and new types of food and drink are regularly appearing. Everything appears fluid – nothing seems permanent and solid. The mainstream culture of modern society is replaced by the fleeting, unstable, fragmented culture of postmodern society.

Postmodern identities In modern societies, people's identities were usually drawn from their class, gender, occupation and ethnic group. In postmodern society, people have more opportunity to construct their own identities and more options to choose from. For example, a woman can be heterosexual, bisexual or lesbian, a business executive and a mother, she can be British, a Sikh *and* a member of Greenpeace. And her lifestyle and consumption patterns can reflect her chosen identity. Brand-name goods such as Gucci and Dolce & Gabbana can be used as statements of her identity.

With all the choices on offer, it is fairly easy for people to change their identities, or to have several identities which they put on and take off depending on their social situation. As a result, postmodern identities are more unstable and fragile. They offer choice, but they don't always provide a firm and lasting foundation.

Loss of faith Exposure to increasingly diverse beliefs, values and lifestyles can lead to a relativist point of view. Nothing is right or wrong, everything is relative. A single truth is replaced by many truths and there is no objective way of choosing between them. Certainty is replaced with uncertainty and there is a loss of faith in rational thinking.

As a result, people are increasingly turning to a range of alternatives in their search for answers and solutions to problems – New Age religions, traditional healers and alternative therapists.

Postmodernity has seen a loss of faith in science and technology. The threat of weapons of mass destruction, the negative side-effects of drugs used to treat physical and psychological problems, global warming and the destruction of the environment caused by pollution, all point to science and technology gone wrong.

Views of reality Some postmodernists claim that our view of reality is largely shaped by the flood of images from the media. These images become as, if not more, real and significant than the things we directly experience in everyday life. For example, the death of Princess Diana resulted in an outpouring of grief across the world – but, for the vast majority, she existed only through the media. The 'unreal' becomes 'real' when a death, a divorce, or a marriage in a soap opera glues millions to the screen and forms a topic of conversation the following day. And, as its name suggests, reality TV brings 'real' people into everybody's homes and lives.

Evaluation Many of these observations of postmodern society are accepted, to a degree, by mainstream sociologists. However, they usually see them as aspects of late modernity rather than postmodernity.

Many sociologists are critical of the picture of society presented by postmodernists. For example, Greg Philo and David Miller (2001) make the following points.

- The claim that people are no longer able to make judgements of right and wrong about different views of the world and different ideologies is incorrect. The vast majority of people would still condemn the fascist ideology of Nazi Germany and the slaughter of millions of Jews, gypsies and gays in Nazi death camps.

- People are well aware that there is a reality beyond the images broadcast by the media. They recognise that media messages are often one-sided, partial and distorted.

- Many people are not free to construct their own identities, choose their own consumption patterns and select their own lifestyles. For example, people living in poverty simply don't have the money to buy Gucci sunglasses or Jean Paul Gaultier fragrance.

Having briefly outlined and assessed the postmodernist view of contemporary society, we now turn to the work of two of the most influential postmodernist writers – Jean-Francois Lyotard and Jean Baudrillard.

Lyotard – a crisis in knowledge

Knowledge in the modern era meant science. Philosophers were, however, unable to agree upon the foundations for such knowledge. Science therefore needed to be justified in terms of a grand story or *metanarrative*. For the Enlightenment, science was justified on the grounds that it would lead to human emancipation and freedom. In view of the contribution of science in creating, for example, weapons of indiscriminate mass destruction, people are now sceptical towards this metanarrative and the status of science has consequently been questioned. And what is true of this metanarrative is true of others. None can be 'objectively' proved or rejected and so we need to be sceptical towards all metanarratives. Hence Lyotard defines the condition of postmodernity as 'incredulity towards metanarratives' (Lyotard, 1992).

This is not to say that knowledge is unimportant. We live in a post-industrial society where, in fact, it is central. Knowledge has, however, fragmented into a series of 'language games' where the rules governing what counts as knowledge differ. The central concern is 'performativity', whether the information produced is efficient and saleable rather than of intrinsic value or serving some human purpose.

Lyotard welcomes the downfall of metanarratives and the emergence of a plurality of language games. Grand stories, with their privileged truth, rode roughshod over many groups and, in the case of Marxism, led to totalitarianism. In the postmodern era, there is a chance to hear the voices of diverse groups previously on the margins, such as women and ethnic minorities.

Baudrillard – a crisis in representation

Baudrillard agrees with Lyotard that we now live in a post-industrial society. His emphasis, however, is different and centres on the production and consumption of signs. Baudrillard's view is that although at one stage signs were a 'reflection of a basic reality' they now often 'bear no relation to any reality whatsoever' (Poster, 1988). Such signs are known as *simulations* and are characteristic of the images we see on our television screens, when stories and items that have no meaningful or logical connection to each other are juxtaposed.

Baudrillard argues that news reporting often involves simulation. For example, business fraud is reported as shocking and scandalous to conceal the fact that is widespread. Sometimes simulations can be experienced as more real than reality. This is the 'hyperreal' where, for example, people write to characters in soap operas. John Storey gives a good example : 'The riots, following the acquittal of the four Los Angeles police officers captured on video physically assaulting the black motorist Rodney King, were headlined in two British newspapers as "LA Lawless", and in another as "LA War"; the story anchored not by historical reference to similar disturbances in Watts Los Angeles in 1965, or to the implications of the words – "No justice, no peace" – chanted by demonstrators during the riots. The editors chose instead to locate the story within the fictional world of the American television series *LA Law*. Baudrillard calls this "The dissolution of TV into life, the dissolution of life into TV" '(Storey, 1993).

Baudrillard is in two minds about his response to this situation where image and reality can no longer be distinguished. At times, he suggests that we live in a society where we are able to construct our own identities in the process of consumption. Clothes and other items of consumption are not only material objects but also are signs which have meaning. By picking and mixing appropriate images we can distinguish ourselves from others. At other times, he suggests the best we can do is to enjoy the meaningless spectacle produced for us and delight in the sensuous pleasure which images can offer us.

Postmodern theory and social change

The work of Lyotard, Baudrillard and other postmodern theorists has been stimulating in raising new questions about social change. Are we witnessing a shift to a new postmodern culture? Have Lyotard and Baudrillard correctly identified the central features of this new culture? Is it true that people increasingly find general theories implausible and are sceptical towards the old political philosophies of liberalism, socialism and social democracy? Do we live in an era where media images are so pervasive that we find it increasingly difficult to distinguish what is real? Does the advent of a postmodern culture signify a shift towards a new social condition of postmodernity? Is it true that we now live in a post-industrial society? Is this a society which allows an increasing diversity of lifestyles to flourish? Is it one where we have much greater freedom to construct our own individual and collective identities, or one which witnesses an increasing fragmentation of our identities? These questions, which were initially raised by postmodern theorists, are central to much contemporary sociology and have stimulated other theorists, including Marxists such as Jameson and Harvey, to develop their theories in order to account for the fact that we are clearly living through an era of massive social change (Thompson, 1992).

Postmodernism and the Enlightenment

The challenge which postmodernism poses for sociological theory results from its rejection of the Enlightenment 'project' – the promise, which underpinned the emergence of sociology, that human beings could use their reason to produce knowledge of the social world and on that basis promote human progress. Postmodernists have put three central arguments forward.

Anti-foundationalism The first argument is known as *anti-foundationalism*. The search by philosophers for indisputable foundations to knowledge has been a failure. There are no general criteria which enable us to distinguish truth and falsity. We therefore have to accept that different communities will use different criteria to distinguish truth and falsity. What's more these communities will look at the world differently. For we are the subjects of language and other sign systems and can't step outside them to discover what things really mean. In short, there is absolutely nothing to guarantee what is true or what things mean.

Anti-totalisation The second argument is known as anti-totalisation. In view of the fact that there are no indisputable foundations to knowledge or firm bases to meaning, it is extremely arrogant of us to put forward general theories which pretend to reveal *the* truth or *the* meaning of things. We need to abandon attempts to produce theories which seek to depict the structure and dynamics of society as a whole and tolerate the coexistence of a diversity of more limited theories.

Anti-utopianism The third argument is known as *anti-utopianism*. In practice, knowledge has not produced the utopia of human freedom and emancipation, but has been used by some to impose one truth and one meaning on others. Knowledge has not so much provided us with the power to do things that we could not otherwise do, as allowed some groups to exert power over others.

These arguments cannot be dismissed lightly. First, we cannot attain certainty over questions of truth and meaning. Second, general theories which claim to reveal the inevitable development of society are flawed. There is no justification for believing that history has a purpose, or that we can predict the future. Third, knowledge has often been used by Western societies to dominate others. (For an outline of postmodernist methodology, see pages 140-141.)

Evaluation

The Enlightenment project, and with it the possibility of sociological theory, cannot be so easily dismissed.

- First, the fact that there are no indispensable foundations to knowledge and meaning does not mean that there are no general criteria of truth and that there is not a connection between sign systems and the world. To assume otherwise is to fall into the trap of relativism. Presumably, the postmodern theorists believe that what they say is meaningful and true or otherwise they would not bother to write books.

- Second, the fact that different societies have different ideas and beliefs of what is true and what things mean does not mean that we should abandon the search for general theories which seek to explain these differences. Indeed, somewhat inconsistently, postmodern theorists do provide such general theories.

- Third, the fact that reason has been used to dominate people does not mean that it did not play a progressive role in the past in combating 'the relative blinkeredness and backwardness of the epoch of pre-modernity' (McClennan, 1992), and that we should abandon the Enlightenment ideal that knowledge might further human emancipation. The arguments of postmodernist theories which challenge the very possibility of sociological theory are unconvincing.

key terms

Metanarrative A grand story or theory which explains and justifies something – for example, scientific theories, political ideologies and religions are seen by postmodernists as metanarratives.
Simulations Signs and images which have no relationship to reality.
Anti-foundationalism The argument that there are no clear, indisputable foundations to knowledge.
Anti-totalisation The argument that there are no general theories which reveal and explain the truth or the meaning of things.
Anti-utopianism The argument that knowledge has not been used to create a utopia – a perfect society. Instead, it has been used by some to exert power over others.

summary

1. Traditionally, the main unit for study in sociology has been the society – a social system with distinct boundaries which separates it from other social systems.

2. Globalisation challenges this view. Societies are becoming increasingly interconnected and cultures increasingly similar.

3. Some sociologists see opposing tendencies in the process of globalisation. They include:
    - Cultural homogenisation versus cultural differentiation
    - Old identities versus new identities
    - Centralisation versus decentralisation.

4. While recognising the impact of globalisation, sociologists have not abandoned the idea of society. The boundaries of societies are sufficiently distinct for them to be studied as social units.

5. Postmodernism rejects the key ideas of the Enlightenment – in particular, the view that it is possible to build a natural or social science on the basis of observable facts.

6. According to postmodernists, postmodern society has the following characteristics.
    - A diversity of images, values and lifestyles
    - Opportunities for people to construct their own identities
    - A loss of faith in rational thinking and in science and technology

    - Views of reality which are largely shaped by the media.

7. Lyotard argues that postmodern society is characterised by the downfall of metanarratives. Knowledge is judged in terms of performativity – whether it is efficient and saleable.

8. Baudrillard argues that members of postmodern society see the world in terms of simulations – images which bear no relation to reality.

9. Postmodernists reject Enlightenment ideas on the basis of three main arguments.
    - Anti-foundationalism
    - Anti-totalisation
    - Anti-utopianism.

10. Criticisms of postmodernism include the following.
    - To claim that there are no foundations to knowledge leads to relativism. In terms of their own argument, postmodernists' views are no better than anybody else's.
    - Just because different societies have different versions of the truth does not mean that their beliefs cannot be studied and explained.
    - Just because rational thinking has been used to dominate people does not mean it cannot be used to free them.

activity 12 postmodern society

Item A Detached identities

The more social life is influenced by the global marketing of styles, places and images, by international travel, and by globally networked media images and communications systems, the more identities become detached – disembedded – from specific times, places, histories and traditions, and appear 'free-floating'. We are confronted by a range of different identities, each appealing to us, or rather to different parts of ourselves, from which it seems possible to choose. It is the spread of consumerism, whether as reality or dream, which has contributed to this 'cultural supermarket' effect.

Adapted from Hall, 1992

Item B I am me

Salima Dhalla: I don't know how to start to describe myself. I feel identity-less but very unique. On paper I'm 'Asian' but in my head I'm a cocky little person with lots of hopes and ambitions.

My parents are East African, their parents are Indian, I was born in Wales. I went to a White middle-class girls' private school and I have brown skin, short Western hair, Western clothes, Eastern name, Western friends. So I guess I'm in an identity wasteland. Now I will only agree to being *me*.

Adapted from Kassam, 1997

Item C A shrinking world

Item D Norman and Norma

Norman on Tuesdays *Norma on Wednesdays*

Norman Horton enjoyed his new hobby of line dancing so much that he decided to go twice a week – once as a man and once as a woman. Mr Horton, aged 58, would set off on Tuesday nights in open-neck shirt, trousers and stetson. But on Wednesdays he transformed himself into Norma, with a frilly blouse, short skirt, gold tights and high heels. A former paratrooper and military policeman, he has been cross-dressing since the age of 12. 'My wife doesn't mind me cross-dressing as long as I don't do it too often and keep it under control.'

Adapted from *The Guardian*,17.4.1998

Item E Bodybuilders

The top three in the women's bodybuilding world championship, 2002

Item F Panjabi MC

Panjabi MC. His music is a fusion of bhangra and hip hop.

Item G Growing up in poverty

questions

1 What does Stuart Hall in Item A mean by 'detached identities'?

2 What support do Items B to F provide for the view of postmodern society given by Stuart Hall in Item A and described in the preceding text?

3 What criticism of this view of postmodern society is suggested by Item G?

5 Crime and deviance

Introduction

We are fascinated by crime and deviance. This is evident from the mass media – from crime series on TV and crime reports in newspapers, from detective novels which are concerned with finding the criminal and explaining the crime, and from movies which often portray the more colourful, lurid and violent aspects of crime.

Why this fascination? Criminal behaviour appears unusual and different. It involves risks which endanger those who commit crimes and their victims. For many people, out-of-the-ordinary behaviour seems much more interesting than their own humdrum activities. And to those of us looking on, the risks and dangers involved are often experienced as exciting and entertaining – from a safe distance!

Crime and deviance break social norms – they deviate or diverge from conventional behaviour. This can be disturbing. We often fear crime and feel worried and anxious when taken-for-granted norms are broken. Why? Because such activities disrupt our sense of social order and threaten our view of the way things should be.

And this adds to our fascination with crime. It should therefore come as no surprise that crime and deviance is one of the most popular topics in sociology.

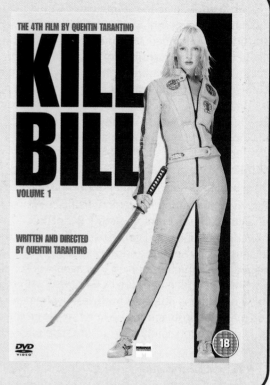

chaptersummary

▶ **Unit 1** looks at the meanings of deviance, crime and social control.

▶ **Unit 2** investigates evidence on the extent of crime, trends in the crime rate, and the identity of offenders.

▶ **Unit 3** examines media representations of crime and deviance.

▶ **Units 4, 5 and 6** outline and evaluate various sociological theories of crime and deviance, including functionalist, interactionist and Marxist approaches.

▶ **Units 7 and 8** examine two opposing theories of crime and social control – right realism and left realism.

▶ **Unit 9** looks at the ethnicity and crime debate.

▶ **Unit 10** considers the relationship between gender and crime.

▶ **Unit 11** examines sociological studies of suicide, focusing on the methodologies they use.

Unit 1 The nature of crime, deviance and social control

keyissues

1 What are crime, deviance and social control?

2 What is distinctive about the sociological approach to crime, deviance and social control?

1.1 Defining crime and deviance

Human social life is governed by norms and values – by norms which define appropriate and acceptable behaviour, and by values which define behaviour as right or wrong.

Sociologists have long been concerned with how society's norms and values are maintained.

However, there is another side to the story – how and why are norms broken and values rejected? In other words, how and why does *deviance* occur?

Deviance

Deviance is usually defined as behaviour which goes against conventional norms and generally accepted values. In terms of this definition, deviance is behaviour which most people would regard as inappropriate, or more strongly, as unacceptable and wrong. As a result, deviance is usually subject to a variety of social controls ranging from mild disapproval to severe punishment.

This view of deviance is reflected in the following definition by Downes and Rock (2003). 'Deviance may be considered as banned or controlled behaviour which is likely to attract punishment or disapproval.' This definition covers acts such as murder and rape which are explicitly banned in most cultures and subject to severe punishment. It also covers relatively trivial acts such as burping and farting in public which usually attract little more than a disapproving glance or a negative comment.

Crime

At first sight, *crime* is a much more specific category than the wide and varied range of activities covered by deviance. Often, crime is simply defined as an infraction of the criminal law – as lawbreaking. Crimes are usually seen as particularly serious and negative forms of deviance – hence laws which ban them and agents of social control such as the police and judges who deal with them. This view of crime is reflected in the following definition. 'Crimes are those actions deemed so disturbing to citizens or disruptive to society as to justify state intervention' (Pease, 2002).

This type of definition has its limitations. We cannot assume that crimes are always more disturbing to citizens or more disruptive to society than non-criminal behaviour. Think of all the non-criminal behaviour that contributes to global warming, global pollution and the destruction of the world's wildlife. In Muncie's (2001) words, 'Any number of damaging events are far more serious than those that make up the "crime problem" '.

What is more, breaking the criminal law covers a vast array of actions from the trivial to the serious. Crime, like deviance, covers a highly varied range of behaviour. This leads some sociologists to talk about crimes in the plural rather than crime in the singular. In other words, there's 'crime and crime'.

There are many different definitions of deviance and crime. None are without their problems as Activity 1 illustrates. It looks at vandalism which the *Concise Oxford Dictionary* defines as the wilful or malicious destruction or damage of property. This destruction or damage may or may not be seen as deviant. It may or may not be defined as criminal damage.

key terms

Deviance Actions which deviate from the norms and values of society.
Crime A form of deviance which breaks the law.

activity1 vandalism

Item A

Item B

Item C

Item D

Item E

Item F

questions

1 Look at the pictures. Which (if any) would you see as examples of vandalism? Give reasons for your answer.

2 Using examples from this activity, briefly discuss the problems of defining crime and deviance.

1.2 The contexts and diversity of deviance

Deviance takes varied forms in society. For example, we can distinguish between secret and private deviance as against open and public deviance, and between individual deviance as against collective deviance.

Secret and private deviance This form of deviance is often concealed – not least due to the heavy personal costs of exposure to the public gaze. It is often undercover and may be hidden in normal settings such as the home or the workplace. Secret deviance may be legal – for example, a group with unusual sexual practices who meet in each other's homes. Or it may be illegal, as in the case of the Gloucester serial killer, Frederick West.

West appeared to be a fairly average family man with a normal occupation as a self-employed builder. Yet, in the privacy of his home, he murdered two members of his family and a number of vulnerable young women. Furthermore, he was able to use his 'normal' skills as a builder to hide the dead bodies in his house and garden.

Open and public deviance This form of deviance often involves conforming to the norms and values of a clearly defined outsider group – norms and values which differ from those of the wider society. Take the example of the so-called New Age Travellers in Britain today. Their lifestyle is very different from that of the mainstream population. They tend to be seen as a deviant group and are viewed with distaste and hostility by some members of society. They are an example of public and collective deviance.

1.3 The relativity of crime and deviance

Crime and deviance are relative to time, place and culture. In other words, what counts as crime and deviance varies from time to time, place to place and culture to culture.

Societal and situational deviance Ken Plummer (1979) captures this point in his distinction between societal and situational deviance. Societal deviance refers to behaviour which breaks the law or which is seen as deviant by most members of society. It is judged to be deviant on the basis of their shared values and beliefs and what 'common sense' tells them. There is general agreement about the identification of societal deviance – for example, most people regard armed robbery as wrong, as deviant and as criminal.

Situational deviance refers to the effect of the context or situation on the classification of deviance. In one situation an act may be seen as deviant, in another situation it may not. People interpret what counts as deviance in their personal worlds of friends, colleagues and acquaintances. Plummer accepts that the beliefs and values of the wider society affect views of situational deviance. However, he argues that in certain contexts people either neutralise or reject the societal version of deviance.

Plummer uses the example of homosexuality to illustrate this point. Homosexuality is societally deviant but not always situationally deviant. In certain contexts, such as gay bars and clubs, homosexuality is no longer deviant – it becomes the norm.

Culture and deviance Crime and deviance are relative to culture. Different cultures have different norms and values. As a result, what is considered normal and deviant will vary from one culture to another. For example, in many non-Western societies marriage is polygynous – a man may have two or more wives. In the West, this is not only deviant, but criminal.

As cultures change, so do definitions of deviance and crime. At certain times in Western societies it was considered deviant for women to use make-up and consume alcoholic drinks in public. Today, this is no longer the case. In the same way, definitions of crime change over time. Sexual relations between men were once a criminal offence in Britain. Since 1969, homosexual acts between consenting adults in private have no longer been illegal.

activity2 deviance is relative

Item A Smoking banned

On Saturday, 29 March 2003, Robert de Niro and Danny de Vito joined 280 guests in the ballroom of the Regent Wall Street Hotel in New York for a $95-a-head Last Smoke dinner. The prime rib steak smoked in tobacco leaves went down well. De Niro and De Vito lit up their Cuban Montecristo cigars.

When the clock struck midnight, the Last Smoke was over. Smoking was banned in 13,000 New York bars and restaurants which were not covered by an earlier smoking ban.

The city hired an army of inspectors to tour bars and restaurants, confiscating ashtrays and issuing warnings in a 30-day grace period before fines of up to $3000 start being slapped on owners.

Adapted from *The Observer*, 30.3.2003

After the ban

and prison service which enforce the law.

The ultimate and most obvious form of social control is physical force. Under certain circumstances, some have the right to use physical force against others in an attempt to control their behaviour. In modern industrial societies, the police are an obvious example. Other formal methods of social control include judicial punishments such as fines and imprisonment.

Informal methods of social control Informal methods of social control involve institutions and social groups which are not directly concerned with enforcing social control and upholding the law. These groups and institutions include the family, schools, religious organisations and significant others.

The family and the school socialise young people, teaching them the norms and values of the wider society. Conformity to these norms and values is usually rewarded, deviance from them is usually punished.

Religious teachings often reinforce the values of society. For example, the Christian Commandments you shall not kill and you shall not steal reinforce the values placed on human life and private property. And, in turn, they back up secular laws protecting life and property. Religions offer rewards to those who follow their teachings and punishments to those who deviate from them. In this way, religion acts as a mechanism of social control.

Significant others are people who matter to an individual. They usually include his or her immediate family, friends, neighbours and workmates. People are concerned about what significant others think about them. Their approval makes them feel good, their disapproval upsets them. Because the opinion of significant others is held so highly, they can play an important part in controlling the behaviour of an individual. People often conform to social norms in order to gain the approval and acceptance of significant others and to avoid their disapproval and rejection.

Many sociologists see informal social controls as more important and effective than the more obvious formal controls.

Item B Endorsing Camels

The late American film star John Wayne advertising Camel cigarettes.

questions

1. Use information from Items A and B to illustrate the point that deviance is relative to time and place.
2. Look at Item B. Why would it be unlikely for a film star today to endorse cigarettes?

1.4 Social control

Every society has methods of making its members toe the line, of making sure that they stick to the straight and narrow. These methods are known as mechanisms or methods of *social control*. They ensure that most of the people, most of the time, conform to society's norms and values. For social order to exist, shared norms and values are necessary and conformity to them must be enforced. Enforcing conformity means discouraging deviant and criminal behaviour – behaviour which breaks social norms and goes against shared values.

Social control takes many forms. Some researchers have distinguished between *formal* and *informal* methods of social control.

Formal methods of social control Formal methods refer to institutions specifically set up to enforce social control. In modern industrial societies, this mainly involves institutions which create and enforce the law – for example, parliament which enacts the law and the police, judiciary

summary

1. The term deviance covers a wide range of behaviour which deviates from the norms and values of society.

2. The term crime also covers a variety of activities – from the trivial to the serious.

3. Crime and deviance may be secret and private or open and public; individual, involving one person, or collective, involving a group of people.

4. Crime and deviance are relative to time, place and culture. What counts as crime and deviance varies from time to time, place to place and culture to culture.

5. Every society has mechanisms of social control which discourage crime and deviance.

6. Formal mechanisms of social control include institutions which create and enforce the law – for example, parliament, the police and the judiciary.

7. Informal mechanisms of social control include the family, schools, religious organisations and significant others. Although not directly concerned with social control, sociologists see them as powerful control mechanisms.

activity3 social control

Item A Police

Item B Family

Item C Friends

Item D Prison

questions

1 Which of the items are examples of a) formal social control and b) informal social control?

2 Briefly suggest how each item may help to enforce social control.

Unit 2 *Crime statistics*

keyissues

I How are the volume and trends in crime measured?

2 How are offenders identified?

3 How valid and reliable are data on crime and offenders?

2.1 Measuring crime

The two main measures There are two main measures of crime in Britain. The first, *police recorded crime*, is based on police records – on records kept by the police of crimes which they have recorded. The second, the British Crime Survey (BCS), is based on interviews with a representative sample of adults. It asks whether they have been victims of particular crimes during the previous year.

Sections 2.2 and 2.3 look at the 'official' picture of crime presented by police recorded crime. Section 2.4 looks at the picture presented by the British Crime Survey.

The official picture Each year statistics produced from police records provide an official account of the volume of crime and trends in crime. In addition, statistics compiled from court records and police cautioning records give an official picture of those responsible for criminal offences – that is the 'criminals'. Together, these statistics present a picture of the 'crime problem' – a picture interpreted for us by politicians and transmitted to us by the mass media.

But are official statistics a valid measure of crime? Do they provide an accurate measure of the extent of crime and of trends in crime? Do they present a true picture of those who commit crimes? The short answer to all these questions is probably not.

2.2 The volume of crime

According to official statistics based on police records, there were 6,468,000 cases of recorded crime in the United Kingdom in 2002/03 (*Social Trends*, 2004). Four-fifths of these were offences against property – theft, handling stolen goods, criminal damage, burglary, fraud and forgery.

These statistics do not represent the total volume of crime. There is a so-called 'dark figure' or 'hidden figure' of unrecorded crime. There are various reasons why the

official picture is incomplete. And there are reasons why this picture may be systematically biased – for example, it may repeatedly underestimate certain kinds of crime.

Recorded versus known offences Official statistics do not even give a complete record of criminal offences known to the authorities. For example, until 1998 they didn't cover *summary offences* – those tried in Magistrates Courts as opposed to Crown Courts. Such offences include driving after consuming alcohol over the legal limit. Nor do statistics on recorded crime cover offences dealt with *administratively* by organisations such as the Inland Revenue. Generally speaking, the Inland Revenue negotiate a monetary settlement with people who commit a tax offence – for example, with a business which does not record all its takings and so pays less tax than it should.

There may be some justification for omitting the above offences if they were trivial. But consider this. Two-fifths of crime statistics are made up of criminal damage and theft from a vehicle or from shops. Often such crimes involve small amounts of damage or loss. It is questionable whether they can be seen as more serious than summary offences or offences dealt with administratively.

Police recording practices A further example of known offences not appearing in official statistics is provided by police recording practices. Over 30% of offences reported to the police in 2002/03 were not recorded (Simmons & Dodd, 2003). While the police have a statutory obligation to record crimes, they also have some discretion over whether a crime is serious enough to warrant their attention.

This discretion can be used in different ways by different police forces. For example, in 1981, Nottinghamshire appeared to be the most criminal area in the country. This was largely due to many more crimes involving £10 or less being recorded in Nottinghamshire than in comparable counties such as Leicestershire and Staffordshire (Holdaway, 1988).

The Home Office provides police forces with 'counting rules' to calculate the extent of crime. The basic rule is that the statistics should indicate the number of victims rather than the number of criminal acts. For example, if a single victim has been assaulted by the same person on several occasions, only the most serious offence is counted (Maguire, 2002). This can make some crimes appear less serious than they are. For example, it can understate the extent of domestic violence which often involves numerous assaults over a prolonged period.

Police priorities The number and type of offences discovered by the police in the course of their operations will vary according to their priorities. And this, in turn, will affect crime statistics.

Police priorities are influenced by the concerns of local and national government, pressure groups, public opinion and the media. For example, in recent years, the police have directed more resources to combat paedophilia, due, in part, to increased media concern with this offence.

An ongoing police priority is to improve their clear-up rate – solve more crimes and catch more offenders. With this in mind, resources tend to be targeted at certain crimes. In the words of a retired police officer, 'If you don't catch a burglar, he will go out and he will commit a lot of crime which will then be reported and it will damage your detection rate' (Davies, 1994).

Reporting and non-reporting Over 80% of all recorded crime results from reports by the public (Bottomley & Coleman, 1981). Some types of crime are more likely to be reported than others. For example, 97% of thefts of vehicles were reported to the police in 2002/03, as an official record of the incident is needed for insurance purposes. This compares with estimates which suggest that only around a third of incidents of vandalism and theft from the person are reported (*Social Trends*, 2004).

There are many reasons why crimes are not reported to the police.

- There may be a lack of awareness that a crime has taken place – eg, fraud.
- The victim may be relatively powerless and frightened of the consequences of reporting – eg, child abuse and domestic violence.
- The offence may seem too trivial – eg, vandalism.
- There is no apparent victim – eg, prostitution.
- A view that the police can't do anything about the incident.
- The matter was dealt with privately.

Crime statistics rely heavily on the public reporting incidents to the police. Since some types of crime are more likely to be reported than others, official statistics will not reflect the overall pattern of crime.

The significance of crime statistics Numbers aren't everything. For example, violence against the person, sexual offences and fraud may form a relatively small proportion of recorded crime, but there are other ways of measuring their significance.

Violent and sexual offences often have a traumatic effect upon victims and their seriousness is evident from the number and length of prison sentences they bring – around a third of prisoners are serving sentences for violent or sexual offences.

Fraud may only account for 6% of recorded crime but its monetary value is far greater than this suggests. In Mike Maguire's (2002) words, 'If one measures the importance of

property offences in terms of the value stolen, rather than the quantity of incidents, fraud comes out as of enormously greater significance than other categories'. If we take any one of the major cases of alleged fraud investigated by the Serious Fraud Office in the early 1990s – Barlow Clowes, Guinness, Maxwell, BCCI, Polly Peck – we find that, by itself, it exceeded the total amount stolen in thefts and burglaries recorded by the police (Levi, 1993).

Conclusion Official statistics on recorded crime are drawn from police records – they are based on data collected by the police. The evidence presented in this section indicates that these statistics fail to provide a reliable and valid measurement of crime. And they may be systematically biased in underestimating the extent of certain crimes.

Official statistics on recorded crime are *not* simple, straightforward facts. Instead, they are a *social construction* – they are constructed during the process of social interaction, they are based on a series of interpretations, definitions and decisions which are influenced by a variety of factors, and vary from situation to situation. In the words of Simon Holdaway (1988), 'Official statistics of crime are not so much the facts about crime, as the end product of a complex series of decisions. An incident occurs and someone decides that it is a crime. A decision is made to telephone a police officer and the police officer receiving the call decides to regard the incident as a crime. Another officer attends the scene and, hearing the various accounts of the incident, makes a further decision about its being a crime, and so on. The official statistics are socially constructed; they are the end product of a range of decisions.'

key terms

Police recorded crime Crimes recorded by the police from which official statistics on crime are drawn.
Summary offences Crimes dealt with by Magistrates Courts as opposed to Crown Courts. They were not included in official statistics until 1998.
Crime dealt with administratively Crimes which are not prosecuted – not taken to court. They are dealt with by organisations such as the Inland Revenue and do not appear in police recorded crime.
Social construction Definitions and meanings constructed in the course of social interaction.

activity4 domestic violence and fraud

Item A Domestic violence

Domestic violence includes violent incidents which involve partners, ex-partners, household members or other relatives. According to the British Crime Survey, only one in three victims of domestic violence report the incident to the police. Reasons for non-reporting include a desire for privacy, fear of reprisals and of family break-up.

Domestic violence often involves a series of incidents over a period of time – for example, a woman may be assaulted many times by her partner. However, the police only record the most serious incident.

A study conducted jointly by the police and the Crown Prosecution Service investigated 465 incidents of domestic violence to which the police were called. There should have been 260 crime reports, but only 118 incidents were recorded. Only 21% of these resulted in charges and there was a conviction in just 11%. In nearly half the cases received by the Crown Prosecution Service, the victim withdrew the complaint.

Adapted from Cowan, 2004

A Women's Aid poster – the organisation helps women who have been victims of domestic violence.

Item B Fraud

In June 2002, WorldCom, the second largest long-distance telephone company in the USA, was forced to admit a $4 billion hole in its accounts. In other words, the company had fraudulently claimed to have $4 billion more than it actually had. WorldCom shares dropped from a peak of $64 to a mere 20 cents. Investors lost a fortune because of this accounting fraud.

Fraud is a difficult crime to define. It ranges from avoiding VAT and alcohol and tobacco smuggling – estimated by the Home Office to be worth around £7 billion a year – to credit card fraud which rose in value by 30% between 2000 and 2001 to an estimated £411 million. The value of cases of fraud in the City investigated by the Serious Fraud Office – for example, illegal share dealing – totalled £1.75 billion in 2001/02. Social security fraud is estimated at £2 billion a year. But the above examples are dwarfed by tax fraud. One estimate, by the accountancy firm Deloitte and Touche, puts the cost of 'tax dodging' between 1976 and 1996 at £2000 billion – the equivalent of six years of government expenditure.

Fraud is difficult to detect – the cases uncovered are probably only the tip of the iceberg. Often they involve a large number of fraudulent acts. But, when they are detected, only one or two 'sample' offences are recorded by the police. And many cases of detected fraud never enter police records. Tax, social security and VAT fraud are usually dealt with administratively. The Inland Revenue rarely prosecutes detected offenders, despite the enormous sums involved.

Adapted from Croall, 2001; Maguire, 2002; *The Guardian*, 12.7.2002

Bernard Ebbers, former WorldCom chief executive officer (centre), escorted by US federal agents after turning himself in to face fraud charges.

question

Police recorded crime statistics present an incomplete picture of crime. They seriously underestimate certain types of crime. They fail to indicate the significance of certain types of crime.

What support do Items A and B provide for these views?

2.3 Trends in crime

Police recorded crime

Each year, when the government publishes statistics on recorded crime, newspapers respond with headlines such as: Violent crime up 20%; Burglary up 10%. These headlines are usually based on a comparison of the present year's figures with those of the previous year. This section looks at trends in crime over longer periods of time.

Official statistics since 1876 show little change in annual crime figures until the 1930s. Then, there is a gradual rise to the early 1950s, followed by a sharp increase until the early 1990s. Since then, the figures have gone up and down, but remained at a high level compared to earlier years – see Activity 5, Item B.

If there are problems with official crime statistics in any one year, these are magnified when we examine trends over time. First, more crimes may be reported as time goes on. Second, new types of crime may be emerging and new opportunities opening up for existing crimes. Third, changes in legislation and law enforcement may result in more crimes being recorded. These are some of the factors which must be considered before drawing any conclusions from trends in crime statistics.

More crimes may be reported Since the mid-1990s, the proportion of crime reported to the police has remained more or less the same – around 44% of all crime. This is significantly higher than in the early 1980s (Simmons & Dodd, 2003). A number of reasons have been suggested for the increase in reporting rate.

- Increased telephone ownership, especially of mobiles, which makes reporting easier.
- The growth of reported burglary between 1981 and 1993 may be related to an increase in valuable goods in the home – for example, TVs and videos – to wider car ownership, and more insurance policies covering house contents and cars. Insurance companies require a police report when a crime has been committed (Mayhew et al., 1994).
- People may be less willing to tolerate certain types of crime. For example, the increase in reported violent crime may, at least in part, be due to less tolerance of violence. Recorded incidents of robbery, rape and theft from the person more than doubled between 1991 and 2000/01 (Maguire, 2002).
- The break-up of traditional, close-knit communities may result in people being more inclined to bring in the police to deal with incidents rather than sorting things out for themselves (Maguire, 2002).

New crimes and new opportunities Trends in crime change. New crimes emerge as do new opportunities to commit existing crimes. The invention of credit and debit cards and computers provides opportunities for theft and fraud which did not exist 50 years ago. Today, thefts of, or from, motor vehicles make up around one fifth of recorded crime. In the 1950s, these offences were relatively rare as there were far fewer cars on the road (Maguire, 2002).

Changes in legislation and law enforcement These changes may result in more crimes being recorded. This can be seen from the following examples.

The decision in 1977 to include offences of criminal damage of £20 or less in police crime statistics raised the annual total by around 7% (Maguire, 2002). And the decision in 1998 to include summary offences, such as common assault, again boosted the total of recorded crime, as well as giving the impression of a major increase in violent crime. It is estimated that this change, plus new counting rules, increased the total number of recorded offences by up to 14% (Maguire, 2002). In 2002, the introduction of a new National Crime Recording Standard, designed to reduce police discretion in recording reports of offences from the public, resulted in the highest proportion of reported crime ever recorded by the police (Simmons & Dodd, 2003).

In the 1970s, the increased use of formal cautions for young people added substantially to the volume of recorded crime. According to one estimate, this change accounted for the whole increase in recorded crime for boys under 14 during the 1970s (Pearson, 1983).

Finally, the increase in the numbers of police officers – an increase of over 50% since the 1980s – coupled with more sophisticated technology, is likely to have resulted in more crimes being recorded.

Conclusion Does the rise in recorded crime mean that more crimes are being committed? The evidence presented in this section suggests that this may not be the case. It shows that at least part of the increase in recorded crime may have nothing to do with changes in the actual volume of crime.

2.4 The British Crime Survey (BCS)

Methodology

The British Crime Survey (BCS) is a *victim study* – it asks people if they have been a victim of particular crimes. The survey was conducted every two years from 1982 to 2000, and since then every year.

The BCS is based on a representative sample of adults (aged 16 and over) living in private households in England and Wales. The response rate – those who agreed to be interviewed – in the 2002/03 survey was 75%. Some 36,500 interviews were conducted. Respondents were asked to recall crimes against themselves or any other member of the household over a 12 month period preceding the interview.

Various crimes are excluded from the BCS – crimes such as murder, where the victim is no longer available for interview, so-called victimless crimes (eg, drug possession or dealing), fraud, and offences against non-domestic targets such as businesses. BCS estimates exclude sexual offences due to the small number reported to the survey and concerns about people's willingness to disclose such offences (Simmons & Dodd, 2003).

The 2002/03 BCS

The 2002/03 British Crime Survey provides the following picture of crime in England and Wales.

The volume of crime On the basis of interviews conducted in 2002/03, the BCS estimates that 12.3 million crimes were committed against adults living in private households. Police recorded crime for England and Wales for the same period was just under 5.9 million. The BCS estimate is, therefore, more than double police recorded crime.

Unreported and unrecorded crime Not all BCS crimes can be directly compared with police figures – for example, thefts involving household and personal property are placed by the police in the same category as thefts of business property and shoplifting, crimes which are not included in the BCS. However, just over 9.5 million BCS crimes are comparable with those in police statistics. Of these, 43% were reported to the police, and of those reported, 68% were recorded by the police. This means that only 29% of all BCS crimes were actually recorded by the police and entered the official statistics of police recorded crime (Simmons & Dodd, 2003).

Since the BCS includes both unreported and unrecorded crime, it gives a more complete estimate of many crimes than police records.

Trends in crime From 1981 to 1995, British Crime Survey estimates show a steady rise in crime. Since then, there has been a steady fall – by 2002/03, the estimates were only slightly above the 1983 level – see Activity 5, Item C.

In general, the BCS trends in the volume of crime are reflected in the trends in police recorded crime. However, they diverged when a new counting rule for recorded crime was introduced in 1998 and the National Crime Recording Standard came into operation in 2002. These

key term

Victim study/survey A study of the victims of crime. Such studies usually ask people to report the crimes that have been committed against them, or any other member of the household, during the previous year.

activity5 the British Crime Survey

Item A The BCS and police recorded crime

	% BCS crimes reported to the police	% of reported BCS crimes recorded by the police	% of all BCS crimes recorded by the police
Vandalism	31	70	22
PROPERTY CRIME	50	75	38
Burglary	65	71	46
Burglary attempts and no loss	49	42	21
Burglary with loss	87	94	81
All vehicle thefts	50	84	42
Thefts from vehicles	47	75	35
Thefts of vehicles	97	84	81
Attempted vehicle theft	36	100	38
Bicycle theft	50	56	28
Thefts from the person	33	59	19
VIOLENCE	41	52	21
Common assault	34	46	16
Wounding	46	57	26
Robbery	53	54	28
ALL COMPARABLE CRIME	43	68	29

Adapted from Simmons & Dodd, 2003

Item B   Police recorded crime trends

Crimes recorded by the police, England and Wales, 1920-2002/03

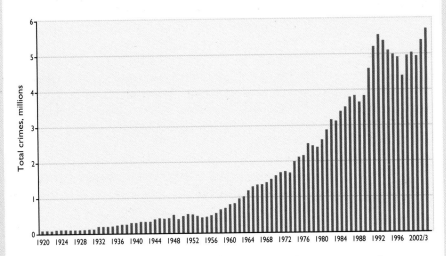

Note: From 1997, the figures are based on the financial year (ie, April to March).
Adapted from Home Office, 2001 and *Annual Abstract of Statistics*, 2004

questions

1 a) Briefly summarise the differences between the police and BCS figures in Item A.

   b) Why are some crimes more likely to be reported to the police than others?

   c) Why are some crimes reported to the police more likely to be recorded than others?

2 a) Briefly summarise the trends shown in Items B and C.

   b) Suggest reasons for the differences in recent trends (2001/02 and 2002/03) between police recorded crime and BCS estimates.

Item C   BCS trends

BCS crime estimates, England and Wales, 1981-2002/03

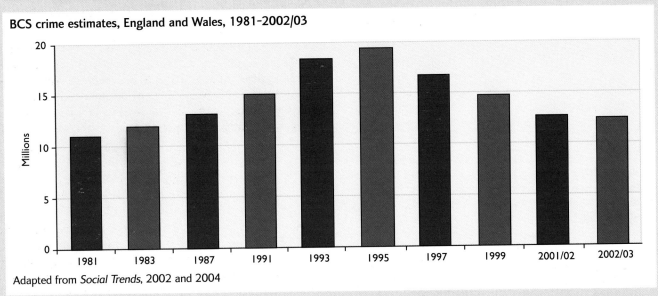

Adapted from *Social Trends*, 2002 and 2004

---

new measures increased the volume of police recorded crime. For example, the National Crime Recording Standard raised the volume of police recorded crime by 10% in 2002/03. This 10% 'increase' was simply due to a change in recording practice, it does not reflect a real increase in crime.

Without these changes in recording practices, the trends in police recorded crime would be similar to the BCS trends – they would show a steady decline in the volume of crime from the mid-1990s (Simmons & Dodd, 2003).

Evaluation of the BCS

Advantages For the crimes it covers, the British Crime Survey provides a more accurate picture of the extent of crime and of trends in crime than police recorded crime. There are two main reasons for this.

- First, BCS estimates include unreported and unrecorded crime.
- Second, the trends identified by the BCS are not affected by changes in recording practices, unlike the trends identified from police records.

Disadvantages There are a number of disadvantages of the BCS. They include the following.

- Only three-quarters of BCS crimes can be directly compared to police recorded crime.

- Because it is a household survey, the BCS does not cover a range of crimes which appear in police statistics. These include crimes against corporate and commercial organisations – such as fraud and shoplifting – motoring offences and so-called victimless crimes – such as possession or dealing in drugs (Maguire, 2002).

- Locally-based surveys of women indicate that the BCS underestimates assaults committed by people known to the victims – for example, partners.

- The BCS is a national survey. However, crime is not spread evenly across the country. In certain inner-city areas, the risks of serious crime are high. A local victim survey in Islington revealed that one-third of all households reported being a victim of burglary, robbery or sexual assault within the previous year (Jones et al., 1986). This is considerably higher than the national figure.

2.5 The social characteristics of offenders

Sociologists often explain behaviour in terms of people's social characteristics – for example, their social class, ethnicity, gender and age. Sociologists are therefore interested in the social characteristics of offenders. For instance, if offenders are primarily young, male and working class, then these factors may help to explain their criminal behaviour.

There are two main sources for identifying the social characteristics of offenders – official sources and self-report studies.

The official picture

Known offenders Statistics compiled from court records and police cautioning records provide an official picture of offenders. It is important to note that the number of 'known offenders' is small compared to the number of recorded offences. For example, in 2000, some 325,000 people were sentenced in court in England and Wales and 151,000 were cautioned by the police. This compares with over 5 million recorded crimes. The proportion of known offenders becomes even smaller when a comparison is made with BCS data. According to one estimate, only 3 in 100 BCS crimes resulted in an offender being convicted or cautioned (Barclay & Tavares, 1999).

We cannot assume that all offenders are similar to this small proportion of known offenders. In other words, we cannot generalise from such a small, and probably unrepresentative, sample.

Social characteristics Of the 476,000 offenders convicted or cautioned in 2000, 80% were male and 41% under the age of 21. Often gender and age are the only characteristics of offenders available from court and police cautioning records.

A fuller picture is provided by the National Prison Survey which was conducted in England and Wales in 1991

(Walmsley et al., 1992). The main findings were as follows.

- 62% of inmates were under 30 compared with 25% in the population as a whole.

- A disproportionate number were from the lower levels of the class system – 41% of males formerly had unskilled or partly-skilled manual jobs compared with 18% of the population as a whole.

- Given their numbers in the general population, a disproportionate number of prisoners came from ethnic minorities – particularly African Caribbean.

Overall, the findings of the National Prison Survey reveal a very different pattern than that found in the wider population.

Mike Maguire (2002) describes the picture presented by official sources of the social characteristics of offenders. 'There are many more males, young people, Black people, poor people, poorly-educated people, and people with disturbed childhoods than one would find in a random sample.'

Self-report studies

Only some 3% of crimes result in a conviction or caution. What about the other 97%? Do those who committed these offences share the same characteristics as the 3%? *Self-report studies* may help to provide an answer to this question.

Self-report studies of crime ask people whether they have committed a series of offences. They are usually based on a self-completed questionnaire or an interview. Respondents are presented with a list of offences and asked which they have committed over a period of time – for example, during the past 12 months or during their lifetime.

Crime is normal Self-report studies suggest that most of us have committed at least one crime at some stage in our lives. This questions the view that a clear distinction can be made between law-abiding people and offenders. Gabor (1994) argues that many of us have done one or more of the following: 'taken home linens, silverware, art and other "souvenirs" from hotels in which we have stayed; made inflated insurance claims following a fire or theft; illegally copied computer software or videos; used prohibited drugs or abused prescription drugs; exhibited disorderly conduct in public; physically struck another person intentionally'.

It is possible to argue that crime is 'normal'. If this is the case, then there is nothing particularly distinctive about the social characteristics of those who break the law. However, there are problems with this view. What kinds of crime are we talking about? Many of the crimes committed by most people can be seen as fairly trivial. And how many crimes do most people commit? Self-report studies indicate that committing one or two criminal acts is a 'normal' part of growing up for most boys. However, frequent lawbreaking is relatively rare (Hood & Sparks, 1970).

Gender Self-report studies indicate that far more males than females commit crimes. This reflects the picture given by official statistics. In a self-report study conducted by the

Home Office, over 30% of 22-25 year-old males admitted a criminal offence within the previous year, compared with only 4% of females in the same age group (Graham & Bowling, 1995).

Social class Most self-report studies suggest a link between social class and criminal behaviour. They indicate that the lower a person's position in the class system, the more likely they are to commit a crime. Again, this reflects the picture given by official statistics (Coleman & Moynihan, 1996).

This link appears strongest in terms of 'street crime' – burglary, robbery, theft of or from a vehicle – and the so-called *underclass* – those at the base of the class system, the long-term unemployed and those dependent on welfare benefits (Farnworth et al., 1994).

However, there are problems with this apparent link between class and crime. Street crimes are the typical crimes of the poor. They are a police priority and are the types of crime which the police are most likely to deal with. And they are the types of crime which tend to be listed by researchers in self-report questionnaires and structured interviews. Other types of crime, such as fraud, domestic violence and child abuse, are less visible and less likely to appear on a list in self-report studies. In view of this, it is not surprising that the poor appear to commit more crimes than their better-off counterparts (Maguire, 2002).

Age Self-report studies, like official statistics, suggest that crime is a 'young person's game'. However, it is important to note that young people tend to offend in groups and in public – they are more visible and more likely to be apprehended. Also the crimes young people commit are more likely to be listed in self-report studies (Coleman & Moynihan, 1996). And they are more likely to be reported to the police – for example, vehicle theft.

Ethnicity There is little difference between Blacks and Whites in self-reported crime. This is at odds with the picture presented by official statistics which shows a relatively high proportion of Black offenders.

Evaluation and conclusion

Official statistics reveal the social characteristics of those who have been processed by the criminal justice system – that is, those who have been cautioned, those found guilty by the courts, and those imprisoned. They reflect the priority given by the police to certain kinds of crime and certain types of lawbreakers. As such, they are useful.

However, official statistics are unlikely to present a picture of the social characteristics of lawbreakers in general. They indicate that young, working-class males are a major crime problem. But this may simply reflect the fact that 'most police resources are devoted to uniformed patrol of public space' where most young working-class males are likely to spend their social lives (Reiner, 1994). And police priorities and perceptions might well be the main reason for the apparent class/crime link. According to William Chambliss (1969) 'The lower class person is (i) more likely to be scrutinised and therefore to be observed in any violation of the law, (ii) more likely to be arrested if discovered under suspicious circumstances, (iii) more likely to spend the time between arrest and trial in jail, (iv) more likely to come to trial, (v) more likely to be found guilty, and (vi) if found guilty, more likely to receive harsh punishment than his middle or upper-class counterpart.'

Self-report studies The results of self-report studies must be approached with caution. Traditionally, they have focused on male juvenile delinquency – the criminal behaviour of young men. And the lists of crimes presented in self-report studies tend to reflect those typically committed by young working-class males – in particular 'street crime'. They tend to omit 'hidden crimes' and adult crimes, such as domestic violence and child abuse, crimes which are likely to be spread more evenly across age and class groups. And they are unlikely to include fraud, often committed by middle-class, middle-aged men. As a result, self-report studies provide only a partial view of crime. And this leads to a one-sided picture of the social characteristics of offenders.

key terms

Self-report study A survey in which respondents report on aspects of their behaviour - in the case of crime, the offences they have committed over a period of time.

Underclass Some sociologists claim that an underclass, a class below the working class, has developed in modern societies. Characteristics of the underclass include dependency on welfare benefits and long-term unemployment.

summary

1. There are two main measure of crime in Britain - police recorded crime based on police records, and the British Crime Survey (BCS), a victim study based on a representative sample of adults.

2. Police recorded crime statistics do not represent the total volume of crime. There is a 'dark figure' or 'hidden figure' of unrecorded crime.

3. Certain offences, for example many tax offences, do not enter police records because they are dealt with administratively by organisations such as the Inland Revenue.

4. Many of the offences reported to the police are not recorded – over 30% in 2002/03. Often this is because the offences are seen as too trivial to record.

5. Police priorities affect the crimes they target, the number and

type of offences they discover, and the crime statistics they produce.

6. Some crimes are more likely to be reported to the police than others. For example, vehicle theft is much more likely to be reported than domestic violence.

7. Police recorded crime provides statistics. It has nothing to say about the significance of crime. For example, in monetary terms fraud is much more significant than other property offences.

8. Police recorded crime fails to provide a reliable and valid measure of crime. It may be significantly biased in underestimating certain types of crime – for example, fraud and domestic violence.

9. Police crime statistics are a social construction. They are constructed during the process of social interaction and based on a series of interpretations, definitions and decisions.

10. Police recorded crime provides the following picture of trends in crime. There is little change in the annual crime figures from 1876 until the 1930s. Then, there is a gradual rise to the 1950s, followed by a sharp increase until the early 1990s. Since then, the figures have gone up and down, but remained high compared to earlier years.

11. The following reasons have been given for the increase in police recorded crime.
   - The proportion of crime reported to the police rose significantly between the early 1980s and mid-1990s.
   - New crimes and new opportunities for crime have developed – for example, credit card fraud.
   - Changes in police recording practices have increased the total of recorded crime.

12. The rise in police recorded crime does not necessarily mean that more crimes are being committed. However, evidence from the British Crime Survey indicates an actual rise in crime from the early 1980s until 1995.

13. The British Crime Survey (BCS) is a victim study based on a representative sample of adults in England and Wales.

14. It estimates that the total volume of crime is more than double the total given by police recorded crime.

15. The BCS indicates a steady rise in crime from 1981 to 1995, followed by a steady fall to 2002/03.

16. Differences between BCS and police recorded crime trends since 1995 are probably due to changes in police recording practices. These changes increased the level of recorded crime.

17. Compared to police recorded crime, the BCS has the advantage of including both unreported and unrecorded crime. Also, it is not affected by changes in recording practices.

18. The BCS has a number of disadvantages. They include:
   - The BCS does not cover certain crimes which appear in police statistics – for example, fraud.
   - It underestimates certain crimes – for example, domestic violence.

19. There are two main sources for identifying the social characteristics of offenders - official sources and self-report studies.

20. Statistics from court records and police cautioning records provide an official picture of offenders. However, the number of 'known offenders' is small compared with the number of recorded offences.

21. This number becomes even smaller when BCS crimes are taken into account. Only around 3 in 100 BCS crimes result in an offender being convicted or cautioned. We cannot generalise from such a small and probably unrepresentative sample.

22. According to official sources, the typical offender is young, male and working class.

23. Self-report studies indicate that most people have committed at least one crime. In this respect, there is nothing distinctive about people who break the law.

24. Self-report studies give the following picture of the social characteristics of offenders. It reflects the picture provided by official statistics.
   - Significantly more males than females commit crimes.
   - The lower a person's position in the class system, the more likely they are to commit crimes.
   - Younger people are more likely to commit crimes than older people.

25. The social characteristics of offenders provided by official statistics reflect the priorities given by the police to certain kinds of crime and certain types of lawbreakers.

26. Self-report studies tend to focus on the types of crime committed by young working-class males. They tend to omit adult crimes, such as domestic violence and fraud, which are likely to be spread more evenly across age and social class groups.

27. Both official sources and self-report studies give only a partial view of crime. This leads to a one-sided picture of the social characteristics of offenders.

activity6 your self report

Incident	Offence	Maximum Penalty
1. Have you ever bought goods knowing or believing they may have been stolen?	Handling stolen property	£5,000 and/or 6 months imprisonment
2. Have you taken stationery or anything else from your office/work?	Theft	£5,000 and/or 6 months imprisonment
3. Have you ever used the firm's telephone for personal calls?	Dishonestly abstracting electricity	£5,000 and/or 6 months imprisonment
4. Have you ever kept money if you received too much change?	Theft	£5,000 and/or 6 months imprisonment
5. Have you kept money found in the street?	Theft	£5,000 and/or 6 months imprisonment
6. Have you taken 'souvenirs' from a pub/hotel?	Theft	£5,000 and/or 6 months imprisonment
7. Have you tried to evade customs duty on a small item bought on holiday?	Intending to defraud	Three times value of goods or £5,000 fine, whichever is greater and/or 3 years imprisonment
8. Have you used a TV without buying a licence?	Using a TV without a licence	£400 fine
9. Have you ever fiddled your expenses?	Theft	£5,000 and/or 6 months imprisonment
10. Have you ever driven a car knowing you are 'over the limit'?	Driving with excess alcohol	£5,000 and/or 6 months imprisonment

questions

1 a) How many of these offences have you committed?

b) Add up the maximum penalties which you could have received.

c) Compare your answers to a) and b) with those of other students.

2 What do your answers to Question 1 suggest about a) the accuracy of official statistics and b) the picture of the 'typical criminal' drawn from official statistics?

Unit 3 Media representations of crime

key issues

1 What pictures of crime do the media present?

2 What factors influence media representations of crime?

3 To what extent do the media shape popular perceptions of crime?

3.1 Media images of crime

The previous unit looked at the pictures of crime and the criminal presented by official statistics, victim studies and self-report studies. This unit looks at the pictures presented by the mass media.

Judging by the output of the media, the public have an enormous appetite for crime. A significant proportion of newspaper articles, broadcast news (TV and radio), films, novels, comics, drama, documentaries and reality TV focuses on crime. And the pictures of crime and the criminal presented by the media are often different from those provided by official statistics, victim studies and self-report studies.

Methodology

Most of the studies of media representations of crime are based on content analysis.

Formal content analysis This method aims to classify and quantify media content in an objective manner. For example, it is used to measure the amount of space devoted to crime and the types of crime covered in newspapers. Researchers usually have a checklist of crimes which they use to classify and quantify newspaper coverage. Formal content analysis can often effectively measure simple, straightforward aspects of content. However, it says little about the meaning of content to the audience.

Thematic analysis This form of content analysis looks for themes which underlie the content. For example, the police may be regularly presented in a positive light – as sympathetic, honest, just and efficient. This theme may underlie many news reports on crime. However, the themes interpreted by sociologists may have little to do with the interpretations of the audience.

Textual analysis This form of content analysis involves a close examination of the 'text' in order to see how it encourages a particular reading and creates a particular impression. Ray Pawson (1995) gives the following example from a newspaper headline, GIRL GUIDE, 14, RAPED AT HELLS ANGELS CONVENTION. This is an example of the 'innocent victim'/'wicked perpetrator' pair which creates the impression of two extremes, one good, the other evil. It is one of the many tricks of the trade used to convey particular messages.

As with thematic analysis, the problem with textual analysis is reading things into the text which may have little or nothing to do with interpretations of the audience.

The extent of crime in the news

Most analyses of crime in the media have focused on the news. The results show that crime forms a significant part of news' content. For example, a study comparing the coverage of ten national daily newspapers for four weeks in 1989 found that 12.7% of the events reported were about crime. The proportion of space given to crime was greater the more down-market the paper – the *Guardian* containing only 5.1%, the *Sun* 30.4% (Williams & Dickinson, 1993).

Another study found that broadcast news devoted even more attention to crime than the press, with commercial stations containing a higher proportion of crime features than the BBC (Cumberbatch et al., 1995).

Studies indicate that the proportion of news devoted to crime has increased over the past 50 years. For example, one study found that the proportion of space given to crime reports in the *Daily Mirror* and the *Times* from 1945 to 1991 rose from 8% to 21% (Reiner et al., 2000).

The pattern of crime news

Content analysis conducted at different times and places reveals the following patterns in crime news.

Types of crime The coverage of violent and sexual crimes is significantly greater than their incidence as measured by official statistics, victim studies and self-report studies. Homicide accounts for one-third of all crime news. Williams and Dickinson's (1993) study of ten national newspapers in 1989 found that 64.5% of crime stories dealt with violence against the person. According to British Crime Survey, only 6% of crimes reported by victims in 1989 were violent.

The proportion of violent and sexual crimes tended to be greater the more down-market the newspaper. Television news coverage is closer to the tabloids (eg, the *Sun*) than the broadsheets (eg, the *Guardian*) (Reiner, 2002).

Social characteristics of offenders Like official statistics and self-report studies, crime news portrays offenders as overwhelmingly male. But here the similarity ends. Offenders in crime news are older and higher status – they are more likely to be middle class. In this respect, the media may present a more accurate picture, since official statistics tend to underestimate the proportion of older, higher status offenders (Reiner, 2002).

Incidents rather than causes Crime news focuses on actual incidents of crime. It tends to describe events and pays little attention to the causes of crime. There are exceptions – broadsheets, such as the *Guardian*, are more likely to contain some analysis of the causes of crime (Carrabine et al., 2002).

The criminal justice system The news media usually present a positive picture of the criminal justice system. For example, the success of the police in detecting crime is often exaggerated. There are stories exposing police corruption and malpractice. However, such wrongdoing tends to be portrayed as the failings of individuals rather than the criminal justice system as a whole (Chibnall, 1977). When the system is clearly to blame, the media usually report that reforms have been made and all is now well. Again, the legitimacy of the criminal justice system is safeguarded.

Crime and reality TV

The emergence of reality TV has blurred the boundaries between news and fiction. *Crimewatch UK* is one of the earliest reality TV programmes – it presents dramatised reconstructions of crime. It aims to both entertain and to help the police solve crimes. And it still continues to attract a far larger audience than the news.

In its portrayal of crime, *Crimewatch UK* is similar to the news – it focuses on murder, armed robbery with violence, and sexual crimes (Dobash et al., 1998). This focus is very different from the picture presented by official statistics, victim studies and self-report studies. In some ways this is nothing new. In Victorian times, today's reconstructions of crime were matched by the popular *Penny Dreadful* – cheap sensational accounts of recent murders which whetted the Victorian appetite for both blood and indignation in a tantalising cocktail.

More recent reality TV programmes such as *Crime Beat*, *Police Camera Action* and *Car Wars* are different. They use CCTV footage as opposed to dramatised reconstructions and highlight 'the "everydayness" of the crimes portrayed and the frequency of their occurrence in "everyday life" ' (Brunsdon et al., 2001). In other words, they portray crime as a routine and regular event and address the viewer 'as a threatened consumer' who must take responsibility for crime prevention (Carrabine et al., 2002).

Crime fiction

The extent of crime fiction Crime has always been a staple ingredient of media fiction. One estimate suggests that between a quarter and a third of paperback novels could be categorised as crime stories (Mandel, 1984). Since 1945, around 20% of all films are crime movies and around 50% have a significant crime content (Allen et al., 1997). And, since 1955, some 25% of the most popular British TV programmes have been crime or police series (Reiner et al., 2000).

Crime in fiction In many respects, the picture of crime in media fiction is similar to that presented by crime news. As such, it is very different from the picture given by official statistics, victim studies and self-report studies.

- Media fiction focuses on murder and other violent crimes. Murder was the most frequent offence in crime movies since 1945 (Reiner, 2002).

- Offenders in crime fiction are mainly middle-aged, middle-class males as opposed to the young, working-class males in official statistics and self-report studies (Reiner, 2002).

- The police clear-up rate is very different from the picture given by official statistics. In crime fiction, the police usually 'get their man'. According to official statistics, they usually don't.

The police tend to be presented in a positive light in crime fiction – as protecting citizens from harm. However, in recent years, there has been increasing criticism of the criminal justice system – in terms of both its effectiveness and its honesty (Reiner, 2002).

activity7 media pictures of crime

Item A Newspaper reports

Murdered by a savage out on bail

A drug addict murdered a widow of 82 for her pension money while on bail for another violent crime.

Wayne Franks, 29, was jailed for life yesterday for a savage attack in which he hit Mabel Whitelam over the head with a hammer, strangled her and stabbed her 22 times.

Financial adviser accused of murdering his client

A financial advisor seduced a lonely and vulnerable elderly woman before stealing £280,000 and murdering her in her bed, a court heard yesterday.

Aged 64, married and father of three, he allegedly began an affair with his client after she contacted him for advice on investing her £500,000 savings. He stole her money to help clear his debts and pay for his affluent lifestyle, Chester Crown Court was told.

The terrifying violence that shames Britain

Mugged, Louisa La Rouche was savagely attacked.

Threatened...Customers cower under a shotgun-wielding raider in a Leeds building society.

From *Today*, 28.9.1994

Terror of 'SAS' rapist

A builder who terrorised a family after convincing them he was a member of the SAS was jailed for 20 years yesterday.

Over 16 months, Nigel Da Costa carried out a series of indecent assaults and rapes and held members of the family prisoner.

The 33-year-old shaven-headed thug subjected them to the degrading attacks, often at gunpoint, telling them they had

threatened national security by searching for his name on the Internet.

He maintained his grip on their lives by threatening to have them killed.

His wife Helen, 29, a former primary school teacher, was jailed for five years for going along with her husband's fantasies. She was present at many of the attacks.

All reports adapted from the *Daily Mail*, May 2004

Item B Crime fiction

questions

1 In what ways are the crime reports in Item A typical of newspaper representations of crime?

2 Judging by Item B, how does crime fiction picture crime?

3 How do the representations of crime in Items A and B differ from those presented by official statistics, victim studies and self-report studies?

3.2 Explaining media representations of crime

Little is known about the production of representations of crime in media fiction. However, there have been a number of studies of the production of crime news.

News values What makes 'news'? In the course of their professional socialisation, journalists are taught what makes a good news story and what events are newsworthy. In other words, they learn *news values*.

In terms of these values, a good news story should include the following:

- Novelty, freshness and surprise
- Drama and excitement
- Titillation
- A focus on personalities (Chibnall, 1977).

Given these news values, it is not surprising that violent and sexual crimes predominate in the news, that the focus is on criminal incidents rather than an analysis of causes, and that the offenders and victims portrayed tend to be well-known personalities, often celebrities.

Sources of crime news The police and the courts are the main sources of crime news. As a result, journalists are largely dependent on official sources for their information. These sources have become *primary definers* – they define

what counts as crime, what counts as justice, and what crimes are significant. And, in doing so, they reflect the concerns of the powerful – the agents of social control and the state (Hall et al., 1978).

What about alternative ways of defining crime and its significance? Human rights organisations such as Amnesty International identify a variety of 'state crimes' for example, the treatment of so-called asylum seekers and suspected terrorists in Britain. Occasionally, their views are reported. But, for the most part, their voices are drowned out by the primary definers. In view of this, it is not surprising that the criminal justice system tends to be presented in a positive light.

key terms

News values Values which define what is newsworthy.
Primary definers Those who have the power to define the way things are – in this context, what counts as crime and justice.

3.3 The media and perceptions of crime

Do media representations of crime influence people's views of crime? Do they amplify people's fear of crime?

The British Crime Survey includes questions about

perceptions of and concerns about crime. It also asks questions about newspaper readership. Findings from the three surveys from 2001 to 2003 indicate the following.

The crime rate Over the three years in question, an increasing proportion of respondents believed that the national crime rate had risen 'a lot' (25% in 2001, 30% in 2001/02 and 38% in 2002/03). However, the BCS indicated a steady fall in crime over these years.

According to the 2002/03 survey, 43% of those who read a national tabloid newspaper thought that the crime rate had risen 'a lot', compared to 26% of broadsheet readers (Simmons & Dodd, 2003).

Concerns about crime The BCS found that concern about particular types of crime was associated with newspaper readership. Compared to broadsheet readers, readers of tabloids were twice as likely to be 'very worried' about burglary, mugging, physical attack and rape (Simmons & Dodd, 2003).

Newspaper readership and perceptions of crime Is there a causal link between newspaper readership and perceptions of crime? As noted earlier, tabloids are more likely to report violent and sexual crimes than broadsheets. And they are more likely to headline the more dramatic and negative aspects of official crime statistics – for example, CRIME SOARS – Muggings up by 28% (*Daily Mail*, 12.7.2002). Since tabloid readers are more likely to be concerned about violent crime, and more likely to believe that the crime rate is rising, it is tempting to argue that their perceptions are influenced by the papers they read.

However, there is another view. Tabloid readers tend to be working class and broadsheet readers middle class. The BCS found that people living in inner-city areas and council estates are particularly concerned about crime, especially violent crime. These are the areas where working-class people are likely to live and the areas where violent crime is probably highest. Rather than causing this fear of crime, tabloid newspapers may simply be reflecting it. As Crawford et al., (1990) put it, 'in inner-city areas, mass media coverage of crime tends to reinforce what people already know'.

summary

1. Most of the studies of media representations of crime are based on content analysis.
2. There are three main types of content analysis, each with its strengths and weaknesses.
   - Formal content analysis
   - Thematic analysis
   - Textual analysis.
3. A significant proportion of space in newspapers is devoted to crime news. The more down-market the paper, the greater the proportion of crime news.
4. Broadcast news tends to devote more attention to crime than the press.
5. News coverage of violent and sexual crimes is significantly greater than their incidence as measured by official statistics, victim studies and self-report studies.
6. Offenders in crime news are more likely to be older and middle class than those who appear in official statistics and self-report studies.
7. Reality TV programmes, such as Crimewatch UK, focus on murder, armed robbery with violence, and sexual crimes. More recent reality TV programmes tend to focus on routine, 'everyday' crimes.
8. Media fiction concentrates on murder and other violent crimes. Offenders tend to be middle-aged, middle-class males as opposed to the young, working-class males who predominate in official statistics and self-report studies.
9. In both crime news and crime fiction, the police are usually portrayed in a positive light.
10. Media representations of crime are largely shaped by news values and official sources – the police and the courts.
11. Despite a recent decrease in the crime rate, a growing number of BCS respondents believe the rate is increasing. Those who read tabloid newspapers are more likely to take this view.
12. Tabloid readers are twice as likely as broadsheet readers to be very concerned about violent crime.
13. Tabloids are more likely to report violent crime and to headline negative trends in official crime statistics than broadsheet newspapers. This may influence tabloid readers' perceptions of crime.
14. There is an alternative argument. Tabloid readers tend to be working class and to live in areas with a high rate of violent crime. The tabloids may simply reflect their concern with crime rather than shaping it.

activity8 definitions and perceptions of crime

Item A *News values*

Cilla Black returning home after the burglary

Thugs target the famous

The vicious gang who struck at Cilla Black's home had earlier robbed Tony Blair's friend Lord Levy it emerged last night. Detectives revealed several chilling similarities, including the degree of violence used.

The armed gang held a hunting knife to the throat of Miss Black's youngest son as they stole jewels, cash and gold worth more than £1 million.

Five months earlier, Lord Levy, the Prime Minister's special envoy to the Middle East, and his wife were handcuffed to chairs and beaten after three masked men broke into their £5 million North London mansion. The gang made off with £80,000 in cash and jewellery.

Adapted from the *Daily Mail*, 24.05.2004

Item B *Violent crime*

Figures show how promise to crack down on thugs is failing

Heat on ministers as violent crimes go up by 20pc

By **Jo Butler**
Home Affairs Correspondent

VIOLENT crime has soared by 20 per cent in a year, official figures are expected to show.

Despite the Government's pledge to crack down on crimi...

increase in violent crime and an overall rise of 8 per cent.

But the latest figures still make

Looking down the barrel of a gun: Violent crime is on the increase

From *Daily Mail*, 26.5.2003

Item C *Concern about crime*

Worry about crime and newspaper readership

Percentages

% very worried about:	National tabloids	National broadsheets
Burglary	17	9
Mugging	16	7
Physical attack	17	6
Rape	18	7
Being insulted or pestered in a public place	9	5

Adapted from Simmons & Dodd, 2003

questions

1 What news values are reflected in Item A?

2 What impression might readers form from the newspaper report in Item B?

3 a) Briefly summarise the table in Item C.

   b) Suggest explanations for the apparent link between newspaper readership and concern with crime.

Unit 4 Explaining crime and deviance: Functionalism, strain theory and subcultural theory

keyissues

1 What is distinctive about the sociological approach to crime and deviance?

2 What are the main sociological explanations of crime and deviance that flow from a functionalist perspective?

3 What are the strengths and weaknesses of these explanations?

4.1 Normalising the criminal

Sociology is not the only subject concerned with crime and deviance. Cesare Lombroso, the first writer who tried to explain crime scientifically, drew on biology. Writing in the 19th century, he claimed that criminals were biologically distinct from non-criminals and that this difference explained their criminal behaviour. Other researchers have drawn on psychology, arguing that there is a psychological basis for criminal behaviour. What these approaches have in common is a picture of the criminal as somehow different from the rest of us.

For some researchers, this difference is mainly due to heredity – to the inheritance of particular genes which predispose individuals to criminal behaviour. For others, the difference arises from people's experiences, particularly childhood experiences, which again are seen to predispose them to crime. In both cases, the criminal is seen as abnormal in a normal population.

Sociologists tend to be sceptical of these views. They insist that a satisfactory explanation of crime and deviance must take the social context into account. As noted earlier, crime and deviance are socially constructed. What counts as crime and deviance is based on meanings, definitions and interpretations of behaviour which develop in the context of social interaction. Even crime statistics are socially constructed – based on countless decisions which, in turn, are based on definitions and interpretations which change from time to time and context to context.

Sociologists look to the social situation for explanations of why people commit criminal acts or are defined as criminal. For example, they look at people's position in the class structure, their power and influence in society, their age, gender and ethnic groups, their culture and subculture for these explanations. There is no suggestion of abnormal genes or abnormal personalities. From a sociological viewpoint, the 'criminal' is as normal as the rest of us.

activity9 criminals are different

Item A Throwbacks

Cesare Lombroso is credited with being the founding father of criminology, a new discipline which sought to explain crime scientifically. From his studies of convicted criminals he claimed to have discovered biological characteristics which were the outward signs of an inborn criminal nature. These included 'enormous jaws, high cheek bones, prominent superciliary arches (eyebrow ridges), solitary lines on the palms, extreme size of the orbits, handle-shaped or sessile ears found in criminals, savages and apes, insensibility to pain, extremely acute sight, tattooing, excessive idleness, love of orgies and the irresistible craving for evil for its own sake'. Lombroso believed that criminals were a throwback to an earlier and more primitive form of human being.

Adapted from C. Lombroso, *L'Uomo Delinquente*, first published in 1876

Item B Cartoon from Punch, 1881

CIVILISATION OF THE ROUGH
Professors of Dancing and Deportment giving Lessons to the Convicts.

Item C *Criminal types*

Typical 'criminal types' identified by the Victorian criminologist Havelock Ellis .

Item D *Personality and crime*

Hans Eysenck argues that personality is largely inherited – that is, genetically based. Certain types of personality are more prone to react to particular environmental factors with criminal behaviour. Personality and environment are equally important. It is the interaction between the two which is probably the most important factor.

Eysenck identified a number of dimensions of personality. One dimension ranged from introversion at one end of the scale to extraversion at the other. Introverts learn the norms and values of society more quickly and effectively than extraverts. They are therefore more likely to respond to mechanisms of social control. Introverts are quiet and reserved, they tend to avoid high levels of stimulation. Extraverts, on the other hand, seek stimulation and excitement, they are impulsive and enjoy taking risks.

Eysenck devised a questionnaire to measure extraversion. He claims that those with a high extraversion score are more likely to commit criminal acts. For example, in one study he found that young men who repeatedly offended had high extraversion scores.

Adapted from Eysenck, 1987

questions

1 The criminal types identified by Victorian criminologists were little different from popular stereotypes of the day. Discuss with reference to Items A, B and C.

2 What similarities and differences are evident in Lombroso's and Eysenck's explanations of criminal behaviour? (Items A and D).

4.2 Functionalism and crime

Sociological theories of crime and deviance are diverse and often competing. But they share one thing in common – they offer social rather than biological or psychological explanations.

In this and the next two units, these theories are grouped under three major perspectives within sociology – functionalism, interactionism and Marxism. It is important to recognise that these perspectives are broad schools of thought which contain many variations, and that a number of sociological theories of crime and deviance straddle different perspectives. Nonetheless, this approach provides a chronological overview which shows how new theories developed from a critique of earlier work.

Functions of crime and deviance

Crime and deviance as 'normal' Functionalists see shared norms and values as the basis of social order and social solidarity. It is not surprising that they consider crime and deviance, beyond a certain level, to be dysfunctional or harmful to society – a threat to social order and to the survival of the social system. What *is* perhaps surprising is the view that a certain amount of crime and deviance is not only 'normal' but also 'an integral part of all healthy societies' (Durkheim, 1964).

A crime-free or a deviance-free society is seen as a contradiction in terms. Writing in 1895, the French sociologist Emile Durkheim asked us to 'Imagine a society of saints, a perfect cloister of exemplary individuals. Crimes, properly so called, will there be unknown; but faults which appear venial (trivial) to the layman will create there the same scandal that the ordinary offence does in ordinary consciousness.'

While too much crime or deviance constitutes a threat to social order, too little crime or deviance is unhealthy. It indicates that the norms and values are so strong and constricting that they prevent the innovation and change necessary for a healthy society.

Crime and deviance as functional How then is a certain amount of crime and deviance functional? For Durkheim, it is functional because of the response such activities draw forth from society. Through *degradation ceremonies* such as criminal trials and public punishment, we are reminded of our shared norms and values. By publicly condemning those who have broken significant rules, not only are norms and values reaffirmed but also we learn the limits of toleration and unite against the condemned. Crime and deviance, or at least the public response to them, are functional because they serve to reinforce social solidarity and integrate society.

Do crime and deviance serve any other functions? Some functionalists believe they do. For example, Kingsley Davis (1961) argued that crime and deviance can act as a 'safety valve'. He claimed that there is a conflict between man's instinctual need for sexual satisfaction and society's need to restrict the legitimate expression of sex to within the family. Prostitution, in this context, is functional because it provides sexual satisfaction without threatening the family as an institution. Another writer has identified a 'warning function' of crime and deviance. They 'may serve as a signal or warning that there is some defect in the social organisation' which may 'lead to changes that enhance efficiency and morale' (Clinard, 1974). For example, truancy from school may indicate unsuspected causes of discontent and the need for changes in the education system.

Evaluation Suggesting functions for crime and deviance, however, is not the same as finding an explanation for them. To argue that crime and deviance have certain social consequences does not explain their presence in the first place. 'It is one thing to assert that crime can be made to serve some social end or other once it has occurred – for example, to heighten solidarity by uniting against the offender. It is another step altogether to explain crime as promoted in advance by society to bring about that end' (Downes & Rock, 2003).

key terms

Dysfunctional Activities which are harmful to society – for example, they weaken social solidarity and disrupt social order.
Degradation ceremonies Ceremonies which degrade and condemn wrongdoers – for example, public punishment.

activity10 functions of crime and punishment

Item A Public execution

Hogarth's engraving of a public execution at Tyburn

Item B Prostitution

A prostitute in New York City

Item C Riots

Bradford, 2001

question

Suggest how the activities in Items A, B and C can be seen as functional for society.

4.3 Strain theory

In the 1930s, the American sociologist Robert K. Merton wrote an article entitled *Social Structure and Anomie*. It became one of the most influential explanations of crime and deviance. Merton's theory was sociological – he offered a social rather than a psychological or biological explanation.

Culture and norms According to Merton, American culture attaches great importance to success – and success is measured in terms of money and material possessions. There are norms which define legitimate means for achieving success. These legitimate means include gaining skills and qualifications and career advancement. The American Dream states that anybody can make it to the top if they try hard enough.

Anomie So much emphasis is placed on material success that many people experience pressure to deviate from accepted norms and values. Deviance occurs when they reject the goal of success and/or the legitimate means of reaching that goal. For example, some people are tempted to use any available means of getting to the top – even if this involves criminal behaviour.

Merton refers to this pressure to deviate as a 'strain to anomie'. *Anomie* means normlessness – it refers to a situation where norms no longer guide behaviour, where 'anything goes'.

Social structure Despite what the American Dream says, not everybody has an equal chance of success. The social structure prevents equal opportunity. In particular, the strain to anomie is most strongly felt by those at the bottom of the class structure. They are less likely to acquire the

skills and qualifications needed to reach the top. As a result, they are more likely to seek alternative routes to success.

Adaptations Merton identifies five possible adaptations or responses to the strain to anomie in American society – see Table 1. The first is conformity – aiming for success and sticking to the rules. The other four are deviant adaptations – they reject the goal of success and/or the norms for achieving it.

Table 1 Goals and means

	Cultural goal	Normative means
Conformity	acceptance	acceptance
Deviant adaptations		
Innovation	acceptance	rejection
Ritualism	rejection	acceptance
Retreatism	rejection	rejection
Rebellion	replacement	replacement

Conformity According to Merton, most people conform despite the strain to anomie. Even if they don't make it, they continue to strive for success and follow the normative means of getting there.

Innovation People who adopt this deviant adaptation accept the goal of success but, in Merton's words, they have 'little access to conventional and legitimate means for becoming successful'. As a result, some innovate – they turn to illegitimate means, to crime. The pressure to select this adaptation is greatest for those in the lower levels of the class system.

Ritualism People who follow this deviant route abandon the goal of success, but stick rigidly to the rules – for example, people in dead-end, white-collar occupations who follow their job descriptions to the letter.

Retreatism This deviant adaptation involves a rejection of both the goal of success and the normative means of achieving it. It applies to people who 'drop out' – tramps, drug addicts and habitual drunkards.

Rebellion This involves a rejection of conventional goals and means and their replacement with alternatives. The revolutionary who seeks to change society illustrates this type of deviant adaptation.

Evaluation of strain theory

Advantages Merton's strain theory was an early attempt to explain crime and deviance in terms of the culture and structure of society. It provided a sociological alternative to biological and psychological theories. In particular, it offered an explanation for working-class crime. Whatever its weaknesses, Merton's work provided a spur for the development of further sociological theories of crime and deviance.

Disadvantages Merton's theory raises a number of unanswered questions.

- First, why do some people but not others adopt deviant adaptations? For example, why do some people in the lower levels of the class system turn to crime but others do not?
- Second, Merton's theory focuses on individuals rather than groups. Crime and deviance are often collective activities. How can this be explained in terms of strain theory?
- Third, crime and deviance are not always motivated by a desire for monetary gain. How can activities such as vandalism and fighting between rival gangs be explained in terms of Merton's theory?

In search for answers to these questions, subcultural theory was born.

4.4 Subcultural theory

Albert Cohen – status frustration

Albert Cohen (1955) was the first sociologist to develop a subcultural theory of working-class crime and deviance. He examined delinquent gangs in low-income, inner-city areas. Delinquency refers to the criminal and anti-social acts of young people.

Cohen agreed with Merton that the mainstream value of success creates problems for young working-class males. Many do badly at school and fail to acquire the skills and qualifications needed for success.

Status frustration Defined as failures by the wider society, many working-class adolescents experience *status frustration*. They are frustrated with their low status as 'losers' and are given little or no respect.

A subcultural solution Faced by a common 'problem of adjustment' – a problem they share – some working-class adolescents develop a deviant solution. They create their own *subculture* – their own norms and values which differ from those of mainstream society. In Cohen's words, 'the delinquent subculture takes its norms from the larger culture but turns them upside down'.

Anti-social and criminal behaviour, which are condemned by the wider society, are valued by the delinquent subculture. And, most importantly, they provide a means by which 'failed' working-class young people can solve the problem of status frustration. By succeeding in terms of the values of the delinquent subculture, they gain respect and admiration from their peers – those in a similar situation.

This is where *collective* deviant activities come in. Gang members require an audience to gain respect. The 'successful' delinquent gains status in the eyes of his peers.

Non-utilitarian crime If status frustration is the main problem, then criminal activities to achieve monetary success – Merton's 'solution' – may not be necessary. Vandalism, joy-riding, fighting, anti-social behaviour such as giving cheek to teachers and disrupting the classroom, can bring respect. These are examples of *non-utilitarian* crime and deviance – not 'useful', not directed to monetary gain.

Acting in terms of the deviant subculture, young men not only gain status in each other's eyes, they also hit back at a society which has denied them the opportunity to succeed and branded them as failures.

Evaluation Cohen's subcultural theory offered explanations for non-utilitarian crime and collective deviance – explanations which Merton's strain theory failed to provide. However, there are other explanations for working-class delinquency, as the following sections illustrate.

Cloward and Ohlin – opportunity structures

The American sociologists Richard Cloward and Lloyd Ohlin (1961) provide an explanation for different types of working-class delinquency. They argue that both Merton and Cohen fail to explain why delinquent subcultures take different forms. Why, for example, are some gangs mainly concerned with theft while others focus on violence?

Cloward and Ohlin agree with Merton that delinquency results from legitimate opportunity structures being largely closed to many young, working-class males. However, their response to this situation varies depending on the social environment in which they grow up. Different social environments provide different opportunities for crime and deviance which, in turn, encourage the development of different delinquent subcultures. Cloward and Ohlin identify three types of delinquent subculture.

The criminal subculture This type of subculture tends to develop in areas where there is a well-established pattern of adult crime. This provides an illegitimate opportunity structure. Young men are presented with role models from whom they can learn the tricks of the trade. They are given the opportunity to climb the professional criminal hierarchy and to become 'successful' by participating in crime which brings monetary gain.

The conflict subculture This type of subculture tends to develop in areas where an *illegitimate opportunity structure* is absent. These areas usually have a high turnover of population and a low level of social cohesion – this prevents established patterns of adult crime from developing.

With little opportunity to succeed by either legitimate or illegitimate means, young men become frustrated and angry. They often respond to this situation with gang violence which gives them the opportunity to gain status and respect from their fellow gang members.

The retreatist subculture This type of subculture tends to emerge among those who have failed to succeed either by legitimate means or as members of either criminal or conflict subcultures. These 'double failures' sometimes form retreatist subcultures based on illegal drug use.

Evaluation Cloward and Ohlin develop both Merton's strain theory and Cohen's subcultural theory. They show that working-class delinquency is not simply concerned with material gain. And they identify, and provide explanations for, a number of delinquent subcultures.

However, Cloward and Ohlin tend to box off the subcultures they identify and ignore the overlaps between them. For example, gangs involved in the conflict subculture often deal in drugs and make large sums of money in the process. The same applies to members of the retreatist subculture – some addicts also 'successfully' deal in drugs (Winlow, 2001).

key terms

Anomie A state of normlessness – where norms no longer direct behaviour.
Delinquency The criminal behaviour of young people.
Status frustration Dissatisfaction and frustration with the status and respect given by others.
Subculture Distinctive norms and values shared by a group within society. These norms and values differ from those of the mainstream culture.
Non-utilitarian crime Crime which is not directed to monetary gain – for example, vandalism.
Illegitimate opportunity structure A structure which provides illegal opportunities for monetary gain.

Lower-class subculture

The theories we've looked at so far present a similar picture of society. They assume that there is a consensus or agreement about values. Members of society are socialised into a common value system and become committed, at least in the USA, to the ideal of success in monetary terms. Criminal and deviant subcultures are seen as reactions by young working-class males to their inability to obtain this goal by legitimate means.

The American sociologist Walter B. Miller (1958) takes a different view. He sees society as consisting of different social classes, each with a distinct set of values. Miller argues that there is a distinctive lower-class subculture which is passed on from generation to generation. It arose partly from the experience of low-skilled labour which involved boring, repetitive, dead-end jobs, interspersed with periods of unemployment. Lower-class subculture provides ways of living with this situation and of finding satisfaction outside of work.

*activity*11 *hispanic gangs*

Item A Hispanic gangs in LA

East Los Angeles is a mainly Hispanic area. Hispanics or Latinos have their origins in Spanish speaking countries in Central and South America. Hispanics in the USA are twice as likely to live in poverty as White Americans.

East LA has at least 800 Hispanic gangs with more than 100,000 members. The level of gang violence is extremely high. LA is known as the murder capital of the USA. Most of these murders are gang-related.

The Hispanic gangs are split into two groups. The *chicanos* are Mexican-Americans born in the USA who often don't speak any Spanish. Their rivals are gangs whose members are recent immigrants from Mexico and other Spanish speaking countries who have evolved a language of their own called *calo*. Older members (*veteranos*) are held in great respect by their 'home boys', having defended the honour of their neighbourhood with fierce urban warfare.

Each gang has its own initiation ceremony. For example, to become a Playboy, a new member has to get 'jumped in' – beaten up – by a minimum of three gang members. While the beating takes place, others look on and count up to 13 slowly. Once initiated, members take on nicknames and adopt the dress codes of their comrades.

Many gang members deal in drugs. At the age of 15, former gang member Luis Rivera was earning 1000 dollars a day selling crack cocaine. 'I had my first car at the age of 16. I had no shortage of money.'

Adapted from the *Observer*, 6.2.94, 7.7.2002 and Winant, 1994

Item B Hand signals and tattoos

Hand signals representing the Playboys

Hand signals and tattoos are important signifiers of gang loyalties. Tattoos are usually done by *carnals* (fellow gang members) often using home-made instruments. They are a symbol of identity and defiance.

Young men who want to escape from gang life sometimes get their tattoos removed with a laser gun. Jose, a former gang member, states, 'The quicker I get 'em off, the quicker I get out of the gang. If I get them removed, then I'll no longer be a gang member.'

Adapted from the *Observer*, 6.2.1994, 7.7.2002

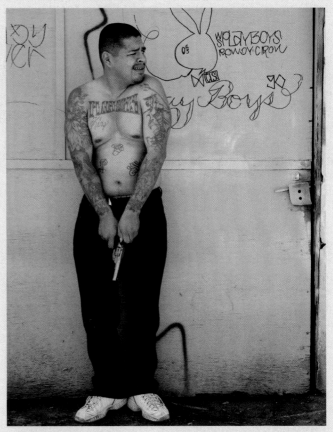

A member of the Playboys

question

Read Items A and B and look at the pictures.

Explain the behaviour of Hispanic gangs in terms of a) Merton's strain theory, b) Cohen's subcultural theory, and c) Cloward and Ohlin's opportunity structure theory.

Focal concerns According to Miller, lower-class subculture has a number of *focal concerns* – major interests and involvements. They include a desire for excitement and thrills, an emphasis on toughness – on a macho form of masculinity – and a concern with 'smartness' – with conning and outwitting others. These concerns are exaggerated by lower-class young men because of their desire for status in the eyes of their peer group.

Lower-class delinquency results from young men acting out the concerns of lower-class subculture. In doing this, they often break the law. The concern with toughness can lead to fights, the concern with excitement can result in a range of criminal activities from joy-riding to robbery, and the concern with smartness can be seen in the repertoires of the hustler and the con man.

Evaluation Miller pictures lower-class subculture as a 'distinctive tradition, many centuries old'. Lower-class young men are seen to act out this subculture with little reference to mainstream society. They appear to live in a world of their own. While accepting that a lower-class

subculture may well exist, it is unlikely that lower-class young men are as insulated from the wider society and its values as Miller suggests (Bordua, 1962).

4.5 Delinquency and drift – David Matza

The theories examined so far tend to see criminal and deviant behaviour resulting from forces beyond the individual's control. For example, in terms of Merton's strain theory, those at the bottom of the class structure are under considerable pressure to turn to crime. And Cohen's subcultural theory suggests that the deviant behaviour of many young working-class males is directed by a delinquent subculture. To an extent, these theories picture people as prisoners of the social structure, acting out predetermined roles with little or no say in the matter.

David Matza (1964) sees three main problems with this approach.

• First, it tends to make deviants more distinctive than

they really are. For example, the idea of deviant subcultures suggests that those involved are very different from members of mainstream society.

- Second, it 'over-predicts' delinquency – it accounts for more delinquency than there actually is. Why doesn't everybody in a particular position in society become a delinquent?
- Third, it suggests that the deviant has little or no freedom of choice – that their behaviour is determined by social forces beyond their control.

How different are delinquents?

Matza rejects Cohen's view that delinquents are different, that they have a distinctive subculture in opposition to mainstream society.

Subterranean values Matza argues that delinquent behaviour is often directed by *subterranean values* which are found throughout society. These 'underground values' are only expressed in particular situations. They include an emphasis on excitement and toughness. In mainstream society they are expressed in competitive sports – for example, on the football field. If, as Matza claims, they often direct delinquent behaviour, then in this respect, delinquents are little different from other young people (Matza & Sykes, 1961).

Techniques of neutralisation How do young people view their delinquent behaviour? According to Matza, many express guilt and shame for their delinquent acts. This suggests at least some commitment to mainstream norms and values. If this is so, why does delinquent behaviour occur? Part of the answer is *techniques of neutralisation* which open the door to delinquency and provide a justification for it. Matza identifies five techniques which neutralise the blame for delinquent acts and make them acceptable (Sykes & Matza, 1962).

- **Denial of responsibility** This technique states the delinquent was not responsible for his own actions. He got in with a bad crowd and came from a poor neighbourhood. As a result, 'It wasn't my fault'.
- **Denial of injury** Nobody was really hurt. For example, stealing from those who could afford it, 'borrowing' a car for joyriding.
- **Denial of the victim** They had it coming to them – the person concerned was not a victim but someone who deserved to be punished.
- **Condemning the condemners** Those who condemn the delinquent are themselves wrongdoers – for example, the police are corrupt and brutal.
- **Appeal to higher loyalties** Criminal behaviour is justified in terms of mainstream values such as duties and obligations to families and friends – stealing to provide food for their family, fighting to defend their friend.

According to Matza, techniques of neutralisation suggest that delinquents largely accept the values of the wider society. They justify their criminal acts in terms of mainstream values. And there is little evidence for a distinctive delinquent subculture. Delinquents are therefore

similar to young people in general.

Drifting into delinquency Subcultural theory suggests that many young males are committed to a distinctive subculture and a deviant lifestyle. In *Delinquency and Drift*, David Matza (1964) rejects this view. He argues that many young men drift in and out of delinquency. Their delinquent acts are casual and intermittent rather than a way of life. This fits with evidence indicating that most young people have little difficulty giving up delinquent activities as they grow older.

Again, the delinquent is pictured as little different from young people in general.

Evaluation of Matza

Advantages Matza provided a view of delinquency which answers the criticisms of strain theory and subcultural theory. Delinquents are no longer seen as prisoners of the social system directed by their position in the social structure and/or their distinctive subcultures.

According to Downes and Rock (2003), Matza's view describes the criminal behaviour of many young men in Britain. The most frequent reason they give for their delinquency is boredom. And delinquency offers plenty of opportunity for risk, daring and excitement to relieve boredom.

Disadvantages

- In seeking to remedy theories which over-predict delinquency, Matza may have gone too far in the opposite direction – and under-predicted. For example, one in three British men born in a single month in 1953 had a criminal record by the time they reached 30 (Carrabine et al., 2002).
- Matza's picture of young men drifting in and out of delinquency with little commitment to a deviant lifestyle does not fit the highly organised gangs in the USA. The life of the young men in the Hispanic gangs described in Activity 11 shows a real commitment to a deviant subculture. If there are over 100,000 Hispanic gang members in Los Angeles, this is hardly casual and intermittent behaviour.
- According to Stanley Cohen (2003), techniques of neutralisation don't necessarily indicate a commitment to conventional norms and values. They may simply be a public justification and excuse for criminal behaviour. For example, at the Nuremburg trials after World War II, neutralisation techniques were used by Nazis in their defence for the murder of millions of Jews.

key terms

Subterranean values Values which are only expressed in particular situations.
Techniques of neutralisation Techniques which neutralise the blame for actions which are defined as unacceptable or wrong by society's norms and values.

4.6 White-collar crime

The starting point for the theories of crime and deviance examined so far is the social pattern reflected in official statistics – that most offences are committed by young working-class males. As a result, these theories have little to say about *white-collar crime.*

Defining white-collar crime

The American criminologist Edwin Sutherland (1949) defined white-collar crime as 'a crime committed by a person of respectability and high social status in the course of his occupation'. He challenged the view that crime was mainly a 'working-class problem', claiming that the financial cost of white-collar crime was probably several times greater than the cost of working-class crime.

Today, many researchers identify two types of white-collar crime – *occupational crime* and *corporate crime.* Occupational crime refers to crimes committed at the expense of the organisation, for example employees stealing money or goods from their employer. Corporate crime refers to crimes committed on behalf of the organisation, such as non-payment of VAT.

Some researchers identify a third type of white-collar crime – *state crime.* This involves crimes committed by the state or agencies of the state such as the police or the military. Such crimes are committed on behalf of the state. For example, many people regard the treatment of suspected terrorists held by the US government at Guantanamo Bay in Cuba as a criminal offence.

Corporate crime

There are many types of corporate crime. They include the following.

Crimes against consumers These include manufacturing or selling food which is unfit for human consumption, manufacturing or selling dangerous goods, and falsely describing the contents of goods – for example, of food.

These crimes can have disastrous consequences. In the 1970s, mechanical defects in the Ford Pinto may have led to between 500 and 900 deaths in the USA. The company was fully aware of these defects (Box, 1983). Again from the 1970s, the deliberate fabrication of test data on the fertility drug thalidomide resulted in the births of thousands of deformed babies.

Many instances of companies harming consumers are not dealt with as a criminal offence. Accidents and 'disasters' for which companies are held to be responsible provide an example. In 1987, the capsizing of the cross-Channel ferry *Herald of Free Enterprise* led to the deaths of 154 passengers and 38 crew members. An official inquiry blamed the owners, P&O Ferries, for failing to provide a safe operating system. However, attempts to prosecute the company for 'corporate manslaughter' failed (Croall, 2001).

Crimes against employees These include failing to meet health and safety regulations which can lead to the injury or death of employees. Between 1965 and the mid-1990s in the UK, around 25,000 people were killed at work. According to the Health and Safety Executive, 70% of these deaths were due to the failure of management to meet safety regulations (Hughes & Langan, 2001).

Environmental offences These include polluting the environment with toxic waste. For example, ICI was fined £300,000 by the Environment Agency in 1999 for polluting groundwater in Runcorn. However, most fines are much lower, averaging £4300 in 1998 (Croall, 2001).

Financial frauds These include false accounting, insurance frauds and the making of false claims by sellers about the benefits of pension schemes and savings plans. Fraud can involve vast sums – over $4 billion in the case of WorldCom's false accounting (see Activity 4, Item B). And the consequences can be extremely serious – in WorldCom's case, 17,000 workers were made redundant and many investors lost their life-savings.

Views of white-collar crime

Compared to more visible and obvious types of crime such as burglary and murder, white-collar crime is often seen and treated differently by the public, police, courts and regulatory bodies. According to Gordon Hughes and Mary Langan (2001), this is due to four main factors.

Low visibility Street crimes and their consequences are highly visible. White-collar crimes are largely hidden from the public gaze. And when they are detected, it is often difficult to pinpoint blame – for example, which individuals were responsible for neglecting health and safety regulations?

Complexity Large-scale frauds are highly complex operations. They are difficult to unravel and it is hard to allocate blame. They involve different companies, various bank accounts, a multitude of transactions, and a variety of individuals who are more, or less, aware of what's going on. Teams of expert investigators spend years attempting to get to the bottom of large-scale frauds.

Diffusion of responsibility Responsibility for corporate crime is often diffused – widely spread. It is difficult to allocate blame to particular individuals. In the case of the *Herald of Free Enterprise* disaster, a variety of people and organisations were blamed – crew members, their commanding officers, the company and the regulatory authorities.

Diffusion of victimisation Many white-collar crimes are described as 'crimes without victims'. In many cases, there is no obvious victim as in cases of murder or robbery. However, there are victims but they are spread out or diffused. For example, environmental pollution can affect thousands of people. And we all have to pay for white-collar crime – in higher prices, insurance premiums and taxes (Hughes & Langan, 2001).

Regulating corporate crime

Compared to many other forms of crime, corporate crime

has a lower rate of detection and prosecution, and more lenient punishments (Croall, 2001).

Regulatory offences Many corporate offences are dealt with by regulatory bodies rather than the criminal justice system. Bodies such as the Health and Safety Executive, the Environment Agency and the Trading Standards Agency deal with violations of health and safety, environmental health and trading standards regulations. They are more likely to issue 'official warnings' to put matters right rather than pursue prosecutions.

In the case of professionals, such as doctors and lawyers, 'misconduct' is usually dealt with by professional associations such as the British Medical Association. Only the most serious cases result in prosecution.

Many private companies operate a system of self-regulation. For example, the London Stock Exchange and Lloyds attempt to regulate their own affairs, even if this means a certain amount of loss through fraud.

Risk of prosecution Regulatory bodies are primarily concerned with securing compliance with regulations rather than identifying offenders. They advise and warn rather than punish.

Organisations such as the Inland Revenue and Customs and Excise tend to deal with offences administratively rather than prosecute. Their main aim is to recover the money lost from tax evasion and VAT fraud rather than charge the offender with a criminal offence.

Lenient punishment When white-collar offenders are prosecuted and found guilty of a criminal offence, their punishment tends to be lenient. Compared to 'ordinary criminals' such as burglars, they are more likely to be 'punished' with community service, a fine, or a short sentence in an open prison.

Explaining white-collar crime

White-collar crime covers a vast array of offences from petty occupational crime, such as fiddling expenses and stealing small items from employers, to corporate crime such as large-scale frauds. It is difficult to find an explanation for this variety of offences.

Strain theory revisited Merton's strain theory has been developed in an attempt to explain white-collar crime. A typical explanation goes as follows. All members of society face the same success goals – there is pressure on all social classes to succeed. When people in white-collar occupations find the routes to pay increases and promotion

summary

1. Sociologists look to society for an explanation of crime and deviance rather than the biological or psychological makeup of the individual.

2. According to Durkheim, a certain amount of crime is not only 'normal' but also an 'integral part of all healthy societies'. Society's values and norms must not be too strong - this would prevent the innovation and change necessary for a healthy society. Crime can be seen as a byproduct of this necessity.

3. Some crimes can be functional for society - for example, they may indicate that something is wrong with the way society is organised.

4. Merton's strain theory argues there is a 'strain to anomie' when the normative means for attaining cultural goals are blocked. This strain is most strongly felt by those at the bottom of the class structure. Some 'innovate' and turn to crime to attain monetary success.

5. Cohen's subcultural theory argues that many young working-class males experience status frustration. Some respond by developing a delinquent subculture in terms of which they can gain status and respect.

6. Cloward and Ohlin provide an explanation for different types of working-class delinquency. They argue that different social environments provide different opportunities for crime and deviance. This encourages the development of different delinquent subcultures.

7. David Matza argues that many sociological theories picture delinquents as more distinctive than they really are. He sees delinquents responding to subterranean values which are found throughout society. They use techniques of neutralisation which indicates that they largely share the values of the wider society. And they drift in and out of delinquency rather than being committed to a delinquent subculture.

8. Many sociological theories of crime and deviance tend to ignore white-collar crime.

9. There are two main types of white-collar crime - occupational crime and corporate crime.

10. Corporate crime includes crimes against consumers, crimes against employees, environmental offences and fraud.

11. Corporate crime is seen and treated differently from crimes such as burglary and murder. Reasons for this include:
   * Its low visibility
   * Complexity
   * The diffusion of responsibility
   * The diffusion of victimisation.

12. Compared to many other forms of crime, corporate crime has a lower rate of detection and prosecution, and more lenient punishments.

13. Merton's strain theory has been adapted to explain white-collar crime. This version states that some middle-class people experience relative deprivation when they make comparisons with those better off than themselves. In the absence of legal means to reach this level of success, some turn to crime.

14. Subcultural theory has been developed to explain middle-class crime. Many corporations have a subculture which emphasises the pursuit of wealth and profit. For some, the pressure to succeed in terms of this subculture leads to criminal acts.

blocked, they sometimes 'innovate', just like members of the working class. In other words, they turn to illegal means to become successful and attain monetary goals. They experience the same strain to anomie, to normlessness. This weakens the mechanisms of social control – the norms which would otherwise restrain criminal behaviour.

But why should middle-class people experience a strain to anomie when they are better off than those at the bottom of the class structure? One suggestion is that deprivation is relative. Middle-class people may feel deprived relative to, that is in comparison to, others who are considerably better off than themselves. And, given the pressure to succeed, they experience a strain to anomie. As a result, they innovate, just like their working-class counterparts.

In much the same way, corporations may find that legal ways of maintaining or increasing their profits are ineffective. As a result, there is a strain to anomie and pressure to turn to illegal means. The desired result may be obtained by fraud or by ignoring health and safety and environmental regulations (Box, 1983).

Subcultural theory revisited The hero of the film *Wall*

Street – the street where the big New York stockbroking firms are located – stated that 'greed is good'. Some sociologists have argued that many corporations, especially financial institutions, have a subculture which emphasises the pursuit of wealth and profit. This so-called enterprise culture places a high value on risk-taking and monetary success. For some, it is a short step to 'success at all costs', even if this means fraud, bribery and corruption.

Further explanations of white-collar crime are examined in Unit 6 which looks at Marxist theories of crime.

activity 12 corporate crime

Item A Enron

Under its president Kenneth Lay, the US company Enron became the world's largest energy trading company. It specialised in contracts to deliver natural gas and electricity to customers at a future date. In December 2001, Enron filed for bankruptcy, billions of dollars in debt.

Investors lost a fortune with Enron shares practically worthless. Enron's 19,000 employees lost both their jobs and their savings because they belonged to a retirement plan based on Enron shares. 20,000 creditors were owed an estimated $67 billion. Most received less than 20 cents for every dollar they were owed.

Investigations revealed fraud on a vast scale. Top executives lined their pockets while concealing massive debts. False accounting practices boosted reported income and lowered reported debt. As a result, share prices remained high, bearing no relationship to the true value of the company.

Shortly before bankruptcy was declared, the company president Kenneth Lay borrowed $74 million and repaid it with company shares. And a number of senior executives were given payments totalling $55 million.

Adapted from various issues of the *Guardian*, 2001, 2002, 2003

An effigy of Enron president Kenneth Lay (right) at an anti-capitalist demonstration in New York

Item B The Piper Alpha disaster

On July 6, 1988, there was an explosion on the oil rig Piper Alpha, 100 miles off the east coast of Scotland. It was caused by an escape of flammable gas and resulted in the deaths of 167 workers. The rig was owned by the Occidental Group.

A public enquiry led by Lord Cullen looked into the causes of the disaster. They included:

- An inadequate assessment by the company of the risks involved
- A failure to put right known deficiencies in the system
- Management neglect of safety standards and regulations.

Adapted from SafetyLine Institute, 1998, www.safetyline.wa.gov.au

Piper Alpha two days after the explosion

Dear G E Rald,

We should like to take this opportunity to inform you that on 12th of March this year you were seen entering empty handed into the private premises of Ms P C Edwards of Convent St, Folkestone, and leaving shortly afterwards with your hands full.

In our opinion, this constitutes a violation of the Theft Act 1968 subsection 32(c) and we would be grateful if you would consider the following advice: please stop going down Convent St and entering houses without the owners' permission.

We should warn you that next March 12th another police constable will be on foot duty in Convent St, and should he notice a repetition of your behaviour, we shall have to consider the possibility of taking even more stringent action than we have on this occasion.

Item C A warning

Many regulatory bodies inspect companies to check that regulations, for example on health and safety, have been followed. Warnings are issued if any regulations have not been met and companies are revisited to check that matters have been put right. On the left is a spoof letter, using similar procedures, written to a young burglar.

From Box, 1983

questions

1 The consequences of corporate crime can be extremely serious. Discuss with reference to Item A.

2 Would you describe the Piper Alpha disaster (Item B) as a crime? Give reasons for your answer.

3 How does Item C illustrate the difference between the way many corporate offences and 'ordinary crimes' are seen?

Unit 5 Interactionism and labelling theory

keyissues

1 What is distinctive about the interactionist approach to crime and deviance?

2 What are the strengths and weaknesses of labelling theory?

5.1 The interactionist approach

To move from functionalism to interactionism is to move to a very different theoretical perspective. Gone are the social systems and social structures which direct behaviour. In their place are small-scale interaction situations in which people act in terms of meanings and definitions of the situation. The interactionist approach to crime and deviance became popular in the 1960s.

The interactionist perspective According to Herbert Blumer (1969) interactionism, or more specifically symbolic interactionism, is based on three central views.

- First, 'human beings act towards things on the basis of the meanings that things have for them'. Human behaviour is not determined by social forces. Rather, people are self-conscious beings who choose what to do on the basis of their subjective perceptions – how they see things.
- Second, 'the meaning of things is derived from, or arises out of, the social interaction that one has with one's fellows'. Meanings are not fixed but are continually modified as people negotiate with each other.
- Third, 'group action takes the form of a fitting together of individual lines of action'. Society is not so much a determinant of human action as a product of human activity. People make society, rather than society making people.

The challenge to functionalism In terms of its approach to crime and deviance, functionalism was challenged on three grounds.

- First, the assumption that there is agreement about what forms of behaviour constitute crime and deviance. What intrigued interactionists was why the same behaviour is defined as criminal or deviant in some contexts but not others.
- Second, the claim that deviants are somehow distinctive, comprising a specific group of the population. We are asked instead to look at the process of interaction and question why certain individuals or groups are more likely to be defined as deviant.
- Third, the search for the causes of deviance is seen to be fruitless. We all commit acts which break rules. What is more interesting is the way that agencies of social control respond to different individuals and the effects of that response on their future actions.

5.2 Labelling theory

From an interactionist perspective, deviance is an act which is labelled as such. There is nothing essentially or intrinsically deviant about any act. It only becomes deviant when it is seen as such and labelled as such.

The classic statement of this view is given by Howard Becker (1963). In his words, 'social groups create deviance by making the rules whose infraction constitutes deviance and by applying those rules to particular people and labelling them as outsiders. From this point of view, deviance is not a quality of the act the person commits but rather a consequence of the application by others of rules and sanctions to an "offender". The deviant is one to whom that label has successfully been applied; deviant behaviour is behaviour that people so label.'

Becker's words are frequently quoted because they represent a new approach within the sociology of crime and deviance. The focus moves away from a concern with

the deviant and the causes of deviance to a concern with the agencies of social control – with the process by which they label certain acts as deviant and the consequences of this labelling. How, then, is deviance created?

Defining deviance Society creates the rules. Deviant behaviour is not a distinctive form of behaviour but behaviour which is seen to contravene these rules. Becker (1963) illustrates this point well. 'The act of injecting heroin into a vein is not inherently deviant. If a nurse gives a patient drugs under a doctor's orders, it is perfectly proper. It is when it is done in a way that is not publicly defined as proper that it becomes deviant.' What applies to the use of drugs also applies to other forms of behaviour. Even the act of taking someone else's life is, in some contexts, considered appropriate. Indeed, in a war it is the refusal to kill which is often seen to be deviant.

Labelling Acts labelled as deviant tend to be committed by certain types of people. For example, the police tend to target specific groups. Studies of policing indicate that 'those who are stopped and searched or questioned in the street, arrested, detailed in the police station, charged, and prosecuted are disproportionately young men who are unemployed or casually employed, and from generally discriminated against ethnic minorities' (Reiner, 1994). For labelling theorists, this is due to the perceptions held by the police of the 'typical criminal'. They are more likely to see the activities of young men from the lower levels of the class structure and from certain ethnic minority groups as suspicious.

Aaron Cicourel's (1976) study of police and juvenile (probation) officers in California illustrates this point. Both groups held a similar picture of the 'typical delinquent' – as 'coming from broken homes, exhibiting "bad attitudes" towards authority, poor school performance, ethnic group membership, low-income families and the like'. As a result, young people who fitted this picture were more likely to be arrested and handed over to the juvenile officers. And, in turn, those who came closest to the picture of the 'typical delinquent' were more likely to be charged with a criminal offence by the juvenile officers. The middle-class minority who were arrested were usually 'counselled, cautioned and released' by the juvenile officers.

In the process, the police and probation officers not only created typical delinquents, they also created the social characteristics of the typical criminal shown in official statistics – young, working class and male.

Primary and secondary deviance

Edwin Lemert (1972) makes a distinction between *primary* and *secondary deviance*. Primary deviance refers to deviant acts which have not been publicly labelled. Most of us have engaged in such acts at one time or another, and for all sorts of reasons. Usually, this has little effect on our identity and status in society, or on our future lives.

Secondary deviance refers to acts which have been publicly labelled as deviant and to the deviance which is generated by this labelling.

Societal reaction The reaction of society – the way others react to someone labelled as deviant – may have a dramatic effect on that person's status and identity and may lead to further deviant acts.

Labelling people as deviant will tend to mark them out. The label may become a *master status* which overrides all other statuses. As a result, the individual is no longer seen as a parent, a friend or a worker but only as a criminal. Rejected by conventional society, they may embark on a deviant career – engage in further deviant acts and ultimately join an organised deviant group. Public labelling may result in a *self-fulfilling prophecy* whereby the person labelled deviant not only commits further deviant acts but also accepts the label.

Jock Young's (1971) study of hippie marihuana users in Notting Hill during the 1960s illustrates this process. The police targeting of a group, whose lifestyle included smoking marihuana, served to widen the differences between the hippies and conventional society. In the process, drug taking, which had been 'essentially a peripheral activity' became 'of greater value to the group as a symbol of their difference and of their defiance against perceived injustices' (Young, 1971). In this context, a deviant subculture developed. Individuals labelled outsiders began to see themselves as different from non-drug takers, all of which made it difficult for them to re-enter the wider society.

Evaluation of labelling theory

Advantages Labelling theory has a number of advantages.

- First, it has drawn attention to the importance of labelling and societal reaction. These processes can, in themselves, generate deviant and criminal behaviour.
- Second, it has shown that certain types of people are singled out for labelling.
- Third, it has shown that this results from the definitions and perceptions of the agents of social control – for example, their perceptions of the 'typical delinquent'.

Disadvantages Critics have pointed to the following weaknesses of labelling theory.

- **Origins of deviance** Labelling theorists see the search for the origin of deviant acts as largely fruitless. But deviance is not simply created by the label. People do not become burglars simply because they are labelled as such. They know that their actions are deviant, they are aware that they are breaking the law. Why do they become burglars? This example suggests that looking for the origins of deviance is an important sociological question.
- **Selection of deviants** Labelling theory fails to explain why certain types of people are selected as likely deviants rather than others. It is not sufficient to say that they fit definitions of likely deviants held by the agents of social control. Where do these definitions come from? They don't appear to be simply created in interaction situations. The picture of the 'typical

delinquent' is common to criminal justice systems in the UK, USA and elsewhere.

- **Who makes the rules?** According to Howard Becker (1963), 'social groups create deviance by making rules whose infraction constitutes deviance'. But who are these people who make the rules? And why do they make these particular rules? For example, are rules made by the powerful for their own benefit? This possibility is examined in the next unit which looks at Marxist approaches to crime and deviance.

key terms

Primary deviance Deviant acts which have not been publicly labelled.
Secondary deviance Acts which have been publicly labelled as deviant and the deviance which is generated by the label.
Societal reaction The reaction of others to an individual. In this case, the reaction of others to someone labelled as deviant.
Master status A status which overrides all other statuses. The status in terms of which a person is seen by others.
Self-fulfilling prophecy A prophecy which comes to pass simply because it has been made. The prophecy therefore fulfils itself.

5.3 Deviancy amplification

A number of sociologists who do not share the same theoretical perspective as the interactionists have also focused on societal reaction. The following study looks at societal reaction to mods and rockers in the mid-1960s.

Mods and rockers Mods and rockers are youth groups who differed from each other in terms of dress, musical tastes and modes of transport – mods rode scooters, rockers rode motor bikes. Stanley Cohen's (1987) study looked at societal reaction to disturbances involving mods and rockers which took place in Clacton over the Easter bank holiday in 1964.

The mass media represented these disturbances as a confrontation between rival gangs 'hell bent on destruction'. On inspection, however, Cohen discovered that the amount of serious violence and vandalism was not great and that most young people who'd gone to the seaside that weekend did not identify with either the mods or the rockers. The mass media had produced a distorted picture of what went on.

Deviancy amplification spiral Media coverage led to considerable public concern with mods and rockers. And this set in motion a *deviancy amplification spiral*. Sensitised to the 'problem', the police made more arrests, the media reported more deviance, and young people were more likely to identify with either mods or rockers. Further disturbances followed on subsequent bank holidays, attracting more police attention, more arrests, increased media interest and more young people reacting to what they saw as heavy-handed and unjustified treatment from the police.

activity 13 labelling theory

Item A *Defining deviance*

Item B *Labelling deviance*

Item C *Secondary deviance*

Stop and search

questions

1 Which act or acts in Item A might be defined as deviant? Give reasons for your answer.

2 If there was trouble at a soccer match, which of the people in Item B would the police be more likely to question and arrest? Give reasons for your answer.

3 How might the police activity in Item C lead to secondary deviance?

The reaction to the initial disturbances over the Easter bank holiday not only exaggerated the amount of deviance, it also generated more deviance.

Moral panics

Stanley Cohen claimed that the reaction of the media to events in Clacton generated a *moral panic*. A moral panic occurs when 'a condition, episode, person or group of persons emerges to become defined as a threat to societal values and interests' (Cohen, 1987). In the above case, mods and rockers were singled out as 'folk devils' whose behaviour constituted a threat to the social order. The 1960s were a decade of widespread social change, in which cherished norms were challenged. The mods and rockers served as symbols of what was wrong with society. In subsequent decades, young people continued to be the focus of moral panics. The 1970s saw the moral panic of mugging, and the 1980s the moral panic of football hooliganism (see Activity 14).

More recently, moral panics have focused on threats to children with concerns over child abuse, paedophilia and the influence of violent films on young viewers (Critcher, 2003).

The media's reaction to deviance may lead to a deviancy amplification spiral, a moral panic and more authoritarian forms of control. This process is illustrated in Figure 1.

Figure 1 A deviancy amplification spiral

Adapted from Muncie, 1987

Evaluation

There is evidence that societal reaction can amplify deviance. And there is evidence that this reaction can reach the level of a moral panic. When it reaches this level, it is out of proportion to the situation – it is 'over the top'.

But who's to say that a so-called moral panic is unreasonable? Jock Young (1986) criticises the concept of a moral panic because it implies that crime is, in large part, constructed by the media. Young accepts that the media may exaggerate the 'crime problem', but it does not create it. He argues that the reality of crime, and the human suffering it produces, must be taken seriously and not reduced to a media construction.

key terms

Deviancy amplification spiral A process in which deviance is increased by societal reaction.
Moral panic According to Cohen (1987), a moral panic occurs when 'a condition, episode, person or group of persons emerges to become defined as a threat to societal values and interests'.

summary

1. From an interactionist perspective, people act in terms of meanings and definitions which arise in social interaction. The interactionist approach to crime and deviance became popular in the 1960s.

2. Interactionists challenge the view that deviants are essentially different from non-deviants.

3. In terms of labelling theory, deviance is behaviour which is labelled as such, a deviant is someone to whom a label has successfully been applied.

4. Labelling theory focuses on the agents of social control, on the way they define certain acts and certain kinds of people as deviant, and the consequences of this.

5. Societal reaction to someone labelled as deviant can lead to a self-fulfilling prophecy. Individuals so labelled may be encouraged to commit further deviant acts and may see themselves in terms of the label.

6. Although it has a number of advantages – for example, showing the importance of societal reaction – labelling theory has been criticised for failing to explain:
   - The origins of deviance
   - Why certain types of people are seen as likely deviants
   - Who makes the rules.

7. Societal reaction can lead to a deviancy amplification spiral in which the response to the initial deviance generates further deviance.

8. Societal reaction can take the form of a moral panic.

9. The idea of a moral panic has been criticised because it implies that crime is largely constructed by the media. According to Jock Young, it tends to ignore the reality of crime.

activity 14 football hooliganism

Item A Moral panics and social control

```
┌─────────────────────────────────────────┐
│         IDENTIFICATION OF A PROBLEM       │
│         (eg football hooliganism)         │
│                     ↓                     │
│      Identification of a subversive minority │
│   (eg the 'few who spoil the enjoyment of millions': identification │
│          by styles - skinheads, etc)      │
│                     ↓                     │
│            Simplification of cause        │
│   (eg decline in moral standards, lack of discipline etc) │
│                     ↓                     │
│        Stigmatisation of those involved   │
│  (Media use of emotive and disparaging significations eg │
│       'morons'; 'animals'; 'savages' etc) │
│                     ↓                     │
│          Stirring of public indignation   │
│  (eg media campaigns calling for 'action': criticism of 'soft' │
│    sentences; evocation of the 'national image', etc) │
│                     ↓                     │
│             Stamping down hard            │
│  (eg government responds to 'public demand' as presented by │
│   the media. Stiffer sentences; more 'anti-hooligan' legislation; │
│           bans on spectators etc)         │
│   MORE AUTHORITARIAN FORMS OF CONTROL     │
└─────────────────────────────────────────┘
```

Adapted from Muncie, 1987

Item E The police response

In the last twenty years increasing attempts by police to control football hooliganism have included separating rival groups at matches in pens surrounded by spiked fences; closed circuit television crowd surveillance techniques; the use of identity card schemes; soccer hooligan group infiltration through police undercover operations and the formation of a National Football Intelligence Unit with computerised data banks on known soccer hooligans.

Adapted from Kerr, 1994

Item F A hooligan's view

We just don't have the time we used to have. The moment a fight starts we're immediately surrounded by dogs and horses. That's why everyone has started using knives. I suppose it might sound stupid but, because the policing has got so good, we've got to the point where we have to inflict the greatest possible damage in the least amount of time, and the knife is the most efficient instrument for a quick injury. In fact the knifings – because there is so little time – have been quite symbolic. When someone gets knifed, it amounts to an important victory to the side that has done the knifing. If the policing was not so good, I'm sure the knifings would stop.

Quoted in Kerr, 1994

Item B Newspaper headlines, 1988

Before the European Championship
Sun Euro hoolies league
Daily Mirror Plague of the Euro yob: Dutch go top of the Thug's Table

During the European Championship
Sun World War III
Star Yobs Plot War

Item C Reaction in Parliament

'We must really eradicate this blot on our reputation. We want those guilty of it caught and convicted, and given a severe sentence as an example to others.'

Margaret Thatcher, 1988, after rowdiness by some English fans at the European championships.

Item D Pictured in the media

Liverpool vs Juventus, European Cup Final, Brussels, 1985

questions

1 To what extent does the societal reaction in Items B to E fit the process outlined in Item A?

2 How might societal reaction generate further and more serious deviance? Refer to Item F in your answer.

Unit 6 *Marxism and radical criminology*

keyissues

1 What is distinctive about the Marxist approach to crime, deviance and social control?

2 What are the strengths and weaknesses of this approach?

6.1 Traditional Marxist approaches

This unit examines two Marxist approaches to crime and deviance which emerged in the 1970s. The first is a fairly traditional development of Marxist ideas. The second – radical criminology – incorporates certain aspects of the interactionist approach.

From a Marxist perspective, crime and deviance in Western society can only be understood in terms of capitalism and the class struggle. Coercion and conflict are seen as the key features of capitalist society in contrast to functionalism's emphasis on consensus and integration. However, like functionalism, Marxism sees the structures and institutions of society as largely determining how people behave.

Causes of crime From a Marxist viewpoint, crime is systematically generated by the structure of capitalist society. Capitalism is an economic system based on the private ownership of the means of production and the maximisation of profit. As such, it emphasises individual gain rather than collective wellbeing. Capitalism is a competitive system which encourages aggression and emphasises the importance of winning. It is also an exploitative system in which some gain at the expense of others.

Given these priorities it is a short step to seeing the end as justifying the means – to be so obsessed with personal gain and coming out on top that breaking the law seems a minor barrier to success. Pressures to break the law will affect people across the social spectrum from wealthy business people to the poverty-stricken unemployed. In this respect, fiddling business expenses and fiddling the dole have similar causes.

From a Marxist perspective, capitalism encourages greed and self-interest, it generates frustration and aggression. Breaking the law can be seen as a rational step in order to satisfy these desires and express these feelings. Crimes motivated by financial gain can be seen as a logical outcome of the priorities of profit. Crimes with no apparent financial motive can be seen as an expression of the frustration, aggression and hostility which the system produces.

The law Laws in capitalist society are seen to reflect the interests of the dominant capitalist class. Thus the many laws protecting private property, which have appeared on the statute books over the past 200 years, reflect the growth of industry and the expansion of trade and commerce. In this respect, private property, the essence of capitalism, is protected.

Laws which appear to protect the interests of workers can be seen as concessions to the working class to maintain, if not its loyalty, then its acceptance of the system. For example, health and safety laws protecting workers can be seen in this light – and they have the additional benefit to capitalism of helping to provide a fit and healthy workforce.

Law enforcement 'There is one law for the rich and another for the poor.' This piece of folk wisdom summarises how many Marxists characterise law enforcement in capitalist society. The law is enforced selectively – there is a systematic bias in favour of those at the top. The crimes of the powerful such as corporate crime – for example, failing to pay business taxes and breaking trading laws – if discovered are rarely prosecuted. By comparison, those at the bottom of the class system who are caught breaking the law are regularly prosecuted. Yet in monetary terms their crimes are a drop in the ocean compared to the vast sums involved in the criminal activities of those at the top. Some of the evidence for this claim can be seen in Activity 15.

Evaluation Marxist approaches have the advantage of combining explanations of crime which cover members of all social classes, a wide variety of offences, the nature of law in capitalist society and the selective enforcement of the law. However, these explanations are very general and depend for their force on an acceptance of a Marxist view of capitalism. Many sociologists reject the view that there is a fundamental conflict of interest between the ruling and subject classes in capitalist society and the exploitation of one by the other.

6.2 Radical criminology

Radical criminology is the most influential attempt to apply a Marxist perspective to the study of crime and deviance. It emerged in Britain in the 1970s out of dissatisfaction with existing theories – including the more traditional Marxist approaches.

Radical criminology focuses on the process by which the state defines certain activities as criminal and thereby criminalises certain groups, particularly the oppressed and disadvantaged. This stress on the process of criminalisation is reminiscent of labelling theory. While accepting that interaction between lower-level agents of social control, such as the police, and deviants is important, radical

activity15 scrounging

Item A Two views of capitalist society

'I got the loot, Charlie, but after bank costs, services and handling charges, we owe them £6.25p.'

Item B 'The real scroungers'

Cost of dole fraud	£500 million	Cost of tax fraud	£5,000 million
Number of prosecutions	14,000	Number of prosecutions	20

In the eyes of the law, all people may be equal but the government's treatment of tax and social security offenders suggests there is one law for the rich and another for the poor. For every individual who is pursued through the courts for tax fraud, about 700 are prosecuted for welfare offences. This disparity cannot be accounted for by arguing that benefit fiddling is a more serious social menace than tax fraud. Official estimates indicate that losses from benefit abuses are dwarfed by losses from tax evasion. The Inland Revenue sees prosecution as a last resort and seeks to secure 'a reasonable settlement by agreement'. As one tax accountant put it, 'You have to be very unlucky, very stupid and very crooked to be done by the Revenue'.

Adapted from the *Observer*, 23.10.1988

questions

1 Using a Marxist perspective, briefly comment on the cartoons in Item A.

2 Read Item B. Suggest reasons for the different treatment of tax fraud and welfare fraud.

---

criminology demands a wider focus. It looks at the process of criminalisation in relation to the state as it seeks to manage the capitalist system.

A 'fully social theory of deviance'

The ambition of radical criminology is evident in the final chapter of *The New Criminology* by Ian Taylor, Paul Walton and Jock Young (1973). There the authors outline a model which they term a 'fully social theory of deviance'. The model has seven dimensions:

1 'The wider origins of the deviant act'

   The radical criminologist needs to locate the deviant act within the wider social system – capitalism and its class divisions.

2 'The immediate origins of the deviant act'

   They then need to look at the immediate social context within which an individual chooses to commit an act of deviance.

3 'The actual act'

   Attention needs to be given to what the deviant act means to the individual concerned.

4 'The immediate origins of social reaction'

   They need to look at the immediate response of other people, such as members of the deviant's family and the police, to the discovery of deviance.

5 'Wider origins of deviant reaction'

   The immediate reaction needs to be located within the wider social system, with particular attention given to the question of who has the power to define certain activities as deviant.

6 'The outcomes of social reaction on the deviant's further action'

While most deviants recognise that there will be a reaction against them, it is important to examine the effects of the labelling process on the deviant.

7 'The nature of the deviant process as a whole'

Finally the six aspects of the deviant process need to be connected together for there to be a 'fully social theory of deviance'.

The closest approximation to a 'fully social theory of deviance' is *Policing the Crisis* by Stuart Hall et al. (1978). It is a study of the moral panic which took place in the early 1970s over 'mugging'. In the following summary, particular attention is given to the way this study illustrates a 'fully social theory of deviance'.

Policing the crisis

The wider origins of mugging Mugging is a term imported from America. It refers to the street crime of robbery or theft involving the threat or actual use of violence. During the early 1970s in Britain, a moral panic developed about the dangers of street crime and, in particular, the threat of the young Black mugger. Stuart Hall et al. (1978) argue that this societal reaction to mugging must be seen in the wider context of capitalism and the class system.

Street crime has traditionally been one 'survival strategy' for those at the bottom of the class system, particularly during an economic crisis.

Partly as a result of racism, the first generation of African-Caribbean migrants were the most disadvantaged members of the working class. The majority found low-paid employment and made the best of their situation.

The immediate origins of mugging Acutely aware of the racism of British society, Black youth were less willing than their parents to accept the situation. This sometimes caused conflict between the generations, resulting in some young people leaving home, taking to the streets and drifting into petty crime. In this context, a small minority of Black youngsters adopted the 'mugging solution' as a survival strategy.

The immediate origins of the social reaction to mugging The media were central in 'orchestrating public opinion' against the Black mugger. Between August 1972 and August 1973, the national daily newspapers reported 60 incidents as 'muggings'. They pictured Black youth creating mindless havoc in the inner cities. Yet mugging was neither a new problem, nor was it growing at an alarming rate – in fact, the rate of growth was less than half the rate in the 1960s. Hall et al. see the societal reaction to mugging as a moral panic.

The wider origins of the social reaction to mugging Hall et al. argue that this moral panic must be seen in the context of the problems that British capitalism was experiencing in the early 1970s.

Since 1945, full employment, rising living standards and the growth of welfare services resulted in the working class accepting the authority of the state. However, an economic crisis in the early 1970s brought rising unemployment, a slowing down of the rise in people's living standards and a halt to the expansion of welfare services. As a result, the authority of the state came under challenge from various groups, especially trade unions. For example, in 1972, there were more workdays lost by strikes than in any year since 1919. (See Chapter 4, Activity 7, pages 178-179.)

The state reacted by presenting this challenge to its authority as a 'law and order' issue. The stability of society was threatened by lawlessness and the state must respond. The focus on the Black mugger served to symbolise this threat to social order. The result was to divide the working class on 'racial' grounds, so weakening any challenge to the state. And, the apparent need to stamp out mugging as quickly as possible justified the state increasing its powers.

The outcome of social reaction Responding to the perceived threat of mugging, the police targeted this crime and Black youth in particular. Increasing numbers of young Black men were randomly stopped, searched and questioned in the street. Many saw this as unjustified and some responded with verbal abuse or violence. This often led to their arrest and appeared to confirm that they were indeed prone to crimes of violence. The result was a process of deviancy amplification. The labelling of Black youth as deviant led to more arrests which, in turn, justified even stronger police measures against so-called Black muggers, all of which provided further headlines for the newspapers.

A fully social theory *Policing the Crisis* looks at the moral panic of mugging from a variety of viewpoints. It analyses the crisis faced by British capitalism in the early 1970s and the resulting threat to the authority of the state. It argues that the state responded to this crisis by mounting a law and order campaign which led to a moral panic over mugging. As a result, Black youth became increasingly criminalised and the state was able to justify its growing powers. This analysis looks at the 'problem of mugging' on various levels – from society as a whole right down to street level.

Evaluation of radical criminology

Advantages Radical criminology combines a number of different perspectives in an attempt to provide a fully social theory of deviance. Within a Marxist framework, *Policing the Crisis* includes labelling theory along with concepts such as societal reaction, moral panics and deviancy amplification. In doing so, it offers a more comprehensive picture than previous perspectives.

Disadvantages In adopting a Marxist framework, radical criminology ultimately explains crime and deviance in terms of the nature of capitalist society, the conflict of interest between social classes and the role of the state in representing the capitalist class. Can all crime and deviance be explained in terms of this framework? Critics argue that many laws and much police activity cannot simply be seen as an expression of the interests of the capitalist class - for example, traffic laws and their enforcement (Rock, 1979).

According to Lea and Young (1993), radical criminology tends to trivialise and underplay the reality of crime. While moral panics do occur and societal reaction can amplify deviance, crime has risen. And the consequences are serious. Both the victims and the perpetrators of street crime are usually working class and, in many inner-city areas, this is a major problem. Radical criminology has little to say about the victims of crime.

According to Downes and Rock (2003), *Policing the Crisis* was a brave but unsuccessful attempt to provide a fully social theory of deviance. In particular, the authors failed to demonstrate that the societal reaction to mugging was caused by a crisis of capitalism. At the very least, they needed to show a link between economic crises and moral panics at other times and places. And this was not done.

summary

1. Marxist theories of crime and deviance became popular in the 1970s.
2. Traditional Marxist approaches argued that:
   - Crime is systematically generated by the structure of capitalist society.
   - Laws reflect the interests of the dominant capitalist class.
   - Laws are enforced selectively - there is a systematic bias in favour of those at the top.
3. Radical criminology adopts a Marxist framework but includes other perspectives - for example, interactionism.
4. It focuses on the process by which the state defines certain activities as criminal and thereby criminalises certain groups, particularly the disadvantaged. It looks at the process of criminalisation in relation to the state's management of the capitalist system.
5. Radical criminology aims to provide a 'fully social theory of deviance' - to explain every aspect of deviance from the activity of the state to crime on the streets.
6. Policing the crisis argued that the state manufactures a crime problem in order to justify strengthening its control over the population.
7. Radical criminology has been criticised for:
   - Seeing the actions of the state and the agents of social control as solely serving the interests of the capitalist class.
   - Downplaying the significance of crime and largely ignoring the victims of crime.

Unit 7 Right realism and social control

keyissues

1 What is distinctive about right realist approaches to crime?

2 What are the strengths and weaknesses of these approaches?

right realism and *left realism*. Both see crime as a major problem in society, especially for its victims, and both claim to take crime seriously and to put forward practical proposals to combat it. 'Realist' approaches can be seen as a reaction to both labelling theory and radical criminology. Neither of these perspectives appeared to show much concern for the victims of crime. Indeed, labelling theory implied that in many cases the 'victim' was the person who had been labelled as 'criminal'.

7.1 Recent developments in the sociology of crime

New approaches to crime and deviance are partly a reaction to the shortcomings of previous approaches, partly a reflection of changing academic and political priorities, partly a response to changing fashions.

In the 1980s and 90s there was increased concern about law and order in Britain and the USA. This was accompanied by a growing awareness of high levels of unreported victimisation, especially amongst the most vulnerable sections of the population. These concerns were reflected in two new approaches to the study of crime –

7.2 The right realist approach

Conservative theorists were the first to adopt a realist approach. James Q. Wilson (1975), an American New Right theorist and policy adviser to President Reagan, was one of the earliest authors to question the predominant liberal and left analyses of law and order which prevailed in sociology. What then are the central features of the right realist analysis of crime?

Poverty, unemployment and crime

First and foremost, right realists question the view that

economic factors such as poverty or unemployment are responsible for the rising crime rate. In the following passage, Wilson makes a telling critique of this view by arguing that affluence and prosperity may go hand in hand with rising crime.

'If in 1960 one had been asked what steps society might take to prevent a sharp increase in the crime rate, one might well have answered that crime could best be curtailed by reducing poverty, increasing educational attainment, eliminating dilapidated housing, encouraging community organisation, and providing troubled or delinquent youth with counselling services.

Early in the decade of the 1960s, this country (the USA) began the longest sustained period of prosperity since World War II. A great array of programmes aimed at the young, the poor and the deprived were mounted. Crime soared. It did not just increase a little; it rose at a faster rate and to higher levels than at any time since the 1930s, and, in some categories, to higher levels than any experienced in this century' (Wilson, 1975).

Explaining rising crime

According to James Q. Wilson and Richard Hernstein (1985), 'crime is an activity disproportionately committed by young men living in large cities'. They explain this in terms of both biological and social factors. In their words,

'It is likely that the effect of maleness and youthfulness on the tendency to commit crime has both constitutional [biological] and social origins: that is, it has something to do with the biological status of being a young male and with how that young man has been treated by family, friends and society.'

Wilson and Hernstein picture young men as 'temperamentally aggressive'. This aggression is partly biologically based and makes them prone to crime.

An increase in the proportion of young men in the population is therefore likely to increase the crime rate. In the USA and Britain in the 1970s, the proportion of young men in the population and the crime rate both increased. Since the early 1980s, the proportion of young men has decreased but the crime rate has continued to increase. Wilson and Hernstein offer a social explanation for this increase.

Culture and socialisation Wilson and Hernstein argue that the way young men are socialised in the family, school and wider community has an important effect on their behaviour. Consistent discipline inside and outside the home encourages individuals to learn and follow society's norms and values and develop self control.

Wilson and Hernstein see the growth of a culture which emphasises *immediate gratification* – the immediate satisfaction of wants and desires – *low impulse control* – less control over desires and emotions, fewer restraints and checks on behaviour – and *self-expression* – the outward expression of feelings. These aspects of culture have produced a less effective learning environment for many young men and reduced the restraints on their behaviour. As a result, they are less likely to conform to society's norms and values and more likely to commit crime.

Costs and benefits Wilson and Hernstein argue that the crime rate will change with changes in the costs and benefits of crime, particularly property crime. The more the benefits rise – for example, the more successful criminals are – and the more the costs fall – for example, the less likely they are to be caught – the more the crime rate will rise.

7.3 Social control

Control theory

Many right realists argue that individuals are more likely to commit crime when the social constraints on their behaviour are weakened. Control theory is mainly concerned with identifying the factors which prevent individuals from committing crimes.

According to the American sociologist Travis Hirschi (1969), none of us is immune from the temptations of crime. What stops most of us from committing crime are strong social bonds which link us together. Social bonds consist of four main elements: attachment, commitment, involvement and belief. The stronger our attachments to key social institutions such as the family and school, the more we develop commitments to those involved – parents and teachers. Such commitments in turn foster involvement in family life and learning, and encourage a belief in conforming to the rules. Effective social bonds mean that we have too much to lose by committing crime. To do so would risk losing the good opinion of significant others – those who matter to us.

In support of his theory, Hirschi reports the findings of a large-scale self-report study of over 4000 young people aged 12-17 in California. Variations in their reported bonds with parents and teachers were much more significant than economic factors in accounting for variations in reported delinquency. Drawing on a range of studies, Hirschi has put forward a general theory of crime. He argues that the primary distinguishing feature of offenders is a lack of self-control. This, in turn, stems from poor socialisation in families and schools (Gottfredson & Hirschi, 1990).

Social control and the underclass

The American New Right theorist Charles Murray (1990, 1996) claims that an underclass is emerging in modern Western societies. For Murray, an underclass does not simply consist of those with the lowest income at the base of the class system. Instead, it consists of those with low income who behave in a certain way. In Murray's words, 'When I use the term *underclass*, I am indeed focusing on a certain type of poor person defined *not* by his condition, eg long-term unemployed, but by his deplorable behaviour in response to that condition, eg unwilling to take the jobs that are available to him'.

Murray sees births outside marriage 'as the leading indicator of an underclass'. Such births often lead to lone-parent families, the majority of which are headed by women. When lone-parent families become widespread, they form the basis of and the 'breeding ground' for an underclass. And 'proof that an underclass has arrived is that large numbers of young, healthy, low-income males choose not to take jobs'.

Inadequate socialisation Many of these young men have grown up in a family without a father and male wage earner. As a result, they lack the male role models of mainstream society. Within a female-headed family dependent on welfare benefits, the disciplines and responsibilities of mainstream society tend to break down. Murray believes that work must become the 'centre of life' for young men. They must learn the disciplines of work and respect for work. And they must learn to become 'real fathers', accepting the responsibilities of parenthood. However, 'Little boys don't naturally grow up to be responsible fathers and husbands. They don't naturally grow up knowing how to get up every morning at the same time and go to work. They don't naturally grow up thinking that work is not just a way to make money, but a way to hold one's head high in the world.' Murray believes that the socialisation and role models required to develop these attitudes are often lacking in female-headed low-income families.

Crime and the underclass According to Murray (1990), crime is a characteristic of the underclass. He argues that 'men who do not support families find other ways to prove that they are men, which tend to take various destructive forms'. Many turn to crime – particularly violent street crime – and to drug abuse. The high crime rate and high levels of victimisation result in fragmented communities which reinforce already inadequate socialisation.

Welfare benefits and family Although Murray appears to blame members of the underclass for their situation, he places most of the blame on government policy. It is the availability of overgenerous welfare benefits which has allowed the underclass to develop. Members of the underclass have become dependent on the state which has funded their unproductive lifestyles. Murray's solution is a sharp reduction or withdrawal of welfare benefits in order to force people to take responsibility for their own lives. In addition, Murray (1996) recommends penalising births outside marriage and reaffirming 'the value of marriage and the nuclear family'.

Without these changes, Murray believes that the underclass will reproduce itself from generation to generation.

7.4 Social order and crime prevention

Right realists are concerned with practical measures to reduce crime and maintain social order. Some of those measures are based on *rational choice theory*.

Rational choice theory As noted earlier, Wilson and Hernstein (1985) argue that there is an important element of choice when deciding whether or not to commit a crime. They picture the individual weighing up the costs and benefits of criminal activity and coming to a rational decision. In terms of this view, crime reduction means increasing the costs of crime and raising the benefits of conformity.

Two measures which increase the costs of crime are *target hardening* and *surveillance*. Target hardening reduces the physical opportunities for offending. Examples include installing tougher coin boxes in phone kiosks, making it more difficult to break into buildings, and gated communities with security guards. Surveillance refers to systems like CCTV (closed circuit television) which can film criminal activities. These measures increase the costs of crime – the cost of failure and the cost of getting caught.

Informal social controls In James Q. Wilson's view, it is not practical to deal with the fundamental causes of crime – the biological and social factors outlined in Section 7.2. The central concern of the criminal justice system should be the maintenance of social order. Since informal controls are fundamental in preventing crime, the police should seek to prevent further deterioration of communities before it is too late.

In a highly influential article, Wilson and Kelling (2003) argue that crime and social disorder are closely connected. Leaving broken windows unmended and ignoring anti-social behaviour can result in a vicious cycle whereby graffiti proliferates, noise levels increase, vandalism grows and more windows get broken. The consequence of inaction is to tip a neighbourhood into decline – property values spiral downwards, respectable members of the community are afraid to go out, they eventually leave the neighbourhood, and crime and disorder become widespread.

The role of the police is to prevent an area from deteriorating by clamping down on the first signs of petty crime and disorderly behaviour. By working with local residents to deal with undesirable behaviour, the police can help to prevent the deterioration of neighbourhoods and reinvigorate informal social controls. Since the police have limited resources, prioritising areas where there is still a possibility of regenerating communities means that there is little point in wasting valuable resources on the worst inner-city areas. The most that can be done there is to contain the crime problem by adopting more punitive measures – for example, longer prison sentences – to deal with 'wicked people' (Wilson, 1975). The prison population in the US has tripled since the late 1970s (from 500,000 to 1.8 million in 1998) and is now the highest per capita in the world (Carrabine et al., 2002).

7.5 Evaluation of right realism

What's 'real' about right realism? Right realists see the rising crime rate as a real indicator of a *real* social problem

– a problem which must be tackled with practical methods. However, as discussed in Unit 2, at least part of the rise in crime indicated by official statistics may result from changes in recording and reporting crime (Walklate, 2003).

Economic change and crime Right realists make an important point when they argue that economic growth and rising living standards have gone hand in hand with rising crime since the 1960s. However, this does *not* mean that social inequality ceases to be an important factor in generating crime. Despite rising living standards, the gap between top and bottom has widened over the past 25 years. This can result in a sense of relative deprivation which may lead to an increase in crime.

Disorder and community deterioration Do signs of disorder – 'broken windows' and anti-social behaviour – lead to a vicious cycle of community deterioration and rising crime? A study of 196 neighbourhoods in Chicago questions this view. It found that economic disadvantage underpinned *both* growing disorder and crime (Sampson & Raudenbush, 1999). Again, this points to the importance of relative deprivation in generating crime.

Young males Right realists focus on young males and street crime. They are the real problem, and the type of crimes they commit are the real threat to social order. This view is questionable. Other types of crime may be equally, if not more harmful – for example, corporate crime and domestic crime.

Right realists assume that young males in inner-city areas are responsible for most crimes. Again, this is questionable. It assumes that official statistics provide a valid picture of the typical offender.

Immediate gratification The immediate satisfaction of wants and desires.
Low impulse control Little control over emotions, few restraints on behaviour.
Self-expression The outward expression of feelings.
Target hardening Reducing the physical opportunities for offending by 'hardening' the targets of crime – for example, more secure buildings.
Surveillance Close observation, particularly of suspected persons.

Crime prevention According to Wilson (1975), 'wicked people exist' and the only thing that works is to 'set them apart from innocent people'. More imprisonment and longer sentences keep wicked people out of circulation and reduce the crime rate. Not only is this a very expensive measure, there is no sound evidence that it works (Walklate, 2003).

Civil liberties The major concern of right realists is to maintain order in society. For some, their prescription for producing order is based on a 'culture of control' – social control, situational control and self-control. This has alarmed some sociologists who see it as a threat to civil liberties – for example, the widespread use of surveillance techniques intruding on people's privacy (Hughes, 2000).

summary

1. Right realists accept the view that the crime rate rose dramatically in the second half of the 20th century.
2. They reject the view that economic factors and social inequality explain this rise.
3. Wilson and Hernstein argue that the rise in crime results from the growth of a culture which emphasises immediate gratification, low impulse control and self-expression. This results in a less effective learning environment for many young men. As a result, they are less likely to conform to society's norms and values.
4. Control theory states that strong social bonds result in high levels of social control. These are the main factors which prevent criminal behaviour.
5. Charles Murray argues that the underclass is a 'breeding ground' for crime. The 'deplorable behaviour' of young males results from inadequate socialisation in female-headed families and a lack of mainstream role models. Murray argues that overgenerous welfare benefits have allowed the underclass to develop.
6. Rational choice theory states that individuals weigh up the costs and benefits of criminal activity. Crime reduction therefore means increasing the costs of crime and the benefits of conformity.
7. Target hardening, surveillance, more imprisonment and longer sentences increase the costs of crime.
8. The primary role of the criminal justice system is to maintain public order. According to Wilson, strong informal social controls are the most effective method for maintaining order.
9. Disorder indicates a weakening of informal controls. The police should clamp down on the first signs of disorder to prevent community deterioration and rising crime.
10. Right realism has been criticised for:
    - Accepting the picture of crime presented by official statistics
    - Rejecting the view that economic factors and social inequality can generate crime
    - Focusing on young males and street crime and largely ignoring other types of offenders and crime.
    - Placing too much emphasis on control which some see as a threat to civil liberties.

activity16 controlling crime and anti-social behaviour

Item A Maintaining order

How to sweep these beggars from our streets

by David Marsland

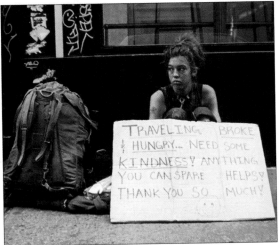

In all of our major cities and larger towns beggars have multiplied over recent years like fungus spreading in a damp cellar. Their aggressive hassling of men, women, and children is an intolerable blot on the complex but orderly copy-book of a modern civilised society.

Their arrogant contempt for the values of most decent, ordinary people - honesty, hard work, and civility foremost among them - is intolerable. Their possessive occupation - like locusts swarming on the harvest - of the most celebrated and attractive streets and squares they can find, is contemptible.

Analysis of historical and international evidence serves to disprove most fashionable explanations of begging. Neither 'capitalism' nor poverty is the cause. Begging on any scale is unheard of in some of the richest countries in the world - such as Switzerland - and some of the poorest - such as Malaysia.

Nor is it unemployment which causes begging. The current scale of begging was unheard of in the Britain of the 1930s, when unemployment was at much higher levels and much crueller in its impact.

Victorian experience provides the clue to the real explanation. Faced with a problem very like today's, politicians, businessmen and community leaders carefully analysed cause and effect, and rapidly set up a practical system which solved the problem in short order.

The Poor Laws and the work-houses were modernised and toughened up.

Help without a return of effort was outlawed. The values of hard work, self reliance and respectability were reinforced and unapologetically defended by a powerful consensus of public opinion in the schools, the churches, the media and Parliament. Begging was shamed out of existence.

What is causing the escalation in modern begging is:
• The hand-out culture of the decaying welfare state.
• The cultivation of tolerance for 'doing nothing' and 'doing your own thing' by teachers, intellectuals and political leaders.
• The impact on established British values of the sloppy, alien thinking of the Sixties.

Adapted from *Daily Mail*, 1994

Item B Controlling crime

Closed circuit television

Gated community

questions

1 In what ways does Item A reflect the right realist approach?

2 How do the pictures in Item B illustrate right realist views on crime control?

Metropolitan Police Chief Sir Paul Condon (centre) promoting the Neighbourhood Watch Scheme

Unit 8 *Left realism*

keyissues

1 What is distinctive about the left realist approach?
2 What are its strengths and weaknesses?

8.1 The left realist approach

The emergence of left realism Left realism developed in the early 1980s. It was a reaction to both right realism and radical criminology. It was led by the British sociologist Jock Young.

Left realism accused the right of over-dramatising the crime problem with its picture of crime rates out of control. It rejected right realism's view of moral decay and sick societies. And it accused the right of failing to understand the real causes of crime.

Marxism and radical criminology were criticised for focusing on the crimes of the powerful and for failing to understand working-class crime. In particular, left realism argued that street crime could not simply be dismissed as a moral panic fuelled by a crisis of capitalism. Left realism accused radical criminology of failing to take working-class crime seriously.

Taking crime seriously Left realism, as its name suggests, claims to focus on the reality of crime. Its rallying cry to sociologists is to 'take crime seriously'. And this means starting from 'problems as people experience them' (Young, 1986). Although left realists do not discount the importance of white-collar and corporate crime, they see street crime as 'the most transparent of all injustices' (Lea & Young, 1993). Its effects can be traumatic, it can leave people living in fear, it can impoverish victims. Left realists see crime committed by working-class people against working-class people as a problem of the first order.

Explaining crime Left realists argue that earlier explanations of crime failed to see the whole picture. For example, they looked at offenders and ignored victims, or focused almost exclusively on the criminal justice system. Left realists argue that an understanding of the reality of crime requires an examination of four basic elements and how they interact (Young, 1997).

- The victims – how they see and experience crime
- The offenders – why they commit crime
- The reaction of the formal agencies of the state – for example, the police and the courts
- The response of the public and the nature of informal methods of social control.

8.2 The victims

Left realists see crime as a real problem and the public's fear of crime as largely rational and justified. And they see the social survey as the main research method for studying the victims of crime.

Victim studies According to Jock Young (1992), victim surveys 'allow us to give voice to the experience of people' and to take their needs seriously. They reveal the extent of victimisation, the concerns and priorities of the victims of crime, and they provide information on which to base policies of crime prevention.

Left realists accept that estimates from national surveys, such as the British Crime Survey, show that the average chance of being a victim of crime is small. However, national surveys underestimate the risks faced by low-income groups in inner-city areas. For example, the Islington Crime Survey found that 36% of local residents saw crime as a major problem, 56% were anxious about being burgled, 46% had been a victim of a street robbery and a third of women avoided going out after dark for fear of sexual harassment (Jones et al., 1986).

In contrast to some earlier approaches, such as labelling theory and radical criminology, left realists highlight the plight of victims. It is disadvantaged groups living in the inner cities who are most at risk from being harmed by street crime. And since these groups are on low incomes, they often suffer more – petty theft is a lot more serious when people are living in poverty.

8.3 The offenders

Left realists largely accept the picture presented by official statistics – that there has been a significant growth in crime, especially working-class crime. They see the increase in working-class crime as a particularly disturbing development – most of the victims are not the rich but the most vulnerable members of society. And most of the offenders come from the same social groups as their victims.

Why do people commit crime? The key concept used by left realists to answer this question is *relative deprivation*.

Relative deprivation Jock Young notes that the rise in crime between 1960 and 1975 occurred at a time of full employment and rising living standards. And since then 'as the West became wealthier, the crime rate rose' (Young, 1999). Deprivation, as such, clearly does not cause a rise in crime. What does, according to left realists, is how people see or perceive deprivation. In other words, what matters is relative deprivation.

People see themselves as deprived in comparison to, or relative to, other people. This comparison may be relative to people in the same social category as themselves – for example, in the same social class or ethnic group – or to people in other social categories – for example, in different social classes or ethnic groups to themselves.

In late modern society – from the 1970s onwards – there has been an increase in relative deprivation. And this increase has been particularly acute for those at the base of the class structure and for those in certain ethnic groups. Reasons for this will be examined shortly.

Relative deprivation does not necessarily lead to crime. It breeds discontent which can be expressed in many different ways – crime is only one of them. It is the combination of relative deprivation and *individualism* that provides a recipe for crime. In Jock Young's (1999) words, 'The lethal combination is relative deprivation and individualism'.

Individualism A number of sociologists see the rise of individualism as one of the main characteristics of late modern society. Individualism refers to a focus on and concern with the self, to a demand for individual freedom and autonomy. It is partly responsible for, and partly a result of, the breakdown of close-knit communities and the break-up of families. It undermines the relationships and values necessary for social order and weakens the informal mechanisms of social control in the community. And it often results in the pursuit of selfish interests.

According to Jock Young (1999), the combination of relative deprivation and individualism is the main cause of crime in late modern society. As a result of this combination, 'the working-class area implodes upon itself', anti-social behaviour is widespread, 'neighbours burglarise neighbours' and 'aggression is widespread'.

Late modern society and rising crime

What are the changes in late modern society that have led to the disintegration of community, the increase in relative deprivation and rising crime rates? Left realists provide the following picture with particular reference to the lower working class.

Changes in the economy There has been a rapid decline in manufacturing and manual jobs, particularly unskilled and semi-skilled occupations. Lower working-class males have been particularly hard hit, as have African Caribbeans in Britain and African Americans and Hispanics in the USA. And within these groups, the young are most likely to experience unemployment – many have never had full-time work. This has led to acute feelings of relative deprivation because of a lack of fit between their situation and what they see as reasonable expectations in terms of jobs and material rewards.

Changes in the economy have led to the disintegration of many lower working-class families and communities, and the informal social controls they provided.

Government policy has not helped. Most Western governments have adopted free-market policies which discourage state intervention in the economy to provide jobs. Alongside this, many governments have reduced welfare benefits.

Exclusion Those at the base of the class structure are increasingly excluded from mainstream society.

- They are largely excluded from the labour market.
- They face increasing social exclusion as the middle classes flee from the inner city to areas where the poor cannot afford to live and, in some cases, cannot enter as the rich increasingly live in gated communities with security guards at the entrance.
- And they are excluded from society, as prison populations increase dramatically. For example, in the USA, 1 in 9 Black males in their 20s are in prison compared to 1 in 135 of the total population (Mauer, 1997).

The mass media and inclusion There is one area where those at the base of the class structure are included – the mass media, especially television. Living in a world which excludes them, they remain 'glued to the television sets which alluringly portray the glittering prizes of a wealthy society' (Young, 1999). And, sharing the materialistic values of the mainstream culture, they are faced every day with comparisons which fuel relative deprivation.

Jock Young (2002) argues that the lower working class live in a *bulimic society* – a society constantly exposed to the material goods taken for granted by most of the population, but unable to consume them. In this sense, they are starving. In Young's words, 'The process is not that of a society of simple exclusion. Rather it is one where both inclusion and exclusion occur simultaneously – a *bulimic society* where massive cultural inclusion is accompanied by systematic structural exclusion.'

8.4 Dealing with crime

The public and informal control

Left realists agree with the right realists that the police and other criminal justice agencies can only play a limited role in preventing crime. Far more important are the forces of informal control. 'It is not the "Thin Blue Line" but the social bricks and mortar of civil society which are the major bulwarks against crime. Good jobs with a discernible future, housing estates that tenants can be proud of, community facilities which enhance a sense of cohesion and belonging, a reduction in unfair inequalities, all create a society that is more cohesive and less criminogenic' (Young, 1992).

On the local level, what's needed is a concerted effort by all the agencies which may have an impact on crime. Left realists refer to this as *multi-agency intervention*. Local authorities must coordinate their various departments – for example, housing, education, social services and planning – in order to rebuild disintegrating communities. On the national level, the state must reduce economic inequalities and create a more just society.

The police and formal control

Left realism accepts that good policing can play an important part in reducing crime. But, low clear-up rates and a decline in public confidence have made members of some communities reluctant to help the police. Where the

activity17 Life at the bottom

Item A Watching TV

A study of a low-income Black ghetto in Philadelphia found that African Americans watch TV half as much again as whites – in the average Black household TV is on for 11 hours a day. By the age of five and six, children are familiar with adult luxury – from Gucci, Evan Piccone and Pierre Cardin, to Mercedes and BMW. By the age of ten they are thoroughly engrossed in Nike's and Reebok's cult of the sneaker.

Adapted from Nightingale, 1993

Item B Dealing in drugs

A study of Puerto Rican immigrants in East Harlem drew the following conclusion.

I want to place drug dealers and street level criminals into their rightful position within the mainstream of US society. They are not 'exotic others' operating in an irrational netherworld. On the contrary they are 'made in America'. Like most other people in the United States, drug dealers and street criminals are scrambling to obtain their piece of the pie as fast as possible. They are aggressively pursuing careers as private entrepreneurs: they take risks, work hard, and pray for good luck. They are the ultimate rugged individualists, braving an unpredictable frontier where fortune, fame, and destruction are all just around the corner, and where the enemy is ruthlessly hunted down and shot.

Adapted from Bourgois, 1995

Item C Riots

Two youths stole a police BMW motorbike in Hartcliffe, Bristol. In the police chase which followed, they crashed and were killed. Trouble ensued – crowds of young people, White and Black, set fire to the local library and community centre, and looted shops. The following night, there were more riots. It is a familiar pattern, repeating what has occurred in depressed estates from Teeside to Salford.

The affluent societies of the West have fostered new expectations. Advertising and the rules of an economy based on mass consumption teach us that if we are truly to belong to our society, we must possess its glittering prizes. Hunger no longer propels riots – in its place are the DVD player, the mobile phone and the BMW.

Adapted from Young, 1992

Looting during a riot in Miami, Florida 1990

Item D Exclusion

US population in prison, on parole or on probation, 1995		
	In prison	In prison, on parole or on probation
Total population	1 in 135	1 in 37
Black males	1 in 24	1 in 13
Black males in 20s	1 in 9	1 in 3

Adapted from Mauer, 1997

Inmates from a maximum security prison, Miami

questions

1 In what way does Item A illustrate Young's view of the bulimic society?

2 How does Item B indicate that those at the bottom share the values of mainstream society?

3 Use the concept of relative deprivation to explain the behaviour outlined in Items B and C.

4 How can Item D be seen as the ultimate form of exclusion?

flow of information from the public – which is crucial to the solution of many crimes – has ground to a halt, the police have responded with more direct methods such as stopping and searching large numbers of people.

This can lead to 'a drift towards military policing' which can make it well nigh impossible to police with the consent of the community (Lea & Young, 1982). In some Black low-income inner-city areas, the police are regarded by some as an army of occupation. And in Brixton in 1981, a police operation, which swamped an area with officers on a stop and search mission, triggered riots.

In line with its concern about what is to be done about law and order, left realism calls for greater democratic control of the police. A genuinely accountable police force will be more efficient since it will restore the flow of information from the public. And it will reflect the concerns and priorities of the community.

In addition, left realism urges the state to decriminalise minor offences such as the possession of cannabis, find more alternatives to imprisonment, and develop multi-agency and community-based forms of crime prevention.

8.5 Evaluation of left realism

Left realism is a genuine attempt to take crime seriously. And it is a comprehensive approach which looks at both victims and offenders, and informal and formal methods of social control. Despite these advantages, it has been criticised in various ways.

Focus on street crime While left realists accept that crime takes place across the class structure, their primary focus is on street crime and lower working-class offenders and victims. In their defence, such crimes loom large in victim surveys and are particularly harmful to victims. However, some sociologists criticise left realists for neglecting white-collar and corporate crime – which may be even more harmful (Walklate, 2003).

Over-predicting crime The view that relative deprivation plus individualism and economic inequality generate crime 'over-predicts the level of crime' (Jones, 1998). Since this explanation appears to fit most people, why isn't there more crime?

A trend towards inclusion Some sociologists question whether the trends identified by left realists are as serious and permanent as they suggest. According to the British Crime Survey, crime rates have been falling since the mid-1990s. And so have unemployment rates.

It is possible to detect trends towards inclusion as well as exclusion in late modern societies (Downes & Rock, 2003). For example, the Labour government in Britain has introduced the minimum wage, raised child benefits, set up the New Deal to help the unemployed return to work, and created the Social Exclusion Unit with the aim of bringing the excluded into mainstream society.

Victim surveys Left realists rely heavily on victim surveys to measure the type, extent and fear of crime in low-income inner-city areas. As outlined earlier, victim studies have their limitations (see pages 212-123). Certain types of crime are under-reported or not reported – for example, domestic violence and child abuse. And victim studies do not capture how people define and experience criminal victimisation – for example, do women define domestic

summary

1. Left realism aims to 'take crime seriously'. It sees street crime as particularly damaging to victims.

2. Understanding crime requires an examination of four basic elements and how they interact – victims, offenders, the police and the criminal justice system, and the public and informal control.

3. Local victim studies reveal the type and extent of crime in low-income, inner-city areas. They present a disturbing picture.

4. Relative deprivation is the key concept used by left realists to explain crime. Relative deprivation is felt most acutely by those at the base of the class structure.

5. In late modern society, the combination of relative deprivation and individualism is the main driving-force generating crime.

6. Changes in late modern society have led to the disintegration of community and informal social controls, an increase in relative deprivation, and rising crime rates. These changes include:
   - Economic change and the loss of many unskilled and semi-skilled jobs
   - The growing exclusion of those at the base of the class structure from mainstream society.

7. One area where those at the bottom are included is the mass media. They are presented daily with expensive goods and lifestyles but are unable to consume them. In Jock Young's words, they live in a 'bulimic society'. The media fuels relative deprivation.

8. Left realists argue that the criminal justice system has only a limited role in preventing crime. Informal mechanisms of social control are far more important.

9. Left realists argue that multi-agency intervention on the local level can help to reduce crime rates.

10. The police have an important part to play but they need the support of the public. This requires an accountable police force under local democratic control.

11. Left realism has been criticised for:
    - Paying too much attention to street crime and largely ignoring white-collar and corporation crime
    - 'Over-predicting' the level of crime
    - Ignoring trends towards inclusion in late modern society
    - Relying too heavily on victim studies as a source for information.

violence by their partner as a crime and, if so, what level of violence? In-depth interviews rather than survey questionnaires are more likely to answer this and similar questions.

Unit 9 Ethnicity and crime

key issues

1 Are some ethnic groups more likely to commit crimes than others?

2 Are some ethnic groups more likely to be victims than other groups?

3 Is the criminal justice system biased?

9.1 The ethnicity and crime debate

Questions of ethnicity and gender were barely looked at by sociologists of crime and deviance until the 1970s. The primary focus was on class. Since the 1970s, sociologists have recognised the need to examine ethnicity and gender. This unit focuses on the ethnicity and crime debate. Issues relating to gender and crime are examined in the following unit.

In the early phase of post-war migration, there was a widespread assumption that members of ethnic minority groups were no more likely to be offenders or victims than the majority White group. It was also assumed that the criminal justice system treated all ethnic groups fairly. Indeed, according to a major investigation into police-immigrant relations in 1972, 'Black people were more law abiding than the general population' and there was little evidence of racist attacks against Black and Asian immigrants (Layton-Henry, 1992). During the following ten years, however, relations between the police and the Black community deteriorated and evidence mounted of increasing racist attacks.

Two reports published in November 1981 signalled the onset of official concerns. The Scarman Report (1981) into the Brixton disorders emphasised how the riots were essentially an outburst of anger and resentment by young African Caribbeans against perceived harassment by the police. And a Home Office report into racial attacks revealed that South Asians were 50 times, and African-Caribbeans 36 times, more likely to be the victims of racially motivated attacks than Whites. There was growing evidence that Black and Asian people were increasingly involved with the criminal justice system.

Two issues in particular have given rise to concern – the racist violence and harassment experienced by ethnic minority groups and the criminalisation of Black people.

Criminalisation The issue which initially attracted most attention concerned the criminalisation of Black people. At the end of the criminal justice process, 'Black people are about six times as likely to be in prison as White people or South Asians' (Smith, 1997). Two broad explanations have been put forward for this. The first sees Black people as disproportionately criminal. This explanation tended to be adopted by the police and other criminal justice agencies and reproduced in the media (Hall et al., 1978). The second sees the criminal justice system as inherently racist and discriminating against Black people. This explanation has received some support from radical sociologists (Gilroy, 1983). Until the 1990s, the ethnicity and crime debate was primarily concerned with this issue.

Victimisation More recently, attention has turned to another question. The murder of Stephen Lawrence, a Black teenager, and the failure of the criminal justice system to convict those responsible, led to an official inquiry, the Macpherson Report in 1999. The report found serious failings with the police investigation into this racially motivated murder. It not only challenged the dominant picture of the criminal justice system as unbiased, but also raised the profile of another question. Are ethnic minority groups more likely to be victimised than the White majority ethnic group?

9.2 Ethnicity and offending

To discover whether there are differences between ethnic groups in rates of offending, we can turn to three sources – official statistics, victim surveys, and self-report studies.

Official statistics

Table 2 presents the official statistics detailing the ethnic groups at different stages of the criminal justice system.

The table indicates that in 2000/01, Black ethnic groups were particularly over-represented at different stages of the criminal justice system. While they comprised only 1.8% of the population, they made up 7.7% of arrests, 6.2% of cautions and 12.1% of the prison population. Asian groups,

Table 2 *Representation of ethnic groups at different stages of the criminal justice process, 2000/01*

	White	Black	Asian	Other	Not known	Total
			Ethnicity			
Population (aged 10 and over)	94.5%	1.8%	2.7%	1.1%	0.0%	100.0%
Stops and searches	82.7%	10.1%	4.9%	1.0%	1.2%	100.0%
Arrests	86.3%	7.7%	4.4%	0.9%	0.6%	100.0%
Cautions	85.7%	6.2%	4.6%	1.0%	2.0%	100.0%
Youth offenders	77.9%	5.8%	2.7%	1.9%	11.6%	100.0%
Prison receptions	85.6%	8.9%	2.4%	3.1%	0.0%	100.0%
Prison population	81.9%	12.1%	2.8%	3.1%	0.1%	100.0%

Adapted from Home Office, 2002

by comparison, were slightly over-represented. Comprising 2.7% of the population, they made up 4.4% of arrests, 4.6% of cautions and 2.8% of the prison population. In contrast to these ethnic minority groups, White ethnic groups were under-represented – they were less likely to be arrested, cautioned or sent to prison.

While the official statistics point to ethnic differences at different stages of the criminal justice system, they do not demonstrate that there are ethnic differences in rates of offending. The higher arrest rate of Black ethnic groups could reflect the fact that these groups are more likely to be targeted by the police. Similarly, the higher rate of imprisonment could reflect the fact that these groups are more severely sentenced by the courts.

Victim surveys

At first sight victim studies, such as the British Crime Survey, provide a more effective way of discovering whether there are ethnic differences in rates of offending, since they include questions asking victims about the ethnic identity of offenders. Unfortunately, victims are usually only aware of offenders when it comes to personal crimes, which account for only 20% of all crimes. These surveys show that, in many cases, both offenders and victims come from the same ethnic group. An analysis of the 1988 and 1992 British Crime Surveys (Mayhew et al., 1993) revealed that 88% of White victims of violence identified the offenders as White. In the majority of violent offences against ethnic minority groups, the offenders were also identified as White (51% in the case of Black victims and 62% in the case of Asian victims). This is to be expected since the general population is overwhelmingly White. Once account has been taken of White offenders, a majority of Black victims of violence identified Black offenders (42%) and the majority of Asian victims identified Asian offenders (19%).

Mugging The offence that has given rise to most controversy has been 'mugging'. Although this term is a criminal label that has no formal legal standing, it has been taken up widely since its arrival from the USA in 1972. It has been

used by the police and the BCS to refer to robbery and some thefts from the person. Victim surveys suggest that Black ethnic groups are significantly more likely to commit this offence than other ethnic groups. Mayhew et al. (1993) point to 42% of muggings being committed by Black offenders in the early 1990s, while Clancy et al. (2001) point to a slightly lower figure of 31% in the late 1990s. BCS figures are similar to police data on the ethnicity of those arrested for robbery and therefore suggest that the Black over-representation amongst muggers indicates a higher Black offending rate (Clancy et al., 2001).

A word of caution is in order, however. 'The effects of stereotyping and prejudice may lead White victims sometimes to say that offences committed against them have been committed by Black people, even when they are not sure who was involved' (Bowling & Phillips, 2002). What is more, mugging constitutes only a small proportion of crime – only 2.8% of offences recorded by the BCS. While Black ethnic groups may have a higher offending rate for this crime, victim surveys do not point to significant over-representation of Black or other ethnic minority groups among offenders for other crimes.

Self-report studies

In contrast to both the official statistics, which measure the outcomes of the actions of criminal justice agencies, and victim surveys, which are only able to reveal the ethnic identity of offenders for a small proportion of crime, self-report studies address the question of offending directly. Self-report studies ask people whether they have been engaged in criminal and disorderly behaviour.

The major study conducted in Britain which expressly pays attention to the question of ethnicity is the Home Office study, *Young People and Crime* (Graham & Bowling, 1995). Based on a large sample of young people, 'this study found that White and Black respondents had very similar rates of offending (44% and 43% respectively), while Asian respondents – Indians (30%), Pakistanis (28%) and Bangladeshis (13%) – had significantly lower rates' (Phillips & Bowling, 2002).

This study challenges the widespread view that the rate of offending of Black ethnic groups is higher than that of White ethnic groups. And it supports the suggestion that the rate of offending of Asian groups is somewhat lower. However, we cannot infer that this study reveals the true rate of offending. Self-report studies rely on the honesty of respondents and exclude from their sample people in institutions who may be more involved in offending. They also underplay the more serious offences.

Evaluation

The evidence from the three sources on the extent and nature of offending by different ethnic groups is inconclusive. The sources of data are all flawed in some way, with self-report studies pointing in one direction and arrest data in the other (Bowling & Phillips, 2002).

However, there are two exceptions to this. Homicide statistics, which are more reliable than other official statistics, do 'indicate that a disproportionate number of homicides involve people from ethnic minorities [especially African Caribbeans] as both victims and suspects' (Bowling & Phillips, 2002). And victim reports do point to the greater involvement of African Caribbeans in robbery. While homicide and robbery represent only a small proportion of recorded crime, the data for these offences suggests somewhat higher rates of offending by African Caribbeans (Phillips & Bowling, 2002).

9.3 Racism and the criminal justice system

Some researchers argue that the greater likelihood for ethnic minority groups, particularly Black ethnic groups, to be criminalised (arrested and imprisoned, for example) reflects their greater involvement in crime. Other researchers argue that ethnic differences in criminalisation stem from institutional racism within the criminal justice system. This view received support from the Macpherson Report.

The Macpherson Report

Institutional racism The 1999 Macpherson Report on the police investigation into the murder of Stephen Lawrence concluded that 'institutional racism' in the police force was widespread. The Macpherson Report agreed with the earlier Report of Lord Scarman into the 1981 Brixton disorders that the police do not 'knowingly as a matter of policy, discriminate against Black people' (Scarman, 1981). However, it did not accept Scarman's view that 'institutional racism does not exist in Britain' (Scarman, 1981).

For Macpherson, the concept of institutional racism does not imply that the policies of organisations are racist. The term instead is defined as: 'the collective failure of an organisation to provide an appropriate and professional service to people because of their colour, culture or ethnic origin. It can be seen or detected in processes, attitudes

and behaviour which amount to discrimination through unwitting prejudice, ignorance, thoughtlessness and racist stereotyping' (Macpherson, 1999, para 6.34).

The Macpherson Report gives official recognition to the fact that the police in particular, and the criminal justice system in general, are biased against ethnic minority groups.

Policing For Macpherson, the failure of the police investigation into the murder of Stephen Lawrence was not due to acts of discrimination by individual officers acting out their personal prejudices. Instead, it stemmed from the occupational culture of the police. In an occupation that may entail danger, great emphasis is placed on teamwork, with jokes and banter being used to cement solidarity. A number of studies have discovered that derogatory stereotypes about ethnic minority groups are prevalent among police officers, the vast majority of whom are White (Smith & Gray, 1995, Holdaway, 1996, Graef, 1990). Jokes and banter often take a racist form and reinforce a negative perception of Black and Asian people.

While we cannot assume that such racism leads to discriminatory policing, it can do so. A case in point is Dwayne Brooks, Stephen Lawrence's companion on the night of his murder. As a Black young man at the scene of a knifing, he was regarded by the police as a suspect rather than a witness. In seeking to protect society from crime and disorder, the police identify certain groups as more likely to mean 'trouble'. Black young men and, more recently, Muslim young men are often viewed in this way. As a result, their actions are more likely to be regarded with suspicion (Kalra, 2003).

Stop and search The Macpherson Report identified the use of stop and search powers by the police as a key factor in contributing to poor relations between the police and ethnic minority groups. In 1998/99, Black people were six times and Asians twice as likely to be stopped and searched as Whites. The police have considerable discretion in the use of these powers, which can be used on the basis of 'reasonable suspicion'. At the time of the inquiry, the BCS revealed that ethnic differences in the likelihood of being stopped and searched could not be accounted for by other factors such as age or social class. This suggests that discrimination may be responsible.

The Macpherson Report's judgement on the use of stop and search powers by the police states: 'we are clear that the perception and experience of the minority communities that discrimination is a major element in the stop and search problem is correct' (Macpherson, 1999). In the immediate aftermath of the report, the use of stop and search powers fell and, at the same time, the ethnic differences declined. In addition, the 2000 BCS indicates that the ethnic differences in foot stops, as opposed to car stops, could now be accounted for by factors other than ethnicity – for example, by social class (Clancy et al., 2001). While this suggests that ethnic discrimination may have fallen, the official statistics in Activity 18 indicate that the fall may have been short-lived.

activity18 stop and search

Item A Stop and search statistics

Stop and search in Brixton, South London

Stops and searches per 1,000 population

[Line graph: x-axis years 1997/98, 1998/99, 1999/2000, 2000/01, 2001/02; y-axis 0–160. Black line starts at ~140, declines to ~82, rises to ~108. Asian line ~45 down to ~38. White line ~20.]

— Black   — Asian   — White

Adapted from Home Office, 2002

Item B 'It makes you feel stigmatised.'

Wesley Walters-Stephenson is a race relations trainer for the police. He is an African Caribbean.

'How many times have I been stopped and searched? It happens so often. I become defensive when I am stopped because I am weary of being pulled up and it makes you feel stigmatised, it makes you feel like a criminal. It can happen any time and I try to stay off the streets as much as possible.

My worst experience was when I got my shoulder busted and went unconscious for a short while after I was stopped and searched. I was 26. It is no wonder they have problems with youth culture when the police have criminalised two generations of Black people.'

Adapted from *The Guardian*, 8.11.2002

Wesley Walters-Stephenson

questions

1 Summarise the trends in Item A.
2 Read Item B. What are the likely effects of being regularly stopped and searched?

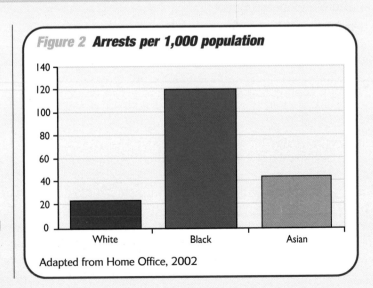

Arrests Figure 2 shows ethnic differences in arrest rates. Black people are approximately six times and Asians approximately twice as likely to be arrested as Whites. Most arrests result from the police responding to reports from the public. However, a significant minority are due to the police targeting particular ethnic minority groups through their use of stop and search powers (Phillips & Bowling, 2002).

Once arrested, and in contrast to other ethnic groups, Blacks are less likely to admit the offence. As a result, they are less likely to escape with a caution and more likely to face formal action (Home Office, 2002). Black juveniles are less likely than other groups to have their cases referred to multi-agency panels and thus more likely to go to court. This holds true even when 'admission of the offence' has been taken into account (Phillips & Bowling, 2002).

Figure 2 Arrests per 1,000 population

[Bar chart: White ~24, Black ~121, Asian ~45; y-axis 0–140]

Adapted from Home Office, 2002

Prosecution Before a case goes to court, the Crown Prosecution Service (CPS) decides whether to proceed with a prosecution. It does so when it believes that there is a 'realistic prospect of conviction' and that it is in the public interest to do so. The CPS is more likely to terminate cases that involve ethnic minority groups. This suggests that the police may, as a result of holding negative stereotypes, put forward cases against ethnic minorities where the evidence is weak (Phillips & Bowling, 2002).

Once the decision to prosecute has been made, the next step is to decide whether to remand a defendant in custody or grant bail. Ethnic minorities are more likely to be remanded before and during a trial 'partly because they have an increased risk of being "of no fixed abode", a key criterion on which courts refuse bail' (Phillips & Bowling, 2002). Those remanded in custody are more likely to be given a custodial sentence if found guilty.

There is a greater likelihood of defendants from ethnic minority groups pleading not guilty and electing for trial in a Crown Court rather than a Magistrate's Court. If found guilty, they are likely to face a more serious sentence than they would if they had entered a guilty plea or opted for trial in a Magistrate's Court.

Ethnic minority defendants are more likely to be acquitted than White defendants (Home Office, 2002). This finding reinforces the suggestion above that cases involving ethnic minorities are more likely to be brought forward by the police where the evidence is weak. It also suggests that the CPS still allows 'a disproportionate number of weak cases against ethnic minorities to go to trial' (Denman, 2001).

Sentencing and imprisonment

Sentencing The most significant study on ethnic differences in sentencing was conducted in five Crown Courts in the West Midlands in 1989. All male ethnic minority defendants found guilty were compared to an equivalent sample of male White defendants. After taking the seriousness of the offence and previous convictions into account, the study revealed that Black men were 5% more likely to be given a custodial sentence. What is more, for defendants who pleaded not guilty and were sent to prison, Asian men were given sentences 9 months longer and Black men 3 months longer than Whites (Hood, 1992). Sentencing is a clear example of discrimination against ethnic minority groups.

Imprisonment In comparison with other ethnic groups, Black people have significantly higher rates of imprisonment. This is illustrated in Figure 3. Some of the reasons for this difference have already been mentioned. Further reasons are given in the following section.

Evaluation

The evidence clearly points to racial discrimination in the criminal justice system. However, an important question still remains. Does discrimination wholly account for the greater criminalisation of ethnic minority groups? The two

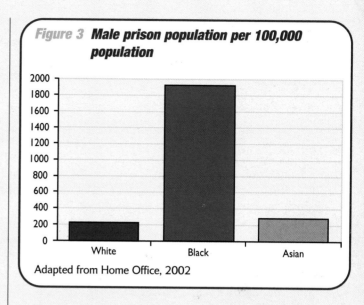

Figure 3 **Male prison population per 100,000 population**

Adapted from Home Office, 2002

most recent overviews that have looked at this question reach somewhat different conclusions.

Evidence of bias The first review acknowledges 'evidence of bias' against Black people at various stages of the criminal justice system – in the use of stop and search powers, in the decision to prosecute juvenile offenders, and in sentencing by the Crown Courts (Smith, 1997). Such bias does not demonstrate, however, that the criminal justice system is institutionally racist. For bias is not evident at all stages in the criminal justice system. What is more, if the criminal justice system were institutionally racist, it is difficult to understand why Black people are much more likely to be criminalised than Asians. The extent of the disproportionate imprisonment of Black people is, in this view, too great to be explained by racial discrimination in the criminal justice system.

Discrimination A more recent review is more sympathetic to the view that discrimination in the criminal justice system has a cumulative effect on Black people and helps to explain their over-representation in the prison population. 'It is not necessary for there to be discrimination at each and every stage in the process in order for the over-representation of Black people in prison to be the result of cumulative discrimination' (Bowling & Phillips, 2002).

The criminal justice system can still be racist even though Black people are treated more harshly than Asians. This may reflect the fact that Black people are more likely to be viewed with suspicion, itself a result of contrasting stereotypes held of Black (violent and dangerous) and Asian people (passive and traditional).

Despite the fact that the two most recent overviews reach somewhat different conclusions, they agree that the available evidence is not able to demonstrate whether the over-representation of Black people in prison is better explained in terms of their higher rate of offending or discrimination by the criminal justice system. There is now widespread agreement among sociologists that we need to move beyond the 'either/or of racist criminal justice vs

Black criminality' (Reiner, 1993). While acknowledging bias at various stages of the criminal justice system, Smith emphasises that 'in large part the difference in rate of arrest and imprisonment between Black and White people arises from a difference in the rate of offending' (Smith, 1997). Similarly, Phillips and Bowling (2002) – after highlighting the discriminatory nature of the criminal justice system – acknowledge 'somewhat "elevated" rates of offending by African Caribbeans'.

Discrimination and criminalisation In short, both discrimination in the criminal justice system and the greater involvement of young Black men in street crime contribute to the criminalisation of Black people (Hudson, 1993). The two are linked – 'discrimination on the one hand, and Black crime on the other, reinforce and feed off one another in a vicious cycle of amplification' (Reiner, 1993).

Lea and Young (1982) illustrate how this vicious circle develops. For there to be policing by consent, a community must act as a source of information to the police so that they can 'catch and/or deter individual lawbreakers'. As unemployment generates an increasing crime rate in inner cities, however, the police begin to adopt a more aggressive policing policy and turn to operations which involve the random stopping of 'suspicious' youth. This inevitably results in large numbers of innocent people being stopped and searched. Once this happens, the community 'begins to become alienated from the police'. It 'comes to see any attempt at an arrest by officers as a symbolic attack on the community' and ceases to provide the police with any information which can help them identify individual offenders. Faced with this situation, the police adopt an even more aggressive policing policy and so the vicious circle continues. In this context, 'whatever racist sentiments exist within the police force are reinforced' (Lea & Young, 1982; Pilkington, 2003).

9.4 Ethnicity and victimisation

Racist incidents

Although racist violence and harassment is by no means new, mounting evidence indicates the scale of the problem in Britain. The police recorded 23,049 racist incidents in 1998/9, a massive increase since 1988 (4,383 incidents) when records of such incidents were first collected. The police statistics – though they cover the majority of the most serious cases – represent the tip of an iceberg if we include all racially motivated crimes. The 2000 British Crime Survey discovered, for example, 280,000 racially motivated offences in 1999. If we also include 'forms of racially insulting and threatening behaviour which are not seen as criminal events in themselves', the extent of racist victimisation becomes even more evident (Modood et al., 1997). The Policy Studies Institute Survey provides an estimate of such low-level racist harassment in 1994. It concludes 'that over a quarter of a million people were subjected to some form of racial harassment in a 12-month period' (Modood et al., 1997).

While all ethnic groups face the risk of being the victim of racist harassment, the risk is significantly greater for members of ethnic minority groups. In 1999, for example, 'the annual risk of being the victim of a racially motivated offence was 0.3% for White respondents, 2.2% for Black groups, 3.6% for Indians and 4.2% for Bangladeshis and Pakistanis' (Clancy et al., 2001). The consequences of such racist harassment are extremely damaging. A range of studies confirms how they can create a climate of continual insecurity for victims and their families (Chahal & Julienne, 1999). Such everyday harassment provides the backdrop to racist violence. The murder of Black teenager Stephen Lawrence at a bus stop by five White youths in 1993 is the most notorious example.

The Macpherson Report considered the reluctance of the police to acknowledge the existence of racially motivated offences and to protect ethnic minority groups from victimisation to be a serious failing. Its conclusion outlined a series of recommendations related to the handling of racist incidents. A plethora of activity has followed. A code of practice on the reporting and recording of racist incidents has been produced by the Home Office (2000); the Association of Chief Police Officers (ACPO, 2000) has produced a guide to identifying and combating hate crime; and Her Majesty's Inspectorate of Constabulary has produced a succession of reports on community and race relations (HMIC, 2001). Whether significant progress has been made in the handling of racist incidents remains to be seen.

Victimisation and fear of crime

Ethnic minority groups also face a higher risk of a range of 'household crimes' such as burglary and theft (Clancy et al., 2001). The same applies to violent crime, although in this case, ethnic minority groups are much more likely to see these incidents as racially motivated.

The 2000 British Crime Survey points out that a significant proportion of the increased risk of victimisation faced by ethnic minority groups is due to factors such as area of residence and age. However, even with regard to these factors, racial discrimination may still play a part in increasing the risk of victimisation – it can influence the area in which people choose to live. And finally, the increased victimisation faced by ethnic minorities is reflected in their increased fear of crime.

summary

1. The ethnicity and crime debate has addressed two key questions:
   - Why are some ethnic groups, especially Black groups, more likely to be criminalised?
   - Are some ethnic groups more likely to be victimised than others?

2. We cannot reach a definite conclusion as to whether there are ethnic differences in the rate of offending. For specific offences, such as mugging, there is some evidence of a higher rate of offending by Black ethnic groups.

3. There is clear evidence of racial discrimination at various stages of the criminal justice system.

4. It is likely that ethnic differences in rates of offending and a discriminatory criminal justice system combine to produce ethnic differences in criminalisation.

5. Ethnic minority groups face a higher risk of victimisation and suffer disproportionately from racially motivated offences. As a result, they are more likely to express fear of crime than other groups.

Unit 10 *Gender and crime*

keyissues

1 Why are there gender differences in crime?

2 Is there a gender bias in the criminal justice system?

10.1 The gender and crime debate

Official statistics indicate that men are much more likely to commit crime than women. For example, in 2002, over 80% of known offenders were men (Home Office, 2003). This ratio is found in other Western countries and has remained remarkably similar over time.

In the past, sociologists paid little attention to these marked gender differences. They tended to take them for granted. Instead, they focused on why some men rather than other men were more likely to commit crime or become labelled as criminals.

Things began to change in the 1970s. Feminists, such as Carol Smart (1977), as challenged what they saw as the male dominance of the subject. They opened up new lines of inquiry into women and crime and asked a new set of questions.

- Why do women commit fewer crimes than men?

- Why are women more likely to conform to social norms than men?

- Is there anything distinctive about women's experience as offenders and as victims of crime?

- Are women treated differently than men by the criminal justice system?

Today, there is widespread agreement that the sociology of crime and deviance must take account of gender. This means examining both women and crime *and* men and crime. And this also means asking a new set of questions about men – for example, what is the relationship between crime and masculinity?

10.2 Gender and offending

In 2002, over 481,000 people in England and Wales were cautioned for, or found guilty of, criminal offences. Just over four-fifths were men (Social Trends, 2004). These figures are drawn from official statistics based on police and court records. As outlined in Unit 2, there are a number of problems with the reliability and validity of official statistics (see pages 207-214).

Self-report studies provide an alternative source of information for gender differences in offending. For example, the 1998/9 Youth Lifestyles Survey, based on 4,849 12 to 30-year-olds, found that males were two-and-a-half times more likely to have offended in the last year than females (Home Office, 2003). However, there are also problems with self-report studies (see pages 213-214).

Despite these problems, all sources of data point in the same direction. As a result, there is now general agreement that:

- Significantly more men than women commit crime.
- Men are more likely to commit serious offences.
- Men are more likely to re-offend (Heidensohn, 2002).

Sex role theory

Sex role theory argues that boys and girls are socialised differently and, as a result, boys are more likely to become delinquent. There are a number of versions of this theory.

Edwin Sutherland According to Sutherland (1949), there are two main gender differences in the socialisation process. First, girls are more closely supervised and more strictly controlled. Second, boys are more likely to be encouraged to take risks and to be tough and aggressive. As a result, boys have more opportunity and more inclination to commit crime.

Talcott Parsons According to Parsons (1955), there are clearly defined gender roles in the modern nuclear family. The father performs the instrumental role of leader and provider, the mother performs the expressive role of giving

activity19 gender and offending

Offenders found guilty or cautioned, 2002

England & Wales					Rates per 10,000 population
	10-15	16-24	25-34	35 and over	All aged 10 and over (thousands)
Males					
Theft and handling stolen goods	86	183	104	17	131.5
Drug offences	18	159	62	9	84.1
Violence against the person	31	77	32	9	51.8
Burglary	29	49	21	2	30.4
Criminal damage	13	18	7	2	12.5
Robbery	6	14	4	0	7.2
Sexual offences	3	4	3	2	5.0
Other offences	11	102	59	12	69.0
All offences	196	606	292	53	391.5
Females					
Theft and handling stolen goods	51	67	32	6	50.1
Drug offences	2	15	9	1	9.8
Violence against the person	11	12	5	1	9.5
Burglary	3	3	1	0	2.1
Criminal damage	2	2	1	0	1.6
Robbery	1	1	0	0	0.9
Sexual offences	0	0	0	0	0.1
Other offences	3	20	13	2	14.4
All offences	74	119	61	12	88.6

Adapted from *Social Trends*, 2004

Shoplifting – according to official statistics, a typical female offence

questions

1 Summarise the data in the table.

2 Briefly outline the problems with official crime statistics.

emotional support and socialising children. These gender roles are rooted in biology since women give birth to and nurse children.

While girls usually have a readily available female role model at home – their mother – boys have less access to a male role model. Largely socialised by their mother, they tend to reject any behaviour seen as feminine and to compulsively pursue masculinity. There is an emphasis on toughness and aggression which can encourage anti-social behaviour and delinquency.

Albert Cohen According to Cohen (1955), socialisation can be a difficult process for boys. Without a readily available male role model, they can experience anxiety about their identity as young *men*. One solution to this is the all-male peer group or street gang. In these social contexts, aspects of masculinity can be expressed and rewarded. Being tough, taking risks and breaking rules can help to confirm a masculine identity. But, they can also encourage delinquent behaviour.

Evaluation Sex role theory is an early sociological theory which attempted to explain gender differences in crime. It has the advantage of explaining these differences in terms of learned behaviour rather than earlier theories which looked for explanations in biological differences between males and females. However, something of this earlier approach remains in the work of Talcott Parsons. He sees women as biologically adapted to a nurturing and caring role. As a result, they are mainly responsible for socialising children.

Feminist writers criticise sex role theory for failing to consider gender differences in power – in particular, the power that men have over women. This view is considered in the following section.

10.3 Feminist perspectives

Feminist perspectives start from the view that society is patriarchal. It follows that the behaviour of women can only be understood in the context of male dominance. In terms of women and crime, this viewpoint leads to new questions and new answers. The research examined in this section combines feminist insights with control theory.

Female crime as rational

Pat Carlen (1990) argues that women's crimes are largely 'the crimes of the powerless'. Many women who commit crimes are powerless in various ways. They often live in poverty with little power to change their situation. As children, many have been harshly supervised, and sometimes abused by their fathers. And as adults, they have often lived under the dominance of male partners who, in some cases, used violence in an attempt to assert control.

Carlen (1988) conducted in-depth interviews with 39 working-class women aged 15-46 convicted of a range of offences. She draws on control theory, arguing that people turn to crime if the advantages outweigh the disadvantages. For the women Carlen interviewed, crime appeared as a rational choice. Their experience of low-paid work and unemployment had not led to the standard of living and lifestyle they had hoped for. And their experience of family life, both as children and adults, had been unhappy and unfulfilling.

Unrewarded in the family and in the workplace and with little power to change their situation by legitimate means, they saw crime as a rational alternative. And the crimes they typically committed were seen as a rational choice. In Carlen's words, 'Property crime was *chosen* because certain types (eg, shoplifting and cheque fraud) were seen to be "easy" '.

Evaluation Carlen's sample of 39 women is too small to generalise from. However, her research suggests that conformity to social norms tends to break down when the rewards for doing so are largely absent. But, as the next section indicates, it may be much more difficult for women than men to deviate from society's norms.

Conformity and control

According to Frances Heidensohn (1996, 2002), the most striking thing about women's behaviour is their conformity to social norms. Drawing on control theory, she argues that women have more to lose than men if they deviate from norms. And drawing on feminism, she argues that in a male-dominated society, the control of women by men discourages deviance from norms.

Home and family Women still have the primary responsibility for raising children and domestic work. Their commitment to raising children and to family life also involves a commitment to conformity – to the traditional mother-housewife role and to socialising children in terms of society's norms and values. From the point of view of control theory, women have more to lose than men by deviating from social norms.

Women have been socialised to conform. Girls are more strictly supervised than boys, given less freedom and expected to perform more household duties. And these controls, duties and expectations continue into adult life. As adults, women are not only controlled by their childhood socialisation but also by their male partners. Women who challenge their traditional roles are often brought into line by men's financial and physical power. According to Heidensohn, wife-battering is an 'assertion of patriarchal authority'.

Women's socialisation and domestic responsibilities plus the controls imposed on them by men discourage deviance from social norms. Their lives are centred on the private sphere of the home and they have less freedom to go out. As a result, they have less inclination, less time and fewer opportunities to commit crime.

Beyond the home Outside the home, women's freedom to come and go as they please and to deviate from social norms is limited in various ways. For example, women are often reluctant to go out after dark, particularly in inner-city areas, for fear of attack or rape by men. And they are less likely to deviate from norms of respectability for fear of being labelled a slag or a bitch.

At work, men are more likely than women to be in control – in managerial and supervisory roles. And surveys indicate that sexual harassment is common in the workplace. This is a further indication of male power and control as it is often experienced as intimidating by women.

Both inside and outside the home, there is pressure for women to conform – pressure which is reinforced by male power.

Evaluation Heidensohn's combination of a feminist perspective with control theory provides an explanation for women's conformity to social norms and for their low crime rate. However, critics have made the following points. First, it presents women as passive, as simply accepting their situation (Naffine, 1987). The feminist movement from the 1960s onwards suggests a rather different picture. Second, Heidensohn makes sweeping generalisations about women and men. In doing so, she fails to recognise the differences between women, and the differences between men (Walklate, 2003).

10.4 Crime and masculinities

Research into gender and crime over the last 25 years has been mainly concerned with women and crime. Feminists focused on women, and men enter the picture in terms of their control over women.

Researchers now recognise that there is another side to the gender issue – men and masculinity. Why are men more likely to commit crime than women? Is there a relationship between male crime and masculinity?

Men, masculinities and crime

James Messerschmidt (1993) has presented the most influential and comprehensive view of the relationship between masculinity and crime.

Accomplishing masculinity Messerschmidt starts from the position that gender identity is a vital part of the individual's sense of self. It is something that people accomplish – they are continuously constructing, expressing and presenting themselves as masculine or feminine. And, in the case of males, crime can be a resource for accomplishing masculinity. It can be used in the construction of masculinity so that men can express their masculinity both to themselves and to others.

Masculinities Messerschmidt identifies a number of different masculinities which are shaped by social class, ethnicity, age and sexual orientation. Men's position in society provides differential access to power and resources which leads to different constructions and expressions of masculinity. And this, in turn, leads to different types of crime.

Messerschmidt refers to the dominant form of masculinity as *hegemonic masculinity*. It is the 'idealised' form which is 'defined through work in the paid-labour market, the subordination of women, heterosexism and the driven and uncontrollable sexuality of men'. This is the form of masculinity that most men seek to accomplish. However, for various reasons, some men are unable to, or do not wish to, accomplish this dominant form.

Messerchmidt calls the alternatives to hegemonic masculinity *subordinated masculinities*. They include masculinities which develop in some ethnic minority and lower-class groups, and homosexual masculinity.

Crime, masculinities and youth Young middle-class White males are usually able to demonstrate some of the characteristics of hegemonic masculinity through success at school and college. However, this comes at a price – subordination to teachers. Some assert their masculinity outside school through vandalism, petty theft and heavy drinking.

White working-class young men are less likely to be successful in education. They sometimes resist school and construct their masculinity around physical aggression, anti-social behaviour, delinquency and, in some cases, violence towards gays and members of ethnic minority groups.

Lower working-class young men from ethnic minority groups with little expectation of educational success or secure employment sometimes assert their masculinity in street gangs. With little chance of accomplishing hegemonic masculinity by legitimate means, they are more likely to turn to robbery and serious property crime.

Social class and masculinities Even middle-class males who have the resources to accomplish hegemonic masculinity use crime to express masculinity. Messerschmidt argues that white-collar and corporate crime are not simply a means for profiting the individual or the organisation. They are also a means of accomplishing hegemonic masculinity – as a successful breadwinner and as an aggressive, risk-taking male.

Working-class crime in the workplace can also be seen as a means of accomplishing masculinity. Workers sometimes resist the authority of management by theft and industrial sabotage.

Ethnicity and masculinities Messerschmidt uses the example of African Americans to illustrate a subordinated masculinity. Lower-class African-American males often lack the resources to accomplish hegemonic masculinity. The pimp and the hustler – long-established roles in African-American subculture – offer an alternative subordinate masculinity.

The pimp dominates a string of prostitutes and lives off their earnings. With his 'pimp walk', soft-top Cadillac, diamond rings, gold chains, and prowess with and power over women, the pimp demonstrates a highly visible alternative masculinity to himself and others.

Evaluation Messerschmidt has provided a sophisticated analysis of the relationship between masculinities, age, class, ethnicity and crime. His focus on accomplishing masculinity is an original explanation of the high level of male crime. However, there are a number of criticisms of his research.

- First, it over-predicts crime (Jones, 1998). For example, pimps are the exception rather than the rule in low-income African-American areas. And why do only a minority of men from all social classes and ethnic groups feel the need to assert their masculinity through crime?

- Second, the claim that hegemonic masculinity is the ideal which all men aspire to is questionable. It can be seen as little more than a popular stereotype. Masculinities may be considerably more complex and diverse than Messerschmidt claims.

- Third, Messerschmidt uses the idea of masculinity to explain practically every crime that men commit – theft, burglary, rape, domestic violence, joy-riding, white-collar and corporate crime. According to Richard Collier (1998), this stretches the explanatory power of the concept of masculinity much too far.

- Fourth, there is an element of tautology in Messerschmidt's argument – in other words, his argument tends to be circular. Masculinity explains male crimes. How do we know? Because males have committed those crimes.

key terms

Hegemonic masculinity The dominant and ideal form of masculinity which most men seek to accomplish.
Subordinated masculinities Less desirable forms of masculinity which some men seek to accomplish because they lack the resourses required for hegemonic masculinity.

Masculinity and crime in late modern society

A crisis of masculinity Late modern societies have seen an economic transformation. There has been a rapid decline in manufacturing industry and a rise in service industries. This has resulted in a fall in unskilled and semi-skilled manual jobs and a rise in working-class male unemployment.

These changes have been particularly unsettling for men who, in the past, were able to express their masculinity through physical labour. In addition, unemployment and intermittent employment mean they can no longer accomplish their masculinity through full-time work and support for their families. This can lead to a *crisis of masculinity* (Campbell, 1993).

According to Jock Young (1999), this crisis is particularly acute for young men who have never had a job and have little prospect of getting one. They are 'cast adrift' and are not even suitable marriage material.

Some respond by creating subcultures of machismo which glorify an exaggerated form of masculinity – toughness, aggression, sexual prowess, and respect for manhood backed up by physical strength and, in some cases, by guns. This can be seen in gangsta rap where women are portrayed as whores, bitches and sex objects to be exploited, where pimping, hustling and gun law are expressions of masculinity, and men earn respect by defending their reputation with violence.

The night-time economy In recent years there has been a massive expansion in the night-time leisure economies of many towns and cities in Britain. Local authorities, anxious to regenerate their communities through attracting private investment to the inner cities, have adopted increasingly liberal attitudes towards alcohol and entertainment licensing. Night clubs have mushroomed, with large numbers of young people flocking to them.

A two year research project studied this development (Hobbs et al., 2003). The researchers used both participant observation and interviews with bouncers, police, council staff, night-club managers, licensees and other key players in order to understand how the night-club economy worked. To facilitate access, three of the project team trained as bouncers and one of the research assistants worked underground as a bouncer.

According to Dick Hobbs, 'The night time economy is currently an unplanned largely unregulated zone where alcohol-related violence and disorder is rife'. Any control that does exist is mainly in the hands of bouncers who fill the void left by the police. The activities of these men (only 7% are women) are not effectively regulated and order is maintained by frequent threat or use of violence. While being a hard man has always been a source of status in many working-class communities, in the night-time economy it becomes a means of earning a living as a bouncer. What is more, being a bouncer provides opportunities for engaging in lucrative criminal activities. These include protection rackets, drug dealing, and importing duty-free cigarettes and alcohol and selling them at cut-price to clubs and pubs. With the loss of many working-class jobs, these men assert their masculinity through being hard, working as bouncers and, in many cases, getting involved in criminal activities.

Joy-riding A study of crime and riots in the early 1990s on two deprived council estates in Newcastle-upon-Tyne and Oxford points to the pleasures gained by working-class young men asserting their masculinity through joy-riding (Campbell, 1993). High unemployment on these estates meant that many young men could not look forward to a secure job that would enable them to support a family. They asserted their masculinity by manufacturing excitement through joy-riding and ram raiding. Brought up in a consumer society where high performance cars are associated with power and status, they drove stolen cars at speed around local estates and in some cases smashed them into shops to gain entry. This often led to a car chase with the police which added to the excitement.

Evaluation The case studies examined above relate to specific contexts. As a result, we cannot generalise from these studies. However, they do suggest that some working-class men turn to crime to accomplish masculinity. While research on masculinities and crime indicates there is a link between the two, it has yet to demonstrate that most, let alone all, male crime can be explained in these terms.

10.5 Gender and the criminal justice system

Is there a gender bias in the criminal justice system? Are women and men treated differently by the police and the courts? There are two schools of thought on this issue.

The chivalry thesis Chivalry means treating others, especially women, with courtesy, sympathy and respect. The *chivalry thesis* states that women are treated more leniently than men by the criminal justice system. Male chivalry means that the police are less likely to charge women and the courts will tend to give women lighter sentences, even when they have committed the same offences as men.

Double deviance This argument states that women are treated more harshly by the criminal justice system. This is because they are doubly deviant – they have deviated from social norms by breaking the law and deviated from gender norms which state how women should behave.

Many women feel they have been treated harshly by the criminal justice system. They see it as a male-dominated institution and feel their treatment has been unsympathetic and unjust (Heidensohn, 2002).

The evidence

Official statistics reveal the following.

- After arrest, women are more likely than men to be cautioned rather than charged.
- They are less likely than men to be remanded in custody or committed for trial.
- Women offenders are more likely than men to be discharged or given a community sentence and less likely to be fined or sentenced to prison.
- Women sent to prison receive shorter sentences than men (Home Office, 2003).

At first sight, these figures suggest that the criminal justice system treats women more leniently. They appear to

activity20 subordinated masculinities

Item A Gangsta rap

Gang members in Los Angeles

Tupac Shakur

The rapper Tupac Shakur died from gunshot wounds at the age of 25. He now sells more CDs dead than alive. He often used to pose with guns and had THUG LIFE tattooed on his stomach.

Gangsta rap reflects the violence of low-income ghetto areas. Rappers boast about using guns to defend their reputation, to settle scores and to avenge murdered 'homies' (friends from the neighbourhood). In one rap, Ice Cube refers to himself as a 'natural born killer' and states:

'When I grab my sawnoff (shotgun)
Niggas get hauled off.'

Women are often referred to as 'hoes' (whores) and bitches. Rappers boast about their sexual exploits and their prowess with women.

When work is mentioned, it is usually pimping, hustling, dealing in dope and the rewards they bring.

Adapted in part from Light, 1998

Item B Bouncers

Bouncers need to present themselves as hyper-masculine. This form of masculinity has the following characteristics: toughness, autonomy, vitality, power, dominance, respect, honour, pride, and of course violence. Body size and shape are accentuated, and stance, clothing, facial expression and general demeanour are often tailored to display the mental and physical toughness required.

A licensee of a pub gives the following description of a bouncer. 'I already knew Jimmy for a few years. I knew he did the doors at some of the pubs in town so I just asked him to call in. I just picked a time when I knew some of the local lads would be in. We talked for about five minutes and you can hear them go quiet then start talking about him. After a few minutes, he just walked over and said 'all right' to them, and that he was working here now. They didn't say a fucking word. They knew who he was obviously, everyone knows Jimmy don't they? It's not like you can miss him. And that's it. I gave him twenty quid that first time, and fifteen quid a week after that. He gave me his mobile number to "phone if there's any bother" and he comes in every now and then. With someone like Jimmy doing that, I don't need a bouncer on at all really. I'm still here all the time and I keep a pickaxe handle behind the bar.'

Adapted from Hobbs et al., 2003

Bouncer outside the Chunnel club in London

questions

1 How do Items A and B illustrate subordinate masculinities?
2 Suggest reasons why these masculinities are developed by men from particular social groups.

provide support for the chivalry thesis. Matters are not that simple, however. To compare like with like, we need to take into account the seriousness of the offence and differences in offending history. The higher cautioning rate for women and the lower likelihood of being remanded in custody or sent for trial mainly reflect differences in the type of offence and past offences (Home Office, 2003). Women's offences tend to be less serious and women are less likely to have a criminal record. This suggests that there is no systematic bias for or against women.

Sentencing The evidence on sentencing is conflicting. Farrington and Morris (1983) examined sentencing in Cambridge City Magistrates Court over a one year period. They found that men and women received similar sentences, once relevant factors such as the seriousness of the offence and the offender's previous record were taken into account. By contrast, Hood's (1992) study of sentencing in Crown Courts in the West Midlands found that women were treated much more leniently, even when relevant factors were taken into account. A review of a range of studies on sentencing found that, on the whole, women and men received similar treatment. However, there is some evidence of women being treated more leniently, including avoiding imprisonment where men would not (Cavadino & Dignan, 2002).

There is evidence that courts treat some women differently than other women. This appears to be based on the view that the primary role of women is as a mother. On the basis of interviews with Scottish sheriffs (judges), Carlen (1983) concludes that women who are considered good mothers are unlikely to be imprisoned. Such leniency towards some women was accompanied by harshness towards others. Women who were not considered good mothers and whose children were in care received harsher sentences, including imprisonment.

Evaluation It is not possible to reach a definite conclusion about gender bias in the criminal justice system. There are clearly differences in the likelihood of men and women being sent for trial and placed in custody. However, many but not all of these differences disappear when the severity of the offence and the offender's record are taken into account. In addition, there is evidence that some women are treated more harshly than others on the basis of how well they are judged to have performed their role as mothers.

10.6 Gender and victimisation

Victim surveys consistently show that men are more likely to be the victim of violent crime than women. The British Crime Survey 2002/03 reveals that 5.3% of adult males and 2.9% of adult females had been the victim of at least one violent crime in the preceding twelve months (Home Office, 2003). The type of violent crime men and women experience tends to differ. Men are more likely to be the victims of violent attacks by strangers and other men in

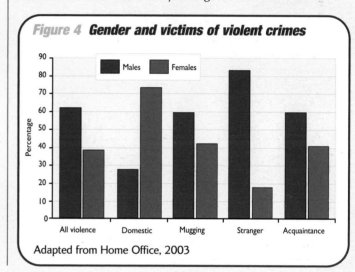

Figure 4 **Gender and victims of violent crimes**

Adapted from Home Office, 2003

summary

1. Available sources of data indicate that:
   - Significantly more men than women commit crime.
   - Men are more likely to commit serious offences.
   - Men are more likely to re-offend.

2. Sex role theory argues that boys and girls are socialised differently and, as a result, boys are more likely to become delinquent.

3. Feminists argue that the behaviour of women can only be understood in the context of male dominance.

4. Pat Carlen argues that women's crimes are largely 'crimes of the powerless'. She draws on control theory, arguing that working-class women turn to crime when the advantages appear to outweigh the disadvantages.

5. According to Frances Heidensohn, the most striking thing about women's behaviour is their conformity to social norms. She explains this in terms of their socialisation and control over their behaviour by men. As a result, women have less inclination, time and opportunity for crime.

6. James Messerschmidt argues that male crime can be seen as an expression and assertion of masculinity.

7. He distinguishes between hegemonic masculinity – the ideal which most men strive for – and subordinate masculinities – constructed by men who lack the resources to accomplish the dominant form.

8. Masculinities are shaped by class, ethnicity, age and sexual orientation. Different masculinities lead to different forms of crime.

9. A number of researchers argue that there is a 'crisis of masculinity' in late modern society. This is due to the decline in manufacturing and the resulting loss of many unskilled and semi-skilled jobs. As a result, some men have turned to crime in order to assert their masculinity.

10. At first sight, it appears that men and women are treated differently by the criminal justice system. However, when the seriousness of offences and the history of offending are taken into account, most of these differences disappear.

11. There is evidence that some women are treated more leniently than others on the basis of how well they are judged to have performed their role as mothers.

12. Men are more likely to be the victims of violent crime. Women are more likely to be the victims of domestic violence and sexual violence.

13. Woman tend to express more fear of violent crime than men. This places constraints on their behaviour.

public spaces. Women, on the other hand, are more likely to know their attacker and to be victimised at home. The British Crime Survey 2002/03 reveals that 73% of domestic violence incidents were against women. In the case of homicide, 46% of female victims were killed by current or former partners compared to only 5% of males. Women are also more likely to be the victims of sexual violence. According to the British Crime Survey 2000, around one woman in 20 has been raped since the age of 16, with strangers accounting for only 8% of those rapes (Home Office, 2003).

Feminism and women's victimisation Feminists have highlighted the extent and seriousness of crimes such as rape and domestic violence. These crimes, which usually involve women as victims, are seen to reflect male power in a patriarchal society. They differ from most other crimes since they often continue over long periods of time. Male violence against women is not limited to the home – it also occurs at work and in public places.

Women tend to express more fear of violent crime than men, despite the fact that they are less likely to be victims. This can place constraints on women's lives. They may avoid going out after dark for fear of being attacked. And they may take measures to dress and behave in ways that prevent them being seen as provocative by men (Stanko, 1994).

Unit 11 *Suicide*

key issues

1 What are the main sociological studies of suicide?

2 What methodologies do they use?

3 What are the strengths and weaknesses of each methodological approach?

Suicide has already been examined to illustrate various methodological approaches in Chapter 3 (see pages 131-132 and 137-139). This unit looks at suicide in more detail. For convenience, some of the material in Chapter 3 will also be covered here.

11.1 Durkheim's study of suicide

Published in 1897, Emile Durkheim's *Suicide: A Study in Sociology* was the first major sociological study of suicide. Keen to establish the value of a sociological approach, Durkheim chose suicide, a highly personal act, which seemed more suited to a psychological rather than a sociological explanation. If he could show that suicide was linked to society, rather than simply to individual psychology, then the value of sociology would be established.

The suicide rate

The *suicide rate* is the number of people who kill themselves in a particular society, or in a group within a society, in a given period of time. Durkheim based his research on the rate of suicide per million inhabitants in different European countries. The statistics revealed a number of patterns.

- First, suicide rates varied between different countries (see Table 3). For example, they were generally higher in Protestant countries than Catholic countries.
- Second, when suicide rates across Europe rose and fell, the differences between countries generally remained (see Table 3).

- Third, the rise and fall in suicide rates appeared to be related to social factors. For example, the rates rose during periods of economic recession and, more surprisingly, during periods of economic prosperity. And they fell during times of war and political upheaval.
- Fourth, there were variations in the suicide rate between different groups within the same society. For example, the unmarried and the childless had higher rates than the married and those with children.

Table 3 Rates of suicide per million inhabitants in European countries

Country	1866-70	1871-75	1874-78
Italy	30	35	38
Austria	78	94	130
Saxony	293	267	334

Adapted from Durkheim, 1970

Explaining suicide rates

Suicide and society According to Durkheim, patterns in suicide rates could not be explained in terms of the psychology of individuals. Instead, the answer lay in society – in the relationship *between* individuals and society and, in particular, the degree to which they were integrated into social groups and the degree to which they were regulated by society.

Integration In a strongly integrated society, individuals are bound together by shared norms and values. The level of integration can be measured by the strength and number of relationships between individuals. In a strongly integrated society, people have powerful duties and obligations to each other. Levels of integration vary between societies and between groups within society.

Regulation Similarly, regulation varies between societies and groups within society. Regulation refers to the control which society has over its members – to the degree to which society regulates their behaviour.

Without regulation, people's desires are limitless. Society places limits on their desires by defining specific goals and the means of obtaining them.

Social order Durkheim, like all functionalists, was concerned with the following questions. How was society held together? How was social order maintained? What constituted a 'healthy' society? Durkheim's answer was appropriate levels of integration and regulation.

Too little integration and regulation would result in social disorder. The norms and values which bound individuals together and the regulations which controlled their behaviour would be weakened. Society would become unbalanced. The results would be 'pathological' or harmful to society.

Durkheim believed that this was happening in modern society. And the rise in suicide rates in European countries was one indication of this trend.

Too much integration and regulation was also harmful to society. If norms and values are too strong, they would prevent the innovation and change necessary for a healthy society.

Types of suicide

Durkheim identified four types of suicide, each of which is related to the level of integration or the level of regulation in society.

- Altruistic suicide occurs when the level of integration is too strong.
- Egoistic suicide occurs when the level of integration is too weak.
- Fatalistic suicide occurs when the level of regulation is too strong.
- Anomic suicide occurs when the level of regulation is too weak.

The relationship between types of suicide and levels of integration and regulation is illustrated in Figure 5.

Altruistic suicide Altruism means acting unselfishly, directed by a concern for others even if this is harmful to oneself. Altruistic suicide occurs when individuals are so strongly integrated into society that they take their own lives out of a sense of duty. They are so powerfully committed to the norms and values of society that they make the ultimate sacrifice.

Altruistic suicide can be seen in traditional Hindu India where a wife would throw herself on to her husband's funeral pyre and burn to death. It can also be seen in some nomadic hunting and gathering bands who followed the seasonal movements of game. Those who were too old and frail to travel stayed behind and died for the benefit of the group. In traditional Inuit (Eskimo) society, the elderly died in the snow as the band moved on in order to survive.

According to Durkheim, altruistic suicide is rare in

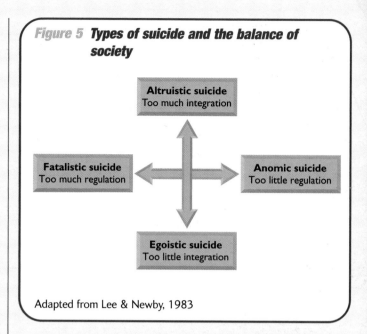

Figure 5 *Types of suicide and the balance of society*

Altruistic suicide
Too much integration

Fatalistic suicide
Too much regulation

Anomic suicide
Too little regulation

Egoistic suicide
Too little integration

Adapted from Lee & Newby, 1983

modern societies. However, it does occur. For example, in World War II, Japanese kamikaze pilots flew planes packed with explosives on to the decks of American warships. They committed suicide for the benefit of their countrymen.

Fatalistic suicide Fatalism is a belief that nothing can be done to change the situation. Fatalistic suicide is characteristic of societies where there is too much regulation, too much control of individuals. Slavery is an example of excessive regulation – often there was little or nothing slaves could do to change their situation. Suicide offered an escape. Durkheim argued that this accounts for the high rate of suicide which occurred when people's hopes and desires were crushed by 'oppressive discipline'.

Egoistic suicide The word ego refers to the self. Egoistic suicide occurs when there is too little integration, when the individual increasingly stands alone. It results from a weakening of the ties which bind individuals to social groups.

Durkheim saw egoistic suicide as characteristic of societies which were making the transition to modernity. These societies have an 'excess of individualism' – people tend to think primarily of themselves, they are less concerned with their duties and obligations to others, and with the opinions of others. The lower their level of integration with social groups, the more likely they will be to commit suicide. They have fewer obligations to others. And there is less moral pressure from others to prevent them from taking their own life.

Durkheim provides the following evidence to support his views. Unmarried people have the highest rate of suicide, followed by married people without children. And the more children married people have, the less likely they are to commit suicide. Thus, the larger the family group, the higher the level of social integration and the less vulnerable people are to suicide.

Protestant countries have a higher rate of suicide than

Catholic countries. According to Durkheim, the Catholic religion integrates its members more strongly into a religious community.

The suicide rate falls during times of war and political upheaval. At times like these, the level of integration in society increases as people draw together to focus on a common cause.

In Durkheim's words, when the level of integration is low, 'The individual yields to the slightest shock of circumstances because the state of society has made him ready prey to suicide'.

Anomic suicide Like egoistic suicide, anomic suicide mainly occurs in modern societies. It results from a lack of regulation of people's desires and expectations.

Modern societies are characterised by rapid social change which disrupts the norms governing behaviour. The result is a situation of anomie or normlessness. There is no ceiling on people's desires, no limits to their expectations. Without norms to govern what people can reasonably expect from life, desires are uncontrolled and can never be satisfied. Living in a moral vacuum without sufficient regulation, people are more vulnerable to suicide.

Anomie is particularly acute in times of rapid economic change – in times of 'boom' and 'bust', prosperity and recession. This leads to changes in people's circumstances which further disrupt the norms governing their behaviour. Durkheim found that suicide rates rose with rapid upturns and downturns in the economy.

Conclusion Durkheim claimed that both suicide rates and types of suicide were shaped by social factors – by the

levels of integration and regulation in society. He concluded that, 'There is therefore, for each people [society], a collective force of a definite amount of energy, impelling men to self-destruction'.

Durkheim's methodology

Social facts In *The Rules of the Sociological Method*, Durkheim outlined the rules that sociologists should follow in order for sociology to become a science. In his words, 'The first and most fundamental rule is: Consider social facts as things'. Social facts include the norms, values and institutions of society (see pages 165-166).

Social facts exist outside individuals – they are over and above them. However, they become part of them via the socialisation process during which they learn society's norms and values. Norms and values are shared, they are

activity21 *classifying suicide*

Item A *Types of suicide*

Death from poison – living alone in a one-room attic

A Baltimore banker who has lost all his money in a recession blows himself up.

A Japanese servant, pretending to be his master, cuts out his entrails and throws them at the enemy, so allowing his master to escape.

Haitians kill themselves and their children to escape from the cruelty of their Spanish masters.

Item B *Problems of classification*

Suicide bombings can be categorised as an extreme form of political protest. They appear to fit into Durkheim's category of *altruistic* suicide – acts by people who are so highly integrated into a group that they are prepared to sacrifice their own lives to further its cause. The hopelessness experienced by some might also give ground for interpreting these suicides as *fatalistic* – the actions of people who feel trapped in a repressive regime, which is how Palestinians would undoubtedly describe the state of Israel. Alternatively, their suicides could also be described as *anomic* – the result of living in a society undergoing dramatic and disorientating social change. They could be *egoistic*, if the desire for reward in Paradise is the bombers' highest motivation.

Adapted from Swale, 2004

A Palestinian suicide bomber

questions

1 a) Match each of the pictures in Item A with one of Durkheim's four types of suicide – altruistic, egoistic, fatalistic and anomic.

  b) Give reasons for your answers.

2 a) How does Item B challenge Durkheim's classification of suicide?

  b) Choose one of the pictures from Item A and suggest how it might fit into more than one of Durkheim's suicide types.

not simply personal beliefs. Because of this, Durkheim argued that 'collective ways of acting and thinking have a reality outside the individuals'. As such, they are social facts and can be studied 'objectively as external things'.

Just as the behaviour of matter is directed by external forces, so the behaviour of human beings is directed by external forces – by social facts. In view of this, human behaviour can be studied using the methodology of natural sciences. And in this way, sociology can become a science.

The social facts of suicide Suicide rates are social facts. And they are determined by other social facts – by levels of integration and regulation in society. These are 'real, living, active forces which, because of the way they determine the individual, prove their independence from him'.

Durkheim found correlations between suicide rates and a range of social facts. He claimed that these correlations indicated causal relationships. For example, an individual's religion, marital status, family size and age can all be used as measures of their level of integration in society. And in each case, the lower the level of integration, the higher the rate of suicide. In Durkheim's words, 'suicide varies inversely with the degree of integration of the social groups of which the individual is a part'.

Durkheim then provided an explanation for this relationship. People are social beings – they have been socialised to participate in society. The lower their level of integration, the less they can do this. Isolated from others, their lives lack meaning and purpose. In Durkheim's words, 'The individual alone is not a sufficient end for his activity. He is too little'. As a result, the individual is vulnerable to suicide.

A science of society Durkheim believed that his research on suicide showed that scientific methodology was appropriate for the study of human society. In his view, he had followed the procedures of the natural sciences and his results showed that 'real laws are discoverable' in the social world, just as they are in the natural world.

Realism or positivism Durkheim's methodology is sometimes described as positivist. Positivists believe that sociology should adopt the methodology of the natural sciences and focus only on directly observable facts. At first sight, this is exactly what Durkheim does. He identifies observable social facts and correlates them with other observable social facts.

However, Durkheim goes further. He identifies other social facts which cannot be directly observed. He refers to these as *social currents*. They cannot be observed and measured in the same way as social facts such as family size and religious beliefs. But they are just as real and they have just as much power over people's behaviour.

Social currents flow through society. In his study of suicide, Durkheim identified four social currents – altruism, fatalism, egoism and anomie. Durkheim's methodology 'involved searching for the invisible underlying causes of the relationships between things that are observed' (Taylor, 1988). In terms of his study of suicide, this meant identifying social currents which were the underlying causes of various types of suicide.

This is a realist rather than a positivist approach. Realists argue that the causes of many of the things we observe lie in underlying structures and processes which cannot be directly observed. From a realist viewpoint, both the natural and social sciences operate in much the same way. In this sense, Durkheim's methodology can be seen as scientific.

Evaluation of Durkheim's research

Many sociologists have enormous respect for Durkheim's study of suicide. However, both his general approach and specific aspects of his research have been criticised.

Suicide statistics Durkheim's study was based on official statistics of suicide. Critics argue that he paid insufficient attention to both their reliability and validity.

Suicide statistics are reliable if coroners – the officials who decide the cause of death – reach the same conclusions. However, one coroner might give a verdict of suicide when the evidence suggests that a person probably took their own life. Another coroner might want more conclusive evidence – for example, a suicide note. Differences in suicide rates between two towns may simply reflect the views of different coroners. The reliability of suicide statistics is therefore questionable (Taylor, 1988).

Statistics are valid if they represent a true and accurate measurement. Coroners have to decide whether a death is a suicide, an accident, or due to natural causes. This can be a difficult judgement. If coroners cannot reach a decision, they give an 'open verdict'. Such verdicts do not form part of the suicide statistics. For these reasons, the validity of suicide statistics is questionable.

The positivist response Positivists accept that much of Durkheim's work is scientific. He quantified a number of social facts. His statistical analysis revealed correlations between them and indicated cause and effect relationships. However, they part company with Durkheim on two main counts.

First, Durkheim sometimes failed to provide an operational definition of social facts – that is a definition which could provide quantifiable data. For example, without an operational definition of social integration, this aspect of Durkheim's theory could not be tested and shown to be true or false (Gibbs & Martin, 1964).

Second, positivists reject Durkheim's realist approach. In particular, they reject his view that causes can be found in underlying structures and processes that cannot be directly observed and measured. From a positivist viewpoint, Durkheim's use of unobservable social currents to explain suicide rates is unacceptable and unscientific.

Further criticisms of Durkheim's methodology are examined in the following sections.

11.2 Suicide – an interpretivist view

The meanings of suicide

From an interpretivist perspective, people act in terms of meanings. Sociologists must therefore interpret the meanings which direct action in order to understand human behaviour.

In *The Social Meanings of Suicide* (1967), Jack Douglas argues that the first step in studying suicide is to interpret how individuals who commit suicide define and give meaning to their action.

Step 1 Douglas admits that this is easier said than done. He suggests the following ways of discovering the meanings which victims give to acts of suicide.

- An analysis of suicide notes if available
- An examination of diaries if kept
- Interviews with those who knew the victim – for example, family and friends

- Building up a biography of the victim
- Analysing the events which immediately preceded the suicide
- Interviews with those who have survived suicide attempts.

According to Douglas, this first step is essential in order to classify suicides into types. He rejects Durkheim's approach, arguing that he imposes definitions on suicides. The resulting classification into types may have little or nothing to do with the meanings that suicide victims give to their actions.

Step 2 The next step is to look for patterns of meaning which are common to a number of suicides. Only if these are found is it possible to classify suicides into different types. Using this method, Douglas claims that the most common types of suicide include the following. In each case, he argues that this is how victims give meaning to their action.

- **Revenge Suicide** is seen as an act of revenge against those who have wronged the victim – for example, to make a former lover feel guilty.
- **A Search for Help Suicide** is seen as a 'cry for help' when all else has failed.
- **Escape Suicide** is seen as an escape from a life which has become unbearable.
- **Repentance Suicide** is seen as an act of repentance, a means of expressing sorrow for wrongdoing and an attempt to put it right.
- **Self-punishment Suicide** is seen as a way of punishing oneself for misdeeds – a self-imposed penalty.

Step 3 The third step is to link these patterns of meaning with the wider beliefs of the culture. For example, in Western culture, suicide is seen as an act of desperation when all else fails. In other cultures it is expected and accepted in certain situations – for example, the suicide of the elderly in nomadic hunting and gathering bands.

Apart from making a few suggestions, Douglas doesn't take Step 3 any further.

Suicide statistics Douglas criticises Durkheim for largely accepting the reliability and validity of official statistics on suicide. He argues that suicide statistics are the result of negotiated meanings and a complex series of social interactions. For example, the family and friends of the victim may do their best to conceal his or her death as suicide. And this, in turn, may influence the coroner to deliver a verdict of accidental death or death by natural causes.

Successful concealment is most likely when the suicide victim is highly integrated into a social group. Friends and family will be concerned to protect the deceased's reputation and standing in the community. As a result, correlations which indicate a relationship between low suicide rates and high integration may simply reflect a link between successful concealment and high integration.

Douglas maintains that an examination of the negotiated meanings which accompany a suicide death are essential for an understanding of suicide statistics. And this, he argues, is what Durkheim failed to do.

Evaluation Jack Douglas offers an alternative view of suicide. It is an act which is defined and given meaning by the victim, their family, friends and acquaintances, and the officials whose job it is to make a judgement on the cause of death. And suicide statistics are socially constructed from these definitions and meanings, and from the negotiations of those involved.

However, as Steve Taylor (1988) argues, there is a contradiction in Douglas's work. At times, Douglas suggests that it is possible for the researcher to discover whether a death really was suicide. If so, it should be possible to produce valid suicide statistics and a valid suicide rate. And from this, it should be possible to discover the causes of suicide.

At other times, Douglas implies that suicide is nothing more than the meanings given to particular deaths. If so, there are no such things as real, objective suicide acts or suicide rates. The job of the sociologist is simply to discover the meanings which people use to define suicide. And there is no reality beyond these meanings.

Discovering suicide

In *Discovering Suicide* (1978), J. Maxwell Atkinson takes the interpretivist position to its extreme. He states quite categorically that suicide is simply a meaning and there is no reality beyond that meaning. This is sometimes known as a *phenomenological* approach. It argues that the phenomenon, the 'thing' being studied, must be studied in its own right. In this case, suicide is nothing more than a meaning and must be treated as such. Suicide statistics are not right or wrong, they simply are. And the job of the sociologist is to discover the meanings used to define suicide and to find out how those meanings are constructed. In Atkinson's words, the question which should direct a sociological investigation of suicide is 'How do deaths get categorised as suicide?'

Research methods Atkinson's research examined the ways in which coroners and coroner's officers classified deaths. It was based on observations of inquests, interviews with coroners in three different towns, an examination of a coroner's records and observations of a coroner's officer at work. Atkinson claims that his findings show that coroners have a 'common-sense theory' of suicide. If the facts fit the theory, then a verdict of suicide is likely.

Primary cues According to Atkinson, coroners begin by looking for 'primary cues' which appear to indicate suicide. They include the following.

- The existence of suicide notes and/or reports of threats of suicide.
- The type of death – 'typical suicide deaths' include gassing, hanging, drowning and drug overdose. Road deaths are unlikely to be seen as suicides.

- The place and circumstances of death – an individual found shot to death in a car parked on a deserted country lane is more likely to be seen as a suicide victim than somebody who shot themselves while climbing over a fence on a pheasant shoot. And gassing is more likely to be seen as suicide if windows and doors have been sealed.

Secondary cues These include the life history of the deceased. According to Atkinson, coroners have a picture of a 'typical suicide biography'. It includes the following.

- A history of mental illness, particularly of depression
- A disturbed childhood
- A recent loss – a divorce or death of a loved one
- Few if any friends
- Financial difficulties
- Problems at work.

Categorising suicide According to Atkinson, if the circumstances of death and the life history of the deceased fit the 'typical suicide death' and the 'typical suicide biography' then a verdict of suicide is likely.

Coroners' common-sense theory of suicide contains an explanation of suicide. For example, if the deceased is friendless, has a history of depression and financial difficulties, then they may feel that life is not worth living and commit suicide. In some respects, this is similar to the theories of suicide put forward by sociologists. For example, Durkheim's socially isolated individual fits neatly into the coroners' theory.

According to Atkinson, this comes as no surprise. Sociologists are simply uncovering the meanings used by coroners to reach a verdict of suicide. Since social isolation is seen by coroners as a reason for suicide, then suicide statistics will contain a high proportion of socially isolated individuals.

Evaluation Atkinson's work is a valuable contribution to the study of suicide. He has indicated how coroners see and define particular deaths as suicide. And he has provided evidence to support his claims. However, there are two main criticisms of his research.

First, how come coroners appear to share the same common-sense theories of suicide? Where do the meanings they use to define suicide come from? Atkinson fails to answer these questions. For example, it could be argued that coroners' theories are derived from ideas about suicide in the wider culture.

Second, as Barry Hindess (1973) argues, if suicide statistics are simply based on the interpretations of coroners, then research findings are simply based on the interpretations of sociologists. In terms of Atkinson's logic, the interpretations of coroners are neither right nor wrong, they just are, and the same applies to the interpretations of sociologists.

According to Hindess, this means that there is no 'possibility of an objective knowledge of society'. If this is the case, sociologists may as well pack up and go home.

activity22 interpreting suicide

Item A **Terminal illness**

A young man jumps to his death suffering from an incurable disease.

Item B **Salvation**

A young woman burns to death praying for forgiveness for her sins.

Item C **Reasons for suicide**

A young man killed himself because his bride of four months wanted a divorce so she could marry his brother. He left a message to his wife which began, 'I used to love you, but I die hating you and my brother too'. The day before he died, he said to his wife and brother, 'I can do you more harm dead than alive'.

Adapted from Douglas, 1967

Item D **Contemplating suicide**

Item E **Homeless, friendless, deserted**

The Maniac Father and The Convict Brother Are Gone - The Poor Girl, Homeless, Friendless, Deserted, Destitute and Gin Mad, Commits Self Murder.

questions

1 Which of Douglas's types of suicide do Items A, B and C illustrate?
2 How does Item D illustrate 'typical suicide deaths'?
3 How does Item E indicate a 'typical suicide biography'?

11.3 Suicide – a realist approach

This section looks at the work of the British sociologist Steve Taylor (1982, 1988). Taylor draws on both Durkheim's realist perspective and the interpretivist approaches of Douglas and Atkinson.

Like Durkheim, Taylor adopts a realist perspective. He argues that sociologists should look for the 'underlying, unobservable structures and causal processes' which lie behind suicide acts. However, he parts company from Durkheim, claiming that 'official suicide rates are a most inappropriate source of data for sociological research'.

Taylor agrees with Douglas that the case study – studies of particular suicide acts – is the most appropriate research method for studying suicide. He argues that suicide cannot be understood 'without reference to the actor's intentions' and their immediate social situations. And this means examining individual cases. However, he parts company with Douglas's implication and Atkinson's claim that suicide is simply a social construction – a meaning which develops from social interaction. People do kill themselves. And it is the sociologist's job to explain their actions.

Persons under trains

Around five people a month die under London Transport trains. London Transport keeps records of each case and files them under 'People under Trains'. Taylor (1982) studied 32 cases, 17 of which resulted in a verdict of suicide. He attended inquests in coroner's courts in order to discover how these verdicts were reached. His evidence shows that coroners focused on the following aspects of the deceased.

State of mind Coroners call one or two witnesses who knew the dead person. If they indicate that the deceased was depressed, anxious or withdrawn, this was seen as a possible reason for suicide. In general, the closer the witness to the deceased, the more likely they were to resist a suggestion of suicide. For example, one witness insisted that his brother had nothing 'preying on his mind'.

Mental and physical health Coroners tend to see suicide as a result of mental or physical illness. There were eight cases where people had been patients in mental hospitals – seven were recorded as suicides. There were two cases of severe physical illness – both were recorded as suicides.

Social problems Coroners looked for social problems – marital difficulties, failing careers, financial problems. On their own, these were not seen as sufficient causes for suicide. However, combined with negative states of mind or serious illness, they may well be seen as a reason for suicide.

Life history Coroners looked for evidence of a broken home, a failure to form lasting relationships, drug taking and crime. Again, on their own, these were not sufficient for a suicide verdict.

Conclusion Taylor argues that coroners attempt to reconstruct a suicide biography on the basis of their beliefs about the likely causes of suicide. If the deceased fits, then a verdict of suicide is likely.

However, Taylor rejects Atkinson's view that suicide is nothing more than a social construction based on coroners' definitions and meanings. Instead, he argues that these meanings produce a systematic bias in official statistics. As a result, deaths officially defined as suicides are an unrepresentative sample. We should therefore be highly sceptical of the reliability and validity of suicide rates. In view of this, sociologists should look to alternative sources of data for studying suicide.

A realist theory of suicide

Steve Taylor (1982) developed a theory of suicide based on case studies. Using a range of specific cases from a variety of sources, he attempted to discover the underlying causes of suicide.

Defining suicide acts The main sociological studies of suicide have focused on 'genuine' and 'successful' suicides – on people who actually killed themselves. Taylor argues for a broader definition. He notes that the vast majority of suicides fall between two extremes.

- At one extreme are people who are determined to die and make every effort to kill themselves.
- At the other extreme are those who make suicidal gestures and ensure there is little chance of death.

Suicide acts are not simply aimed at death. For example, they may be designed to communicate the person's feelings to others with a real possibility of survival.

Taylor argues that a wider definition of suicide is needed in order to explain the broad spectrum of suicidal behaviour. He therefore defines a suicide act as 'any deliberate act of self-damage, or potential self-damage, where the individual cannot be sure of survival' (Taylor, 1988).

Taylor's realist theory argues that the *underlying* motivation for suicidal behaviour arises from imbalances in individuals' sense of their own identity and in their relationships with others.

Certainty and uncertainty Taylor argues that for an individual to lead a normal life – that is without thoughts of suicide – they require a balance between certainty and uncertainty about themselves and the world around them. Certainty is about stability and the predictability of events,

uncertainty is about change and the unexpected. Taylor hypothesises that suicide is more likely in situations of complete certainty and complete uncertainty.

Submissive suicides/certainty suicides Taylor uses the term *submissive suicide* to refer to suicide acts where the individual feels they know everything worth knowing. They are *certain* about the future – there is no hope, no light at the end of the tunnel. In one sense they are already dead, life is already over.

Suicide acts which stem from certainty are wholehearted, determined attempts to die. The individual is 'embracing death from a firm conviction that nothing further remains in life'. For example, a 62-year-old woman with a terminal illness said, 'I'm through, I'm whipped. I can't take it any longer. I will not die a lingering death'. And an elderly widower who committed suicide to rejoin his dead wife felt that without her he *was* dead.

Thanatation/uncertainty suicide Uncertainty suicides, which Taylor calls Thanatation, are the opposite end of the spectrum from submissive suicides. The individual is tortured by uncertainty – about themselves, their identity, what others think about them and the meaning of their existence. They feel that it's impossible to go on living until this uncertainty is resolved. The individual demands an answer from suicide to reveal whether they are intended to go on living.

Suicide acts which stem from complete uncertainty are a gamble with life. For example, the poet Sylvia Plath deliberately drove her car off the road knowing it *might* kill her. She survived and felt validated, qualified to live – she felt really alive. Similarly, the novelist Graham Greene felt exhilarated when he survived a game of Russian roulette – 'I remember an extraordinary sense of jubilation, as if carnival lights had been switched on in a dark drab street'.

Ectopia and inner-directed suicides Thanatation and submissive suicide result from a state of mind which Taylor calls ectopic. It involves a psychological detachment or moral insulation from the feelings, opinions and actions of others. Sylvia Plath described her sense of detachment as being trapped in a bell jar. In a famous case study of suicide, Ellen West says, 'I feel excluded from all real life. I sit in a glass ball'.

In cases of submissive suicide, this detachment means that others cannot dissuade the individual from what they already know – they cannot shake their certainty. And in Thanatation, detachment means that others cannot tell the individual what they want to know – they cannot remove their uncertainty. Detachment means that Thanatation and submissive suicide are inner-directed acts. They are private and self-contained since those concerned have no sense of attachment to others.

Taylor argues that suicide acts result from 'a *combination* of detachment from others *and* uncertainty about one's existence, *or* a certainty that one's life is over'.

Symphysis and other-directed suicides In situations which Taylor calls symphysic, suicide acts are directed by an overriding attachment to others. The individual has no real existence apart from others, requiring their love and respect as a basis for their sense of self.

Suicide acts directed by symphysic situations are other-directed – they are a communication to somebody. There are two types – appeal suicides and sacrifice suicides.

Appeal suicides These are a cry for help to those to whom they are strongly attached. Appeal suicides are accompanied by considerable uncertainty – the individual has serious doubts about the significance of their existence to others. Appeal suicides are often preceded by warnings, threats and pleas. To end the uncertainty, the individual gambles with their life.

Appeal suicide is illustrated by the following case study. A 19-year-old girl was having an affair with a married man. When he returned to his pregnant wife, she became very distressed and took an overdose of barbiturates. She wandered out on to the street and was taken to hospital. Later, when asked if she intended to kill herself, she said, 'I don't know. Not really I suppose, but I couldn't see any other way of getting through to him.'

Sacrifice suicides Like appeal suicides, sacrifice suicides are directed by a powerful attachment to others. However in this case, there is no uncertainty. The individual is certain that they have no alternative to suicide – they are therefore determined to kill themselves. They have either done something which makes it impossible to live with a person to whom they are deeply attached. Or, the other person has done something to them which completely destroys the relationship.

Taylor illustrates sacrifice suicide with the example, given in Activity 22, of the young man whose wife of four months wanted a divorce so that she could marry his brother. He loved and trusted both his wife and his brother. He saw no way of repairing his relationships with either of them. In his words, left in a note, 'I sentence myself to die for having been fool enough to ever have loved anyone as contemptible as my wife has proven to be'.

Conclusion and evaluation

Steve Taylor has taken a realist approach which seeks to reveal the 'underlying rules of suicidal action'. He tries to show how a wide and complex variety of suicide acts result from four 'general states of meaning' – a sense of certainty or uncertainty and a sense of attachment to others or detachment from others. The four possible combinations of these states of meaning result in four types of suicide – Thanatation, submissive, appeal and sacrifice. This is shown in Figure 6.

Evaluation Taylor's theory has the advantage of covering both completed and attempted suicide. It includes the contribution of others to the suicide act and the communication to others of the intention to commit suicide. His theory is comprehensive in the sense that it claims to cover all types of suicide.

Taylor identifies two main problems with his research

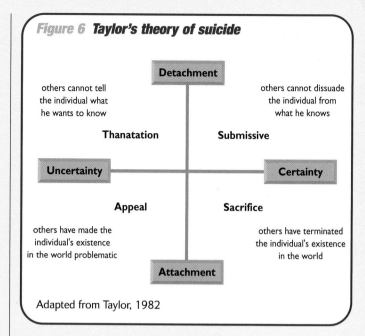

Figure 6 **Taylor's theory of suicide**

Adapted from Taylor, 1982

(Taylor, personal communication, 2004). First, case studies do not provide a representative sample of suicide acts. Second, he fails to develop his theory to include the wider society. To move to the societal level of causality, Taylor needs to ask what kinds of society produce high levels of certainty and uncertainty, attachment and detachment. Including the wider society would complete his theoretical model.

Despite these problems, Taylor has produced an elegant and original theory.

key terms

Submissive suicide A type of suicide that arises from certainty and detachment. The individual is certain that there is no hope for the future.

Thanatation A type of suicide that arises from uncertainty and detachment. The individual demands an answer from suicide to resolve their uncertainty.

Appeal suicide A type of suicide that arises from uncertainty and attachment. The individual has serious doubts about the significance of their life to others.

Sacrifice suicide A type of suicide that arises from certainty and attachment. A deep attachment has been broken and the individual is certain that they cannot live with this situation.

summary

1. On the basis of official statistics, Emile Durkheim found that suicide rates varied between different countries, between different groups within the same country and over time.

2. Durkheim identified four types of suicide, each of which is related to the level of integration or the level of regulation in society.
   - Altruistic suicide occurs when the level of integration is too strong.
   - Egoistic suicide occurs when the level of integration is too weak.
   - Fatalistic suicide occurs when the level of regulation is too strong.
   - Anomic suicide occurs when the level of regulation is too weak.

3. Durkheim claimed that both suicide rates and types of suicide were shaped by social facts – by the levels of integration and regulation in society.

4. Durkheim's methodology is usually seen as a realist approach. He looked for the invisible underlying causes of the relationships between the things he observed.

5. Critics argue that Durkheim paid insufficient attention to the validity and reliability of official statistics.

6. Positivists reject the realist view that causes can be found in underlying structures and processes that cannot be directly observed and measured.

7. From an interpretivist viewpoint, Jack Douglas argues that the first step in studying suicide is to interpret how individuals who commit suicide define and give meaning to their action.

8. Douglas argues that this is essential in order to classify suicides into types.

9. Douglas sees suicide statistics as the result of negotiated meanings within a complex series of social interactions.

10. J. Maxwell Atkinson states that suicide is simply a meaning and there is no reality beyond that meaning.

11. His research indicates that coroners have pictures of a 'typical suicide death' and a 'typical suicide biography'. The closer the death and the life history of the deceased to these pictures, the greater the likelihood of a suicide verdict.

12. Barry Hindess argues that the logic of Atkinson's methodology means that there is no 'possibility of an objective knowledge of society'.

13. Steve Taylor adopts a realist perspective, arguing that sociologists should look for the 'underlying, unobservable structures and causal processes' which lie behind suicide acts.

14. Taylor agrees with Douglas that the case study is the most appropriate research method for studying suicide.

15. Taylor's theory argues that the underlying motivation for suicide acts arises from imbalances in individuals' sense of their own identity (too much certainty or too much uncertainty) and in their relationships with other (too much attachment to, or too much detachment from, others).

16. Taylor identifies two main problems with his research.
    - Case studies do not provide a representative sample of suicide acts.
    - He fails to develop his theory to include the wider society – for example, what kinds of society produce high levels of certainty or uncertainty.

References

Abel-Smith, B. & Townsend, P. (1965). *The poor and the poorest*. London: G. Bell & Sons.

ACPO (Association of Chief Police Officers) (2000). *A guide to identifying and combating hate crime*. London: ACPO.

Ahmed, L. (2000). Women and gender in Islam: Historical roots of a modern debate. In L. Woodhead & P. Heelas (Eds.), *Religion in modern times: An interpretive anthology*. Oxford: Blackwell.

Allan, J., Livingstone, S. & Reiner, R. (1997). The changing generic location of crime in film. *Journal of Communication, 47*, 4, 1-13.

Althusser, L. (1969). *For Marx*. London: Penguin.

Althusser, L. (1971). *Lenin and philosophy and other essays*. London: New Left Books.

Alvesson, M. (2002). *Postmodernism and social research*. Buckingham: Open University Press.

Ammerman, N.T. (2003). Re-awakening a sleeping giant: Christian fundamentalists in late twentieth-century US society. In G. ter Haar & J.J. Busuttil (Eds.), *The freedom to do God's will: Religious fundamentalism and social change*. London: Routledge.

An-Na'im, A. (2003). Islamic fundamentalism and social change: Neither the 'end of history' nor a 'clash of civilisations'. In G. ter Haar & J.J. Busuttil (Eds.), *The freedom to do God's will: Religious fundamentalism and social change*. London: Routledge.

Annual abstract of statistics (2004). London: TSO.

Atkinson, J.M. (1978). *Discovering suicide*. London: Macmillan.

Bachrach, P. & Baratz, M. (1962). The two faces of power. *American Politics Science Review, 56*.

Barclay, G. & Tavares, C. (1999). Digest 4: *Information on the criminal justice system in England and Wales*. London: HMSO.

Barker, E. (1983). New Religious Movements in Britain: *The context and the membership*. *Social Compass, XXX/1*, 33-48.

Barker, E. (1984). *The making of a Moonie*. Oxford: Blackwell.

Barker, E. (1999). New Religious Movements: Their incidence and significance. In B. Wilson & J. Cresswell (Eds.), *New Religious Movements: Challenge and response*. London: Sage.

Barthes, R. (1973). *Mythologies*. London: Paladin.

Bauman, Z. (1992). *Intimations of postmodernity*. London: Routledge.

Beck, U. (1992). Risk society: *Towards a new modernity*. London: Sage.

Becker, H.S. (1963). Outsiders: *Studies in the sociology of deviance*. London: Macmillan.

Becker, H.S. (1970). Whose side are we on? In H.S. Becker, *Sociological work*. New Brunswick: Transaction Books.

Beckford, J.A. (1975). *The trumpet of prophecy: A sociological study of Jehovah's Witnesses*. Oxford: Blackwell.

Beckford, J.A. (2003). Religion: Consensus and conflict. *Sociology Review*, November.

Bell, D. (1987). The world and the United States. *Daedalus, 116*, 1-32.

Bellah, R.N. (1967). Civic religion in America. In R. Richey & D. Jones (Eds.), *American civic religion*. New York: Harper & Row.

Bennett, T. (2001). Sociology and government. In P. Hamilton & K. Thompson (Eds.), *The uses of sociology*. Oxford: Blackwell.

Bentley, R., Dobson, A., Dorey, P. & Roberts, D. (2004). *British politics in focus: AS level*. Ormskirk: Causeway Press.

Bentley, R., Dorey, P. & Roberts, D. (2002). *British politics update: 1999-2002*. Ormskirk: Causeway Press.

Berger, P. (1970). *A rumour of angels: Modern society and the rediscovery of the supernatural*. London: Allen Lane.

Berger, P. (1973). *The social reality of religion*. Harmondsworth: Penguin.

Berger, P., Berger, B. & Kellner, H. (1974). *The homeless mind*. Harmondsworth: Penguin.

Bhaskar, R. (1978). *A realist theory of science* (2nd ed.). Hassocks: Harvester.

Birnbaum, N. (1955). Monarchs and sociologists: A reply to Professor Shils and Mr Young. *Sociological Review*, July.

Blaikie, N. (1993). *Approaches to social enquiry*. Oxford: Polity Press.

Blumer, H. (1962). Society as symbolic interaction. In A.M. Rose (Ed.), *Human behaviour and social processes*. London: Routledge.

Blumer, H. (1969). *Symbolic interactionism: Perspective on method*. Englewood Cliffs: Prentice Hall.

Blumler, J.G. & MacQuail, D. (1968). *Television and politics*. London: Faber & Faber.

Bogdanor, V. (2003). Asymmetric devolution: Toward a quasi-federal constitution? In P. Dunleavy, A. Gamble, R. Heffernan & G. Peele (Eds.), *Developments in British politics 7*. Basingstoke: Palgrave

Bordua, D. (1962). A critique of sociological interpretations of gang delinquency. In M.E. Wolfgang, L. Savitz & N. Johnston (Eds.), *The sociology of crime and delinquency*. New York: John Wiley & Sons.

Bottomley, A. & Coleman, C. (1981). *Understanding crime rates*. Farnborough: Saxon House.

Bottomore, T. & Rubel, M. *Karl Marx: Selected writings*. Harmondsworth: Penguin.

Bourgois, P. (1995). *In search of respect*. Cambridge: Cambridge University Press.

Bowling, B. & Phillips, C. (2002). *Racism, crime and justice*. London: Longman.

Box, S. (1983). *Power, crime and mystification*. London: Tavistock.

Brecht, B. (1980), *Life of Galileo*.

Brierley, P. (2000). *Religious trends*. Christian Research Association.

British Social Attitudes Survey 2001-02 – see Park, A. (Ed.), 2001.

Brittan, S. (1983). *The role and limits of government*. London: Temple Smith.

Bronner, S.E. & Kellner, D.M. (Eds.). *Critical theory and society*. London: Routledge.

Broughton, D. (2000). Political participation in Britain. *Politics Review, 9*, 4.

Brown, D. (1975). *Bury my heart at Wounded Knee*. London: Pan Books.

Bruce, S. (1992). The twilight of the gods. *Sociology Review*, November.

Bruce, S. (1995). *Religion in modern Britain*. Oxford: Oxford University Press.

Bruce, S. (2001). *Fundamentalism*. Oxford: Polity Press.

Bruce, S. (2002). *God is dead: Secularisation in the West*. Oxford: Blackwell.

Brunsdon, C., Johnson, C., Moseley, R. & Wheatley, H. (2001). Factual entertainment on British television. *European Journal of Cultural Studies, 4*.

Bryant, A. (1953). *The story of England: Makers of the realm*. London: Collins.

Budge, I. (1999). Party policy and ideology: Reversing the 1950s? In G. Evans & P. Norris (Eds.), *Critical elections: British parties and voters in long-term perspective*. London: Sage.

Budge, I. et al. (1983). *The new British political system*. London: Longman.

Butler, D. & Kavanagh, D. (1997). *The British general election of 1997*. Basingstoke: Macmillan.

Butler, D. & Kavanagh, D. (2002). *The British general election of 2001*. Basingstoke: Palgrave.

Butler, D. & Stokes, D. (1974). *Political change in Britain*. London: Macmillan.

Callinicos, A. (1989). *Against postmodernism*. Cambridge: Polity.

Callinicos, A. (2003). *An anti-capitalist manifesto*. Cambridge: Polity.

Campbell, B. (1993). *Goliath: Britain's dangerous places*. London: Macmillan.

Carlen, P. (1983). *Women's imprisonment*. London: Routledge.

Carlen, P. (1988). *Women, crime and poverty*. Buckingham: Open University Press.

Carlen, P. (1990). *Alternatives to women's imprisonment*. Buckingham: Open University Press.

Carrabine, E., Cox, P., Lee, M. & South, N. (2002). *Crime in modern Britain*. Oxford: Oxford University Press.

Castells, M. (1983). *The city and the grass roots: A cross-cultural theory of urban social movements.* London: Edward Arnold.

Castells, M. (1996). *The rise of the network society.* Oxford: Blackwell.

Cavadino, M. & Dignan, J. (2002). *The penal system* (3rd ed.). London: Sage.

Chahal, K. & Julienne, L. (1999). *'We can't all be white!' Racist victimisation in the UK.* York: York Publishing Services.

Chambliss, W. (1969). *Crime and the legal process.* New York: McGraw-Hill.

Chibnall, S. (1977). *Law and order news.* London: Tavistock.

Chitty, C. (2002). *Understanding schools and schooling.* London: RoutledgeFalmer.

Cicourel, A.V. (1976). *The social organisation of juvenile justice.* London: Heinemann.

Clancy, A., Hough, M., Aust, R. & Kershaw, C. (2001). *Crime, policing and justice: The experience of ethnic minorities: Findings from the 2000 British Crime Survey, Home Office Research Study 223.* London: Home Office.

Clinard, M. (1974). *Sociology and deviant behaviour* (4th ed.). New York: Holt, Rinehart and Winston.

Cloward, R. & Ohlin, L. (1961). *Delinquency and opportunity.* Glencoe: The Free Press.

Coates, D. (1984). *The context of British politics.* London: Hutchinson.

Coates, K. & Silburn, R. (1970). *Poverty: The forgotten Englishmen.* Harmondsworth: Penguin.

Cohen, A. (1955). *Delinquent boys.* Glencoe: The Free Press.

Cohen, P. (1968). *Modern social theory.* London: Heinemann.

Cohen, S. (1987). *Folk devils and moral panics* (2nd ed.). Oxford: Blackwell.

Cohen, S. (2003). Human rights and crimes of the state: The culture of denial. In E. McLaughlin, J. Muncie & G. Hughes (Eds.), *Criminological perspectives: Essential readings* (2nd ed.). London: Sage.

Cohn, N. (1957). *The pursuit of the millennium.* London: Secker and Warburg.

Cole, W.O. (Ed.) (1991). *Moral issues in six religions.* Oxford: Heinemann.

Coleman, C. & Moynihan, J. (1996). *Understanding crime data.* Buckingham: Open University Press.

Collier, R. (1998). *Masculinities, crime and criminology.* London: Sage.

Collison, M. (1996). In search of the high life: Drugs, crime, masculinity and consumption. *British Journal of Criminology, 36.*

Cook, G. (2000). *European values survey.* Gordon Cook Foundation.

Cowan, R. (2004). Police failing to tackle domestic abuse. *Guardian,* 19 February.

Cowe, R. (2001). The acceptable face of anit-capitalism. *The Observer,* 6 May.

Craib, I. (1984). *Modern social theory.* London: Harvester Wheatsheaf.

Craib, I. (1992). *Anthony Giddens.* London: Routledge.

Craig, F.W.S. (1989). *British electoral facts 1832-1989.* Aldershot: Gower.

Crawford, A., Jones, T., Woodhouse, T. & Young, J. (1990). *Second Islington Crime Survey.* London: Middlesex Polytechnic.

Crenson, M. (1971). *The unpolitics of air pollution: A case study in non-decision making in the cities.* London: John Hopkins Press.

Crewe, I. & Thompson, K. (1999). Party loyalties: Dealignment or realignment? In G. Evans & P. Norris (Eds.), *Critical elections: British parties and voters in long-term perspective.* London: Sage.

Crewe, I. (1992). Why did Labour lose (yet again)? *Politics Review, 2, 1.*

Critcher, C. (2003). *Moral panics and the media.* Buckingham: Open University Press.

Croall, H. (2001). *Understanding white collar crime.* Buckingham: Open University Press.

Crook, S., Pakulski J. & Waters, M. (1992). *Postmodernisation: Changes in advanced society.* London: Sage.

Cumberbatch, G., Woods, S. & Maguire, A. (1995). *Crime in the news.* Birmingham: Aston University.

Curtice, J. & Park, A. (1999). Region: New Labour, new geography? In G. Evans & P. Norris (Eds.), *Critical elections: British parties and voters in long-term perspective.* London: Sage.

Dahl, R. (1957). The concept of power. *Behavioural Science, 2.*

Dahl, R. (1961). *Who governs? Democracy and power in an American city.* London: Yale University Press.

Dahl, R. (1973). A critique of the ruling elite model. In J. Urry & J. Wakeford (Eds.), *Power in Britain.* London: Heinemann.

Dahl, R. (1989). *Democracy and it critics.* New Haven: Yale University Press.

Dalton, R.J. & Wattenberg, M. (Eds.) (2002). *Parties without partisans.* Oxford: Oxford University Press.

Davidman, L. (1991). *Tradition in a rootless world: Women turn to orthodox Judaism.* Berkeley: University of California Press.

Davie, G. (1994). *Religion in Britain since 1945: Believing without belonging.* Oxford: Blackwell.

Davies, N. (1994). Dirty business: Red light for Blue Squad. *The Guardian,* 29 November.

Davis, K. (1961). Prostitution. In R. Merton & R. Nisbet (Eds.), *Contemporary social problems.* New York: The Free Press.

Deacon, D., Golding, P. & Billig, M (2001). Press and broadcasting: 'Real issues' and real coverage. In P. Norris (Ed.), *Britain votes 2001.* Oxford: Oxford University Press.

Delamont, S. (2003). *Feminist sociology.* London: Sage.

Denman, S. (2001). *The Denman report – Race discrimination in the Crown Prosecution Service,* London: Crown Prosecution Service.

Denver, D. & Hands, G. (1990). A new gender gap. *Talking Politics, 2, 3.*

Denver, D. (1994). *Elections and voting in Britain* (2nd ed.). London: Harvester Wheatsheaf.

Denzin, N.K. (1970). *The research act in sociology.* London: Butterworths.

Dobash, R., Schlesinger, P., Dobash, R. & Weaver, C. (1998). Crimewatch UK. In M. Fishman & G. Cavender (Eds.), *Entertaining crime.* New York: Aldine De Gruyter.

Dobson, A. (1992). Ideology. *Politics Review, 1, 4.*

Donnison, D. (2001). The changing face of poverty. In M. May, R. Page & E. Brunsdon (Eds.), *Understanding social problems: Issues in social policy.* Oxford: Blackwell.

Dorey, P. (2002). A languid landslide: The 2001 general election. In S. Lancaster (Ed.), *Developments in Politics, Vol 13.* Ormskirk: Causeway Press.

Douglas, J. D. (1967). *The social meanings of suicide.* New York: Princeton.

Downes, D. & Rock, P. (2003). *Understanding deviance* (4th ed.) Oxford: Clarendon Press.

Downton, J. (1979). *Sacred journeys: The conversion of young Americans to the Divine Light Mission.* New York: Columbia University Press.

Dunleavy, P. & O'Leary, B. (1987). *Theories of the state: The politics of liberal democracy.* Basingstoke: Macmillan.

Dunthorne, H. (1991). *The enlightenment.* London: The Historical Association.

Durkheim, E. (1933). *The division of labour in society.* New York: The Free Press.

Durkheim, E. (1964). *The rules of sociological method.* New York: The Free Press.

Durkheim, E. (1968). *The elementary forms of the religious life.* London: Allen & Unwin.

Durkheim, E. (1970). *Suicide: A study in sociology.* London: Routledge & Kegan Paul.

Eichler, M. et al., (1988). *Non-sexist research methods.* London: Allen & Unwin.

Eisenstadt, S.N. (1967). The Protestant Ethic Thesis in analytical and comparative context. *Diogenes, 59.*

Equal Opportunities Commission (2004). *Sex power: Who runs Britain?* Manchester: Equal Opportunities Commission.

Evans, G. (2003). Political culture and voting participation. In P. Dunleavy, A. Gamble, R. Heffernan & G. Peele (Eds.), *Developments in British politics 7.* Basingstoke: Palgrave.

Evans, G., Heath, A. & Payne, G. (1999). Class: Labour as a catch-all party. In G. Evans & P. Norris (Eds.), *Critical elections: British parties and voters in long-term perspective.* London: Sage.

Evans, M. (1997). Political participation. In P. Dunleavy et al. (Eds.), *Developments in British politics 5*. Basingstoke: Macmillan.

Eysenck, H.J. (1987). Personality theory and the problem of criminology. In B. McGurk, D. Thornton & M. Williams (Eds.), *Applying psychology to imprisonment*. London: HMSO.

Farrington, D. & Morris, A. (1983). Sex, sentencing and reconviction. *British Journal of Criminology, 23*.

Finch, J. (1993). 'It's great to have someone to talk to': Ethics and politics of interviewing women. In M. Hammersley (Ed.), *Social research: Philosophy, politics and practice*. London: Sage.

Foucault, M. (1967). *Madness and civilisation*. London: Tavistock.

Foucault, M. (1977). *Discipline and punish: The birth of the prison*. London: Tavistock.

Fowler, D. (1997). Secularisation in the English context. *Independent Saturday Magazine*, December 6.

Franklin, J.H. & Starr, I. (Eds.) (1967). *The Negro in 20th century America*. New York: Vintage.

Gabor, T. (1994). *Everybody does it*. Toronto: University of Toronto Press.

Gay, P. (1973). *The enlightenment: An interpretation Vol 2: The science of freedom*. London: Wildwood House.

Geerz, C. (Ed.) 1973. *The interpretation of cultures*. New York: Basic Books.

Gibbs, J. & Martin, W. (1964). *Status integration and suicide*. Oregon: University of Oregon Press.

Giddens, A. (1974). Elites in the British class structure. In P. Stanworth & A. Giddens (Eds.), *Elites and power in British society*. Cambridge: Cambridge University Press.

Giddens, A. (1985). Jurgen Habermas. In Q. Skinner (Ed.), *The return of grand theory in the human sciences*. Cambridge: Cambridge University Press.

Giddens, A. (1985). *The nation state and violence*. Cambridge: Polity Press.

Giddens, A. (1990). *The consequences of modernity*. Cambridge: Polity Press.

Giddens, A. (1991). *Modernity and self-identity: Self and society in the late modern age*. Cambridge: Polity Press.

Giddens, A. (1998). *The Third Way: The renewal of social democracy*. Cambridge: Polity Press.

Giddens, A. (2000). *The Third Way and its critics*. Cambridge: Polity Press.

Giddens, A. (2001). *Sociology* (4th ed.). Cambridge: Polity Press.

Gillborn, D. (1990). *'Race', ethnicity and education: Teaching and learning in multi-ethnic schools*. London: Unwin Hyman.

Gilroy, P. (1983). Police and thieves. In Centre for Contemporary Cultural Studies *The empire strikes back*. London: Hutchinson.

Glock, C.Y. (1964). The role of relative deprivation in the origin and evolution of religious groups. In R. Lee & M. Marty (Eds.), *Religion and social conflict*. Berkeley, CA: University of California Press.

Glock, C.Y. & Stark, R. (1965). *Religion and society in tension*. Chicago: Rand McNally.

Goffman, E. (1959). *The presentation of self in everyday life*. Harmondsworth: Penguin.

Goffman, E. (1968). *Asylums*. Harmondsworth: Penguin.

Gottfredson, M. & Hirschi, T. (1990). *General theory of crime*. Stanford: Stanford University Press.

Gouldner, A.W. (1971). *The coming crisis of Western sociology*. London: Heinemann.

Gouldner, A.W. (1975). *For sociology*. Harmondsworth: Penguin.

Graef, R. (1990). *Talking blues*. London: Fontana.

Graham, J. & Bowling, B. (1995). *Young people and crime, Home Office Research Study,145*. London: Home Office.

Gramsci, A. (1971). *Selections from the Prison Notebooks: Notebooks of Antonio Gramsci*. London: Lawrence & Wishart.

Grant, W. (2000). *Pressure groups and British politics*. Basingstoke: Palgrave.

Grove-White, R. (1997). Brent Spar rewrote the rules. *New Statesman*, 20 June.

Hadaway, C.K. & Marler, P.L. (1999). Did you really go to church this week? Behind the poll data. www.religion-online.org

Hadden, J.K. (2003). The Religious Movements Page. http://religiousmovements.lib.virginia.edu/cultsect/concult.htm

Halfpenny, P. (1984). *Principles of method*. York: Longman.

Hall, S. (1992). The question of cultural identity. In S. Hall et al. (Eds.), *Modernity and its futures*. Cambridge: Polity.

Hall, S., Critcher, C., Jefferson, T., Clarke, J. & Roberts, B. (1978). *Policing the crisis*. London: Macmillan.

Hallsworth, S. (1994). Understanding new social movements. *Sociology Review*, September.

Hamilton, M. (2001). *The sociology of religion: Theoretical and comparative perspectives*. London: Routledge.

Hamilton, P. (1992). The enlightenment and the birth of social science. In S. Hall & B Gieben (Eds.), *Formations of modernity*. Cambridge: Polity.

Hanson, S. (1997). The secularisation thesis: Talking at cross purposes. *Journal of Contemporary Religion, 12*, 2.

Haralambos, M. (1995). *Right on: From blues to soul in Black America*. Ormskirk: Causeway Press.

Harvey, D. (1989). *The condition of postmodernity*. Oxford: Blackwell.

Heath, A., Jowell, R. & Curtice, J. (1985). *How Britain votes*. Oxford: Pergamon Press.

Heelas, P. (1996). *The New Age Movement: The celebration of the self and the sacralisation of modernity*. Oxford: Blackwell.

Heelas, P. (1998). Introduction. In P. Heelas (Ed.), *Religion, modernity and postmodernity*. Oxford: Blackwell.

Heelas, P. (2000). Religion and postmodern difference. In Woodhead & Heelas (Eds.), *Religion in modern times*. Oxford: Blackwell.

Heelas, P. & Woodhead, L. (2003). The Kendal Project: Testing the 'spiritual revolution thesis'. *Sociology Review*, November.

Heelas, P. & Woodhead, L. (2004). *The spiritual revolution: Why religion is giving way to spirituality*. Oxford: Blackwell.

Heidensohn, F. (1996). *Women and crime* (2nd ed.). London: Macmillan.

Heidensohn, F. (2002). Gender and crime. In M. Maguire et al. (Eds.), *The Oxford handbook of criminology* (3rd ed.). Oxford: Clarendon Press.

Heilbut, T. (1971). *The gospel sound*. New York: Simon & Schuster.

Held, D. (1992). The development of the modern state. In S. Hall & B. Gieben (Eds.), *Formations of modernity*. Cambridge: Polity.

Held, D. (1993). *Democracy and the new international order*. London: IPRR.

Herberg, W. (1960). *Protestant-Catholic-Jew: An essay in American religious sociology*. Chicago: University of Chicago Press.

Herbert, D. (2001). Representing Islam: The 'Islamisation' of Egyptian society, 1970-2000. In G. Beckerlegge (Ed.), *From sacred text to internet*. Milton Keynes: Open University Press.

Heritage, J. (1984). *Garfinkel and ethnomethodology*. Cambridge: Polity Press.

Hewitt, C. (1974). Elites and the distribution of power in British society. In P. Stanworth & A. Giddens (Eds.), *Elites and power in British society*. Cambridge: Cambridge University Press.

Heywood, A. (2002). *Politics* (2nd ed.). Basingstoke: Palgrave.

Hindess, B. (1973). *The use of official statistics in sociology: A critique of positivism*. London: Macmillan.

Hirschi, T. (1969). *Causes of delinquency*. Berkeley CA: University of California Press.

Hirst, P. (1990). The state we're in. *New Statesman and Society*, 19 October.

HMIC (Her Majesty's Inspectorate of Constabulary) (2001). *Winning the race: Embracing diversity*. London: Home Office.

Hobbs, D., Hadfield, P., Lister, S. & Winlow, S. (2003). *Bouncers*. Oxford: Oxford University Press.

Holdaway, S. (1988). *Crime and deviance*. London: Macmillan.

Holdaway, S. (1996). *The racialisation of British policing*. London: Macmillan.

Holden, A. (2002). Witnessing the future? Millenarianism and postmodernity. *Sociology Review*, February.

Home Office (2000). *Code of practice on reporting and recording racist incidents*. London: Home Office.

Home Office (2002). *Statistics on race and the criminal justice system*. London: Home Office.

Home Office (2003). *Statistics on women and the criminal justice system*. London: Home Office.

Hood, R. (1992). *Race and sentencing*. Oxford: Clarendon Press.

Hoyle, C. (2000). Being 'a nosy bloody cow': Ethical and methodological issues in researching domestic violence. In R.D. King & E. Wincup (Eds.), *Doing research on crime and justice*. Oxford: Oxford University Press

Hudson, B. (1993). Racism and criminology: Concepts and controversies. In D. Cook & B. Hudson (Eds.), *Racism and criminology*. London: Sage.

Hughes, G. & Langan, M. (2001). Good or bad business?: Exploring corporate and organised crime. In J. Muncie & E. McLaughlin (Eds.), *The problem of crime* (2nd ed.). London: Sage.

Hughes, G. (2000). What are the futures of crime control? *Sociology Review*, 9.

Hunt, S. (1992). *Religion in Western society*. Basingstoke: Palgrave.

IMF (2004). *About the International Monetary Fund*. www.imf.org

James, O. (2003). So George, how do you feel about your mom and dad? *Guardian*, 2 September.

Jenkins, J. (1987). *Contemporary moral issues*. Oxford: Heinemann Educational.

Jessop, B. (1990). State theory: *Putting capitalist states in their place*. Oxford: Polity.

Johnston, R.J. & Pattie, C.J. (1992). The changing electoral geography of Great Britain. In D. Denver & G. Hands (Eds.), *Issues and controversies in British electoral behaviour*. London: Harvester Wheatsheaf.

Jones, I. (1974). A critique of Murdock and Phelps' 'Mass media and the secondary school'. Unpublished dissertation, School of Education, University of Leicester.

Jones, K. (1998). Death of a Princess. *Sociology Review*, September.

Jones, P. (1993). *Studying society: Sociological theories and research practices*. London: Collins Educational.

Jones, S. (1998). *Criminology*. London: Butterworth.

Jones, T., McLean, B. & Young, J. (1986). *The Islington Crime Survey*. Aldershot: Gower.

Judah, J.S. (1974). *Hare Krishna and the counter culture*. New York: John Wiley.

Kalra,V. (2003). Police lore and community disorder: Diversity in the criminal justice system. In D. Mason (Ed.), *Explaining ethnic differences*. Bristol: The Policy Press.

Kaluzynska, E. (1980). Wiping the floor with theory. *Feminist Review no. 7*.

Kassam, N. (1997). *Telling it like it is*. London: Women's Press.

Katz, E. & Lazarfeld, P. (1955). Personal influence. New York: *The Free Press*.

Kerr, J. (1994). *Understanding football hooliganism*. Buckingham: Open University Press.

Khasala, K. (1986). New religious movements turn to worldly success. *Journal for the Scientific Study of Religion, 25*, 233-247.

Kincaid, J.C. (1973). *Poverty and equality in Britain*. Harmondsworth: Penguin.

Kuhn, T.S. (1962). *The structure of scientific revolutions*. Chicago: University of Chicago Press.

Lakatos, I. (1970). Falsification and the methodology of scientific research programmes. In I. Lakatos & A. Musgrave (Eds.), *Criticism and the growth of knowledge*. Cambridge: Cambridge University Press.

Langley, P. (1988). *Discovering sociology*. Ormskirk: Causeway Press.

Layton-Henry, Z. (1990). The Black electorate. *Contemporary Record, 3, 3*.

Layton-Henry, Z. (1992). *The politics of immigration*. Oxford: Blackwell.

Lea, J. & Young, J. (1982). The riots in Britain: Urban violence and political marginalisation. In D. Cowell, T. Jones & J. Young (Eds.), *Policing the riots*. London: Junction Books.

Lea, J. & Young, J. (1993). *What is to be done about law and order?* (2nd ed.). London: Pluto Press.

Lee, D. & Newby, H. (1983). *The problem of sociology*. London: Hutchinson.

Lemert, E.M. (1972). *Human deviance, social problems and social control* (2nd ed.). Englewood Cliffs NJ: Prentice Hall.

Levi, M. (1993). *The investigation, prosecution and trial of serious fraud, Research Study, 14*. London: Royal Commission on Criminal Justice.

Lévi-Strauss, C. The structural study of myth. In W.A. Lessa & E.Z. Vogt (Eds.), *Reader in comparative religion* (2nd ed.). New York: Harper & Row.

Light, A. (Ed.) (1997). *Tupac Ama Ru Shakur, 1971-1996*. London: Plexus.

Lilleker, D., Negrine, R. & Stanyer, J. (2003). *Media malaise*.

Linton, M. (1996). Was it the Sun wot won it? Oxford: Nuffield College. *Politics Review, 12, 3*, February.

Lombroso, C. (1876). *L'uomo delinquente*. Milan: Hoepli.

Long Lance, Chief Buffalo Child. (1956). *Long Lance*. London: Corgi.

Longley, C. (1986). Robin Hood and liberation theology. *The Times*, 27 January.

Luckmann, T. (1970). *The invisible religion: The problem of religion in modern society*. New York: MacMillan.

Lukes, S. (1974). *Power a radical view*. London: Macmillan.

Lupton, T. & Wilson, S. (1974). The social background of top decision makers. In J. Urry & J. Wakeford (Eds.), *Power in Britain*. London: Heinemann.

Lyon, D. (2000). *Jesus in Disneyland: Religion in postmodern times*. Cambridge: Polity Press.

Lyotard, J.F. (1984). *The postmodern condition*. Manchester: Manchester University Press.

Lyotard, J.F. (1992). Abandoning the metanarratives of modernity. In S. Hall et al. (Eds.), *Modernity and its futures*. Cambridge: Polity.

Macdonald, K. & Tipton, D. (1993). Using documents. In N. Gilbert (Ed.), *Researching social life*. London: Sage.

MacGregor, S. (2001). The problematic community. In M. May, R. Page & E. Brunsdon (Eds.), *Understanding social problems: Issues in social policy*. Oxford: Blackwell.

Macpherson, W. (1999). *The Stephen Lawrence Inquiry*. London: HMSO.

Maduro, O. (1982). *Religion and social conflicts*. New York: Orbis.

Maguire, M. (2002). Crime statistics. In M.Maguire et al. (Eds.), *The Oxford handbook of criminology* (3rd ed.). Oxford: Clarendon Press.

Malinowski, B. (1954). *Magic, science and religion and other essays*. New York: Anchor Books.

Mandel, E. (1984). Delightful murder: *A social history of the crime story*. London: Pluto.

Mann, M. (1986). *The sources of social power, vol 1*. Cambridge: Cambridge University Press.

Mann, M. (1993). *The sources of social power, vol 2*. Cambridge: Cambridge University Press.

Marsh, D. (1985). Power and Politics. In M. Haralambos (Ed.), *Developments in Sociology, vol 1*. Ormskirk: Causeway Press.

Marshall, G. (Ed.) (1994). *The concise Oxford dictionary of sociology*. Oxford: Oxford University Press.

Martin, B. (2003). The Pentecostal gender paradox. In R.K. Fenn (Ed.), *The Blackwell companion to the sociology of religion*. Oxford: Blackwell.

Martin, D. (1969). *The religious and the secular*. London: Routledge & Kegan Paul.

Matza, D. & Sykes, G.M. (1961). Juvenile delinquency and subterranean values. *American Sociological Review, 26*, 5.

Matza, D. (1964). *Delinquency and drift*. London: Wiley.

Mauer, M. (1997). *Intended and unintended consequences: State racial disparities in imprisonment*. Washington DC: The Sentencing Project.

May, M., Page, R. & Brunsdon, E. (2001). Social problems in social policy: An introduction. In M. May, R. Page & E. Brunsdon (Eds.), *Understanding social problems: Issues in social policy*. Oxford: Blackwell.

Mayhew, P., Aye Maung, N. & Mirrlees-Black, C. (1993). *The 1992 British Crime Survey, Home Office Research Study, 132*. London: HMSO.

Mayhew, P., Mirrlees-Black, C. & Aye Maung, N. (1994). *Trends in crime : Findings from the 1994 British Crime Survey, Home Office Research and Statistics Department Research Findings, 18*. London: HMSO.

McAuley, J.W. (2003). *An introduction to politics, state and society*. London: Sage.

McClennan, G. (1992). The Enlightenment project revisited. In S. Hall et al. (Eds.), *Modernity and its futures*. Cambridge: Polity.

McCullagh, C. (2002). *Media power*. Basingstoke: Palgrave.

McGuire, M. (1981). *Religion: The social context*. New York: Orbis.

McGuire, M. (2003). Ritual healing in suburban America. In S.J. Sutcliffe (Ed.), *Children of the New Age: A history of spiritual practices*. London: Routledge.

Merton, R.K. (1968). Social structure and anomie. In R.K. Merton *Social theory and social structure*. New York: The Free Press.

Messerschmidt, J. (1993). *Masculinities and crime*. Lanham: Rowman & Littlefield.

Mies, M. (1993). Towards a methodology for feminist research. In M. Hammersley (Ed.), *Social research: Philosophy, politics and practice*. London: Sage.

Miliband, R. (1969). *The state in capitalist society*. London: Weidenfeld & Nicholson.

Miller, W.B. (1958) Lower class culture as a generating milieu of gang delinquency, *Journal of Social Issues,14*.

Miller, W.L. (1991). *Media and voters: The audience, content and influence of press and television in the 1987 general election*. Oxford: Clarendon Press.

Mills, C.W. (1956). *The power elite*. New York: Oxford University Press.

Miner, M. (1965). Body ritual among the Nacirema. In W.A. Lessa & E.Z Vogt (Eds.), *Reader in comparative religion: An anthropological approach* (2nd ed.). New York: Harper & Row.

Modood, T., Berthoud, R. et al. (1997). *Ethnic minorities in Britain*. London: Policy Studies Institute.

Morgan, C. (1997). Vicars inflate attendance figures. *The Sunday Times*, 1 June.

Mosca, G. (1939). *The ruling class*. New York: McGraw-Hill.

Muncie, J. (1987) Much ado about nothing? The sociology of moral panics, *Social Studies Review, 3*.

Muncie, J. (2001). The construction and deconstruction of crime. In J. Muncie & E. McLaughlin (Eds.), *The problem of crime*. London: Sage.

Munck, R. & Rolston, W. (1987). *Belfast in the 30s: An oral history*. Belfast: Blackstaff Press.

Murdock, G. & Phelps, C. (1973). *Mass media and the secondary school*. London: Macmillan.

Murray, C. (1990). *The emerging British underclass*. London: Institute of Economic Affairs.

Murray, C. (1996). *Charles Murray and the underclass: The developing debate*. London: Institute of Economic Affairs.

Naffine, N. (1987). *Female crime*. Sydney: Allen & Unwin.

Nelson, G.K. (1986). Religion. In M. Haralambos (Ed.), *Developments in Sociology, Volume 2*, Ormskirk: Causeway Press.

Niebuhr, H.R. (1929). *The social sources of denominationalism*. New York: World Publishing.

Nightingale, C. (1993). *On the edge*. New York: Basic Books.

Nisbet, R. (1967). *The sociological tradition*. London: Heinemann.

Nordlinger, E.A. (1981). *On the autonomy of the democratic state*. Cambridge, MS: Harvard University Press.

Norris, P. (Ed.) (2001). *Britain votes 2001*. Oxford: Oxford University Press.

O'Connell Davidson & Layder, D. (1994). *Methods, sex and madness*. London: Routledge.

O'Toole, R. (1984). *Religion: Classic sociological approaches*. Toronto: McGraw-Hill.

Oakley, A. (1981). Interviewing women: A contradiction in terms. In H. Roberts (Ed.), *Doing feminist research*. London: Routledge.

Offe, C. (1982). Some contradictions of the modern welfare state. *Critical Social Policy, 2, 2*.

Page, R. (2001). The exploration of social problems in the field of social policy. In M. May, R. Page & E. Brunsdon (Eds.), *Understanding social problems: Issues in social policy*. Oxford: Blackwell.

Page, R.M. (2002). New Labour and the welfare state. In M. Holborn (Ed.), *Developments in Sociology, Volume 18*. Ormskirk: Causeway Press.

Pareto, V. (1963). *A treatise on general sociology*. New York: Dover Publications.

Park, A. (Ed.) (2001). *British Social Attitudes, 18th Report*. London: Sage.

Parry, G. & Moyser, G. (1993). Political participation in Britain. *Politics Review, 3, 2*, November.

Parry, G., Moyser, G. & Day, N. (1991). *Political participation in Britain*. Cambridge: Cambridge University Press.

Parsons, G. (2002). *Perspectives on civil religion*. Milton Keynes: Open University and Aldershot: Ashgate Publishing.

Parsons, T. (1951). *The social system*. New York: Free Press.

Parsons, T. (1955). The American family: Its relations to personality and social structure. In T. Parsons & R. Bales (Eds.), *Family, socialisation and interaction process*. New York: The Free Press.

Parsons, T. (1965). Religious perspectives in sociology and social psychology. In W.A. Lessa & E.Z. Vogt (Eds.), *Reader in comparative religion: An anthropological approach* (2nd ed.). New York: Harper & Row.

Parsons, T. (1967). *Sociological theory and modern society*. London: Collier-Macmillan.

Pateman, C. (1988). *The sexual contract*. Cambridge: Polity.

Pawson, R. (1989). 'Methodology'. In M Haralambos (Ed.), *Developments in sociology, Volume 5*. Ormskirk: Causeway Press.

Pawson, R. (1992). Feminist methodology. In M. Haralambos (Ed.), *Developments in sociology, Volume 8*. Ormskirk: Causeway Press.

Pawson, R. (1995). Methods of content/document/media analysis. In M. Haralambos (Ed.), *Developments in sociology, volume 11*. Ormskirk: Causeway Press.

Pearson, G. (1983). *Hooligan: A history of respectable fears*. London: Macmillan.

Pease, K. (2002). Crime reduction. In M. Maguire et al. (Eds.), *The Oxford handbook of criminology* (3rd ed.). Oxford: Clarendon Press.

Phillips, C. & Bowling, B. (2002). Racism, ethnicity and criminal justice. In M. Maguire et al. (Eds.), *The Oxford handbook of criminology* (3rd ed.) Oxford: Clarendon Press.

Philo, G. & Miller, D. (Eds) (2001). *Market killing: What the free market does and what social scientists can do about it*. Harlow: Longman.

Philo, G. & Miller, D. (2002). Circuits of communication and power: Recent developments in media sociology. In M. Holborn (Ed.), *Developments in Sociology, Vol. 18*. Ormskirk: Causeway Press.

Pilkington, A. (2003). *Racial disadvantage and ethnic diversity in Britain.* London: Palgrave.

Plummer, K. (1979). Misunderstanding labelling perspectives. In D. Downes & P. Rock (Eds.), *Deviant interpretations.* Oxford: M. Robertson.

Polsby, N. (1963). *Community power and political theory.* London: Yale University Press.

Popper, K.R. (1959). *The logic of scientific discovery.* London: Hutchinson.

Poster, M. (Ed.) (1988). *Jean Baudrillard: Selected writings.* Cambridge: Polity.

Poulantzas, N. (1975). *Classes in contemporary capitalism.* London: New Left Books.

Puwar, N. (2001). Problematising, seeing, listening and telling: Reflections on the research enterprise. In M. Haralambos (Ed.), *Developments in Sociology, Volume 17.* Ormskirk: Causeway.

Reeves, R. (1999). Inside the world of the global protestors. *The Observer,* 31 October.

Reiner, R. (1993). Race, crime and justice: Models of interpretation. In L. Gelsthorpe (Ed.), *Minority ethnic groups in the criminal justice system.* Cambridge: Institute of Criminology.

Reiner, R. (1994). Policing and the police. In M. Maguire et al. (Eds.), *The Oxford handbook of criminology* (1st ed.). Oxford: Clarendon Press.

Reiner, R. (2002). Media made criminality. In M. Maguire et al. (Eds.), *The Oxford handbook of criminology* (3rd ed.). Oxford: Clarendon Press.

Reiner, R., Livingstone, S. & Allen, J. (2000). No more happy endings? The media and popular concern about crime since the Second World War. In T. Hope & R. Sparks (Eds.), *Crime, risk and insecurity.* London: Routledge.

Roberts, D. (Ed.) (1999). *British politics in focus.* Ormskirk: Causeway Press.

Robertson, R. (1970). *The sociological interpretation of religion.* Oxford: Blackwell.

Rock, P. (1979). Sociology of crime. In D. Downes & P. Rock (Eds.), *Deviant interpretations.* Oxford: M. Robertson.

Roseneil, S. (1995). *Disarming patriarchy: Feminism and political action at Greenham.* Buckingham: Open University Press.

Rowbotham, S. (1973). *Woman's consciousness: Man's world.* Harmondsworth: Penguin.

Sachs, J. (1990). The persistence of faith. *The Listener,* 15 November.

Saggar, S. (1997). Racial politics. In P. Norris & N.T. Gavin (Eds.), *Britain votes 1997.* Oxford: Oxford University Press.

Saggar, S. (2001). *Race and political recruitment: Ethnic pluralism and candidate selection in British political parties.* London: Hansard Society.

Sampson, R. & Raudenbush, S. (1999). Systematic social observation of public spaces: A new look at disorder in urban neighbourhoods. *American Journal of Sociology.*

Sanders, D. (1997). Voting and the electorate. In P. Dunleavy et al. (Eds.), *Developments in British politics 5.* Basingstoke: Macmillan.

Sarlvick, B. & Crewe, I. (1983). *A decade of dealignment.* Cambridge: Cambridge University Press.

Saunders, D. (2001). Bush's Christian guru Marvin Olasky aims to reshape America. *Toronto Globe & Mail,* 13 January.

Sayer, A. (1992). *Method in social science: A realist approach.* London: Routledge.

Scammell, M. & Harrop, M. (1997). The press. In D. Butler & D. Kavanagh (Eds.), *The British general election of 1997.* Basingstoke: Macmillan.

Scammell, M. & Harrop, M. (2002). The press disarmed. In D. Butler & D. Kavanagh (Eds.), *The British general election of 2001.* Basingstoke: Palgrave.

Scarman, L. (1981). *The Scarman Report: The Brixton disorders.* London: HMSO.

Scott, J. (1991). *Who rules Britain?* Cambridge: Polity.

Sewell, T.A. (1993). *Black tribunes: Black political participation in Britain.* London: Lawrence and Wishart.

Simmons, J. & Dodd, T. (2003). *Crime in England and Wales 2002/2003.* London: ONS.

Sklair, L. (2003). Globalisation, capitalism and power. In M. Holborn (Ed.), *Developments in Sociology, Vol. 19.* Ormskirk: Causeway Press.

Skocpol, T. (1979). *States and social revolutions.* Cambridge: Cambridge University Press.

Skocpol, T. (1985). Bringing the state back in: Strategies of analysis in current research. In P. Evans, D. Rueschemeyer & T. Skocpol (Eds.), *Bringing the state back in.* Cambridge: Cambridge University Press.

Smart, B. (1992). *Modern conditions, postmodern controversies.* London: Routledge.

Smart, C. (1977). *Women, crime and criminology.* London: Routledge.

Smiles, S. (1859). *Self help.* Harmondsworth: Penguin (republished, 1986).

Smith, D. & Gray, J. (1995). *Police and people in London.* Aldershot: Gower.

Smith, D. (1994). Race, crime and criminal justice. In M. Maguire et al. (Eds.), *The Oxford handbook of criminology* (1st ed.). Oxford: Clarendon Press.

Smith, D. (1997). Ethnic origins, crime and criminal justice. In M. Maguire, R. Morgan & R. Reiner (Eds.), *The Oxford handbook of criminology* (2nd ed.). Oxford: Oxford University Press.

Stanko, E. (1994) Challenging the problem of men's individual violence. In T. Newburn & E. Stanko (Eds.), *Just boys doing business?* London: Routledge.

Stanworth, P. & Giddens, A. (Eds.) (1974), *Elites and power in British society.* Cambridge: Cambridge University Press.

Stark, R. (1999). Micro-foundations of religion: A revised theory. *Sociological Theory, 17,* 264-289.

Stark, R. & Bainbridge, W.S. (1985). *The future of religion.* Berkeley, CA: University of California Press.

Stark, R. & Bainbridge, W.S. (1987). *A theory of religion.* New York: Lang.

Starrett, G. (1998). *Putting Islam to work: Education, politics and religious transformation in Egypt.* Berkeley CA: University of California Press.

Stone, D. (1976). The human potential movement. In C.Y. Glock & R.N. Bellah (Eds.), *The consciousness reformation.* Berkeley, CA: University of California Press.

Storey, J. (1993). *An introductory guide of cultural theory and popular culture.* London: Harvester Wheatsheaf.

Stradling, R. (1988). *The politics of law and order.* London: Longman.

Strinati, D. (1992). Postmodernism and popular culture. *Sociology Review,* April.

Sutherland, E. (1949). *White collar crime.* New York: Holt, Rinehart & Winston.

Swale, J. (2000). Women's role in religion. *Sociology Review,* April.

Swale, J. (2004). Suicide: A synoptic approach, *Sociology Review,12.*

Sykes, G.M. & Matza, D. (1962). Techniques of neutralisation: A theory of delinquency. In M.E. Wolfgang, L. Savitz & N. Johnston (Eds.), *The sociology of crime and delinquency.* New York: John Wiley & Sons.

Taheri, A. (1987). *Holy terror: The inside story of Islamic terrorism.* London: Sphere.

Tawney, R.H. (1938). *Religion and the rise of capitalism.* Harmondsworth: Penguin.

Taylor, I., Walton, P. & Young, J. (1973). *The new criminology.* London: Routledge.

Taylor, S. (1982). *Durkheim and the study of suicide.* London: Macmillan.

Taylor, S. (1988). *Suicide.* London: Longman.

Tester, K. (1995). Postmodernism. In M. Haralambos (Ed.), *Developments in sociology vol 11.* Ormskirk: Causeway Press.

Thatcher, M. (1993). *The Downing Street years.* London: Harper Collins.

Thompson, K. (1992). Social pluralism and postmodernity. In S. Hall et al. (Eds.), *Modernity and its futures.* Cambridge: Polity.

Touraine, A. (1983). *Anti-nuclear protest.* Cambridge: Cambridge University Press.

Touraine, A. (1995). *Critique of modernity.* Oxford: Blackwell.

Troeltsch, E. (1931). *The social teachings of the Christian Churches.* London: Allen & Unwin.

Tumin, M. (1967). *Social stratification: The forms and functions of social inequality.* Englewood Cliffs: Prentice-Hall.

Utley, R.M. (1963). *The last days of the Sioux nation.* New Haven: Yale University Press.

Walby, S. (1990). *Theorising patriarchy.* Oxford: Blackwell.

Walby, S. (1997). *Gender transformations.* London: Routledge.

Walklate, S. (2003). *Understanding criminology: Current theoretical debates* (2nd ed.). Buckingham: Open University Press.

Wallis, R. (1974). Ideology, authority and the development of cultic movements. *Social Research*, 41, 299-327.

Wallis, R. (1975). Scientology: Therapeutic cult to religious sect. *Sociology, 9*, 89-100.

Wallis, R. (1984). *The elementary forms of the new religious life.* London: Routledge & Kegan Paul.

Wallis, R. (1985). The sociology of the New Religions. *Social Studies Review*, September.

Wallis, R. & Bruce, S. (1989). Religion: The British contribution. *British Journal of Sociology, 40*, 3.

Weber, M. (1958). *The Protestant ethic and the spirit of capitalism.* New York: Charles Scribner's Sons.

Weber, M. (1963). *The sociology of religion.* Boston, MA: Beacon Press.

Weber, M. (1964). *The theory of social and economic organisations.* New York: The Free Press.

Weber, M. (1978). *Economy and society: An outline of interpretative sociology.* Berkeley CA: University of California Press.

Welsh, I. (1997). Power and Globalisation. In M. Haralambos (Ed.), *Developments in Sociology, Vol. 13.* Ormskirk: Causeway Press.

Westergaard, J. & Resler, H. (1976). *Class in a capitalist society.* Harmondsworth: Penguin.

White, J. (1981). The summer riots of 1919. *New Society*, 13 August.

Whiteley, P., Seyd, P. & Richardson, J. (1994). True Blues: *The politics of the Conservative Party.* Oxford: Oxford University Press.

Whitely, R. (1974). The city and industry. In P. Stanworth & A Giddens (Eds.), *Elites and power in British society.* Cambridge: Cambridge University Press.

Whyte, W.F. (1955). *Street corner society* (2nd ed.). Chicago: University of Chicago Press.

Williams, K.M. (1981). *The Rastafarians.* London: Ward Lock Educational.

Williams, P. and Dickinson, J. (1993) Fear of crime: Read all about it? *British Journal of Criminology, 33.*

Wilson, B.R. (1966). *Religion and secular society.* London: C.A. Watts.

Wilson, B.R. (1970). *Religious sects.* London: Weidenfeld & Nicolson.

Wilson, B.R. (1976). *Contemporary transformations of religion.* London: Oxford University Press.

Wilson, B.R. (1982). *Religion in sociological perspective.* Oxford: Oxford University Press.

Wilson, J. & Kelling, G. (2003). Broken windows: The police and neighbourhood safety. In E. McLaughlin et al. (Eds.), *Criminological perspectives* (2nd ed.). London: Sage.

Wilson, J.Q. (1975). *Thinking about crime.* New York: Basic Books.

Wilson, J.Q. & Hernstein, R. (1985). *Crime and human nature.* New York: Simon & Schuster.

Winant, H. (1994). Racial formation and identity. In A. Rattansi & S. Westwood (Eds.), *Racism, modernity and identity.* Cambridge: Polity Press.

Woodhead, L. & Heelas, P. (Eds.) (2000). *Religion in modern times: An interpretive anthology.* Oxford: Blackwell.

Wright, C. (1986). School processes – An ethnographic study. In S.J. Eggleston, D. Dunn & M. Angali (Eds.), *Education for some.* Stoke on Trent: Trentham Books.

Wright, C. (1992). Early education: Multiracial primary classrooms. In D. Gill, B. Mayor & M. Blair (Eds.), *Racism and education: Structures and strategies.* London: Sage.

Yeo, A. (1988). Is there anybody out there? *Midweek*, 28 July.

Yinger, M. (1970). *The scientific study of religion.* London: Routledge.

York, M. (1995). *The emerging network: A sociology of the New Age and Neo-Pagan networks.* Lanham, MD: Rowman & Littlefield.

Young, J. (1971). *The drugtakers.* London: Paladin.

Young, J. (1986). The failure of criminology: The need for a radical realism. In R. Matthews & J. Young (Eds.), *Confronting crime.* London: Sage.

Young, J. (1992). Ten points of realism. In J. Young & R. Matthews (Eds.), *Rethinking criminology: The realist debate.* London: Sage.

Young, J. (1997). Left realist criminology. In M. Maguire et al. (Eds.), *The Oxford handbook of criminology* (2nd ed.). Oxford: Clarendon Press.

Young, J. (1999). *The exclusive society: Social exclusion, crime and difference in late modernity.* London: Sage.

Young, J. (2002). Crime and social exclusion. In M. Maguire et al. (Eds.), *The Oxford handbook of criminology* (3rd ed.). Oxford: Clarendon Press.

Zeitlin, I. (1971). *Ideology and social theory.* Glencoe Illinois: The Free Press.

Author index

Holden, A. 24
Home Office 212, 252, 254-257, 261-264
Hood, R. 255, 263
Horkheimer, M. 176
Hoyle, C. 129
Hudson, B. 256
Hughes, G. 230, 245
Hunt, S. 27, 39, 40, 42, 47, 49, 51, 54
Husserl, E. 188

J
James, O. 30
James, W. 180
Jenkins, J. 15
Jessop, B. 92
Johnston, R.J. 111
Jones, I. 146
Jones, K. 5
Jones, P. 159
Jones, S. 250, 260
Jones, T. 213, 247
Jowell, R. 108
Judah, J.S. 46
Julienne, L. 256

K
Kalra, V. 253
Kaluzynska, E. 144
Kassam, N. 198
Katz, E. 124
Kavanagh, D. 74, 75, 107, 113
Kelling, G. 244
Kellner, D.M. 177
Kellner, H. 22
Kerr, J. 238
Khasala, K. 51
Kincaid, J.C. 147
Kuhn, T.S. 132-135

L
Lakatos, I. 133
Langan, M. 230
Langley, P. 138
Layder, D. 148-150
Layton-Henry, Z. 85, 251
Lazarsfeld, P. 124
Lea, J. 242, 247, 250, 256
Lee, D. 159, 265
Lemert, E.M. 234
Levi, M. 208
Lévi-Strauss, C. 186, 192
Light, A. 262
Lilleker, D. 125
Linton, M. 124
Lockwood, D. 174
Lombroso, C. 222
Long Lance 149
Longley, C. 15
Luckmann, T. 53
Lukes, S. 63, 65, 67, 68, 87
Lupton, T. 74
Lyon, D. 23, 26
Lyotard, J.F. 23, 47, 58, 196-198

M
Macdonald, K. 128
Macgregor, S. 152
Macpherson, W. 85, 251, 253, 256

MacQuail, D. 124
Maduro, O. 14-16, 27
Maguire, M. 207-210, 213, 214
Malinowski, B. 8-10, 25, 28, 172
Mandel, E. 218
Mann, M. 65
Marcuse, H. 176, 177
Marler, P.L. 60
Marsh, D. 69
Marshall, G. 187
Martin, B. 17
Martin, D. 54
Martin, W. 268
Marx, K. 12, 13, 15-17, 19, 25, 27, 33, 51, 52, 57, 60, 67, 74-76, 79, 87, 89, 101, 132, 147, 150, 151, 157, 159-164, 167, 170-172, 175, 176, 186
Matza, D. 228, 229, 231
Mauer, M. 248, 249
May, M. 154
Mayhew, P. 210, 252
McAuley, J.W. 89
McClennan, G. 198
McCullagh, C. 123
McGuire, M. 12, 32, 33, 42
McRobbie, A. 153
Mead, G.H. 180, 181, 183, 184
Merton, R.K. 173, 174, 184, 225-228, 231
Messerschmidt, J. 259, 260. 263
Mies, M. 144
Miliband, R. 77-79, 87, 89, 94, 123
Millar, J. 180
Miller, D. 124, 196
Miller, W.B. 227, 228
Miller, W.L. 124, 125
Mills, C.W. 73, 74, 87
Miner, M. 142, 143
Modood, T. 256
Morgan, C. 53
Morris, A. 263
Mosca, G. 71-73, 87
Moynihan, J. 214
Moyser, G. 105, 106
Muncie, J. 202, 237, 238
Munck, R. 128
Murdock, G. 146
Murray, C. 243-245

N
Naffine, N. 259
Negrine, R. 125
Nelson, G.K. 32
Newby, H. 159, 265
Niebuhr, H.R. 35, 48-50
Nightingale, C. 249
Nisbet, R. 159
Nordlinger, E.A. 91
Norris, P. 109

O
O'Connell Davidson, J. 148-150
O'Leary, B. 88
O'Toole, R. 11
Oakley, A. 143, 144, 146
Offe, C. 89, 94
Ohlin, L. 226-228, 231

P
Page, R.M. 151, 152

Paluski, J. 119, 120
Pareto, V. 71-74, 87
Park, A. 111
Parry, G. 105, 106
Parsons, G. 10
Parsons, T. 9, 10, 15, 25, 29, 65, 172-174, 184, 187, 189, 257, 258
Pateman, C. 83
Pattie, C.J. 111
Pavlov, I. 180
Pawson, R. 139, 140, 143, 144, 217
Payne, G. 108, 109
Pearson, G. 210
Pease, K. 202
Phelps, C. 146
Phillips, C. 252-256
Philo, G. 124, 196
Pierce, C. 180
Pilkington, A. 83, 84, 256
Plummer, K. 204
Polsby, N. 63
Popper, K.R. 97, 132, 135
Poster, M. 196
Poulantzas, N. 78, 79, 87, 89, 94, 178
Puwar, N. 129

R
Radcliffe-Brown, A.R. 172
Raudenbush, S. 245
Reeves, R. 122
Reiner, R. 214, 217, 218, 234, 256
Resler, H. 69, 75
Roberts, D. 75, 84, 107, 110, 115-119, 124, 126
Robertson, R. 36
Rock, P. 202, 224, 229, 242, 250
Rolston, W. 128
Roseneil, S. 66
Rowbotham, S. 143
Rubel, M. 162-164

S
Sachs, J. 171
Saggar, S. 85, 110, 113
Sampson, R. 245
Sanders, D. 109
Sarlvick B. 108
Saunders, D. 30
Saussure, F. de, 185, 186
Sayer, A. 133, 134
Scammell, M. 124
Scarman, L. 251, 253
Schutz, A. 188, 189
Scott, J. 78
Sewell, T.A. 75, 85
Silburn, R. 154
Simmons, J. 207, 210-212, 220, 221
Sklair, L. 92, 94
Skocpol, T. 91
Smart, B. 159, 160
Smart, C. 257
Smiles, S. 98
Smith, A. 180
Smith, D. 251, 253, 255, 256
Spencer, H. 172, 173
Stanko, E. 264
Stanworth, P. 73
Stanyer, J. 125

Subject index